BENEFICIAL OWNERSHIP IN TAX LAW AND TAX TREATIES

This book explores the concept of beneficial ownership in equity law, the domestic tax laws of the United Kingdom, Canada and the United States, as well as its varied and increasing uses in international tax law. By analysing the evolution of beneficiary rights in equity and the use of beneficial ownership wording in tax law, the book draws a roadmap for dealing with beneficial ownership in both national and international tax law. This approach highlights those common misconceptions that can be avoided by understanding the origins of the concept and its engagement with equity, as well as the differences with tax law. However, the book does not limit itself to dealing with theoretical discussion, but also offers an instructive and detailed practical case study. Offering both academic commentary and a practitioner focus, the book will be of the utmost interest to scholars and practitioners from common and civil law countries dealing with tax and estate law, particularly given beneficial ownership's increasing relevance.

Beneficial Ownership in Tax Law and Tax Treaties

Pablo A Hernández González-Barreda

•HART•
OXFORD • LONDON • NEW YORK • NEW DELHI • SYDNEY

HART PUBLISHING

Bloomsbury Publishing Plc

Kemp House, Chawley Park, Cumnor Hill, Oxford, OX2 9PH, UK

1385 Broadway, New York, NY 10018, USA

HART PUBLISHING, the Hart/Stag logo, BLOOMSBURY and the Diana logo are trademarks of Bloomsbury Publishing Plc

First published in Great Britain 2020

A catalogue record for this book is available from the British Library.

Library of Congress Cataloging-in-Publication data

Names: Hernández González-Barreda, Pablo Andrés author.

Title: Beneficial ownership in tax law and tax treaties / Pablo A Hernández González-Barreda.

Description: Oxford ; New York : Hart, 2020. | Based on author's thesis (doctoral – Universidad Pontificia Comillas, Facultad de Derecho, 2014) issued under title: El concepto de beneficiario efectivo en los convenios tributarios sobre la renta y sobre el patrimonio. | Includes bibliographical references and index.

Identifiers: LCCN 2019056009 (print) | LCCN 2019056010 (ebook) | ISBN 9781509923076 (hardback) | ISBN 9781509923083 (Epub)

Subjects: LCSH: International business enterprises—Taxation—Law and legislation. | Double taxation—Treaties.

Classification: LCC K4475 .H47 2020 (print) | LCC K4475 (ebook) | DDC 343.07—dc23

LC record available at https://lccn.loc.gov/2019056009

LC ebook record available at https://lccn.loc.gov/2019056010

ISBN: HB: 978-1-50992-307-6
ePDF: 978-1-50992-309-0
ePub: 978-1-50992-308-3

Typeset by Compuscript Ltd, Shannon

To find out more about our authors and books visit www.hartpublishing.co.uk. Here you will find extracts, author information, details of forthcoming events and the option to sign up for our newsletters.

To my parents

To my brother

Because this book is a result of their unconditional and unlimited support and love no matter what.

What is it that unites this time and place we share, Jesús Ricardo?

The word, the word brings us together one minute and then tears us apart the next, the word that, whether friend or enemy, in the end acquires an independent meaning. And it's that transience that drives us, my young and beloved friend, in this hopelessly polluted and pigeon-shit-covered stoa, to utter the next word, knowing that it too will slip from our grasp and enter into the great realm of reason that engulfs us.

'Don't ever stop talking. Don't ever say the last word.'

(C. FUENTES, *The Eagle's Throne*, Bloomsbury, London, 2006, p. 137.)

FOREWORD

It gives me much pleasure to welcome this book. The concept of beneficial ownership should never have been incorporated into tax treaties and, as I have argued, although Pablo Hernández disagrees, it was never necessary anyway. But it is far too late in history to say that and we must live with the consequences.

Beneficial ownership is truly the mythological beast on the cover. It is a perfect example of Humpty Dumpty's famous saying, 'When I use a word it means just what I choose it to mean – neither more nor less'. It is amazing that the same expression can have such different meanings in (i) equity; (ii) domestic tax law, where it tends to be used in relation to the capital, and even in UK tax law it seems to have different meanings depending on the context; (iii) tax treaties, where it is used in relation to income, and the position gets worse when different languages and legal systems are involved as the expression is essentially untranslatable and inapplicable in a different legal system; (iv) EU law, where it is applied to permanent establishments; and (with an entirely different meaning) (v) exchange of information instruments.

We in the UK think we know what beneficial ownership means, although the author is right in saying that we cannot explain it, and we think we know what it must have been intended to mean in tax treaties, but it required Pablo Hernández from Spain to make us see all the contradictions that are involved and make sense of them by including interesting civil law comparisons.

The earliest reference to beneficial ownership in relation to income in treaties that I have been able to find is in the negotiations for the US–UK treaty of 1945, where a UK memorandum outlining proposals to be communicated to US representatives mentioned that 'regard is to be had, of course, to the position of the beneficial owner of the shares etc where the nominal shareholder etc is not the beneficial owner'.[1] One assumes that the US negotiators agreed with the 'of course' and neither side suggested that it needed to be stated specifically in the treaty, nor that its precise meaning needed to be discussed. Indeed, the memorandum was not written by a lawyer and the wrong expression had been used, but its meaning was obvious. It was not until 1966 that beneficial ownership was expressly added to that treaty, but I doubt if either side thought it was that important other than being superior for charities and pension funds to the subject to tax test that it replaced. The problem was then that the OECD thought it was a good idea to include beneficial ownership in the Model Tax Convention (the Model) for use in treaties where neither side was familiar with the concept for which it was translated in various different ways. Since then, many court cases have examined its meaning and many books, including this one, have been written about it.

[1] UK National Archives IR63/167, 510.

I remain of the simplistic 'of course' view that beneficial ownership was something that was implied – as it still is for all treaty articles except for Articles 10, 11 and 12 of the Model, which unwisely use the expression 'paid to'. If one must read these words literally (which is a wrong approach to treaty interpretation anyway), there is a case for the inclusion of beneficial ownership so that the withholding tax reduction applies only to the real owner of the income rather than someone else, who might be a nominee or trustee. Surely one can determine whether income really belongs to someone or not without needing to analyse the expression 'beneficial ownership'? I would favour applying the 'of course' test; if the recipient is 'of course' not the real owner of the income, then the treaty reduction does not apply.

I am sure most of us would agree with the author's conclusion and his final words that the term should be interpreted in the narrow sense that gives legal certainty.

John Avery Jones
July 2019

PREFACE

As John Avery Jones writes in his foreword to this book, the concept of beneficial owner is a perfect example of Humpty Dumpty's famous saying: 'When I use a word it means just what I choose it to mean – neither more nor less.' Therein lies the difficulty of Pablo Hernández's work: since the beginning of his doctoral research he has endeavoured to unravel the reasons why a concept could be interpreted so differently. Like Alice, he wondered, 'whether you can make words mean so many different things'. Reality shows, as Pablo Hernández shows in detail, that in different jurisdictions tax authorities and courts can have different views about the meaning of beneficial ownership, because what finally matters is, as Humpty Dumpty said, 'which is to be master – that's all'.

After several years of discussions, scholars, administrative practice and courts still maintain significant differences on the concept of beneficial owner in international taxation. However, there are not many cases in which the technical meaning of those terms has been discussed in depth, and references to case law, apart from some domestic cases and other cases of little significance, are normally to the following: the Court of Appeal decision (2006) in the UK in *Indofood International Finance Ltd v JP Morgan Chase Bank NA*, which is not technically a tax case; the French Conseil d'Etat decision in *Bank of Scotland v Ministre de l'Economie, des Finances et de l'Industrie* (2006); the *Prévost Car Inc.* (2008) and the *Velcro Canada Inc.* (2012) cases in Canada; and the recent decisions of the Court of Justice of the European Union (CJEU) in the so-called Danish Beneficial Ownership cases (2019) (Case C-115/16 *N Luxembourg 1*, Case C-118/16 *X Denmark A/S*, Case C-119/16 *C Danmark I*, Case C-299/16 *Z Denmark ApS*, Case C-116/16 *T Denmark* and Case C-117/16 *Y Denmark Aps*).

Those rulings summarise the doctrine around a term whose interpretation, taking into account the context, according to Article 3(2) of the OECD Model Tax Convention, otherwise requires; so it cannot be understood under the meaning that it has under the law of the state applying the treaty. However, not even the Commentaries to the OECD Model Tax Convention – at least until the 2014 amendments – managed to set an international autonomous meaning of the term 'beneficial owner', which was added to address potential difficulties arising from the use of the words 'paid to … a resident'. For this reason, following the Commentaries, one cannot refer to any technical meaning that the term could have under the domestic law of a specific country when interpreting it, because 'beneficial owner' is not used in a narrow technical sense, and should be understood – at least since the 2003 Commentary – in the light of the purpose of the tax treaties, notably the prevention of fiscal evasion and avoidance.

Consequently, as Pablo Hernández states in analysing case law, the main trend is to interpret 'beneficial owner' as a broad anti-avoidance rule, related to the determination of the actual legal facts – an anti-abuse rule whose interpretation varies from the formal views given by some, referring to a legal obligation to pass on the payment received to another person, to those that use the term to refer to the facts and circumstances showing, in a substance-over-form analysis, that the recipient does not have the right to use and enjoy the income.

The view of the 'beneficial owner' rule as an anti-abuse clause has been emphasised by the CJEU in the so-called Danish Beneficial Ownership cases that, once again, addressed numerous controversies not only over the meaning of that term in the Interest and Royalties and Parent–Subsidiary Directives, but also about the use of the OECD Commentaries for its interpretation and the meaning of the general anti-abuse principle in tax law, especially in areas that are subject to a limited harmonisation.

After the CJEU decisions in the beneficial ownership cases, it is pretty clear who should be considered the 'master', in Humpty Dumpty terms, because from now on the concept of 'beneficial owner' should be interpreted taking into account the Commentaries to the OECD Model Tax Convention, which are 'relevant when interpreting Directive 2003/49' (Cases C-115/16, C118/16, C-119/16 and C-299/16, para 90). This statement is controversial because, although the Proposal for the Directive was drafted upon Article 11 of the OECD 1996 Model Tax Convention and pursues the same objective, it is debatable whether it can be interpreted in accordance to subsequent commentaries with a significantly different content to the 1996 Commentaries, as the court does, especially taking into account that the commentaries used regarding the interpretation of 'beneficial owner' were issued later than the adoption of the Directive.

All in all, the most relevant issue in the Danish Beneficial Ownership cases is the value given to the general principle on prohibition of abuse, from which unforeseen consequences are derived in the light of previous case law, notably Case C-321/05 *Kofoed*. In that case, the CJEU stated that 'the principle of legal certainty precludes directives from being able by themselves to create obligations for individuals. Directives cannot therefore be relied upon per se by the Member State as against individuals' (para 42).

According to such case law, national tax authorities were not able to apply the anti-abuse reservation of Article 15 of the Merger Directive directly against a taxpayer if no domestic rule or general principle was found. Notwithstanding, in the Danish cases the CJEU took a different approach, emphasising that the (unwritten) general principle of prohibition of abuse implies that any right or advantage can be denied based on this EU general principle, regardless of any specific EU or domestic law provision (Cases C-115/16, C-118/16, C-119/16 and C-299/16, para 111; Cases C-116/16 and C-117/16, paras 89–90). As Haslehner and Koefler have pointed out, in light of the general anti-abuse rule in Article 6 of the Anti-Tax Avoidance Directive, this issue might have little practical relevance in the future, but seems to be quite important from the perspective of the constitutional separation of powers. This is because, if the parliament in a Member State decides not to issue legislation to implement a directive's anti-abuse reservation, tax authorities and courts could still, according to the CJEU case law, deny benefits considered as abusive in application of the EU general principle of prohibition of abuse.

It is still rather early to analyse the outcomes of this ruling, which reopens the debate on the usefulness of the 'beneficial owner' rule, as similar results may be achieved through the application of other anti-abuse rules or principles, special or general, whose multiplication carries several inconveniences from the perspective of legal certainty.

This work contributes to the debate and to a better understanding of the obscure 'beneficial owner rule'. Its publication is the brilliant culmination of the author's academic education that started as an undergraduate and master student in the Faculty of Law of the Universidad Pontificia Comillas – ICADE, and continued with his doctoral studies and successive pre- and post-doctoral research trips abroad. The academic maturity of the author and the process of intense redrafting of the original work of his doctoral thesis has brought about the final result the reader holds in their hands, a monograph that establishes Pablo Hernández González-Barreda as an authoritative voice in a particularly complex area of international taxation, who is, in our view, able to successfully take on any issue in the future, in this or any related field.

We trust that his determined academic vocation, both in research and lecturing, is reinforced with fruits such as this book, and that he is encouraged to continue along the path on which he has already taken such strong steps, without prejudice, to also continue the highly committed public service that is at the very heart of his legal and academic vocation.

Francisco Javier Alonso Madrigal
Juan Zornoza Pérez
August 2019

ACKNOWLEDGEMENTS

This book, even though it has been subject to significant changes in the four years since I finished my doctoral studies,[1] has its roots in the doctoral thesis I defended at the Universidad Pontificia Comillas – ICADE on 12 March 2015 before a panel made up of Prof María Teresa Soler Roch (University of Alicante), Prof Rainer Prokisch (Maastricht University), Prof Luís Eduardo Schoueri (University of Sao Paulo), Prof José Manuel Almudí Cid (Complutense University of Madrid) and Prof Ramón Casero Barrón (Universidad Pontificia Comillas – ICADE). I would therefore like to thank them for their invaluable comments, as well as for their support during the defence and in the first steps of my academic career.

However, this work could not have been undertaken without the support of my alma mater, Universidad Pontificia Comillas – ICADE, who first awarded me a doctoral research grant and then appointed me as lecturer. In particular, I would like to thank Profs Concepción Molina Blázquez and Íñigo Navarro, as successive Deans of the Faculty of Law, for their support and trust.

I would like to thank my former supervisors, Profs Alonso Madrigal (Universidad Pontificia Comillas – ICADE) and Zornoza Pérez (Universidad Carlos III de Madrid), for their dedication. Without their trust, amity and continuous support, it would have been impossible to finish this work. The amount of time devoted to reviewing the original drafts of the thesis, and the time they have invested in supporting my academic career, deserves all my gratitude. I would especially like to thank them for continually pushing me to take the extra step. Whether or not I achieved them, any good ideas the reader may perceive are due to their continuous encouragement of my academic growth. More importantly, I could not be more thankful for their backing as I started out on my academic life, which, although sometimes tough, has provided me with some of the moments of my life for which I am so far most grateful.

I would also like to thank Prof Judith Freedman (Oxford University), Prof Michael Lang (Wirtschaftsuniversität Wien), Prof Pasquale Pistone (Wirtschaftsuniversität Wien and IBFD), Prof Stephen Shay (Harvard Law School), Prof Edoardo Traversa (Université Catholique de Louvain) and Prof Joao Pinto Nogueira (IBFD), for their academic support and trust during my academic residencies and during the first steps of my academic career.

[1] The content of the doctoral thesis on beneficial owner in tax conventions has been condensed into what are now Chapters 4 and 5 of this book, and new content has been added. The resulting book now includes a comprehensive analysis of beneficial ownership in different fields and their relationship to each other, including beneficial owner in equity law (Chapter 2), beneficial owner principles in the domestic tax law principles of the United Kingdom, United States and Canada (Chapter 3), beneficial owner in European Union law (Chapter 6) and beneficial owner in exchange of information (Chapter 7).

Dr John Avery Jones deserves my extraordinary gratitude for having the patience to discuss with me some of the points of this work, as well as for reading parts of the piece, making really thorough comments, and kindly agreeing to write the foreword. For a lawyer, dealing with a foreign jurisdiction is always a complex matter, and even more so if one is educated in a civil law environment and tries to delve into a common law jurisdiction, and he kindly provided me with feedback that undoubtedly improved the piece. In any case, any mistakes the reader may see are entirely mine.

I especially wish to thank the OeAD (Austrian Agency for International Cooperation in Education and Research) for awarding me the Ernst Mach Grant in 2012–2013, which enabled me to undertake a research stay at the Vienna University of Economics and Business that boosted this research and enabled me to get in touch with a wonderful academic family. In addition, it should be noted that this work is framed within the Research project 'Post-BEPS International Taxation: Are the New Rules and Proposals Suitable for Every Jurisdiction?' (DER2017-85333-P), led by Prof Juan Zornoza Pérez (Universidad Carlos III de Madrid). My thanks too to the silent contributors to academic works in the common services in the universities and archives I have been in, especially those of the libraries (my apologies for my weakness for accumulating books). Among all, Renee Pestuka (WU) deserves special gratitude for her patience dealing with all the administrative work I required regarding my stays at the Institute for Austrian and International Tax Law.

I have to thank Prof María Cruz Barreiro Carril, Prof Félix Vega Borrego, Prof Domingo Jiménez Valladolid and Prof César Martínez for helping me with the steps to follow in my academic career. I extend also my gratitude to Dr Ricardo García Antón, with whom I shared the first steps of my academic career at the IBFD in Amsterdam.

Special thanks are also due to the 2013–2014 Year of Visiting Researchers and Doctoral Students at the Institute of Austrian and International Tax Law, who are now academic colleagues, with whom I shared so many rewarding academic moments and discussions, and with whom I have started an academic network that reaches even beyond university: Alessandro Roncaratti, Dr Alice Pirlot, César Alejandro Ruiz Jiménez, Felipe Vallada, Dr Giulio Allevato, Dr José Manuel Castro, Dr Markus Seiler, Dr Raffaele Pettruzzi, among others.

Similar thanks go to my former doctoral colleagues in Madrid, Dr Aitor Navarro, Dr Eva Escribano, Dr Félix Daniel Martínez Laguna and some other young professors who, in one sense or another, were involved in the process of writing this book.

Dr Adam Dubin, Dr Antonio Pérez Miras, Prof Blanca Sáenz de Santa María, Prof Bruno Martín, Prof Ignacio Paredes Pérez, Dr Miguel Martínez Muñoz, Dr Pablo Sanz and Prof Paula García Andrade, colleagues at my alma mater, deserve their own recognition for listening to all my comments on this work irrespective of whether or not it was related to their work, for their comments on my work and academic career, and for their friendship beyond the walls of academia.

Some friends (Alonso, Dácil, Elena, Fernando, Gloria, Luis, Leandro, Ignacio, José, also Alejandro, Álvaro, Cristina, Daniel, Diego, Javier, Lola, Marta among others and, very especially, Ana, to whom this book is somehow specially dedicated) also carried a significant weight of the process of writing this book, so even though most of them remain outside the academic community, their contribution in supporting and listening to my heavy conversations on beneficial ownership should be recognised, especially taking into account that, if the topic is heavyweight for tax lawyers, it is even more so for non-tax lawyers. I also want to say sorry for all the times I have not been there because of this work, for the personal support given to my academic career and for the unconditional friendship, as well as for insisting and requesting to spend the needed leisure time without which one cannot carry such a work like this.

Finally, I have to thank my family for their support and patience during this period. For respecting my research and study times, and for forgiving me for all the times I was not able to attend relevant events. To my parents and grandparents for permanently sustaining me in all senses, but specially for their unconditional and unlimited love. To my brother, for his continual invitation to critical thinking, as well as for his trust and unconditional affection. To Paola González-Barreda (and indirectly to José María and Álvaro), for her invaluable help in the original English draft of the thesis and for being one of the few people who have read the whole initial work, even more not being a (tax) lawyer. Moreover, for being one of my strongest supports through every tough time.

To everybody who contributed to making my recent years working on this piece so unforgettable, and to my being able to bring this book to publication. Thank you, *gracias*.

Pablo A Hernández González-Barreda
La Orotava, Canary Islands,
7 August 2019

TABLE OF CONTENTS

TABLE OF CASES

Argentina

Australia

Canada

Czech Republic

Denmark

France

India

Indonesia

Italy

Mexico

Netherlands

Poland

Republic of Korea

Russia

Spain

Sweden

Switzerland

United Kingdom

United States

Court of Justice of the European Union

International Court of Justice

1

Introduction

It is said that the Governor of the Bank of England stated in 1987 that beneficial owners 'are like elephants; you know them when you see them'.[1] The statement has its roots in the famous *Jacobellis v Ohio* test, but beneficial ownership has little to do with obscenity.[2]

The phrase reminds the author of somebody speaking about a myth. Myths have been seen by few or many, they claim they can recognise one when they see it, but still the description of what happened or the animal they saw varies significantly from one witness to the other. In fact, the comparison with elephants is probably wrong. It is easy to describe an elephant because of the exaggerated proportions of the animal and their different body parts, but to describe beneficial ownership is very difficult.[3] Myths derived from literature are just that: literature. Beneficial ownership is a sort of mythological animal seen by few and extensively written about in the literature. As in the case of the seahorse on the cover of this book, some claim it is a fish with the head of a horse. Others claim it is a horse with the tail of a fish. And probably both are true to some extent.

The myth or tale of beneficial ownership is a long one that covers a significant period of history and different fields of law, and is continually expanding. Much literature has surrounded the myth throughout its history. As the seahorse can swim and run, some claim the same, or similar, can be said of beneficial ownership in equity law, tax law and international tax law, and it can be applied in the same way as an allocation or income, or an anti-avoidance rule.

To some extent, beneficial ownership is a shadow overlying all the economic law of legal systems. It departs from the philosophy of law, going on to influence ownership rights, affect tax law and enter international tax law. The issue departs from how rights on property and ownership are considered from a political and economic perspective. It is a label defining certain property or ownership rights that have worth in society, so that only once such concepts are defined may one look at beneficial ownership. And then tax law must be taken into account, the purpose of which is to raise revenue by taxing a subject's ability to pay. Because ability to pay depends on ownership, tax law has to consider it in determining whether a subject should be taxed. Finally, there is international tax law, where different tax systems, which all aim to collect revenue from a subject's ability to pay, have to coordinate with each other. Beneficial ownership again

[1] M Reinhard-DeRoo, *Beneficial Ownership* (Springer, 2014) 3.
[2] *Jacobellis v Ohio* (1964) 378 US 184 (US) 197 (Stewart J, concurring).
[3] Reinhard-DeRoo (n 1) 5.

comes into play. Because at each level beneficial ownership is a sort of myth, and one is related to the other, so the myth becomes even greater.

These beneficial ownership myths are probably the result of the evolution of the term through its history. From a kings' and queens' jurisdiction based in conscience, beneficiary rights developed a stable case law, albeit still based on the prerogative of judges. The term appeared in the nineteenth century only as a colloquial term, but once revolutions had strengthened ownership rights, it entered into law, at which point it developed significantly to achieve the more or less consistent lines of definition it has today. From there, it was taken into tax law, as with the development of contemporary tax law in the early twentieth century, as tax law wanted to catch such wealth. Tax law developed a new line of reasoning, connected to equity law, but not always attached to it.

As can be seen here, beneficial ownership is a matter of history. This is the reason why this book is largely based on historical reasoning, and its structure is based on the historical timeline. Consequently, the chapters are structured to delve into the myths on beneficial ownership, analysing case law and academic discussion to answer the questions surrounding it and giving a significant importance to the historical perspective.

Probably the first myth is that beneficial ownership is a term of art;[4] almost every lawyer in common law countries tend to think of it as such. However, if you ask them to define it, they answer with vague, ambiguous and, especially, with variable definitions. If the large majority cannot provide and answer, and even courts fail to define it, it can hardly be said to be a term of art. Conversely, there are some authors who claim beneficial ownership is defined on a case-by-case basis. It is true that beneficial ownership adapts itself to different cases, especially if one takes into account its origin as derived from pure equity law case-by-case jurisdiction. Today, however, there is a consistent corpus that enables provision of a definition of beneficial ownership to serve as guidance, although obviously, as with any other rule, this is subject to its application, context and functions in the diverse rules in which it is included.

The second chapter deals with those issues on beneficial ownership that arise in equity law, and how the evolution in the concept of ownership in the UK has impacted its meaning. From an imprecise and case-by case meaning, the term is nowadays closer to continental law ownership than ever.[5] This does not mean it is the same as continental ownership, and it depends on the case, although, at its greatest intensity, the approximation of beneficial ownership to full legal ownership is surprising. The French revolution, and reforms to ownership that took place in England at the nineteenth century probably had something to do with such approximations.

[4] Considering is not a term of art: C Brown, 'Tax, Trusts and Beneficial Ownership: Perils for the Unwary Practitioner' (2003) 23 *Estates, Trusts and Pensions Journal* 9, 51; R Speed, 'Beneficial Ownership' (1997) 26 *Australian Tax Review* 34, 50.

[5] See *Baker (Inspector of Taxes) v Archer Shee* [1927] AC 844 (HL); *Saunders v Vautier* (1841) 42 ER 282 (Ct of Chancery); *FHR European Ventures LLP and others v Mankarious and others* [2014] Ch 1 (CA); *Shell UK Ltd and others v Total UK Ltd and others Total UK Ltd v Chevron Ltd* (2010) 180 EWCA Civ (CA). See the discussion on whether some principles, especially those in *Saunders v Vautier* or *Baker v Archer-Shee*, deviated beneficiary rights in equity towards strong rights close to common law rights, in Kam Fam Sin, *The Legal Nature of the Unit Trust* (Oxford University Press, 1997) 114 et seq and 264 et seq. See also J Getzler, 'Transplantation and Mutation in Anglo-American Trust Law' (2009) 10 *Theoretical Inquiries in Law* 355, 369.

Another myth, this time in tax law, is that beneficial ownership is the person to whom income or assets have to be allocated in tax law. As previously stated, beneficial ownership of course follows ability to pay, and if property is defined by the beneficial owner in equity, income has to be allocated to him or her. But there are several cases where equity does not provide the answer as to who is the owner of the income or assets at large.[6] And there are some cases in which taxpayers arrange their contracts to try to take advantage of allocation rules. The question is how do tax law allocation rules apply to such cases and how do they relate to beneficial ownership in equity?

The third chapter deals with those cases in the tax law of the UK, the USA and Canada, countries which have developed allocation of income principles that try to overcome the issues of beneficial ownership being suspended or being uncertain. The result is a corpus of beneficial ownership tax principles. However, this chapter does not aim to analyse all the tax rules in relation to equity cases. Instead; the objective is to analyse the main rationales behind the tax rules in those cases in order to shed light on the principles applicable to allocation of income in equity cases.

The next myth is the meaning of beneficial ownership in international tax law.[7] The issue is actually a clash of legal traditions and the consequence of a legal transplant. When the USA and the UK started to discuss their first tax treaties, beneficial ownership was a key – but non-explicit – concept in their tax law systems, relating to the important matter of taxing according to ability to pay. On the other side, civil law countries did not know what such a concept was. There was also an increasing concern in countries from both legal systems about tax avoidance. The interposition of subjects, to which beneficial ownership relates, was a key issue for avoidance purposes. In the end, beneficial ownership in equity law was a matter of the interposition of subjects. The issue is, how was beneficial ownership transplanted to international tax law? Has it carried its meaning over from common law countries?

The fourth chapter is the bridge connecting beneficial ownership in the domestic law of common law countries and in international tax law. The chapter explains how the concept departed from those countries and was then reshaped to serve international tax law. This helps in understanding the different conceptions of the term in those countries and in international matters.

The fifth chapter deals with the meaning of beneficial ownership in tax treaties. Because the term departed from common law countries and was adapted to serve the ownership and tax systems of civil law countries, and was aimed at intermediaries, its meaning achieved a new dimension.

In the European Union, the myth deals with how beneficial ownership contained in the Interest and Royalties Directive relates to the concept as defined in the OECD Model Tax Convention and its Commentary, and how the interpretation of the Directive may influence the interpretation of tax treaties. The sixth chapter deals with this issue.

[6] Apparently following equity, though subject to criticism and controversy for a long time, *Baker (Inspector of Taxes) v Archer Shee* (n 5); following an anti-avoidance principle in the USA, *Moline Properties Inc v Commissioner of Internal Revenue* (1943) 319 US 436.

[7] For a good picture of the discussion, see D Oliver et al, 'Beneficial Ownership' (2000) 54 *Bulletin for International Taxation* 310.

Also in international law, beneficial ownership has been used for some decades in instruments for obtaining and exchanging information in the prevention of crimes such as drug trafficking, terrorism, proliferation and money laundering.[8] From there it has entered into exchange of information for tax matters. The myth questions how beneficial ownership as a concept linked to some extent to ownership/ability to pay is related to identification in the prevention of crime.

Finally, the seventh and last chapter considers such an issue. Because the concept definitions are taken from such instruments for prevention of crimes, it is doubtful they can serve their purpose. In addition, because the terms are not properly serving their purpose, proportionality concerns regarding the right to privacy arise.

The last myth, connecting all the previous ones, is beneficial ownership as a single concept. Analysis of the previous ones may allow us to answer this one.

[8] See Global Forum on Transparency and Exchange of Information for Tax Purposes, *Exchange of Information on Request: Handbook for Peer Reviews 2016–2020*, 3rd edn (OECD Publishing, 2016) 19 et seq. See also ss 1.1(e) and 2.2(a) of the Multilateral Competent Authority Agreement for the Common Reporting Standard, signed in Berlin on 29 October 2014. OECD, *Standard for Automatic Exchange of Financial Account Information in Tax Matters*, 2nd edn (OECD Publishing, 2017) 57.

2

Beneficial Ownership: From Conscience to Liberalism and Law

I. The Historical Evolution of Beneficial Ownership and Relation to Other Concepts

A. From Conscience to Law: Thirteenth to Eighteenth Centuries

It is widely accepted that current beneficial ownership principles are derived from equitable ownership in trusts and the *cestui que* use in uses, as were developed by the Court of Chancery between the fourteenth and nineteenth centuries.[1] What is less clear is its primary origin.

Some authors consider beneficial ownership to be based on the fiduciary rights in Roman law, as was widely accepted until the end of the nineteenth century; others consider it to be derived from German *Treuhand*.[2] More doubtful origins or relationships considered by some authors are Roman law usufruct, Islamic waqf, term of years, lease and other similar rights on estate or chattels.[3] A final group of scholars consider it to be the evolution of different institutions to serve the same social need.[4] In the author's view, most of these relationships are dubious, as the historical analysis is simply based on the common structure and wording, which may well be founded on historical mistakes or deviations.[5] Moreover, most studies on the origin of the trust were done in the nineteenth century, following a significant increase in its use for estate planning. Thus, it is highly likely that such studies are biased by the liberal trends and Romanistic inclinations of that century, triggered in continental Europe by the Historical School of Jurisprudence.

[1] R Pearce, J Stevens and W Barr, *The Law of Trusts and Equitable Obligations*, 5th edn (Oxford University Press, 2010) 56; GG Bogert and AM Hess, *Trust and Trustees*, vol 1, 3rd edn (West, 2007) 17; JH Baker, *An Introduction to English Legal History* (Butterworths, 2002) 248 et seq.

[2] On the controversial ultimate origin of trusts see OW Holmes Jr, 'Early English Equity' [1885] *Law Quarterly Review* 162, 163–70; FW Maitland, 'The Origin of Uses' (1894) 8 *Harvard Law Review* 127; JB Ames, 'The Origin of Uses and Trusts' (1908) 21 *Harvard Law Review* 261; AVW Thomas, 'Note on the Origin of Uses and Trusts – WAQFS' (1949) 3 *Southwestern Law Journal* 162.

[3] W Blackstone, *Commentaries on the Laws of England*, vol 1 (Bancroft-Whitney, 1915) 1156; Thomas (n 2).

[4] V Vasey, 'Fideicommissa and Uses: The Clerical Connection Revisited' (1982) 17 *The Jurist* 201.

[5] For arguments on its coincidence of structure and wording see Holmes (n 2); Maitland (n 2). Questioning the arguments of structure and words on which Maitland and Holmes, among others, based their arguments for the Roman or Germanic origin, see DWM Waters, 'The Nature of the Trust Beneficiary's Interest' (1967) 45 *Canadian Bar Review* 219, 220 et seq.

Beneficial ownership as it stands today is probably related to some extent to all of the above-mentioned concepts in that it is derived from common legal ideas to answer a common social need, but not directly comparable to any of them.[6] It is only in relation to trusts and uses that it seems there is a strong direct relationship shown by primary sources. This connection can be traced as far back as the thirteenth or fourteenth century but no further, and even with uses and trusts, the concept has gone through so many social, economic and political changes since the thirteenth century that it may well be sceptical even to assert that beneficial ownership bears any resemblance to how uses interests and beneficiary rights were understood at the time. From a soft obligation in conscience in the thirteenth century, with little or no legal force, the concept has evolved into beneficial ownership today, implying some *in rem* rights.[7] This evolution may be better understood in parallel to the evolution of ownership rights since then.

The Norman Conquest of England developed a significant evolution of ownership rights. In this period, feudal rights to land by tenants in demesne, or copyholders, mesne, tenants in chief or the king himself have some resemblance with the split of ownership under beneficial ownership today.[8]

In a feudal property structure, tenants in demesne have immediate rights to use and enjoy. Whilst to qualify this as ownership may be doubtful, its character of interest in the land is beyond any doubt.[9] However, this tenure was acquired upon a broad legal relationship with the lord or the king that goes beyond the right in the land, being in several cases the right to land subject to others or at least tied. Kings and lords also had simultaneous interests or incidents in the land of different intensity that were linked to the rights of the tenant, and were sometimes able to withdraw the rights from the tenant under certain circumstances.[10] Nevertheless, far from an absolute right, it seems that excessive exercise of lordship over the rights of the tenant to the land was not considered an act according to a legal conscience, more a matter of force.[11] All in all, according to common law or custom, upon failing to comply with incidents, treason, voluntary surrender of the land to the lord or other reasons, the land may return to the lord – or king in royal demesne – the lord himself thus having some beneficiary rights.[12] But even in some of these cases, such as in the case of death or voluntary surrender, the tenant was regarded as having some kind of primitive right to suggest that the lord give livery of seisen to his son or another person and, even in later times, inheritability and

[6] Stating nobody has traced directly the origin Vasey (n 4) 204.

[7] See Blackstone (n 3) 1159–69; F Bacon, *The Reading Upon the Statute of Uses* (William Henry Rowe 1804) 5 et seq; JB Ames, *Lectures on Legal History* (Harvard University Press, 1913) 238; F Pollock and FW Maitland, *History of English Law*, vol 2, 2nd edn (Cambridge University Press, 1968) 232; Pearce et al (n 1) 80–81; GG Bogert and HS Shapo, *Trust and Trustees*, vol 3, 2rd edn (West, 2012) 512. And compare to *Shell UK Ltd and others v Total UK Ltd and others Total UK Ltd v Chevron Ltd* (2010) 180 EWCA Civ (CA); *Saunders v Vautier* (1841) 42 ER 282 (Ct of Chancery); *Baker (Inspector of Taxes) v Archer Shee* [1927] AC 844 (HL).

[8] E Jenks, *A Short History of English Law* (Methuen and Co, 1949) 101.

[9] ibid 26 et seq; Baker (n 1) 223–43; F Pollock and FW Maitland, *History of English Law*, vol 1, 2nd edn (Cambridge University Press, 1968) 2–8, 232 et seq.

[10] Baker (n 1) 230–36, 237–38; Pollock and Maitland (n 9) 236–238; Jenks (n 8) 44. On the doubtful character of ownership in feudal tenure see Pollock and Maitland (n 7) 2–8.

[11] Baker (n 1) 231–35.

[12] ibid 237–39; Jenks (n 8) 36 et seq; AWB Simpson, *An Introduction to the History of Land Law*, reprint from 1st edn (Oxford University Press, 1964) 46 et seq.

alienation of certain free tenancies would be recognised.[13] In addition, in certain cases of abuse of the lord, some rights of appeal to the king were available, in a form of a basic set of actions that in time would end up forming common law.[14] Further, some feudal incidents attached to the land provided the lord and/or king with beneficiary rights over the land, its production or certain services.[15] This was not too different to the structure of European feudalism and was probably derived from barbarian invasions that took place all around Europe in medieval times.[16]

From this perspective, it can be said that the tenant, the mesne, the tenant in chief or the king had certain beneficiary rights on the land, and at the same time it might be said that the king, tenant in chief or mesne had some kind of formal or legal ownership of the land during the time the tenant was in possession of the land.[17] However, any similarity between such a structure of tenure and beneficial ownership only follows our biased contemporary view on ownership as the relationship between subjects and land. The relationship at that time was very different and tenure in feudal society was part of a complex set of relationships that bound lords and vassals in different ways, while ownership after the nineteenth century is a much simpler, independent, comprehensive and more absolute concept compared to such feudal relationships.[18] While feudal tenure was difficult or impossible to understand without other social and feudal bonds, current liberal ownership is largely regarded as a stand-alone concept, and while feudal tenure was not a pure right *in rem* – probably because there was no proper development of rights *in rem* – liberal ownership is built as an *erga omnes* direct relationship with the object.[19]

After a set of rights similar to proprietary rights today were progressively recognised around the twelfth and thirteenth centuries, some limits still applied to tenure of land. Among them, it seems that the main disruption in the economic and social system, based on land ownership, was the prohibition of devising land upon will.[20] In addition, uses were also probably used to allow the transfer of property to persons who were limited in their rights to property, such as religious communities, infants or women, to avoid feudal incidents, to protect property, to avoid creditors and even for other fraudulent purposes.[21] The obsolete concepts of interest in properties of medieval times did not fit modern needs, triggering uses upon uses or modern age trusts: precedents of contemporary trusts.[22] This contributed to the move towards contemporary ownership,

[13] Jenks (n 8) 35–37, 106–07; Simpson (n 12) 16–17, 112 et seq; Baker (n 1) 239, 248.

[14] Baker (n 1) 230–37; Pollock and Maitland (n 7) 2–8.

[15] Baker (n 1) 226–29, 237; Simpson (n 12) 7–23; Pollock and Maitland (n 9) 240 et seq.

[16] J Castán Tobeñas, *Derecho Civil Español, Común y Foral*, vol 2, decimocuarta edición (Reus, 1992) 109.

[17] Simpson (n 12) 44–46; Pollock and Maitland (n 7) 6–9.

[18] Baker (n 1) 230; Simpson (n 12) 44–45; J Christman, *The Myth of Property: Toward an Egalitarian Theory of Ownership* (Oxford University Press, 1994) 17–18.

[19] Pollock and Maitland (n 7) 77.

[20] Baker (n 1) 249.

[21] Simpson (n 12) 164, 171–72; Jenks (n 8) 95–97. Hudson mentions fraud and fear as driving uses and trust: A Hudson, *Equity and Trusts* (Routledge, 2017) 50.

[22] As uses became prohibited by the Statute of Uses, 1536, it seems trusts became the word for referring to surviving uses, such as terms of years for the use of another person, uses upon uses or active uses, and uses became the word for those repealed by the statute.

as well as building in parallel immediate types of provisional solutions, uses and trusts to deal with those cases. The relationship of the uses with trusts today, however, has to be carefully considered.

To solve the inconveniences of limits of interest in land, tenants would convey the land to the hands of another person – feoffee to uses – and bind them by solemn oath to hold the land for the benefit of another person – *cestui que* use – to transfer it, in turn, at a certain event to another person, or to manage it under certain instructions.[23]

The protection of the use and effects of the obligation by the transferee to fulfil its commitments was only a conscience and social obligation at first instance. Its strength was confined to the breach of uses as against ecclesiastical conscience.[24] However, given the lack of protection under common law, the Court of Chancery soon gave protection to such beneficiary rights.[25] Entrusting the Great Seal to ecclesiastics introduced conscience to the Chancery and beneficiary rights of *cestui que* use progressively gained the protection of the Court of Chancery.[26] Although not homogeneous and *erga omnes* in the first stage, a well-established set of principles gave enough grounds to foster the expansion of uses. A progressive recognition by legislation and common law courts in the fourteenth and fifteenth centuries consolidated the uses as a legal concept.[27] Within this period, uses lived in a permanent state of tension between its recognition by the Court of Chancery on the one hand and parliamentary and royal attempts to set limits on its use for fraudulent purposes on the other.[28] It was precisely this tension that eventually led to the end of uses in the sixteenth century with the Statutes of Uses, triggered by a sharp decrease in the Crown and lords' revenues due to the inability to collect incidents and other levies on lands enfeoffed for the use of another.[29]

Nonetheless, the prohibition of uses and conversion of *cestui que* uses rights to common law property did not cover terms of years for the use of another person or uses upon a use, and it seems it was never intended to cover active uses.[30] Thus, after the initial decrease in uses, the doctrine regained interest, but not to enable wills, now permitted, but to avoid creditors, to plan succession, to preserve secrecy, to allow estate planning and land ownership, and, more recently, to evolve into the modern concept of trust.[31] In the sixteenth century, chancellor jurisdiction evolved from a Court of Conscience to a Court of Equity, from an ecclesiastical court to a court of law, highly influenced by the common law origins of new chancellors.[32] Thus, in the sixteenth to eighteenth centuries, the Court of Chancery developed a set of principles on trust and beneficial ownership that, even though based on previous uses, could be regarded as rules and law as compared to conscience and case-by-case previous uses.[33] These principles

[23] Simpson (n 12) 163; Blackstone (n 3) 1156 et seq.
[24] Jenks (n 8) 97; Baker (n 1) 250.
[25] Simpson (n 12) 166; Baker (n 1) 250–51.
[26] Jenks (n 8) 211–12.
[27] Baker (n 1) 251; Simpson (n 12) 173–74; Jenks (n 8) 98.
[28] Simpson (n 12) 172–175.
[29] Baker (n 1) 253–57; Simpson (n 12) 173; Jenks (n 8) 99–100; Pearce et al (n 1) 56–57; Blackstone (n 3) 1168.
[30] Jenks (n 8) 100–01; Simpson (n 12) 182–86; Baker (n 1) 290–92.
[31] Baker (n 1) 291.
[32] Jenks (n 8) 213–15.
[33] Simpson (n 12) 194; Jenks (n 8) 222–23; Baker (n 1) 309.

of trusts would form the basis of modern-day beneficial ownership, even though several distinctions may be found between them.

Comparing uses with modern-day beneficial ownership, the former seems to have little to no resemblance other than being the latter's historical precedent. While nowadays beneficial ownership is enforceable before courts in general upon its relevant rights, rights of *cestui que* uses had little enforceability in their initial stages, and recently no enforceability in regular jurisdiction. Only in equity was the right enforceable, although subjected to conscience on a case-by-case basis. It was still not recognised as a formal legal right in the contemporary sense, although it could be considered as a primitive legal right. Most scholars consider uses were never meant to have any right over the object or right *in rem* other than an obligation in conscience, while current beneficial ownership is frequently regarded as an *in rem* right, an *in rem* interest or having a partial *in rem* right, and in some cases even an *erga omnes* right.[34] Where they largely resemble modern-day trusts is in their effect and late function in avoiding incidents and taxes on the land. In this regard, history shows a constant swing movement from the fourteenth century to today, from the protection of trusts and the extension of its use to attempts to limit its fraudulent and tax avoidance effects.

As per the modern age trust, current beneficial ownership is based on equitable interest as developed on the basis of uses by the Court of Chancery in the late seventeenth and early eighteenth centuries. The resemblance between the two of them is obvious as an immediate precedent. However, there are several differences. It is doubtful whether the *in rem* character of beneficial ownership was clear before the nineteenth century. The doubtful *in rem* or *in personam* character is probably due to the fact that this distinction was not embraced by English law until the revival of Roman law and the influence of the civil law revolution in the nineteenth century, in part due to the works of John Austin.[35] Until then, beneficiary rights were probably not defined as an *in rem* right, nor an *in personam* right, but as an action in equity upon which the *cestui que* use was given executory court rights to prevent other persons from acting on the object, or to oblige the trustee to perform.[36] This is proven by the fact that before the nineteenth century there was no reference to beneficial ownership at all but to the expressions *cestui que* trust, benefit or, at most, beneficiary or interest.[37] It was not until the late nineteenth and early twentieth centuries that beneficial ownership wording gained use.

B. Liberal Sense of Ownership and Beneficial Ownership

The French Revolution was paramount to the progression of law, and in particular ownership rights, that took place through the medieval and modern ages. It was a major

[34] Baker (n 1) 309; Pollock and Maitland (n 7) 226. See discussion in Waters (n 5).

[35] Waters (n 5); Maitland (n 2) 131; J Austin, *Lectures on Jurisprudence*, vol 1, 5th edn (John Murray, 1911) 364 et seq.

[36] For a summary on the discussion of the *in rem* or *in personam* character of beneficiary interest, see Waters (n 5). See ss II.A(iv) and II.B(i) below.

[37] H Godefroi, *The Law of Trusts and Trustees* (Stevens & Sons, 1879) ia 353, 358 et seq; T Lewin, *A Practical Treatise on The Law of Trusts and Trustees*, 2nd edn (Maxwell & Son, 1842) ia 759–64; FW Maitland and J Brunyate, *Equity* (Cambridge University Press, 1936) 331.

disruption on all aspects of law and in all developed legal systems. This even affected England and Wales, regardless of the uniqueness of its legal system in comparison to continental law.

Proprietary rights and ownership were at the very core of the revolutionary principles and legal developments of the nineteenth century.[38] Ownership was understood by revolutionaries as a major means for achieving the moral objectives of equality and freedom of individuals, so the protection against any interference by others or the state was a priority in revolutionary legal developments.[39] The revival of Roman law also played a major role – or was used as an argumentative tool – in establishing a liberal understanding of ownership. Ownership became a much simpler, more absolute and stronger idea compared to previous modern age ownership or ancient ownership, which was complex, intricate and related to other relationships.[40]

Beneficial interest was also affected by the revolutionary winds. Legal works in the nineteenth century, especially those by Blackstone and Austin, influenced a change in the English legal view of ownership.[41] This change ultimately led in the nineteenth century and beginning of the twentieth century to the abolition of the last medieval legal characteristics of ownership, although most of them were already not enforced. In 1925, estate in fee simple was established as the paramount single and absolute ownership concept in England's legal system.[42] The expansive effects of the liberal view on property probably influenced nineteenth-century developments on beneficiary rights, leading courts to progressively reinforce beneficiary interests in the nineteenth and early twentieth centuries.[43] In addition, the merging of common law and equity law jurisdictions in 1873 contributed to the progressive development of a harmony between beneficial entitlement and legal ownership.[44] Even though two different proprietary rights were recognised, a common body of proprietary rules could be identified.

In the meantime, the nineteenth century saw a sharp increase in the use of trusts to hold property or for estate planning purposes, probably due to the new understanding of ownership, economic industrialisation, change in capital conceptions and maybe

[38] See TE Kaiser, 'Property, Sovereignty, the Declaration of Rights of Man, and the Tradition of French Jurisprudence' in D Van Kley (ed), *The French Idea of Freedom: The Old Regime and the Declaration of Rights of 1789* (Stanford University Press, 1994).

[39] ibid 330.

[40] Christman (n 18) 18–19; Castán Tobeñas (n 16) 135–36.

[41] The importation of revolutionary liberal and absolute ownership into common law has been attributed to Blackstone as he defines ownership as 'that sole and despotic dominion which one man claims and exercises over the external things of the world in total exclusion of the right of any other individual in the universe'. This is not surprising, as his quotes show he is following liberal works by Bentham, Locke, Mill Grotius or Montesquieu that inspired the French Revolution. By doing so, it seems he departs from the previous medieval propriety system to blend French absolute ownership and the common law proprietary system. See Blackstone (n 3) 707 et seq; J Austin, *Lectures on Jurisprudence*, vol 2, 5th edn (John Murray, 1911) 790.

[42] The final abolition of services such as military services and other remaining feudal incidents during the nineteenth century that eventually led to final repeal under the Law of Property Act 1925 is seen as the result of revolutionary and liberal developments in ownership concepts. From that time on, legal ownership and fee simple in absolute would be regarded as synonymous with common law systems unless otherwise provided for.

[43] Waters points out that courts have been asserting beneficiary interest in trust property since the first half of the 19th century, matching the legal influence of liberal developments in most legal systems, even though the proprietary nature of such interest may be controversial. Waters (n 5) 281.

[44] Supreme Court of Judicature Act, 1873, s 24.

the development of contemporary taxes.[45] Ultimately this increase in the use of trusts attracted the attention of scholars.[46] The author's view is that it is highly likely that change in how ownership was understood, together with the increase in the use of trusts, led to an evolution of beneficiary interests, including certain *in rem* and *erga omnes* effects in some cases.[47] The increase in the use of beneficial ownership wording at this time, incorporating the strong connotation of ownership to beneficiary interests, is probably a proof of this evolution.

Not surprisingly, the *in rem–in personam* binomial from which Maitland derived the controversy on beneficiary interest was brought to common law by Austin, also considered one of the early supporters of the new liberal understanding of ownership in common law, and whose works are absolutely influenced by Roman law.[48] Even though Maitland was trying to convince that beneficial interest was not an *in rem* right, by framing the issue in the *in rem–in personam* and absolute ownership Austinian frame to which the concept did not pertain, he led the path to the contemporary partial *in rem* characterisation of the concept.[49] Thus, *Archer-Shee v Baker*, at the very beginning of the twentieth century, has been seen by some as a recognition of the *in rem* character of beneficiaries' interest, but not without heavy criticism.[50]

This does not mean beneficial ownership – or beneficial interest in some cases – has lost its flexible and casuistic character, nor that English law has lost its singularity in splitting ownership between legal and beneficial ownership. However, it is beyond any doubt that the concept has clearer definition lines today and has wider and stronger effects than its immediate ancestor.

II. Beneficial Ownership Nowadays

A. Contemporary Ownership

The definition of ownership has always been considered to be a highly complex social, economic and legal phenomenon.[51] The main discussion lies, broadly speaking, in considering ownership as a more or less absolute and comprehensive concept, or different sets of rights, privileges, claims and others that may be disaggregated.[52] The revival

[45] Pearce et al (n 1) 57.

[46] Maitland (n 2); Holmes (n 2); Maitland and Brunyate (n 37). The fact that independent treatises on the topic were published in the nineteenth century gives an idea of the importance the issue attracted. Baker (n 1); Godefroi (n 37); Lewin (n 37).

[47] For an excellent explanation of the issue and the development of the discussion in the late 19th century and early 20th century see Waters (n 5).

[48] Austin (n 35) 364 et seq; Waters (n 5); Maitland and Brunyate (n 37) 106 et seq; Austin (n 41) 790.

[49] Waters (n 5) ia 224.

[50] *Baker (Inspector of Taxes) v Archer-Shee* (n 7). HG Hanbury, 'Periodical Menace to Equitable Principles' (1928) 44 *LQR* 468.

[51] Christman (n 18) 17; S Munzer, *A Theory of Property* (Cambridge University Press, 1990) 15–17.

[52] Christman (n 18) 16–22; Munzer (n 51) 17–27. Many authors frame ownership analysis in Hohfeld's distinction between rights, privileges, power and immunities. However, some of them regard ownership as one of them while others tend to see ownership as not fully attainable to one of them, though its incidents qualify under such normative categories. In this regard, see Munzer (n 51) 17–27; Reinhard-DeRoo (n 1) 31–37.

of the liberal view of ownership during the eighteenth and nineteenth centuries moved the discussion on again to the position it is in today.[53]

Defence of a more liberal and comprehensive bulk concept, or a disaggregated view, largely follows the positions taken on the main issues that surround ownership. This includes: (i) essential characteristics, incidents or rights that define ownership; (ii) how ownership is projected onto subjects and objects; (iii) the difference between ownership rights and other types of rights, such as contractual rights; and (iv) whether claims or contractual rights are able to be owned. A final position – whether ownership rights are derived or constitute natural rights – falls outside the scope of this study.[54] As a ground for our work, it is the author's view that nowadays understanding of ownership can only be justified on a social positive ground.[55]

Regarding the first issue, beneficial ownership is usually defined from a legal perspective by its three classic characteristics: *ius utendi*, *ius fruendi* and *ius dispondendi* or *ius abutendi*.[56] The spread of this view follows the liberal interpretation of ownership developed in the nineteenth century through the (re)interpretation of Roman property law. The political framework of the nineteenth century developed such an understanding of property that it needed a strong concept. From this viewpoint, early liberal ownership normally refers to the three legal rights to be vested in a subject almost in an absolute manner.[57] Divided rights on a property were – and still are to some – not seen as proprietary rights themselves, but as incidents on the property of another person.[58] This view tends to see that there is only one property and not a broader concept that may cover different rights which can be vested in different persons. However, it is an oversimplification of the issue, probably from a deviated Roman understanding of ownership,[59] and, if it ever had any existence, this was probably only for a brief period immediately after the revolutionary waves.[60]

[53] Christman (n 18) 18–19.

[54] Among the leading discussions in this matter are those by Locke and Hegel: J Locke, *Second Treatise of Government* (Harlan Davidson, 1982) 17 et seq; GWF Hegel, *Hegel's Philosophy of Right* (Oxford University Press, 1952) para 41 et seq. More recent discussions took place in the 1990s following the fall of the Soviet Union. See these more recent discussions in Christman (n 18) 47 et seq; S Buckle, *Natural Law and the Theory of Property: Grotius to Hume* (Oxford University Press, 1993); Munzer (n 51); CM Rose, 'Property as the Keystone Right' (1995) 71 *Notre Dame Law Review* 329; JW Harris, *Property and Justice* (Oxford University Press, 1996).

[55] See, eg Harris (n 54); L Murphy and T Nagel, *Myth of Ownership* (Oxford University Press, 2002) 45.

[56] Christman (n 18) 19; Pearce et al (n 1) 46; Castán Tobeñas (n 16) 180. See also Lawson and Rudden as quoted by Pearce et al (n 1).

[57] Even though absolute ownership is controversial as no legal system ever seemed to recognise property without taxation, subjection to public interest or right to expropriation. Christman (n 18) 15, 22. On the current view of a comprehensive ownership see S Van Erp and B Akkermans (eds), *Cases, Materials and Text on Property Law* (Hart Publishing, 2012) 219.

[58] Austin (n 41) 847–48.

[59] Ownership did not have any absolute characteristics even in Rome, as in such ancient times incidents on property such as taxes or state abilities on the property were recognised. Christman (n 18) 17. Stating that Roman ownership was subject to limitations, absolute reference being in relation to excluding other people, the concept having a unity and being disengaged from superiority, P Birks, 'The Roman Law Concept of Dominium and the Idea of Absolute Ownership' [1985] *Acta Juridica* 1.

[60] Christman (n 18) 16–19.

(i) The Basket Approach and Control as Commanding Key

Conversely, AM Honoré's well-known work better considers ownership as a broader and complex concept that may include: (i) right to possess; (ii) right to use; (iii) right to manage; (iv) right to the income; (v) right to the capital; (vi) right to security; (vii) the incident of transmissibility; (viii) the incident of absence of term; (ix) prohibition of harmful of use; (x) liability to execution; and (xi) its residuary character rights.[61] In theory, most of these characteristics may be referred to using the classic three characteristics,[62] but defining property as a bulk of those three characteristics is a broad-brush painting that loses many nuances of property, leading to misunderstandings. Conversely, disaggregating ownership rights may lead to a blurred understanding of ownership and possible loss of its social and economic importance, even making it unable to perform important roles, such as measuring wealth in order to be able to build a redistributive structure.[63]

It is clear that, even if it is a complex concept, any individual in the world can talk to another about things they 'control', 'benefit from' or 'own', and they would have a common core idea in their minds.[64] Any contemporary society recognises the ability of subject to deal with objects as 'owners', and globalisation may be driving a progressive convergence between different systems. There should be a common central core that, with several shades, defines ownership.

Honoré leaves this question open to a degree by defining ownership as *the greatest interest in a thing which a mature law system recognises.*[65] An analysis of the above-mentioned characteristics within the relevant legal system and the case at stake will lead to a consideration of ownership. The definition recognises the possibility of holding ownership without having one or more of the mentioned characteristics, rejecting a bulk approach.[66] On the other hand, by pointing to the greatest interest, he recognises that ownership should comprise a large or the largest part of such rights.

The question is whether such rights should be balanced quantitatively (the holder of most of those rights) or qualitatively (some of those rights weigh more than others), or both. For Honoré, it seems the key characteristic is control, including the right to decide on use, the right to exclude others, the right to alienate and immunity to expropriation.[67] Similarly, Christman points to primary functional control and the primary right to income flows as ownership-defining characteristics.[68] This does not mean the rest of the above-mentioned rights are not able to define ownership or

[61] AM Honoré, 'Ownership' in P Smith (ed), *The Nature and Process of Law: An Introduction to Legal Philosophy* (Oxford University Press, 1993) 371–75.

[62] Christman (n 18) 29.

[63] Munzer (n 51) 31–36; Christman (n 18) 20–23.

[64] Honoré (n 61) 370.

[65] ibid; Christman (n 18) 25–26. Similarly, D Greenberg, K Banaszak and Y Greenberg (eds), *Jowitt's Dictionary of English Law*, vol 2, 4th edn (Sweet & Maxwell, 2015) 1729.

[66] Honoré (n 61) 370.

[67] ibid 370–71.

[68] Christman (n 18) 22. See also FH Lawson and B Rudden, *The Law of Property* (Clarendon Press, 1982) 8, although they divide right to income. Although obscure and adding nuances in a view that is critical towards Honoré, it seems that Harris argues in a similar vein, at least from a preliminary and social perspective: Harris (n 54) ch 8. On property, see Pearce et al (n 1) 45.

are irrelevant. However, at least from a strictly legal view, rights to control and income define the primary premise of ownership and are preliminary clues to understanding ownership, a proper analysis of all the rights at stake in the relevant legal system being necessary. Thus, in most legal systems, the rights to primary control and income would, prima facie, define ownership, unless the rest of the characteristics vested in another person outweighed such rights. In addition, primary rights to control and income may be divided into positive and negative rights, the first being the ability to positively control and decide or enjoy the property, the latter being the ability to exclude third parties.[69]

(ii) The Relationship of Ownership with Objects and Subjects

Ownership, as an *in rem* right, is commonly defined as the right falling, the subject of the right being or the right deriving from the object itself.[70] This is connected to the idea that rights *in rem* are normally negative rights before third parties, while rights *in personam* are positive rights or duties to perform in a certain way or, in a negative sense, not to harm.[71] The premise of proprietary rights falling on objects is absolutely misleading as objects cannot be subjects of rights, nor can they derive any right per se, as rights necessarily refer to persons as instruments for regulating social living.[72] Ownership rights, as *in rem* rights, are characterised as being vested in a subject, against other persons, most frequently any person, and in relation to a thing.[73] Thus, where the right actually falls is on the passive persons of the right, even though the fact refers to an object. Conversely, the fact or object of an *in personam* right is a certain behaviour. The confusion lies in the second case, where the fact is mixed with the subjects, as the legal pattern refers to the subjects as both subjects entitled and part of the fact pattern. Moreover, *in rem* rights not only give negative rights by limiting third parties' use or control of the property or estate, but may also oblige the owner to perform certain duties, such as to use the property in a certain way, urban planning or administrative coercion – or to pay taxes. It is true that this last argument has been heavily criticised under the reasoning that those are general obligations and absolute, not being a government legal right against its subjects,[74] but from the author's view, following Murphy and Nagel, a general principle of developed legal systems in relation to ownership is the duty to pay taxes. The legal system regulates how ownership is acquired and regulated, but at the same time and on an equal footing with ownership regulation, the law requires the taxee to pay taxes in relation to his estate or income position as part of the social contract, and even law may

[69] R Nolan, 'Equitable Property' (2006) 122 *LQR* 232, 236–37.

[70] Austin (n 41) 786; Christman (n 18) 16–17; Castán Tobeñas (n 16) 37.

[71] Classical medieval–Roman distinction refers to *in rem* and *in personam* rights; more recent distinctions referred to real rights, contractual rights and civil liability. Austin (n 41) 784 et seq; Christman (n 18) 21; Pearce et al (n 1) 47; Austin (n 35) 370 et seq; Castán Tobeñas (n 16) 33 et seq; A Colin and H Capitant, *Cours Élementaire de Droit Civil Français*, vol 2, dixième edn (Dalloz, 1948) 6.

[72] Christman (n 18) 16. Harris, despite recognising that ownership is essentially a social idea, at least from a legal perspective, argues that the layman reference to ownership of the thing directly is not completely incorrect as it serves to organise ideas and principles. Harris (n 54) 120.

[73] Christman (n 18) 23 et seq; Pearce et al (n 1) 45.

[74] Austin (n 41) 785.

enable the seizure of property in some cases if taxes are not paid.[75] Not understanding the relationship between taxes, property and their attachment within the same legal and political system derives from an idea surviving from the old regime of taxes as a power relationship which does not stand up in contemporary liberal legal systems that base taxes on the idea of obligations.[76]

The misunderstanding on how *in rem* rights relate to third parties and to the object is one of the reasons why ownership is largely misinterpreted as an absolute right. The understanding of the right of the owner as falling directly on the object to satisfy his or her will and without intermediary logical steps, and not framed within a constitutional order or social contract – with several nuances – leads to a consideration that ownership overrides any other legal relationship. In the author's view, *in rem* rights and ownership rights can only be understood as negative rights in most cases, with certain positive obligations imposed by the relevant legal system and framed within the set of rights and obligations defined by the relevant political, legal and social order.

(iii) Joint Ownership and Legal Persons

Active subjects of ownership may be persons in the widest sense, including individuals and corporations.[77] Ownership could also be held jointly by different subjects without any incorporation, even though the arrangements on how property should be controlled and managed may add nuances to the characteristics of ownership. Under a liberal view, it may be said that each owner's right in a joint ownership cannot be considered as a full liberal and independent ownership.[78] However, once the absolute view is discarded, such arrangements and rules on managing joint property are seen as not limiting ownership rights themselves, but how decisions are made. Such rules fall on a prior step on how decisions are taken, but not on the ability to take decisions about the property. Such rules define how decisions are achieved within the co-ownership, but, once achieved, there is only one decision in relation to the property that affects all owners – both those agreeing with the decision and those not. But that does not mean the ones who disagree do not have control. The decision taken is also within their control, but achieved through consensus or votes. The control is jointly held by the co-owners, with the consequence that decisions on control have to be taken jointly. However, ownership is not required to be vested in a single subject. The same issue, with the same conclusion, arises on publicly owned property or assets, such as parks or roads.[79] It is a matter of

[75] Nagel and Murphy (n 55) 44. In a similar vein, some authors, such as Rigaud, claim that *in rem* rights against the world are public law rights and not private rights, thus falling within the same sphere of taxes: Castán Tobeñas (n 16) 37.

[76] As Baez Moreno points out in the relationship between private law and taxes, protection against taxes no longer lies in private law and ownership as a prominent right over taxes seen as a power of the king, but in the legality and legal certainty as to the taxable event. Turning this idea to the taxes–ownership puzzle, a guarantee on property lies in the constitutional guarantees and procedures to establish taxes, not in the defence of an absolute ownership: A Baez, *Los Negocios Fiduciarios En La Imposición Sobre La Renta* (Aranzadi, 2009) 122.

[77] Christman (n 18) 23.

[78] See RJ Smith, *Plural Ownership* (Oxford University Press, 2005) 28 et seq. See in France, Arts 915 and 1873 of the *Code Civil*; in Spain, Art 392 of the *Código Civil*; and in Italy, Arts 1100 et seq of the *Codice Civile*.

[79] On public ownership see Christman (n 18) 23.

how the decisions are made, and not a matter of ownership, that is totally subjected to the control achieved through the system upon which decisions are made.

From an economic or social perspective, the issue could be more controversial. In the case of corporations, where the company owns assets or holds rights that, in turn, are owned by an individual, it might be said that the individual holds the ownership of the asset.[80] The case is of significant importance for closed and private corporations, especially if wholly or majority owned by a single individual.[81]

In the case of legal bodies, legal protection of the asset is usually not given directly to the individual, but to the company or body. The shareholder is not protected in relation to his or her rights on the property but on his or her right to control, manage and decide in relation to the corporation, while the rights on income and assets of the corporation, along with other rights, are given to the corporation. From a legal point of view, the individual shareholder is not the owner of the company assets. He or she has to follow certain steps to enforce his decision, and once that decision has turned into a company decision, it is executed in relation to the assets. Consequently, ownership rights have to be analysed carefully in each relationship. If one owns shares, those shares give certain specific rights, namely economic and political rights, to the corporation, but not directly to the underlying rights and duties held by the corporation. On the other side of the coin of limiting responsibility, management independence and other rights depending on the specific corporation or non-corporate vehicle, independence of the corporation also works to limit the right of the shareholder to corporation rights and assets, even though shareholders frequently misunderstand this dividing line.

This point on joint ownership and legal persons is relevant for beneficial ownership. An individual, in certain cases, may be said to have equitable ownership of property held by his or her wholly owned company. In this case, he or she has legal ownership of the shares and equitable ownership of the company assets. The legal system recognises both rights. This does not contradict the author's assertion. Equitable ownership will be recognised under certain requirements. If ownership is seen not as a whole but as a set of different rights, the shareholder will have certain rights on the shares and other rights on the assets of the company, without conflict.

(iv) In Rem *or* In Personam *Rights*

In relation to the previous answer, there is a question as to whether ownership rights are different from any other types of rights, such as contractual rights, as they derive from the Roman distinction of *in rem* and *in personam* rights.[82] As has been said, the discussion arises due to the revival and probably misunderstanding of liberal ownership in the nineteenth century.[83] As mentioned, rights *in rem* fall on objects, while rights

[80] Munzer (n 51) 320–45.

[81] See the extensive analysis on ownership, control and rights involved in relation to property and business corporations in ibid 317–79.

[82] Austin (n 41) 784; Castán Tobeñas (n 16) 34.

[83] Austin (n 35) 382. Castán argues that in Rome only actions *in rem* and *in personam* were considered, with glossators in medieval law being the ones that established the distinction between rights *in personam* and rights *in rem*. Castán Tobeñas (n 16) 34. On how these terms were improperly attributed Roman origins, see ibid 54. See also Austin (n 35) 369; Waters (n 5) 223.

in personam refer to another person performing or refraining from performing a certain action, or compensating an action.[84] Broadly speaking, *iura in rem* are considered to be against any person, and generally a negative right of prohibiting or limiting other persons' behaviour, whereas *iura in personam* refer to specific persons and not to the world at large, and could be positive or negative, ie they display a certain behaviour or not.[85] A third category may comprise both rights *in rem* and rights *in personam*.[86]

Some authors have challenged such distinctions in what has been called the unitary theory. The argument is that some flexible rights, as contractual-basis rights, cannot be easily distinguished from *in rem* principles.[87] They also argue that some rights, such as the right not to be harmed, have enforceable claims that are similar to those of property rights.[88] From this view, there is no significant distinction between the compensation from the infringement of the prohibition to enter my property and liability following a personal harm. Critics to such an approach state that it ignores the control element of property and just focuses on the income, use and enjoyment rights of ownership.[89] When control is a central element of ownership, property rights are significantly different for those critics. In this sense, one can legally protect and prevent the property from being used as much as one can, as a preliminary right which nobody can neither legally oppose nor interfere with – a privilege – while compensation from harm is just a legal consequence of illegal behaviour: a right to the owner, a duty to the trespasser.

From my viewpoint, both perspectives have inconveniences.[90] There is no doubt that there is a difference between personal rights and rights *in rem*, insofar as one provides a person to control and enjoy, and limit the rights of third parties, involving both privileges and claim-rights, while the other constitutes either an obligation to perform in a certain way or, in the case of liability for harm, an ex post compensation for a misbehaviour – a claim-right against a duty.[91] However, there might be several exceptions or cases where the two rights are similar or when one may follow the other in such a way that their differences may be blurred. As in almost all legal rules, exceptions are needed to maintain coherence. In the case of a car being used by a non-authorised third party, which triggers the obligation to compensate, there is no doubt the owner has the right of controlling and limiting use by third parties.[92] However, the owner has a personal right against such person for liabilities when they have unduly used the car. In this case, personal right is not a substitute for the real right and is clearly different from the ability of the holder to legally try to avoid the use of third parties or interference in his or her property as much as he or she can, but without entering into other prohibited behaviours against rights that will override his right, such as the right to life of others, but indeed supplements the right *in rem* in order to contribute to its enforcement, as well as the right to compensation for the harm caused.

[84] Austin (n 35) 370; Castán Tobeñas (n 16) 37.
[85] Austin (n 35) 370 et seq; Castán Tobeñas (n 16) 35.
[86] See Munzer (n 51) 25. See also the discussion on *universitas* in Austin (n 41) 784–85.
[87] TC Grey, 'The Disintegration of Property' (1980) 22 Nomos 69, 71.
[88] ibid 72.
[89] Christman (n 18) 21–22.
[90] For intermediary positions see Castán Tobeñas (n 16) 36 et seq.
[91] Following Hohfeld's well-known distinction. Munzer (n 51) 17–27.
[92] Example used by Grey (n 87) 72; Christman (n 18) 21.

However, more importantly, *in rem* rights fall within public order and may be considered to pertain to the public law sphere. Thus, the state may enforce *in rem* rights *ex officio*, while private law liability or personal rights can only be enforced by the creditor himself.[93] In the previous example of the car being used by a third person, if the trespasser does not bring the car back, public officers may stop him or her and bring the property back. However, public officers will not normally enforce the compensation.

In addition, a third category of rights on rights has been considered: *universities* of rights and duties.[94] Those rights could hardly be categorised as rights *in rem* or as rights *in personam*, because the right comprises a different set of rights that, in turn, may be *in rem* or *in personam*. Thus, the right may in some cases be exercised against any person and in other cases be exercised against a single person, and may sometimes be a negative prohibition and at other times be an obligation to perform.[95] However, in the author's view, this is not actually a third category. The fact that the right is tied together with other rights within a legal fiction does not alter its characteristics. In a different scenario, the right of the person to the *university* may, however, be considered independent from the right of the *university* itself.[96]

Within rights *in rem*, *dominium* and servitudes or *iura in re aliena* may be distinguished.[97] The difference is based on the absolute concept of ownership. *Dominium* is considered as the only *actual* ownership; improper rights on objects, such as mere use or enjoyment, are simply a right on somebody else's property.[98] This is the consequence of understanding that only a person can own, although other persons may have rights over the ownership. The problem is that if control and income are the main abilities of ownership, and use is with a different person, the bare owner can be regarded as the owner only with difficulty. That is precisely why incidents are shown as exceptions.

In the author's view, the biased absolute understanding of ownership elicits this mistake. Once rights are seen against others, and not falling on the object, and once ownership is seen to comprise different sets of rights, there is no such issue. Rights on use and enjoyment as opposed to the right to naked ownership – or reversionary interests – are just different rights that may fall at the same time over the same object, but do not exclude each other, nor limit its protection against third parties.

In sum, conversely to what has been argued, it is the author's view that the *in rem–in personam* distinction, although subject to several conflicts and exceptions, may serve as a yardstick to move between different rights of ownership. Generally speaking, a right that can be broadly exercised against the general public, normally in a negative sense of prohibiting third parties from exercising or impelling the right, and that is exercised in relation to an object, whether tangible or intangible, that is considered valuable, can be regarded as *iura in rem*.

As to whether it is possible to own claims, strong arguments can be sustained on both sides.[99] It is the author's view that, philosophically, there is no objection to considering

[93] Rigaud argues that the external dimension of ownership falls within public law. Castán Tobeñas (n 16) 37.
[94] Austin (n 41) 784–85.
[95] ibid 785.
[96] Taking into account that *universities* may be considered the origin of corporations, and, as already said, it might be considered that the right in the corporation is different from corporation rights.
[97] Austin (n 41) 847–48; Castán Tobeñas (n 16) 64.
[98] Austin (n 41) 847–48; Castán Tobeñas (n 16) 227 et seq.
[99] Van Erp and Akkermans (n 57) 369.

claims as capable of being owned. To some extent, shares represent rights and claims against corporations, and are widely recognised as a subject that is owned. From a practical point of view, however, this will depend on the legal system and the specific rules governing a claim. Thus, if the subject is able to control, has the right to the income, can sell the claim and can make any other decision on how to deal with the claim, it would be possible to consider it as capable of being owned. However, personal claims which are not transferable or controllable could not be regarded as property.

To sum up, nowadays, ownership has to be understood in the following terms:

(i) Ownership is the greatest interest in a thing which a mature law system recognises, with special weight given to primary control and primary right.[100]

(ii) Ownership generally refers to a negative right of an individual, corporation, or public or social entity or group against third parties to oppose the will of the owner with reference to his abilities in relation to the property, even though a positive obligation may also be derived in relation to the state or third parties.

(iii) Ownership rights are different from rights *in personam* insofar as such rights are normally exercised with broad *erga omnes* effects, and normally in a negative way, while personal rights usually refer to a person or a group of persons, as a duty to perform in a certain way or to indemnify in case of misbehaviour. In addition, such rights have to be analysed through time, insofar as rights vested in a person over a thing may change in time, thus overriding previous rights guaranteed by the same legal system.[101]

This view recognises the influence of liberal understanding of ownership in contemporary legal systems, as well as defining its complex nature.[102] In addition, on a broader understanding, this view not only recognises direct rights on a thing, but may also cover legal rights on a certain aspect of a property, such as being the owner of a usufruct, as the person would have the control and primary right to income on the servitude, but not on the whole thing itself.[103] It also covers rights on tangibles and intangibles. This view also reconciles civil law and common law ownership legal systems as, under a classical understanding of ownership, beneficial ownership in trust could, strictly speaking, only be recognised as such with difficulty.

Ultimately, albeit through different sets of rules, characteristics and understanding of ownership in different legal systems, almost all ownership rules of almost all legal systems usually refer to the same social phenomenon and to a same legal basic core and function.[104] Ownership concepts in different legal systems are converging, especially following the current state of economic globalisation, although they are still subject to significant differences. As different as common law and civil law systems are, and without denying their many nuances, their understandings of ownership are

[100] Honoré (n 61) 370; Christman (n 18) 25–26.

[101] On the issue of the temporary power on the property as regards the shift from the feudal system of property to liberal ownership, see Christman (n 18) 18. See also Austin (n 41) 796.

[102] Christman points out the tension between the liberal (absolute) view of ownership and the complex definition in law and economics. He therefore takes an intermediate position, recognising that even though it has a complex nature, it has a particular though variable structure: Christman (n 18) 15, 26–27.

[103] Austin (n 41) 825.

[104] Honoré (n 61) 370.

getting closer. As we will see, this is largely due to beneficial ownership, paramount to the English property system, being strengthened in its proprietary character since the nineteenth century, bringing the system closer to a more liberal view of ownership and so closer to civil law systems. As has been said, it may be considered that the *Saunders v Vautier* and *Archer-Shee* cases turned beneficiary interest in a trust early on from its conscience and quasi-contractual origins closer to a proprietary interest in the nineteenth and early twentieth centuries.[105] All in all, we will come to see whether we are attending a new switch in global understanding of ownership due to recent trends in the sharing economy.

B. Contemporary Proprietary Rights and Beneficial Ownership

Beneficial ownership – or beneficial owner – wording was not used, or at least not frequently used, in medieval and modern trust law.[106] Instead, medieval law used the term *cestuy que* use or *cestuy que* trust. Beneficial owner, on the other hand, seems to have gained extensive use in the late nineteenth and early twentieth centuries.

The concept was first used in section 1 of the UK Larceny Act 1868, the heading of section 58 of the UK Merchant Shipping Act 1894, section 7 of the UK Conveyancing and Law of Property Act 1881 and, in tax law, section 55 of the UK Finance Act 1927.[107] However, it started to have a wider use in tax law, securities law and rules related to control and confiscation of property in the twentieth century during times of war or economic crisis, especially in the USA.[108] Especially in relation to shares, their movable character and difficulty in tracing them made frequent the interposition of subjects and the custody in nominees or banks. Regulators reacted by requiring beneficial ownership to be disclosed or, in the case of corporate or tax benefits, the abilities to be vested in the beneficial owner and not the custodian or nominee. Beneficial ownership was probably a colloquial phrase adapting the new revolutionary understanding of ownership to property held in trust, which had started to be used by lawyers, and at some point appeared in legislation without any proper definition.

What is surprising is that sources today, ie equity casebooks, do not use the term beneficial ownership extensively;[109] they normally use beneficiary, beneficial interest or beneficial entitlement. This may be indicative of its illegitimate origin or improper use. It is more likely that the term is used by lawyers who are not experts in equity practising in fields outside equity, and that equity lawyers are not fully comfortable with it because it does not express the multiple nuances of equity.

[105] *Baker (Inspector of Taxes) v Archer-Shee* (n 7); *Saunders v Vautier* (n 7). Criticising this turn from contractual character to proprietary interest, see Hanbury (n 58).

[106] Godefroi (n 37) ia 353, 358 et seq; Lewin (n 37) ia 759–64; Maitland and Brunyate (n 37) 331; W Blackstone, *Commentaries on the Laws of England*, vol 2 (Bancroft-Whitney, 1915) 1157; Bacon (n 15) 48.

[107] R Speed, 'Beneficial Ownership' (1997) 26 *Australian Tax Review* 34, 41.

[108] See, eg SR Bross, 'The United States Borrower in the Eurobond Market – A Lawyer's Point of View' (1969) 34 *Law and Contemporary Problems* 172, 200; 'Trust Shares and the Nominee Problem in New York' (1938) 48 The Yale Law Journal 106, 108; D Partridge, 'Simplification of Securities Transfers by Trustees' [1958] *ABA Section Real Property Probate & Trust Proceedings* 44, 46.

[109] Pearce et al (n 1) lvii, 53–60, 456–58; Hudson (n 21) 153 et seq; Bogert and Shapo (n 7) 281 et seq; AW Scott, W Franklin Fratcher and M Ascher, *Scott and Ascher on Trusts*, vol 3, 4th edn (Aspen, 2007) 803.

Concepts of beneficial interest in a trust, beneficiary and beneficial owner are usually equated or, at least, related, because of their imprecise character. The question is how beneficial ownership and beneficiary interest concepts relate to each other and if there is any difference between them.

A trust relationship, where beneficial ownership may arise, is built upon the transfer of property by a person, the settlor, to another subject, the trustee, who will hold legal ownership for the benefit or use of another, which may be a third party or the settlor himself – the beneficiary.[110] As simple as a trust relationship is, the flexibility of trust and equity law enables the modification of many aspects of such a relationship. The interest of the beneficiary may be limited, leaving the remainders to another person, for instance; it may be for the benefit of a person decided by the trustee within a certain group – a discretionary trust; or it may be a trust derived from the facts of the case and not by express settlement – a constructive or resulting trust. There may be an almost infinite number of modifications to the way the trust respects the main principles of equity law.[111] Beneficial ownership, at this first stage, is identified with the beneficiary of the trust.

Statutory provisions do not provide for an explicit definition of beneficial ownership, and neither does case law in equity law, probably because equity is more interested in the specific rights of the objects involved rather than in its label, and because the term may be stranger to equity as used in other fields of law. This may explain why most beneficial owner definitions are provided in tax law cases.

One of the few definitions of the concept in case law is found in the US tax law case of *Montana Catholic Missions v Missoula County*:

> The expression, beneficial use or beneficial ownership or interest, in property is quite frequent in the law, and means in this connection such a right to its enjoyment as exists where the legal title is in one person and the right to such beneficial use or interest is in another, and where such right is recognized by law, and can be enforced by the courts, at the suit of such owner or of someone in his behalf.[112]

This concept does not distinguish the infinite differences of beneficiaries' interest in equity law, such as those reflected by beneficial use, ownership and interest, mere *spes*, vested or contingent, and does not distinguish where ownership rights are exercised by the beneficiary or by the trustee. The concept seems to equate beneficial ownership to any beneficiary right, leaving the issue wide open.

Similarly, the UK House of Lords ruled in *Ayerst v C & K (Construction) Ltd*:

> My Lords, the concept of the legal ownership of property, which did not carry with it the right of the owner to enjoy the fruits of it or dispose of it for his own benefit, owes its origin to the Court of Chancery. The archetype is the trust. The 'legal ownership' of the trust property is in the trustee, but he holds it not for his own benefit but for the benefit of the *cestui que* trust or beneficiaries. On the creation of a trust in the strict sense as it was developed by equity the

[110] See Maitland and Brunyate (n 44) 44; GJ Virgo and EH Burn, *Trusts and Trustees*, 7th edn (Oxford University Press, 2008) 7 et seq.

[111] Certainty, beneficiaries and compliance with perpetuity rules are needed for a trust to be valid: see Virgo and Burn (n 110) 75 et seq.

[112] *Montana Catholic Missions v Missoula County* (1905) 200 US 118 (Supreme Court) 127–28.

> full ownership of the trust property was split into two constituent elements, which became vested in different persons: the 'legal ownership' in the trustee and what came to be called the 'beneficial ownership' in the *cestui que* trust.[113]

In *Sainsbury*, Nourse LJ stated:

> It means ownership for your own benefit as opposed to ownership as trustee for another. It exists either where there is no division of legal and beneficial ownership or where legal ownership is vested in one person and the beneficial ownership or, which is the same thing, the equitable interest in the property in another.[114]

Again, these definitions in UK tax law are vague, merely referring the concept to equity law trust and not defining what characteristics define a beneficial interest as beneficial ownership. Even the definition proposed by Nourse LJ in *Sainsbury* blends beneficial ownership and equitable interest. It does not distinguish the difference of intensity between ownership and interest.

Similarly, *Jowitt's Dictionary* defines beneficial owner as 'the individual who enjoys the benefits of owning, in equity, a security or property, regardless of whose name the title is in'.[115]

Black's Law Dictionary, in turn, broadly follows lawyers' understanding of beneficial ownership, defining it as 'one recognized in equity as the owner of something because use and title belong to that person, even though legal title may belong to someone else'.[116]

Beneficial ownership is defined by *Black's Law Dictionary* as a beneficiary's interest in trust property.[117]

More accurate, as it distinguishes beneficial ownership from other types of beneficial interests in equity, is the definition found in the Canadian *MacKeen* case:

> It seems to me that the plain ordinary meaning of the expression 'beneficial owner' is the real or true owner of the property. The property may be registered in another name or held in trust for the real owner, but the 'beneficial owner' is the one who can ultimately exercise the rights of ownership in the property. I believe that the other expression 'beneficially entitled to' has a slightly different meaning from that of 'beneficial owner'. The person beneficially entitled to property may be further removed from the exercise of ultimate ownership of the property than the 'beneficial owner', but as long as that person has the right to legally establish the exercise of the rights of ownership over the property then it may be said that he is beneficially entitled thereto.[118]

Beneficial ownership is a subtype of beneficial interest or beneficiary rights where the characteristics of ownership rights may be allocated to the beneficiary or entitled person. Once ownership is defined as the largest set of rights on a thing, normally including control and income, a beneficiary interest may easily fit within the definition if the set of rights included in the equitable interest are strong enough. Taking into account those

[113] *Ayerst (Inspector of Taxes) v C & K Construction Ltd* [1975] STC 345 (CA) 349.

[114] *Sainsbury v Inland Revenue Commissioners* [1970] Ch 712 (Ch D).

[115] D Greenberg, K Banaszak and Y Greenberg (eds), *Jowitt's Dictionary of English Law*, vol 1, 4th edn (Sweet & Maxwell, 2015) 254.

[116] B Garner (ed), *Black's Law Dictionary*, 10th edn (West – Thomson Reuters, 2009) 1280.

[117] ibid.

[118] *MacKeen* (1977) 36 APR 572.

rights defining ownership, the negative character against third parties and being an *in rem* right, beneficial ownership in equity could be defined as *the greatest interest in a thing recognised in common law countries under equity law, usually comprising a primary right to income and control, and even with overriding abilities over legal ownership and any other interest in the thing from third parties, though the latter be subject to third party bona fide acquirers.*[119]

The main problem with such a definition is that the flexibility of equity does not match the strong core of abilities of ownership rights. Primary rights to control and income may be vested in the trustee or the beneficiary or beneficiaries, or all together; they may refer to either negative or positive obligations of the trustee in relation to the beneficiary, also depending on the specific characteristics of the trust; and they are not always opposable or claimable against third parties or with *erga omnes* effects. From this point of view, beneficial ownership seems to be a *contradictio in terminis*, as ownership rights appear, even though variable, as a concept with some strength, with relatively intense and defined characteristics, and more or less easy to identify. Beneficiary rights in equity deal with flexible concepts, are variable from case to case and are somehow complex to identify in many cases. In this sense, the beneficial ownership concept carries a tension that can only be solved once equilibrium between the strong characteristics of ownership and the flexibility of trusts is achieved.

C. The Never-Ending Question: Contemporary Trusts' Beneficiary Rights, *In Rem* or *In Personam* Rights?

It is well known that Maitland framed the *cestui que* trust rights in Austin's *in rem–in personam* distinction of rights taken from Roman law, fanning the discussion of the character of the trust.[120]

On the one hand, Maitland in the first instance, and later Stone, among others, argued in favour of the contractual or *in personam* character of beneficiary rights.[121] On the other hand, Austin and Scott, among others, defended the *in rem* character of the *cestuy que* trust.[122]

The first group defend this status based on the fact that the beneficiary only has rights against the trustee, but not against third parties. The main arguments are summarised by Scott as follows: (i) the trustee is owner and two persons cannot be owners; (ii) equity is a jurisdiction of persons; (iii) *in rem* duties are always negative and beneficiaries do

[119] Similarly, but referring to beneficial ownership in international tax, mismatching the UK domestic definition in equity and international tax meaning, C Du Toit, *Beneficial Ownership of Royalties in Bilateral Tax Treaties* (IBFD, 1999) 200–01.

[120] Maitland and Brunyate (n 37) 106; Waters (n 5) 220.

[121] Maitland (n 2); HF Stone, 'The Nature of the Rights of the "Cestui Que Trust"' (1917) 17 *Columbia Law Review* 467. It seems, however, that Maitland changed his mind in later works: HAL Fisher, *The Collected Papers of Frederik W Maitland* (Cambridge University Press, 1911) 349.

[122] AW Scott, 'The Nature of the Rights of the Cestui Que Trust' (1917) 17 *Columbia Law Review* 269; Waters (n 5) 221.

not always have negative rights only; and (iv) if a person obtains the *res* from the trustee without notice of the trust, it receives property free of any incident.[123]

The second group of academics argue that the beneficiary has *in rem* rights as actual rights on the object, and that the trustee is a mere buffer, as in some cases he or she can claim his or her rights against the world at large.[124]

Scott argues that the beneficiary rights may be called ownership rights at the time, even though they may not have been called so before. For him, equity is not only a jurisdiction of personal rights, with examples such as imprisonment. The duty under the trust to refrain from using the property against the conditions of the trust is for the 'world at large', and the protection of the third party bona fide conveyer from the trustee is a matter of history derived from economic interest to protect commercial traffic, as equity jurisdiction is a conscience jurisdiction that will not interfere in cases where subjects are both equally innocent, as the beneficiary and the third party may be.[125] Scott maintains that the set of rights and claims between the beneficiary, the trustee and third parties on conveyances for a fair amount or without a payment, and with or without notice, are, broadly speaking, the result of historical and practical evolution and not because of the *in personam* characteristics of the trust.[126] In sum, Scott argues that the beneficiary has a claim not only against the trustee, but also against the rest of the world not to interfere in the trustee–beneficiary relationship, even though such claims or rights may cede in some cases for historical or practical reasons.[127]

In his answer to Scott, Stone defends the right of the beneficiary not to be interfered with in its relationship with the trust and the trustee, which constitutes property itself or an identical economical right, but such a right does not fall on the trust property itself.[128] He also argues that the beneficiary's interest does not limit the trustee's legal ownership to property. Consequently, the transfer of property to the third party is completely valid. Stone justifies the liability of the third party purchaser in certain cases of negligence.[129] For that author, the third party is responsible under a personal claim for interfering in another personal right that might be considered personal property – movable property.[130]

These authors, especially those defending the contractual character of beneficiary rights, seem to blend or even equate *in rem* rights and ownership.[131] It is probable that the discussion being framed immediately after the liberal waves of the nineteenth century led all these authors to misunderstand the issue and follow an *in rem* and ownership absolute understanding of rights as all or nothing. Such views fall into the trap of considering ownership as a right on the thing.[132] Taking into account the historical

[123] Scott (n 122) 275–80.
[124] ibid 290.
[125] ibid 275–80.
[126] ibid 280–89.
[127] ibid 274.
[128] Stone (n 121) 470 et seq; Waters (n 5) 221. Regarding whether claims are able to be owned, see Van Erp and Akkermans (n 57) 369.
[129] Stone (n 121) 477 et seq.
[130] ibid.
[131] See Ames et al in Scott (n 122) 269, 275–76, 278; Stone (n 121) 468.
[132] For references to rights on the thing, rights to *res* itself and similar phrasing referring the right directly to the thing, see Scott (n 122) 278; Stone (n 121) 469,470, 472, 474, 476, 484.

context, this discussion took place at the time when equity and common law jurisdiction merged, so the interaction of both systems probably also added confusion to the matter. Trying to fit English equitable rights into Roman and revolutionary simplistic concepts led to the rejection of the beneficial interest *in rem* character.

More recently, authors have rejected the *in personam–in rem* distinction and adopted a pragmatic approach, focusing on the content of the rights.[133] Similarly, McFarlane and Stevens have argued that equitable rights are rights upon rights.[134] To this group, framing trusts in an *in personam–in rem* discussion does not help to solve trust cases, but adds confusion, as it is derived from an improper revival of Roman law. Thus, what matters is the specific solution given in the case at hand, no matter the classification taken under the Roman distinction.

The view of the author, in line with a contemporary view, is that beneficiary rights will pose ownership and/or *in rem* characteristics in some cases, while in others only personal claims may be found.[135] In some cases, it may even comprise both. However, the distinction may be helpful as it could help to define the extent to which trust rights apply just against the trustee or *erga omnes* against any person. In other words, some trust rights may be claimable against the world because either equity or common law guarantees the beneficiary's rights on the object against the world – the *in rem* right – and not just because current rules recognise a claim against a third party in certain cases. Following trust case law developed since the nineteenth century, it is clear that there is a pattern to grant certain rights on the subject matter against the world, and thus such pattern defines a core right, not just being a matter of fact.[136] Even in the case of third parties interfering with the trust, damages rights, even though personal, seem to arise from the interference with the right of the object to the subject matter, thus being derived from proprietary rights, as I will argue later in relation to bare trusts. In other cases, equity law denies the ability of a beneficiary to claim proprietary rights in certain conditions, its rights only being claimable against the trustee because of the breach of the trust duties, and not because of the damage to the property right, falling within *in personam* rights characteristics. And even though it may be rights that matter in the specific solution of the case, as with any other legal classification, this characterisation serves as a map for equitable rights, serving to compare and find the reasoning and the failures, and ultimately serving to improve equity law.

As Davies and Virgo pointed out, to defend only a contractual nature of trusts is not in line with case law, fails to explain the proprietary nature of the beneficiary's interest and cannot explain why, if a trustee declines to serve, the beneficiary may request another trustee to be appointed by the court.[137] The question is when is a beneficiary's interest closer to the *in rem* ownership definition, including key rights, and when is it closer to mere personal rights? The first case concerns beneficial ownership.

[133] See Waters (n 5). See the Opinion of Kitto J in *Livingston v The Commissioner of Stamp Duties* (1960) 107 CLR 41.

[134] B McFarlane and R Stevens, 'The Nature of Equitable Property' (2010) 4 *Journal of Equity*.

[135] Munzer (n 51) 25; Pearce et al (n 1) 456; Scott et al (n 109) 803–12.

[136] *FHR European Ventures LLP and others v Mankarious and others* (n 5); *Shell UK Ltd and others* (n 7); *Twinsectra v Yardley* (2002) 2 AC 164 (UKHL); *Saunders v Vautier* (n 7).

[137] Even though they end up by giving some value to McFarlane and Stevens's thesis: PS Davies and G Virgo, *Equity and Trusts* (Oxford University Press, 2016) 59–61.

Because of the economic importance of ownership, to talk about a right upon a right does not serve to define in which cases beneficiary interest would exclude a large group of persons against its economic interest on the subject, and when it must exercise its rights, forcing the trustee to perform certain activities. This can only be explained by labelling different trust rights within the *in rem* and *in personam* categories.

In sum, as somehow flexible as equity is, the contemporary understanding is that beneficiary rights may sometimes be *in personam* rights and sometimes *in rem* rights, even appearing together within the same contract, fiduciary obligation or trust, defining a really specific and *sui generis* configuration that can only be categorised in the specific right on a case-by-case basis.[138] However, we will see that in most cases, if beneficiary rights are strong enough, they can be qualified as proprietary interest or extremely close to *in rem* rights if beneficiaries can be fully ascertained.[139]

(i) Bare Trusts

In a bare trust with a single beneficiary, the trustee – sometimes called a nominee[140] – holds legal title but has no active duties other than to hold the property, protect it and manage it for the benefit of the beneficiary.[141] The trustee has no discretion or any substantive ability to take significant decisions other than to hold the property for the benefit of the beneficiary and to follow his instructions, the beneficiary holding all the rights to both the income and the capital.[142] In this case, the beneficiary can instruct the trustee in any sense, and even, if of full age and sound of mind, can ask the trustee to transfer all the assets or funds to them even against the will of the settlor or the trustee.[143]

These wide abilities of beneficiaries to even override settlor, will and trustee powers reflect the impact of *Saunders v Vautier*, where the court decided that the decision of a beneficiary of a trust old in age and sound of mind may override a breach of trust, including the transfer of the interest to third parties or even to the beneficiaries themselves.[144] Even when beneficiaries are unknown, underage, unborn or incapable,

[138] In a similar vein, arguing equitable interests are negative (proprietary) rights against a wide group of persons and positive rights against few persons, see Nolan (n 69). See also Davies and Virgo (n 137) 11. In Canada, arguing for a primary contractual character that in some cases may be proprietary, see C Brown, 'Tax, Trusts and Beneficial Ownership: Perils for the Unwary Practitioner' (2003) 23 *Estates, Trusts and Pensions Journal* 9, 33.

[139] Davies and Virgo (n 137) 61; Nolan (n 69) 234. *Baker (Inspector of Taxes) v Archer-Shee* (n 7).

[140] Even though nominee, strictly speaking, refers to the intermediary in a common law contract, a trustee in a bare trust frames within an equity relationship.

[141] The concept of bare trust as provided was defined following the definition proposed by Dart and Barber in JH Dart and W Barber, *A Treatise on the Law of and Practice Relating to Vendors and Purchasers of Real Estate*, 5th edn (Stevens & Sons 1876) because of the controversy regarding undefined use in s 48 of the Land Transfer Act 1875 in *In Re Cunningham and Frayling* (1891) 2 Ch 567 (Ch) 572; *Christie v Ovington* [1875] Ch 1873 C. 25, 1 Ch D 279, 281.

[142] *Christie v Ovington* (n 141) 281; *In Re Cunningham and Frayling* (n 141) 569–70; Davies and Virgo (n 137) 31.

[143] Pearce et al (n 1) 704. *Timpson's Executors v Yerbury (Inspector of Taxes)* [1936] KB 645 (CA) 668–69; *In Re Pain Gustavson v Haviland* [1919] Ch 38 (Ch); *Saunders v Vautier* (n 7); Law of Property Act 1925, c 20.

[144] On the transfer of the equitable interest, see s 53 of the Law of Property Act 1925; see also *Vandervell Appellant v Inland Revenue Commissioners Respondents* [1966] Ch 261 (CA) 296–98. The transfer can be done through different mechanisms, such as the assignment of equitable interest, the direction to a trustee

variation of trust rules, upon approval by the court, may be allowed in certain cases to deal with trust property in an extensive way, as rules on protections of the incapable and minors allow in common law.[145]

Compared to the protection of the will of the settlor before *Saunders v Vautier*, this decision appears to the author as the zenith of the influence of new nineteenth-century understanding of property in trust law. As Getzler pointed out, *Saunders v Vautier* resulted in the 'final recognition of beneficiaries under a trust as holding beneficial title mirroring the plenary title of a common legal owner, save for the interposition of a nominee as legal titleholder'.[146]

The result is that, since then, the beneficiary of a bare trust has almost all known powers related to ownership, outweighing any right from the trustee or third parties to the property.[147] So far, it seems clear that beneficiaries in bare trusts have beneficial ownership in the property, really close to a single legal owner or holder of fee in estate simple in common law, or the single owner in continental law. However, are these rights *in rem* rights?

Nolan, even though recognising the mixed nature of equitable rights, seems to recognise a core of negative proprietary interest against the world, or at least a very large group of persons, as characteristic of beneficiary rights, and positive rights or actions against the trustee and other beneficiaries.[148] Brown, conversely, argues for a primary contractual character that in some cases may be proprietary.[149] Harris, similarly but on leaseholder cases, sustains he has a right against the world.[150]

The author's view is that this last case is so insofar as the beneficiary may claim in court their rights on the property against any third party who uses it against their will or bought it from the trustee in breach of trust.[151]

The main argument for holding that the beneficiary has no *in rem* right is that the beneficiary cannot claim the subject matter upon their beneficial ownership rights if the trustee sells it to a third party good faith buyer.[152]

to hold on trust for another, the conveyance of legal estate by a nominee or the declaration of a sub-trust. On the ability of beneficiaries to override settlors' intents and even ask to transfer property to them, see *Saunders v Vautier* (n 7). See also J Getzler, 'Transplantation and Mutation in Anglo-American Trust Law' (2009) 10 *Theoretical Inquiries in Law* 355, 367 et seq.

[145] See ss 53 and 57 of the Trustee Act 1925; s 1 of the Variation of Trusts Act 1958, c 53. In case law, see *In Re Suffert's Settlement* [1961] Ch 1 (Ch). See also Davies and Virgo (n 137) 721 et seq.

[146] Getzler (n 144) 369.

[147] Except in some cases, eg third party bona fide purchasers. And even in these cases, beneficial owner rights do not significantly differ from a good faith third party who buys from a non-owner in common law. See Fisher (n 121) 349; Pearce et al (n 1) 81; Getzler (n 144) 369.

[148] Nolan (n 69) 236.

[149] Brown (n 138) 33.

[150] Harris (n 54) 130.

[151] On the ability of beneficiaries to hold proprietary rights, to trace and follow property, and apparently giving priority to the proprietary rights of the beneficiary, see *FHR European Ventures LLP and others v Mankarious and others* (n 5). See also *Twinsectra v Yardley* (n 136). On the ability of the beneficial owner to directly sue for damages, even sometimes against third parties, provided certain requirements are met, and with much academic controversy, see *Shell UK Ltd and others* (n 7). On the many nuances of proprietary remedies of beneficiaries, see Davies and Virgo (n 137) 845–972; Pearce et al (n 1) 962–63; AW Scott, W Franklin Fratcher and M Ascher, *Scott and Ascher on Trusts*, vol 5, 4th edn (Aspen, 2007) 1937; GG Bogert and G Taylor Bogert, *Trust and Trustees*, vol 16, 2nd edn (West, 1995) 109 et seq; D Salmons, 'Claims against Third-Party Recipients of Trust Property' (2017) 76 *CLR* 399.

[152] *Burgess v Wheate* (1759) 1 Eden 177 (Ch) 195. On a third party good faith acquirer and if such breach of trust may derive in constructive trust, answering it cannot, see *Akers and others v Samba Financial Group*

In these cases, the beneficiary will just have remedies in common law or equity against the trustee or persons involved in bad faith in the breach of trust and, in some cases, only to damages, equivalent amounts or substitute property, and not the property itself.[153]

However, the solutions are not far from the one provided in civil law countries in cases of acquisition from non-owner or double sell cases.[154] In some countries, the new bona fide owner acquiring in good value from a non-owner may acquire actual *in rem* rights depending on the requirements of consent, contract and *traditio* of the relevant system.[155] Where one of these cases come to court, both the original owner and the new bona fide purchaser have valid titles to property.[156]

Broadly speaking, although differing on the preferred criteria and requirements, civil law countries solve those issues in favour of a third party good faith buyer.[157] The main reason is that commerce and legal certainty principles are considered, as a policy matter of the rules involved, as being above the specific right of the subject. The original owner, in turn, is given compensation rights.

Even in common law, some protection is given to third party bona fide acquirers, although the cases to which it applies may be restricted.[158] The main reason why some

[2017] AC 424 (UKSC) 463–64. See Ames et al in Scott (n 122) 279; Stone (n 121) 484; Hanbury (n 58) 471–72.

[153] *AIB Group plc v Redler* [2014] AC 1503 (UKSC) 1544–46; *Target Holdings v Redferns* [1996] AC 421, ia 436. See Pearce et al (n 1) 961 et seq; Hudson (n 21) 737 et seq; Davies and Virgo (n 137) 797 et seq and 845 et seq; Bogert and Bogert (n 151) 93 et seq; Scott et al (n 15) 1937 et seq.

[154] See Arts 1599 and 2276 and 2277 of the Code Civil and *Hispano-Suiza* (Cour de Cassation civ 1e). In Spanish law, see Art 34 of the Ley Hipotecaria Ruling from the Supreme Court of 12 January 2015 (465/2014); in Germany, see ss 890 et seq and 932–35 of the Bürgerliches Gesetzbuch (BGB) and s 366 of the Handelsgesetzbuch (HGB); in the Netherlands, see Arts 3:86–3:90 of the Burgerlijk Wetboek. See Van Erp and Akkermans (n 57) 916 et seq. On the evolution of protection of third parties, see B Kozolchyk, 'Tranfers of Personal Property by a Nonowner: Its Future in Light of Its Past' (1986) 61 *Tulane Law Review* 1453. It must also be taken into account that sales derived from theft may differ from those derived from non-ownership but pacific possession, such as by an agent, from land to personal property, and from market to private transactions. Comparative views, even though sometimes oversimplifying the view of different countries, can be found in G Dari-Mattiacci and C Guerriero, 'Law and Culture: A Theory of Comparative Variation in Bona Fide Purchase Rules' (2015) 35 *OJLS* 543; A Schwartz and RE Scott, 'Rethinking the Laws of Good Faith Purchase' (2011) 111 *Columbia Law Review* 1332, 1378 et seq.

[155] The French transfer system relying on the title does not allow the sale of non-owned property, thus a sale by a non-owner is not valid and the third party is not protected. However, prescription upon that non-valid title is given if the buyer performed in good faith and was given value. In addition, courts have recognised protection of third parties buying from non-owners in good faith in certain cases. See Arts 1599, 2276 and 2277 of the Code Civil and *Hispano-Suiza* (n 154). In Spanish or German law, the fact that transfer of property takes place under a dual system requiring title and *traditio* enables the recognition of contracts of sale from a non-owner. However, the recognition of the contract does not imply transfer of property to the third party as the transaction lacks the second part, *traditio*. All in all, protection is also given to good faith third parties in certain cases, such as buying from the owner recognised in the public register, by presuming the validity of the invalid title from the seller. In Spanish law, see Art 34 of the Ley Hipotecaria, and Ruling from the Supreme Court of 12 January 2015 (465/2014); in Germany, see ss 890 et seq and 932–35 of the Bürgerliches Gesetzbuch (BGB) and 366 of the Handelsgesetzbuch (HGB); in the Netherlands, see Arts 3:86–3:90 of the Burgerlijk Wetboek. See M Cuena Casas, 'La Validez de La Venta de Cosa Ajena Como Exigencia de Sistema' [2008] *Nul: estudios sobre invalidez e ineficacia* 1; Van Erp and Akkermans (n 57) 916 et seq.

[156] M Franklin, 'Security of Acquistion and of Transaction: La Possession Vaut Titre and Bona Fide Purchase' (1931) 6 *Tulane Law Review* 589, 591.

[157] On different possible solutions, such as protecting the owner, protecting the buyer or splitting the burden, see Schwartz and Scott (n 154).

[158] In the UK, this principle was largely developed for personal goods during the late 18th and 19th centuries following economic, industrial and liberal developments. In equity case law see *Burgess v Wheate* (n 160) 195;

authors claim that equitable rights are not proprietary rights is because in equity the priority of the good faith third party is greater than in common law. However, in the author's view, this derives not from the fact that the equitable title is necessarily, and in all cases, a worse title against the world than an owner in common law or the title of the third party, but from the historical development of case law in this matter and because of the not fully transparent and public nature of beneficial interest.

Because of historical development as a jurisdiction of conscience, equity law cannot interfere with two innocent persons, which the beneficiary and third parties are.[159] Moreover, protection of the beneficial owner in such cases would jeopardise legal certainty – and subsequently trade – as buyers would never have full certainty that they were buying from an absolute owner and in the absence of a third party with more interest in the thing.[160] This is why, in civil law countries, protection to third party good faith buyers usually applies in the case of the buyer acquiring from the person who appears to hold the title in the register.[161] For common law countries, this greater protection of third parties in equity perfectly matches the hidden – or at least imprecise, not public and never absolutely certain – nature of beneficial ownership that lies at the very core of beneficiary rights.[162] To make buyers' ownership conditional on putting on them the burden of proof of unravelling actual ownership beyond reasonable due diligence, where a subject appears in public registers and is publicly regarded as the owner, would render a simple buy-and-sell as a high-risk activity.[163]

The point being made here is that the protection of third parties does not, per se, alter the proprietary condition of the original owner, including beneficial owner cases. In these cases, purported beneficial ownership weakness is not derived from it being personal in character or being worse title than the common law third party bona fide purchaser title, as it is not in the case of double sale or acquisition from a non-owner in civil law countries or common law, but a matter of relativity of title.[164] To some extent, he or she has better right than the rest of the world, but worse than the third party good faith acquirer. In this regard, the trustee could not have sold what he or she does not have, ie beneficial ownership, and consequently the third party could not have acquired full ownership by means of the sale of the trustee. However, the theoretical weaker title of the third party does not per se confer full ownership, but by law, given certain conditions, its weakness is fixed and ownership rights of the original owner against him or her are destroyed, conferring on him or her full ownership by law, just because

Akers and others v Samba Financial Group (n 160). Codification of these principles are found, inter alia, in ss 25 of The Sale of Goods Act 1979, c 54, and ss 8 and 9 of the Factors Act 1889 c. 45. See A Burrows (ed), *English Private Law* (Oxford University Press, 2007) 383. In the USA, see s 2-403 of the Uniform Commercial Code. For a criticism on favouring the third party buyer in terms of protection of property and economics behind it, see Schwartz and Scott (n 154).

[159] Scott (n 122) 279.

[160] ibid.

[161] See, eg Art 34 of the Spanish Ley Hipotecaria.

[162] On the relationship between bona fide purchaser doctrine and registers, see G Ferris, How Should a System of Registered Title to Property Respond to Fraud and Sharp Practice?' in H Conway and R Hickey (eds), *Modern Studies in Property Law*, vol 9 (Hart Publishing, 2017).

[163] ibid.

[164] On the relativity of title, see L Katz, 'The Concept of Ownership and the Relativity of Title' (2011) 2 *Jurisprudence* 191.

law prioritises legal certainty of commerce in these cases. As has been shown, neither ownership nor beneficial ownership is as absolute as it was supposed to be, and neither of them loses its proprietary character, but ownership ends at the time when the new title comes into being, similarly to how it would end if the property were physically destroyed. In such a case, the ownership former right is not questioned, and neither should that of beneficial ownership be.

On the limited personal action against the trustee in case of a good faith third party buyer, this solution again does not significantly differ in civil law countries' solutions in cases of eviction responsibility or sale by a non-owner, countries where only full ownership, and not beneficial ownership, is recognised, and such solution does not diminishes its character.[165] In addition, the case is obviously similar to that of property being destroyed by a third party both in civil law and common law countries. In such a case it is obvious that the ownership can no longer be exercised against the world, thus the property right enables a claim for damages against the person who destroyed the object or disabled the owner from exercising his or her right. Ownership as the right does not disappear but, because it cannot be exercised due to the behaviour of a person, has to be compensated.

In sum, from a case law perspective, there is no doubt since *Saunders v Vautier* there is a clear tendency to strengthen beneficiary abilities in relation to property that shows an increasing *in rem* proprietary understanding by the courts, probably following or influenced by the revolutionary and liberal view of ownership since the nineteenth century.[166] The *in rem* character probably appears most obviously in the case of bare trusts.

Finally, on the limits of minors, unborn or incapable persons, the author's view is that this rule does not limit ownership as such, but constitutes a control mechanism precisely to guarantee the beneficiary property because of his or her inability to accurately understand the consequences of legal decisions.[167] Moreover, a court may substitute the minor's or incapable person's will in order to enable the trustee to devise land to each beneficiary, including a minor, or devise land allocating the minor's interest to a new trust.[168] However, these rules do not significantly differ from those applicable to the ability of a minor or incapable person to deal with property he or she holds on both legal and beneficial ownership but subject to trust property because of legal capacity limitations, guardianship or another required legal representation or substitution.[169]

[165] *AIB Group plc v Redler* (n 153) 1544–46; *Target Holdings v Redferns* (n 153) ia 436.

[166] *Saunders v Vautier* (n 7); *Shell UK Ltd and others* (n 7); *FHR European Ventures LLP and others v Mankarious and others* (n 5) 14. Arguing on the increasing proprietary understanding of beneficiary rights, Brown (n 138) 11. For the evolution and influence of liberal winds in trust law, see Getzler (n 144).

[167] Regarding persons lacking mental capacity, see above, n 137. See also s 3(1) of the Mental Incapacity Act 2005, c 9.

[168] See above, n 137.

[169] For example, children are forbidden from holding legal ownership in property or real estate. Thus, children's property is held in trust for their benefit by the transferor or another adult conveyee if it has been conveyed to the children jointly with other over-age persons. By doing so, there is an *ex lege* protection system, thus the trustee exercises the protection and is able to transfer or manage the property for the benefit of the children under relevant conditions. See s 1(6) of the Law of Property Act 1925 and s 2(1) of the Trusts of Land

(ii) Brief Reference to Nominees

In the UK, nominees and bare trusts are frequently equated. Case law, academic works and even statutory legislation use both wordings as synonymous, or at least very close.[170] However, it seems that, strictly speaking, a nominee is an intermediary in a contractual arrangement, such as custody or very limited agency, characterised by having very little or no power at all in relation to the assets or income involved, but just holding it for the benefit of the other contracting part.[171] In contrast, a bare trust derives from a settlement of property or by operation of the law, such as in a constructive or resulting trust resulting from transactions with property.[172]

Probably due to the fact that an agency or similar intermediary contract relationship may derive an implicit trust, the use of the word 'nominee' to define an intermediary both in equity and in common law is frequent.[173] It is likely that the word 'nominee' is used to note the few abilities of the trustee in bare trusts. In any case, when interpreting the word 'nominee' in the UK, the context has to be analysed carefully to check whether one is facing a bare trust, a pure common law intermediary contract or a common law contract with implicit equitable obligations.

In the USA, contrarily, a nomineeship is framed within common law obligations and the use of the word 'nominee' to refer to equitable obligations is less frequent, although not nonexistent.[174]

and Appointment of Trustees Act 1996. In the case of patients, a court can take decisions or appoint a deputy to take them: s 16 of the Mental Incapacity Act 2005, c 9.

[170] Pearce et al (n 1) 477; A Hudson, *Equity and Trusts* (Routledge, 2013) 54, 482. In case law, Sir GJ Turner LJ seems to equate trustee and nominee in *In Re Tempest* (1866) 1 ChApp 486 (Ch), as quoted by R Clements and A Abass, *Equity and Trusts*, 2nd edn (Oxford University Press, 2011) 169–70. See also *Vandervell Appellant v Inland Revenue Commissioners Respondents* (n 152) 295, 298; *Tomlinson (Inspector of Taxes) v Glyns Executor and Trustee Co and Another* [1970] Ch 112 (Court of Appeal) 124–26.

[171] Matthews argues, and the distinction in former s 22(5) of the Finance Act 1965, c 25 and in the *Vandervell* case seems to support this, that nominee does not refer to a trustee in a trust relationship but falls within common law agency: P Matthews, 'All About Bare Trusts: Part 1' [2005] *Private Client Business* 266, 266–67; Bogert and Hess (n 9) 171 et seq. See also M Lupoi, *Trusts: A Comparative Study* (Cambridge University Press, 2000) 157–58.

[172] Matthews (n 171).

[173] Note that agency and trusts differ in that trusts need entrustment of property and are bound by the trust document, while agency may involve entrustment of property and/or power, and is bound by the principal's control, making it possible to have broader powers and discretion.

[174] Some authors note that agency and nomineeship are equivalent or very similar: see CE Falk, 'Nominees, Dummies and Agents: Is It Time for the Supreme Court to Take Another Look?' (1985) 63 *Taxes* 725, 725; JE Miller, 'The Nominee Conundrum: The Live Dummy Is Dead, but the Dead Dummy Should Live' (1978) 34 *Tax Law Review* 213, 223. MA Turner, 'Agent vs Nominee: A Suspended Decision for Dummy Corporations' (1989) 67 *Taxes* 263, 267. However, the difference seems to lie in the nominee having almost no freedom of decision or being severally limited as compared to an agent, which has some freedom of decision, even though it is always in line with the instructions, and to his or her best knowledge and in good faith. See ibid 268. See also, noting the very limited abilities of a nominee within fiduciary relationships, RA Wilson, 'Unincorporated Business Activity for 1980' (1982) 2 *Statistics of Income Bulletin* 15, 16. In case law, the very limited abilities of a nominee are reflected in the *Turk* case: 'a *nominee* is essentially a proxy, or even a decoy, for someone else'. *Turk v Internal Revenue Service*, D Mont [2000] 127 F 2d, 1165. *Black's Law Dictionary* also supports the ability of nominee to be interpreted as an agent or representative with very limited powers: 'One designated to act for another as his representative in a rather limited sense': HC Black, *Black´s Law Dictionary*, 6th edn (West, 1990) 1050.

(iii) Simple Trusts with Several Beneficiaries

In a simple trust with several beneficiaries, overriding the instructions in the settlement needs the agreement of all beneficiaries, following the *Saunders v Vautier* principle.[175] In cases of a minor, who is unable to give consent, or especially of unidentifiable, unborn or successive beneficiaries, the beneficiaries are not able to act together on the property at their will.[176] Worse, if beneficiaries, though existent and identified, have different views on how to deal with the property or one or some oppose the agreement, the proprietary interest of the rest of the beneficiaries would be limited as they cannot deal with the property as they would wish to do. Such cases are controversial as they must conclude whether each beneficiary has any ownership *in rem* rights or has limited beneficial interest against the trustee and the rest of the beneficiaries.[177]

In the case of a defined group of beneficiaries, it is the inclination of this author to also consider each beneficiary to have an *in rem* beneficial ownership interest in the property, with regard to both the income and the capital. In cases of breach of trust, each beneficiary may claim to protect the property against third parties, other beneficiaries or even the trustee. By doing so, he or she is protecting his right on the property against the world. However, as the beneficiary's right is not defined as a part of the property, he or she has to protect the whole trust property so that his or her part may be protected. Even in the case where the beneficiaries want the property to be transferred, they may claim for substitution. Such a decision will be subject to control as conflicting with the rights of others, but such substitution does not mean he or she has no intense right on the property. Compared to third parties, he or she has a truly great right.

On the right to occupy or use, the issue is not whether beneficiaries have a proprietary interest in the land or chattel, but how the interest has to be arranged insofar as they cannot exercise it at the same time.[178] Regarding land, trustees may reasonably arrange the right to occupy the land, but cannot deprive all of the beneficiaries of their right to occupy, and where it is allocated to one of them against the rest, they should be compensated through appropriate payments or through the occupant renouncing the income or profit derived from the trust for it to be allocated to the excluded beneficiary.[179] Trustees can also divide the land, maintain it within the trust or convey it to a new trust to the beneficiaries with their consent.[180] Consequently, there is clearly an implicit recognition of the beneficiaries' simultaneous interest in the right to occupy and use the land, but as several rights may collide in time, the law allocates a third party with the ability to decide on a solution that enables effective realisation of respective rights without depriving any of the beneficiaries of their rights on the property.

In this respect, joint tenancy in English law provides solutions for those cases that resemble co-ownership in civil law countries.[181] Under joint tenancy, issues on rights

[175] See *Re Sandeman's Will Trust* (1937) 1 All ER 368; *Brown v Pringle* (1845) 4 Hare 124, 125; *June Goulding, Marcus Geoffrey Goulding v John Michael James, Peter James Daniel* (1997) 2 All R 239 (SCJCA).

[176] Pearce et al (n 1) 552.

[177] Brown (n 138) 13.

[178] See ss 12 and 13 of the Trusts of Land and Appointment of Trustees Act 1996, c 47.

[179] See s 13(6) of the Trusts of Land and Appointment of Trustees Act 1996, c 47.

[180] See s 7 of the Trusts of Land and Appointment of Trustees Act 1996, c 47.

[181] In joint tenancy, two or more persons hold property or land and, in case of death, the survivors acquire the part or parts of the deceased. In tenancy in common, each party holds their portion of property, and in

to control, occupy or use may arise.[182] Conflicting use or control of joint tenancy – in trust – as in the common house in the case of divorce, may end up in a sale order by the court and the allocation of the proceeds to both beneficiaries or, where physically possible, the splitting up of the property.[183] Tenancy in common of chattels could also end in such way. Similarly, in civil law, co-ownership, where a conflict in the control or use of the property arises, co-owners may make a claim in court either to divide the property, if possible, or to sell it and distribute the proceeds.[184] Thus, both *in rem* civil law proprietary undivided rights and tenancy in common and equitable co-ownership resort to trustees or court powers to sell and distribute the benefits in cases of conflict.

There are several differences in ownership rights and the division of ownership in such cases in equity and in civil and common law. However, the important point is the lack of immediate control, and the decision of the joint beneficiary alone does not per se exclude the proprietary character of its right. Thus, its proprietary character will depend on the specific limitation his or her rights has and, in the case of joint beneficiaries with no other limitation, it is the author's view that there is no doubt as to its proprietary character. The limitation on its right is not a matter of being an *in personam* right, but a solution by operation of the law to enable effective fulfilment of each of the conflicting or concurring rights or sub-rights both or several beneficiaries have on the property. If one were not speaking about proprietary *in rem* rights in these cases, ownership would somehow be in limbo or, even worse, a sort of *res derelictae*.

Some have argued in favour of a suspended ownership, and case law has sometimes supported such approach.[185] In the author's view, cases of joint ownership differ from discretionary trusts, where beneficial ownership has been considered as suspended, as in those cases there are no defined beneficiaries yet, while in joint ownership they exist and have a right against the trust property, although colliding with others rights. In discretionary trusts, it is a matter of all, part or nothing; in a joint ownership, it is always a part. This does not exclude the existence of large proprietary rights to control and income, even though the allocation of it may be shifted until some event occurs. Being subject to such an event, ownership has to be exercised on behalf of, or for the account of, the potential owner or owners.

case of decease, it is devised to their heirs. However, tenancy in common of land is forbidden in English law. Thus, co-ownership is usually arranged through a trust where a single owner or joint tenants hold the land for the benefit of the co-owners. However, in civil law countries, ownership of undivided parts of land is widely accepted. See s 36 of the Law of Property Act 1925, c 20. Smith (n 78) 28 et seq. In France, see Arts 915 and 1873 of the Code Civil; in Spain, see Art 392 of the Código Civil; in Italy, see Art 1100 et seq of the Codice Civile. On the similar approaches in civil law countries, see Van Erp and Akkermans (n 57) 241.

[182] Smith (n 78) 120.

[183] ibid 124–25; *Jones v Challenger* (1961) 1 QB 176, 184–85; s 7 of the Trusts of Land and Appointment of Trustees Act 1996, c 47. However, in some cases of non-express trust it may end up in a deadlock if no power to sale is given.

[184] See Arts 815 and 815-5-1 of the French Code Civil; Arts 1111 et seq of the Italian Codice Civile; Arts 400 and 404 of the Spanish Código Civil.

[185] Even though, in a tax case, their arguments were doubtful in equity law as taking into account nuances derived from the interpretation of tax statutes: see Nourse LJ and Lloyd LJ in *Sainsbury v Inland Revenue Commissioners* (n 114). See also Donovan and Widgery in *Wood Preservation Ltd v Prior (Commissioner)* (1969) 1 WLR 1077. Arguing for a limited use of suspended beneficial ownership, maybe just for estates of deceased persons, *Ayerst (Inspector of Taxes) v C&K (Construction)* (1975) 3 WLR 16 (HL). On the beneficial ownership being in suspense as a controversial statement, see A Rowland, 'Beneficial Ownership in a Corporate Context: What Is It? When Is It Lost? Where Does It Go?' [1997] *British Tax Review* 178, 181.

On the other hand, saying the property is owned by the trustee against the world does not accurately define the case, as precisely such trustees' powers cannot be opposed to everybody but to everybody on behalf of the beneficiaries, and except the beneficiaries as they may act against the trustee to defend their rights and even override trustee decisions if acting all together. It is true that cases of joint ownership may somehow conflict with ownership *strictu sensu* characteristics, such as primary control, but this only arises if ownership is understood as a unique bulk concept.[186] As already noted, ownership rights do not necessarily preclude joint ownership, even though some characteristics of ownership rights are adjusted depending on the case, establishing rules to manage conflicts in control, right to use, income and other rights.

In the case of *non sui juris*, for the above-mentioned arguments, it also feels right to consider that limitation does not deprive the rest of the beneficiaries of the proprietary character of their right, as they can protect it before third parties, request division in some cases, have the right to occupy it or to be indemnified, or can request court substitution.[187] The substitution, being a matter of protection, does not seem to the author to be an obstacle that would override the proprietary rights of the rest of beneficiaries. It is just ownership rights being subject to control to guarantee the rights of certain persons who cannot themselves understand their decisions. However, the case of undefined or unknown beneficiaries seems more controversial, as here the substitution could be more difficult, albeit not impossible.

(iv) *Interests in Possession and Remaindermen's Rights*

Turning to the case of a fixed trust with remainder, or where a settlor transfers his right to a trustee, for the benefit of a person fully entitled to the income or interest in possession – whether lifetime or vested with successive beneficiaries and in reversion – it is much more controversial to say that beneficiaries or remaindermen have ownership rights.[188] In this case, they may all together have ownership rights, and the remaindermen and the beneficiary or beneficiaries together may lay claim to the property as they wish to do, or even allocate it to the beneficiaries in a certain way.[189] However, neither the beneficiaries nor the remaindermen have full individual control over the property itself, nor over a part of it, but the beneficiaries are beneficiaries to the benefits, use or occupation, and the remaindermen are beneficiaries to the remainders.

It may be said that the beneficiary has an *in rem* right to the benefits as they arise, and to the potential benefits or profits, or to use or occupation, for the relevant period.

[186] See above, nn 49–52 and accompanying text.

[187] See above, nn 137 and 159.

[188] Pearce et al (n 1) 703. Even though frequently used by practitioners in both equity and tax law contexts, interest in possession seems to derive from tax law, and in the author's view should not, strictly speaking, be used in equity law, as it has been interpreted in relation to certain tax provisions. It was so defined in *Pearson v IRC* as present right of present enjoyment: *Pearson v Inland Revenue Commissioners* [1980] AC 753 (HL) 773. In addition, HMRC's Inheritance Tax Manual defines it, relying on the above-mentioned *Pearson* case, as '"present right of present enjoyment" or an immediate right to the income or enjoyment of property (irrespective of whether the property produces income). In contrast, the beneficiary (or object) under a non-interest in possession settlement has only the right to be considered by the trustees if and when they distribute any income or benefits': IHTM16062. See also *Gartside v Inland Revenue Commissioners* [1968] AC 533 (HL).

[189] Brown (n 138) 33. See *Ayerst v C&K* (n 185).

He or she may oppose his rights to the whole world if they obtain the profit, income, use or enjoyment. However, as to the original asset or property from which they derive, the beneficiary has the right to income for a period, but may have limited control depending on the conditions of the trust, as he or she can only exercise it in a manner that is compatible with remainderman rights, or with the latter's consent against the settlor intentions.

Remaindermen have no actual ownership nor *in rem* right on the capital or asset, as they cannot primarily control it, nor do they have a right to the income. They do, however, have a suspended right to acquire the land or chattel in the future. Thus, they have no current *in rem* or ownership right on the property, but have an *in rem* title to acquire the property in the future, a vested contingent interest in reversion, but they may be able to oppose third parties or even transfer in certain cases.[190] This is a matter of timing as, in the future, the remainderman may become legal owner or beneficial owner, the issue being to define each time who holds the greatest interest in the property. Consequently, in trusts with remaindermen, at first instance, rights are a mix of direct and derivative, suspended or more or less potential rights, but *in rem* rights, depending on the specific relation at stake. It could be said, not without controversy, that the beneficiary with interest in possession is a beneficial owner with some limitations, and remaindermen have future, interest in reversion or contingent equitable interest.

(v) Discretionary Trusts

In discretionary trusts, the settlor transfers to the trustee for the benefit of the person or persons upon the decision of the trustee, normally among a certain group of persons.

Again, all beneficiaries or potential beneficiaries together hold a joint *in rem* right, but separately hold just a *spes* interest.[191] However, considered separately, beneficiaries have no current right to the property, nor can they oppose it to the world.[192] They can only jointly or individually protect the property and claim against third parties, this being a characteristic of property rights, and make the trustee hold, protect and maintain the property in a manner in accordance with the trust until their discretionary powers are exercised.[193] They cannot, however, sell their right, rendering their interest so soft that it cannot be considered as an *in rem* or proprietary right.[194]

Conversely, the trustee is exercising all of his or her abilities for the benefit of the future beneficiary, which may be any one of the potential beneficiaries. One view is that beneficial ownership is suspended until the trustee exercises his or her discretion to

[190] See, as the main historical source of analysis of vested and contingent rights, C Fearne, *An Essay on the Learning of Contingent Remainders and Executory Devises* (RH Small, 1845). On the historical development and 20th-century discussion in the USA on vested and contingent rights of remaindermen, see ME Brake, 'The Vested vs Contingent Approach to Future Interests: A Critical Analysis of the Michigan Cases' (1946) 9 *University of Detroit Law Journal* 61.

[191] *In Re Smith Public Trustee v Aspinall* [1928] Ch 915 (Ch). In Canada, see Brown (n 138) 33.

[192] MD Brender, 'Symposium: Beneficial Ownership in Canadian Income Tax Law: Required Reform and Impact on Harmonization of Quebec Civil Law and Federal Legislation' (2003) 51 *Canadian Tax Journal* 311, 318.

[193] *Sainsbury v Inland Revenue Commissioners* (n 114) 724; *Gartside v Inland Revenue Commissioners* (n 188) 617.

[194] *Schmidt v Rosewood Trust Ltd* (2003) 709 AC (UKPC) [51, 54]; Davies and Virgo (n 137) 493–94.

allocate the trust benefit or appoint a fixed beneficiary, or until reversion or remainder.[195] Here, there is no current beneficial ownership, but it also cannot be said that the trustee has no *in rem* or ownership right. He or she has ownership in common law. Potential beneficiaries have a potential right or *spes* that cannot be absolutely considered *in rem*; however, a blend of a personal right to be taken into account when allocating the benefit and against the trustee as per management and access to documents, among others, together with the negative right to exclude third parties, means that it may be converted into an *in rem* beneficiary right upon the future exercise of proprietary rights. Waters arranges the beneficial ownership rights around a 'sufficient direct interest'.[196] Under this approach, potential beneficiaries will fail to have something more than what Waters frames as a personal right. The problem with this approach is the definition of what is a 'sufficient interest'.

Nolan, in turn, argues that beneficiaries have negative proprietary rights, while they do not have positive rights.[197] This approach seems to be the most reasonable and is in line with the author's view on ownership with reference to different sets of rights and of different intensities. Their intensity is less than full beneficial ownership, equal to other potential beneficiaries, but certainly more than the rest of the world.

(vi) Non-charitable Purpose Trusts and Charities

Non-charitable purpose trusts are in principle forbidden because they lack a necessary certainty in beneficiary or beneficiaries, or at least potential identifiable beneficiaries, and also because of what perpetuity purposive trusts may entail.[198] However, case law has recognised the validity of purposive trusts in a very small number of cases because they benefit a specific public or group interest, or they rely on an ethical interest.[199] In addition, charities are also recognised, even though they have to be aimed at one of the recognised public interest objects and satisfy the public benefit test in order to prevent the use of charities for tax avoidance because of their exempted status.[200]

[195] See Lord Millett's analysis in *Twinsectra v Yardley* (n 136), even though this referred to a case of contractual rights raising equitable proprietary rights.

[196] Waters (n 5) 175, 281.

[197] Nolan (n 69) 256–57.

[198] This was especially due to the odd nature of perpetuity estates and to the fact that without beneficiaries decree performance seems difficult. See *Morice v Bishop of Durham* (1804) 9 Ves 399 (Ch) 658–59; *In Re Flavel's Will Trusts* [1969] WLR 444 (Ch) 448. However, more recently, such rules seem to have proved to serve to protect trusts from being unduly used to avoid taxes by settling a trust on a purported general public interest while serving their trustees or settlors. For an analysis of the historical rule and current function of the beneficiary requirement see J Getzler, 'Morice v Bishop of Durham (1805)' in in C Mitchell and P Mitchell (eds), *Landmark Cases in Equity Law* (Hart Publishing, 2012).

[199] Such as trusts for a particular animal, for maintenance of (public) monuments and graves, or for the saying of private masses if it does not breach the perpetuity requirement. However, courts have ruled that non-charitable purpose trusts cannot be accepted in general and have rejected, for instance, trusts for the erection and maintenance of private monuments or similar. See *In Re Dean Cooper-Dean v Stevens* (1889) 41 Ch 552 (Ch) 559–60; *Musset v Bingle* [1876] WN 170 (Ch); *In Re Endacott* [1960] Ch 232 (Ch) 248–50; *In Re Hooper Parker v Ward* (1932) 1 Ch 38 (Ch) 40–41.

[200] To be recognised, charities have to fall within a recognised charitable purpose and to satisfy the public benefit interest. Even though historically developed through case law and administrative decisions from the Charity Commission, charitable purposes are now defined in s 3 of the Charities Act 2011, c 25. This includes

In all of these cases, no *in rem* ownership rights, nor beneficial ownership, can be found in a singular person or defined group of persons, but can potentially be found in any person or all persons that may benefit from the objective of the charity, and are exercised by the trustee, the Charities Commission, the Advocate General or the Crown to the account of the relevant purpose.[201] As these cases are an equity 'anomaly', being against the general principles of equity, ownership refers not to a subject, but to an object or purpose. There is no doubt that beneficial ownership exists, as the use, control, enjoyment and benefit of property belonging to these types of trusts excludes any other person in the world from controlling or benefiting from them directly and not through the charity.

As noted in relation to the ownership of public goods, this is a matter of how decision powers regarding the property are organised or attributed. In this sense, beneficial ownership is in the charity or trust, although the decision is subject to a process.

Connected to non-charitable purpose trusts, unincorporated associations are also frequently used to hold and manage property for the benefit of a group of persons. As this cannot be done through a purposive trust, it is normally performed through a charitable trust, on trust for present and future members, as a contract or in agency.[202] The specifics of the characteristics of these cases have to be analysed because proprietary and contractual rights are involved, as in many cases they are not trusts but common law reciprocal contracts.

(vii) Revocable and Settlor-Interest Trusts

In addition, revocable trusts or trusts where the settlor reserves the power to appoint beneficiaries may take the type of any of the above types of trusts, if valid, but they are special, as in these the settlor reserves the right to the benefit from them for their life or revokes it.[203] In these cases, control and benefit is split among the beneficiaries, the settlor and the trustee. Thus, it is highly likely that rights may be a mix of direct or contingent and *in rem* or *in personam* rights.

The author's view is that proprietary rights may be considered to be held by the beneficiary even if the settlor has revocable rights, but only revocable rights and not any other beneficiary right, if the beneficiary can control and has the primary right to the property in any aspect other than deciding whether to revoke the trust. The point here is that ownership is a matter of right at the time, being the right of the beneficiary entitled at any time, which ends if the settlor exercises his power. As in a sale subject to

relief of poverty, advancement of education, advancement of religion, advancement of health or the saving of lives, advancement of citizenship or community development, advancement of arts, culture, arts heritage or science, advancement of amateur sports, advancement of human rights, conflict resolution or reconciliation, the promotion of religious or racial harmony or equality and diversity, the advancement of environmental protection or improvement, the relief of those in need because of youth, age, ill-health, disability, financial hardship or other disadvantage, advancement of animal welfare, the promotion of the efficiency of the armed forces of the Crown or of the efficiency of the police, fire and rescue services or ambulance services, and any other purpose that is considered charitable under recreational or similar trusts, analogous to those included or within the spirit of the law. On charities see Davies and Virgo (n 137) 175 et seq.

[201] See s 13 of the Charities Act 2011.

[202] Davies and Virgo (n 137) 205 et seq.

[203] On the effects of revocable trusts, see *Glen v Watson* [2018] EWHC 2016 (Ch).

resolutive condition, ownership rights are transferred but, if a certain event takes place, ownership reverts to the original owner. For the time being, however, the transferee is the owner. As suggested by some authors, it seems that revocable trusts in England are not frequent, at least in an express form and excluding sham trusts, probably due to the loss of tax advantages they may imply.

(viii) Constructive and Resulting Trusts

Finally, constructive or resulting trusts must be mentioned. Leaving aside the discussion on the difference between them, it is generally considered that resulting trusts derive from the transferor implicitly assuming not to transfer beneficial interest to the transferee, thus a trust being set by operation of the law, while constructive trusts are the legal result of unconscionable conduct or as a court remedy for an unfair situation where property has been transferred to the transferee.[204] As in any other type of trust, beneficial interest may be difficult to allocate and qualify, but the fact that an implicit trust is not explicitly recognised adds to the complexity of recognising it.[205] Moreover, the trust may be only recognised at a later time after a conflict between the parties arises, may be raised as a remedy in court or may even never be recognised but remains hidden. Timing then becomes relevant. For instance, there is significant controversy as to when an implicit trust arises in a sale or when beneficial ownership passes in an implicit trust, or even if it stays and how long it is suspended for.[206]

In a resulting trust, beneficial ownership is never transferred, so an in rem right characteristic may be inferred. In constructive trusts rights, an institutional or declarative constructive trust would include large proprietary rights, but could be just a personal right in some remedial constructive trusts, depending on whether the objects are traceable and identifiable.[207] However, if one follows this argument by saying that the theory

[204] In constructive trusts, courts just limit to recognise the existence of the trust, not being conditional on the courts' declaration. Some jurisdictions recognise the ability of the court to discretionally create a constructive trust as a remedy in unfair situations. However, this approach has been rejected in England: see *Halifax Building Society v Thomas and Another* [1996] Ch 217 (Ch) 229; *Westdeutsche Landesbank Girozentrale v Islington LBC* [1996] AC 669 (UKHL) 714–15. Resulting trusts arise when somebody transfers property to a person, the transferor implicitly not transferring beneficial interest or failing to transfer beneficial interest. In this regard, see *Vandervell Appellant v Inland Revenue Commissioners Respondents* (n 152); *In Re Vandervell (2)* [1974] Ch 269 (Ch). For a comprehensive and clear analysis of resulting and constructive trusts, see Davies and Virgo (n 137) 327–427, and the case law quoted therein. On the controversy of the main and definitory characteristics of constructive and resulting trusts, see Virgo and Burn (n 118) 197–208. See also T Frankel, *Fiduciary Law* (Oxford University Press, 2010) 267. However, some authors claim that constructive trusts are just remedies and not a proper trust.

[205] See the analysis of a constructive trust in a sale in *Lysaght v Edwards* (1876) 2 Ch D 499; *Rayner v Preston* [1881] Ch D 1.

[206] *Parway Estates, Ltd v IRC* (1958) 45 TC 135 (CA); *English Sewing Cotton Co v IRC* (1947) 1 All ER 679 (CA); *Jerome v Kelly (Inspector of Taxes)* [2004] UKHL 25 (UKHL); *Wood Preservation Ltd v Prior (Commissioner)* (n 185); *Ayerst (Inspector of Taxes) v C&K (Construction)* (n 185).

[207] Implicitly recognising proprietary rights in constructive trusts, even though obscure as derived from quoting other sources, Nolan (n 69) 238–39. In the *Twinsectra* case, concerning a Quistclose constructive trust (a trust in favour of the lender in a loan for a purpose that becomes impossible to perform), Lord Millett analysed the beneficial interest to be vested in the lender, the borrower, a contemplated beneficiary or in suspense. However, as per Lord Millett's analysis, it seems even the court resolved in favour of a suspended interest, it giving a proprietary remedy to the lender unless the purpose is fulfilled: *Twinsectra v Yardley* (n 136).

of the constructive trust is just a remedy and not a proper trust, as some authors argue, then rights would be just personal rights in every case.[208] Because these cases depend on the arrangements at stake, careful consideration of each right involved is needed.

Finally, if ownership leaves a subject but has not reached another, implicit trusts or equitable performance obligations may leave proprietary rights in suspense, as beneficial ownership in these cases is not vested until certain activities are performed by the parties.[209]

(ix) Common Law Arrangements with Implicit Trusts

Equity rights may overlap with other common law rights. In this regard, it is important to bear in mind that an agency, a partnership or any common law intermediary contract significantly differs from a trust and should be identified properly. The main difference is that trust obligations derive from the trust document or legal origin, whereas common law obligations normally derive from the instructions of the principal. Another difference is that trust property is entrusted, while in intermediary contracts property is not always entrusted.[210]

However, in certain cases, an agency contract in common law may derive equitable proprietary rights through constructive or resulting trust rights. The same may be said for purchase and sales, partnerships, mandates, custody, and almost any contract in common law where assets are involved and where confidence plays a role in the reason why property is conveyed and/or there is a misbalance of rights.[211] A proper separation of both the arrangement and the equity rights is needed before defining beneficial ownership.

(x) Other Trusts

Many other types of trusts may be found, such as custodian trusts, unit investment trusts or protective trusts. In addition, as flexible as trusts are, each type may be redefined in several ways. The point that the author is attempting to make by analysing the different types of trusts is that, contrary to what most scholars have argued, beneficial interest characterisation as *in rem* or *in personam* rights cannot be predefined and absolute, but depends on the specific characteristics of the trust, the assets involved and the relevant legal systems, as they differ from one common law country to another. In addition, in some cases, rights may be regarded as a blend of them. It must be admitted that in many cases, the main core of beneficial interests would be closer to proprietary

[208] Some interesting contributions to the discussion are M Cope, *Constructive Trusts* (Law Book Co, 1992) 24 et seq; JL Dewar, 'The Development of the Remedial Constructive Trust' (1982) 60 *Canadian Bar Review* 265; L Rotman, 'Deconstructing the Constructive Trust' (1999) 37 *Alberta Law Review* 133; DWM Waters, *Constructive Trusts: Case for a New Approach in English Law* (Athlone Press, 1964).

[209] *Parway Estates, Ltd v IRC* (n 206); *English Sewing Cotton Co v IRC* (n 206); *Ayerst (Inspector of Taxes) v C&K (Construction)* (n 185); *Wood Preservation Ltd v Prior (Commissioner)* (n 185). See also Rowland (n 193).

[210] Frankel (n 204) 5–6.

[211] On how a buy and sale may derive equitable obligations on performance see *Parway Estates, Ltd v IRC* (n 206). See also the cases in n 209 above.

rights; however, this should not be considered to be an absolute truth, as it could mislead the analysis in some, although admittedly few, exceptions, in which beneficiaries cannot be said to have proprietary interests.[212]

In any case, characterisation of each right remains relevant as it will define the core characteristics as to how the parties involved relate to each other, the objects involved and the world.

III. Beneficial Ownership and the Tension between Ownership as a Strong Right and Beneficiary Rights as a Flexible Matter

As already said, ownership is a word of some strength as a result of the evolution of the concept in the nineteenth century. Once its absolute character is properly balanced, it is the greatest right in a thing against the world at large, with the ability to exclude third parties, and usually comprising the primary rights to income and control. On the other hand, beneficiary rights in equity comprise infinite sets of rights, as many different rights can be allocated in different configurations in trusts. To balance both definitions, beneficial ownership in equity is located in the intersection where beneficiary rights match those strong characteristics of ownership. In this regard, beneficial ownership in equity could be defined as the present right in equity against the world at large over assets or property of a trust, outweighing any other rights and usually including the primary right to control and the primary right to income. In addition, it is important to bear in mind that beneficial ownership is a subtype of beneficial interest.

Beneficial interest, in turn, is a right in equity in a broad sense, including an expectation or right to be taken into consideration, a vested right and beneficial ownership. Thus, only when beneficiary interest qualifies as a proprietary interest may one speak of beneficial ownership. This would be the case of most beneficiaries in trust, where beneficiaries may be more or less certain in relation to a certain income or assets, or, at least, there is a group within them from which future beneficiaries will be appointed. However, in some cases, beneficial ownership cannot be said to be held by beneficiaries, as they will only have a hope or a loose right to be considered as potential beneficiaries, or the right is conditional on performance. In these cases, if nobody holds beneficial ownership or beneficiary interest, those rights might be seen in the trustee, though limited, or in suspense.

It is also important to bear in mind that a subject might be considered as the beneficial owner of a certain item of income or asset insofar as they have a primary right against the world to income and control, even though they are not considered the beneficial owner of all a trust's assets, as the beneficiary of an interest in possession may be. In that regard, they might be considered as the beneficial owner of the income when arising, but not the beneficial owner of the capital of the trust.

[212] Holding that the main core of beneficial interest are proprietary rights, see Nolan (n 69) 234; Davies and Virgo (n 137) 61.

In addition, where there are different beneficiaries, even of different types of rights, beneficial ownership is held by all of them together, as happens in joint ownership or ownership in common, subject to the specific rules governing the relevant trust.

Finally, differentiation must be made between the above-mentioned legal beneficial ownership definition and loose common parlance usage, where the term is employed to refer to any subject that relates to a property as in fact controlling something, irrespective of the legal title it holds.

3

Beneficial Ownership in Tax Law

I. Ability to Pay, Allocation of Income and Beneficial Ownership

In contemporary income and capital taxes, liability to tax is defined by a subject matter of wealth being allocated to an object. Both elements – subject and object – and the relationship between them are equally important in defining taxation, as an object without an owner is not taxable, and neither is a subject without an object. This is derived from the ability to pay and personal taxation principles, which require taxes to be levied in the hands of the subject to whom the wealth is available.[1] However, despite the importance of defining liability to tax, it has not received the treatment it deserve in statutes.[2] And even though it has been behind a significant number of conflicting cases, it has received little attention by the courts and by scholars, with the issue in many cases being directly framed in anti-avoidance and sham rules.[3]

In the first instance, allocation of income is normally defined by reference to the right to the income in income taxes, or the right to the assets in capital taxes or inheritance taxes.[4] Similarly, some countries define tax rules on the person legally entitled to, or the owner of, the asset or income.[5] However, such broad definitions do not define

[1] Taxation is built upon ability to pay, as each person should contribute from the wealth they enjoy under the protection of the state. Following such a premise, taxes are defined by the connection of a subject to the relevant subject matter. Even though this principle has been recognised since the beginning of times, Adam Smith is considered one of the main advocators of this principle in modern tax systems. AG Buehler, 'Ability to Pay' (1945) 1 *Tax Law Review* 243; A Smith, *Wealth of Nations : An Inquiry into the Nature and Causes of The Wealth of Nations* (Mobilereference.com, 2009) 1084 et seq.

[2] J Wheeler, 'General Report', *Conflicts in the Attribution of Income to a Person* (Kluwer, 2007) 20; A Baez, *Los Negocios Fiduciarios En La Imposición Sobre La Renta* (Aranzadi, 2009) 58, 62 et seq.

[3] Wheeler (n 2) 20; C McAree, 'United Kingdom' in J Wheeler (ed), *Conflicts in the Attribution of Income to a Person* (Kluwer, 2007) 647. See, as an example, *Tomlinson v Miles* [1963] 5th Circuit 316, F 2d 710, where, even though the court seems to recognise ownership is on the shareholders, it relies on anti-avoidance rules or general tax principles to allocate the income: *Tomlinson v Mile*. See also the *Real Madrid* and *Goldman Sachs* case ruled by the National Court (Audiencia Nacional) in Spain. In those cases, tax consequences were allocated following a substance over form or business purpose approach without a proper analysis of allocation rules. For an explanation in English, see A Martín Jiménez, 'Beneficial Ownership as a Broad Anti-Avoidance Provision: Decisions by Spanish Courts and the OECD's Discussion Draft' in M Lang et al (eds), *Beneficial Ownership: Recent Trends* (IBFD, 2012); A Martín Jiménez, 'Beneficial Ownership as an Attribution-of-Income Rule in Spain: Source and Residence Country Perspectives' in M Lang et al (eds), *Beneficial Ownership: Recent Trends* (IBFD, 2012).

[4] See Germany, Norway or Japan in Wheeler (n 2) 21.

[5] ibid 20–21. Germany and Austria are two of the few countries with a specific allocation rule based on private law ownership and a specific subsidiary effective and economic control allocation. See s 39 of the

the type of right or ownership rights that the subject should have in order to be liable for taxation. These simplistic definitions leave aside many cases in which contractual or real rights to the income or assets are split among different subjects, or are even vested in a single subject, such rights being offset for the economic benefit of a third party. This may be the case where ownership is split between a naked ownership or a reversionary interest being vested in one person and the use and enjoyment being held by another person. In this case, should the ability to pay be allocated to, and tax paid by, the former, the latter or both? A similar case may be that of a bank deriving income from shares bought at the request of a client, while it is committed by a derivative contract to pay an equivalent amount to that client. Should income be attributed to the bank or directly to the derivative creditor?

Although subject to significant controversy during the twentieth century, it is widely accepted that such tax relationships should be defined in the first instance by reference to private law.[6]

If allocation of income can sometimes be controversial, defining tax liability on the person with 'right' or 'ownership' leads nowhere when it comes to trusts. As Thomas and Hudson rightly point out, the 'advantage of trusts is the possibility of more than one person owning at one and the same time such that the question of which of them is to bear liability to pay tax is a complex one'.[7] After all, one of the main original objectives of trusts, which continues to be so, was to avoid taxes and incidents on land and property.

The split of ownership in trusts made development of some principles to deal with them necessary. Beneficial ownership is, to some extent, the result of the need of tax law to deal with the split of ownership in trusts in order to tax the ability to pay that is held in the trust. The rise of trusts, the strengthening of equitable proprietary rights and the development of the modern tax system led case law to develop allocation of tax principles in relation to trusts in the last part of the nineteenth and early twentieth centuries.[8] As tax treatment of trusts gained attention and beneficial ownership was used

Abgabenordnung of Germany and s 24 of the Austrian Bundesabgabenordnung. In the UK, the historical evolution of the income tax relying on different tax types, without a comprehensive tax liability, meant that the system lacked allocation of income rules and relied on anti-avoidance rules. See McAree (n 3).

[6] Wheeler (n 2) 20. In Canada, see C Brown, 'Tax, Trusts and Beneficial Ownership: Perils for the Unwary Practitioner' (2003) 23 *Estates, Trusts and Pensions Journal* 9, 25. However, the debate on the relationship between private law and tax law, and the role of what has been called economic interpretation, is well known. See, on legal interpretation, economic interpretation and avoidance, G Marín Benítez, *¿Es Lícita La Planificación Fiscal?* (Lex Nova, 2013) 144–61; A Hensel, *Steuerrecht* (NWB Verlag, 1986); Baez (n 2); V Combarros Villanueva, 'La Interpretación Económica Como Criterio de Interpretación Jurídica (Algunas Reflexiones a Propósito Del Concepto de "Propiedad Económica" En El Impuesto Sobre Patrimonio)' [1984] *Civitas. Revista española de derecho europeo* 485; F Geny, *Méthode d'interpretation Eet Source En Droit Privé Positif: Essai Critique*, vol II (Librairie générale de droit et de jurisprudence, 1919); J Ramallo Massanet, 'Derecho Fiscal Frente a Derecho Civil: Discusión En Torno a La Naturaleza Del Derecho Fiscal Entre L Trotabas y F Geny' [1973] *Revista de la Facultad de Derecho de la Universidad Complutense de Madrid* 7. See also C Grimm, 'Das Steuerrecht Im Spannungsfeld Zwischen Wirtschaftlicker Betrachtungsweise Und Zivilrecht' [1978] *Deutsche Steuer-Zeitung* 283, quoted by Combarros Villanueva.

[7] GJ Virgo and EH Burn, *Trusts and Trustees*, 7th edn (Oxford University Press, 2008) 31; GW Thomas and A Hudson, *The Law of Trusts* (Oxford University Press, 2004) 50.

[8] In England, see *William v Singer* (1921) 1 AC 65; *Baker (Inspector of Taxes) v Archer-Shee* [1927] AC 844 (HL); *Pool v Royal Exchange Assurance* (1921) 7 TC 387; *Kelly (Inspector of Taxes) v Rogers* (1935) 2 KB 446; *Reid's Trustees v Inland Revenue Commissioners* [1929] SC 439; *Timpson's Executors v Yerbury (Inspector of Taxes)* [1936] KB 645 (CA).

to deal with them in taxation, so the concept was also used to deal with cases where, although no trust was found, the interposition of corporations or other subjects led to an economic or factual pattern similar to an equitable ownership. This was especially true when defining the applicability of certain exemptions and reliefs.

Consequently, beneficial ownership is used nowadays in the tax law of common law countries as part of the set of principles of allocation of income or assets.[9] The concept defines the relationship that exists between the objects of income or assets and taxable subjects in order to trigger or set tax liability, or for an exemption or relief to be applicable in cases where proprietary rights may be split or, confusingly, are diverted to different subjects.

However, as it developed from equity law and tax law, the concept also carried equity flexibility and imprecise character. Strictly speaking, one cannot talk about a concept of beneficial ownership in tax law. The term refers to a set of principles, and several concepts were derived from them depending on the context and cases in which they appear, often not necessarily in accordance with equity or private law, but providing their own meaning derived from the context.[10] Thus, the lawyer faced with beneficial ownership in tax law must be very careful as, even though the concept uses the same or similar wording, it relies heavily on context, which, together with its function, which is by nature obscure and flexible, leads to frequent misunderstandings. To analyse all of them would be a titanic feat and, worse still, usually leads to pessimistic impractical conclusions.[11] Although case law and some scholars have tried to find a uniform definition, no consistent solution has been found and different results and nuances have been reached.[12] Despite this, in tax law, a central premise comprising two principles may be identified. The aim of these two principles and four sub-principles of beneficial ownership is to balance equity law principles with the collection of tax revenue on ability to pay.

The first principle, the main principle in the UK until the 1980s, is the certainty and absolute entitlement principle. Under this principle, first developed in its current form in the *Archer-Shee* case, if a person is almost absolutely entitled in equity to an object or income, such as in a bare trust, tax liability will be defined on him or her. In a negative sense, if there are doubts regarding to whom income or assets have to be allocated in equity, if it is subject to future decisions or is split into different levels, such as in discretionary trusts, taxation will be defined as falling upon the trustee or legal owner, even

[9] The leading case defining tax liability in relation to beneficial ownership is *Baker (Inspector of Taxes) v Archer-Shee* (n 8). For statutory reliefs or exemptions, see, eg s 351 of the Income Tax Act 2007, c 3; ss 237 and 241 of the Corporation Tax Act 2010, c 4; s 85.1(2) of the Income Tax Act, RSC, 1985, c 1 (5th Supp) (Canada). Noting the relevance of beneficial ownership in common law countries for defining tax liability and in relation to reliefs, A Rowland, 'Beneficial Ownership in a Corporate Context: What Is It? When Is It Lost? Where Does It Go?' [1997] *British Tax Review* 178, 179–80; M Stone and V Lesnie, 'Some Thoughts on Beneficial Interests and Beneficial Ownership in Revenue Law' (1996) 19 *University of New South Wales Law Journal* 181, 182; J Wheeler, 'The Attribution of Income in the Netherlands and the United Kingdom' (2011) 3 *World Tax Journal* 39, 72.

[10] Brown (n 6) 27, 51; R Speed, 'Beneficial Ownership' (1997) 26 *Australian Tax Review* 34, 50. Rowland (n 9) 180 notes that to reach the conclusion of beneficial ownership having a different meaning in different contexts is unsatisfactory, but implicitly recognises that this is the current case law outcome.

[11] Rowland (n 9) 180.

[12] ibid; Brown (n 6) 51–52; C Brown, 'Symposium: Beneficial Ownership and the Income Tax Act' (2003) 51 *Canadian Tax Journal* 401, 452.

though future beneficiaries may also have secondary tax liability to adjust it to their personal tax conditions, ie the certainty principle in a negative sense: uncertain or split rights leading to the uncertainty subprinciple. The fact that taxation is defined on the trustee follows as, in the absence of a certain beneficiary, he is the person with the greatest rights against the world, though not absolute.[13]

In addition to the certainty principle, the broad use of trusts to reduce or defer taxation requires the certainty principle to be supplemented with an anti-avoidance principle. The first anti-avoidance sub-principle, specifically the settlor benefit principle, places taxation on the settlor if he or she retains control or interest. The second, a general anti-avoidance sub-principle, states that if ownership rights are shifted for the purpose of defeating the purpose of a rule, without a business purpose or artificially, income or assets will be allocated to the person factually controlling the income or assets. Under this line of reasoning, it may be said that in some cases tax law defines a kind of 'implicit tax constructive or resulting trust' solely for tax purposes in cases where no express trust is defined, or even where equitable constructive or resulting trusts are doubtful, but where tax law principles require the reallocation of ownership in order to follow the economic rationale of the transaction or for anti-avoidance purposes.

These principles have been developed in case law, largely in the UK, and have followed in the other common law countries, and in some cases have been codified in statutory law, especially in relation to trusts, although some principles, such as the general anti-avoidance principle, were developed earlier in the USA.

However, these principles are not absolute. In many cases, specific rules depart from the above-mentioned principles. Nevertheless, such principles play a major role, as anti-avoidance principles are applied directly as judiciary tools, even on top of some specific rules, or, because statutory rules leave the question open by referring to 'beneficial ownership', submitting the issue to this set of principles and leaving the final answer to the judges.

Although the UK, Canada and the USA follow those principles in a similar way, the specifics of how each system implements them are different. For instance, following the principle of certainty, the UK tax system may allocate tax consequences both to the trustees and to the beneficiaries, giving to the latter a credit on the tax paid by the former once the beneficiaries have been defined.[14] Meanwhile, in Canada, taxation is defined on the trustee but, if income is paid or due to the beneficiaries, it will be allocated to the latter and deducted from the trust income.[15] This does not, however, distort the validity of the principles. These cases may be seen as withholding taxes as in payrolls, so what matters is who actually carries the burden upon the action of the whole system.

[13] See ss II.B and C in ch 2 above.

[14] J Wheeler, *The Missing Keystone of Income Tax Treaties* (IBFD, 2012) 150–52.

[15] See s 104(2) and (6) of the Income Tax Act, RSC 1985, c 1 (5th Supp) (Canada). However, no deduction is allowed if the income is distributed to a person different from the spouse in a spousal trust, a beneficiary other than the settlor in an alter ego trust, and other than the settlor or the spouse or common law partner in the case of a joint spousal or joint common law partner trust. ibid 152–153; ES Roth et al, *Canadian Taxation of Trusts* (Canadian Tax Foundation, 2016) 119 et seq. On the use of beneficial ownership as an allocation principle and starting point based on UK case law, see Brown, 'Symposium: Beneficial Ownership' (n 12) 30 et seq and the reference to the *Archer-Shee* case as the basis for Canadian jurisprudence therein, namely *Ontario (Minister of Revenue) v McCreath* (1977) 1 SCR 2.

In US tax law, equitable principles on allocation of income have been blended with anti-avoidance principles under the third principle, influencing or distorting the first principle.[16] Consequently, the USA has been seen as following an economic ownership allocation. However, the blurred view of the principles in the USA does not diminish their value, as they serve as main guidance, although one must be careful as it is full of exceptions.

The result of the combination of these principles referring to private law ownership or entitlement, specific rules referring to partial rights in private law, and anti-avoidance or economic rules or principles is important as a way of guaranteeing state taxing rights, in tension with private law flexibility under freedom of will that enables tax planning opportunities.[17] This is even more important in common law countries, where equity and trust law enables the rearrangement of rights on income and assets with great flexibility. Thus, the tax law of common law countries both resorts to ownership rights in common law and in equity law as well as anti-avoidance principles, guaranteeing that tax falls on the person benefiting from the ability to pay to be taxed.

II. The Two Principles

A. Certainty, Absolute Entitlement and Uncertainty

(i) The Archer-Shee Principle: Certainty and Uncertainty

In cases where abilities or rights to the income and control of the property are split among different subjects, such as trusts, ordinary allocation rules based on private law may fail or be difficult to apply. This was especially true of the UK, where the lack of a comprehensive income tax and non-subjection of capital gains until 1965, together with the fact that UK tax law 'heavily' relied on withholding the tax at the payer level, made allocation relatively unnecessary.[18] The result was a lack of statutory rules on the issue, and nor did it receive enough academic attention. That made reduction of the tax burden through tax planning relatively easy by allocating income to an overseas trustee, or even a local trustee subject to a reduced rate. To solve this issue, case law dealt with it early on, providing judicial solutions for the allocation of income in trust cases and anti-avoidance principles, although the use of anti-avoidance rules was

[16] See C Du Toit, *Beneficial Ownership of Royalties in Bilateral Tax Treaties* (IBFD, 1999) 126. This blend derives from the so-called nominee and disregard theories in relation to allocation of income in cases dealing with intermediary entities. See *Moline Properties Inc v Commissioner of Internal Revenue* (1943) 319 US 436. See also the analysis of the case and its relation with beneficial ownership in JE Miller, 'The Nominee Conundrum: The Live Dummy Is Dead, but the Dead Dummy Should Live!' (1978) 34 *Tax Law Review* 213, 219, fn 13.

[17] Wheeler (n 2) 20–21.

[18] Even though it has been argued since 2007 that the system has been changing from a tax at source to a tax at the payee system, Wheeler argues that this was never the case, as the withholding tax was never applied to the full system and only applied for the basic rate: Wheeler (n 9) 47; McAree (n 3) 647. In case law, on the fact that statutory tax law did not dealt with title, see Viscount Sumner in *Baker (Inspector of Taxes) v Archer-Shee* (n 8) 749.

significantly limited following the narrow tax law interpretation approach provided in *Duke of Westminster*.[19]

The leading case on the use of equitable rights as a starting point in defining tax liability is the *Archer-Shee* case.[20] In this case, Lady Archer-Shee was entitled to the income derived from an estate composed of a significant amount of shares, securities and stock held by a New York trustee in a trust that she inherited from her father. The bank remitted some income to the UK, the rest being credited to the bank account of Lady Archer-Shee in her New York bank, and also used part of the income to fulfil duties in the USA and for their management fees. The question was whether the income derived was income from the stocks, securities and shares held in possession by Lady Archer-Shee indirectly through the trust, or whether the stocks, securities and shares were not held by her but she had a general unspecific right to the trust income. The former would fall under income from foreign possessions in shares, stock and securities under the Income Tax Act 1918, and so would be taxable in the UK, while the latter would be considered as foreign income derived from possessions different from stocks, shares and securities, and would not be taxable in England unless remitted.[21] In sum, the issue was to define whether Lady Archer-Shee had a proprietary right to the shares, stocks and securities under the trust, or if it was another type of right.

Although there were different arguments throughout the appeal stages, the House of Lords finally ruled in favour of the Commissioners of the Inland Revenue, considering that Lady Archer-Shee held possession of the income through the trust and was therefore liable to tax on the whole income, including the proceeds remaining in the US Bank.[22]

The main argument of the Lords Justice who opposed assessment of the unremitted income referred to the inability of the beneficiary to instruct on the amount to receive or the time upon which the income was submitted.[23] However, this may be an imprecise conclusion. First, under *Saunders v Vautier*, she had the ability, jointly with her niece and New York College as beneficiaries in case of death of Lady Archer-Shee, to override settlors' instructions and limitations to the trustees.[24] She had no absolute control, but she had a right to joint control. Secondly, once the income was assigned to Lady Archer-Shee, as the income was credited in the New York bank account, she could fully claim the income in court. The issue, as stated in the previous chapter, is a matter of timing. Before the trustee has exercised discretions, equitable ownership to the income does not yet exist but is a potential right. On the capital and potential income, however, she has

[19] *Commissioner v Duke of Westminster* [1936] AC 1 (HL).

[20] *Baker (Inspector of Taxes) v Archer-Shee* (n 8). This principle was also dealt with later for purposes of capital gains taxes in *Tomlinson (Inspector of Taxes) v Glyns Executor and Trustee Co and Another* [1970] Ch 112 (Court of Appeal). See M Gammie, 'The Archer-Shee Cases (1927): Trusts, Transparency and Source' in J Snape and D de Cogan (eds), *Landmark Cases in Revenue Law* (Hart Publishing, 2019); M Gammie, 'The Origins of Fiscal Transparency in UK Income Tax' in J Tiley (ed), *Studies in the History of Tax Law*, vol 4 (Hart Publishing, 2010); KF Sin, *The Legal Nature of the Unit Trust* (Oxford University Press, 1997) 264 et seq.

[21] See Cases IV and V, Sched D to the Income Tax Act 1918, c 40.

[22] See the different arguments through the different stages in Gammie, 'The Origins of Fiscal Transparency' (n 20); Gammie, 'The Archer-Shee Cases' (n 20). See Lord Atkinson, Lord Wrenbury and Lord Carson in *Baker (Inspector of Taxes) v Archer-Shee* (n 8) 861–63, 866, 871–72 against Viscount Sumner and Lord Blanesburgh.

[23] Lord Blanesburgh in *Baker (Inspector of Taxes) v Archer-Shee* (n 8) 873.

[24] *Saunders v Vautier* (1841) 42 ER 282 (Ct of Chancery).

a joint ownership under *Saunders v Vautier*. But from then on, the income is owned by Lady Archer-Shee as if she has obtained the income from the securities. If the property entrusted had been apple trees, and apples had been assigned, what would the case have been? Would the apples have been qualified as neutral 'income' from a right in the trust, or would the apples continue to be apples as sourced from the trees, despite being income in kind? The author's view is that the fact that the income is entrusted does not change its nature with regard to 'rights', but just suspends its enjoyment until the trustee exercises its powers.

Finally, as the powers of the trustee may be limited by Lady Archer-Shee's performance claims and may be subject to a joint instruction by Lady Archer-Shee and the remaindermen, to say the trustee has 'full' legal ownership misunderstands the roles of legal ownership and beneficiary rights.[25] Legal ownership cannot be full unless misunderstood as absolute ownership, and less so if understood as a set of rights co-existing in parallel to beneficiary rights in equity.

Another argument against allocating the income to Lady Acher-Shee was that the income remaining in New York was retained to fulfil US law requirements and US tax liabilities, and there was no certainty on the income to be paid until it was effectively remitted, the resulting income remitted to the UK not being the income obtained from the portfolio.[26] It was also argued that Lady Archer-Shee's income did not accrue to her but to the trustee, and she only had a right in the USA to claim that the trust funds be executed in her favour or performance.[27] These arguments also fail insofar as income was accruing to the trustees, taxes were falling on them, and they were paying and fulfilling legal obligations in their condition of trustees, not as a different matter from the beneficiaries, but for the benefit of Lady Archer-Shee.

Also, the fact that an additional burden may arise is a matter of how tax is collected in the UK on the trust and on the beneficiary, not one of the income being different.

Contrary to what Viscount Sumner argued, it is for the interpreter to match how the tax burden is allocated in the law and how rights to income are arranged in a will, the will not being irrelevant.[28] If what Viscount Sumner argued were the case, it would mean tax law disregards private arrangements, and avoiding taxes would be as easy as it was before the Statute of Uses tried to tackle trusts, contrary to tax principles that were developed in the nineteenth century. However, the fact that the UK tax system in the early twentieth century was highly susceptible to tax avoidance by giving preference to private arrangements before the tax law, and by interpreting tax liability narrowly, must be taken into account; it was more than half a century after *Archer-Shee* that the *Ramsay* case fully recognised the balance between private law freedom of will and the duty to contribute to public expenses.[29]

Gammie explains the case differently. He argues that the decision is grounded in the implicit distinction contained in the Income Tax Act 1842 between property and

[25] *Baker (Inspector of Taxes) v Archer-Shee* (n 8) 850.

[26] Lord Blanesburgh in ibid 873.

[27] ibid 855–56 (Viscount Sumner).

[28] ibid 851 (Viscount Sumner).

[29] On a narrow interpretation of tax liability doctrine that was in force in the UK for more than half a century, see *Commissioner v Duke of Westminster* (n 19). Regarding overturning such doctrine and providing for the ability to interpret law and private arrangements in the light of the duty to contribute and providing for an anti-avoidance approach, see *Ramsay v Inland Revenue Commissioner* (1981) 1 All ER 865 (HL).

activities that are 'income producing' classified by schedule and case, and rights not falling within any schedule or case which represent an entitlement to income.[30] As previously mentioned, the UK tax system at the time was collecting tax at source, so whom the income was benefiting was almost irrelevant.[31] The main criterion was source taxation. Rights as entitlement to income from property or activities were not seen as sources themselves, but as entitlements to share in the income sourced in a particular property or activity.[32] For Gammie, the issue in *Baker* was that the rules for taxing foreign income depended on two issues: whether the income was sourced in foreign property or activity, or was a right to participate; and who could be assessed in respect of it.[33]

Under his reasoning, the second question was the key issue. As the foreign trustee was not assessable, the question was whether the entitlement of Lady Archer-Shee as beneficiary was enough to support the assessment. The nature of the entitlement was to some extent irrelevant, the point being whether she was assessable under her title. Gammie's view is that the House of Lords ruled that the *in rem–in personam* debate was irrelevant for income tax purposes, but whether the type of income was chargeable was. Once the income was defined as chargeable under general provisions of the law, her entitlement was only relevant in defining whether she was assessable. With those two elements, tax could be charged on her.[34] For Gammie, the qualification of the type of income at its source – shares or other income – was only relevant in defining the income as something Income Tax Act aimed to charge under a particular schedule and case – who had the right to the income and under which title was irrelevant.

Gammie's approach, although appealing, does not fully convince this author. First, his claim is built upon the argument that the Income Tax Act 1842 (ITA 1842) generally gave almost no relevance to the person entitled to the income.[35] The tax system at the time of the ruling, likely in transition from real and schedular taxes towards income taxes, put the spotlight on collecting tax at source to guarantee revenue. The reasoning behind this was that if the income was due to another person, the burden would pass on. Gammie assumes, and is right to some extent, that some rules of the ITA 1842 were based merely on income arising – source rules – while others (namely those dealing with foreign income) were dependent on a subject to be assessable, and income falling within a certain type of income was considered as chargeable.[36] However, the fact that some rules put more emphasis on the source does not necessarily mean the subject was irrelevant; rather, it shows a mixture of practical reasons and historic evolution. Probably he is right on how ITA 1842 was understood at the time when it was passed in Parliament, but this was maybe not the case at the time of the ruling. Because the system was progressively evolving to one of comprehensive personal taxation, to put the burden on the subject implied a risk to collection.[37] On the other hand, to put it at source was a

[30] Gammie, 'The Archer-Shee Cases' (n 20) 151.

[31] ibid 150.

[32] Gammie, 'The Origins of Fiscal Transparency' (n 20) 36–40; Gammie, 'The Archer-Shee Cases' (n 20) 150–51.

[33] Gammie, 'The Archer-Shee Cases' (n 20) 151; Gammie, 'The Origins of Fiscal Transparency' (n 20) 47–49.

[34] Gammie, 'The Archer-Shee Cases' (n 20) 152.

[35] ibid 150.

[36] ibid 151; Gammie, 'The Origins of Fiscal Transparency' (n 20) 47–49.

[37] See the failure of collection under Pitt's Income Tax 1799, which some claim was due to the system of collection, in Gammie, 'The Origins of Fiscal Transparency' (n 20) 33–34.

guarantee of collection.[38] This does not necessarily mean the person was irrelevant, but that the system established a primitive withholding system to guarantee tax collection. Taxpayers were in several cases obliged or able to fulfil their tax obligations, deducting the tax collected at source. There was an implicit assumption behind the ITA 1842 that taxes have to be charged on a person, although this was not explicitly mentioned, and for practical reasons they were collected at source. The specific mechanism should not be confused with the architecture. Implicit charging rules defined the income to be charged, and rules on rights representing entitlement to income – rights on partnerships, trusts, etc – established special provisions so that taxes could be quantified and advanced. However, both the charging rules and the special provisions provide an implicit reference to subjects, as income in personal taxes to which the act refers, ie income tax, cannot exist without a subject – there is, and there was, no income for tax purposes if there is no subject.

In *Archer-Shee*, Gammie seemingly blends assessment and allocation of income. It is true that charging provisions and assessment rules are different, but he seemingly derives a sort of allocation rule from assessment rules.[39] He states that general charging provisions and assessment rules work differently, and radically divide the issue. Charging provisions will look at the income, defining whether it should be chargeable, while assessment rules will define who has to pay. He argues that Sir Archer-Shee was considered as chargeable because the income was chargeable, and he was assessable. But once we have defined that there is an implicit subjective element of the charging provision that does not necessarily match the assessment provisions, this reasoning fails. If the subject does not fulfil the subjective element of the charging provision – the income to be his or her income – then no charge can arise. Precisely, *Archer-Shee* defines that implicit subjective element of the charging provision. A different issue is how income tax is going to be assessed and who is going to fulfil the assessment conditions. Gammie forgets about the implicit subjective element of income tax, not clear at the time and under development, and derives it from a totally different rule, the mechanics on how it is assessed; however, the income tax subjective element does not necessarily depend on who is assessed, but on who performs the charging event. For the income to be charged, income has to arise, and it has to arise in the hands of a subject who is a resident in the UK. Only then is it chargeable, because otherwise there is no income, and no chargeable event occurs. Once the event is defined, who is to be assessable will be considered.

Another point that does not fully convince this author is that Gammie relies on an implicit assumption of tax legislation against the wording of Viscount Dunedin in *Archer-Shee v Garland*, which explicitly explains the majority view in *Archer-Shee* as stating that 'there was in the beneficiary a specific equitable interest in each and every one of the stocks, shares, etc, which formed the trust fund'.[40] One may not agree with the Court, but it clearly explained the ratio decidendi of *Archer-Shee*, supporting the assessment that the unremitted income in the person of Lady Archer-Shee's husband was Lady Archer-Shee's equitable ownership of the shares. The use of the wording 'equitable interest' leaves little doubt that the court was grounding taxation on the income as derived

[38] ibid.
[39] ibid 47, 56.
[40] *Archer-Shee v Garland* [1930] AC 212.

from ownership of the shares in equity.[41] What this author would criticise about the court ruling is that it asserts equitable interest in the shares. To the author's view, what is relevant is the interest on the income, and only indirectly and jointly in the shares as the origin of the income for qualification purposes.

The actual issue behind *Archer-Shee* was that the ITA 1842 provisions on foreign income divided types of chargeable income into income from foreign possessions in shares, stock and securities, or income derived from possessions different from stocks, shares and securities.[42] The author's view is that those rules were adapting charging provisions to international taxation. Was the idea behind this that active income should be taxable immediately, while passive income had to be taxed upon remittance, advancing international tax rules allocating taxing rights on active income to residence and on passive income to source? At the time, though, it was not a matter of taxing rights, as the UK will always tax, but of timing.[43] The rules probably paid little or no attention to allocation, especially regarding foreign income. The assumption, then, was that the beneficiaries of foreign income who were residents in the UK were to be taxed.[44] But nothing was said on the type of entitlement of the beneficiary to be charged as an implicit assumption. *Archer-Shee* was precisely filling such a gap.

Archer-Shee cannot be understood without looking at the full picture with the benefit of hindsight. Tax legislation at the time of the ruling was trapped between consolidation of the beneficiary's proprietary rights and the shift from a real or impersonal tax system towards a personal one based on the concept of income.[45] Gammie is probably right that at the time the tax system, namely statutory tax legislation, was not explicitly looking at who the income was benefiting, but the whole system was moving in that direction. Precisely because the system lacked the allocation rules needed for personal taxes, the rules were failing where the source was not within the UK, as legislation heavily relied on such a mechanism to fill the gap. *Archer-Shee* made such a connection and set down the next milestone in defining equitable ownership.

On that point, Gammie, following learned commentators contemporaneous to the *Archer-Shee* ruling, such as Hanbury, seemingly argued that the reasoning in *Archer-Shee* is confined to 'income tax law' or is simply a tax law principle, and cannot be regarded as defining equitable ownership as being vested in beneficiaries where discretion of trustees is needed.[46] However, that view follows the resistance of scholars of the time to the evolution of beneficiary proprietary rights that was taking place. Nowadays, to oppose the partial proprietary character of beneficiaries' rights does not fit in with the way

[41] Sin (n 20) 277.

[42] See Cases IV and V of Sched D to the Income Tax Act 1918, c 40.

[43] See the resemblance with the UK position in J Avery Jones, 'The History of the United Kingdom's First Comprehensive Double Taxation Agreement' in J Tiley (ed), *Studies in the History of Tax Law*, vol 3 (Hart Publishing, 2009) 237.

[44] Gammie, 'The Origins of Fiscal Transparency' (n 20) 48.

[45] Gammie precisely points that the Income Tax Acts of 1842 and 1853 were heavily reliant on land and activities related to land, as the concept of economic income was not yet fully achieved: ibid 38–39.

[46] Gammie, 'The Archer-Shee Cases' (n 20) 41–42; Gammie, 'The Origins of Fiscal Transparency' (n 20) 148; HG Hanbury, 'Periodical Menace to Equitable Principles' (1928) 44 *LQR* 468, 469. Sin implicitly considers this view as the narrow interpretation of *Archer-Shee*: Sin (n 20) 276. This also seems to be the view of Brown (n 6) 31.

in which equity law has developed.[47] Between then and now, equitable rights against third parties have been strengthened and beneficiaries' interests are today strong enough in a number of instances, as was shown in the previous chapter. Even Maitland changed his view on the matter to support beneficiary rights imply proprietary rights and not mere contractual rights.[48] In this regard, *Archer-Shee* can be seen as one of the last rulings dealing with the problem of the lack of proprietary rights of beneficiaries and impersonal taxes, while, at the same time, being one of the first rulings providing for proprietary rights and establishing the conditions for personal taxes, though legislation in force at the time was still influenced by previous views. The case probably forced the law or interpreted it into the new personal taxes ideas.

Consequently, and despite the criticism from some authors, this author stands by his view regarding the wording of the majority of judges. The case can be said to raise two ideas. First, it contributed to the idea, which was increasing in favour at the time, of beneficiary rights being proprietary rights, where there is a single beneficiary who has strong enough rights against the trustee.[49] Secondly, it demonstrated that tax liability in equitable cases is defined by reference to equitable ownership if there is enough certainty and strength of rights in equity with reference to who benefits from the trust property. However, each trust case has to be assessed carefully to ascertain whether the beneficiary's right is enforceable enough to reach a proprietary interest character.[50]

In the end, *Archer v Shee* was probably another milestone in the consolidation of the proprietary character of beneficiary interest in certain cases where the beneficiary was absolute and had been ascertained which took place at the beginning of the twentieth century. Interest in possession to the income was fully ascertained, although subject to the performance of the trustee, but the compelling abilities of the beneficiary made it enough to consider it an equitable interest – almost an equitable ownership. Thus, all these arguments against the *Archer-Shee* view were probably not fully incorrect, but are outdated, residing in the old understanding of trusts as a contractual and confidence contract where the beneficiary had little more right than claims against the trustee but nothing to the property, reasoning that was superseded in the late nineteenth century and beginning of the twentieth century. Also outdated as it took into consideration the original view on ITA 1842 based on taxes as an impersonal matter. If one looks at more recent judgments, such as *Sainsbury*, beneficial ownership is clearly equated to equitable ownership if the beneficiary can be ascertained, as was developed throughout the twentieth century.[51]

In any case, to take the view of the critics does not change the author's point that *Archer-Shee* recognised the certainty principle. It may be said that the ratio decidendi of the case was tax law, that the case confined its effects to taxation or it is just a tax law principle and the beneficiary had no equitable ownership in the entrusted assets,[52] but

[47] Gammie states beneficial interest may pose ownership rights, but he seemingly denies equitable content to one of the cases that most contributed to such development: see Gammie, 'The Origins of Fiscal Transparency' (n 20) 41.

[48] On Maitland's change of view see fn 121 in ch 2 above.

[49] Sin (n 20) 276. On the author's argument on the switch of understanding of beneficiary interest qualification at the beginning of the twentieth century, see ch 2 above.

[50] Sin (n 20) 279.

[51] *J Sainsbury Plc v O'Connor (Inspector of Taxes)* (1991) 1 WLR 963 (CA).

[52] Sin (n 20) 277. See s II.A in ch 2 above.

the authors claiming those theories do not deny in any case that the tax effects lie on the beneficiary. Still, the consequence would be that *Archer-Shee* provided taxation of trusts where it was ascertained that a beneficiary right would fall on the beneficiary.

Previous cases such as *William v Singer* or *Pool v Royal Exchange Assurance* dealt with a similar issue, although in both cases the trustee was resident and the beneficiaries were non-residents, and also contributed to the development of the certainty principle.[53] In those cases, the issue was whether income could be assessed in the hands of trustees who were resident in the UK when income was remitted abroad for the benefit of overseas residents. The conclusion, along the same line of reasoning as the later *Archer-Shee* case, was that no liability could be imposed as the income was beneficially owned by non-residents, thus it was not subject to UK taxation. In the end, what those cases advanced, and what was later confirmed in *Archer-Shee* and subsequent jurisprudence building the allocation of income in relation to equitable rights, is that the relevant rights for defining tax liability in tax cases should be drawn by equity law as regards the person to whom the relevant trust conditions allocate the benefit of possession, the right to the income and the potential right to control, if such rights can be ascertained.

In Canada, *Trans-Canada Investment* followed *Archer-Shee*, and the ruling contained a similar reasoning, introducing the beneficial owner principle into Canadian tax law.[54] However, the context was slightly different as the question was whether dividend income paid by a trustee to a beneficiary retained its dividend qualification. The issue was of importance because if the income were a dividend it would be deducted from the beneficiary's taxable income, and thus not being taxable.[55]

In the USA, it seems that case law was much more active in analysing the issue than in the UK, and the topic of the allocation of income attracted the early attention of some scholars.[56] The *Young v Gnichtel* and *Shellabarger* cases recognised as early as the 1930s that income tax liability has to be defined upon the equitable owner of the interest – in those cases, an assignee – and not the trustee.[57] See also the *Moore* case, where dividends paid upon shares held in guarantee for the payment of notes issued for buying the shares themselves were taxable on the beneficial owner, that is, the transferee, as the beneficial interest passed to him.[58] However, early case law held that where assignments of stock were held in trust, with dividends passing to the beneficiary, the taxable person was the assignor if he was to keep the stock, or the assignee if both the stocks and the dividends

[53] *William v Singer* (n 8); *Pool v Royal Exchange Assurance* (n 8).

[54] *Minister of National Revenue v Trans-Canada Investment Corp Ltd*, [1953] CTC 353; *Minister of National Revenue v Trans-Canada Investment Corp Ltd*, [1955] CTC 275; *Minister of National Revenue v Trans-Canada Investment Corp Ltd*, (1955) 5 DLR 576; *Minister of National Revenue v Trans-Canada Investment Corp Ltd*, [1955] DTC 1227; *Minister of National Revenue v Trans-Canada Investment Corp Ltd*, [1953] Ex CR 292; *Minister of National Revenue v Trans-Canada Investment Corp Ltd*, [1956] SCR 49. Brown (n 6) 31.

[55] Brown (n 6) 31–32.

[56] See S Surrey, 'Assignments of Income and Related Devices: Choice of the Taxable Person' (1933) 33 *Columbia Law Review* 791 and the large number of cases cited therein.

[57] *Young v Gnichtel, Collector of Internal Revenue* 789 (F2d); *Shellabarger v Commissioner* (1930) 38 F (2d) 566. See also *O'Malley-Keyes v Eaton* (1928) 24 F2d 436 (D Conn). For a commentary of the early jurisprudence on allocation of income, see Surrey (n 56).

[58] *Moore v Commissioner* (1930) 19 BTA 140.

were for the benefit of the beneficiary.[59] In the end, tax liability was defined upon the equitable owner of the dividend or interest as derived from the right to the stock or bonds. In other words, if the beneficiary had a right to the income itself but not to the stock, he was the equitable owner not of the dividend or interest itself, as that character was linked to holding ownership of the stock or bonds, but to an equivalent amount.

In *National Bank of Commerce in Memphis v Henslee*, the court held for the computation of property as if it were in the hands of the settlor-beneficiary in the case of a trust settled within a divorce agreement for the husband to enjoy a house.[60] As far as the settlor-beneficiary retained broad powers of decision in relation to the property, even revoking powers, the court ruled that the property should be included in the decedent's estate following Treasury Regulations 105, section 81.18 in relation to section 811(c)(1)(B) of the Internal Revenue Code 1939, insofar as the exclusion of section 811(i) was not applicable as the property was not transferred to the trust for consideration in money or money's worth. In other words, property was allocated in this case following beneficial ownership, jointly with the consideration of the retained powers of the husband, and not legal ownership. However, this case also deals with the settlor-benefit anti-avoidance sub-principle, as will be explained later on.

In the case of *Central Life Assurance Society, Mutual v Commissioner of Internal Revenue*, the Eighth Circuit analysed whether a mutual insurance company was bound by contract to pay all the income from the non-participating business acquired by contract to the shareholders of the stock company who span off its business to the mutual.[61] Here, the court ruled that the case was close to a trust case under a substance over form analysis, so allocation had to follow trust rationale. Thus, income was to be allocated to the stockholders and not the mutual company. This development was a deviation of the anti-avoidance principle that misled the certainty and absolute entitlement principle, blending the equitable entitlement of the corporation with an anti-abuse analysis. At this point, following this and many other cases, US tax law started to develop a constructive tax trust doctrine in tax law that blended entitlement and anti-abuse doctrines, resulting in significant confusion.[62] I will return to the issue later, in the analysis of the second anti-avoidance principle.

Finally, the certainty principle, as construed in *Archer-Shee*, underlies the uncertainty sub-principle where the person with control of the income or assets is subsidiarily responsible for tax liability where no person is fully entitled to a primary right to income and control of the income or assets, either in common law or in equity. Recognised early on, in *Williams v Singer*, the House of Lords made it plain that clear control of income or assets commanded tax liability in cases where beneficiaries were not ascertainable or where beneficiaries were not *sui juris*.[63] Conversely, the same ruling recognises this principle as opposed to cases where the beneficiary is in possession (having a primary right to income and enjoyment) and control, where (under the certainty principle) the income would be taxable on the beneficiary.[64]

[59] Surrey (n 56) 800 et seq.
[60] *National Bank of Commerce in Memphis v Henslee* (1959) 179 FSupp 346.
[61] *Central Life Assur Soc, Mut v Com'r of Internal Revenue* (1931) 51 F2d 939 (8th Circ).
[62] See Miller (n 16).
[63] William v Singer (n 8).
[64] ibid 72–73.

Later, the *Dawson v Inland Revenue Commissioners* decision also dealt with the uncertainty sub-principle in a case where all the beneficiaries and two of the trustees were resident overseas, while one of the trustees was resident in the UK.[65] In this case, the Commissioners assessed all the income obtained by the trust and taxed it in the hands of the only resident trustee, irrespective of the income being obtained abroad and not being remitted to the UK. The issue was whether the trust income was 'arising or accruing' to the resident trustee, as the relevant statutory rule required for it to be taxable in the UK. Contrary to the Crown argument of the trustees being joint tenants, with each of them having the right to call on all of the income, the court held that joint trustees were only jointly entitled to the income and, consequently, the income could not be said to 'arise or be accrued' on the resident trustee, but on all of them together, so it was not taxable in the UK according to the relevant section of the Income Tax Act.[66]

The case, following the uncertainty sub-principle, allocated the income and assets to the person controlling, irrespective of the lack of a right to income or enjoy, as the assets and income cannot be considered to be controlled by each trustee individually, but by all of them together. Therefore, as beneficial ownership in equity cannot be defined in discretionary trusts or joint tenancies, income is allocated under the uncertainty sub-principle to all of the trustees together, and if beneficial ownership for tax purposes is to be by the person to whom the income should be allocated, in these cases beneficial ownership for tax purposes lies with the trustees or persons with the right to control, but not with the primary absolute right to income or control.

(ii) The Certainty and Absolute Entitlement Principle: Bare Trusts and Interest in Possession

In summary, early in the twentieth century, the UK, Canada and the USA recognised under the *Archer-Shee* principle that tax liability had to be analysed and defined with reference to the beneficiary of the trust, the equitable owner or the person with primary rights to income and control if there was an unconditional and certain right of some strength in equity to the income and capital or just the capital, and not necessarily directly to the legal owner. Subsidiarily, if no person is sufficiently entitled in equity, tax liability should be referred in first instance to the legal owner, to guarantee collection, and later adjusted if the beneficiary is appointed after the first assesment on the trustee.

(a) United Kingdom

Following this approach, English tax law laid down such principles for bare trusts and interest in possession. In this sense, bare trusts, nominees,[67] trusts with joint

[65] *Dawson v Inland Revenue Commissioners* (1990) 1 AC 1 (UKHL).

[66] ibid 10–12.

[67] In the UK, nominees seem to refer to bare trusts for the most apart, even though they may also comprise agents acting in their own name but for the benefit of another. See above fns 170–74 in ch 2 and accompanying text.

beneficiaries equally and absolutely entitled (even though technically not a bare trust), other passive trusts where the beneficiaries are fully entitled to capital and/or income, and other arrangements similar to trusts but not strictly speaking trusts are disregarded and income and capital are directly allocated to the beneficiaries, with charges due accordingly.[68] However, on income tax, the trustee and the beneficiary may opt for the former to fill the tax return and pay due tax, with the beneficiary then being able to deduct the income taxed at the trustee level on his tax return.[69] On this point, it is important to note that trusts are considered as an independent body from trustees for income tax purposes if they are charged or chargeable.[70] In the case of minors or vulnerable people, income tax is charged on the settlors unless no income is distributed.[71] Regarding capital gains tax, as it is considered that the property is owned directly by the beneficiary, no tax is due when the property is transferred between the trustee and the beneficiary.[72]

Constructive or resulting trusts where the beneficiary is absolutely entitled, as is usually the case, would be disregarded under the bare trusts rule.[73] However, in some of these cases, even where, from a legal point of view, the trust exists, it may be difficult to recognise, and its declaration may not be seen or even be controversial until settled in court. Thus, the application of such a rule to constructive or resulting trusts may not be applied from the birth of the trust, raising timing and retroactive application issues. Finally, sham trusts, as they are regarded as being non-existent, would be disregarded and, consequently, income would be taxed in the hands of the actual owner of the property, or according to the underlying actual trust or equitable relation.[74]

Similarly, in trusts with an interest in possession or current and absolute entitlement to income as it arises, the ultimate income tax liability rests on the beneficiary.[75] In such cases, even though the ultimate liability is on the beneficiaries of the interest in possession, the trustees are also liable for tax upon receipt of the income at the so-called basic rate – generally 20 per cent, and 7.5 per cent for dividends – for the benefit of the beneficiary, who will be taxed at his or her applicable rate and can apply a credit for the amount of tax paid by the trustee on his or her tax liability on the income derived from

[68] See ss 250, 357 and 666 of the Income Tax Act 2007, c 3. See s 60 of the Taxation of Chargeable Gains Act 1992, c 12. On absolute entitlement and taxation in the hands of the beneficiary see inter alia *Tomlinson (Inspector of Taxes) v Glyns Executor and Trustee Co. and Another* (n 20); *Cochrane v IRC* [1974] STC 335; *Figg v Clarke* (1997) 247 STC; *Hoare Trustees v Gardner* (1978) 89 STC (Ch D). See also the text and other cases in N Eastaway, J Kimber and I Richards, *Tax Advisers' Guide to Trusts* (Bloomsbury, 2016) 357–61.

[69] But this option does not modify beneficiary liability, as they will still be liable to tax on the trust income even when it is not distributed. See *Tax Bulletin*, Issue 27, February 1997, p 395; *Tax Bulletin*, Issue 32, December 1997, p 487, as quoted by Eastaway et al (n 68) 360–61.

[70] See s 474(3) of the Income Tax Act 2007, c 3; s 69(1) of the Taxation of Chargeable Gains Act 1992, c 12.

[71] See s 629 of the Income Tax (Trading and Other Income) Act 2005, c 5.

[72] See s 60(1) of the Taxation of Chargeable Gains Act 1992, c 12.

[73] On resulting and constructive trusts and their tax treatment, see Trusts, Settlements and Estates Manual, HMRC internal manuals, TSEM9700, namely TSEM9705; and TSEM9600, namely TSEM9620.

[74] For the trust to be considered a sham trust, the parties shall never have intended to give rise to the trust or to deal with the assets in accordance with the intentions of the deed. In this regard, all parties should consider it so, as if one of the parties does not consider the trust as inexistent, there might be a different equitable relationship, but not a sham. Also, there might be partial shams, referring to just parts of the trust deed. As the HMRC manual right points out, sham trusts are a matter of fact: Trusts, Settlements and Estates Manual (HMRC internal manuals, TSEM1007).

[75] See *Baker (Inspector of Taxes) v Archer-Shee* (n 8); *William v Singer* (n 8). For Scottish trusts, see s 464 of the Income Tax Act 2007, c 3. See also Eastaway et al (n 68) 361 et seq.

the trust on which the trustees paid such tax.[76] However, this is not a modification of the certainty principle, but is done to advance collection. If, on the other hand, trustees mandate the income directly to the beneficiary, such as instructing the payer to pay the amounts directly to the holder of the interest in possession, then the trustees will not be liable for tax and the beneficiary will be taxed directly without being able to apply any deductible tax credit.[77] An exception applies in cases of income being allocated in the trust as capital, such as in the application of the accrued interest system, where tax would be assessed according to those rules in the hands of the trustee, and the beneficiary would not be liable to tax at all if he benefited from such funds.[78]

For the purposes of capital gains taxation, the principle was incorporated much later, as capital gains taxation was established in the UK relatively recently. Thus, it was the *Tomlinson* case where the principle was probably first recognised in regard to capital gains tax (CGT).[79] Following that principle, charges are normally not due for transfers between settlor-beneficiaries and trustees and beneficiaries from a bare trust, as the property is considered to be that of the beneficiary-settlor himself. However, certain cases, such as transfer to a bare trust for the benefit of a third party, will trigger capital gains taxation. In addition, in interest in possessions, a transfer to a trustee and/or a remainderman is deemed to take place upon the end of the interest by death in order to update values.[80] However, if the transfer of the interest in possession takes place by sale, the capital gains would be taxed in the hands of the beneficiary if he acquired interest for consideration in money or money's worth.[81] On the other hand, if the beneficiary received his or her interest as a gift, he or she will not be liable to chargeable gains tax on the sale of his interest.[82] On inheritance tax payable upon interest in possession pre-existent to the death (as opposed to immediate post-death interest and as in discretionary trusts), the property is not allocated to the estate subject to inheritance tax, and is generally consequently not subject to taxation.[83] It must, however, be borne in mind that this does not usually apply to settlor-interested trusts. As can be seen, CGT normally arises where there is a change in the beneficiary of the assets, following the certainty principle.

In implied trusts, case law has frequently considered the case to be a sale where the contract has not been completed and a constructive trust arises.[84] In case law on taxation, beneficial ownership is considered to be vested in the beneficiary once the contract is completed, while in suspense in the meantime.[85] Thus, income and capital gains will be allocated to the seller or buyer if beneficial ownership is split at first instance where the contract has not been yet been completed and there is no implicit trust yet; will be

[76] See ss 493–98 of the Income Tax Act 2007, c 3. Note that trustees are not individuals and cannot apply personal reliefs, the relief being applicable to the beneficiary, who can claim the deduction of the tax paid by the trustee, thus adjusting the tax on the income to his or her personal tax situation.

[77] See s 76 of the Taxes Management Act 1970 c. 9.

[78] See s 667(1) of the Income Tax Act 2007, c 3.

[79] *Tomlinson (Inspector of Taxes) v Glyns Executor and Trustee Co and Another* (n 20).

[80] See s 72 of the Taxation of Chargeable Gains Act 1992, c 12.

[81] See s 76 of the Taxation of Chargeable Gains Act 1992, c 12.

[82] ibid.

[83] See ss 89B, 49A–49E of the Inheritance Tax Act 1984, c 51. On the right of the remainderman or reversionary interests of such trusts, normally no tax is due as per consolidation of the full right.

[84] In equity law, see *Lysaght v Edwards* (1876) 2 Ch D 499; *Rayner v Preston* [1881] Ch D 1. In tax law, see *English Sewing Cotton Co v IRC* (1947) 1 All ER 679 (CA).

[85] *Jerome v Kelly (Inspector of Taxes)* [2004] UKHL 25 (UKHL).

allocated to the trustee but for the charge of the beneficiary if beneficial ownership is in suspense; and will be allocated to the beneficiary if the implied trust is already in place.

(b) Canada

Canadian tax treatment of bare trusts and interests in possession also follows the certainty and absolute entitlement principle. Trusts' tax liability is defined upon the tax definition of settlement, which in turn is based on the trust definition of private law.[86] Bare trusts and other similar arrangements are excluded from the definition.[87] The result is that bare trusts are not treated as trusts for tax purposes, and the income is directly taxed in the hands of beneficiaries.

In interest in possession trusts, the trust is subjected to taxation as a settlement.[88] The general treatment of settlements in Canada makes the trust liable for all the income, but allows the income distributed or to be distributed to the beneficiaries to be deducted.[89] The beneficiary, in turn, is liable for the income paid or to be paid to him or her.[90] Thus, as a person with interest in possession is entitled to the income as it arises, the income would generally be taxed in his or her hands, irrespective of whether the income is actually distributed to him or her, and allowing a deduction of the income taxed at the trust level. The same result – taxation of the income in the hands of the beneficiary with a strong entitlement in equity to the income – is achieved, even though it is arrived at via a different mechanism from UK tax law.

Income from bare trusts will normally retain its qualification from the source it is derived from as it is directly considered to be income from the source to the beneficiary, whereas in interest in possession, income may lose its original qualification. Generally, income from an interest in possession would take the character of property income, except for capital gains, dividends, capital dividends, foreign source pension benefits, death benefits, foreign source income and others, if proper designation is made.[91]

[86] See s 104(1) of the Income Tax Act, RSC 1985, c 1 (5th Supp) (Canada). See Roth et al (n 15) 55 et seq.

[87] See s 104(1) of the Income Tax Act, RSC 1985, c 1 (5th Supp) (Canada). There was significant controversy surrounding the treatment of bare trusts until 2001, namely how tax liability should be allocated. This was solved at the time through an amendment, and the Income Tax Act now provides for consideration of beneficial ownership as the relevant entitlement for defining tax liability. Amendments included in Bill C-22, An Act To Amend the Income Tax Act, the Income Tax Application Rules, Certain Acts Related to the Income Tax Act, the Canada Pension Plan, the Customs Act, the Excise Tax Act, the Modernization of Benefits and Obligations Act, and Another Act Related to the Excise Tax Act, first reading 21 March 2001; SC 2001, c 17. Brown, 'Symposium: Beneficial Ownership' (n 12) 423–24; Roth et al (n 15) 86 et seq.

[88] See s 104(1) of the Income Tax Act, RSC 1985, c 1 (5th Supp) (Canada).

[89] See s 104 (2), (6) and (13) of the Income Tax Act, RSC 1985, c 1 (5th Supp) (Canada). See also Roth et al (n 15) 119 et seq. However, no deduction is allowed in the cases of spousal, alter ego, joint spousal or joint common law partner trusts if the income is distributed to a person different from the spouse in a spousal trust, a beneficiary other than the settlor in an alter ego trust, and anyone other than the settlor or the spouse or common law partner in the case of a joint spousal or joint common law partner trust.

[90] See s 104(13) and (24) of the Income Tax Act, RSC 1985, c 1 (5th Supp) (Canada); C Brown, 'The Taxation of Trusts: Reconciling Fundamental Principles' (2001) 21 *Estates, Trusts and Pensions Journal* 1, 29 et seq; G Chow and I Pryor, *Taxation of Trusts and Estates* (Thomson Reuters, 2018) 161; Roth et al (n 15) 198 et seq.

[91] See ss 108(5), 104 (19), (20), (21), (22), (27), (27.1) and (28) of the Income Tax Act, RSC 1985, c 1 (5th Supp) (Canada).

In constructive trusts, case law suggests that income and capital shall be allocated to the person for whom income or property is held.[92] However, as has already been stated in relation to the UK, as constructive trusts are not always asserted until they have been analysed by the courts, it may be difficult to define tax liability in advance, and allocation may be confused by facts not properly framed within a constructive trust.[93]

(c) United States

The same principle is followed in the USA, even though the mechanism is again slightly different. This largely depends on the main distinction made by US taxation of trusts between grantor trusts and non-grantor trusts. Because of the use of trusts to avoid taxes while retaining control of the property, US tax law largely focuses on tackling such cases. Grantor trusts for the benefit of resident US citizens will sometimes shift the tax incidence to the settlor.[94] The rule, settled by the Supreme Court in *Helvering v Clifford*, states that if the grantor of a trust fails to divest sufficient incidents of ownership over trust property, any income from that property is included in his or her taxable income.[95]

Bare trusts, largely matching what is known in US tax law as fixed or simple trusts (with a single or several beneficiaries), will not always be excluded from trusts' taxation regime as in the UK and Canada, unless they are settled for the benefit of the grantor.

The tax treatment of simple, bare or fixed trusts may be divided in two groups. The first group includes fixed or bare non-grantor trusts where the beneficiary:

> has a power exercisable solely by himself to vest the corpus or the income therefrom in himself, or has previously partially released or otherwise modified such a power and after the release or modification retains such control as would, within the principles of sections 671 to 677, inclusive, subject a grantor of a trust to treatment as the owner thereof.[96]

In those cases, income will be treated as directly owned by the beneficiary. However, the trust will still remain taxpayer for control purposes.

The second group comprises other fixed trusts, where income is fully allocated to a beneficiary or a group of beneficiaries but where those subjects cannot claim the object or income absolutely, including interest in possession. In these cases, income and gains

[92] *Holiziki v The Queen* 95 DTC 5591 (FCTD); *Kostiuk v The Queen* 93 DTC 5511 (FCTD); Brown, 'Symposium: Beneficial Ownership' (n 12) 426.

[93] C Brown and CL Rajan, 'Constructive and Resulting Trusts: Challenging Tax Boundaries' (1997) 45 *Canadian Tax Journal* 659.

[94] See ss 671–79 of the Internal Revenue Code, 26 USC. Trust property and income are taxed normally on the grantor if the settlor is a resident or citizen of the USA and retains any reversionary interest exceeding 5% of trust value; the power to control the beneficial enjoyment of trust property; the power to revoke the trust; certain administrative powers, including the power to borrow trust funds and vote stock of closely held companies; and any interest in trust income. In the case of non-residents, the trust would be treated as a grantor trust and disregarded if the settlor has the power to revoke the trust without the consent of any other person or with the consent of a person who is considered 'related or subordinate' to the settlor and not adverse to the settlor's wishes; or if the only amounts distributable (whether income or corpus) during the lifetime of the settlor are distributable to the settlor or to the spouse of the settlor. See DD Kozusko and SK Vetter, 'Trusts: United States' [2012] *IBFD* 16; JA Miller and JA Maine, *The Fundamentals of Federal Taxation*, 4th edn (Carolina Academic Press, 2017) 569–70.

[95] *Helvering v Clifford* (1940) 309 US 331.

[96] See s 678 of the Internal Revenue Code, 26 USC. See also JG Blattmachr, MM Gans and AH Lo, 'A Beneficiary as Trust Owner: Decoding Section 678' [2009] *ACTEC Journal* 106.

would be taxable at trust level, with a similar treatment of an individual, allowing for deduction of the income or gain paid or to be paid to the beneficiary (distributable net income, or DNI).[97] The beneficiary, in turn, will be liable for the income paid or to be paid to him or her. As in simple trusts, where all income is distributed or is to be paid, trust income will usually amount to zero as all the income will be included in the trust tax return. It will then be deducted under the DNI rule, and the tax will be paid by the beneficiary.[98] In sum, even though in the USA bare trusts are not always directly disregarded for tax purposes as in the UK and Canada, the overall result of the system jointly considered is similar and allocates the tax burden to the beneficiary, who is sufficiently entitled, following the certainty principle.

Regarding capital gains, tax is generally paid by the trust and no deduction is made insofar as capital gains usually do not qualify as DNI.[99] However, if the capital gain is effectively distributed to the beneficiaries in the year of the capital gain, it will be taxed in the hands of the beneficiaries and will be deducted as DNI at the trust level.[100] In the case a capital gain of a grantor trust, it will be allocated to the settlor.[101]

(d) Nominees

As was argued above, nominee in a loose sense is used to refer to bare trusts or fixed simple trusts, and principals in agency contracts.[102] However, in a strict sense, a nominee is probably framed within common law contracts, while bare trusts are framed within equity law. In this regard, there is no doubt under a nominee arrangement in an agency sense: income will be allocated to the principal for tax purposes if the agent activity is done in the name and on account of the principal. As nominee implies little to no powers, this will be true of most cases of nomineeships. However, the case of a nominee derived from an agency may also be redirected to the treatment of a bare trust in the USA if an implied trust is found to arise from the arrangement. In addition, as the agent may be responsible for certain tax duties in some cases, consequences may somehow be close.

Regarding nominee interpreted as bare trusts in equity or as an implicit trust derived from agency, the treatment in the UK and Canada is different from that in the USA. In the UK and Canada, the trustee will be disregarded, while in the US the trustee will be liable to tax even though a deduction of the income paid or to be paid will be available. This makes the different usage of the term nominee relevant for tax purposes.

In summary, in a case involving nominees, it is important for tax purposes in the USA to define whether an agent–principal relationship, a trust–beneficiary relationship or both overlapping relationships exist. Consequently, the context must be analysed

[97] See ss 641, 643, 651, 652, and 661 of the Internal Revenue Code, 26 USC.

[98] Miller and Maine (n 94) 570; Wheeler (n 14) 152. However, in the case of foreign trusts, other relevant rules apply and adjustments may be needed. In relation to Puerto Rican trusts, which are treated as domestic trusts for US Internal Revenue Code purposes, and the result of the DNI being nil if benefiting residents in Puerto Rico, see 'Foreign Trusts – Proposed amendments relating to (1) possible removal of dividend and interest withholding tax, and (2) Puerto Rican trusts', Box 52, Office of the Tax Policy, subject files, [RG 56-90-73 131-14-7-4], National Archives at College Park, College Park, MD.

[99] Kozusko and Vetter (n 94) 18–19, 36.

[100] ibid 17–18.

[101] ibid 36. Above, n 94.

[102] See fns 170–74 in ch 2 above.

carefully. In the UK or Canada, on the other hand, whether a nominee is framed within an equitable or a common law frame, the tax treatment remains almost the same.

(iii) Uncertainty or Split Rights: Discretionary Trusts, Split Rights, Interest in Possession and Others

A negative consequence arising from the *Archer-Shee* case is that where there is no person significantly or largely entitled to the income or assets, then tax liability has to be allocated to the person who, in principle, is legally entitled to the property. In trust cases this is normally the trustee who legally owns the property, even though in equity he or she has to use it or control it according to the settlement conditions. In most cases, however, such trusts will allocate the property to a certain person in a later step, or it will even be allocated from the beginning to certain subjects, but splitting rights to the property in different ways. Consequently, tax law will not disregard the fact that such income, in principle allocated to the trustee, is indeed ability to pay of the later beneficiaries, and will adjust the tax liability to the latter persons once the final assignment in equity to them occurs. In other words, taxation on the trustees is a matter of timing in order to advance tax collection, and a matter of guarantee of the right of the state to collect taxes.

Statutory tax law in the UK and other common law countries follows such principles for discretionary trusts, accumulation trusts, trusts with remainders, trusts with several beneficiaries benefiting from different types of rights and many others where beneficiaries are not fully ascertained or benefits are split.

To define taxation of trusts, statutory tax rules of the UK, as well as in the USA and Canada, provide for a specific tax definition for trusts.[103] This concept – in the UK settlement is defined broadly as any property held in trust other than by a nominee or bare trustee – covers most trusts in an equity sense where beneficiaries are uncertain or rights are split. However, it also includes other settlements that may not qualify as trusts in equity law and that may also have some common characteristics with uncertain or split trusts, such as an unincorporated estate or vehicle without absolute certainty of rights for a specific subject.[104] In a negative sense, those definitions in the UK and Canada normally exclude trusts in an equity sense where there is a certain and absolute beneficiary, such as bare trusts. The result is that trusts falling within that definition will be taxed, so the uncertainty principle applies to all tax settlements where the intermediary performs active duties, such as both discretionary trusts and trusts with split rights in equity, but also to other common law contracts with underlying fiduciary characteristics.

It is only in the USA that the trust definition includes bare and fixed trusts, although, as the system deducts distributed income from taxable income, the result is that income will only be taxed in the hands of the trustee if there is no defined right to income, following the uncertainty principle.

[103] See s 466 of the Income Tax Act 2007, c 3; s 620 of the Income Tax (Trading and Other Income) Act 2005, c 5; s 68 of the Taxation of Chargeable Gains Act 1992, c 12; s 43 of the Inheritance Tax Act 1984, c 51. In Canada, trust is defined with reference to ownership and control. See s 104(1) of the Income Tax Act, RSC 1985, c 1 (5th Supp) (Canada).

[104] I Maston, *Tolley's UK Taxation of Trusts 2018–2019* (Relx – Tolley, 2018) 9.

Under those systems, trusts will normally be taxable, and only where a beneficiary is later defined will the beneficiary be taxed. If there is no beneficiary, the trust will be taxable under the uncertainty principle. If there is a beneficiary, the trust will still be taxed, but subsequent credit or deduction mechanisms will allocate the tax burden to the beneficiary under the certainty principle. In the end, ability to pay will at some point be with the beneficiary, so the uncertainty principle works as a sort of collection mechanism, rather than as a full definitive allocation, even though in some cases it would act in that way. Trustees do not normally have ability to pay for themselves, but are provisionally the ones with the largest interest in the assets and income. In the end, potential beneficiaries are waiting, as otherwise, unless under exceptions, there would be no trust if it lacks object certainty.

(a) United Kingdom

In discretionary trusts, the uncertainty as to who will benefit from the income makes trustees fully liable for the trust income – except for settlor-benefited trusts – as the persons entitled to control, with legal ownership and in the absence of a person significantly entitled to the income and control in equity. This follows the need to guarantee tax collection and to prevent tax mitigation or avoidance schemes.

Trustees are taxable on all the income due to the trust, normally at special rates – 38.1 per cent for dividends and 45 per cent for all other income – irrespective of who receives it, even if the trustee instructs the payer to pay directly to a certain beneficiary.[105] Once the income is directed to a beneficiary, the beneficiary will be taxed on the income and will deduct the taxes paid by the trust as a credit.[106]

However, if the income or assets are assigned or appointed to an accumulation trust, the income obtained before the assignment or appointment may be considered capital and not income, so taxation will not always arise in the hands of the beneficiary for the previously obtained income.[107] On the income or the assets obtained after the appointment, if the trust now turns into an interest in possession or bare trust, subsequent income will be treated as such. In the latter case, income will be directly allocated to the beneficiary, whereas in the first case it will be taxed at both the trust and beneficiary level unless payments are directed to the beneficiary directly.[108]

Regarding capital gains, transfer by the settlor to the trustee will trigger capital taxation on the settlors.[109] Mere assignment of income does not trigger capital gains liability, but appointment of capital may. This will depend on whether the appointment results in a sub-trust, or if capital leaves the settlement to the beneficiary.[110] In the latter case, capital gains taxation will be charged in the hands of the trustee, following the uncertainty principle and on a deemed gain to market value, while no tax will be levied in the former case.[111] Similarly, a person becoming absolutely entitled will draw a charge of CGT on a deemed disposal by the trustees.[112]

[105] See s 9 of the Income Tax Act 2007, c 3, as modified by s 1(3)(b) and (c) of the Finance Act 2012, c 14.
[106] See ss 493–98 of the Income Tax Act 2007, c 3; Maston (n 104) 9.
[107] A Hardy, 'Trusts: United Kingdom' [2012] *IBFD* 48.
[108] See above, nn 68 and 75.
[109] Maston (n 104) 85.
[110] ibid 89. However, in some cases taxation may be deferred or not taxable at all.
[111] ibid 305.
[112] See s 71 of the Chargeable Gains Act 1992, c 12; Maston (n 104) 86.

It is clear that taxation is due in the hands of the beneficiary where there is certainty, but falls on the trustee where there is no beneficiary yet.

(b) Canada

The uncertainty principle regarding discretionary trusts and divided-interest trusts is reflected in the Canadian tax law of trusts through the fiction of treating the trust as an individual.[113] Treated as such, income received by the trust will be, in principle and leaving aside bare trusts as mentioned above, taxed in the hands of the trustee.

The main issue with the system is that income may be taxed twice, as income allocated to the trust as a person may also be taxed in the hands of the beneficiary, once paid, payable or allocated upon benefit, as income from that individual. To integrate the uncertainty and certainty sub-principles, the deduction mechanism allows an optional deduction at the trustee level of the income paid or payable to the beneficiary.[114] This means income and capital gains will be taxed in the beneficiary's hands where certain and the income is actually paid or is payable (irrespective of whether it is actually paid or not), but in the trustee's hands where the beneficiary is uncertain.

However, in some cases, it will be possible to designate income as deemed to be not paid or payable in order to be taxed in trustees' hands, and excluded from beneficiary income, even though assigned or paid to the beneficiaries.[115] After 2016, this is only possible if the trust has losses against which profits may be offset.[116]

In addition, the preferred beneficiary regime provides for a special allocation to the highly likely beneficiary in certain cases – namely, disabled people – irrespective of the trustee retaining the control and not actually assigning or paying.[117]

Also, in some cases, the trust property may be allocated to the person who effectively controls the trust for tax purposes, such as for the purpose of meeting stockholding requirements.[118]

(c) United States

Following the deductible net income rule mentioned above, a discretionary trust, as a non-grantor complex trust, will be assessed on its received income less the distributed income. Thus, it will be liable insofar as it does not distribute nor has to assign the income to a beneficiary.[119] However, if the trustee assigns or transfers the income, the beneficiary will be liable to tax and the trust may deduct the income.[120] Regarding capital gains, insofar as the gain is not distributed to the beneficiaries, it will only be taxed at the trust level.[121] In the final liquidation of the trust or consolidation of the

[113] See s 104 (2) of the Income Tax Act, RSC 1985, c 1 (5th Supp) (Canada).

[114] See s 104(6(b)), (13) and (24) of the Income Tax Act, RSC 1985, c 1 (5th Supp) (Canada); Roth et al (n 15) 198 et seq.

[115] See s 104 (13.2) and (13.3) of the Income Tax Act, RSC 1985, c 1 (5th Supp) (Canada).

[116] Chow and Pryor (n 90) 169–70.

[117] See s 104(12) and (14) of the Income Tax Act, RSC 1985, c 1 (5th Supp) (Canada). ibid 174 et seq; Roth et al (n 15) 258 et seq.

[118] CCRA, Technical Interpretation (external) 2001-0104745, 'Associated Corporations' (23 October 2001), cited by Brown (n 6) 46.

[119] See s 641(4) of the Internal Revenue Code, 26 USC.

[120] See s 661 of the Internal Revenue Code, 26 USC.

[121] Kozusko and Vetter (n 94) 36.

rights, capital gains taxation may fall on the beneficiaries, even though rollover may be available in some cases.[122]

(d) Charities and Purposive Trusts

Under the uncertainty principle, tax liability on income derived by charities and purposive trusts is allocated to the trust itself. This is because the nature of such trusts makes defining who benefits from the trust impossible, as they are set for the benefit of an undefined or broad group or whole society and, from a tax policy perspective, because taxation of beneficiaries in charities contradicts the objective of the activities recognised by the law as within the scope of action of charities.[123] However, it is important to bear in mind that such charities are broadly exempted from most taxes if they fulfil certain requirements.[124]

B. The Anti-avoidance Principle: The Settlor-Interest Trust and the General Beneficial Ownership Anti-avoidance Sub-principles

Because trusts were used from the very beginning to avoid taxes, modern tax systems soon took measures to prevent the most obvious avoidance schemes. To do so, all tax systems of common law countries include or have developed two anti-avoidance sub-principles: a specific one and a general one.

The first one, as already mentioned, is the settlor-interest trust sub-principle, which is aimed at preventing most gross tax avoidance schemes through trusts that work by the grantor or settlor transferring income or assets to a trustee, while retaining control over the income or assets. To solve the problem, the specific anti-avoidance principle simply disregards the trust and allocates the income to the grantor or settlor.[125] In these cases, although beneficial ownership in equity may be in the beneficiaries or in suspense, the settlor simply retains a small portion of equitable interest, or ownership, income and/or capital is allocated to him or her. Even in revoking trusts, he or she cannot be said to have beneficial ownership in equity, because he or she only has the option to revert the property to him- or herself, with the effective day-to-day control and benefits being

[122] Note that in grantor trusts, taxation of capital gains accrued during the existence of the trust will fall on the grantor, thus the liquidation does not have such effect. However, income obtained in the last year before liquidation will be taxed on the grantor: ibid 39, 54.

[123] On the purposive character of charities for the benefit of public as opposed to trusts for people see PS Davies and G Virgo, *Equity and Trusts* (Oxford University Press, 2016) 175–76. A quick look at s 3 of the Charities Act 2011 shows how absurd it would be to allocate income to beneficiaries of charities. This would make income on charities assessable on poor people receiving aid from charities, people receiving education on services received from educational charities, people receiving sanitary attention, armed forces or other public security services, or even the Crown for the charities for the promotion of the efficiency of armed forces, police, fire or ambulance services.

[124] Subchapter F, Chapter 1, Subtitle A of the Internal Revenue Code, 26 USC; Pt 10 of the Income Tax Act 2007, c 3; s 256 of the Chargeable Gains Act 1992, c 12; s 149(1)(f) of the Income Tax Act, RSC 1985, c 1 (5th Supp) (Canada).

[125] In the UK, see Maston (n 104) 27 et seq.

invested in other persons. It cannot therefore be said that tax allocation follows equitable interests; rather, it follows a sort of anti-avoidance principle defined by the distrust of tax legislation regarding those instruments where the settlor retains any interest, namely a nuclear button.

The second, much more complex, anti-avoidance principle is derived from the evolution of case law about beneficial ownership in tax law. As was shown in the previous chapters, contemporary trusts and current tax law systems were parallel developments in the nineteenth and early twentieth centuries. In this situation, the increasing tax pressure of contemporary welfare states incentivised the transfer of assets into trusts to avoid or reduce taxes. As a reaction to such moves, tax law started to locate the tax burden on the beneficiaries following the above-mentioned principles, using the beneficial owner term to refer to those principles.[126] As a counterreaction to such tax rules, trusts and other fiduciary arrangements became more and more complex in order to escape taxation. The question, then, was whether beneficial ownership in tax law was covering such situations in which a person was factually controlling trust property, even though the complex legal equitable situation was properly structured to avoid being considered owner or beneficiary in common and equity law, so no beneficial ownership could be allocated to him or her, and consequently no tax liability could arise on him on her.

Those cases were dealt with early on in case law, leading to an expansion of the beneficial ownership principle in an anti-avoidance sense, to cover those abusive situations. At the same time, a broadening of the concept and its increasing use in tax case law led to the increasing use of the concept in statutory law. The result was that beneficial ownership, which had been spreading throughout tax law, included this broadened economic or anti-avoidance concept, thus expanding the effect of the rule from its original scope, which largely followed proprietary rights in equity under the certainty principle.

(i) The Self-Benefit, Settlor-Interest or Grantor Trust Principle

(a) United Kingdom

When discussing settlement tax treatment, an important set of preliminary rules are those derived from the settlor-interest anti-avoidance principle that apply to complex or active trusts, differing from bare trusts in favour of settlors that will be treated as bare trusts.[127] According to these rules, if the settlor or his or her spouse reserves any interest in the property, directly or indirectly, or even a *spes* indicative of an interest, income or capital gains are taxed in the hands of the settlor, or the property is not considered as settled at that time for inheritance tax purposes.[128] This includes revocable

[126] On the development of allocation rules following beneficial ownership blended with anti-avoidance purposes in the USA, see PN James, 'Aiken Industries Revisited' (1986) 64 *Taxes* 131; Miller (n 16). On how beneficial ownership in the UK may be dangerously moving towards being defined in relation to a 'just' result, see Rowland (n 9) 187.

[127] Maston (n 104) 27 et seq.

[128] See ss 622–27, 629–32 of the Income Tax (Trading and Other Income) Act 2005, c 5; s 77 of the Taxation of Chargeable Gains Act 1992, c 12. Similarly taxing in the hands of the settlor but for transfers to settlements outside the UK for tax avoidance purposes if the settlor retains power to enjoy, see ch 2 of Pt 13 to the Income Tax Act 2007, c 3; s 80 of the Inheritance Tax Act 1984, c 51.

trusts – which is why revocable trusts are infrequently encountered in the UK, as it makes the transfer ineffective for tax purposes, or even more burdensome.[129] However, the settlor may in some cases have the right to recover from trustees, so the tax is effectively charged on trust resources.[130] Conversely, the settlor must return the taxes paid to the trustees or beneficiaries if such settlor was not liable at the basic rate.[131]

However, the fact that tax is allocated on the beneficiaries does not prevent the income from also being taxable for income tax purposes in the hands of the trustees as receivers of the income – unless income is mandated to the beneficiaries – even though subsequent reliefs, adjustments or refunds may be claimed if taxes were paid at both trust and beneficiary levels.[132] All in all, many exceptions apply, such as commercial valid transactions, heritage maintenance trusts, trusts for the benefit of minor children (subject to their specific tax treatment), divorce settlements, pension rights and charities.[133]

(b) Canada

For trusts for the benefit of the spouse or common law partner, joint partner, alter ego and self-benefit trusts, leaving aside the main benefits of inheritance taxes and putting the spotlight on allocation of the income, the general system is used, so in many cases the trust would be disregarded and income and property would be allocated directly to the beneficiaries.[134] However, some nuances are added, such as a limitation on the deduction if income is paid to a third party.[135] Regarding deemed transfers at the termination of these types of trust, taxation may occur at the trust level at higher marginal rates and there is no right to deduction.[136]

In addition, an anti-abuse principle or purposive interpretation leads to beneficial ownership not being considered as transferred, and property may, in certain cases, be considered to remain with the settlor for tax purposes if he or she retains any interest, as was held in the *McCreath* case.[137] In that case, the Supreme Court of Canada ruled that the ability of a settlor to appoint a beneficiary or legatee by will made property subjected to such appointment to be considered as property passing upon her death and subject to inheritance tax. The issue was whether retaining a power of appointment could define the settlor as retaining 'property' in the subject matter in order to be subject to inheritance tax.[138] The court, even though recognising that there was technically no direct and specific interest in a discretionary trust under trust law, ruled that the retained power should be considered as property upon a purposive interpretation

[129] Eastaway et al (n 68) 220.
[130] See s 646(1) of the Income Tax (Trading and Other Income) Act 2005, c 5.
[131] See s 646(5) of the Income Tax (Trading and Other Income) Act 2005, c 5.
[132] See s 646(8) of the Income Tax (Trading and Other Income) Act 2005, c 5. Maston (n 104) 44.
[133] See ss 626–28, 630 of the Income Tax (Trading and Other Income) Act 2005, c 5.
[134] Brown, 'Symposium: Beneficial Ownership' (n 12) 425; CCRA document no 2000-0048735, 24 May 2001.
[135] D Stevens, 'Taxation of Trusts in Canada' 1–6 https://store.lsuc.on.ca/Content/pdf/2017/CLE17-00205/CLE17-00205-pub.pdf.
[136] ibid.
[137] *Ontario (Minister of Revenue) v McCreath* (n 15) 22–24.
[138] ibid 7–8.

of the broad definition of property in the inheritance tax regulations.[139] In addition, in considering whether exemption of gifts made more than five years prior to the death was applicable, the court ruled that it was not applicable as the donor did not divest herself of the control of the property and the disposition retaining interest was not a bona fide one, which the exemption is intended to apply to.[140] To sum up, retaining an interest in a discretionary trust may allocate the property for certain tax purposes, namely inheritance tax, to the settlor.

(c) United States

Similarly to settlor-benefit treatment in UK tax law, US federal tax law may shift taxation to the settlor from the trustee and/or beneficiaries if he or she retains an interest in the trust, such as the right to revoke the trust, the right to change beneficiaries, the right to substantial reversion, the right to borrow from the trust without security and the right to control income or principal.[141]

Those principles are found for inheritance tax purposes in *Helvering v Mercantile-Commerce Bank & Trust Co.*[142] In this case, a man transferred assets to a trust for the benefit of and to be used by his wife for family expenses and her own maintenance and support. Upon her survival of the husband, she was to receive $100,000. The issue was whether the inherited money was part of the deceased estate as it was held in trust. The court ruled that the trust was giving effect to the husband's civil liabilities to a retaining interest, thus falling within the decedent's taxable estate.

(ii) The Development of the General Beneficial Owner Anti-avoidance Principle

As was briefly mentioned earlier, the broad and increasing use of beneficial ownership in tax law in the twentieth century led to a blending of the term with other concepts or principles to adapt it to its diverse functions. Those uses do not follow equity law use of beneficial ownership, but blend ordinary tax principles of beneficial ownership – certainty and settlor-interest – with other principles in order to fit a rule to a desired result in the context of a specific case before the courts, or to adapt allocation rules to specific events in some statutory rules.

These developments followed different reasoning in the USA and the UK, probably because of their different attitudes in domestic tax law towards tax avoidance. In the UK, beneficial ownership certainty principles broadened their scope through contextual interpretation of the statutes where the term was used, employing an imprecise understanding of sham as part of that context, although not fully distorting the certainty principle. In the USA, beneficial ownership principles were absolutely mixed with anti-avoidance doctrines such as substance over form or the business purpose test, leading to a sometimes improperly considered economic allocation. Comparing both approaches,

[139] ibid 15–16.
[140] ibid 21–22, 24.
[141] See s 671 et seq of the Internal Revenue Code, 26 USC.
[142] *Helvering v Mercantile-Commerce Bank & Trust Co* (1940) 111 F2d 224 224 (8th Cir).

the concept in the UK is still largely attached to equity law, simply requiring contextual adaptation in certain cases, whereas in the USA the concept broadly embraced an anti-avoidance purpose to its core.

(a) United Kingdom: Control, Enjoyment and Legal Shells

Beneficial ownership interpretation in case law during the twentieth century mainly dealt with two issues. The first was the meaning of beneficial ownership. The interpretation of beneficial ownership in the UK, especially when the wording is interpreted as part of a statutory rule, may be divided into two periods. The first one, from the beginning of the century until the 1980s–90s, used a quite formal approach, largely following the certainty principle and defining beneficial ownership in tax law by reference to equity law.[143] The second period, from the 1980s–90s and probably framed by a new substantive approach to tax law, apparently widened the concept to include cases where, even though absent beneficial ownership in equity, there are reasons to consider an object as beneficial ownership according to the context of the relevant rule.[144] However, even though this second tendency opened the door to a broadening of the concept, the actual scope of the expansion still remains uncertain.

The second issue was whether beneficial ownership may be in suspense or, if it is not found in a person, to whom it has to be vested. This issue also evolved during the twentieth century. It seems that earlier in the century it was held that beneficial ownership may be in suspense, while later on it was considered that beneficial ownership always had to be vested in somebody for tax law purposes. Finally, in recent cases, beneficial ownership was again considered to be in suspense.

In one of the first UK tax law cases on beneficial ownership, *English Sewing Cotton Co v Inland Revenue Commissioners* (1947), the Court of Appeal analysed whether a corporation was the beneficial owner of 90 per cent of stock in a US company mortgaged to the US Government by an Act of Parliament.[145] Dividends were payable to the mortgagor in the USA, and the government was obliged to pay an amount equivalent to the dividends paid by the US company to the corporation. The court ruled that the corporation was the beneficial owner irrespective of the mortgage for the purposes of the excess profit tax.

However, even though it is fully clear that the corporation remained the beneficial owner in relation to the stock for such tax purposes, it was less clear whether the corporation was to be considered the beneficial owner of the dividends if the tax rules also required the corporation to be beneficially entitled to them in order to apply reliefs. One of the main reasons why the court considered the company to be the beneficial owner was because the Mortgaging Act provided indications that this was the case. However, it is unclear whether the corporation would have been considered the beneficial owner

[143] See Lloyd LJ's analysis of the evolution of beneficial ownership in case law in *Sainsbury v O'Connor*, where he shows how beneficial ownership was historically interpreted as referring to beneficiary rights in equity, even though switching previous jurisprudence and concluding beneficial ownership shall not be interpreted in a strict equity sense: *J Sainsbury Plc v O'Connor (Inspector of Taxes)* (n 51) 969–77.

[144] *Sainsbury v O'Connor* (n 51); *BUPA Insurance Ltd v Commissioners* [2014] STC 2615 (UT); *Gemsupa Ltd v Commisioners* (2015) 3 WLUK 67 (FTTTC).

[145] *English Sewing Cotton Co v IRC* (n 84).

for this or other rules if the Act did not explicitly provide support for saying so. What is significant from this case is that it considers beneficial ownership cannot be considered as gone unless it has gone somewhere else, rejecting the view that beneficial ownership may be suspended.[146]

Relief for intra-group transfer of shares in stamp duty is the field where beneficial ownership has been discussed the most. In 1958, *Parway Estates Ltd v Commissioners of Inland Revenue* dealt with a case where a company agreed to sell their shares in a subsidiary to an individual, but certain assets were to be transferred to the seller before the transfer and payment.[147] The main issue was whether Parway was the beneficial owner of more than 90 per cent of the shares for the exemption for intra-group asset transfer to be applicable during the time between the agreement and the effective transfer after the assets had been withdrawn from the subsidiary. The Court of Appeal decided in favour of the Commissioner, arguing that the contract was an unconditional one, even though it was subject to specific performance in the form of withdrawing certain assets, the vendor being a trustee for the buyer of the shares with specific duties following the transfer and the purchaser being enabled to claim that the agreement was fulfilled by his will and able to get legal ownership of the shares and the performance. As a consequence, the seller was not the beneficial owner of the subsidiary shares and relevant intra-group transfer relief was not applicable. In this sense, the case seems to identify beneficial ownership in tax law with beneficial ownership in equity law by identifying an implicit trust where equitable ownership is in the buyer, as it was earlier defined for sales with performance by equity case law in the nineteenth century.[148]

Also dealing with stamp duty relief, *Homleigh Holdings Ltd v IRC* concerned a sale of shares made by an agent on behalf of the directors and the parent company.[149] Following the reasoning of *Leigh Spinners Ltd* – in turn based on the above-mentioned doctrine of implicit equitable performance developed in the nineteenth century[150] – it was ruled that once there is an agreement to sell the shares and the parties are bound, there is an equitable obligation of the original shareholder to transfer them to the acquirer.[151] By identifying a constructive or implied trust in a sale, those cases denied beneficial ownership being vested in the seller even before receiving the price or before conveyance. Similar to *Parway*, those cases identify beneficial ownership in tax law with beneficial ownership in equity law, even though they reached controversial results through determining the existence of implied trusts.[152] However, what is not clear from those cases is whether beneficial ownership was to be in the buyer even before paying, or whether it was suspended.[153] It also remains unclear whether such implied trusts are only considered for tax purposes or also in equity.

[146] Rowland (n 9) 185.
[147] *Parway Estates, Ltd v IRC* (1958) 45 TC 135 (CA).
[148] *Rayner v Preston* (n 84); *Lysaght v Edwards* (n 84).
[149] *Homleigh Holdings v IRC* (1958) 37 ATC 406.
[150] Above, n 148.
[151] *Leigh Spinners v IRC* (1956) 35 ATC 58.
[152] JG M, 'Beneficial Owner' [1962] *British Tax Review* 343; JG M, 'Transfers between Associated Enterprises' [1959] *British Tax Review* 142; JG M, 'Relief from Stamp Duty on Inter Company Transfers' [1956] *British Tax Review* 184.
[153] M, 'Relief from Stamp Duty on Inter Company Transfers' (n 152) 186–87.

A similar case concerning stamp duty relief was *Escoigne Properties, Ltd v IRC*, but in this case it was considered that beneficial ownership was to be vested in the buyer before the property was conveyed but after the price was paid, as there was an equitable obligation for the seller to convey the subject matter.[154] This case did not solve whether beneficial ownership passed to the buyer before the price was paid; although the case caused significant controversy at the time, it is probable that the majority thought this to be the case.[155]

Another case, and probably the most quoted one on beneficial ownership in tax law, is *Wood Preservation v Prior* (1968).[156] In this case, Company A sold the shares in Company B to a purchaser Company X, subject to the condition made by a German corporation, whose products were being marketed by B, to honour the pre-existing marketing agreement between the German company and Company A. After some months, Company X waived the condition. Company B made a claim to offset losses from A derived from expenses incurred in marketing the German products after the subscription of the buy and sell agreement but prior to the waiver of the condition. The argument was that beneficial ownership did not to pass to X before the condition was fulfilled.

The Chancery Court ruled in this that, insofar as the condition performance was absolutely available to Company X, beneficial ownership for the purpose of offsetting losses was in the hands of the buying company following the subscription of the agreement, and not from the waiver of the condition.[157] Thus, Company A's losses were not for the benefit of Company B because that corporation was already beneficially owned by Company X following the purchase and sale agreement.

At first instance, the court's ratio for the decision relied on the object and the purpose of the loss offsetting rule and, specifically, on the fact that Company X was fully able to decide and benefit from the corporation at their will upon their ability to waive the condition. Company A had no power remaining to control the corporation, so the court excluded its beneficial owner condition. Because all control was in X and no power was in A, and in accordance with the spirit of the loss offsetting rule, there was no other solution but to say A had no beneficial ownership. A's only obligation was to reimburse and take the shares back in case of no performance, but no right to the shares. It was clear the seller had no right and, the condition being dependent on the buyer, the effect of the contract was to give rights to control and income to the new owner following the agreement. In other words, as the condition was dependent on the acquirer and there was no power or benefit available to the seller, equitable ownership was not available to the seller but to the acquirer and, to some, held upon trust by the seller.[158] Millett J argued in the judgment, with slightly different arguments but equal consequences, that the seller had the ability to sell the shares to another party but, given the contract, it was not able to do so it for its own benefit, so its beneficial ownership condition was excluded.[159]

[154] *Escoigne Properties v IRC* (1956) 1 WLR 980.
[155] M, 'Relief from Stamp Duty on Inter Company Transfers' (n 152) 186–87.
[156] *Wood Preservation v Prior* (1968) 2 All ER 849; *Wood Preservation Ltd v Prior (Commissioner)* (1969) 1 WLR 1077.
[157] *Wood Preservation v Prior* (n 156).
[158] Rowland (n 9) 182.
[159] *Wood Preservation v Prior* (n 156).

The Court of Appeal reached a similar conclusion, even though the ruling does not show a clear reasoning because each judge provided a different view, with little clarity in most of them.[160] In the Court of Appeal judgment, Lord Donovan and Harman LJ did not agree that beneficial ownership had reached the buyer, and following previous case law supported the ability of beneficial ownership to be suspended. They argued that as A had something that it could not use, control or enjoy, it could not be said to be the beneficial owner, and beneficial ownership was regarded as suspended as, pending the condition, it could not be said to be in the purchaser either.[161] Goff and Widgery argued on the contrary, saying that beneficial ownership could not be suspended but had to be in somebody if it was to leave the vendor.[162] As was argued in *English Sewing Cotton* and contrary to the trend in the above-mentioned stamp duty relief cases, beneficial ownership could not be considered as leaving the vendor unless it was vested in another person.[163]

In any case, despite the judges reached no agreement on the ability of beneficial ownership to be in suspense, the case was decided against offsetting losses either on a purposive interpretation of the rules involved or on the fact that the seller retained no beneficial ownership. It would seem to this author that the ruling spotlights the existence of an implied trust by the fact that all the judges recognised that beneficial ownership left the vendor, although they were unclear on whether or not it reached the buyer. Recognising an implied trust, *Wood Preservation* still leaves beneficial ownership in tax law as referred to in equity law.

Harman LJ casts doubt on this by introducing reference to the 'mere legal shell' test, which will later be expanded by the *Sainsbury* case. In this sense, Harman seemed to consider legal ownership to be irrelevant to the case as the owner had no benefit, thus ownership of the shares was a 'mere legal shell'. However, the important reason for reaching the result in this case was that beneficial ownership was not considered as being in the seller as it had no ability to deal with the property as its own, rather than because of the more or less artificial character of the transaction or ownership in the seller, which was just a consequence and not the cause of the subject not being the beneficial owner. The use of an avoidance reasoning in the interpretation was there, and thus entered the universe of beneficial ownership in UK tax law, although it did not reach the ratio decidendi.

In *Pritchard (Inspector of Taxes) v M H Builders (Wilmslow) Ltd*, the issues were whether preferred creditors had a sole beneficial interest in the trade business of a corporation in liquidation, and whether they continued to have beneficial ownership solely or jointly with ordinary creditors from the original corporation if such trade was transferred to another corporation.[164]

The Chancery Division ruled in the first issue in favour of a unique beneficial interest of the preferred creditors, while in the second it stated that the beneficial ownership was shared by preferred creditors jointly with ordinary creditors. However, what is

[160] Goff J, Harman LJ and Widgery LJ in *Wood Preservation Ltd v Prior (Commissioner)* (n 156) 1094, 1096–97. See commentaries on JG M, 'Beneficial Ownership' [1969] *British Tax Review* 64; JG M, 'Conditional Contracts and Beneficial Ownership' [1968] *British Tax Review* 267.

[161] *Wood Preservation Ltd v Prior (Commissioner)* (n 156) 1095–97.

[162] GoffJ and Widgery LJ in ibid 1094, 1096–97.

[163] Rowland (n 9) 185.

[164] *Pritchard (Inspector of Taxes) v MH Builders (Wilmslow) Ltd* (1969) 1 WLR 409 (Ch).

relevant for this purpose is that beneficial ownership was understood in the sense of the subject being entitled to control and especially to compel. This seems to match the *Wood Preservation* majority view on beneficial ownership as it was understood there, following the right of the owner to compel or the right to performance on the shares. Not surprisingly, some authors at the time interpreted the beneficial owner from *Pritchard* and from *Wood Preservation* as the person who is free to deal with the assets as they wish – ie control.[165] In this regard, this view largely matches my above-proposed definition on beneficial ownership in equity as the right to primary control and income.

In 1976, another leading case, *Ayerst (Inspector of Taxes) v C & K (Construction) Ltd*, discussed beneficial ownership and tax law, in this case in the context of transfer of losses in liquidations.[166] The appellant bought a corporation from a company in liquidation. The sellers sought to offset the taxable profits against losses incurred by the parent in liquidation in running the business before it was acquired by the new owners. In this case, after a long analysis of whether corporations in winding up or liquidation are able to retain legal and beneficial ownership, the House of Lords ruled against the parent having beneficial ownership of its assets at the time of being liquidated.

But leaving aside the question of whether beneficial ownership is in suspense or lost in liquidation, which seems to be the subject of great controversy, *Ayerst* continues recognising beneficial ownership in tax law as attached to its equity meaning.[167]

Another case where beneficial ownership in tax law was discussed is *Burman (Inspector of Taxes) v Hedges & Butler Ltd*.[168] In the case, BC Group wanted to sell its subsidiary, Bushmills, to Seagram's, a Canadian company. If they had done so directly, a significant taxable capital gain would have arisen. Instead, they incorporated Vostoka, the latter issuing around 76 per cent of its shares in the form of preference shares to be subscribed to by BC and 24 per cent as ordinary shares to be subscribed to by Seagram's. Vostoka, in turn, incorporated a second subsidiary, Zagal, all of whose shares were directly or indirectly owned by Vostoka. Seagram's then granted a loan to Zagal, which was used to buy the Bushmills shares from BC Group holding. As Zagal was part of the BC Group, tax on capital gain was electable for rollover. Once the Bushmills shares were owned by Zagal, Vostoka was wound up, the BC Group holding received £76 and Seagram's received all the shares in Zagal.

Section 532 of the Income and Corporation Taxes Act 1970 provided a definition of group that was based on beneficial ownership. The first issue was to define if BC was the beneficial owner of 75 per cent of Zagal's shares, so that Zagal could be considered part of the group, making the rollover regime applicable. The court ruled, against the Commissioners, that BC holding was the beneficial owner of Vostoka and, indirectly, of the Zagal shares, insofar as they would have been able to deal as they wished with them. Irrespective of whether the arrangement could have been agreed in advance and whether to do any other thing would have been disadvantageous, BC was legally able

[165] RS Nock, '"Hiving off" and Stamp Duty Exemption' [1971] *British Tax Review* 254, 257–58.

[166] *Ayerst (Inspector of Taxes) v C & K Construction Ltd* [1975] STC 345 (CA); *Ayerst (Inspector of Taxes) v C&K (Construction)* (1975) 3 WLR 16 (HL).

[167] On the controversy of beneficial ownership in liquidations see J Coombes, 'A Beneficial Decision? *Ayerst v C&K Construction Ltd*' [1975] *British Tax Review* 302.

[168] *Burman (Inspector of Taxes) v Hedges & Butler Ltd* (1979) 1 WLR 160 (Ch D).

to do whatever they wished with their shares until the winding up without Seagram's being able to claim. Consequently, they were beneficial owners of the shares in Vostoka and Zagal, and the rollover regime was applicable as both companies were part of the same group.

The second issue raised was whether Zagal was acting as a principal or as an agent or nominee for Seagram's. The court again ruled against the Commissioner, arguing that an agency relationship for tax purposes was a matter of fact, the loan and the shares were included in the accounts and all had legal effects for Zagal, and there was no document or proof showing any fact different to a parent–subsidiary relationship.

The approach taken by the court was extremely formal, probably framed on the formal understanding of tax law taken in the UK from the 1930s until the 1980s as a result of the *Duke of Westminster* case.[169] In this sense, it did not actually scrutinise the meaning of beneficial ownership in tax law as in other cases, but simply maintained the previous equity law understanding. However, even if one does not delve into the legal duty of explaining the court's interpretation, it may be derived from the assumptions of the ruling that, contrary to more recent interpretations, the *Burman* case continues to assume that beneficial ownership refers to the legal ability to claim control and enjoy.

What is different from previous cases is that the *Burman* case does not resort to considering an implied trust as derived from the previous agreement between the holding and Seagram's and the subsequent loan transaction. However, it seems possible to this author that Seagram's may have claimed equitable remedies in certain cases against Zagal, Vostoka and even BC if BC would have taken decisions on the use of the loan which were different from buying Bushmills and the subsequent winding up. Although *Burman* continues to define beneficial ownership in an equity sense, it departs from previous cases as not delving into equity law to solve the issue in a material sense.

Summarising the cases analysed so far, stamp duty rulings tended to recognise the ability of beneficial ownership to be suspended, while rulings on other statutory rules, especially on the second period, established the need to reach the buyer in order to leave the vendor. With regard to its meaning, the majority view was that beneficial ownership in tax law had to be interpreted in accordance with equity law, even though in some cases a constructive or implicit trust may show the underlying economic rationale of the arrangements, with the exception of *Burman*.

However, even though, in this first period, an overwhelming majority supported such an equity law view of the concept, it was not an absolute view, and some justices were arguing early on in favour of understanding the concept in tax matters in a broader sense, opening the path to the second period.[170]

In *Parway Estates*, Upjohn J argued in favour of defining beneficial ownership in its 'ordinary or popular sense', seemingly heading to a colloquial use that may imply anti-avoidance effects.[171] However, Upjohn's argument was a minority view, and the Court of Appeal explicitly denied such an approach. Pennycuick J, in *Brooklands Selangor Ltd* (1970),

[169] *Commissioner v Duke of Westminster* (n 19); *Commissioner v Duke of Westminster* [1935] All ER 259.

[170] Probably the best summary of dissenting opinions and the evolution of beneficial owner until the liberal construction developed by the *Sainsbury* case is Lloyd's opinion in the case *Sainsbury v O'Connor* (n 51) 969–77.

[171] *Parway Estates, Ltd v IRC* (n 147) 142.

also moved towards a similar conclusion by saying beneficial ownership is not the same as equitable ownership as it is understood in equity law, despite recognising that they match in several cases.[172]

Another case taking a broader view on beneficial ownership was *Rodwell Securities Ltd v Inland Revenue Commissioners*, where it was held that beneficial ownership should be defined liberally.[173] The case denied a corporation from having beneficial ownership, despite controlling two subsidiaries, and therefore group exemption from stamp duty on property transfer.

A liberal and broad understanding of beneficial ownership was also followed in the *Andrea Ursula* case in 1973.[174] Even though it was not a tax case, it attracted significant attention from equity and tax lawyers because of the possible effects of such doctrine. The case concerned whether a company performing repairs on a vessel may or may not arrest it where the subscriber of the repairs is not the legal and/or equitable owner but a demise charterer or any other person in possession and control. The relevant rule, contained in the 1952 International Convention relating to the Arrest of Sea-Going Ships, applied to beneficial ownership of the boat. The court concluded that it shall be construed liberally to include both a charterer and any other person in possession and control. However, the arguments for reaching such a conclusion largely rely on the International Convention relating to the Arrest of Sea-Going Ships from which the relevant rules derive, which include demise charters and any other title. Thus, beneficial ownership in this case is derived from a contextual interpretation to give effect to UK international commitments, and not from a proper UK statutory understanding of the concept.

From such previous formal approaches, the *J Sainsbury* case of 1990 went a step further, and could be regarded as founding today's broader liberal understanding of tax law beneficial ownership.[175] The case involved a joint venture between Sainsbury and GB, in which they held 75 per cent and 25 per cent of the stock, respectively. However, at the time of the incorporation, an option to purchase 5 per cent of the stock was given by the former to the latter, and GB gave Sainsbury an option to require the purchase of the 5 per cent, in both cases no earlier than five years hence. The options were never exercised and Sainsbury requested the offsetting of the joint venture losses, which was rejected by the tax authorities on the grounds that Sainsbury was not the beneficial owner of the 5 per cent subject to the option and thus was not eligible for offsetting the subsidiary losses.

After an extensive analysis of previous cases, Lloyd LJ relied on *Wood Preservation* to deem that the definition of beneficial ownership should not be constructed strictly with reference to equity law, but should depend on the nature and extent of the rights involved.[176] In accordance with this, if the taxpayer lacks all ownership characteristics despite holding beneficial and legal ownership, it cannot be said to hold beneficial ownership; rather, its rights are a mere legal shell. The court followed the arguments of

[172] *Brooklands Selangor Holdings Ltd v IRC* (1970) 1 WLR 429 (ChD) 450.
[173] *Rodwell Securities Ltd v Inland Revenue Commissioners* (1968) 1 All ER 257 (Ch D).
[174] *Medway Drydock & Engineering Co Ltd v MV Andrea Ursula* [1973] QB 265 (QB) 269–74.
[175] *Sainsbury v O'Connor* (n 51).
[176] ibid 972–77.

the Crown representative: (i) whether or not the company has the right to sell the shares; (ii) whether it has the right to dividends; and (iii) whether the price of the exercise of the option was the amount agreed, less dividends and 1 per cent interest, excluding any gain on the value of the shares. This quantification meant that the buyer was receiving the profits of the company, which was close to a loan. On the first two points, the court decided that the limitation to the 5 per cent derived from the need for agreement between the two parties to jointly decide on dividends and a change of capital structure was not different from the remaining 70 per cent, and there was no doubt Sainsbury was the owner of the 70 per cent. On the third point, the court ruled that the fact that dividends were deducted from the price did not mean Sainsbury was not beneficially entitled to them, even though little explanation was given on this point. Finally, a last attempt by the Crown to call for a 'balanced judgment' of beneficial ownership in what seems to be not a liberal, but a fully free, analysis was rejected by the Court as the taxpayer retained all the legal attributes of ownership. In the end, the court decided in favour of the taxpayer insofar as the rights held by the taxpayer were not considered to be a mere legal shell.

As stated above, *J Sainsbury* was the first case where a liberal interpretation of beneficial ownership was completely supported, despite Nourse LJ's rejection.[177] However, the case did not go as far as providing for a broadest material fairness analysis underlying beneficial ownership. What the ruling did provide was for a release from equity law conclusions and for a linking of the concept to the analysis of the specific rights involved in the whole set of arrangements at stake. What is surprising is that such a view is considered not to be a new perspective, but to derive from *Wood Preservation*. To this author, such a conclusion might be a misinterpretation of the *Wood Preservation* case. Although *Wood Preservation* has been considered as broadening understanding of beneficial ownership, this author cannot agree.

First, Lord Donovan's argument in *Wood Preservation*, that the seller who owns a tree can neither cut it down nor obtain the fruits is somehow misleading. It cannot be said that you can own something you cannot control or enjoy, because such rights will not fall within the characteristics of ownership.[178] It is precisely the case that ownership requires primary rights to control or enjoy. Thus, the person holding the tree cannot be said to be an owner, but is entitled to or holds an interest or duty.

Secondly, the reasoning behind the approach of the appealed ruling and the other judges' arguments seems to follow a constructive trust in which the buyer has beneficial ownership, as was argued by Goff J, excluding the seller's beneficial ownership.[179] Moreover, Donovan's reference to injunctions available to the buyer in case of sale by the seller to a third party probably includes equitable remedies for implied trusts.[180] And even though the three judges disagreed on whether beneficial ownership reached the buyer, they simply agreed on a controversial assertion that it was not in the seller.[181] If beneficial ownership suspense is only recognised in a limited sense, it cannot be said

[177] ibid 977–80.

[178] See s II.A in ch 2 above.

[179] *Wood Preservation v Prior* (n 156); *Wood Preservation Ltd v Prior (Commissioner)* (n 156) 1094.

[180] *Wood Preservation Ltd v Prior (Commissioner)* (n 156) 1095.

[181] Rowland (n 9) 182.

that it may leave the vendor without reaching the purchaser. As stated in previous chapters, it is likely that the buyer had negative ownership rights, but beneficial ownership cannot fully disappear, otherwise there is no trust.

Of more relevance, it cannot be said that the judgment defines beneficial ownership in a broad sense just because the ruling excludes beneficial ownership rights being vested in the seller in a contract and without resorting to the arguments of the judges, who differ on whether beneficial ownership is in the acquirer. Finally, it is important to bear in mind that *Sainsbury* largely relies on the 'mere legal shell' wording used by Harman LJ. The shell character seems to derive simply as the consequence of the vendor not having beneficial ownership as having no right to benefit, but not the cause of beneficial ownership not being on it. In other words, saying beneficial ownership is not in the subject because he has no right to benefit is to take the part as the whole. In the end, if somebody holds legal ownership but their abilities are limited by the contractual or equitable rights of somebody else, it is not a matter of having a mere legal shell, but simply having plain legal ownership and not having beneficial ownership. As stated, beneficial ownership is probably reduced in force in the beneficiary, and in a negative sense.

All in all, and despite the case law grounds of *Sainsbury* possibly being controversial, there is no doubt that the case set a new line of reasoning for beneficial ownership, ultimately leading to the current liberal understanding of the concept. However, the case explicitly denied an absolute anti-avoidance free interpretation of beneficial ownership derived from a search of material tax justice or 'balanced judgment'.[182] As properly argued by some authors, to search for a 'just' result given the possibility of the lack of definition of beneficial ownership is highly risky.[183] In addition, it does not explicitly support a variable contextual interpretation of statutory beneficial ownership that is dependent on the circumstances in which the wording is used by the legislature, as it may be accepted today.[184]

Sainsbury interpreted beneficial ownership in tax law as largely referring to equitable ownership, even though, in referring to other cases, the court did not clarify this. However, *Sainsbury* boosted the mere legal shell analysis that was simply recognising in *Wood Preservation* what was obvious – that legal ownership does not imply beneficial ownership – and misleadingly induced later jurisprudence to connect beneficial ownership with soft anti-avoidance ideas. As will be seen, anti-avoidance derived from beneficial ownership in the UK has not been as hard as in the USA, maintaining a major connection to equity law.

Jerome v Kelly solved the issue of whether beneficial ownership for tax purposes is able to be in suspense.[185] Indeed, what the case did was to apply in tax law what was said before in *Chang v Registrar of Titles*.[186] In that case, following *Lysaght v Edwards* or *Rayner v Preston*, it was held that an implied trust in a sale only exists insofar as the remedy of specific performance is available. In that sense, transfer of beneficial ownership depends on when the contract is considered to be complete. Thus, if the contract

[182] *Sainsbury v O'Connor* (n 51) 976.
[183] Rowland (n 9) 187.
[184] *cf Sainsbury v O'Connor* (n 51). See also *BUPA Insurance Ltd v Commissioners* (n 144) fourth argument.
[185] *Jerome v Kelly (Inspector of Taxes)* (n 85).
[186] *Chang v Registrar of Titles* (1976) 137 CLR 177.

is completed upon the payment of the price, then beneficial ownership is transferred to the buyer only after payment. On the other hand, if the completion is upon agreement, beneficial ownership is transferred at that time. In any case, before the event considered as completion of the agreement, beneficial ownership is not considered to be transferred as there is no implied trust in force. From such an assertion, *Jerome v Kelly* derives that there is a period until the completion of the contract and the availability of specific performance when beneficial ownership has not yet arrived in the buyer, but where the seller has no absolute powers on the subject matter. In this sense, it seems that the ruling recognises that beneficial ownership is split between the seller and the buyer, contrary to the suspense theory that was held hitherto.[187] For the purposes of beneficial ownership interpretation in tax law, this means that when tax law requires full beneficial ownership to be vested in a person, it cannot be said that it is in the seller or in the vendor in the period between a contract being agreed and the completion of the contract.

In the author's view, to state beneficial ownership is in suspense is not fully accurate. As stated previously, beneficial ownership is heavily attenuated in those cases, and potential beneficiaries only retain negative ownership rights against the trustee and the rest of the world at large. Otherwise, it cannot be said that there is a trust, as if there is no certain or potential beneficiary to whom the trust will benefit, then there is no trust, so there is no equitable ownership and mere legal ownership. As soon as there is a potential beneficiary, he or she holds rights against the world, although in this case only very weakly and in a negative sense.

In 1997, in *Inland Revenue Commissioners v Willoughby*, the House of Lords analysed the effect of anti-avoidance provisions and allocation of income in relation to property underlying financial instruments.[188] In that case, two individuals resident in Hong Kong purchased a bond in the Isle of Man representing underlying investments in unit trusts, later moved to the UK and became residents, and after becoming residents bought two new bonds.[189] In both cases, the first bonds were acquired with proceedings from the retirement benefits as a professor of the University of Hong Kong, and from the proceeds of an earlier offshore policy that was funded by the earnings of the subject as professor. The main issue was whether income derived from underlying investments and paid to the insurance corporation who was the bonds' debtor was to be attributed to the individuals, as the transfer of the bonds was just an arrangement to take advantage of the non-subjection of the income to the offshore policies tax regime.[190] The House

[187] *Jerome v Kelly (Inspector of Taxes)* (n 85) 32.

[188] *Inland Revenue Commissioners v Willoughby* (1997) 1 WLR 1071 (UKHL).

[189] ibid 1073–74.

[190] In s 739, the Income and Corporation Taxes Act 1988 provides for taxation in the hands of UK residents if property is transferred to non-residents for the purposes of avoiding UK tax rules while continuing to enjoy the benefits of such property: '(1) Subject to section 747(4)(b), the following provisions of this section shall have effect for the purpose of preventing the avoiding by individuals ordinarily resident in the United Kingdom of liability to income tax by means of transfers of assets by virtue or in consequence of which, either alone or in conjunction with associated operations, income becomes payable to persons resident or domiciled outside the United Kingdom. (2) Where by virtue or in consequence of any such transfer, either alone or in conjunction with associated operations, such an individual has, within the meaning of this section, power to enjoy, whether forthwith or in the future, any income of a person resident or domiciled outside the United Kingdom which, if it were income of that individual received by him in the United Kingdom, would be chargeable to income tax by deduction or otherwise, that income shall, whether it would or would not have been chargeable to income tax apart from the provisions of this s, be deemed to be income of that individual for all purposes of the Income Tax Acts.'

of Lords did not consider so, and upheld the application of the special regime to the taxpayers. What is remarkable for the interpretation of beneficial ownership is that the Lords explicitly denied that the bondholders had in substance any legal or equitable interest in the underlying investments, as argued by the Commissioners. In the words of the court, the right on the bonds remains a 'mere contractual right to the benefits promised by the policy, no more and no less', insofar as if the bond debtor fails, the subject will not have any right on the investments.[191] By saying so, the court confirmed that the allocation of income remains attached to equitable ownership, so beneficial ownership as the person to whom income should be allocated continues to be referred to the substantive owner who holds the property in equity law.

Yet, the court's reasoning is based on the fact that the transaction cannot be regarded as abusive; as a consequence, allocation remains within the ordinary allocation rules, ie to beneficial ownership in equity on the bonds and not the underlying property. Hence, it does not clarify whether prevention of avoidance principles being applicable and underlying property being assigned to the bondholders would imply beneficial ownership of the individuals for tax purposes to be referred to underlying property, or whether anti-avoidance rules are just exceptions independent from beneficial ownership principles.

Finally, and following in the steps of *Sainsbury*, the Upper Tribunal consolidated and compiled current understanding of beneficial ownership in tax law in the *BUPA Insurance* case of 2014.[192] The case concerned whether a corporation was the beneficial owner of the shares in a subsidiary, beneficially entitled to the distributions and beneficially entitled in the winding-up of the subsidiary, in order to apply group relief as required by section 403C(2) of the Income and Corporation Taxes Act 1988, where the agreement upon which the shares on the subsidiary were bought included the obligation to pay the seller amounts equivalent to the distribution received from the subsidiary up to $171 million, and 95 per cent of distributions after such amount. The Upper Tribunal ruled that the corporation was the beneficial owner of the shares and entitled to the distribution, being the relief applicable. The main arguments in reaching this conclusion were: (i) lack of beneficial ownership in Scottish law, hence the rule not being applied in Scotland;[193] (ii) the context in which the concept appears refers to beneficial ownership being held directly or through another body corporate, making it clear that the assets of a company in whose stock a shareholder participates cannot be considered to be held by the shareholder in equity, the statutory rule explicitly recognising such approach by broadening beneficial ownership for such purposes;[194] and (iii) applicable case law regarded beneficial ownership as distinct from equity law.[195] In this regard, what is interesting from the ruling is the clear compilation of beneficial ownership principles as they were understood in *Sainsbury*, as well as the express clarification of some other points that had not been dealt with before.

[191] *Inland Revenue Commissioners v Willoughby* (n 188) 1080.
[192] *BUPA Insurance Ltd v Commissioners* (n 144).
[193] ibid 54.
[194] ibid 53.
[195] ibid 55.

Among the clarifications or consolidations of previous doctrines, *BUPA* first defines beneficial ownership in tax law as different from beneficial ownership in equity law.[196] Secondly, the analysis has to be done on the relevant object in search of the relevant attributes of beneficial ownership in relation to the subject matter.[197] Thirdly, beneficial ownership in the context of group relief means ownership with benefit.[198] Fourthly, the right to dispose of an asset and enjoy the fruits confers beneficial ownership, while the complete absence of them deprives the owner of 'beneficial ownership'.[199] Fifthly, if legal rights are just a legal shell without any rights, it cannot be said that there is beneficial ownership.[200] And finally, beneficial ownership in equity law normally implies beneficial ownership in tax law, but if the incidents of equitable ownership constitute a 'mere shell' of ownership rights, the relevant object would lack such beneficial ownership.[201]

Following such principles, the definition of beneficial ownership in *BUPA* may be summarised as follows: in the first instance, full control and ability to dispose, and right to enjoyment, will define beneficial ownership. Secondly, in a negative sense, an object lacks beneficial ownership if such rights enabling disposal and enjoyment derive from a mere legal shell. From such principles, *BUPA* seems to leave statutory beneficial ownership in tax law unclear.

On the first point, it does not express how such abilities should be. It clarifies that absolute absence precludes beneficial ownership and full ability defines it. However, it does not define where the point between those two limits is where beneficial ownership is lost. This leaves beneficial ownership still close to private law ownership as it largely follows the common definition on ownership seen in chapter two.[202] On this point, Rowland relates the concept to deciding who holds the value of the assets, apparently linking it to economic allocation doctrines.[203]

On the other hand, a negative definition connected to a legal shell apparently links the concept with sham or anti-avoidance doctrines. But again, it does not define upon or opposed to what principle or doctrine such shell legal rights are defined. In the author's view, the case references to the actual legal relationships involved seem to link legal shells to sham doctrines. If this were the case, the link between beneficial ownership and sham is irrelevant, as sham doctrine – or even private law substance over form – could be applicable on shell legal rights arrangements in any case, even in the absence of a beneficial owner requirement.[204] As said, *Wood Preservation* simply points out legal

[196] ibid 53.
[197] ibid 56.
[198] ibid 58.
[199] ibid 59–60.
[200] ibid 59.
[201] ibid 61.
[202] See ss II.A and B in ch 2 above.
[203] Rowland (n 9) 186.
[204] Zornoza and Báez point out the distinction between sham in civil law countries, which applies in the step of definition of the facts, and anti-avoidance rules. However, sham in common law countries does not refer to definition of facts but to qualification within the law. In any case, substance over form or sham in common law countries and sham (simulation/simulación) in civil law countries are applicable irrespective of beneficial ownership requirements if the transaction is abusive in the first case, redirecting the consequences to the avoided rule and, if the transactions contained in the arrangements are false but covering a hidden transaction, redefining the facts and thus leading to a different tax consequence in the latter case of civil law countries. See J Zornoza Pérez and A Báez Moreno, 'The 2003 Revisions to the Commentary to the OECD Model on Tax

ownership as a 'mere legal shell' – it does not necessarily imply beneficial ownership. However, resorting to the sham transaction doctrine is not a consequence of the application of beneficial ownership, but serves as a tool to define legal facts – if the legal owner lacks beneficial ownership – only after legal facts are defined under the sham transaction doctrine, beneficial ownership may be identified on actual legal facts.

BUPA does actually add new remarks that are helpful for the understanding of the concept of beneficial ownership. First, it states that beneficial ownership may be in suspense. Even though this had been previously stated in *Wood Preservation* and *Sainsbury*, it was highly controversial and collateral in those rulings, while *BUPA* makes it plainly clear.[205] Moreover, such assertions coming from *Wood Preservation* and *Sainsbury* were derived from equity law, while beneficial ownership is regarded in *BUPA* as having its own tax scope. Thus, beneficial ownership departing from equity law may leave behind controversy around such characteristics and allow denial of beneficial ownership without the need to identify a new beneficial owner for tax law purposes. Still, as previously stated, the author considers this view of beneficial ownership being in suspense as controversial.

Another important point is that *BUPA* distinguishes between beneficial ownership and beneficial entitlement, the former referring to actual right and the latter being a right to, for instance, future distributions.[206] Finally, even though it was also implicit in previous cases, it is clearer in *BUPA* that beneficial ownership has to be interpreted in the context of the statutory provision in which it appears.[207]

The last point is possibly the most important one. As the right to control and enjoyment and the mere legal shell principle simply define the core of beneficial ownership and are close to ordinary applicable principles in private law, so, continuing with a formal understanding of the concept, the important point in the second period is its contextual adaptability. The ability of beneficial ownership to adapt itself to the statutory context will help the interpreter to add nuances and let the concept deviate from its understanding of equity.[208] To date, the limits of such adaptability and the scope of the new liberal understanding are still unclear.

In this regard, it is important to bear in mind that the concept is used in different forms, such as beneficial owner, beneficiary or beneficially entitled. Following *BUPA*, the specific wording used should be balanced against the specific context to unravel which specific characteristics the rule allocates to the income or asset, or how it defines the relief event.

For example, section 138 of the Income and Corporation Taxes Act 1988 used the expression 'full beneficial ownership'.[209] In this case, it seems that the 'full' requires both legal and beneficial ownership to be vested in a single person, or requires beneficial ownership to be held through a bare or simple trust, apparently excluding any other equitable interest or any case where a contract may withdraw any ownership characteristics.

Treaties and GAARs: A Mistaken Starting Point' in M Lang et al (eds), *Tax Treaties: Building Bridges between Law and Economics* (IBFD, 2010). See also Frederik Zimmer, 'General Report', *Form and Substance in Tax Law* (Kluwer, 2002) 29–36.

[205] Rowland (n 9) 181.

[206] *BUPA Insurance Ltd v Commissioners* (n 144) 57.

[207] ibid 51, 55, 58.

[208] Against, Rowland (n 9) 180.

[209] See s 138 of the Income and Corporation Taxes Act 1988, c 1.

In Canada, examples of the use of words related to beneficial ownership in statutory law are found in sections 74(4)(4) and 94.1 of the Canadian Income Tax Act. The first refers to transfers of loans to corporations, not considering a transfer for the benefit of a designated person related to the transferor if certain requirements are met, and the latter to investments in offshore investment funds.[210] In those rules, reference is made to interest in property. In that regard, Canadian tax authorities apparently define beneficiary interest in a discretionary trust to be, in substance, interest in underlying property, and not trust property.[211] In this case, different wording is used and is defined in a sense which deviates from the principle of allocating tax interest in discretionary trusts in the trust or trustee. The rationale for using a concept significantly broader for tax effects is to prevent certain avoidance schemes, even though does it not leave the definition open as a general anti-avoidance rule.

It is the same with the company reconstruction regime in the UK.[212] Even though beneficial ownership here seems to refer to a trust, the use of interest in most parts of the sections governing the regime suggests the concept should be understood in a broader sense.[213]

The relationship between anti-avoidance doctrines and beneficial ownership was not clarified in *BUPA*, so the *Gemsupa* case, decided in 2015, dealt again with the issue and ruled, based on *Sainsbury* and *BUPA*, that beneficial ownership has to be interpreted in accordance with a purposive interpretation of the rules involved.[214] However, it repudiated group relief rules requiring some form of commercial economic unity.[215]

Gemsupa makes an important clarification of *Sainsbury*, stating that the latter did not consider the options as sham or that the *Ramsay* principle was applied to prevent group relief.[216] Even though including beneficial ownership, sham and the beneficial ownership in the same phrasing may confuse the issue by mixing beneficial ownership, determination of the facts and anti-avoidance doctrines, in the author's view *Gemsupa* clearly differentiates beneficial ownership, sham and the *Ramsay* doctrine. This confirms that beneficial ownership still retains equitable ownership at its core. Because it says that neither doctrine applies to the case, while implicitly recognising the applicability of beneficial ownership, it settles that there are rules of different content. Thus, the definition of the legal arrangements involved and the possible implied trusts remains at the heart of the analysis of allocation of income or assets for relief purposes in tax matters. However, as *Sainsbury* recognised, beneficial ownership in tax law being greater than in equity law, there is still a doubt as to whether other cases are covered that are not regarded as beneficial ownership in equity law and, if so, what the definition of beneficial ownership in such cases is. The answer is probably linked to economic allocation, with unpredictable results. However, the author's view is that beneficial ownership

[210] A similar broad use of interest may be also found in the UK in former s 138 of the Income and Corporation Taxes Act 1988.

[211] Brown (n 6) 30.

[212] See s 940 et seq of the Corporation Tax Act, c 4, specially s 941(8).

[213] Interpreting beneficial ownership as referred to trust relationships, G Loutzenhiser, *Tiley's Revenue Law*, 8th edn (Hart Publishing, 2016) 1172.

[214] *Gemsupa Ltd v Commisioners* (n 144) para 121.

[215] ibid 122.

[216] ibid 112.

has to stick to equity rules and, as previously stated, the main issue in controversial cases lies in the definition of implicit trusts.

In sum, following case law, beneficial ownership in tax law has to be interpreted in the context of the relevant provision, according to abilities to dispose and enjoy. This being so, beneficial ownership is not applicable in cases where ownership rights are simply a mere shell. In this regard, it is the author's view that beneficial ownership has not changed dramatically since *Sainsbury* and *BUPA*, and even less so since *Wood Preservation*, and continues to rely largely on equity law.[217] In the end, beneficial ownership leads, in the author's view, to an analysis of the ownership abilities involved in the context of the relevant provision, especially taking into account rights in equity and being careful with regard to formal rights that may give a different appearance to the case. However, this does not differ significantly from the application of tax rules in general to cases where ownership abilities are split, as there has to be a careful analysis, and rules always have to be interpreted in a contextual sense.

As a conclusion, recent case law definition adds confusion that may be framed within the move from a formal literal approach of UK tax law derived from *Duke of Westminster* to a contextual purposive interpretation that followed the *Ramsay* case.[218] However, framing beneficial ownership by the application of general principles of interpretation, ability to pay principles and contextual and purposive interpretation in relation to complex equity and split of rights cases adds nothing but confusion, as they may lead some to consider that they are strongly connected. Although jurisprudence actually explicitly denies such a connection, such arguments being so close leads to mistakes.

Thus, it must be said that beneficial ownership wording should also be avoided in statutory law, as it may lead lawyers with little expertise in both fields to misleading results because of the use of identical wording. On the other hand, other concepts, such as creditors with economical rights similar to those or persons who benefit economically, should, in the author's view, be preferred. In addition, avoidance cases should be left to the application of general anti-abuse rules (GAARs) – especially now that the UK has codified a GAAR – if ownership or private rights have been maintained or shifted artificially, through a transaction without a business purpose or with the principal purpose of avoiding tax law provisions, but far from beneficial ownership.[219]

However, this author recognises that such a recommendation is extremely difficult, if not impossible, to achieve. It is impossible to remove it from statutory law, and in any

[217] Regarding s 941 of the Corporation Tax Act 2010, c 4, Loutzenhiser seems to interpret beneficial ownership as referring to equity law by calling on its effects on trusts. That section resembles ss 344(4) and 838 of the Income and Corporation Taxes Act 1988, c 1, the latter being the one interpreted in *Sainsbury*.

[218] On interpretation of tax statutes, see J Freedman, 'Interpreting Tax Statutes: Tax Avoidance and the Intention of the Parliament' (2007) 123 *LQR* 53.

[219] On the evolution of anti-avoidance principles in the UK, the proposal for a statutory GAAR and its current content, see J Freedman, 'Defining Taxpayer Responsibility: In Support of a General Anti-Avoidance Rule' [2004] *British Tax Review*; J Freedman, 'The UK GAAR', *General Anti-Avoidance Rules (GAARs) – A Key Element of Tax Systems in the Post-BEPS Tax World?* (IBFD, 2016); G Aaronson (ed), *GAAR Study: A Study to Consider Whether a General Anti-Avoidance Rule Should Be Introduced into the UK Tax System* (2011) https://webarchive.nationalarchives.gov.uk/20130402163458/www.hm-treasury.gov.uk/d/gaar_final_report_111111.pdf. See the GAAR in Pt 5 and schs 43–43C of the Finance Act 2013, c 29, and its guidance in HMRC, 'General Anti-Abuse Rule (GAAR) Guidance' www.gov.uk/government/publications/tax-avoidance-general-anti-abuse-rules.

case it is already considered by most lawyers to be part of the tax system. Beneficial ownership will continue to be construed as referring to equity law balanced against the context of the relevant rule that may, in some cases, enable the application of such rule to other cases lacking beneficial ownership in equity. Thus, the first step should be to interpret the concept within its context to verify whether it attaches to equity law or includes other cases; the second step, and the main issue, requires a proper analysis of the arrangements involved and possible implied trusts in order to define the framework; and the third step, interpreting the rule within its context and the legal arrangements involved, will finally analyse whether beneficial ownership is vested in one subject or another for the purposes of such tax rule. In a separate note, anti-avoidance rules may be applied, but only on their own terms – purpose, artificiality, etc – at a later step, and after the legal facts under beneficial ownership have been defined.

(b) USA: Economic Allocation in Financial Instruments and Disregard of Intermediary Entities

In the USA, the development of beneficial ownership allocation principles under anti-avoidance premises was done in two main contexts. The first was the use of bearer shares and bank nominees to hold shares for customers, as well as the later development of complex financial products and derivatives. Secondly, case law developed a set of principles to deal with the effects of intermediary corporations for tax law purposes. These two sets ultimately led to the current understanding of beneficial ownership in US tax law. The principles developed under those two groups are considered to form a key principle governing US tax law providing for economic allocation, although beneficial ownership and allocation principles in relation to anti-avoidance principles also appear in other contexts. However, because intermediary corporations and financial instruments are most frequently used in tax avoidance, as well as because of the importance of case law and practice around them in defining tax allocation of income, this analysis will be confined to these two issues.

In the early stages of development of these anti-avoidance beneficial ownership doctrines, the wording was rarely used in statutory law, and even when it started to be used it was not explicitly used in case law but was derived from the judiciary and the administrative set of allocation principles. Contrary to the UK, where case law explicitly used beneficial ownership wording, US case law does not refer to the concept very often. Nevertheless, the relationship between these doctrines on allocation of income and beneficial ownership is clear. Regarding the development of the doctrine of intermediary entities in particular, the use of concepts related to beneficial ownership in several such cases, the reference to the concept in many commentaries and the subsequent application of the principles of those cases to allocation of income cases make clear that these doctrines, and especially the intermediary entities doctrine, lay at the heart of the beneficial ownership concept in tax law.[220]

[220] Miller points out how 'beneficial ownership' relates to the allocation cases he discusses on intermediary corporations, even though he rejects the use of such wording as its loose and improper use has led to confusion: 'The less than meticulous use of the term "beneficial owner" to cover two radically different concepts – substantive law owner and common speech owner – is responsible for most of the confusion

As we will see, the early stages of allocation of income in conflictive cases followed beneficial ownership in equity. At that point, the reasoning of income being allocated to the beneficial ownership probably led to beneficial ownership being thought of conversely as the person to whom income is allocated. Consequently, once the concept started being used in that sense in tax law, it attached to the evolution of allocation of income derived from the development of anti-avoidance rules and separated it from its original meaning. After decades of consolidation, however, beneficial ownership wording and the principles related to it have spread all around the tax code both explicitly and implicitly, and it will now be analysed with reference to the set of allocation rules and principles used in tax law, including the certainty and uncertainty principles, but also the anti-avoidance reasoning.

Allocation of Economic Effects of Financial Transactions and Instruments

Regarding financial transactions, the use of contracts such as nominee and custodian accounts, portfolio management, securities loans, repurchase agreements, futures and many others may split or divert ownership abilities in different subjects.

Among the cases that have dealt with financial splitting or shifting of tax ownership, *Helvering v Horst* is probably one of the most relevant. In that case, interest coupons were shifted from the holder of the bonds to his son before the due date.[221] The issue was whether the income was assessable on the son, as holder of the coupon of interest, or on the father, who, by retaining the main bond from which the interests were derived, had the original right to the income. The Supreme Court ruled that the power to deal with the right to the income led to the father as the owner being considered as having the economic benefits of the bonds, including the interest, irrespective of locating them in the son.[222] In this regard, it was held that the purpose of tax rules is to tax the income of those who earn or otherwise create the right to receive and enjoy it.[223] Following the classic legal doctrine of the tree and the fruit, the court held that income cannot be considered as separated from the source from which it is originated, and as the interest was derived from the bonds, its tax ownership characteristics have to be connected to the bondholder.[224] Thus, the Supreme Court held that tax ownership was vested in the father.

This case settled that economic benefits and the right to control income as connected to the source of income defines the person to whom income has to be allocated. In this regard, even though not connected to beneficial ownership directly, the case introduced these economic references to allocation of income in US tax law.

Regarding custodians and nominees, it was soon understood and widely held that allocation shall refer to the principal and not to the financial institutions or custodians

in the dummy corporation field. "Beneficial ownership" when used in contradistinction to a term meaning title ownership, usually means substantive law ownership, while, when used in contradistinction to a term meaning substantive law ownership, usually means common speech ownership. It is because of this built-in ambiguity of the word "beneficial" that its use is avoided here': Miller (n 16) 219, fn 13. See also the reference to beneficial ownership in the Board of Tax Appeals ruling in *Moline Properties*, a leading case in allocation of income in intermediary corporations: *Moline Properties v Commissioner* (1941) 45 BTA 647, 650.

[221] *Helvering (Commissioner of the Internal Revenue) v Horst* (1940) 311 US 112 (USSC).

[222] ibid 118.

[223] ibid 119.

[224] ibid 120.

holding the shares or bonds for the client.[225] Those principles and rules largely follow equity law and the certainty principle, as it is clear that the beneficiary may claim the securities and income from them at any time. In some cases, however, tax has been assessed on the intermediaries if it was not possible to identify or reach the principal in order to guarantee tax collection.

In the case of securities loans, the main question was whether the lender was able to claim tax benefits for income derived from dividends and capital gains reserved for the owners of the shares.[226] In these cases, the fact that the lender has no actual right to the financial assets, even though it has the right to receive homogeneous assets, required tax law to allocate ownership rights for tax purposes on the debtor.[227]

Futures and forwards, in turn, have been regarded as not conferring ownership status to the underlying asset for tax purposes until they are exercised.[228] Equity swaps, on the other hand, seem to be more complex, and there is some doubt as to their ability to confer ownership for tax purposes to the underlying assets. From a private law perspective, such swaps do not directly confer rights to the underlying assets, but as the economic effects are transferred through those instruments and may serve for tax avoidance purposes, tax authorities may be tempted to consider swap creditors as owners – or non-owners, depending on the case – of the preferred shares or bonds.[229] A final example could be that of employees and other limited shares or financial assets where the title-owner may have voting rights and right to income, but the selling attributes are limited.[230] In these cases, it seems tax rules would treat the shareholder as a non-owner because of the lack of control abilities.[231]

Many other financial instruments may pose difficulties regarding the consequences of tax allocation, but the brief examples above demonstrate that the main principle of allocation under US tax law is defined by reference to the subject with the right to benefits and burdens associated to the assets, as well as to their control, rather than formal ownership by submission to private law.[232] However, several rules try to tackle cases where such attributes are allocated in other persons in order to avoid tax liability, while

[225] See DS Miller, 'Taxpayers' Ability to Avoid Tax Ownership: Current Law and Future Prospects' (1998) 51 *Tax Lawyer* 279, 310, quoting, among others, *Bettendorf v Commissioner* (1931) 49 F2d 173 (8th Circ); *Shellabarger v Commissioner* (n 57); *Commissioner v Bollinger* (1988) 485 US 340 (USSC); Revenue Ruling 72-514, 1972-2 Cumulative Bulletin 440; Revenue Ruling 70-469, 1970-2 Cumulative Bulletin 179. See also ss 1.6041-5 and 1.6042-2 of IRC USC 26, where the obligations on information to supply on payments refer to the actual owner and not the nominee as the relevant person to be reported. See Miller (n 16) 223–24, and the footnotes therein, where he states and summarises cases and decisions on allocation of tax consequences to actual owners and not to nominees. See also United States in Meindl-Ringler, *Beneficial Ownership in International Tax Law* (Kluwer, 2016).

[226] Miller (n 225) 290.

[227] ibid. Solicitors Memorandum 4281, IV-2 Cumulative Bulletin 187 (1925), s 1058 Internal Revenue Code, 26 USC.

[228] ibid 305.

[229] ibid 295–97.

[230] ibid 302.

[231] See s 83(a); Reg s 1.83-1(a)(l); Reg s 1.1361-I(b)(3). ibid.

[232] On the several arrangements that may be used to avoid tax ownership, such as unfunded or deferred compensation, instalment sales, variable annuity life insurances, tracking stock, non-grantor trusts, contingent payment debt instruments, DECS, income assignments, reverse repurchase agreements, secured lendings, leases, licences, guaranteed pass-through certificates or voting trusts, see ibid 209–314.

holding the economic effects or control of the assets or income.[233] This is the case of, for instance, derivatives with value referred to partnerships, and options or derivatives in certain cases.[234] In addition, such a principle may be overridden by anti-avoidance principles, such as substance-over-form, or economic ownership or control.[235] In many of these cases, such allocation rules may be regarded as related to beneficial ownership, even though they normally provide for their own specific references to control, benefits or enjoyment, or to business purpose or artificiality in anti-avoidance doctrines, so beneficial ownership references may be mismatched in many cases.

Intermediary Entities: From Nominee Theory to the Disregard-Business Purpose Test

The development of anti-abuse doctrines in the USA in the 1930s blended with allocation of income rules to deal with intermediary entities early on.[236] The development of modern tax systems at the same time soon led to strategies to avoid payment of taxes, and parallel progress of anti-avoidance principles and rules. At the same time, there was significant growth in the use of trusts and other common law contracts with equitable consequences, such as agency, custodianship or partnership in the early twentieth century, probably to some extent to avoid increasing taxation.[237] This led to the interaction of the principles of equity law and tax law, with equity principles being used to define private law effects of certain equity structures and tax law principles being applied on equity law structures with avoidance objects, both in order to achieve a consistent tax result. The ultimate consequence was that certain private and equity law and tax principles blended with each other.

From these, one can see how the analysis of the validity of corporations and their business purpose, derived from the corporate business purpose requirement, merged with ability to pay, substance tax principles and duty to contribute. The result mutated initially into the tax business purpose, and later, and relevantly for the purposes of this work, to the well-known anti-avoidance principle against intermediary entities set in *Moline Properties.*[238] However, as *Moline Properties* was decided at an early stage in the development of anti-avoidance doctrines, the evolution of broad initial sham principles to economic substance, economic sham, the business purpose test itself and other

[233] ibid 314–25.

[234] ibid 314–16.

[235] ibid 322–23.

[236] It is well known that the business purpose test as an anti-avoidance tax principle started with *Gregory v Helvering* (1935) 293 US 465 (USSC).

[237] Langbein said that in the 19th century trusts still existed only for conveyance purposes, and the use of trusts for commercial purposes only gained popularity after World War II: J Langbein, 'The Secret Life of the Trust: The Trust as an Instrument of Commerce' (1997) 107 *Yale Law Journal* 165, 188–89. However, Langbein did not mention trusts as a tax avoidance structure, but as instruments for investment funding and other commercial purposes. In this regard, see early cases on tax avoidance through the use of trusts in *Bullen v Wisconsin* (1916) 240 US 625 (USSC); *Weeks v Sibley* (1920) 269 F 155 (ND Tex); *Langley v Commissioner* (1932) 60 F2d 937. A letter to the editor of the *New York Times* in 1932 shows how the increasing tax pressure of the Hoover administration led to an increase in the trust business to avoid taxes. See A Likhovski, 'The Duke and the Lady: *Helvering v Gregory* and the History of Tax Avoidance Adjudication' (2004) 25 *Cardozo Law Review* 953, 1000.

[238] See *Moline Properties* (n 16). On the relationship between beneficial ownership (even though not explicitly mentioned), intermediary corporations and business purpose test, see Miller (n 16).

related doctrines continued to influence the allocation of income and beneficial ownership doctrines, as will be seen later.[239] Among the evolution of such anti-avoidance judiciary principles can be seen the nominee and disregard doctrines.

Due to the inconsistency of beneficial ownership wording, the use of beneficial ownership, economic ownership or control is not recommended at this point. Precisely because of the evolution of its usage, mistakes in analysis may occur. To avoid misunderstandings, Miller's analysis will be used, dividing the legal title to which tax liability may be attached into four categories: record ownership; title ownership; substantive law ownership; and common law ownership.[240] Record ownership is the title recognised in a register or office. Title ownership is the right dependent upon delivery of or written in the deed. Substantive law ownership is the ownership that can be enforced in court in common law or equity law. This may be the case of the title of a beneficial owner against a nominee, who may hold the title and record ownership but has no substantive legal right to, for instance, the shares.[241] Miller also clarifies that a split of rights may allocate full substantive law ownership of each of the split rights to different persons.[242] Finally, common speech ownership is what laypersons would think of as ownership. As an example, the person behind a corporation controlling a building would be regarded as the owner of the building. In conclusion, Miller recognises that these labels are not strict legal categories and may be misleading if used as legal definitive terms, and that they only serve for the purposes of the nominee corporation doctrines.

Under these categories and following the above-mentioned taxation principles, taxation will normally follow substantive ownership as the person who can legally claim control and enjoyment of a subject matter is the person with the relevant ability to pay.[243] However, in certain cases, anti-avoidance rules may allocate tax liability to common speech ownership insofar as in some cases, such as corporate arrangements,

[239] On how early broad sham doctrine evolved and now comprises a broad range of anti-avoidance doctrines, see PF Postlewaite, 'The Status of the Judicial Sham Doctrine in the United States' (2016) 15 *Revenue Law Journal* 140. On probably the first anti-avoidance doctrine, substance over form, see *Southern Pacific v Lowe* (1918) 247 US 330 (USSC). On sham, see *Higgins v Smith* (1940) 308 US 473 (USSC). On the well-known business purpose test, see *Gregory v Helvering* (n 236). On the modern main doctrine for anti-avoidance, economic substance, see *Frank Lyon v United States* (1978) 435 US 561 (USSC). Interestingly, it was held in *Long Term Capital Holdings v United States* (2004) 330 F Supp 2d 122 that the difference between all those doctrines is blurred and difficult to draw, the important point being to analyse the subjective purpose of the taxpayer and the objective economic substance or rationale of the arrangement. On anti-avoidance doctrines in the USA, their evolution, content and differences, see H Fuller, 'Business Purpose, Sham Transactions and the Relation of Private Law to the Law of Taxation' (1962) 37 *Tulane Law Review* 355; Robert Summers, 'A Critique of the Business Purpose Doctrine' (1961) 41 *Oregon Law Review* 38; DA Ward et al, 'The Business Purpose Test and Abuse of Rights' [1985] *British Tax Review* 68; J Libin, 'Congress Should Address Tax Avoidance Head-On: The Internal Revenue Code Needs a GAAR' (2010) 30 *Virginia Tax Review* 339; TA Kaye, 'United States' in KB Brown (ed), *A Comparative Look at Regulation of Corporate Tax Avoidance* (Springer, 2012); WJ Kolarik II and SNJ Wlodychak, 'The Economic Substance Doctrine in Federal and State Taxation' (2014) 67 *Tax Lawyer* 715; L Lederman, 'W(h)ither Economic Substance' (2010) 95 *Iowa Law Review* 389. On the use of early broad sham transactions doctrine to analyse tax allocation in an intermediary company case, see *Moro Realty Holding Corp v Commissioner* (1932) 25 BTA 1135. More recently, using economic substance doctrine, *Matter of Sherwin-Williams Company v Tax Appeals Tribunal of Department of Taxation and Finance of State of New York* (2004) 12 AD3d 112 (NY Tax App Trib).

[240] Miller (n 16) 216–18.

[241] See ss 1.6041 and 1.6042-2 of IRC USC 16, requiring to report information of the actual owner, and not the nominee, as the person to whom income has to be allocated. See ibid 223–24.

[242] ibid 217.

[243] ibid 220.

the subjects behind such legal structures are socially and factually able to control and enjoy the relevant ability to pay.

The first theory on intermediary corporations, the nominee theory, largely follows the general rule of allocating income to the substantive legal owner. To understand the nominee theory, it is important to bear in mind that they appear in the context of circumvention of usury rules.[244] The limited rate under which banks were allowed to lend to individuals barred individuals from access to credit for real estate development. The solution was simple: incorporate a company to apply for the credit, simply to avoid usury laws. In many such cases, the developer of the real estate was not looking for limitation or responsibility, or any other corporate characteristic, behaving ordinarily as the owner of the property. The tax problem arising from this was obvious: if the only effect intended was to avoid usury laws, it would be unnecessary and inconsistent to allocate tax effects to the corporation. On the contrary, to fully disregard a corporation that legally existed was also controversial apropos where to put the limit where a corporation does not derive tax effects. If tax liability is defined in principle with reference to substantive legal ownership, the issue in this case is the definition of who holds such ownership.[245]

Under the nominee theory, if one sees the intermediary corporation as a mere nominee, agent or trustee for the individual, substantive ownership lays in the shareholder, to whom taxable effects will be allocated.[246] This does not disregard the entity, as it recognises its full existence and independence for tax purposes, but qualifies its activity between the corporation and the shareholders within an agency or trust relationship and not within the company–shareholder relationship. The issue is not whether the corporation is valid, but if it is acting on its own behalf or for the benefit of the shareholders or partners.[247]

Several cases were decided in the 1930s under the nominee theory, including *Stewart Forshay*, *Moro Realty*, *Greenleaf Textile Corp* and *112 West 59th St Corp v Helvering*.[248] Analysing the relationship between the corporation and the shareholders, these cases held that the corporation powers in relation to the assets were negligible and were acting for the benefit of the stockholders, resolving in favour of allocating tax effects to the latter.[249]

[244] ibid 219–20. On the agency theory and allocation of tax consequences in straw corporations to beneficial owners, see S Lainoff, S Bates and C Bowers, 'Attributing the Activities of Corporate Agents Under US Tax Law: A Fresh Look from an Old Perspective' (2003) 38 *Georgia Law Review* 143; BN Liebmann, 'Disregarding The Corporate Nominee: *Commissioner v Bollinger*' [1989] *Tax Lawyer* 371; RA Knight and LG Knight, 'Disregard of the Corporate Entity and Nominee Corporations after Bollinger' (1989) 21 *University of Toledo Law Review* 203; BH Hulsey, 'Tax Aspects of the Nominee Corporation: *Roccaforte v Commissioner of Internal Revenue*' (1986) 22 *Tulsa Law Journal* 61; LJ Griffiths, 'New Life for the Agency Theory: *Commissioner v Bollinger*' (1989) 17 *Florida State University Law Review* 127; CE Falk, 'Nominees, Dummies and Agents: Is It Time for the Supreme Court to Take Another Look' (1985) 68 *Taxes* 725; Miller (n 16); J Kurtz and CG Kopp, 'Taxability of Straw Corporations in Real Estate Transactions' (1968) 22 *Tax Law* 647; LG Bertane, 'Tax Problems of the Straw Corporation' (1975) 20 *Villanova Law Review* 735; R Case, 'Disregard of Corporate Entity in Federal Taxation – The Modern Approach' (1943) 30 *Virginia Law Review* 398.

[245] *Commissioner v Bollinger* (n 225) 345.

[246] Miller (n 16) 221; Lainoff et al (n 244) 152; Kurtz and Kopp (n 244) 652.

[247] Bertane (n 244) 752–53.

[248] *Stewart Forshay* (1930) 20 BTA 537; *Moro Realty* (n 239); *Greenleaf Textile Corp* (1932) 26 BTA 737; *112th West 59th St Corp v Helvering* (1933) 58 F2d 397.

[249] See Miller (n 16) 225–27.

The analysis sometimes refers to facts that anticipate an anti-avoidance analysis, even though not fully entering the ratio decidendi. The case of *Stewart Forshay*, even though it was solved by resorting to the nominee theory, considering the corporation as a mere intermediary, refers to the fact that the corporation was not holding directors' meetings, declaring dividends or having any activity, in what resembles a business purpose or activity test.[250] Similarly, in *Moro Realty*, the corporation was considered a mere legal shell.[251] In both cases, although the solution was not based on the anti-avoidance principle, it led to questioning the validity of the corporation although trying to reinforce the agency consideration, and it showed how the validity of intermediary corporations from a corporate view were at the core of the allocation analysis from early on.

However, it was clear that allocation of income followed beneficial or substantive law ownership in this early stage. This is plainly clear in *112 West 59th St Corp v Helvering*, where it was stated that if the case were a private law case nobody would doubt the beneficial interest and real ownership of the shareholder.[252]

Following such approaches, tax authorities recognised the nominee theory, as in Revenue Ruling 70-469, even though in a reverse case.[253] The ruling stated that stock held by a corporation through an individual who apparently exercised voting rights and held a directorship was held by the corporation as owner for the purposes of a rule requiring 80 per cent of the stock to be owned directly.[254] What is surprising is this ruling was so clearly resolved on the nominee theory, even after disregard theories took over and allocation of income was blended with anti-avoidance rules.

These court and administrative rulings were of utmost importance, as allocating property to the corporation or the shareholder would imply at first instance allowance or disallowance of deductions, reliefs or offsets for the shareholder, and later, transfers from the company to the shareholder would or would not trigger capital gains taxation.[255]

First, allocation of tax consequences was defined by reference to the underlying private law situation, as was seen in the above-mentioned early UK beneficial ownership doctrine.[256] Thus, the key issue was to define the facts of the case, ie whether there was an agency or trust relationship, the consequence of deriving tax allocation according to equitable or beneficial ownership being automatic, and not a matter of tax law.[257]

Secondly, references to the legal shell character of intermediary corporations, such as that of Moro Real Estate, bring to mind an early and primitive sham transactions doctrine.[258] Nevertheless, these rulings regard corporations as real and existent, the corporation performing agent functions and not being assets held for the shareholder within the company–shareholder relationship. The consequence of the nominee theory is that a difference must be distinguished between where a corporation holds assets on

[250] Bertane (n 244) 749.
[251] Miller (n 16) 225.
[252] ibid 226.
[253] 1970-2 CB 179.
[254] Miller (n 16) 224.
[255] ibid 213–16.
[256] See above, s II.B(i)(a).
[257] Case (n 244) 432.
[258] Postlewaite (n 239) 142.

its business activity, not being held in trust or agency for the shareholders and being substantive owners, and the case where a corporation holds in trust or agency for their shareholders, overlapping with their shareholder–corporation relationship. Legal shell references, in turn, should be understood in a loose sense as referring to the empty character of the corporation not performing activities on its own rather than in a strict legal sense as related to the legal empty consideration of the incorporation following anti-avoidance reasonings.

Comparing such an approach to the UK, the references to private law together with comments on the shell character of the corporations may bring to mind the UK beneficial owner doctrine in *Wood Preservation*, *Sainsbury* and *BUPA*.[259] Also, the UK distinction between the corporation holding on trust for the shareholders and the corporation–shareholder relationship not being considered a trust or equitable relationship itself is similar to the nominee US approach. However, if the shell references in the US nominee theory are understood in the above-mentioned loose sense, the two approaches lose similarities. Even if the definition in relation to defining actual intermediary, agency or trustee relationships upon private law seems to be familiar to the UK *Sainsbury* doctrine referring to control and enjoyment abilities in equity law, it does not provide for contextual adjustment of the concept as the UK doctrine does – at least, not explicitly. Thus, the nominee theory is more closely related to the early development of beneficial ownership in the UK, in following private law considerations, than to the later broad understanding of the concept.

However, as anti-avoidance principles were being developed at the time, the nominee theory soon blended with such principles.[260] It is well known that there might be cases where substantive ownership does not refer to the relevant subject for tax purposes, but the tax system should tax because, although the person entitled does not actually show ability to pay, not taxing it will lead to tax avoidance. Thus, an overriding principle, such as the need to preserve the tax system from attempts at avoidance, will lead to tax liability being governed by another type of ownership, namely common speech ownership.[261]

One of the first cases combining the analysis of a corporation being an agent for the shareholders with anti-avoidance considerations is *Burnet v Commonwealth Improvement*.[262] In that case, shares in an estate were transferred to a corporation. Some time later, the corporation exchanged securities with the estate, leading to a loss that was claimed by the corporation on its tax return. The court, even though it recognised the possibility of disregarding the entity for tax purposes if the case required it to do

[259] See above, nn 156, 175 and 192 and accompanying text.

[260] The formalist approach to tax law that was predominant in the 19th and early 20th centuries saw a switch in the 1930s to a more substantial approach. This has been attributed to a cultural change towards tax avoidance, from first being considered a moral issue, to later being defined as a technical matter insofar as taxpayers did not have a duty to pay more taxes. In the second sense, taxpayers may apply a self defence against defective and discriminatory legislation and laws derived from constituency biased legislators, so certain tax avoidance was considered as supported by legislation itself. Tax avoidance may also indirectly help to improve defective legislation. Finally, the economic depression as opposed to the economic boom of the 1920s made tax avoidance irrelevant during that period. The well-known JP Morgan assertion summarises this switch in the view towards tax avoidance: 'taxation is a legal question … not a moral one'. See A Likhovski, 'The Story of Gregory: How Are Tax Avoidance Cases Decided?' in S Bank and K Stank (eds), *Business Tax Stories* (Foundation Press, 2005).

[261] Miller (n 16) 220.

[262] *Burnet v Commonwealth Improvement Co* (1932) 287 US 415 (USSC).

so, held that the corporation was independent and valid for tax purposes following the accepted general rule of the independent character of a corporation and insofar as the corporation and the estate behaved and fulfilled their obligations independently for a long time.[263] Some authors have claimed this is a pure disregard case.[264] However, it seems to this author that the case may be blending the previous approach with such new trends, as it not being clear whether the decision is indicating the independent performance and fulfilment of obligations of the corporation as proof of acting on its own, as derived from the nominee theory, or if it is proof of the business activity of the corporation, as the disregard theory may require. In this sense, the ruling seems to find that the behaviour of the corporation and the estate cannot render the former a mere agent, even though the reasoning is mixed with considerations of 'unusual cases' to be disregarded, seemingly referring to anti-avoidance reasoning, although probably not entering the ratio decidendi. In any case, what is relevant from the case is that the ruling is one of the first in which the Supreme Court recognises the possibility of balancing the existence of the corporation for tax purposes against other principles, implicitly recognising the link between the existence of the entity and the avoidance purposes of its incorporation.

In *Higgins v Smith*, the transfer of an asset by the shareholder to its fully owned corporation was considered as fully tax driven in order to obtain a loss.[265] In that case, the court settled for disregarding the transfer of the ownership to a controlled corporation as ineffective for triggering and computing a loss.[266]

Some authors have argued that the court was not defending the fact that the corporation was to be disregarded for all purposes, but that an overriding principle of public interest prevented the taxpayer from enjoying a tax benefit where there is no change in 'common speech ownership'.[267] This does not mean the corporation is disregarded, nor that the transfer has not taken place, but that tax legislation may disregard the effects of the transaction for tax purposes, in this case the loss.[268] In this regard, the circuit ruling makes clear that it was proved that the corporation had other activities and its existence was of no doubt, which was confirmed by the Supreme Court.[269] It remains unclear whether disregard of the transfer had only tax effects or also had other effects, but the corporation was fully valid. What is relevant is that the court speech starts to use anti-avoidance wording referring to sham or unreal transactions, approaching a new anti-avoidance understanding of allocation of income.[270] In this sense, *Higgins v Smith* does not go as far as disregarding the corporation for tax purposes, as was later done in *Moline Properties*, probably due to the fact that the corporation had been engaged in other economic activities, but disregarded the sale of the shares to the corporation.

[263] ibid 286–87.
[264] Griffiths (n 244) 132.
[265] *Higgins v Smith* (n 239).
[266] ibid 478.
[267] Miller (n 16) 230.
[268] GE Cleary, 'The Corporate Entity in Tax Cases' (1945) 1 *Tax Law Review* 3, 8.
[269] *Smith v Higgins* (1939) 102 F2d 456 (2d Circuit) 457–58.
[270] *Higgins v Smith* (n 239) 477.

Two years later, *Palcar Real Estate* also analysed a case of an intermediary corporation, even though in this case the commanding fact was that the corporation was arranging all the business on its own.[271] Some scholars doubt whether it was a kind of economic substance test framed within the disregard theory.[272] However, to my view, it was clearly a nominee case, as the key issue was that the corporation was dealing with the property as its own, and not for the direct benefit of the shareholders but through their stockholder condition.[273] Thus, even though avoidance-related wording was used, the result seems to derive from the fact that the corporation was not a nominee but was holding the property as its own, and not due to the transaction being disregarded or requalified due to its abusive character.

Other cases continued to apply the nominee theory jointly with references to anti-avoidance principles.[274] But *Moline Properties* is considered the leading case on the switch of treatment of wholly owned corporations – or jointly owned straw corporations – to analyse them under the business purpose test in order to set out their existence for tax purposes.[275] The case concerned the gain from a sale of an asset by a corporation, where the single shareholder wanted the taxation of the gain to be in his hands and not in the hands of the corporation. His argument was that the company was a mere agent incorporated to satisfy the creditors. The Supreme Court ruled that the corporation was to be treated as independent and the income allocated to the company for tax purposes on the basis of four arguments.

First, the company was not the shareholder's alter ego, especially because his control of the corporation was at first sight negligible, as the stock was held by third parties on guarantee.[276] Secondly, the argument that the incorporation was requested by the creditors does not support the taxpayer's argument but reinforces the independent character of the corporation.[277] There was a business necessity which was advantageous to the shareholder, and not a mere interposition with no effect. Thirdly, after the mortgages had been repaid and the shareholder had apparently regained control of the corporation, he took out a new mortgage in the name of the corporation, discharged that new mortgage, sold portions of property, filed tax returns on the corporation with these transactions and became engaged in business transactions, such as a rental agreement for a parking lot, giving effect to the independent business character of the corporation.[278] Finally, after fully recognising the independent existence of the corporation on those three arguments, the court held that there was no agency relationship that may allocate the assets to the shareholders.[279]

[271] *Palcar Real Estate Co v Commissioner* (1942) F.2d 131 210 (8th Cir).

[272] Miller (n 16) 235–36.

[273] Palcar Real *Estate Co v Commissioner* (n 271) 212–13.

[274] See *United States v Brager Bldg & Land Corp, Sheldon Bldg Corp v Commissioner*, quoted by Miller (n 16) 232–36.

[275] *Moline Properties* (n 16). Previous cases seemingly applied earlier a disregard principle, even though not setting a general principle of disregarding of entities for tax purposes for later cases, as *Moline Properties* included *Southern Pacific v Lowe* (n 239).

[276] *Moline Properties* (n 16) 439–40.

[277] ibid 440.

[278] ibid.

[279] ibid.

The principles derived from the ruling are of utmost importance and have been the basis of corporations' independent tax treatment ever since. First, the Supreme Court settled corporate independence as a general rule, making disregard an exception.[280] Secondly, for tax purposes, the exception would be if the corporation were to be disregarded if sham or unreal.[281] The new *Moline* doctrine departs from previous nominee theory insofar as it defines the presumption of corporate independence of intermediary corporations unless it is legally empty as a sham transaction. Conversely, previous nominee theories did not question the validity of the corporation as provided by corporate law, but questioned who the actual owner of the assets or income was. This case recognises that a corporation holding substantive ownership may be disregarded for tax purposes and, obviously, that a corporation not holding substantive ownership may be disregarded and does not always have to be treated as the owner of the property for tax purposes.[282] Thus, the new point was not who the substantive owner was, but if the corporation was valid for tax purposes or was just tax-driven. This does not make substantive ownership irrelevant, but the doctrine locates it in a second row, as the disregard theory may reallocate ownership for tax purposes irrespective of where such substantive ownership in private law is vested.

The court performs an analysis in line with economic substance, the business purpose test or business activity doctrines.[283] By doing so, the disregard theory enables the corporation to be omitted where there is no business activity, even though the corporation may be legally existent from the perspective of facts derived from private law, and would regard the corporation as existent for tax purposes if it performs a commercial activity or gets involved in valid contracts.

However, unlike some civil law countries, the US approach to tax avoidance under the sham, economic substance, substance over form and, lastly, the business purpose test used in *Moline Properties* directly derives the tax consequences from the facts, blending legal qualification and pure factual considerations.[284] To do so, *Moline Properties* departs from *Gregory v Helvering* and states that the validity of the corporation has to be analysed, not from a corporate law perspective, where it could be valid, but as if it had other effects and purpose apart from the tax advantages or its tax-driven character.[285] Conversely, the tax law system of some civil law countries would first define whether the apparent contracts actually define the legal reality intended to be created by the

[280] ibid 438–39.

[281] ibid 439.

[282] Miller (n 16) 238.

[283] *Moline Properties* (n 16) 439. On the development and relationship between different anti-avoidance doctrines in the USA, see Postlewaite (n 239).

[284] Note that sham in most civil law countries refers to a definition of actual facts as opposed to possible 'fake' facts shown in documents by the taxpayer. Conversely, in some countries such as the USA it also refers to actual avoidance cases where the taxpayer does not hide any facts but effectively performs a transaction with more advantageous tax consequences but in an artificial way, forcing the construction of the arrangement, or without a proper purpose. The difficulty in drawing a line between avoidance and sham/simulation (in a civil law understanding) is normally attributed to the element of deceit present in both sham and anti-avoidance rules. However, it seems, at least in civil law countries, that sham/simulation is derived from the taxpayer hiding or lying about certain aspects of the contract, such as price or object, in the documents or proofs, while in avoidance cases the taxpayer actually wishes to perform the contract because of the more advantageous tax consequences. See Zimmer (n 204) 31–32; Zornoza Pérez and Báez Moreno (n 204) 135–38.

[285] *Gregory v Helvering* (n 236) 470; *Moline Properties* (n 16) 440.

parties, then define the tax law consequences. From the latter perspective, disregarding the corporation could either come from the contract being just an appearance, even though the parties never intended to establish the entity (sham/simulation), or from tax law defining ordinary consequences as not applicable and redirecting its consequences upon artificial, abusive or economic considerations, even though recognising the existence of the corporation.

Taking into consideration the current formal private law approach to corporations, where little more than consent is needed to incorporate an entity, the US tax law approach seems to fit the picture better as it leaves aside private law considerations that may confuse rather than clarify the issue. However, the recent expansion of anti-avoidance statutory rules in civil law countries seems to have led to a convergence in the consequences of the two approaches.[286]

Moline Properties differs from other cases such as *Higgins v Smith*. In the former, the corporation was disregarded, while in the latter, the transaction (losses) was disregarded after *Gregory v Helvering*.[287] Even though both analyse the issue under a business purpose test of validity of contracts, the subject of the analysis is different: corporation in *Moline Properties*, sale in *Higgins v Smith*. The reasoning poses no difference as it is to analyse the purpose of a contract or arrangement, but the misunderstanding of the different scope of the analysis, combining disregarding of the corporation under the business purpose test and subsequent allocation of income, was probably what led to misinterpretation in *Moline Properties*.

This is not true, as *Moline Properties* reasoning performs two steps: (i) to analyse the validity of the corporation; and (ii) to allocate the assets.[288] Also, the second step is not dependent on the first one, it even being possible to allocate the assets under the second step to the shareholders if beneficial owners. However, if the corporation is disregarded in the first step, then it is clear that allocation has to be made to the only other subject standing for tax purposes.

In conclusion, *Moline Properties* makes validity of corporations for tax purposes dependent on an activity or substance to be performed, and once validity of the corporation has been settled, tax consequences would be allocated either to the corporation or to the subject, depending on who holds substantive ownership of the assets or income, making it possible for the corporation to be an agent or nominee for the shareholders. Moreover, even where the corporation has been considered as valid, and substantive ownership is found to be vested in the corporations, it would be possible under the *Higgins v Smith* reasoning to disregard the sale between the shareholders and the corporation and to allocate it to the former.

[286] As general anti-avoidance rules in several civil law countries and the European Court of Justice follow a purpose test based on artificiality that resemble *Gregory v Helvering*, approaches by different jurisdictions seem to be converging. Moreover, the inclusion of the principal purpose test as a minimum standard of BEPS Action 6 will certainly lead to a progressive harmonisation, even though application will not be absolutely homogeneous because of the influence of social and economic context on interpretation of law.

[287] James (n 126) 145, fn 169.

[288] *Moline Properties* (n 16) 440 states the corporation was not acting as an agent, explicitly recognising the possibility but rejecting it in the case at hand.

However, *National Investors*, another leading case in the treatment of intermediary corporations, slightly misunderstood the steps of the analysis set in *Moline*.[289] The case concerned the incorporation of a subsidiary and the transfer of portfolio investment to it by a corporation as a first step towards merging some related investment trust corporations. However, the merger plan failed and the corporation, after receiving some dividends from the portfolio, was liquidated, resulting in losses for the parent corporation. The tax authorities claimed the subsidiary was a sham corporation and a mere agent, and losses could not be taken into consideration. The court decided that the corporation could not be considered a sham transaction as it was the first step for the legitimate transaction of the merger of all the related investment trust corporations, thus having a business purpose, and had been fully operative for a year, so was fully valid for tax purposes.[290] The court in addition ruled that the fact the liquidation was performed in a tax advantageous way did not override the validity of the corporation.

The problem with this case is that the ruling combines the analysis of the validity of the corporation with the ability of the entity to be acting, or acting in fact, as an agent for the shareholders, or not holding substantive law ownership. In this sense, the court rejected its agency consideration by asserting it:

> had a business purpose and actually functioned as a business enterprise for over a year; its separate existence during this period was carefully maintained and protected by the plaintiff. Under these circumstances, there is no basis for holding that the corporation should not be recognized as a separate entity.[291]

By doing so, the court rejected ownership being vested in the shareholders because of the validity of the corporation, combining the analysis of the validity of the corporation and the allocation of the assets. Because of this misunderstanding, *National Investors* stood in the path of understanding allocation of income under an anti-avoidance reasoning. This does not mean *National Investors* did not recognise the ability of a corporation to be an agent for its shareholders, but that it mismatched the two-step analysis set in *Moline Properties*.

Paymer v Commissioner of Internal Revenue also asserted that the corporation was not a dummy for the shareholder, with an analysis based on the activity of the corporation.[292] The case continued the tendency of eroding the proper disregarding test and leading the nominee theory to the irrelevance, and of defining the agency condition of a corporation based on anti-avoidance considerations.

Many other cases dealt with this issue at the time following the *Moline* doctrine, even though many of them showed confused reasoning with regard to the activity or business test and the ability of the corporation to act as nominee for the shareholders.[293] However, *National Carbide* (1949) is considered the case that unintentionally dealt the final blow to the nominee theory, even though it was probably the case where the two-step *Moline* test appears more clearly.[294] In this case, where a corporation was performing

[289] *National Investors Corporation v Hoey* (1943) 52 F Supp 556 (SDNY).
[290] ibid 557–58.
[291] ibid 558.
[292] *Paymer v Commissioner of Internal Revenue* (1945) 150 F2d 334 (2d Cir).
[293] See cases quoted in Bertane (n 244) 745 et seq; Miller (n 16) 241–47.
[294] *National Carbide Corp v Commissioner* (1949) 336 US 442 (USSC) 422; Miller (n 16) 247–63.

business through three subsidiaries with whom it entered into an agency contract, the court ruled that it could not be held that the subsidiaries were not the owners of the assets just because they bought them with funds advanced by the parent corporation and because of the appearance of contracts, or that the facts were analogous to the case of the parent company contributing the assets in exchange for shares.[295] In addition, the case distinguishes the facts of the case from a 'true corporate agent'.[296]

The case was apparently resolved by a substance over form analysis, which recognised the existence of the corporation and redirected the facts of the agency contended by the corporations to the shareholder-corporation relationship.[297] However, it still recognises the ability of a corporation to have a 'true corporate agency' relationship with their shareholders.[298] Therefore, to determine the existence of a corporate agency: (i) the corporation shall operate in the name and for the account of the shareholders; (ii) the principal shall be bound; (iii) the income shall be transferred to the principal; (iv) its relationships shall not depend on the fact that it is owned by the principal; (v) the income shall be derived from the activity of the employees of the principal and to the assets belonging to the principal;[299] and finally, and most importantly, (vi) it is made clear that the business purpose must be performing an agency on behalf of the principal.[300] This reference may be confusing insofar as it apparently blends business purpose and nominee theories,[301] but this is done only to define the limits of each analysis. If there is no business purpose, no corporation exists for tax purposes, and once the corporation validity is held, the business purpose analysis of the relevant arrangement involved – except the corporation validity already analysed in the first step – may lead to locating the income and assets within an agency relationship with shareholders or within the corporation's normal trading activity. Taking this into account, it is surprising, as Miller pointed out, how *National Carbide* has been frequently quoted by subsequent cases as denying validity to the nominee theory, even though it explicitly recognises the possibility.[302]

Later, the *Schlossberg* case was one of the last consistent cases with the two-step analysis of *Moline*.[303] In that case, a limited partnership incorporated a straw corporation to avoid usury laws in order to obtain a loan. The issue was whether interest paid by the corporation was deductible by the corporation as the beneficial owner. The Eastern District Court of Virginia applied the *Moline Properties* reasoning and held, first, that the corporation was valid for tax purposes insofar as it had sufficient valid commercial reasons to obtain the credit and avoid usury law, and secondly, that the corporation was a mere shell, which as soon as it had obtained the credit passed the loan

[295] *National Carbide Corp v Commissioner* (n 294) 434–35.
[296] ibid 436–38.
[297] The court held on the contention of the subsidiary being an agent: 'Undoubtedly the great majority of corporations owned by sole stockholders are "dummies" in the sense that their policies and day-to-day activities are determined not as decisions of the corporation, but by their owners acting individually': ibid 433.
[298] ibid 436–38. See also Knight and Knight (n 244) 209; Lainoff et al (n 244) 152.
[299] *National Carbide Corp v Commissioner* (n 294) 437–38.
[300] ibid.
[301] Miller (n 16) 249.
[302] ibid.
[303] *Schlossberg v United States* (1981) 81-1 USTC 9272 (EDC Va).

to the partnership.[304] Consequently, property and the loans had to be allocated to the person beneficially entitled to the loan, which could only be the partnership. The court allocated the interest for tax purposes following the nominee theory and consequently using substantive law ownership – in this case, the subjective condition of debtor in substantive law – in equity.

Surprisingly, and contrary to the recognition given by the Supreme Court to the nominee theory in *National Carbide*, subsequent rulings and lower courts started to resolve these cases by denying practical applicability of the nominee theory.[305] For instance, in *Tomlinson v Miles*, the court rejected the allocation of tax consequences to the shareholders despite beneficial ownership, and even legal ownership, in private law being recognised to be in the stockholders, following an anti-avoidance analysis, which was probably more goal-oriented than policy or legally consistent.[306]

Similarly, *Carver v US* rejected the relevance for tax purposes of the equitable or legal ownership in private law.[307] Later, *Harrison Property Management* denied a valid corporation for the purposes of taxes from being able to be an agent for its shareholders as this could be a mere device to avoid the rules of allocation in favour of the taxpayer.[308] In the relevant *Roccaforte* case, the Fifth Circuit held that the corporation agency consideration was dependent on the shareholders' relationship with the corporation, as in most corporations, and such agency could not be taken into consideration for tax purposes as shareholders should not be allowed to change their investment relationship with an agency relationship for tax avoidance purposes.[309]

In summary, even though most of these rulings recognised the ability of a corporation to be an agent, they dismissed the applicability of such an approach under an anti-avoidance analysis and the narrow approach of the agency test developed by *National Carbide* that renders it almost impossible to apply. The result is in line with the reasoning in *Carver*, which was qualified at an early stage by Miller as a 'Taxpayer-always-loses' analysis with no policy or legal ground.[310]

At the same time, and contrary to the judiciary's actions, the tax court applied the disregard theory in recognising the ability of corporations to be a nominee in a more consistent way, even though the cases in which they recognised an agency relationship were reversed by the Fifth and Fourth Circuits.[311]

The disregard theory as it was understood by the judiciary switched allocation of income to come from the person holding substantive law ownership unless the transactions are aimed at tax avoidance, in such cases allocating tax results to the colloquial owner or what has improperly been called the economic owner.[312] The main failure of

[304] For a comment, see '*Schlosberg v United States*: Straw Corporations and the Interest Deduction' (1982) 2 *Virginia Tax Review* 131.

[305] Probably due to the fact that it held that most corporations are dummies for their corporations. *National Carbide Corp v Commissioner* (n 294) 433.

[306] *Tomlinson v Miles* (n 3); Miller (n 16) 250.

[307] *Carver v United States* (1969) 412 F2d 233 (United States Court of Claims); Miller (n 16) 253.

[308] *Harrison Property Management v United States* (1973) 475 F2d 623; Miller (n 16) 256.

[309] *Roccaforte v Commissioner* (1983) 708 F2d 986 (5th Circ). For a comment on the case see Hulsey (n 244).

[310] Regarding the Court of Claims and the *Carver* case, see Miller (n 16) 255. On the significant amount of cases decided by the Fifth Circuit, see Griffiths (n 244) 137–46.

[311] See Griffiths (n 244) 137–46.

[312] On the *Carver* case, see Miller (n 16) 253.

such an approach was that the election between the different titles was done inconsistently, guided by the courts' willingness to curb tax avoidance at any cost.

The excesses of the disregard theory being interpreted in such a loose and imprecise way was later corrected in 1988 in *Commissioner v Bolinger*, which has since then been the respected authority for allocation of income and expenses in cases dealing with intermediary corporations.[313] The case, involving real estate development with a nominee company to avoid usury law, held that a corporation was able to be an agent for the partnership holding the substantive ownership to the assets if, from all the facts, a true agency at arm's length was discovered, as was the case.[314] Even though the result of the case did not significantly differ from *Moline* or *National Carbide*, the case made it clear that the dummy corporations test has to first analyse the validity of the corporation for tax purposes under the business purpose test, then turn to the analysis of the existence of an actual agency, taking account of the *National Carbide* six-factors test, as a helpful framework and denying the corporation a governing statute validity.[315] This restored the ability of corporations to be agents for their shareholders, as opposed to the rigour with which lower courts had rejected agency relationships in the period between *National Carbide* and *Bollinger*.

More recently, *Sherwin-Williams* (2002) again dealt with the issue of wholly owned and controlled corporations and the allocation of income and expenses.[316] The case concerned the deductibility of payments to two subsidiaries located in Delaware who were holding the group's patents and trademarks after they were first transferred to them from other companies in the group through a reorganisation. Relying on *Moline Properties*, the Massachusetts Supreme Judicial Court held that a proper analysis of the corporation's transactions and activity should be undertaken in order to determine if they were valid for tax purposes. The court also held that close corporations deserved special and careful analysis. However, it ruled that despite the fact that a corporation owns a subsidiary, even following a reorganisation, it does not per se follow that the corporation lacks economic substance or business purposes. What is relevant for the purposes of this analysis is that the court confirmed the need to first analyse and state the validity of corporations and transactions for tax purposes, then determine where the assets and income are.

The court first analysed whether the subsidiaries and/or the reorganisation could be regarded as a sham. After an in-depth analysis of the sham doctrine, it held that to hold the trademarks through a corporation could not be regarded as artificial and could have been done directly after the start of the corporation without any doubt about its validity.[317] Moreover, there was no doubt that it would have been tax-oriented if located in a low-tax jurisdiction, but definitely not artificial if the trademark was developed there. It follows that the case in point did not substantially differ from that and could not be regarded as sham.

In a second step, the court analysed the business purpose and economic substance of the transaction. In the court's view, the subsidiaries were effectively holding the

[313] *Commissioner v Bollinger* (n 225); Lainoff et al (n 244) 155.
[314] *Commissioner v Bollinger* (n 225) 348–49.
[315] ibid 349.
[316] *Sherwin Williams v Commisioner* (2002) 78 NE2d 504 (Mass).
[317] ibid 514.

industrial property because they were transferred to them for full consideration – subsidiary shares in exchange. Moreover, and contrary to the argument of the Board of Tax Appeals that the subsidiaries were not adding any substantial value to the property, the court held that the case was the same as if the property had been bought from a third party without adding any value. These arguments led it to consider that the organisation was not a sham for tax purposes. The court then turned to the second step of the *Moline* two-step analysis, concluding in substance and in law that the trademarks were in the subsidiary, allowing for the deduction of payments to the subsidiaries.[318]

The ruling has been criticised for coming to the conclusion that the corporation has a business purpose from the fact that the reorganisation was not a sham for private law purposes.[319] In this sense, it is clear that both tests are different and that the reorganisation passing a sham test does not render it valid for tax business purpose test reasons. However, what is more relevant for our analysis is that the ruling may lead to error, as the phrase mixes the *Moline Properties* two-step analysis and brings about the allocation of the property to the subsidiaries from the fact that the reorganisation was not a sham.[320] In the author's view, although the phrasing was probably not the best, the court was actually deciding that the analysis leads to the conclusion that the corporation was fully valid, having economic substance, and also that the transfer of the property to the corporation was completely valid for tax purposes, the transaction satisfying both tests. The phrasing is probably simply derived from the fact that, in the opinion of the court, both the corporation validity and the property effectively being in the subsidiary were derived from the same transaction: the reorganisation. In this regard, the actual mistake is in mixing the business purpose and economic substance test and the validity of the reorganisation under the sham test. But once the corporation and reorganisation have been defined as valid for tax purposes, there is no issue regarding allocation of the asset to the subsidiary if substantive ownership is not vested in the parent corporation.

At the same time, the *Sherwin Williams* structure was also challenged in New York against the companies of the group marketing *Sherwin-Williams* products in that state.[321] In this case, the facts were also similar, even though the legal challenge was slightly different. Under NY applicable laws at the time, corporations of a group could be requested to fill combined returns if, among other reasons, 'a distortion of income would result if the corporations reported separately'.[322] In addition, distortion was presumed if 'substantial intercompany transactions among the corporations' exist.[323] If the Sherwin Williams Company was requested to file a combined return with SWIMC and DIMC (Delaware corporations), royalty payments were not deductible as a payment to the same tax subject.

The court's discussion turned again to the issue of whether the transactions with the Delaware corporations had economic substance and business purpose in order to

[318] ibid 516–17.

[319] Kolarik and Wlodychak (n 239) 802.

[320] 'Because we have concluded that the reorganization of Sherwin-Williams's intangible assets was not a sham, the answer to the question who had the right to the value of the marks, as a matter of law and substance, is the subsidiaries': *Sherwin Williams v Commisioner* (n 316).

[321] *Matter of Sherwin-Williams Company v Tax Appeals Tribunal* (n 239).

[322] See 20 New York Codes, Rules and Regulations, subpart 6-2.

[323] See 20 New York Codes, Rules and Regulation, subparts 6-2.3[a], [b], 6-2.5.

be considered as distorting the income.[324] In this case, the court ruled, largely based on the Division of Taxation witness, that the transaction of transferring and licensing back the trademarks lacked economic substance and business purpose, concluding that the royalties were not deductible.[325]

However, the arguments of the ruling are confusing insofar as it starts discussing whether the payments were distorting income, but ends up disregarding the transfer of the trademarks and, consequently, the payments. If the payments do not exist for tax purposes, they cannot be distorting the income, but are simply not deductible. The reasoning was probably arrived at by arguing that artificial payments to subsidiaries distorted the income to be reported by the parent. However, it is precisely this situation at which the joint reporting is aimed, not needing to disregard the payments, but just to declare that the payment was a distortion and required a joint return, thus the payments will not be deductible as a payment to the same subject. In any case, the result is similar as both cases lead to non-deduction. What is relevant for the purposes of this work is that the same case led to a different conclusion from the Massachusetts Court: by denying validity to the transfer, it allocated the property for tax purposes in the *Sherwin Williams* corporation and not in the Delaware subsidiaries.[326] In other words, allocation followed economic substance.

In addition, a set of Maryland Court rulings on similar cases held that IP boxes lack economic substance, so are not valid for tax purposes, so expenses and income are allocated to the parent or the active-trading corporation.[327] Again, as the corporations are disregarded for tax purposes, the assets are allocated to the parent corporation or the group, and the expenses are non-deductible.

The NY *Sherwin Williams* case and the Maryland set of rulings did not contradict the *Moline Properties* and *National Carbide* two-step reasoning. As far as the subsidiaries are disregarded, there is no option other than to allocate the assets or income to the parent corporation or the corporation that existed before the reorganisation. Similarly, if the transfer is disregarded, even though the subsidiaries might be recognised for other tax purposes in some cases, the assets are not considered as passing to them, which means the assets must be allocated to the subject in which they were vested before the transfer. However, this does not mean that allocation has to be done directly through anti-avoidance rules on the subject holding the economic substance or business purpose, but simply that if the subject or the transaction does not exist, the assets remain in the original corporation for tax purposes. Conversely, if the corporation has economic substance and business purpose, this should not automatically mean that the assets are allocated to them, as beneficial ownership of the assets could be in the parent corporation, and consequently assets should be attributable to them for tax purposes. This is the case, for example, if a corporation transfers to its subsidiary certain assets to manage them on account of the parent.

Finally, more recently (in 2017), the Fifth Circuit Court of Appeals, in *Barnhart Ranch Company*, dealt with a similar issue in a case where the shareholder of a

[324] *Matter of Sherwin-Williams Company v Tax Appeals Tribunal* (n 239) 115–19.
[325] ibid 117–19.
[326] Kolarik and Wlodychak (n 239) 804.
[327] See rulings quoted in ibid 807–08.

corporation argued his corporation should be considered as an agent of his cattle business. The case was that the corporation held ownership of the cattle.[328] In this case, the court allocated losses incurred in the course of business to the corporation and not the shareholder, mainly following the reasoning that the subject had benefited for a long time from the corporation's independence, and had not sufficiently argued how the corporation was an agent of their activity.[329] Although the case did not seek to analyse the agent condition and validity of the corporation because of the lack of argumentation by the taxpayer, it seems to recognise the possibility of the corporation becoming an agent and allocating the assets to the principal shareholder, even when the corporation is valid.

To summarise, the evolution of the doctrine of allocation of income in intermediary entities in the USA, despite its importance, has been highly inconsistent and still poses several risks.

Early on, before the *National Carbide* case, allocation of income was first done by following substantive law ownership, largely following beneficial ownership in equity. However, in the last part of this first period, the use of anti-avoidance wording started to cause some misconceptions, leading to misunderstanding the allocation of income in cases of split ownership and the application of anti-avoidance doctrines.

Secondly, in the period between *National Carbide* and *Bollinger*, allocation of income was made, largely following anti-avoidance reasoning, to the person holding common speech ownership or economic ownership. This was due to a misunderstanding of the role of anti-avoidance rules and an inconsistent interpretation of allocation rules.

Finally, in the period after *Bollinger*, allocation of income largely followed substantive ownership, without prejudice to the application of anti-avoidance rules but separating both rules in different steps. However, some courts still misunderstand the *Moline* and *Bollinger* doctrines and mix allocation of income with the application of anti-avoidance rules.

Because, at first, the person to whom income should be allocated was the beneficial owner in an equity sense, the term came to mean, reversely and mistakenly, the person to whom income has to be allocated. The consequence was that beneficial ownership was defined in the USA at first as the person holding substantive law ownership.[330] This would, in turn, be defined as the person who can claim in common law or equity control over and the right to income or assets.

However, as anti-avoidance rules took over, beneficial ownership was to be referred to the person holding the title ownership, record ownership or common speech ownership.[331] The main issue is that if one takes the beneficial owner to be the person to whom income is allocated for tax purposes, the concept is then defined by reference to such anti-avoidance principles. This is the reason why beneficial ownership is frequently misunderstood as an anti-avoidance tool.

In the author's view, this was a great mistake that, even though corrected in recent times, still needs clarification. In this sense, beneficial ownership cannot be regarded as

[328] *Barnhart Ranch Co Commissioner* [2017] 5th Circ 16-60834.
[329] ibid II-A.
[330] Miller (n 16) 219, fn 13.
[331] ibid fn 13.

a proper anti-avoidance rule on its own because it lacks its own content, but such anti-avoidance reallocation constitutes exceptions defined by reference to different sets of anti-abuse rules depending on the case. Moreover, from a historical point of view, the concept of beneficial ownership at an early stage of development of tax law was plainly dependent on substantive law, later being improperly combined with anti-avoidance doctrines following their development. The mistake, in the author's view, was that such anti-abuse rules were not seen, as they should have been, as an exception, reallocating income only in certain circumstances and not as part of the general set of allocation of income rules.[332]

Precisely as Miller pointed out in 1977, beneficial ownership being used in a loose sense made the concept refer either to substantive ownership or to colloquial ownership. He criticised in that way how

> the less meticulous use of beneficial ownership wording leads its use to two different opposite contexts, making the concept to lose its practical function as a conceptual reference and ultimately leading to better to avoid its use if a precise analysis is to be performed.[333]

And it was precisely the abuse of anti-avoidance doctrines that made the concept lose its early significance.

III. What is Beneficial Ownership in Tax Law of Common Law Countries? A Set of Allocation Principles and Rules Balancing Substantive Law Ownership as a Primary Right to Income and Control Claimable before Court, and the Duty to Pay Taxes and Prevention of Avoidance

Having summarised the state of the art, the author's opinion is that the inconveniences of beneficial ownership outweighs its usefulness.

The first reason, and contrary to many authors who claim beneficial ownership in tax law is a term of art, is because the concept is nothing but an imprecise general principle.[334] Beneficial ownership was not developed in legal workshops but as a colloquial, undefined wording – probably also because of the informal sense arising from its trust origins – that gained use among lawyers in the twentieth century.[335] Since then, it has been continually evolving and, even though its usage is becoming more consistent, it still has a significant vagueness. Moreover, on its move towards tax law, the concept again underwent transformations in adapting to its new function and serving in a different context. In this regard, such vagueness in defining tax rules that establish economic

[332] On a tendency to deal with allocation of income through anti-avoidance rules, see Wheeler (n 2) 20–21.
[333] Miller (n 16) 219, fn 13.
[334] Speed (n 10) 41, 50.
[335] See Hanbury (n 46).

duties before the state is not admissible, even more so in relation to such an essential element of taxes as the relation between wealth and the subject.

Secondly, because equity lawyers have progressively attributed to the concept one technical meaning and/or another that could be attributed in tax law, the merging of the concept with allocation of income rules, leaving the meaning as the person to whom income is allocated, would lead to lawyers with little expertise in both trusts and tax matters becoming somewhat confused.[336] As discussed extensively in the previous chapter of this work, ownership is a word of some strength as it may refer to control and benefit. On the other hand, in tax law, even though it could largely follow equity law ownership, such as in bare trusts, it does not have a precise meaning and it may also allocate the income or capital to a person with few ownership attributes for practical reasons, such as suspended, potential or contingent rights, or colloquial owners.[337] Therefore, to use the same wording both in cases where a strong right to control and benefit is referred to and in cases where such rights are absent could lead to a distortion of private law rights and even tax law liability, such as enlarging private rights of subjects with little actual entitlement.

Finally, especially in the case of the use of beneficial ownership under anti-avoidance principles, the link to imprecise doctrines, such as economic sham or the business purpose test, poses the risk of beneficial ownership wording carelessly hiding the use of highly controversial tools. Conversely, if those doctrines and beneficial ownership are separated, the explicit use of such doctrines ensures that those applying the law handle them with care.

It is the author's view that beneficial ownership wording should be avoided in defining the person to whom income is allocated, and definition of tax liability should not refer to beneficial ownership but to the specific characteristics that would define it in tax law cases, such as control or benefit, or trustee or beneficiary status. All in all, this solution remains impractical, as beneficial ownership already occurs in several tax statutes and is frequently used by courts and practitioners.

Therefore, it may well be said that, under the current state of the art, beneficial ownership is not a specific rule, nor does it have any specific definition. As a consequence of an early merging of beneficial ownership in equity law and allocation rules, today it refers to a set of principles that guide allocation of income, or a relationship between assets and subjects in exemptions and reliefs. This is recognised in the USA, albeit only in relation to withholding tax rules, by Treasury Regulation §1.1441-1(c)(6), where beneficial ownership is defined as 'the person who is the owner of the income for tax purposes'.[338]

[336] As has already been said, and it is important to remember, this is a historical development from the fact that in an early stage, allocation was largely done to the beneficial ownership in equity, defining allocation of income with reference to such words. As allocation of income rules switched, beneficial ownership in tax law changed its meaning to include new allocation principles, namely the uncertainty principle and anti-avoidance principles.

[337] Even though some authors consider it a term of art: Lord Diplock in *Ayerst (Inspector of Taxes) v C&K (Construction)* (n 166); *Sainsbury v O'Connor* (n 51); Du Toit (n 16) 210; Brown (n 6) 12. On the contrary, Speed (n 10) 50.

[338] Even though the rule adds 'and who beneficially owns the income', which makes the reasoning circular and adds nothing to the definition, making this second part, in the author's view, irrelevant. Y Brauner,

This set of principles leads to a general principle, or certainty principle, and a subsidiary and overriding one, the anti-avoidance principle.

First, following the certainty principle, beneficial ownership will allocate income generally to the substantive owner, if a defined subject holds an absolute and non-contingent right and has a primary right to income and control, either in equity or common law, that could be claimed before a court against the world.[339] This would imply allocation of income to the beneficiaries as substantive law owners in the case of bare trusts, assignments of income, and constructive or implied simple trusts. Despite its simplicity, the certainty principle may be of relevance in cases of transfer of property to third parties as an implied trust may be derived, thus allocating assets or income to the transferee.

The certainty principle is the solution provided by the nominee theory in the early intermediary entities cases in the USA that, because of its simplicity and effectiveness, still deserves a relevant position in allocation cases. However, the main flaw of this solution is that proving the existence of an implied trust may be difficult in several cases. An additional issue would be if beneficial ownership were in suspense for a certain period, as courts have recognised in some controversial cases. In those cases, the certainty principle applies in a negative sense.

The second definition of beneficial ownership derived from the certainty principle is the uncertainty sub-principle. This subsidiary principle allocates the income to the person controlling and/or legally entitled to the income or assets if there are doubts about the person with substantive ownership having the primary right to income and control, or if that person is not identifiable or is only a beneficiary in equity with negative ownership rights at stake.[340] Consequently, in the case of discretionary or accumulation trusts or trusts with certain contingent rights, or where beneficiary rights are uncertain and not falling under the previous tax principle, the beneficial owner for tax purposes will be the trust or trustee. In these cases, it may be said that beneficial owner refers to the title owner with control of the income or assets. However, this sub-principle is only applicable if no subject has an actual right to substantive law ownership as the primary right to income and control of the specific item of income or assets. This seems to be a logical solution as, in the absence of such a person, the person with legal title and control, although having very few powers, is the person with the greatest rights to the asset or income in the world.

Thirdly, there is the beneficial owner as defined following the second anti-avoidance principle. In these cases, tax beneficial ownership will be vested in the person controlling the property, with revoking powers, or in whom the economic substance resides.

In property transferred to a trust to reduce or avoid tax liability, the person controlling the property, with revoking or assignment rights, will be considered as the beneficial owner for tax purposes and will be taxed accordingly. This will be normally based on

'Beneficial Ownership in and Outside US Tax Treaties' in M Lang et al (eds), *Beneficial Ownership: Recent Trends* (IBFD, 2013) 144–45.

[339] *Baker (Inspector of Taxes) v Archer-Shee* (n 8); *BUPA Insurance Ltd v Commissioners* (n 144); *Sainsbury v O'Connor* (n 51).

[340] On control commanding allocation principles in case of the absence of a person fully entitled to income and control as, for example, discretionary trusts, see *Dawson v Inland Revenue Commissioners* (n 65).

the fact that the settlor retains an interest in the property, even though the asset is being transferred into a trust, to reduce progressivity, to allocate benefit into several beneficiaries of the same family, thus splitting tax liability, or to avoid inheritance tax, among other reasons.

In relation to the interposition of entities or transfer to third parties for purposes of avoiding taxes, allocation of assets or income will follow the person in which income or assets are vested once a transaction has been recharacterised following the economic substance, business purpose test or any other applicable anti-avoidance principle. With this, however, one must be careful to highlight that beneficial ownership should not refer to an anti-avoidance rule, or define per se an anti-avoidance rule, but should refer to the person to whom income is allocated after the application of an anti-avoidance rule.[341] Only consequently, and once the anti-avoidance rule is applicable, will beneficial ownership as the person to whom income is allocated be defined as the colloquial owner, common speech owner or economic owner.

Fourthly, beneficial ownership in tax law has to be interpreted in the context in which it appears in order to serve the object and purpose of the rule in which it is used, even though this last principle adds nothing, but is a reminder of the general rules for interpretation of the law.[342]

Fifthly, it is important to bear in mind that beneficial ownership may refer to a certain partial item of income or assets, and not necessarily to the whole set of assets or income at stake. Assets and income in a single trust or corporation may derive different beneficial owners on different items.

Finally, as derived from previous principles, beneficial ownership in tax law cannot be equated to beneficial ownership in equity. This does not mean beneficial ownership in equity is irrelevant, as it may define beneficial ownership in tax law in cases such as under the certainty principle. However, an immediate correlation cannot be established, as many cases differ from equity solutions.

In brief, beneficial ownership in tax law is, as a general principle and in first instance, that the person holding substantive law ownership, as the person with the primary right to claim income and control before a court either in common law or in equity, is the person to whom income should be allocated. Only when balancing other principles, such as duty to contribute and the prevention of avoidance against such a principle, leading to the conclusion that the first one prevails, will the beneficial owner be defined as the person controlling the income or assets or holding the legal title – as in discretionary trusts – or by the person standing after the application of anti-avoidance rules, normally the colloquial or common speech owner. However, these principles are not absolute and do not imply that all allocation rules are based on them, as legislators may depart from them; rather, they are simply general guidelines for lawmakers and those who apply the law.

[341] On how allocation of income rules has not received enough attention and that cases solved through anti-avoidance rule could have been solved through a proper construction of allocation rules, see Baez (n 2).

[342] *Sainsbury v O'Connor* (n 51); *BUPA Insurance Ltd v Commissioners* (n 144); Brown (n 6) 12; Speed (n 10) 50.

4

From Domestic Tax Law to Tax Treaties: How Beneficial Ownership Jumped from US and UK Tax Treaty Policy into the Worldwide Tax Treaty Network

I. US and UK Tax Treaty Policy Towards Intermediaries (1930–1977)

A. Early Uses of Beneficial Ownership in Tax Treaties: The Interaction of Beneficial Ownership as a Domestic Allocation Principle and Tax Treaties

The beneficial ownership concept was used in tax treaties from an early date, especially in the USA.[1] It was not explicitly included in income tax treaties, thus beginning the wide use of it that is seen today, until 1966, although it was considered as being implied in previous treaties.[2] As the person holding the right to the ability to pay and the taxable

[1] Regarding inheritance tax treaties, see, eg Arts 2 and 2(d) of the 1950 Convention between the United States of America and Canada Modifying and Supplementing the Convention of June 8, 1944 for the Avoidance of Double Taxation and the Prevention of Fiscal Evasion in the Case of Estate Taxes and Succession Duties. On income tax treaties regarding subsidiary participation requirement, see, as an example, s 6 of the Protocol to the 1942 Convention between the United States of America and Canada, providing for the avoidance of double taxation and prevention of fiscal evasion in the case of income taxes. On the use of the property tax exemption provided by the treaty with Finland, see Art 7(2) of the Convention between the United States of America and the Republic of Finland for the avoidance of double taxation and the prevention of fiscal evasion with respect to taxes on income. Most of these treaties, jointly with their legislative history, are included in Joint Committee on Internal Revenue Taxation, *Legislative History of United States Tax Conventions, vol 1 – Income Tax Conventions Sec 1–11* (US Government Printing Office, 1962); Joint Committee on Internal Revenue Taxation, *Legislative History of United States Tax Conventions, vol 2 – Income Tax Conventions Sec 12–25* (US Government Printing Office, 1962).

[2] On the implicit consideration of the beneficial ownership test regarding income tax treaties, see the section concerning Article 4 of the Technical Memorandum of Treasury Department Concerning Proposed Protocol Amending the Income Tax Convention between the United States and the United Kingdom, 1966-2, Cumulative Bulletin 1127, Senate Report No 89-3. See also the commentary on the Dividends Article in the Technical Explanation to the 1980 Tax Convention between the United States and Hungary, 1980-1 C B 354, where the Treasury recognised having substituted the beneficial owner requirement with the OECD wording at the Hungarian delegation's request, which apparently makes no difference as the explanation gives it no relevance.

person in trusts or similar situations would be the beneficial owner, the consequences arising from a tax treaty should, in principle, be attributed to the beneficial owners in equity, so that the elimination of multiple taxation was related to the person to whom the tax consequences were attributed in domestic law.

However, as has been seen previously, beneficial ownership in US tax law evolved to adapt to different cases, so that it came to define the person to whom income or assets were allocated. This included the person with the primary right and control in equity law and, subsidiarily, it also came to define the person holding control or the common speech owner if no beneficial ownership in equity law was found, or if arrangements were found to be artificial or with no business purpose.[3] US tax treaties evolved in this way, and tax treaty consequences sought to some extent to be attached to this beneficial owner, although not always successfully. If the beneficial ownership principle is regarded as the set of rules defining allocation of income under domestic law, it makes sense that the tax treaties were linked through it to a definition of domestic liability, as otherwise mismatches would arise. However, because allocation was not explicitly dealt with in US tax treaties, and because domestic principles were assumed rather than properly designed and were not necessarily aligned to the law of the other contracting states, many mismatches have arisen.[4]

Four main early uses bringing allocation principles to tax treaties are found before 1966: (i) to define tax jurisdiction and credit in relation to the location of assets in inheritance tax treaties;[5] (ii) in relation to tax liability of estates or undivided

[3] See above, ch 3.

[4] Decades of allocation mismatches and the residence of hybrid entities such as trusts and partnerships, both in the USA and in every country, have led to several reports from the OECD and studies from academics, without any clear solutions. Solutions such as following the allocation of the state applying the treaty, residence allocation rules or source allocation rules had been proposed, without solving the issue. Action 2 of the OECD Base Erosion and Profit Shifting Action Plan seems to be the most convincing proposal so far, even though it still leaves inconsistencies and gaps. See OECD, *The Application of the OECD Model Tax Convention to Partnerships* (OECD Publishing, 1999); OECD, *Action 2. Neutralising the Effects of Hybrid Mismatch Arrangements – Final Report* (OECD Publishing, 2015); M Brabazon, 'BEPS Action 2: Trusts as Hybrid Entities' [2018] 2 *British Tax Review* 211; L Parada, *Double Non-taxation and the Use of Hybrid Entities: An Alternative Approach in the New Era of BEPS* (Kluwer, 2018); R Danon, *Switzerland's Direct and International Taxation of Private Express Trusts* (Université de Genève, Schulthess, 2003); R Danon, 'Conflicts of Attribution of Income Involving Trusts under the OECD Model Convention: The Possible Impact of the OECD Partnership Report' (2004) 32 *Intertax* 210; M Lang, *The Application of the OECD Model Tax Convention to Partnerships, A Critical Analysis of the Report Prepared by the OECD Committee on Fiscal Affairs* (Kluwer, 2000); P Baker, 'The Application of the Convention to Partnerships, Trusts and Other, Non-corporate Entities' (2002) 2 *GITC Review* 1; J Wheeler, 'General Report', *Conflicts in the Attribution of Income to a Person* (Kluwer, 2007) 48 et seq; J Wheeler, *The Missing Keystone of Income Tax Treaties* (IBFD, 2012); E Reimer and A Rust (eds), *Klaus Vogel on Double Taxation Conventions*, vol 1, 4th edn (Kluwer, 2015) 106 et seq, 249.

[5] See Arts 2 and 2(f) of the 1950 Convention between the United States of America and Canada Modifying and Supplementing the Convention of June 8, 1944 for the Avoidance of Double Taxation and the Prevention of Fiscal Evasion in the Case of Estate Taxes and Succession Duties; Arts III.2 and III.2(d) of the 1949 Convention between the Government of the United States of America and the Government of Ireland for the Avoidance of Double Taxation and the Prevention of Fiscal Evasion with Respect to Taxes on the Estates of Deceased Persons; ss III.2 and III.2(d) of the 1945 Convention between the United States of America and the United Kingdom of Great Britain and Northern Ireland for the avoidance of double taxation and the prevention of fiscal evasion with respect to taxes on the estates; ss III.2 and III.2(d) of the 1947 Convention between the Government of the United States of America and the Government of the Union of South Africa with Respect to Taxes on the Estates of Deceased Persons; ss 2 and 2.D of the 1952 Convention between United States of America and Finland on Estate and Inheritance Taxes; ss II.1 and II.1(d) of the 1954 Convention between the Government of the United States of America and the Government of the Commonwealth of

inheritances;[6] (iii) as regards extra reduced taxation rate at source for subsidiaries' dividends;[7] and (iv) under a procedural rule to collect taxes from the improper application of tax treaties in relation to an implied rule preventing nominees, agents, trustees and/or other fiduciaries from accessing treaty benefits.[8] This would be the predecessor of the current use of beneficial ownership in relation to dividends, interests and royalties.

(i) Allocation of Tax Jurisdiction in Inheritance Tax Treaties: Location of Property and Rights

The first frame in which beneficial ownership appears is for defining the situs of the property and rights in order to determine which contracting state has jurisdiction to tax and to grant tax credits in accordance with inheritance tax conventions. This is the case, among others, of sections III.2 and III.2(d) of the 1945 United States and United Kingdom Inheritance Tax Convention or Articles 2 and 2(f) of the 1950 Protocol to the 1944 Canada–United States Inheritance Tax Convention.[9] Both treaties use beneficial ownership in an implied sense and in an explicit way.

In the first sense, the treaty links the credit for the tax paid in the other contracting state to the situs of the property. The treaty refers to legal or equitable rights or interests to make clear it does not matter whether tax liability on inheritance or estates arises on legal or beneficial ownership for the purposes of providing treaty relief insofar as one or both contracting states include such property as part of the inheritance tax subject matter.[10] This results from both the USA and the UK recognising equitable rights as part of a deceased estate and normally including most such rights within the taxable scope, so relief was needed.

In the second sense, the treaty defines the situs of shares for tax treaty purposes assuming they are located in the place of incorporation of the corporation to which they refer. Beneficial ownership is used to confirm that shares held by nominees and allocated by scrip certificates are still considered to be located in such places of incorporation.[11]

Australia for the Avoidance of Double Taxation and the Prevention of Fiscal Evasion with Respect to Taxes on the Estates of Deceased Persons.

[6] See s XI of the 1944 Convention between the United States of America and Canada for the Avoidance of Double Taxation and the Prevention of Fiscal Evasion in the Case of Estate Taxes and Succession Duties.

[7] See s 6 of the Protocol in relation to Art XI of the 1942 Convention between the United States of America and Canada providing for the avoidance of double taxation and prevention of fiscal evasion in the case of income taxes; s VI of the 1960 Convention between the United States of America and Israel for the Avoidance of Double Taxation of Income and for the Encouragement of International Trade and Investment.

[8] See s XX.2(d) of the Convention and s 6 of the Protocol of the 1942 Convention between the United States of America and Canada providing for the avoidance of double taxation and prevention of fiscal evasion in the case of income taxes.

[9] See above, n 5. In this regard, see R Vann, 'Beneficial Ownership: What Does History (and Maybe Policy) Tell Us' in M Lang et al (eds), *Beneficial Ownership: Recent Trends* (IBFD, 2013) 274.

[10] See Art 2 of the 1950 Protocol to the United States–Canada Tax Convention on Estates and Inheritance Taxes and matching articles in other treaties referred to in n 5 above.

[11] See Art 2(f) of the 1950 Protocol to the United States–Canada Tax Convention on Estates and Inheritance Taxes and matching articles in other treaties referred to in n 5 above. On this point, see Vann (n 9) 274. See also 'Quatrieme Rapport Concernant les Impots sur les Successions' [Fourth Report on Inheritance Taxes], 2 octobre 1962, Groupe du Travail N° 17 du Comite Fiscal [FC/WP17(62)3], Comite Fiscal, OECD, p 5.

This rule was designed to prevent tax avoidance by the owner of shares transferring the shares before death to a nominee, who would hold them in his name or her name, and then after the death of the decedent would pass them on to the beneficiary without disclosing to the tax authorities that the shares were beneficially owned by the decedent.[12] The point of this was that if the shares were in the name of the nominee at the time of the death, they were not part of the estate of the decedent and thus subject to tax, and thus the state of residence of the issuer corporation could not tax it under the treaty. The rule recognised that such shares were in fact part of the deceased estate and the state of residence of the issuer corporation was thus able to tax them.

Such a parenthetical reference is simply a reminder that, under general certainty beneficial ownership principles, tax rules allocate rights or property on the beneficial owner and not on the nominee. However, there might be a case where the explanation is in doubt. In the case of the interposition of an intermediary corporation to hold the shares, it would be doubtful as to whether the situs of the shares was in the place of incorporation of the second corporation, and not where the intermediary is incorporated.[13] Regardless, usually the main problem that would have been faced by the cases the rule was aimed at would be a problem of evidence.

(ii) Relief in Relation to Inheritance Taxes on Estates and Undivided Inheritances and Exemptions on Income Derived from Estates or Undivided Inheritances

Article XI of the 1944 United States–Canada Inheritance Tax Treaty and Article VII of the 1954 United States–Japan Inheritance Tax Treaty granted fiduciaries and beneficiaries the right to apply for relief if double taxation arises.[14] The rule provided support for discretional relief by states after consulting with each other. Different systems of taxing fiduciaries made it difficult to provide a single rule, so the treaties gave support on a case-by-case basis. For similar purposes, but on income derived from such undivided inheritances or estates, the beneficiaries concept is used in several income tax treaties to define the tax jurisdiction of both contracting states in relation to the different subjects involved, such as in Article 4 of the Protocol to the 1939 United States–Sweden Income Tax Treaty.[15]

[12] See the minutes of the negotiation between the United States and Finland, 'January 25, 1951 – 2:30 PM, Room 3408, Internal Revenue Building', p 3; Foreign Taxation: Finland; Box 39; Office of the Legislative Council, subject files 1936–1972, Asst Secretary Tax Policy [RG 56 NN3 56 94 005], National Archives at College Park, College Park, MD.

[13] Under the nominee theory. See the discussion in ch 3 above on the nominee theory. See also *Moline Properties Inc v Commissioner of Internal Revenue* (1943) 319 US 436; *Commissioner v Bollinger* (1988) 485 US 340 (USSC); *National Carbide Corp v Commissioner* (1949) 336 US 442 (USSC).

[14] See s XI of the 1944 Convention between the United States of America and Canada for the Avoidance of Double Taxation and the Prevention of Fiscal Evasion in the Case of Estate Taxes and Succession Duties; s VI of the Convention between the United States of America and Japan for the Avoidance of Double Taxation and the Prevention of Fiscal Evasion with Respect to Taxes on Estates, Inheritances and Gifts.

[15] See the references 'Part A: Treaties Using "Beneficiary" for Certain Types of Income' and 'Part B: Treaties Referring to "Beneficiaries" of Deceased Estates' in Vann (n 9). On the mentioned rule in the Protocol to the 1939 United States–Sweden Income Tax Treaty, see Joint Committee on Internal Revenue Taxation, *Legislative History of United States Tax Conventions* (n 1) vol 2, 2348.

In both cases, the terms are used to deal with a situation where the tax liability of estates or undivided inheritance in cross-border situations arise at different levels on beneficiaries, the estate or both, and in both countries, so exemptions and credits may not match.[16] If beneficiaries have an almost absolute entitlement to the income or the inheritance property, tax rules will normally allocate the tax burden to them as the person with the ability to pay, so there should not be taxation at the estate, trust or undivided inheritance level in the other state; or, if there is, a credit to the beneficiary should be granted. For example, in the case of 1939 Sweden–United States Tax Convention and Protocol, the term beneficiaries was used to grant exemption from Swedish taxation to income derived by a US beneficiary from an estate or undivided inheritance insofar as such income was subject to US tax liability. As Swedish tax rules probably allocated income from the estate to the estate itself – even though it was also likely to be exempted under domestic law – whereas US tax rules were allocating income from a Swedish estate to the beneficiary resident in the USA, the potential for double taxation arose.[17] The solution was likely to prevent Sweden from taxing the income at the estate level. Similarly, as per the 1944 United States–Canada Inheritance Tax Treaty, the solution granted if the subject applied and the contracting states so decided was to give the credit to the beneficiary if he or she was liable to tax on the estate or inheritance, and a tax on the estate property was paid at the estate level in the other contracting state.

In both cases, the term beneficiary is used, not beneficial owner. One reason for such use may be that the term beneficiary, being broader than the latter, covers rights against the property in the deceased's estate or inheritance of different intensity. In addition, it also covers cases where there are no equitable rights at stake. This is especially important in the case of the treaty with Sweden, as Swedish law does not recognise a split between legal and beneficial ownership.[18] Without knowing the details of Swedish inheritance law, in civil law countries the person entitled to the estate or inheritance may sometimes have a general right to part of the inheritance as in co-ownership, while others may directly have ownership rights if no complex distribution of the inheritance is needed, such as in the case of a single heir and a single or few assets without charges.[19]

In the case of the 1944 Inheritance Tax Treaty with Canada, the term appears jointly with the word fiduciary.[20] This confirms the broad sense of the term, so it includes any

[16] On s 4 of the Protocol to the 1939 United States–Sweden Income Tax Treaty see Vann (n 9) 270.

[17] Vann points out three effects of the rule: to turn off the domestic law exemption for the estate in Sweden if the beneficiary was taxed in the residence country; to give the source country exemption from or reduction of tax to the income in Sweden under the treaty if the income was allocated to the beneficiary in the other country, even in the case where Swedish rules do not allocate the income to him or her; and to provide double tax relief to the beneficiary if he or she was an American resident for any tax paid in the USA. Vann also points out that this rule was also used in other treaties with Scandinavian countries as they have similar rules on allocation of income and taxation in relation to income from deceased estates. ibid.

[18] See D Kleist, 'Sweden: Trusts and Foreign Foundations in Swedish Tax Law' (2011) 17 *Trusts and Trustees* 622.

[19] In several civil law countries, the heir is considered to succeed from the death, even though some steps may be followed before the heir can access full ownership. In this regard, an undivided estate may hold allocation to the heir in suspense. However, contrary to common law countries, undivided estates are not considered to derive an implicit trust relationship or equitable ownership in favour of the heir, but simply a potential right until the estate is divided, allocated and accepted. In Sweden, it seems that the income of undivided estates is taxed as a separate entity, which probably led to the issue under discussion.

[20] See s XI of the 1944 Convention between the United States of America and Canada for the Avoidance of Double Taxation and the Prevention of Fiscal Evasion in the Case of Estate Taxes and Succession Duties.

beneficiary in an estate with a more or less defined right to property in the estate or undivided inheritance either through equitable or common law rights.[21] This could be as a result of the need to cover the Québécois civil law tradition, which does not understand a split between legal and beneficial ownership and where inheritance rights do not derive beneficial ownership as understood in equity law.

However, even if it seems that the terms in both the Swedish and Canadian treaties should be interpreted in a broad sense, the context adds more nuances as to how the rules should be interpreted.

On the one hand, in the 1939 United States–Swedish treaty, the term beneficiary appears to define exemption from taxation in Sweden at the estate level only if such beneficiary is liable to tax. Thus, the main issue is not who is a beneficiary, but whether a beneficiary will be liable to tax in the USA. In this sense, if the author is right about the conclusions of previous chapters, the beneficiary of a Swedish estate or undivided inheritance should be subject to US taxation insofar as he has a large interest in the estate or undivided inheritance with primary rights to control and income, either in equity or common law, as a matter of principle and without prejudice to specific rules applicable at the time. The point is that such a view is consistent with the treaty. The exemption is connected to the allocation of income and liability in the USA, so the treaty follows domestic principles. The question raised by this rule is whether the treaty will exempt a non-beneficiary, such as a fiduciary, that is liable to tax in the USA under the uncertainty beneficial owner principle. If the rule was intending submission to domestic rules, it will cover liability in persons other than the beneficiary under the uncertainty or anti-avoidance principles.

The 1944 United States–Canada Inheritance Tax Treaty does not offer guidance as to whether fiduciaries who may claim the relief include fiduciary debtors, creditors or both. The wording alone clearly refers to a fiduciary debtor such as a trustee, even though from the context it could well be construed as referring to the fiduciary creditor, as the beneficiary is mentioned in the same phrase.[22] As the rule provides for a right to claim a relief that will be discretionally granted, it probably includes both insofar as they are affected by multiple taxation. As the rule only provides for the right to apply to the relief, but does not define the relief itself, what is relevant is that tax authorities will analyse the case at stake on the specifics of the different subjects involved and possible multiple tax burdens.

(iii) Participation in Subsidiaries for Extra Reduced Rate at Source

The third context in which beneficial ownership may be found in early tax treaties is in section 6 of the Protocol to the 1942 United States–Canada Income Tax Treaty, as a requirement to access a reduced rate of taxation at source of 5 per cent for dividends

[21] On the problems of applying beneficial ownership rules to Quebec because of its civil law tradition, see MD Brender, 'Beneficial Ownership in Canadian Income Tax Law: Required Reform and Impact on Harmonization of Quebec Civil Law and Federal Legislation' (2003) 51 *Canadian Tax Journal* 311.

[22] According to *Blacks' Law Dictionary*, fiduciary is the debtor. See B Garner (ed), *Black's Law Dictionary*, 10th edn (West – Thomson Reuters, 2009) 743.

derived from subsidiaries, instead of the ordinary 15 per cent limit provided by the treaty.[23] The corporation receiving the dividend has to be the beneficial owner of a percentage of shares in the subsidiary.

Little guidance exists as to how beneficial ownership should be interpreted. The only commentary on the subject notes that the reduced rate was only available to a 'bona fide' parent–subsidiaries relationship.[24] In this regard, the relationship between the beneficial owner rule in the protocol defining a subsidiary and the principal purpose test in Article XI of the convention remains unclear. Was the bona fide explanation referring simply to the principal purpose test or the beneficial owner test, or to both?

The elimination of the main purpose test in a matching rule in the 1946 United Kingdom–Canada Treaty leads one to consider whether the USA was thinking about beneficial ownership in the sense of its domestic allocation principles, jointly with the principal purpose test, in the misunderstood sense following the *Moline Properties* doctrine.[25] If this was the case, then it could be that it was eliminated because it was unknown to the UK. This may be confirmed by the set of requirements included in relation to Article XI of the 1942 United States–Canada Income Tax Treaty, including the principal purpose, the beneficial owner test and the income-flow test, which were probably targeted at conduit and straw corporations. If one notes how beneficial ownership was used in *Moline Properties*, decided only a year before, and similar cases, as well as Treasury regulations at the time governing the application of tax treaties, the conclusion seems consistent, as those rules in such a context were aimed at straw and conduit companies.[26] In this sense, if a bank nominee or custodian or a straw corporation was used to hold shares in a corporation in the other contracting state and dividends were paid to the nominee, allocation of income under US tax law and subsequent tax liability were to be found with the beneficial owner. In that sense, only if such beneficial owner was found to have the percentage of shares required was the limited tax rate applicable.

This context is slightly different to the use of beneficial ownership in inheritance tax treaties. In those cases, beneficial ownership was used to match allocation of income and exemption or credit to relieve double taxation, while in this case it was used in order

[23] See above, n 7. For that rule to be applicable, the parent–subsidiary relationship has to fulfil three requirements. First, the corporation has to be wholly and beneficially owned by the corporation receiving the dividends, as well as having the voting rights. Secondly, no more than a quarter of the subsidiary income can be derived from dividends and interests. In addition, a principal purpose test was included in the reduced rate provision, so the benefit was not available if the subsidiary condition was arranged for the principal purpose of obtaining the parent–subsidiary reduced rate. See Art 6 of the Protocol to the 1942 Convention between the United States of America and Canada providing for the avoidance of double taxation and prevention of fiscal evasion in the case of income taxes. See Art X.2 of the 1942 Convention between the United States of America and Canada providing for the avoidance of double taxation and prevention of fiscal evasion in the case of income taxes: Joint Committee on Internal Revenue Taxation, *Legislative History of United States Tax Conventions* (n 1) 460. The wholly owned requirement was amended by the 1950 Canada–US Convention, reducing the percentage of required beneficial ownership to 95% of the voting stock to access the reduced rate for subsidiaries. This was subsequently reduced again in the 1956 amendment to the convention to require a 51% beneficial ownership of the voting stock.

[24] ibid; Vann (n 9) 271–72.

[25] On the elimination in the 1946 United Kingdom–Canada Tax Treaty, see Vann (n 9) 272–73.

[26] See the section on the anti-avoidance principle in the USA in ch 3 above, and see references to nominees and agents as negative definitions in, amongst other Treasury regulations, Art 4 of Treasury Decision 4766, 1937-2, Cumulative Bulletin 158; s 7.15 of TD 5157, 1942-2, CB 137; s 7.507 of the TD 5532, 1946-2, CB 73.

to grant a special tax limitation because of the special relationship that exists between a corporation and a subsidiary as opposed to an individual shareholder.

First, tax liability on the dividends will again normally only arise if the corporation holds beneficial ownership as per the above-mentioned tax principle, so it only makes sense to reduce the source taxation to the subject receiving the dividends if it holds such a predefined and large right. However, if a subject controlling the shares, such as a fiduciary in a discretionary trust, were to receive the dividends, they would be allocated tax liability, though it is more difficult to fit such a case within the context of this rule if such beneficial ownership requirement is interpreted in the sense of a person to whom income is allocated.

In this sense, beneficial ownership balanced against the context in which it appears seems to require the ownership of the corporation to enable the corporation to control the subsidiary in a manner similar to how it would control its own business units, so that it can carry out that part of the subsidiary's activities as if it were its own. The idea seems to mitigate economic double taxation, as the subsidiary will be taxed and the dividends will also be taxed, while in a permanent establishment only juridical double taxation will arise. This seems to be what the extra reduction is trying to solve by considering the subsidiary to be almost part of the corporation's own business structure, even though it is an independent person. And this can only be beneficial ownership in the sense of a strong ownership and *erga omnes* rights, as it is difficult to imagine any other limited shareholding, such as a fiduciary in a discretionary trust, fitting within such a corporation–subsidiary relationship that enables the first to perform its activities through the second as part of its business structure. It is very unlikely that a corporation will perform part of its core activities through a corporation over which it cannot keep strong control.

Considering this view and the historical context, the rule can probably only be understood in the context of bank nominees and straw corporations, and not in the context of discretionary trusts. In the case of a straw corporation, the reduced rate will be applicable only if shares are considered to be held by the ultimate parent under the *Moline Properties* test. And as, under the *Moline Properties* test, shares income would be allocated to such ultimate parent as the beneficial owner of the stock, the reduced rate and domestic allocation will match the same taxable person.

It is likely that beneficial ownership was used in the sense of a person with the greatest interest in the shares against the world at large who can claim in court primary rights to income and control, either in common law or equity law. Contrary to this, it may well be said that it excludes nominee or intermediary corporations, and nominees, fiduciaries or other subjects, irrespective of income or assets being allocated to such fiduciaries under anti-avoidance or uncertainty principles.

(iv) Summary: Matching Allocation of Income in Domestic Tax Law and Tax Treaties, and Contextual Interpretation

In the author's view, the use of the words 'beneficiaries' and 'beneficial owner' in such treaties, and in many others using those words in a similar context, seemingly relates to beneficial ownership developments in the USA as per the above-mentioned allocation principles.

In the case of inheritance tax treaties or income derived from estates or inheritances, if the beneficiary resident in the USA was entitled in general to a part of the result of the foreign inheritance and not to specific income or property, under principles shown in previous chapters – although there are several nuances of specific rules – it would be unlikely that the USA would tax it, as it requires some intense degree of primary right to income and control. Therefore, if the USA is not taxing it, no double taxation arises. The other contracting state may be able to tax it at the estate or inheritance level, or the USA would not need to grant a credit. Conversely, if income or property was to be allocated to a fiduciary resident in the USA and tax liability arises following the uncertainty principle or right to control, relief or exemption should be granted in order to avoid double taxation as the subject is clearly liable to tax in the USA.

What seems more clear is the relationship between beneficiary for tax purposes, tax liability and exemptions. If exemptions and reliefs were connected to liability as shown in some previous examples, and liability was defined upon beneficial ownership principles, then exemptions and reliefs would be dependent on beneficial ownership. This is clear in the 1939 United States–Sweden Inheritance Tax Treaty, where exemption is connected to the beneficiary as tax is liable in the USA, as otherwise no double taxation would arise; in the 1944 United States–Canada Inheritance Tax Treaty, where fiduciaries are mentioned to grant them the right to apply for the exemption if double taxation arises; or in the 1944 United States–Canada Inheritance Tax Treaty and the 1945 United States–United Kingdom Tax Convention, where indicating nominees as irrelevant and putting the spotlight on the equitable or beneficial owner for tax purposes is seemingly derived from domestic allocation principles.

For the author, the use of beneficial ownership in these treaties seems to progressively incorporate into tax treaties the principles developed at domestic level, so double tax relief is connected to allocation of property or income under domestic tax law.

In any case, this preliminary analysis, given that beneficial owner principles were subject to several specific rules at the time, and given that there is some doubt as to whether this was done intentionally or unintentionally in being considered part of the ordinary set of application of tax rules, offers enough evidence – with further evidence discussed below – to suggest that the drafters were somehow incorporating their domestic thinking into treaties. What is less clear is whether such incorporation was done for a specific meaning. As beneficial ownership principles were under development at the time and it is likely that the drafters were highlighting double taxation, and as allocation under beneficial ownership was a secondary step in such reasoning, it is more likely that a rather broad connection to domestic developments on tax liability being connected to ability to pay was made. However, no specific domestic meaning for tax treaty purposes was given. Not surprisingly, considering these treaties were early developments of the models that would later be adopted, a broad connection and a lack of definition of the relationship between tax liability and tax treaties has come down to us today.[27]

[27] On treaties paying little attention to the allocation issue, see Wheeler, *The Missing Keystone of Income Tax Treaties* (n 4) s 2.4.1.

B. The Use of Beneficial Ownership for Nominees and Other Intermediaries in Relation to Passive Income: From US Treaty Policy to the UK

The early uses of beneficial ownership mentioned above referred to assets, property or rights, rather than to income. Conversely, the most frequent use in income tax treaties is as a requirement to access source tax limits rules for passive income, namely dividends, interest and royalties.[28]

It is accepted that the 1966 Protocol to the 1945 United Kingdom–United States Tax Convention is the first explicit inclusion of the concept of beneficial ownership in articles referring to dividends, interest and royalties.[29] However, the US Treasury already considered that the beneficial owner requirement was implicit in previous treaties, so the explicit inclusion made no change.

Following domestic allocation of income principles in cases of shares or securities held by nominees or custodians, benefits or limitations of tax treaties signed between 1936 and 1966 were only granted if beneficial owners were fulfilling treaty requirements, and not if mere legal owners or intermediaries on behalf of beneficial owners were fulfilling those requirements but beneficial owners were not. This was shown in some IRS Decisions and answers concerning the application of tax treaties to intermediaries from as far back as the 1930s, more than 30 years before the concept was explicitly included.

An IRS Decision issued in 1936 concerned the application of the tax treaty between the USA and the UK to dividends paid to UK partnerships as nominees for subjects who were non-resident in the UK.[30] The decision provided that the reduced rate was not available in such cases, and that the nominee shall withhold a 10 per cent statutory tax rate instead of the treaty rate and submit it to the Treasury.

In relation to trusts, a ruling answered some questions raised by a UK law firm concerning an Englishman who was receiving income through a trust in Canada, part of which derived from bonds of a US company.[31] The Commissioner answered that 'a trust is considered a mere conduit insofar as the beneficiary is concerned, and the beneficiary is taxable on his or her distributable share of the trust income', and concluded that the case could not take advantage of the reduced rate of the United States–Canada

[28] See Arts 10, 11 and 12 of the OECD Model Tax Convention. According to the IBFD Tax Research Database, at least 1,790 income tax treaties include the beneficial owner requirement in relation to dividends, interest and articles following the OECD Model Tax Convention.

[29] See Arts 4, 5 and 7 of the 1966 Protocol amending the Convention for the Avoidance of Double Taxation and the Prevention of Fiscal Evasion with respect to Taxes on Income, signed at Washington on the 16th April, 1945, as modified by the Supplementary Protocol signed at Washington on the 6th June, 1946, by the Supplementary Protocol signed at Washington on the 25th May, 1954, and the Supplementary Protocol signed at Washington on 19 August, 1957; modifying Arts VI, VII and VIII to introduce beneficial ownership. J Avery Jones et al, 'The Origins of Concepts and Expressions Used in the OECD Model and Their Adoption by States' (2006) 60 *Bulletin for International Taxation* 220, 249.

[30] TD 1936-2, CB 106, 1936 WL 65998.

[31] Letter from the Commissioner to Mr William H Taylor, US Treasury Representative in London, 25 January 1945; Box 38; Office of the Legislative Council, subject files 1936–1972, Asst Secretary Tax Policy [RG 56 Entry 67A1804], National Archives at College Park, College Park, MD.

Tax Convention insofar as the beneficiary, as the relevant subject for tax liability, was not resident in Canada.

Both statements, even though they did not mention beneficial ownership, refer to nominee, trust or actual ownership wording, and apply the logic derived from domestic tax law to cases involving nominees, bare trusts and beneficial or actual ownership. This reasoning seems logical, as it links tax treaty limits with tax liability under domestic law, which in turn is defined by beneficial ownership principles. Both set of rules are linked to the same condition on ability to pay: beneficial ownership. It is highly likely that, while tax authorities were thinking about tax treaties, they did not actually carry out an in-depth analysis of allocation of income at treaty level and possible mismatches, but simply carried over their domestic assumptions and made beneficial ownership applicable to tax treaties, even though it was not explicitly included or well thought out.

In addition, negotiations from the UK mention 'other countries did in fact apply the OECD text as if it meant the beneficial owner'.[32] Could it be that these countries were the USA and New Zealand?[33]

Finally, an early report of the OECD on improper use of tax conventions notes that one of the factors that define tax avoidance through the use of tax treaties is that 'the beneficial owner of the income must either not be taxed at all on such income in his home country or must be free of tax until the income is repatriated'.[34] As the rapporteurs were from the USA and Denmark, it is highly likely that the USA introduced its view on the beneficial owner rule as being implicit, although the OECD model did not include the term at the time.

(i) The Withholding Mechanism as Proof of an Implicit Beneficial Owner Principle Excluding Agents, Nominees and Other Intermediaries

The main evidence of the US policy of considering beneficial ownership principles as inherent to any tax treaty derives from the special withholding system the USA had until withholding taxes on dividends and interests were repealed in 1984.[35] Since the 1936 Revenue Act reform, the USA was probably one of the few countries where treaty withholding reduced rates were applicable directly by the withholding agent and where no tax authority's intervention was needed, as opposed to most countries that applied statutory rates, and the difference with tax treaty limited rates was subject to a refund claim. It was not until the 1960s–70s that most countries of the world started to adopt such a system, but the USA already had it.[36]

[32] Negotiation of new Double Taxation Convention with Finland, Helsinki – 27th February to 11th March 1968, m no 13, in Origin papers of the renegotiation of double taxation agreement with Finland (TNA Ref IR 40/17812).

[33] Vann (n 9).

[34] 'Third Report on Tax Avoidance through the Improper Use or Abuse of tax Conventions', 21 December 1967, p 5 [FC/WP21 (67) 1].

[35] See s 127(a) of the Deficit Reduction Act of 1984, Pub L No 98-369. On the reasons for the elimination of any withholding tax on the repeal of the Treaty with Netherlands Antilles and the need to guarantee US corporations access to financial markets and its effects, see RS Avi-Yonah, 'Globalization, Tax Competition, and the Fiscal Crisis of the Welfare State' [2000] *Harvard Law Review* 1573, 1579 et seq.

[36] See s 143.1(a) and (b) of the Revenue Act 1936, 49 Stat 1648; s 143.1(a) and (b) of the Internal Revenue Code 1939; ss 871 and 1441 of the Internal Revenue Code 1954. Conversely, most countries at the

Under this system, payees needed to know in each case whether the statutory or tax treaty rate was applicable. To clarify and provide certainty, the Treasury Department issued regulations with certain presumptions to allow withholding agents to know which rate was applicable in which case.[37] Under such regulations, any individual or corporate payee whose address was in the other contracting state was presumed a resident of that state, so the payor-withholding agent could apply the treaty reduced rate.[38] Those regulations worked on the assumption that the payee was the actual owner and the address was evidence of his or her residence.[39] The weakness of the system appears obvious regarding the chances of tax avoidance, because the application of reduced rates was only based on the person receiving the payment giving an address in the other contracting state.[40] This allowed persons residing in third countries or even US citizens to put their securities in the hands of, for instance, Canadian or UK banks, and be taxed at a reduced rate instead of the statutory rate if the Canadian bank as payee provided its address to the withholding agent.[41]

time required previous tax authorities' certification before reduced rates were applied by payors, or withholding tax was charged at the full statutory rate and non-residents were to apply for a refund to the tax authorities. See 'Methods Used To Reduce Tax At The Source (Report received on 15th January, 1972)', Working Party No 1 of the Committee on Fiscal Affairs on Double Taxation – Working Group No 26 (United States, France, Netherlands) [CFA/WP1(72)1)], 21 January 1972, Committee of Fiscal Affairs, OECD, p 1; 'Memorandum on Exchange of Information under United States Tax Treaties', p 2; Office of the Legislative Council, subject files 1936–1972, Asst Secretary Tax Policy [RG 56 NN3 56 94 005], National Archives at College Park, College Park, MD.

[37] See Treasury Decision 4766, 1937-2, Cumulative Bulletin 158 on the 1935 United States–Canada Tax Convention; TD 5157, 1942-2, CB 137 on the 1942 United States–Canada Tax Convention; TD 5532, 1946-2, CB 73 on the 1945 United States–United Kingdom Tax Convention; TD 5957, 1953-1, CB 238 on the 1948 United States–New Zealand Tax Convention; TD 5690, 1949-1, CB 92 on the 1948 United States–Belgium Tax Convention; TD 5692, 1949-1, CB 104 on the 1948 United States–Denmark Tax Convention; TD 5897, 1952-1, CB 89 on the 1951 United States–Ireland Tax Convention; TD 5867, 1951-2, CB 75 on the 1951 United States Switzerland Tax Convention; TD 6108, 1954-2, CB 614 on the 1953 United States–Australia Tax Convention; TD 6215, 1956-2, CB 1105 on the 1955 Italy United States Tax Convention; TD 6056, 1954-1, CB 132 on the 1952 United States–Belgium Tax Convention; TD 6437, 1960-1, CB 767 on the 1958 Protocol of extension to United Kingdom territories of the 1945 United States–United Kingdom Tax Convention; and TD 6898, 1966-2, CB 567 on the 1966 Protocol to the 1945 United States–United Kingdom Tax Conventions. See AA Ehrenzweig and FE Koch, *Income Tax Treaties* (Commerce Clearing House, 1949) 55 et seq and 134 et seq.

[38] On the address presumption in relation to the 1942 and 1945 United States Tax Conventions with Canada and the UK, see ibid.

[39] See Art 3 of Treasury Decision 4766, 1937-2, Cumulative Bulletin 158 on the 1935 United States–Canada Tax Convention.

[40] On the different problems arising, see 'Problem of allocating the amount of dividends paid to non-resident alien individuals and corporations by countries', 2 June 1937; Withholdings, Non-resident aliens and foreign corporations; Box 12/44; General record of the Department of Treasury, Office of the Tax Policy, subject files [RG 56 NN3 56 94 005]. 'Canadian Bank Problems', 13–16 March 1953; Box 38; Office of the Legislative Council, subject files 1936–1972, Asst Secretary Tax Policy [RG 56 NN3 56 94 005] [56-90-41]. 'Proposals Regarding the Problem of Foreign Capital Inflow', 19 January 1937, p 5; Box 12/44; General record of the Department of Treasury, Office of the Tax Policy, subject files [RG 56 NN3 56 94 005] [56-90-41]. All of them at National Archives at College Park, College Park, MD. At an international level, see the analysis on the issues and advantages of the address system, basically easiness to avoid versus simplicity in treaty application in 'Methods Used to Reduce Tax at the Source (Report received on 15th January, 1972)', Working Party No 1 of the Committee on Fiscal Affairs on Double Taxation – Working Group No 26 (United States, France, Netherlands) [CFA/WP1(72)1)], 21 January, 1972, Committee of Fiscal Affairs, OECD, pp 1–3.

[41] See Joint Committee on Internal Revenue Taxation, *Legislative History of United States Tax Conventions* (n 1) 541; EP King, 'Tax Conventions to Which United States Is a Party' (1960) 1 *Proceedings of the Institute on Private Investments Abroad* 479, 490; 'Withholding on discount element of bankers' acceptances and

It was also possible for a bank or intermediary resident in a treaty partner country to carry out dividend stripping or make bond-washing transactions to benefit from the convention at the time of the distribution, or to make a back-to-back loan from an intermediary treaty partner.[42] In many cases, tax avoidance may not even be the main purpose of putting the securities in the hands of a resident of a US contracting state, but a mere consequence of ordinary business, and still be problematic.[43] The problem was progressively solved, between the 1950s and the 1970s, by requiring the payee to show ownership certificates in order to apply treaty reduced rates on the basis of his or her address, but the flawed system remained in many cases for almost 40 years.[44]

The system back-up until the payee address presumption was abolished was to require the payee resident in the other contracting state to withhold the difference between the reduced rate and the applicable rate if he or she was not the actual owner but an intermediary acting on behalf of a subject who was not resident in the contracting state.[45]

commercial paper', p 4, 6 November 1961; Withholding tax – Foreign; Box 85; Office of the Tax Legislative Council, subject files 1936–1972, Asst Secretary Tax Policy [RG 56 NN3 56 94 005]. See 'CIEP Questions. I. What is the impact on investment decisions of the administrative burdens of the withholding taxes? Are the administrative burdens the same for all countries? How can they be reduced?', p 1, Nov 15, 1973; Withholding tax – Foreign; Box 85; Office of the Tax Legislative Council, subject files 1936–1972, Asst Secretary Tax Policy [RG 56 NN3 56 94 005]. 'Conference in Ottawa – September 21, 22 and 23, 1953' 1 October 1953, pp 2–3; Foreign Taxation – Canada; Box 37; Office of the Tax Legislative Council, subject files 1936–1972, Asst Secretary Tax Policy [RG 56 NN3 56 94 005]. All of them at National Archives at College Park, College Park, MD.

[42] See 'Withholding on Discount Obligations', 4 March 1966; 'Withholding of tax on Discount element of treasury bills, bankers acceptances and commercial papers', 5 December 1961; 'Withholding of tax on Discount element of treasury bills, bankers acceptances and commercial paper- conference with Mr. Deane', 17 November 1961; 'Withholding on Discount element of bankers' acceptances and commercial paper', 6 November 1961; 'Integration of domestic and foreign withholding', 10 July 1961; 'CIEP Interagency Group on the International Competitive Position of US Financial Markets Institutions', p 2. All of them in Withholding tax – Foreign; Box 85; Office of the Tax Legislative Council, subject files 1936–1972, Asst Secretary Tax Policy [RG 56 NN3 56 94 005]. All of them at National Archives at College Park, College Park, MD.

[43] Tax Treaties general; Box 39; Office of the Tax Legislative Council, subject files 1936–1972, Asst Secretary Tax Policy [RG 56 NN3 56 94 005]; National Archives at College Park, College Park, MD.

[44] 'Tax withholding tax on Deutsches mark – denominated United States Government obligations' 23 August 1979; Withholding Foreign (repeal of WHT on interests); Box 52; Office of the Tax Policy, subject files [RG 56-90-73 131-14-7-4]; 'Notice of proposed rule making containing withholding regulations with respect to amended United States–Canada income tax convention', 2 July 1953; Foreign Taxation – Canada; Box 37; Office of the Tax Legislative Council, subject files 1936–1972, Asst Secretary Tax Policy [RG 56 NN3 56 94 005]; 'US withholding Tax Procedures', 6 December 1973; and 'Procedures for Treaty benefits on Treasury Notes', 18 June 1968; both in Withholding tax – Foreign; Box 85; Office of the Tax Legislative Council, subject files 1936–1972, Asst Secretary Tax Policy [RG 56 NN3 56 94 005]; 'Income Tax Treaty Policy', pp 3-4, 12 December 1972; Foreign Taxation – Treaties – General; Box 26; Office of the Tax Policy, Subject files [RG 56-90-73 131-14-6-3]. All of them at National Archives at College Park, College Park, MD.

[45] See Joint Committee on Internal Revenue Taxation, *Legislative History of United States Tax Conventions* (n 1) 541; King (n 41) 490. As an example, s 7.507 of TD 5532, 1946-2, CB 73, s 7.507: 'Addresse not actual owner. – If the recipient in the United Kingdom of the dividend is a nominee or agent through whom the dividend flows to a person other than the person … such recipient in the United Kingdom will withhold an additional tax equivalent to 15 per cent of the gross … The amounts so withheld by the withholding agent in the United Kingdom will, … be deposited with the United Kingdom Board of Inland Revenue, … The Board of Inland Revenue have arranged that they will, on or before the end of the calendar month in which such deposit is so made with the Board, remit by draft in United States dollars the amounts so deposited to the collector of internal revenue, Baltimore, Md., …'. Similar rules are found in Art 4 of TD 4766, 1937-2, Cumulative Bulletin 158 in relation to 1935 Canada–United States Tax Convention, even though such tax convention does not enable such collection mechanism; s 7.15 of TD 5157, 1942-2, CB 137 on Art XX.II of the 1942 United States–Canada Tax Convention; s 7.507 of TD 5532, 1946-2, CB 73 on 1945 United States–United Kingdom Tax Convention, even though this convention does not include collection mechanism;

In such cases, the payee had to submit the difference to the US Treasury.[46] As Treasury decisions applied to payees who were residents in the other contracting states where the USA had no jurisdiction, tax treaties included an assistance in collection clause dealing with 'persons not entitled' to benefits derived from the convention, as well as exchange of information clauses with some special references to persons not entitled.[47]

During negotiations concerning the 1945 Double Taxation Treaty (DTT), the USA saw that the problem in concluding a DTT with the UK was the tax secrecy prevailing in that country. Thus, a nominee or record owner could act in favour of a non-resident beneficial owner not entitled to treaty benefits, and even the UK lacked the mechanisms to see who was the real owner of the asset or the income itself; and the USA would have even less of a possibility of accessing such information.[48] The system thus relied on the bona fides of custodian and nominee payees. The USA probably did not pay much attention to this issue because it recognised that 'withholding provisions and our collection at source (despite unusually good administration of these provisions of

s 7.607 of TD 5957, 1953-1, CB 238 on Art XVII of 1948 United States–New Zealand Tax Convention; s 7.807 of TD 5690, 1949-1, CB 92 on Art XXII of 1948 Netherlands–United States Tax Convention; Arts XVII and XXII of 1952 Finland–United States Convention; s 7.906 of TD 5692, 1949-1, CB 104 on Art XVII of 1948 Denmark–United States Tax Convention; s 7.1007 of TD 5897, 1952-1, CB 89, on 1951 United States–Ireland Tax Convention, even though such treaty does not include collection mechanism habilitation; s 7.307 of TD 5867, 1951-2, CB 75 on Art XVI of 1951 Switzerland–United States Tax Convention; s 501.8 of TD 6108, 1954-2, CB 614 on Art XVI of 1953 United States–Australia Tax Convention; s 512.3 of TD 6215, 1956-2, CB 1105 on Art XVIII of 1955 United States–Italy Tax Convention; s 7.1107 of a TD 6056, 1954-1, CB 132 on 1953 United States–Belgium Tax Convention; s 507.503 of TD 6437, 1960-1, CB 767 on the 1945 Protocol to the United States–United Kingdom Tax Convention; s 507.23 of TD 6898, 1966-2, CB 567 on Art XIX A of the 1945 United Kingdom–United States Tax Convention as amended by the 1966 Protocol. See also 'Technical Memorandum of the Federal Tax Administration of Switzerland at Berne to The Commissioner of Internal Revenue at Washington, DC', p 4; Switzerland; Box 39; 'Conference in Ottawa – September 21, 22 and 23, 1953' 1 October 1953, pp 2–3; Foreign Taxation – Canada; Box 37; 'Notice of proposed rule making containing withholding regulations with respect to amended United States–Canada income tax convention', 2 July 1953, p 4; Foreign Taxation – Canada; Box 37; 'Treasury decision – Withholding regulations under the income tax convention with the United Kingdom', 13 October 1966; United Kingdom; Box 39. All of these in Office of the Tax Legislative Council, subject files 1936–1972, Asst Secretary Tax Policy [RG 56 NN3 56 94 005], at National Archives at College Park, College Park, MD. However, some Regulations on Tax Conventions did not have the collection mechanism, such as the TD 6109, 1954, on the 1954 Tax Convention between United States and Greece.

[46] The submission by the intermediary-withholding agent in the other contracting state was in some cases made directly to the US Treasury, while in other cases it was submitted to the other contracting state, which, in turn, submitted it to the United States Treasury. See s 7.507 of TD 5532, 1946-2, CB 73 on the 1945 convention with United Kingdom; s 7.17 of TD 5157, 1942-2, CB 137 on the 1942 Convention with Canada.

[47] See treaty articles mentioned above in n 45. The Senate raised several concerns on the constitutionality and public order compatibility of assistance in collection provisions for the enforcement of foreign taxes. Also, taxpayers complained about such rules. The result was that collection provisions in treaties signed after 1949 only applied to improper use of the convention. This was mainly the use of intermediaries to improperly access tax treaty reduced rates, so such provisions remain applicable to the cases dealt with here. In this regard, see Joint Committee on Internal Revenue Taxation, *Legislative History of United States Tax Conventions* (n 1) 523–83; EA Owens, 'United States Income Tax Treaties: Their Role in Relieving Double Taxation' (1962) 17 *Rutgers Law Review* 450.

[48] See the claims on the matter by EP King, Special Deputy Commissioner of the Bureau of Internal Revenue, in the debate on the United States–United Kingdom DTTs: Joint Committee on Internal Revenue Taxation, *Legislative History of United States Tax Conventions*, vol 2 (n 1) 2622–23. 'Article XX'; United Kingdom; Box 39; Office of the Legislative Council, subject files 1936–1972, Asst Secretary Tax Policy [RG 56 NN3 56 94 005], National Archives at College Park, College Park, MD. See also, on the British side, Hansard of the House of Commons Debates, 14 February 1967, vol 741, 365; Hansard of House of Commons Debates, 23 June 1966, vol 730, 1095.

our tax laws) do not work effectively as regards interest and dividends paid to foreign taxpayers'.[49] It thus did not care much about source taxation and probably paid more attention to residence taxation.[50]

Those systems concerned with withholding, collection and exchange of information to deal with intermediaries referred to actual owners, and there was no express use of beneficial owner wording. So, what is the connection with beneficial ownership in tax treaties?

Such regulations are based on the concept of actual owner as opposed to nominee, agent, representative or fiduciary.[51] Considering the abundant Treasury discussions, memorandums, treaty negotiations and other documentation related to US tax treaties signed between 1936 and 1966, the Treasury refers indistinctly to actual owner and beneficial owner, as well as nominees, agents, fiduciaries or representatives as being the antonym to both wordings actual owner and beneficial owner.[52] In addition, the Regulations to the 1954 United States–Greece Double Tax Convention explicitly equate beneficial and actual owners.[53]

Outside of the primary sources, most authoritative US scholars at the time would place these mechanisms within the framework of the concept of beneficial ownership

[49] Joint Committee on Internal Revenue Taxation, *Legislative History of United States Tax Conventions* (n 1) 20.

[50] ibid.

[51] See the use of actual owner in Treasury decisions before 1966 at n 45 above.

[52] See the use of actual owner, beneficial owner, nominee, agents, fiduciaries or representatives in Treasury decisions at n 37 above. See also 'Collection' in the Technical Memorandum of the Treasury Department on the 1966 United States–United Kingdom Protocol giving an example of how the assistance in collection and this withholding burden on intermediaries work by referring to a bank acting on behalf of a non-resident beneficial owner. The examples define the beneficial owner as the relevant person upon which the treaty conditions have to be checked in order to apply their benefits, and excludes nominees or intermediaries as relevant persons for such purposes. That example of assistance in collection was also used in relation to pre-1966 treaties, even though in some cases they used the wording actual owner in exactly the same context. See also the use of beneficial ownership as opposite to nominee, in the same sense as the terms actual owner and nominee were used in relation to previous tax treaties with Canada, Sweden and France in 'Article XX'; United Kingdom; Box 39; 'Conference in Ottawa – September 21, 22 and 23, 1953', 1 October, 1953 pp 2–3; Foreign Taxation – Canada; Box 37; Office of the Tax Legislative Council, subject files 1936–1972, Asst Secretary Tax Policy [RG 56 NN3 56 94 005]; 'Interview on the case of bearer shares in France. Monday, Augusta 26 5 p.m'; France; Box 38; 'Custodian Accounts'; Withholding Tax; Box 84. All of them in Office of the Legislative Council, subject files 1936–1972, Asst Secretary Tax Policy [RG 56 NN3 56 94 005]; 'Proposals Regarding the Problem of Foreign Capital Inflow', 19 January 1937, p 5; Box 12/44; General record of the Department of Treasury, Office of the Tax Policy, subject files [RG 56 NN3 56 94 005] [56 -90-41]. All of them at National Archives at College Park, College Park, MD. See also Joint Committee on Internal Revenue Taxation, *Legislative History of United States Tax Conventions* (n 1) 540; 'Exhibit III: Non Resident Individuals Not Engaged In Trade Or Business In The United States; Filing Compliance', p 10; Switzerland; Box 39; Office of the Legislative Council, subject files 1936–1972, Asst Secretary Tax Policy [RG 56 NN3 56 94 005], National Archives at College Park, College Park, MD. In that document, dated in the 1950s, more than 10 years before the 1966 protocol, the collection mechanism is explicitly explained on the basis of the beneficial owner–nominee antonym. In addition, not surprisingly, such references to nominees and actual owners appear in relation to dividends, interest and royalties, precisely the scope of application of the concept in the 1966 Protocol and later OECD Model Tax Convention. Finally, and probably the most relevant, the commentary on Art 4 of the Technical Memorandum to the 1966 Protocol explicitly states that the inclusion of beneficial ownership in the 1966 Protocol makes no difference as it was already considered as implicitly included in previous tax treaties. If no similar word was there and only actual owner was used in such pre-1966 regulations on tax treaties, it is clear it was the same concept.

[53] s 502.10 (b) of TD 6109 (18 October 1954) on the 1954 Tax Convention between United States and Greece.

to be applicable to tax treaties.[54] This was confirmed when, in 1966, the words 'actual owner' and 'beneficial owner' were used indistinctly in the Treasury Decision to the Protocol between the United States and the UK.[55] Insofar as beneficial owner was used in that treaty in the same articles and sense, as well as being regulated in exactly the same way in the Treasury Regulation as actual owner was used in Treasury decisions of previous treaties, it is clear that the 1966 Protocol just made explicit what was already being implied by actual owner.[56] It is probably because the term beneficial ownership was used more colloquially than legally in the early half of the twentieth century that it was not consistently and explicitly used.[57] The 1966 Protocol is considered the first tax treaty to use beneficial ownership in relation to dividends, interest and royalties in the same way as it is used in most modern treaties. By using beneficial ownership in relation to such mechanism rules on nominees, agents and actual owners, such withholding tools become the primary origin of modern beneficial ownership.[58]

Whilst it is clear that beneficial ownership was used in such Treasury decisions to refer to the person with whom tax treaties requirements shall be verified, the question is whether beneficial or actual ownership in such decisions was an additional domestic requirement enacted through Treasury decisions or was an implicit treaty requirement that the treaty simply implemented.

The Technical Memorandum to the 1966 Protocol notes that the explicit inclusion of beneficial ownership made no difference, as it was considered implicit in previous treaties and was not derived from the collection mechanism itself.[59] Moreover, the Protocol introduced authorisation for the collection mechanisms that the USA was already using, and the Technical Memorandum explicitly uses the terms beneficial ownership and nominee to explain the functioning of such mechanisms. As the mechanism was meant to correct withholding to persons not entitled, and such persons not entitled were exemplified with reference to nominees and beneficial ownership, it was clear that

[54] See MB Carroll, 'Evolution of US Treaties to Avoid Double Taxation of Income Part II' [1968] *The International Lawyer* 129, 165; MB Carroll, 'New Tax Convention between the United States and Canada' (1942) 20 *Taxes* 459, 464; MB Carroll, 'Tax Convention with France' (1948) 26 *Taxes* 952, 953; EP King, 'Fiscal Cooperation in Tax Treaties' [1948] *Taxes* 889, 893; AB Rado, 'The Tax Conventions between the United States and Italy' (1959) 14 *Tax Law Review* 203, 220. The comparison between nominee and real owner performed by Surrey is particularly of note, especially in his capacity as Assistant Secretary of the Treasury. S Surrey, 'The United States Tax System and International Tax Relationships' (1964) 17 *Tax Executive* 104, 139.

[55] s 507.30 (c) of TD 6898, 1966-2, CB 567.

[56] See 'Article 4. Dividends' in the Technical Explanation to the 1966 Protocol to the 1945 United States–United Kingdom Convention, where it explicitly states that adding beneficial ownership to the convention adds nothing as it was previously considered as implicit.

[57] See s II.B in ch 2 above.

[58] In this sense, the examples given at the OECD in the UK proposal that led to the introduction of the concept in the OECD Model resemble the examples given by the USA in this early period. See the concern on nominees in third countries in 'Observations of Member Countries on difficulties raised by the OECD Draft Convention on Income and Capital' [TFD/FC/216], Fiscal Committee, OCDE, 9 May 1967, p 14, OECD Archives, Paris, and compare it to the references in n 52 above. Especially compare the references to 'acting on account' in 'Report on suggested amendments to Articles 11 and 12 of the Draft Convention, relating to interest and royalties respectively' [FC/WP27 (70) 1], Working Party 27, Fiscal Committee, OECD, 16 February 1970, p 14; OECD Archives, Paris; 'Conference in Ottawa – September 21, 22 and 23, 1953', 1 October 1953, pp 2–3; Foreign Taxation – Canada; Box 37; Office of the Tax Legislative Council, subject files 1936–1972, Asst Secretary Tax Policy [RG 56 NN3 56 94 005]; National Archives at College Park, College Park, MD.

[59] See above, n 56.

treaty entitlement was dependent on beneficial ownership principles.[60] The well-known *Aiken Industries* case proves the application of beneficial owner principles to US tax treaties – even though it followed the later anti-avoidance understanding of the term, as will be seen later.[61] To sum up, the collection mechanism using beneficial ownership or actual ownership was a consequence of the requirement to be implicit in the treaty, and not a stand-alone requirement.

This makes a withholding scheme and the set of regulations governing it relevant for two reasons. First, these Treasury regulations serve as proof of the assumption that beneficial owner domestic principles are implicitly included in tax treaties, as they explicitly provide for the treaty to apply under the beneficial/actual owner condition and the nominee/agent/fiduciary antonym is excluded. Note that such Treasury decisions do not introduce the concept, but simply reflect what is considered to be common practice. Secondly, because these withholding regulations will be the base from which beneficial ownership will be explicitly included in the 1966 Protocol to the 1944 United States–United Kingdom Double Tax Convention, they connect modern beneficial ownership with its early origin. In this sense, it provides proof of its meaning.

(ii) The First Period: Exclusion of Nominees and Agents and the Certainty Principle in Tax Treaties

The first set of regulations on those mechanisms, those referring to treaties signed between 1936 and 1945, provide a narrow negative definition of actual owners that excludes agents and nominees from limited withholding tax at source provided by the treaty.[62] The definition of agents and nominees is the commanding issue.

In a loose sense, the term nominees probably referred to financial custodians holding shares for the benefit of their clients.[63] During the period when these regulations were approved, the word nominee was widely used in this context in relation to such financial intermediaries because of the increased use of these arrangements to hold and manage stock investment.[64]

[60] See 'Article 13. Assistance in Collection' in the Technical Explanation to the 1966 Protocol to the 1945 United States–United Kingdom Convention, in connection to s 507.23 of TD 6898, 1966-2, CB 567. See also matching provisions in n 45 above.

[61] Even though the applicable treaty did not explicitly include the beneficial owner test, the ruling seemingly derives implicit beneficial ownership from the interpretation of income being 'received'. *Aiken Industries, Inc v Commissioner* (1971) 56 TC 925 (USTC). See Y Brauner, 'Beneficial Ownership in and Outside US Tax Treaties' in Lang et al (n 9) 146; PN James, 'Aiken Industries Revisited' (1986) 64 *Taxes* 131, 137.

[62] As an example, see s 7.507 of TD 5532, 1946-2, CB 73 on the 1945 United States–United Kingdom Tax Convention: 'SEC. 7.507. Addressee not actual owner.–If the recipient in the United Kingdom of the dividend is a nominee or agent through whom the dividend flows to a person other than the person … such recipient in the United Kingdom will withhold an additional tax equivalent to 15 per cent of the gross … The amounts so withheld by the withholding agent in the United Kingdom will, … be deposited with the United Kingdom Board of Inland Revenue, … The Board of Inland Revenue have arranged that they will, on or before the end of the calendar month in which such deposit is so made with the Board, remit by draft in United States dollars the amounts so deposited to the collector of internal revenue, Baltimore, Md'. Similarly, Art 4 of TD 4766, 1937-2, CB 158 in relation to 1935 Canada–United States Tax Convention; s 7.15 of TD 5157, 1942-2 CB 137 on Art XX. II of the 1942 United States–Canada Tax Convention.

[63] See the nominee account in Garner (n 22) 22.

[64] 'Trust Shares and the Nominee Problem in New York' (1938) 48 *Yale Law Journal* 106; JO Kamm, 'American Trading in Foreign Securities' (1951) 6 *Journal of Finance* 406; SR Bross, 'The United States

From a legal technical point of view, however, the term nominee seems to have no universal meaning.[65] *Black's Law Dictionary* notes it is a person designated to act in place of another in a very limited way, or a party who holds bare legal title for the benefit of others who receives and distributes the funds.[66] However, this does not define which legal title defines a nominee, leaving the issue open. As stated before, whether the term nominee refers to both trust and agency cases or just the latter is controversial.[67]

A clear departure point is that a nominee refers to intermediaries with very few powers.[68] This might be the case of a bare trust or a very limited agency. Even though the majority view in US private law is that nominee refers to agency arrangements, the different context in which it appears in tax treaties raises doubts as to whether it is applicable to treaties.

The options for interpretation of the nominee exclusion in such Treasury decisions would be arrangements where the intermediary has very few powers (i) only in agency arrangements or (ii) in agency, trust and other arrangements. A third option may be that a nominee could be a mere registered owner with no legal ownership.[69]

The second part of the definition, referring to agents, leaves it unclear as to whether it supplements or just clarifies the nominees' exclusion. If one takes the exclusion under the test to refer to the common characteristics of agents and nominees, this would only limit agencies to common law contracts, and does not include trust cases. A second option is for agency wording to supplement nominee exclusion so that agents with broader powers than a mere nominee-agent are also excluded. However, this does not clarify whether trust cases are excluded or not upon the nominee exclusion as independent from the agency word.

Such regulations do, however, exclude agents and nominees to the extent 'through whom income flows to a person non-entitled'.[70] What seems to be relevant is that the arrangement allows a third party to derive the income where the intermediary holds few or no powers other than holding the securities and passing the income.[71] The rule will

Borrower in the Eurobond Market – A Lawyer's Point of View' (1969) 34 *Law and Contemporary Problems* 172, 200. See also Van Weeghel, quoting *Macmillan v MNR* in S Van Weeghel, *The Improper Use of Tax Treaties* (Kluwer 1998) 58. References to the problem of nominees in the sense of bank custodians at the time are also found in the National Archives. Disclosure of beneficial ownership of shares held by nominees, in Royal Commission on the Press (1961–1962): Evidence and Papers (TNA 252/6); 'Disclosure of Beneficial Ownership of Shareholdings Registered in Names of Nominees', Draft Amendment of Defence Regulation 80A, War Cabinet: Home Policy Committee, later Legislation Committee, and Sub-Committees: Minutes and Papers (HPC and Other Series) (TNA CAB 75/9/32).

[65] Van Weeghel (n 64) 58.

[66] Garner (n 22) 1211.

[67] See notes above and accompanying text.

[68] See fn 171 and accompanying text in ch 2 above. See also C Du Toit, *Beneficial Ownership of Royalties in Bilateral Tax Treaties* (IBFD, 1999) 215, especially the reference to how a nominee may have little power and bear some risk.

[69] However, registration can provide ownership evidence with *erga omnes* effects, so in many cases registered ownership may be equated to legal ownership except that the former cannot be argued against actual legal ownership with legal title in common law. In addition, equity law may be vested in the common law owner or in a third party. See the distinction used between registered, legal, title and colloquial ownership in fn 241 and accompanying text in ch 3 above.

[70] See above, n 62.

[71] See the references in nn 41 and 52 above, where treasury negotiators are clearly afraid of the intermediary just passing the income to third countries with no role.

exclude both bare trustees and nominees, but only where they have no powers and they pass the income, or have the obligation to do so. It is likely that the issue was dealing with intermediaries acting in their own name, but on behalf of third parties and with few or no powers, as shown by the translation of nominees in the Treasury Regulation with the Netherlands, where the Dutch version notes that nominees are persons acting as intermediaries 'in their own name'.[72] The specific arrangement would be less relevant, so the rule would cover indirect agencies, bare trusts and any other arrangements, but in the latter only where they perform duties like agents or nominees. The key issue is the limited powers. The treatment of fiduciaries and partnerships under those Treasury regulations confirms this view.

Treasury decisions also exclude fiduciaries and partnerships from treaty benefits and make them withhold the difference between the treaty rate and the statutory rate only if they act as a nominee or agent.[73] The decisions also clarify that fiduciaries and partnerships receiving the income in their own right and passing it under the trust deed or partnership agreement conditions do not need to withhold the difference between the statutory rate and the reduced treaty rate.[74] Taking into account the fact that fiduciaries could include trusts – and the decisions explicitly refer to trust deeds – this confirms that the agent and nominee exclusion refers to both intermediary arrangements in common law and equity, where the agent, nominee or trust has no powers so their role is to merely hold and pass the income. Conversely, it does not exclude other active fiduciaries or intermediaries that are resident in the contracting state and receive income in their own right – that is, in the right of the trust – and distribute under the trust deed to third country beneficiaries from tax benefits. This would be the case of, for instance, discretionary trusts.[75]

Slightly differently, the Treasury decision on the 1945 United States–United Kingdom Convention made fiduciaries' and partnerships' treaty entitlement dependent on whether they are subject to tax on the income in the other country – the UK.[76] However, as far as the USA interpreted the subject to tax definition of the Treasury decision in the sense of their domestic allocation rules, it would have made little difference. In addition, because active fiduciaries were normally taxed in the UK in the hands of the trustee, those fiduciaries would be able to access treaty benefits on their own residence conditions.[77]

Historical documents also confirm this interpretation. Most negotiation documents, Treasury internal memorandums and other documentation locate the issue in banks and financial custodians holding securities for their clients.[78] In many of these cases

[72] Nominee is translated as *op eigen naam handelend tussenpersoon*, literally acting intermediary in his own name. See s 7.807 (b) of TD 5690, 1949-1, CB 92 on the 1947 United States–Netherlands Tax Convention.

[73] See Art 4(a) of TD 4766, 1937-2, CB 158 in relation to 1935 Canada–United States Tax Convention; ss 7.11 and 7.15 of TD 5157, 1942-2, CB 137 on Art XX.II of the 1942 United States–Canada Tax Convention; s 7.507 of TD 5532, 1946-2, CB 73 of the 1945 United States–United Kingdom Tax Convention.

[74] See Art 4(a) of TD 4766, 1937-2, CB 158 in relation to 1935 Canada–United States Tax Convention; ss 7.11 and 7.15 of TD 5157, 1942-2, CB 137 on Art XX.II of the 1942 United States–Canada Tax Convention.

[75] Ehrenzweig and Koch (n 37) 55.

[76] See s 7.507 of TD 5532, 1946-2, CB 73 on 1945 United States–United Kingdom Tax Convention.

[77] See s II.A.iii in ch 3 above.

[78] See references to banks and custodian accounts as the problem the withholding obligations wanted to tackle. See 'Custodian Accounts'; Withholding Tax; Box 84; 'Canadian Bank Problems'; 'Report of Proceedings

the use of such custodians was to solve problems with transfers, with the need to make non-transmissible shares transmissible, with the need to speed up transmissions that directly would take weeks, or, in relation to trusts and partnerships, who had some limitations on holding securities directly.[79] The issue had made the use of nominees for holding shares extensive for both domestic and foreign investors since the 1930s.[80] Conversely, domestic nominee cases posed few problems because financial regulation was increasingly requiring US banks and other financial institutions to provide information on the beneficial owner. If there were domestic non-nominee agents, they would probably be required to include the income in their tax return.[81] Historical documents directly show banks located abroad, where the USA had little or no information, and even counterparties' countries had no information in many cases.[82]

The result is that Treasury decisions and treaties were dealing with indirect agents or simple trusts with no powers over the assets or income, such as banks, while active trusts or other intermediary arrangements did not come within the purview of such rules. On the contrary, active intermediaries were probably able to access treaty benefits.

To sum up, the beneficial ownership principle in tax treaties – or actual ownership – was defined in this early period as the person with the greatest interest over a thing opposed to the world at large, including primary rights to income and control, which can be claimed either in common law or equity. In other words, beneficial ownership is interpreted in Miller terms as substantive law ownership.[83] If equitable rights to control and income override a common law right, substantive law ownership on the relevant

at Berne, March 13–16, 1953'; Switzerland; Box 38; 'Treasury decision – Withholding regulations under the income tax convention with the United Kingdom', 13 October 1966; United Kingdom; Box 39. All of them in Office of the Tax Legislative Council, subject files 1936–1972, Asst Secretary Tax Policy [RG 56 NN3 56 94 005], National Archives at College Park, College Park, MD; Joint Committee on Internal Revenue Taxation, *Legislative History of United States Tax Conventions* (n 1) 651, 1008; s 7.501. (d) of TD 5532, 1946-2, CB 73 on 1945 United States–United Kingdom Tax Convention. See also, more recently, 'Article 10: Dividends' in Technical Explanation to the 1975 Tax Convention between the United States and United Kingdom as amended by the 1976 and 1977 Protocols.

[79] 'Custodian Accounts'; Withholding Tax; Box 84; Office of the Tax Legislative Council, subject files 1936–1972, Asst Secretary Tax Policy [RG 56 NN3 56 94 005]; 'Tuesday, September 24, 1945'; Foreign Taxation: Luxembourg; 'September 23, 1946'; Foreign Taxation: Belgium. Both in Box 26; Office of the Tax Policy, subject files [RG 56-90-73 131-14-6-3]. All of them at National Archives at College Park. On the development of the nominee mechanism to speed up transfer, avoid costs, avoid certain limitations and acquisitions of shares, see Brauner (n 61).

[80] Brauner (n 61) 106; JM Niehuss, 'Foreign Investment in the United States: A Review of Governmental Policy' (1975) 16 *Virginia Journal of International Law* 65, 77 et seq; Kamm (n 64).

[81] 'Proposals Regarding the Problem of Foreign Capital Inflow', 19 January 1937, p 6; Box 12/44; General record of the Department of Treasury, Office of the Tax Policy, subject files [RG 56 NN3 56 94 005] [56 -90-41]; National Archives at College Park, College Park, MD.

[82] See n 48 above. See also 'Notes on Memorandum Dated January 31,1951 Prepared by the Swiss Federal Administration and Accompanying Papers, Including Proposed Swiss Regulations Under the Pending United States–Switzerland Income Tax Convention'; Switzerland; Box 38; Office of the Tax Legislative Council, subject files 1936–1972, Asst Secretary Tax Policy [RG 56 NN3 56 94 005]; references to lack of information in relation to bearer shares or nominees in France or Belgium in Foreign Taxation: Belgium, in Box 26; Office of the Tax Policy, Subject files [RG 56-90-73 131-14-6-3]; France; Box 38; Office of the Legislative Council, subject files 1936–1972, Asst Secretary Tax Policy [RG 56 Entry 67A1804]. All of them at National Archives at College Park, College Park, MD.

[83] JE Miller, 'The Nominee Conundrum: The Live Dummy Is Dead, but the Dead Dummy Should Live!' (1978) 34 *Tax Law Review* 213, 216–220. Seefn 241 and accompanying text in ch 3 above.

item will lay with the equitable owner; while if there is no overriding equitable right, equitable and common law rights would, in principle, be vested in the single and unique owner.

During this first period, discretionary trusts, partnerships where partners have no direct right to assets or income, and other similar arrangements where beneficiaries lack such a direct and great interest were considered to be beneficial owners for tax treaty purposes and, under prescribed regulations, had the right to enjoy reduced rates if their address was in the other contracting state, irrespective of the arrangement deriving the income later to a resident in a third country. As the only ascertained person at the time of the income to be received is the fiduciary, irrespective of whether he or she only has the right to control but no right to enjoy the assets or the income, no other person has any overriding right over his or her right. He or she has the greatest right. It follows, therefore, that he or she should be the beneficial owner in these cases.

If, however, a person holds a life interest, for instance, even though it cannot be said that he or she is the beneficial owner of the trust property, that person is the beneficial owner of the income as holding the primary right to income and the control of such income – but not the assets – so they could be able to enjoy treaty benefits insofar as they are resident in the relevant contracting state.[84] The result is clearly consistent with the allocation of income under the principles developed in the previous chapter. As the Treasury explicitly stated at an early stage, it considered agents or trusts to be performing as 'mere conduits', and not as trusts or intermediaries with active roles.[85] The problem was with the exchange of information, which, in the case of indirect agencies and bare trusts, was clearly disregarded from a US tax perspective, and tax consequences were directly allocated to the beneficiaries.

(iii) The Second Period: Exclusion of Agents, Nominees, Trusts and Fiduciaries Distributing Income, the Uncertainty Principle and the Economic Principle in Tax Treaties

The US view soon changed, as reflected in Treasury decisions. The scope of exclusion of treaty entitlement under the beneficial owner–actual owner principle was broadened. First, Treasury regulations on treaties signed after 1949 excluded nominees and representatives from treaty benefits.[86] The change of the wording from agent to

[84] J Avery Jones and et al, 'The Treatment of Trusts under the OECD Model Convention – II' [1989] *British Tax Review* 65, 70.

[85] Letter from the Commissioner to Mr William H Taylor, US Treasury Representative in London, 25 January 1945; Box 38; Office of the Legislative Council, subject files 1936–1972, Asst Secretary Tax Policy [RG 56 Entry 67A1804], National Archives at College Park, College Park, MD.

[86] As an example, s 7.607 of TD 5957, 1953-1, CB 238 on 1948 United States–New Zealand Tax Convention: 'Sec. 7.607. Addressee not actual owner: If the recipient in New Zealand of any dividend from sources within the United States, … is a nominee or representative through whom such dividend flows to a person other than one described in s 7.601(a) as being entitled to such reduced rate, such recipient in New Zealand shall withhold an additional amount of United States tax …'. With the same wording: s 7.906 of TD 5692, 1949-1, CB 104 on 1948 United States–Denmark Tax Convention; s 7.1007 of TD 5897, 1952-1 CB, 89, on 1951 United States–Ireland Convention; s 7.307 of TD 5867, 1951-2, CB 75 on 1951 United States–Switzerland; s 501.8 of TD 6108, 1954-2, CB 614 on 1953 Australia–United States Convention; s 512.3 of TD 6215, 1956-2, CB 1105 on 1955 Italy–United States Convention; s 7.1107 of TD 6056, 1954-1, CB 132 on 1953

representatives apparently widens the persons excluded from the category of beneficial owner for tax treaty purposes.

In addition, the Treasury decisions point out that fiduciaries and partnerships who distribute income to their beneficiaries acting differently from an agent or representative – that is, under their agreement or in any other form – also do not qualify as beneficial owners or actual owners, and their residence does not count for tax treaty purposes, so, if the beneficiaries are not resident in the contracting state, additional withholding up to the statutory rate is required.[87] As previous regulations allowed such fiduciaries or partnerships to act on their own and to pass the income under their respective deed or agreement, and still access treaty benefits, it follows that these second period decisions broadened beneficial owner exclusions.

In addition, these regulations recognise that non-resident beneficiaries of US trusts and estates may qualify as actual owners, but to qualify for treaty benefits they have to fulfil the rest of the requirements, and the item of income has to be included in their distributive share of income of such estate or trust.[88] The requirement connects treaty entitlement to the distributed income as defined by the Internal Revenue Code, that is, as the income that has to be allocated to the beneficiary, and as opposed to the income allocated to the trust that will be deducted.[89]

Under these regulations, non-resident beneficiaries of US discretionary trusts distributing income will be entitled to treaty benefits insofar as assigned income

United States–Belgium Convention; s 507.503 of TD 6437, 1960-1, CB 767 on the Protocol of extension of the 1945 United States–United Kingdom Convention to territories; and s 507.23 of TD 6898, 1966-2, CB 567 on the 1945 United States–United Kingdom Convention as amended by the 1966 Protocol. Within this period, only the Regulation on the 1947 United States–Netherlands tax convention maintains the wording 'nominee or agents' to define intermediaries excluded from beneficial ownership condition to access treaty tax limitations at source. However, the rest of such regulation on fiduciaries and partnerships also fits within this second period as compared to the first period. The use of agents instead of representatives as with the other regulations of this second period probably is due to the specific type of intermediaries covered in the Netherlands and mentioned in the regulation as *gemachtigde*. See s 7.807 (b) of TD 5690, 1949-1, CB 92.

[87] See, as an example, s 7.607 of TD 5957, 1953-1, CB 238 on 1948 United States–New Zealand Tax Convention: 'Sec. 7.607. Addressee Not Actual Owner. … In any case in which a fiduciary or partnership with an address in New Zealand receives, otherwise than as a nominee or representative, a dividend from sources within the United States with respect to which United States tax at the reduced rate of 15 percent has been withheld at source pursuant to s 7.601(d), if a beneficiary of such fiduciary or a partner in such partnership is not entitled to the reduced rate of tax provided in Article VI(1) of the convention, the fiduciary or partnership shall withhold an additional amount of United States tax with respect to the portion of such dividend included in such beneficiary's share of the distributed or distributable income, or in such partner's distributive share of the income, of such fiduciary or partnership, as the case may be. The amount of the additional tax is to be calculated in the same manner as under the immediately preceding paragraph. …'. See respective sections on the same issue in decisions with other countries mentioned in n 86 above.

[88] As an example, s 7.609 of TD 5957, 1953-1, CB 238 on 1948 United States–New Zealand Tax Convention: 'Sec. 7.609. Beneficiaries of a Domestic Estate or Trust.–A nonresident alien who is resident in New Zealand for the purposes of New Zealand tax and who is a beneficiary of a domestic estate or trust shall be entitled to the exemption from, or reduction in the rate of, United States tax provided in Articles VI, VIII, and XII of the convention with respect to dividends and film rentals to the extent such item or items are included in his share of the distributed or distributable income of such estate or trust. In order to be entitled in such instance to the exemption from, or reduction in the rate of, withholding of United States tax such beneficiary must otherwise satisfy the requirements of these respective Articles of the convention and must, where applicable, execute and submit to the fiduciary of such estate or trust in the United States the letter of notification prescribed in s 7.604(b)'. See respective sections on the same issue in decisions with other countries mentioned in n 86 above.

[89] See s 162 (b) of the Internal Revenue Code, 1939.

is considered as distributed income and allocated to that beneficiary under Internal Revenue Code rules, and that those beneficiaries meet treaty requirements. Conversely, if a discretionary trust does not distribute an item of income, or distributions are not considered as distributed income under the Internal Revenue Code, income would not be entitled to treaty reduced tax rates dependent upon the residence of the beneficiary. This makes sense, as following the same principles as internal law makes treaty application and domestic allocation consistent.

Therefore, these regulations recognised the introduction of the anti-avoidance or economic principle in the allocation of income in tax treaty cases, allocating income and treaty consequences to the person factually benefiting from the income if it is possible to define them.[90] Previously, the use of the certainty or uncertainty principle allocated income and tax treaty consequences to the person benefiting from the trust or partnership if it could be defined in advance – such as in bare trusts – or to the person controlling the income if it could be not be ascertained – discretionary trusts. However, the introduction of the economic principle made it possible to allocate treaty consequences to the person effectively benefiting from the trust or partnership irrespective of his or her ability to actually control the income as it arises.

The use of the factual or economic benefit principle as supplementing the uncertainty principle is confirmed by *Maximov v US*.[91] In the case of a trustee resident in the USA for beneficiaries resident in the UK, the court held that as the income was retained in a – presumably accumulation – trust and was not distributed to the beneficiaries, the exemption of source taxation was not applicable.

However, because these regulations follow US domestic allocation principles, they led to several mismatches. For instance, following the general rule on those regulations on fiduciaries and partnerships, if a trust distributes income under the relevant deed, the trust would be disregarded because the relevant income and treaty requirements have to be fulfilled by the beneficiary in order to apply the treaty. However, if the other contracting state taxes the trust, multiple taxation will not be eliminated, and it is possible that triple taxation may arise if the beneficiary is resident in a third state.

This happened under the 1942 Canada–United States Income Tax Treaty, where the USA was applying the economic or anti-avoidance principles in the case of a discretionary trust in Canada deriving income from the USA whose income was allocated for US tax purposes and tax treaty purposes to a resident in a third state. In that case, the USA wold tax the income at source, as it derived from sources in the USA of a resident of a non-contracting state insofar as such income would be distributed income under their rules.[92] However, Canada would also tax it as derived by a non-resident alien.[93]

[90] See s II.B in ch 2 above.

[91] *Maximov v US* (1963) 373 US 49 (USSC).

[92] See 'Income from Trusts' in the Memorandum accompanying the Proposal of the 1957 Protocol, 1957-2, CB 1014, 1957. See also '(4) Foreign income of an estate or trust for distribution to a foreigner' pp 3–4; Foreign Taxation – Canada; Box 37; Office of the Tax Legislative Council, subject files 1936–1972, Asst Secretary Tax Policy [RG 56 NN3 56 94 005]; National Archives at College Park, College Park, MD.

[93] ss 96 and 98 of the Income Tax Act, 1948, c 52 (11-12 George VI) (Canada). Now ss 212(1) and 215(1) of the Income Tax Act, RSC 1985, c 1 (5th Supp) (Canada). However, some treaties, such as the current 1980 United States–Canada Tax Convention provides for the elimination of withholding tax for Canadian taxation on income derived by non-residents in Canada from a Canadian trust if the income was originally

Conversely, if a trust in Canada for the benefit of a US resident derived income from the UK, Canada would tax the trust and the USA would not give a credit for the tax paid as the income would be derived from the UK as far as the USA would be concerned.[94] The problem was solved by including a new paragraph in the Convention stating that Canada would follow the principles of US law for tax treaty purposes on allocation of income to trusts.[95] But this is just an example of the mismatches generated by the US application of their domestic allocation principles, namely beneficial ownership, to tax treaty scenarios for both inbound and outbound income.

In the 1950s, slight changes were made to Treasury regulations governing treaty entitlement of beneficiaries from US trusts and estates. Now it was explicitly stated that beneficiaries of domestic trusts may be entitled to treaty benefits if items of income were included in the gross income of the beneficiaries and they fulfil treaty requirements.[96] The rule follows what was already mentioned in relation to fiduciaries and partnerships, connecting treaty entitlement to allocation of income to the beneficiary under US allocation principles. It may be considered doubtful whether the rule simply clarifies what was already clear under the previous rules on fiduciaries or introduces a new rule. The author's view, as shown by US case law and practice, is that the allocation requirement in both cases referred to already applicable US principles.

The 1966 Protocol to the 1945 United Kingdom–United States Tax Convention may be considered as the final step in consolidating the evolution of beneficial ownership towards allocation of income principles. Treasury regulations to the Protocol followed the scheme developed after 1949, including the requirement for the income of beneficiaries of domestic trusts to be included in their gross income.[97] To this extent, the regulation of this tax treaty was the same as for previous ones.

What was new was that beneficial ownership wording and the assistance in collection mechanism were explicitly included in the treaty itself.[98] However, as the Technical Memorandum recognised, this made no change to the USA, as it already considered the principle to be implicit in previous treaties, so the inclusion was not actually new to the

sourced outside Canada. See ES Roth et al, *Canadian Taxation of Trusts* (Canadian Tax Foundation, 2016) 891, 904–07.

[94] See n 92 above.

[95] See Art XIII E of the 1942 United States–Canada Tax Convention as amended by the 1957 Protocol. See also 'Income from Trusts' in the Memorandum accompanying the Proposal of the 1957 Protocol, 1957-2, CB 1014, 1957.

[96] See s 501.8 (2) of TD 6108, 1954-2, CB 614, 1954 on the 1953 United States–Australia Tax Convention. In the same sense, see corresponding sections of subsequent Treasury decisions on treaties with Australia, Italy, Switzerland and the UK in n 37 above. See also s 507.509(a) of TD 6437, 1960-1, CB 767, 1959 on the 1945 United States–United Kingdom Tax Convention as amended by the 1957 Protocol; and s 517-6 of the TD 6431, 1960, on the 1959 Tax Convention between Pakistan and the United States. In such cases it is also required, in addition to the income being included in the gross amount, that it is *paid, credited, or required to be distributed by the estate or trust to the beneficiary.* However, the first requirement probably made little difference, as the relevant point for tax treaty entitlement was to allocate the income. That is probably the reason why such a second requirement was eliminated.

[97] See s 507.23 of TD 6898, 1966-2, CB 567, 1966 on the 1945 United States–United Kingdom Tax Convention as amended by the 1966 Protocol.

[98] See Arts VI, VII and VIII of the 1945 United States–United Kingdom Tax Convention as amended by the 1966 Protocol.

US application of the treaty.[99] Nevertheless, these explicit references made a real change to the UK side of the Convention.

It is interesting that the Technical Memorandum clarifies that a trust cannot qualify as the beneficial owner of dividends received if it is not required to distribute, and does not in fact do so.[100] The question here is whether there is a two-test requirement for a fiduciary with some powers, such as a discretionary trust. For beneficial ownership, should a fiduciary both not be obliged to and not distribute in fact, or is there simply a single test of not distributing or assigning the income? From the Treasury regulations, the latter seems to be the case. The relevant point here is to assign the income or distribute it in fact as otherwise, if the fiduciary is obliged to pass the income, it will fall within the exclusion of the general agent or representative passing the income. If this were the case, the treaty understanding of the Treasury would follow the economic or anti-avoidance domestic beneficial ownership principle.

So far, it seems that beneficial ownership was understood in this second step on the US side to be following US domestic allocation principles, thus excluding intermediaries under the certainty principle, and the uncertainty sub-principle subject to the overriding economic or anti-avoidance principle. By doing so, the beneficial ownership principles in tax treaties were broadened to include in some cases colloquial or common speech ownership as per the Miller terms.[101]

If income was assigned to the beneficiary under discretion or power, particularly in the case of foreign fiduciaries, the beneficiary would be taken as the beneficial owner for tax treaty purposes, irrespective of whether he or she had no power over the income when it arose to the fiduciary, or whether the other country taxes the income or even allocates the income to him or her. In these cases, the beneficiary has a colloquial or factual power on the income once assigned but, at the time the income was paid to the fiduciary, they had no right, as if they claimed from the original payor his or her right to the income, it would not be granted as subject to the fiduciary decision, as the actual right against the original income payor is in the fiduciary. Conversely, in some cases where fiduciaries cannot be regarded as equitable or legal owners, they may be treated as such for tax treaty purposes if the income is effectively retained in their hands, even in cases where income is taxed on the beneficiaries, such as in the case of grantor trusts.[102] By doing so, tax law was following what was happening or how the income was flowing factually, irrespective of the tax treatment in the other contracting state, but matching the principles the USA was using in its domestic rules to allocate income.

However, these rules do not refer treaty allocation directly to domestic allocation of income principles, but to fiduciaries distributing or not distributing income. As domestic allocation rules also refer to fiduciaries distributing or not distributing income, both refer to the same events. What is relevant is that the US Treasury was looking at treaty application through its domestic allocation glasses.

[99] See n 56 above.
[100] See n 56 above.
[101] See n 83 above.
[102] However, it is doubtful if the USA would allocate the income to the grantor in these cases also following their domestic allocation rules. In any case, there still might be cases where USA tax law taxes income in the hands of beneficiaries in the other country even though the trustee retains the control of the income.

(iv) *The Moline Properties Test in Tax Treaty Cases: The Beneficial Ownership Anti-avoidance Allocation Principle in Tax Treaties*

More proof of how beneficial ownership principles in US tax treaties were interpreted as following domestic allocation principles is the way case law treated intermediary corporations. In the cases with intermediary companies in treaty counterparties countries, the Treasury based their arguments on the nominee and disregarded theories developed for allocation of income in domestic intermediary companies cases.[103] Internal Treasury memorandums on treaty cases held that closely held corporations or wholly owned corporations were disregarded by the Treasury for tax treaty purposes as straw corporations having no business purpose or as sham, using the same wording as used in domestic case law on interposed companies.[104]

One case showing the application to tax treaties of domestic beneficial ownership principles as combined with the business purpose test was the 1961 case *USA v Johansson*.[105] In the case, Ingemar Johansson, a Swedish professional heavyweight boxer, was assessed on the income obtained in the USA from prizes from competitions or performances, and other income from his public appearances or the use of his name in shows, exhibitions and commercials. Among other issues, income from the use of Johansson's name and appearance was allocated to a corporation in Switzerland.[106] The District Court held, and the Circuit Court confirmed, that the corporation had no business purpose and was a mere sham, following the domestic disregard theory, and Johansson was retaining the full economic benefit of it and exercised complete control, so the income had to be allocated to Johansson and not the corporation.[107] It followed that the application of the tax treaty between the USA and Switzerland had to be verified on the boxer and not his company.

In *Perry Bass*, in 1968, an individual and his wife, both residents and citizens of the USA, incorporated a Swiss corporation and transferred to it their undivided interest in oil-producing properties.[108] As a consequence, even though the ruling does not explicitly mention it, presumably payments to the corporation were exempted or enjoyed USA–Switzerland tax treaty reduced withholding rates. The Commissioners challenged the corporation on the basis of lacking any business purpose so as to avoid taxation, and challenged the corporation as having no business activity as their directors had no experience in the sector even though the shareholders did.[109] The Tax Court, however, ruled, on the basis of *Moline Properties* and *National Carbide*, that the corporation was valid as it was performing an actual business activity, and that the fact that the owner retained direction of the activity was not sufficient to disregard it.[110]

[103] See ch 3 above.

[104] Memorandum by Stanley S Surrey, p 9; Tax Treaties general; Box 39; Office of the Legislative Council, subject files 1936–1972, Asst Secretary Tax Policy [RG 56 NN3 56 94 005], National Archives at College Park, College Park, MD.

[105] *Ingemar Johansson, et al v US* (1964) 64-2 USTC 9743 (USCA, 5th); *US v Ingemar Johansson et al* (1961) 62-1 USTC 9130 (USDC Fla).

[106] *US v Ingemar Johansson et al* (n 105) paras 17–18.

[107] ibid Facts 18, 19, 20, Concl 4; *Ingemar Johansson, et al v US* (n 105).

[108] *Perry R Bass et al v Commissioner* (1968) 50 TC 595.

[109] ibid 600.

[110] ibid 600–01.

However, the most quoted case, and the one that most scholars consider a reflection of how beneficial ownership was applied in US tax law as implicitly contained in tax treaties, is *Aiken Industries*. In the case, Ecuatorian Corp Ltd (ECL), a Bahamian corporation, owned Aiken Industries, which in turn owned Mechanical Products Inc (MPI), a resident of the USA.[111] ECL gave a loan to MPI, indirectly its subsidiary, in exchange for promissory notes to be paid upon request.[112] However, there was no tax treaty at the time between the USA, where MPI was resident, and the Bahamas, so the interest paid on such promissory notes was subject to full withholding tax. To avoid such withholding, ECL indirectly incorporated another subsidiary, Industrias Hondureñas (Industrias), in Honduras, all of its capital being owned by Compañía de Cervezas Nacionales (CCN), resident in Ecuador and owned by ECL.[113] Subsequently, ECL assigned the promissory notes from MPI to Industrias in exchange for promissory notes from the latter.[114] The result was that the interest from the former promissory notes were now payable to Industrias (Honduras), instead of to ECL (Bahamas), so the interest payments were not subject to withholding tax but were exempted from source taxation under the United States–Honduras Tax Convention in force at the time.[115] Industrias, in turn, paid the same interest to ECL on the promissory notes given in exchange for the original promissory notes from MPI.[116]

First of all, the court recognised the validity of the Hondurian corporation and did not disregard it.[117] The court argued that the treaty defines who is able to access treaty reduced rates, and if the treaty states a validly constituted Hondurian corporation is a resident for tax treaty purposes and able to access treaty provisions, the Commissioners cannot disregard it.[118]

However, the court questioned whether the payments made to Industrias were 'received by' Industrias as a resident of Honduras as required under the United States–Honduras Tax Convention to access treaty reduced rates.[119] For such interpretation, the court held, following *Maximov v US*, the wording of a treaty had to be given a meaning consistent with the genuine shared expectations of the contracting parties, including in the analysis the whole context of the agreement.[120] It followed that 'received by' as a requirement to access treaty provisions had to be interpreted as the creditor receiving the income on its own and not with the obligation to transmit it to another.[121] From this perspective, the court analysed whether Industrias received the income on its own or for the benefit of ECL.

On this point, the court resorted to *Gregory v Helvering* and *Higgins v Smith*, and held that the transfer of promissory notes from ECL to Industrias lacked any valid

[111] *Aiken Industries, Inc v Commissioner* (1971) 56 TC 925, 926. See the commentary on the case in James (n 61).
[112] *Aiken Industries, Inc v Commissioner* (n 111) 926.
[113] ibid.
[114] ibid.
[115] ibid 927–29.
[116] ibid 934.
[117] ibid 932.
[118] ibid 931–32. The arguments are based on the interpretation of the treaty according to the sense given by the parties following *Maximov v US* (n 91).
[119] *Aiken Industries, Inc v Commissioner* (n 111) 933.
[120] ibid; *Maximov v US* (n 91).
[121] *Aiken Industries, Inc v Commissioner* (n 111) 933.

economic or business purpose, and that the only objective of such transaction was to take advantage of the Honduras–United States tax treaty.[122] The main question here is why the corporation could not be disregarded under business purposes as protected by the treaty while the transaction itself was considered to be disregardable. The key point was that 'received by' was not defined by the treaty, so the USA could define it under its domestic law, this including the *Gregory v Helvering* doctrine. Contrary to this, what a corporation was for treaty purposes was defined by the treaty itself, so domestic doctrines affecting qualification of the corporation, such as *Moline Properties*, were not applicable.

On these grounds, the court continued by saying that Industrias acted as a mere agent and did not received the interest on its own behalf.[123] It explicitly held that Industrias had no beneficial interest in the income and that such beneficial interest was to be found in ECL.[124] The court recognised Industrias as fully valid, but held that the transactions had no business purpose, so beneficial ownership remained in ECL. The result was that Industrias was held as not having 'received' the income in the terms of the treaty and consequently was not entitled to the treaty exemption, but MPI was subject to statutory withholding tax on the interest paid.

The combination of the agency theory and the disregard theory is also present in this case, matching domestic evolution of allocation rules.[125] The corporation was regarded as an intermediary for the payment, but the transaction was void as invalid, following the disregard line of cases. This is not surprising, as the court explictly recognised interpreting 'received by' as following domestic law, this seemingly including such anti-avoidance doctrines. In any case, what the court probably did, despite mentioning both disregarding and agency theories, was to requalify the transactions as an agency following their substance, disregarding the conveyance of beneficial ownership and not completely disregarding the transaction. In other words, it made a partial disregarding of the transaction under a sham doctrine that led to consideration of the transaction as an agency.

In *NIPSCO*, another leading case in US allocation of income in tax treaties, a similar approached was followed.[126] Northern Indiana Public Service Corporation (NIPSCO), established a corporation in Curaçao, Netherlands Antilles, named Northern Indiana Public Service Finance NV (Finance). The purpose of such entity was to issue notes in the Eurobond market to fund a construction project.[127] Finance issued notes to the value of approximately $70 million, which were sold in the Euromarket and listed in London and Dublin.[128] Subsequently, NIPSCO issued notes to a value of approximately $70 million, which were acquired by Finance with the proceeds from the Eurobond issuance. Some important points are that the Eurobonds issuance prospect was jointly subscribed by NIPSCO and Finance, and NIPSCO agreed not to reduce the net worth of Finance below a certain threshold to guarantee a minimum debt–equity ratio.[129]

[122] ibid 934.
[123] ibid.
[124] ibid.
[125] See s II.B.ii.b in ch 3 above.
[126] *Northern Indiana Public Service Co v Commissioner* [1995] USTC 24468-91, 105 TC 341; *Northern Indiana Public Service Co v Commissioner* [1997] USCA 7th Circ 96-1659, 96-1758, 115 F3d 506.
[127] *Northern Indiana Public Service Co v Commissioner* (n 126) 342.
[128] ibid 344.
[129] ibid.

In addition, NIPSCO assigned credits against its customers to Finance and agreed to perform as a mere collection agent for those customers to pass the income to Finance.

The main issue arising from the case was whether interest paid by NIPSCO to Finance was exempt from taxation at source under the United States–Netherlands Tax Convention as Finance was a resident of the Netherlands Antilles or if it was subject to ordinary withholding as interest was to be allocated to the bondholders around the world and Finance was a mere intermediary.[130] The Commissioners argued that Finance should have been disregarded and income allocated directly to the bondholders because Finance was a mere conduit or agent for the Eurobond issuance.[131] The court analysed the validity of Finance under the business purpose test as applied in *Moline Properties*, and held that Finance should be recognised as the recipient of interest paid to it by the petitioner because it was engaged in the business activity of borrowing and lending money at a profit.[132] However, it is the author's view that, even though it can be said that Finance should be considered the recipient of the interest at this very first point, the court probably meant that the corporation was valid and was able to be the recipient, even though this was subject to further analysis of its tax effects. The analysis of whether the income was actually to be allocated to Finance continued exactly from the point of the corporation being valid, but focused on whether the transaction was valid or Finance was to be a mere agent.

All subsequent arguments by the Commissioners that Finance was a mere conduit and income was allocated to the bondholders were denied by the Tax Court. The Tax Court held that Finance could not be a conduit on grounds of low capitalisation, as argued by the Commissioners, because there was no legal reference on proper capitalisation and more capital would change nothing regarding the business activity or finance arrangements performed by Finance.[133] In other words, capitalisation was of little help on its own in determining the validity of the business purpose of a corporation. In addition, it held that Eurobond holders entered into the bonds precisely under the used structure, and it is doubtful they would have lent their money if the issuance had been done directly by NIPSCO.[134] However, an important point that was finally made was that the court distinguished *NIPSCO* from *Aiken* in that in the former the bonds were acquired by third parties while in the latter all the arrangements were intra-group transactions. Moreover, Finance obtained a spread between the interest received and the interest paid to the bondholders, seemingly leading the court to conclude that Finance had a business activity and was acting on its own because it was profiting from the activity.[135]

At Appeal, the Commissioners held that the subsidiary was to be disregarded as a sham corporation following *Gregory v Helvering* or *Aiken Industries*, and abandoned the argument of considering the corporation as a mere conduit. However, the Court of Appeals held that the corporation had an actual activity and that disregarding under the

[130] ibid 347.
[131] ibid 347–48.
[132] *Northern Indiana Public Service Co v Commissioner* (n 126) 348.
[133] ibid 350.
[134] ibid 353.
[135] ibid 355.

business purpose test could only take place 'for lack of meaningful economic activity if the corporation is merely transitory, engaging in absolutely no business activity for profit – in other words, it is a "mere skeleton"'.[136] In addition, transactions could only be disregarded if the corporation 'lacks dominion and control over the interest payments it collects'.[137]

As Finance had actual activity, was managed as a viable concern, not simply as a lifeless façade, and derived a profit, it was fully valid under such doctrines. Even though the court conceded that Finance had minimal activity, it held that such activity was enough to consider it valid.[138] Finally, on the validity of the transaction, the Court of Appeals held that as Finance had the control, obtained benefit from its position and was independent from the lending parties – the opposite to *Aiken* – it was to be considered as valid.[139]

The case law mentioned above, especially that from the 1960s to 1970s, confirms that the allocation of income under tax treaties followed the beneficial ownership principles in domestic tax law as defined in the previous chapter, namely on the intermediary corporations doctrine. Looking at *Johansson*, the court relied on the subject retaining benefit and control, and the corporation being a sham, as held in *Moline Properties* and related jurisprudence. Similarly, in *Aiken*, it was held that ECL retained beneficial interest in the bonds, clearly connecting the issue to beneficial ownership. Even in *Perry Bass*, even though the court ruled in favour of the taxpayer, it was shown that the Treasury was using arguments developed in the case law dealing with straw corporations under domestic tax law to deal with tax treaties. In all these cases there was a parallelism in the use of intermediary corporations as in *Moline Properties*, *Bollinger* and *National Carbide*, and the arguments raised by the Treasury were not coincidentally the same; it is probable that the same principles were followed.

This is also confirmed by some internal Treasury memorandums arguing for the application of beneficial owner limitation to other cases not explicitly dealt with within the regulations. A significant memorandum states: 'If our laws are to be meaningful, assets of a corporation with no business purposes and controlled by the decedent must be treated as though legal title were in a nominee'.[140] Even though referring to estate tax treaties, it confirms the view that the Treasury had in mind of the straw corporations beneficial owner doctrine when it looked into tax treaties.

However, the *Aiken* argument about the inability of the business purpose test to reach corporations protected by the treaty may limit direct application of the business purpose test to the validity of foreign corporations. The solution was to requalify the relevant transaction at stake, which was not protected by the treaty as 'received by' was not defined by the treaty or subject to domestic definition, and to allocate the income to a different subject, with similar consequences. In all of the above cases, the parallelism between the evolution of domestic allocation of income principles under *Moline*

[136] *Northern Indiana Public Service Co v Commissioner* (n 126).
[137] ibid.
[138] ibid.
[139] ibid.
[140] Memorandum by Stanley S Surrey, p 10; Tax Treaties general; Box 39; Office of the Legislative Council, subject files 1936–1972, Asst Secretary Tax Policy [RG 56 NN3 56 94 005], National Archives at College Park, College Park, MD.

Properties and the subsequent jurisprudence and jurisprudence on allocation of income in treaty scenarios is self-evident.

(v) *Beneficial Ownership of What?*

From the previous analysis, it follows that beneficial ownership as an allocation of income principle in tax treaties differs from its uses in estate tax treaties or other reliefs. The main point of difference is that beneficial ownership on estate duties deals with assets, so when it is defined with reference to private law it refers to the person with outweighing primary rights to control and income either in common law or equity. However, in this use, beneficial ownership of income is required to reside in nominees, agents, trusts and other intermediaries in relation to the income. Therefore, it might be doubtful whether beneficial ownership in this use includes such primary rights to control and income over the asset, the income or both.

In the earlier period, when beneficial ownership referred to the income, we only need say that beneficial ownership must refer to the primary right to control the income as it arises.[141] Otherwise, treaty benefits will only be available to persons holding both the assets and the right to the income, and not cases where the bare or naked property may be vested in one person while the profits are assigned to another person.

In the second period, similarly, beneficial ownership could only refer to the income and not the assets from which it derived because Treasury regulations in cases like discretionary trusts provide for precise allocation of the income to the beneficiary – and the treaty entitlement test – if the income is assigned to him or her irrespective of the asset rights remaining with the trustee or to a third party.

Similarly, where beneficial ownership is defined by anti-avoidance rules, the business purpose test has to be performed on how the income is allocated, and speech or colloquial ownership has to be properly assessed on the income as different from the abilities on the subject matter. The *Aiken* case, referring the business purpose test to allocation of income and denying the ability to act on the validity of the corporation, confirms the US translation of the anti-avoidance business purpose test to treaty allocation of income and not the assets. However, the definition of dividends, interests, royalties or the relevant type of income may require the creditor to hold the assets for the income to qualify as such. But this derives from the definition of the relevant type of income and not from the beneficial owner principle.

(vi) *Beneficial Ownership in Tax Treaties: From Beneficial Ownership in Equity Law to Allocation of Income under Source State Domestic Law*

Taking the approach of both periods, one may wonder whether US tax treaty policy carried beneficial ownership from domestic policy into international tax agreements. The USA seemingly interpreted beneficial ownership as the person to whom income

[141] On the OECD beneficial owner meaning but clearly showing a common law sense of the concept in line with this early interpretations, Avery Jones et al (n 84) 70.

had to be allocated for tax purposes, who was the person holding the ability to pay.[142] In the author's view, there is a close resemblance between the interpretation of beneficial ownership and the evolution of the domestic tax position towards intermediaries. As the certainty and uncertainty principle and the anti-avoidance principle were being developed in domestic law, it was reflected in the application of international tax treaties.

Summarising the evolution of allocation in tax treaties to this point, in the author's view, in the first period, beneficial ownership in tax treaties as an allocation principle followed substantive law ownership, as shown by Treasury decisions implementing treaties from 1936 to 1945. Conversely, in the second period after 1949, beneficial ownership in tax treaties was understood as colloquial or common speech ownership following who was factually receiving the income under the certainty principle, and especially regarding intermediary corporations, as shown by Treasury decisions implementing treaties signed after 1945 and case law on the topic from the 1960s to the 1970s.

However, there remained issues, as using allocation principles for intermediaries resident in foreign jurisdictions led to multiple taxation or non-taxation, as argued above in the case of trusts in Canada.[143] Even though this specific issue with Canada was resolved through the amendment of the treaty, it did not resolve many other allocation mismatches derived from the USA allocating income under its domestic rules for tax treaty purposes, especially in cases where the USA was the source country.[144]

This is probably why the USA changed its view on the allocation of income in tax treaties. In the Technical Explanations issued in the 1970s, the USA started to define the treaty residence requirement in relation to trusts, estates and partnerships upon the income being subject to tax in the hands of the fiduciary or the beneficiaries resident in the other contracting state.[145] In the Technical Explanation to the 1975 United Kingdom–United States Tax Convention, the Treasury recognised that under US law partnerships will never be subject to tax and that trusts and estates will sometimes not be subject to tax, but, contrary to previous regulations, it recognised the failure of these rules to define the tax liability of fiduciary arrangements resident in other contracting states.[146] From the new view, only the law of residence could define whether beneficiaries and/or fiduciaries or partnerships were liable on the relevant income.

These explanations were made in connection to Article 4 on residence, and not in relation to dividends, interests and royalties, where the beneficial owner wording was used.

[142] The relationship between allocation of income, taxation and tax treaties may be seen in the beneficial ownership use in 'Third report on Tax Avoidance through the improper use or abuse of tax conventions', 21 December 1967, p 5 [FC/WP21 (67) 1], where the USA points to the beneficial owner as the person who reduces their tax burden through tax avoidance. Implicitly, it recognises the beneficial owner as the person showing the ability to pay.

[143] See n 92 above.

[144] See n 95 above.

[145] Amongst most of the treaties signed by the USA after 1975, see 'Article 4: Fiscal Residence', in Technical Explanation to the 1975 Tax Convention between the United States and United Kingdom as amended by the 1976 and 1977 Protocols; the same article in the Technical Explanation to the 1976 Tax Convention between the United States and Korea, 1979-2, CB 435; the same article in the Technical Explanation to the 1980 Tax Convention between the United States and Hungary, 1980-1, CB 354; the same article in the Technical Explanation to the 1980 Canada–United States Tax Convention, 1987-2, CB 298; and the same article in the Technical Explanation to the 1980 Tax Convention between the United States and Jamaica as amended in 1981, 1982-1, CB 291.

[146] See 'Article 4: Fiscal Residence' in Technical Explanation to the 1975 Tax Convention between the United States and United Kingdom as amended by the 1976 and 1977 Protocols.

But, given the words used (estates, trusts and partnerships), the explanation – that access to treaty benefits depended on the beneficiary or the trust being taxable in the other contracting state – and given that the consequences were the same as the ones given in previous treaties to actual owners and beneficial owners in relation to articles on dividends, interests and royalties – this Technical Explanation implicitly recognises how the USA linked beneficial ownership tax treaties principles and allocation rules. The Technical Explanation to the Treaty with Canada recognises the relationship between the residence requirement of trusts and the beneficial ownership test.[147] What is more surprising is how beneficial ownership is connected to a subject to tax requirement even though the subject to tax requirement was eliminated from the United States–United Kingdom Tax Conventions in the 1966 Protocol.[148] The relationship between the subject to tax test and the beneficial owner requirement will be revisited later.

Some time later, the USA would define beneficial ownership as it is referred to alongside domestic allocation rules in Technical Explanations. This simply confirms what has been shown in relation to the practice. What will not be entirely clear from the US treaty policy from the 1980s until 2006 is which country's allocation rules define beneficial ownership.

Initially, treaties would leave it to the domestic law of the contracting state, without specifying which one.[149] In turn, some treaties, such as the 1992 Netherlands–United States Treaty, specified that the beneficial owner is the person to whom income is allocated under the rules of the source state.[150] The argument was that the concept has to be defined by the contracting state applying the treaty, and in the case of reduced rates at source that is the source country. However, the 1996 Technical Explanation to the United States Model Convention defined beneficial ownership as the person to whom income is allocated under the rules of the state of residence.[151] In addition, the commentary to the residence article also defined the beneficial owner in relation to trusts as being the beneficiary if the state of residence treats the trust as fiscally transparent and allocates the income to such beneficiary, confirming beneficial ownership as residing in the person to whom income is allocated under the state of residence.[152] Technical Explanations to treaties signed by the USA after this date and until 2006 also followed this definition.[153]

However, the US position towards beneficial ownership changed again in the Technical Explanation to the 2006 United States Tax Convention and defined beneficial

[147] 'Article 4: Fiscal Residence' in the Technical Explanation to the 1980 Canada–United States Tax Convention, 1987-2, CB 298.

[148] See Arts VI, VII and VIII of the 1945 United States–United Kingdom Tax Convention before and after the amendments.

[149] See 'Article 10: Dividends', in Technical Explanation to the 1989 Tax Convention between the United States and Finland.

[150] Commentary to Art 10 of the Technical Explanation to the 1992 DTT between the United States of America and the Kingdom of the Netherlands and its 1993 Protocol.

[151] See Commentary to para 2 of Art 10 of the 1996 Model Technical Explanation to the United States Model Tax Convention.

[152] See commentary to para 1 of Article 4 of the Model Technical Explanation to the 1996 United States Model Tax Convention.

[153] Technical Explanations to the 1996 Treaty between the United States of America and Switzerland, the 1996 Treaty with Thailand, the 1998 Treaty with Estonia, the 1999 Treaty with Italy and the 1999 Treaty with Venezuela.

owner as the person to whom income was attributable under the laws of the source state.[154] Technical Explanations to treaties signed after that date defined the concept as such.[155]

This switch is probably related to the inclusion of paragraph 6 in Article 1 to deal with allocation mismatches, as the Commentary to Article 4 drops the references to beneficial ownership and the Commentary to Article 1 includes examples similar to those that were included in relation to such words in the Commentary to Article 4 of the Technical Explanation to the 1996 Model, even though the solutions achieved under the new Article 1.6 are different.[156] Beneficial owner is consequently left as a rule matching reduced rate access with domestic allocation rules, as taxation at source was probably considered a matter of domestic law and not liability in the other state, while solutions to multiple taxation or non-taxation derived from possible mismatches are left to Article 1.6.

II. Crossing the Atlantic: From US Tax Treaty Policy to the UK[157]

From US practice, the beneficial owner principle in tax treaties made the leap to UK tax treaty policy in 1966. This step is highly relevant as from the UK it would jump to the OECD Model Tax Convention and afterwards would be extended throughout the global treaty network.

As already stated and well known, the 1966 United States–United Kingdom Tax Treaty was the first to include beneficial ownership as an explicit requirement for articles dealing with dividends and interest in royalties, as it would only later be included in the Model and in most tax treaties.[158] The author has already stated that it was clear that the USA considered the concept implicit, but it could also be plausible that the UK also considered it implicit to some extent.[159] This is derived from the likely possibility that the UK Treasury already knew the previous US regulations prior to 1966 and

[154] See commentaries to para 2 of Art 10, para 1 of Art 11 and para 1 of Art 12 of the 2006 United States Model Technical Explanation.

[155] See, eg commentaries to Arts 10, 11 and 12 of the Technical Explanation of the proposed Protocol to the 2007 Tax Convention between the United States of America and Canada; Technical Explanation of the proposed Protocol to the 2007 Tax Convention between the United States of America and Bulgaria; Technical Explanation of the proposed Protocol to the 2007 Tax Convention between the United States of America and Iceland.

[156] See Art 1.6 of the 2006 US Model Tax Convention, and commentaries to para 6 of Art 1 and para 1 of Art 4 of the 2006 Model Technical Explanation and compare them with the commentary to para 1 of Art 4 of the 1996 United States Model Technical Explanation.

[157] On the analysis of the UK view on the issue, the author acknowledges with great thanks Dr John Avery Jones CBE, for his invaluable comments on preliminary drafts, even though the text and outcomes are solely the author's and possible mistakes can only be attributed to him.

[158] See Arts VI, VII and VIII in the 1945 United States–United Kingdom Tax Convention and compare it to articles on dividends, interests and royalties in previous treaties, such as those mentioned in n 45 above. See above, n 29.

[159] The consideration on the beneficial ownership condition by the UK in the negotiation of the 1945 United Kingdom–United States convention may suggest so. See Vann (n 9) n 23 and accompanying text.

collaborated on the collection and submission of the difference of rates as the system was sometimes dependent on the collaboration of the counterparty.[160]

In addition to being the first treaty containing this concept, the Protocol is relevant because it included an explicit authorisation to establish the collection mechanism on intermediaries resident in the other contracting states who improperly enjoyed treaty reduced rates on their receipts,[161] and because the Technical Memorandum to the Protocol shows a definition of beneficial ownership that slightly differs from what previous Treasury decisions considered as intermediaries not entitled to treaty benefits, as it links beneficial ownership with factual distribution of income.[162]

Those changes were not significant for the USA as it was already applying them, but the change was of much more importance on the UK side.

Until 1965, because the income tax paid by a corporation was considered to be an advanced payment of the shareholder income tax, non-residents were not subject to additional tax – at least on their basic rate, as some were also paying surtax – and income tax paid by the corporation on their share of the profits was considered to be their final income tax liability.[163] The UK international tax policy at the time held that tax rights should primarily pertain to residence countries and not source countries, for obvious economic reasons derived from the capital exporting status of the UK, but also because the UK was one of the first countries to adopt comprehensive income taxes. The lack of withholding tax on non-residents was consistent with such a view.[164]

However, the system changed with the Finance Act of 1965, and corporate income tax was separated from shareholder liability, so a new withholding tax on dividends of 41.25 per cent was established as an advanced collection mechanism for shareholder income tax liability.[165] As non-resident shareholders were affected by this 41.25 per cent withholding tax and the treaty provided for a reduced rate for dividends of 15 per cent, a mechanism was needed to ensure access to treaty benefits by US residents receiving

[160] It is clear that the USA negotiated the collection mechanism of the 1966 Protocol. See in that regard 'Treasury decision – Withholding regulations under the income tax convention with the United Kingdom', 13 October 1966; United Kingdom; Box 39, in Office of the Tax Legislative Council, subject files 1936–1972, Asst Secretary Tax Policy [RG 56 NN3 56 94 005], at National Archives at College Park, College Park, MD. However, from the negotiations and documents, it seems likely the UK at least knew of the existence of the regulations. What is less clear is whether it accepted their content. Knowing they lodged no complaint, it seems plausible they knew it and considered that the concept could be an implicit principle. See also references to negotiations of the 1945 United States–United Kingdom Tax Convention in ibid and accompanying text.

[161] See XIXA in the 1945 United States–United Kingdom Tax Convention.

[162] See n 100 above and accompanying text.

[163] Before the Finance Act 1965, corporations paid a profits tax of 15%, and an additional income tax that was variable but was usually around 40%. But when profits from the corporation were distributed as dividends from such, income tax paid by the corporation was credited to the shareholder and he or she had only to pay the difference at his personal tax rate. As non-residents were not subject to the personal rate in the UK, income tax paid by the corporation was considered as final income tax as per the basic rate of the shareholder. Foreigners were nevertheless sometimes subject to surtax. See ss 184 and 362 of the Income Tax Act 1952, c 10. See also 'Proposed Protocol with The United Kingdom of Great Britain and Northern Ireland', Senate Report on the Tax protocols with the United Kingdom and the Netherlands, 1966-2 CB 1127, S Rep No 89-3.

[164] On the UK preference for residence taxation as their international tax policy position, see J Avery Jones, 'The UK's Early Tax Treaties with European Countries' in *Studies in the History of Tax Law*, vol 8 (Hart Publishing, 2017); J Avery Jones, 'The History of the United Kingdom's First Comprehensive Double Taxation Agreement' in J Tiley (ed), *Studies in the History of Tax Law*, vol 3 (Hart Publishing, 2009).

[165] See Pt IV of the Finance Act 1965, c 25; see also n 100 above and accompanying text.

dividends from the UK.[166] Even though the UK suggested that Americans apply for a refund of the difference between the rates, US negotiators managed to obtain from the UK the direct application of reduced rates on withholding, as the Americans already had.[167] But the UK requested a guarantee that the reduced rate would only benefit American residents, and this was the reason why the collection mechanism, very similar to the system the Americans had already applied for decades, was explicitly included in the 1966 Protocol.

This change was also probably the reason why beneficial ownership was explicitly included in the 1966 Protocol and not contained in the previous 1945 treaty. Under the pre-1965 UK income tax rules, dividends paid to both residents and non-residents were generally not taxed because income tax on the shareholders was already collected at corporation level, so the UK had no concerns regarding source taxation being avoided through the treaty.[168] Now, as there was a significant difference between the 41.25 per cent statutory withholding tax that would normally be applicable after the Finance Act 1965 and the 15 per cent treaty withholding tax, and because the reduction was directly applicable without intensive intervention by the tax authorities, beneficial ownership was explicitly included jointly with the collection mechanism to put the spotlight on the need to apply reduced withholding only to persons resident in the other contracting state to whom income attained as the persons entitled to treaty benefits.[169] In case the reduction was improperly applied, the treaty provided that the UK could ask the USA to collect the tax and submit it to the Crown Treasury. Because the USA had experience with direct reduced rate applicable that was not applied by any other country and the UK entered this new mechanism, and because both parties were familiar with the US system as already applied by the UK to the US side, it is likely that the UK followed the US protective rules. Later negotiations with Finland confirmed this point, as the UK negotiators asked whether a collection assistance would be possible in relation to payments to a non-resident beneficial owner who benefited from reduced withholding tax in the first instance, similar to what the USA had been proposing for a long time in their treaties.[170]

However, with the beneficial owner principle and collection mechanisms being recognised in the 1966 treaty, two main doubts arose. The first one was how beneficial

[166] Previously, the USA was giving relief to both withholding tax and the part of taxes paid by the US corporation to a resident in the UK, while the UK was not charging surtax and refunding the part of the tax of the corporation. After the Finance Act 1965 and the new 1966 Tax Convention, both countries were charging both corporate income tax, without any right to refund, and withholding tax, limited by the treaty. See 'Double Taxation Relief, Motion for Address' PS 2160/65, 6 and 7, in Negotiations with USA on withholding tax and a double tax agreement – Treasury: Finance, Home and General Division: Registered Files (2FH Series). Negotiations with USA on withholding tax and a double tax agreement (TNA T 326/432 and T 326/433).

[167] See Pt IV of the Finance Act 1965, c 25; 'Proposed Protocol with The United Kingdom of Great Britain and Northern Ireland', Senate Report on the Tax protocols with the United Kingdom and the Netherlands, 1966-2 CB 1127, S Rep No 89-3.

[168] See ss 184 and 362 of the Income Tax Act 1952, c 10.

[169] See the concern on giving a reduced rate and the need to recover the unduly attributed treaty reduced rate in 'm no (13) Paragraph (1) "Beneficially owned", and m nos (58)–(62) "Other matters discussed in the negotiations"' in 'Double Taxation Negotiations in Oslo – 4th–8th March 1968', 'Double taxation agreement with Norway' (TNA Ref IR 40/17262).

[170] Ibid.

ownership was defined in this treaty as the common agreed understanding of both countries. The second was whether the definition was in line with previous US developments on the issue and if, and to what extent, the UK adopted them. In addition, the fact that the subject to tax test that had been included in the previous 1945 tax treaty was dropped from the article referring to dividends, interest and royalties in the 1966 Protocol while beneficial ownership was included has led some authors to wonder if there is any relationship between them.[171]

A. Liable to Tax, Subject to Tax and Beneficial Ownership: Beneficial Ownership was not Included Because of the Dropping of the Subject to Tax Test

It is nowadays accepted that the distinction between the subject to tax test and the liability to tax requirement in order to access the treaty benefits lies in the former referring to the particular item of income while the latter refers to the general liability of the subject.[172] What is more controversial is whether subject to tax requires effective taxation. To some, it means effective taxation; to others, it just means within the scope of charge.[173] At this time, the issue of the meaning of subject to tax was even further from being solved.[174]

The historical origin of the distinction between the subject to tax test and the liable to tax requirement follows the disparity between the tax criteria of the different states, especially in the early stages of development of international tax rules.[175] While some states – such as the UK, although divided into schedules – used comprehensive taxes,

[171] See, arguing respectively that the subject to tax test and beneficial ownership tests were aimed at nominees in the UK who were not taxed on their income remitted to beneficiaries abroad, and that beneficial ownership encompassed a subject to tax test and extended its scope of application, JF Avery Jones, 'The Beneficial Ownership Concept Was Never Necessary in the Model' in M Lang et al (eds), *Beneficial Ownership: Recent Trends* (IBFD, 2013); A Meindl-Ringler, *Beneficial Ownership in International Tax Law* (Kluwer, 2016) 333. Noting subject to tax as an alternative to the beneficial owner test, JF Avery Jones, 'The United Kingdom's Influence on the OECD Model Tax Convention' (2011) 6 *British Tax Review* 653, 678.

[172] JF Avery Jones, '*Weiser v HMRC*: Why Do We Need "Liable to Tax" and "Subject to Tax" Clauses?' [2013] *British Tax Review* 9, 9–12; B Cleave, 'The *Weiser* Case: UK Pension Income Not Subject to Tax in Israel under the Israel–United Kingdom Income Tax Treaty (1962)' (2013) 67 *Bulletin for International Taxation* 280; Reimer and Rust (n 4) 248; DA Ward et al, 'A Resident of a Contracting State for Tax Treaty Purposes: A Case Comment on Crown Forest Industries' (1996) 44 *Canadian Tax Journal* 408, 419 et seq.

[173] On the one hand, there is a tendency to think subject to tax means effectively charged. See Reimer and Rust (n 4) 722. See *Weiser v HMRC* [2012] First Tier Tribunal (Tax) TC/2010/3902, UKFTT 501; Avery Jones (n 172). On the other hand, certain instruments, such as the EU Interest and Royalties Directive, use subject to tax as the income being within the scope of charge, irrespective of being effectively taxed. See J Lopez Rodriguez, 'Beneficial Ownership and EU Law' in Lang et al (n 9). However, recent cases switched that view and have interpreted the directive as meaning effectively taxed. See Court of Justice of the European Union (Grand Chamber) Joined Cases C-115/16, C-118/16, C-119/16 and C-299/16*N Luxembourg 1 and others v Skatteministerie (and joined cases)* [2019] ECLI:EU:C 134 [146 et seq].

[174] In the 1946 United Kingdom–Canada Tax Convention there is a liable to tax requirement in relation to copyright royalties, while other investments are subject to a 'subject to tax test'. In the view of Avery Jones, this is a mistake, and in the author's view probably reflects the poor understanding or early stage of division between both concepts at the time. Avery Jones (n 171) n 23. On the term subject to tax being 'confusing', see Mr Marshall, Double Taxation: Spain, T/1169/204/41, in Double Taxation Agreement with Spain Board of Inland Revenue (TNA ref IR 40/18058).

[175] Avery Jones (n 172) 11–12.

other states – such as most European countries – had scheduler, analytical and/or impersonal taxes.[176] Thus, in the field of income tax treaties, those countries understanding tax policy as comprehensive income taxes had to link source tax treaty reductions to the treatment of the income and subject in the residence state as the latter country was so entitled, being the residence state. Otherwise, if no tax existed on the relevant type of income in the hands of the subject in the other contracting state because it was a type of income that was subject to no *impôt réel* or real tax, there was no potential double taxation to be prevented.[177]

However, the view from the UK was unique. Contrary to most other countries, the UK's double tax relief policy was dependent at an early stage not only on the income to be subject to tax in theory, but also on that effectively taxed in the other state, as otherwise no double taxation arises (most other countries used tax treaties to allocate jurisdictions irrespective of effective taxation and whether the other country effectively taxed the income).[178] The UK's use of comprehensive taxes and the view that double tax relief was only necessary in case of actual taxation in the other state led the British to a dual requirement tax treaty policy for certain types of income – dividends, interest and royalties – requiring the subject to be subject to taxation in the state of residence (liable to tax) and the income to be subject to taxation in the hands of such subject (subject to tax).[179] However, the interpretation of the subject to tax test from the UK perspective was doubtful and posed several inconsistencies.

On the US side, the Treasury was interpreting the subject to tax requirement as meaning within the scope of tax liability, and not necessarily effectively taxed.[180] This is in line with post-1957 Treasury regulation requirement in relation to trusts that the income was to be included in the gross income of the relevant subject upon whom residence is tested, but without requiring effective taxation or inclusion in the net income.[181] However, the UK initially interpreted the subject to tax test as requiring income to be effectively taxed in order to access treaty limited tax rates at source.[182]

[176] ibid.

[177] ibid 12.

[178] See 'The effect of the new United Kingdom/United States Double Taxation Agreement on United Kingdom Charities and Pension Funds', 20 January 1966, para 3 in Double Taxation Bill with United States of America (TNA Ref IR 40/16680); 'Subject to Tax' test in Section B of the Note on Details in 'Protocol amending the Double Taxation Convention with the United States', 10 May 1966, PS 210/65, pp 10–11 in Negotiations with USA on withholding tax and a double tax agreement – Treasury: Finance, Home and General Division: Registered Files (2FH Series); Negotiations with USA on withholding tax and a double tax agreement (TNA T 326/432 and T 326/433). See also 'Subject to Tax Test' in Abuse of Tax Conventions OECD (TNA Ref IR 40/17049).

[179] Avery Jones (n 172) 13–14.

[180] 'The fact that the payee of the dividend is, owing to the application of reliefs or exemptions under United Kingdom revenue laws, not required to pay United Kingdom tax on such dividend does not prevent the application of the reduction of the rate of United States tax with respect to such dividend. If the dividend would have been subject to United Kingdom tax had the payee thereof derived sufficiently large an income to require payment of tax, then liability to United Kingdom tax exists for the purposes of the reduction in the rate of United States tax': s 7.501 of TD 5532, 1946-2, CB 73 on 1945 United States–United Kingdom Tax Convention.

[181] See above, n 96.

[182] See 'The Effect of the New United Kingdom/United States Double Taxation Agreement on United Kingdom Charities and Pension Funds', 20 January 1966, in Double Taxation Bill with United States of America (TNA Ref IR 40/16680); 'Subject to Tax Test' in Abuse of Tax Conventions OECD (TNA Ref IR 40/17049).

An example of these differences in views was the application of treaties to investment funds and charities. The UK did not allow them to fulfil the subject to tax test, and consequently restrained their access to treaty benefits, whereas the USA considered them able to access treaty benefits to the extent that the income was allocated to those subjects and broadly speaking subject to taxation or included in gross taxation, although they were eventually not taxed due to the application of subjective or objective exemptions.[183]

However, although, in the case of the treaty between the USA and the UK and other contemporaneous treaties, the UK concluded that treaty benefits were not applicable if the relevant income was not effectively taxed, the UK Treasury conceded, by agreement with the other contracting state or specifically to certain taxpayers, that it would apply treaty benefits even though the entity or entities at stake receiving dividends were exempted.[184] This was the case, for example, of investment funds in the Netherlands under the UK–Netherlands treaty, where a reciprocal agreement provided for a look-through approach to see whether the beneficiary from the fund was subject to tax on the income, rather than testing the liability of the vehicle.[185]

Therefore, some time later, and probably due to several problems arising from the subject to tax test being interpreted as requiring effective taxation, HM Treasury changed its view and recognised subject to tax as meaning being *within the scope of charge*, rather than being subject to effective tax payment.[186] In this sense, even in cases where income was offset against deductions, the UK took the view that the income was subject to tax if it was included in the gross income or came under subjective exemptions.[187]

[183] See 'The Effect of the New United Kingdom/United States Double Taxation Agreement on United Kingdom Charities and Pension Funds' (n 182) para 3.

[184] See '3. Legal Considerations' and '4. Miscellaneous Cases' in 'Subject to Tax Test' in Abuse of Tax Conventions OECD (TNA Ref IR 40/17049).

[185] '4. Miscellaneous Cases' in 'Subject to Tax Test' in Abuse of Tax Conventions OECD (TNA Ref IR 40/17049).

[186] 'We have generally taken the line that "subject to tax" means "within the scope of charge" rather than "actually burdened with a payment of tax" and in pursuit of this line we recently felt constrained to express the view that emoluments who offset by a deduction under paragraph 1 (3) of Schedule 2 FA 1974 were "subject to tax" for agreement purposes': Internal note by the UK Treasury entitled OECD Working Group No 21 Working Party No 1: Tax Avoidance (R/81NW), p 2, in OECD Fiscal Committee Working Party on Tax Avoidance (TNA Ref IR 40/17049). 'The [UK] delegate doubted whether the UK, in any event, could claim much success for the "subject to tax" test. Difficulties had arisen over the treatment of collective investment institutions regarded as legally transparent and therefore unable to satisfy the test, and in addition the UK had recently felt constrained to take the view that emoluments wholly off-set by a 100% deduction were subject to tax for double taxation agreement purposes': Note II, Draft Report on Tax Avoidance through the Improper Use and Abuse of Tax Conventions', in OECD Fiscal Committee Working Party on Tax Avoidance (TNA Ref IR 40/17049). On the term subject to tax being 'confusing', see Mr Marshall, Double Taxation: Spain, T/1169/204/41, in Double Taxation Agreement with Spain Board of Inland Revenue (TNA Ref IR 40/18058).

[187] 'The [UK] delegate doubted whether the UK, in any event, could claim much success for the "subject to tax" test. Difficulties had arisen over the treatment of collective investment institutions regarded as legally transparent and therefore unable to satisfy the test, and in addition the UK had recently felt constrained to take the view that emoluments wholly off-set by a 100% deduction were subject to tax for double taxation agreement purposes': 'Subject to Tax Test', para 4 in Abuse of Tax Conventions OECD (TNA Ref IR 40/17049). Nowadays the controversy remains. On the one hand, there is a tendency to think subject to tax means effectively charged. See Reimer and Rust (n 4) 722. See also *Weiser v HMRC* (n 173); Avery Jones (n 172). On the other hand, certain instruments, such as the European Union Interest and Royalties Directive, use subject to tax as the income being within the scope of charge, irrespective of being effectively taxed. See Lopez Rodriguez (n 173). However, recent cases switched that view and have interpreted the Directive

Once this view was adopted, the UK recognised the test was of very little worth as an anti-avoidance tool.[188]

What is surprising is that, although the UK had historically adopted such a view, HMRC and the Tax Courts recently went back to the original interpretation of effectively charged that caused significant problems, even though it went against the current view of several other countries.[189]

In the treaty with the USA, British negotiators justified the elimination of the subject to tax test in the 1966 Protocol, on the basis that foreign charities and funds could not pass the test whenever they obtained income from their investments in the UK.[190] Apparently, the subject to tax test prevented such entities from accessing treaty reduced rates given that they were exempted from taxation in their states of residence.

UK charities were exempted in the USA from withholding tax on their US investment dividends, while investments in the UK by US charities would be subject to 41.25 per cent withholding after the 1965 reform, so UK charity investments in the USA were more attractive than US charity investments in the UK.[191] The US Treasury's concern was that this mismatch imbalanced the balance of payments; removing the subject to tax test would improve it.[192] It is true that other considerations were taken into account, such as married women receiving income not being subject to tax on their own account but on their husband's, or even equity considerations to give access to charities and funds themselves.[193] However, the Treasury explicitly recognised that the balance of payments was the main reason why the subject to tax test was dropped.[194]

as meaning effectively taxed. See *N Luxembourg 1 and others v Skatteministerie (and joined cases)* (n 173) para 146 et seq.

[188] '4. I doubted whether the UK could claim much success for this test … In our experience the test does not therefore seems to be worth very much as a check on tax avoidance and in re-negotiating dividend articles, we have, on occasion, accepted the "beneficial ownership" test instead.' See 'Subject to Tax Test' and 'II Draft Report on Tax Avoidance through the Improper Use and Abuse of Tax Conventions' in Abuse of Tax Conventions OECD (TNA Ref IR 40/17049); 'OECD Working Group No 21 of Working Party No 1: Tax Avoidance, Inspector of Foreign Dividends', FD T2100/34/66, p 2, in OECD Fiscal Committee Working Party on tax avoidance (TNA Ref IR 40/17049).

[189] *Weiser v HMRC* (n 173); Avery Jones (n 172). A similar discussion, with different results, was considered by the French Conseil D'Etat, where taxable was distinguished from effectively taxed: *Société Thollon Diffusion v Ministre des finances et des comptes publics* [2014] Conseil D'Etat 362800. The author wonders whether the *Weiser* case may be influenced by recent trends giving support to the single taxation principle.

[190] See 'The Effect of the New United Kingdom/United States Double Taxation Agreement on United Kingdom Charities and Pension Funds' (n 182) para 3; 'Subject to Tax' (n 178); Negotiations with USA on withholding tax and a double tax agreement (TNA T 326/432 and T 326/433). 'Speaking Notes. Double Taxation Orders Relating to New Zealand, Sweden, the Falkland Islands and Luxembourg', p 2, in Luxembourg (TNA IR 40/18362).

[191] See 'The Effect of the New United Kingdom/United States Double Taxation Agreement on United Kingdom Charities and Pension Funds' (n 182) para 4; 'Subject to Tax' (n 178); Negotiations with USA on withholding tax and a double tax agreement (TNA T 326/432 and T 326/433).

[192] Ibid.

[193] See Subject to Tax Clause in Double Taxation Agreements. Husband 'subject to tax' in respect of wife's Income, WEP. 37DR, T/169/137 1968 Ref 10537 (TNA Ref IR 40/17357); 'OECD Working Group No 21 of Working Party No 1: Tax Avoidance, Inspector Of Foreign Dividends, FD T2100/34/66, p 2, in OECD Fiscal Committee Working Party on tax avoidance (TNA Ref IR 40/17049).

[194] See 'The Effect of the New United Kingdom/United States Double Taxation Agreement on United Kingdom Charities and Pension Funds' (n 182) para 4; 'Subject to Tax' (n 178). Negotiations with USA on withholding tax and a double tax agreement (TNA T 326/432 and T 326/433); '"Subject to Tax" Test', in OECD Fiscal Committee Working Party on tax avoidance (TNA Ref IR 40/17049); 'Mr Bryce, Luxembourg', in Amendments to the double taxation agreement with Luxembourg (TNA Ref IR 40/18362).

The UK Treasury recognised that the elimination may have had other effects, as now funds would benefit from the exemption in both directions that they had not hitherto enjoyed, which would also affect the balance of payments, but they expected that the benefits would be larger on the UK side, as the reduction in UK taxation would be larger than that in the USA because in the latter charities already enjoyed exemption, so the UK would improve its balance of payments.[195]

This did not mean that the UK gave up with the subject to tax test in relation to all countries. Apparently, the UK wanted to maintain it in some cases where the state of residence of the person receiving dividends was applying territorial taxation or when, if the subject was exempted in his or her residence state, he or she would have had anti-avoidance legislation applied if he or she would have been resident of the UK.[196] However, pressure from EFTA negotiators following exemption regimes on certain companies established by some European countries caused the UK to progressively decline to use the subject to tax test.[197] Also, the progressive understanding of the subject to tax test as coming within the scope of charge and not effective taxation caused the rule to become of little help against tax avoidance.[198]

It is clear from historical documents why the subject to tax test was dropped, but it is less clear why it was substituted by the beneficial owner test, or what the relation is between the two tests.

The UK recognised the elimination of the subject to tax test to be a relaxation of the treaty access requirement, implicitly recognising beneficial owners, and did not cover all the cases covered by the former test.[199] This is confirmed by the fact that the beneficial owner test needed to be supplemented by other rules, such as those for remittance taxation.[200] On the USA side, however, this did not seem to be the case, as Americans continued to require in some cases income to be included in the gross income or to be liable in theory in respect of the relevant income, even though not necessarily effectively taxed, as if the subject to tax test remained. But the United States already interpreted the term as meaning within the scope of charge and not effectively taxed even when the test was explicit in the treaty.[201] Obviously, the difference was derived from the different interpretation given to the subject to tax test by both countries.[202] However, the important outcome is that the beneficial ownership test and the subject to tax test did not have equal meanings and the first one covered less potential abusive cases than the second, at least from the UK viewpoint at the

[195] See 'The Effect of the New United Kingdom/United States Double Taxation Agreement on United Kingdom Charities and Pension Funds' (n 182) para 4; 'Subject to Tax' (n 178); funds benefiting now 5406.

[196] 'Double Taxation Relief – Mirror image treatment of dividends', 25 February, 1966, p 5, in Double taxation agreements British subjects abroad (TNA IR 40/17357).

[197] See 'The Effect of the New United Kingdom/United States Double Taxation Agreement on United Kingdom Charities and Pension Funds' (n 182) para 3; Negotiation of new Double Taxation Convention with Finland, Helsinki – 27th February to 11th March 1968, p 4, in Origin papers of the renegotiation of double taxation agreement with Finland (TNA Ref IR 40/17812).

[198] See above, n 188.

[199] 'Double Taxation Relief Motion for Address' in Origin papers of the renegotiation of double taxation agreement with Finland (TNA Ref IR 40/17812); 'Double Taxation Relief Motion for Address. Mr Chancellor of the Exchequer. T.1169/326/67' in Double taxation agreement with Austria (TNA Ref IR 40/17260).

[200] ibid.

[201] See s 507.28 of TD 6898, 1966-2 CB 567.

[202] See above, nn 180 and 182.

time they were interchanged.[203] The concepts, even though related, have different meanings, but what is the meaning of beneficial owner?

The US view on beneficial ownership is already known, but the view from the UK side is lacking. The most accepted view is Avery Jones's argument that the beneficial owner concept was aimed at a very specific UK problem and was never necessary in the OECD Model Tax Convention. In a paper presented at the 2012 Vienna University of Business and Economics Conference on Beneficial Ownership, Avery Jones held that the UK proposal for including a beneficial owner or subject to tax test in tax treaties was targeted at nominees dealing for the benefit of non-residents because of the interaction of UK domestic rules on nominees and trustees.[204] The 1963 OECD Draft Model led those intermediaries to access treaty reduced rates at source, whereas no taxation was arising in the residence of the nominee.

On the domestic side, trustees for the benefit of non-residents were only taxed under UK revenue law from sources within the UK, and not on income from overseas.[205] The 1963 OECD Draft Model Tax Convention, on the other hand, defined its scope of application in relation to the residence requirement as:

> 1. For the purposes of this Convention, the term 'resident of a contracting state' means any person who, under the law of that State, is liable to taxation therein by reason of his domicile, residence, place of management or any other criterion of a similar nature.[206]

The residence definition did not explicitly require worldwide liability at the time as the Model would later require after the 1977 Model, even though the requirement was defined in the Commentary.[207] In Avery Jones's view, the aim of the beneficial owner requirement was to avoid trustees accessing treaty benefits as they were liable to tax in accordance to the residence requirement, but were only so on domestic income, so foreign income was not taxable in their hands.[208] This made it possible for foreign residents to put their assets deriving income from UK treaty partners in the hands of trustees or nominees who were residents of the UK, reducing the tax burden in the source country even though no tax liability arose in the UK.[209] However, as the Model Tax Convention was amended in 1977 to limit the scope of application of the treaty by excluding persons liable to tax only from sources within the contracting state, the issue was solved in the view of Avery Jones, so the beneficial owner test became unnecessary.[210]

Under that view, the result varies depending on whether beneficial ownership is seen as a general rule derived from this specific problem or a specific rule only for this problem. Depending on the view, beneficial ownership would be defined as: pertaining to the person to whom income is specifically allocated for tax purposes, as it is clear

[203] See above, n 199.
[204] Avery Jones (n 171).
[205] See s 369 of the Income Tax Act 1952, c 10; Avery Jones (n 171) 335–38.
[206] Art 4 of the 1963 OECD Draft Model Tax Convention.
[207] Compare Art 4 of the 1963 OECD Draft Model Tax Convention and Art 4(1) of the 1977 OECD Model Tax Convention, where the latter excludes resident condition from the tax treaty, and thus access to treaty provisions, to persons liable to tax only on income from sources within the relevant country. See also para 10 of the Commentary to Art 4 of the 1963 OECD Draft Model Tax Convention.
[208] Avery Jones (n 171) 338.
[209] ibid.
[210] ibid 339.

no effective taxation was required; a requirement denying access to treaty benefits to subjects liable to tax only with respect to income from sources within or outside the contracting state; or a requirement denying access to treaty benefits specifically to trustees, nominees or other intermediaries not liable to tax on income derived from sources outside the contracting state. However, leaving aside which definition fits the concept interpretation better under this viewpoint, the author cannot fully agree with this view.

First, it is not entirely clear why the issue was a priority for the UK. This would imply UK domestic tax rules and treaties were being used to avoid foreign taxes, because third-country residents deriving income from third countries would not be taxed in the UK, so the case would have no impact at all on UK tax revenue.[211] On this point, it could be argued that the UK may have been afraid of other countries having the same limited tax jurisdiction rules on income from third countries derived by intermediaries for the benefit of non-resident subjects so that those countries could be exploited, jeopardising UK tax revenue.[212] However, it seems unlikely that any country other than the UK would have such rules.[213] On this point, Avery Jones suggested that it was in the UK's own interest not to leave loopholes in treaties that would give the country a bad reputation and limit its ability to subscribe to new tax treaties. Because of the uniqueness of the UK tax system, the UK's tax negotiation position was taking care of issues that may arise to counterparties from their own tax rules, as it would be difficult for them to understand the risks of the system. However, such an assumption seems to the author quite large, and the author has found no record of it in the treaty negotiations undertaken by the UK at the time, which, if it were the case, would seem surprising.[214] Moreover, not explaining and framing the issue as such at the OECD when the UK suggested introducing the concept in the model (they did not refer to the issue at any time) would not have made sense, as other countries would have been highly worried about the issue.[215] On the contrary, some other countries meeting in the OECD Committee and in some of the negotiations pointed out that the problems that the beneficial owner test and the subject to tax test were trying to tackle were not problems at all for them.[216] If the other countries' revenue was the UK's concern, it is extremely strange that there is no reference to the issue in any of the OECD negotiations

[211] *William v Singer* (1921) 1 AC 65.

[212] Avery Jones (n 171) 680; Vann (n 9) 285.

[213] In the first version of my doctoral thesis that started my research on the topic I argued that the UK may have been concerned about other countries also having limited jurisdiction to tax for intermediaries obtaining overseas income. However, it seems highly likely no such country existed. See Avery Jones (n 171) n 14.

[214] See Negotiation of new Double Taxation Convention with Finland, Helsinki – 27th February to 11th March 1968, in Origin papers of the renegotiation of double taxation agreement with Finland (TNA Ref IR 40/17812); Double Taxation Negotiations in Oslo – 4th–8th March 1968, in Double taxation agreement with Norway (TNA Ref IR 40/17262); Double Taxation Negotiations in Madrid, Monday 25th–Friday 29th November, 1968, in Double taxation agreement with Spain Board of Inland Revenue (TNA Ref IR 40/18058).

[215] 'Observations of Member Countries on difficulties raised by the OECD Draft Convention on Income and Capital' [TFD/FC/216], Fiscal Committee, OCDE, 9 May 1967 p 14; Report on suggested amendments to Articles 11 and 12 of the Draft Convention, relating to interest and royalties respectively, Working Party 27, Fiscal Committee, OCDE, 16 de febrero de 1970 [FC/WP27 (70) 1], pp 13–14.

[216] See Report on Suggested Amendments to Articles 11 and 12 of the Draft Convention, Relating to Interest and Royalties Respectively, Working Party 27, Fiscal Committee, OECD, 16th February 1970, [FC/WP27(70)1], p 14. See also Double Taxation Negotiations in Oslo – 4th–8th March 1968, marginal number 24 in Double Taxation Agreement with Norway (TNA Ref IR 40/17262).

or most UK treaty negotiations of the time introducing the test. Finally, this theory fails in relation to trustees that derive foreign income for a resident and a non-resident at the same time under a single deed.[217] In these cases, it was explictly recognised by the UK that beneficial ownership is still needed, so the theory seems somehow weak.[218]

In contrast, and in favour of this theory, records point out that the subject to tax test worked properly where the UK was the residence country, but not in the opposite case.[219] However, this author's view is that the point the UK was thinking of was the UK as source and where the agents were in treaty countries for the benefit of third parties in third countries, where the income was not allocated to such agents, but where those intermediaries were liable to tax on worldwide income and the income was paid to them. This is similar to the agency treatment in the UK, and probably came up due to knowledge of the agents' domestic treatment, but had nothing to do with territorial liability on intermediaries. This issue will be revisited later.

Secondly, the point is inconsistent with treaties signed at the time by the UK. The tax treaties signed with the Netherlands in 1967, Norway in 1969, Japan in 1969, Austria in 1969 and Finland in 1969 included both the limitation on the scope of application of the treaty to residents excluding subjects liable to tax only on income from sources within the country and the beneficial ownership test.[220] Also, in the 1967 United Kingdom–Australia Tax Convention, the definition of residents excluded non-residents who were taxable in one of the contracting states only on the income derived from sources within the country.[221] Even this definition does not explicitly deal with trustees or nominees, as these were residents with limited liability and not non-residents with limited liability. It may well be argued that the rule can be construed as excluding them, as their liability may be considered a collection mechanism to put the tax burden on the beneficiaries and not their own liability.[222] As the relevant liability is that of the beneficiary – even though assessed on the trustee – and not the liability of the trustee him- or herself, the non-resident will only be assessed on their domestic income and not their worldwide income, and the treaty is not applicable as they cannot be considered a resident. In any case, and even leaving aside the Australian treaty case, if the UK problem with trustees' and nominees' liability was solved by amending Article 4, why was the beneficial owner test also included in such treaties? As negotiations show, Article 4 was aimed at diplomats and similar residents with limited liability, it could be that the UK did not know Article 4 could also solve nominee cases.[223]

[217] Avery Jones (n 171) n 27.

[218] ibid.

[219] 'Double Taxation Relief – Mirror image treatment of dividends', 25 February, 1966, p 5, in Double taxation agreements British subjects abroad (TNA IR 40/17357).

[220] See Arts 4.1, 11.2, 12.1 and 13.1 of the 1967 Netherlands–United Kingdom Income and Capital Tax Treaty; Arts 4.1, 11.1, 12.1 and 13.1 of the 1969 Norway–United Kingdom Income and Capital Tax Treaty; Arts 4.1, 11.1, 12.1 and 13.1 of the 1969 Japan–United Kingdom Income and Capital Tax Treaty; Arts 4.1, 10.1, 11.1 and 12.1 of the 1969 Austria–United Kingdom Income and Capital Tax Treaty; and Arts 4.1, 11.1, 12.1 and 13.1 of the 1969 Finland–United Kingdom Income and Capital Tax Treaty.

[221] See Art 4.1(c) and (d) of the 1967 United Kingdom–Australia Income Tax Treaty.

[222] As, in the UK, trustees for non-residents were charged 'in the name' of the trustee or agent: s 369 of the Income Tax Act 1952, c 10.

[223] Claiming the new wording of Art 4 was to prevent diplomats from being considered as UK residents because of their territorial liability. 'Double Taxation Negotiations in Oslo – 4th–8th March 1968', m no 8, in Double taxation agreement with Norway (TNA Ref IR 40/17262).

In addition, from a policy perspective, it makes sense that the UK turned to worrying about source taxation because of the 1965 change from not withholding tax for non-residents to withholding tax on them.[224] Previous treaties, such as the 1945 United States–United Kingdom Tax Convention or the 1946 United Kingdom–Australia Tax Treaty, only included the subject to tax test as a limitation to the sourcing of taxation on the US side, but not on the UK side, insofar as the treaty limitation to UK surtax made no difference to the pre-1965 domestic exemption on surtax for non-residents.[225] In those treaties, source taxation by the other contracting state was only applicable if the recipient was subject to UK taxation, probably because the UK was interested in a reduced rate at source at the counterparty only if there was taxation in residence because of their policy of granting relief for the tax paid in the other country.[226] In other words, limitation was connected to taxation in the UK, so only a limited amount of relief was given in the UK. Otherwise, under unlimited taxation at source, the UK would have had to give a larger relief. Also, if there was no subjection in the UK, unlimited taxation at source would be irrelevant, as the UK was not subject to giving relief. It follows that the concern about beneficial ownership was the position of the UK not as an intermediary country, but as a source country, derived from the 1965 change introducing source taxation, in line with the policy of most other countries.

Thirdly, a practical reason also sheds doubt on this viewpoint. At the time – and even today – the main issue on international taxation was the lack of information on who the owner receiving the income actually was.[227] If there was no information on who the owner was, it would be impossible to define his or her tax liability scope. If the nominee limited tax liability theory on beneficial ownership is right, avoiding beneficial ownership limitation after the subject to tax test was overridden would have been as simple as putting the income in the name of another person and making a collateral independent agreement to pass the income. In addition, if the beneficiary was not reported and the custodian or nominee was liable to tax for the income derived from sources outside the UK as if the income was his or hers, they would be able to take improper advantage of the treaty despite perhaps paying an additional burden in their own country. In this case, it was widely argued at the time that some subjects were willing to pay an additional burden in exchange for privacy, or even to pay the UK burden as it was lower than in some Nordic countries.[228]

The final reason why such arguments about the UK intermediary position seem unconvincing to the author is because negotiation documents from the National Archives of the UK on several treaties signed in the 1960s and 1970s clearly show that the UK concern related to the beneficial ownership proposal was giving up source

[224] See above, nn 163 and 165.

[225] Compare Arts VI.1 and VI.2 of the 1945 United Kingdom–United States Income Tax Treaty.

[226] See Schs 16 and 17 to the Income Tax Act 1952, c 10.

[227] See above, nn 48 and 82.

[228] See US memorandums dealing with withholding at statutory rates in European countries enabling purchase of non-disclosure at the cost of higher burdens, 'Memorandum on Exchange of Information under United States Tax Treaties', p 2; Office of the Legislative Council, subject files 1936–1972, Asst Secretary Tax Policy [RG 56 NN3 56 94 005], National Archives at College Park, College Park, MD. At the OECD, on the later discussion of improper use of tax conventions, see on bearer shares 'Notes on Discussion of Dividends and Abuse of Tax Conventions during the 32nd Session of the Fiscal Committee Held From 16th to 19th September, 1969', 20 October 1969, p 7 [DAF/FC/69.13].

taxation in cases where custodians were holding shares for the benefit of third countries' residents, specifically mentioning the issue of French nominees holding Swiss firms.[229] This author does not know of a single reference in several negotiations to a UK intermediary receiving income from a third country and acting for the benefit of a resident in the other contracting state which, even though it could mean that they thought about it without making it explicit, seems at least surprising.

In summary, first, on the relationship with the subject to tax test, beneficial ownership does not equate to subject to tax as it is clear it implied a relaxation of the subject to tax test and did not require effective taxation, because it was used to overcome subject to tax inconveniences.[230] Secondly, beneficial ownership was targeting arrangements used to exploit tax treaties' source reduced tax rates by putting shares or securities in the hands of an intermediary who would not be assessed on the income because it is actually owned by a third party resident in a third country.[231]

B. The Meaning of Beneficial Ownership in UK Tax Treaty Practice between 1966 and 1977

One may be tempted to interpret beneficial ownership in accordance with how the same wording was interpreted in UK domestic tax law.[232] At the time that beneficial ownership was introduced in British tax treaties, cases such as *English Sewing Cotton*, *Parway Estates* and *Wood Preservation* dealt with the term.[233] These rulings largely interpreted beneficial ownership in tax law in accordance with equity law.[234] However, even though the UK perhaps understood the concept in accordance with their domestic rules, such interpretation has to be balanced against the treaty context being different from domestic tax rules.[235]

[229] Negotiation of new Double Taxation Convention with Finland, Helsinki – 27th February to 11th March 1968, m no 13 and 60-62, in Origin papers of the renegotiation of double taxation agreement with Finland (TNA Ref IR 40/17812).

[230] See above, n 199.

[231] Double Taxation Negotiations in Oslo – 4th–8th March 1968, m no 24 and 72, in Double taxation agreement with Norway (TNA Ref IR 40/17262); Negotiation of new Double Taxation Convention with Finland, Helsinki – 27th February to 11th March 1968, núm M no 13 and 60–62, in Origin papers of the renegotiation of double taxation agreement with Finland (TNA Ref IR 40/17812); above, n 215.

[232] See the use and evolution of beneficial owner test in UK domestic tax law in chapter 3 above.

[233] *English Sewing Cotton Co v IRC* (1947) 1 All ER 679 (CA); *Parway Estates v Inland Revenue Commissioners* (1957) 1 WLUK 322 (HC); *Parway Estates, Ltd v IRC* (1958) 45 TC 135 (CA); *Wood Preservation v Prior* (1968) 2 All ER 849; *Wood Preservation Ltd v Prior (Commissioner)* (1969) 1 WLR 1077. See comment on these cases above in s II.B.ii a in ch 3.

[234] See mentioned case law and above, s II.B.ii a in ch 3.

[235] See, *mutatis mutandis*, on the need to interpret beneficial ownership independently from domestic definitions because of the different context in treaties based on the OECD Model Tax Convention, Reimer and Rust (n 4) 718–19; K Vogel, *Klaus Vogel on Double Taxation Conventions*, 3rd edn (Kluwer 1997) 562; L De Broe, *International Tax Planning and Prevention of Abuse* (IBFD, 2008) 672; Meindl-Ringler (n 171) 297; D Oliver et al, 'Beneficial Ownership' (2000) 54 *Bulletin for International Taxation* 310, 314–16; A Martín Jiménez, 'Beneficial Ownership: Current Trends' (2010) 2 *World Tax Journal* 35, 50; P Baker, *Double Taxation Conventions*, loose-leaf edn (Sweet & Maxwell) 10–17. In case law, see *Indofood International Finance Ltd v JP Morgan Chase Bank NA* 158 (EWCA Civ) 42. However, as those arguments are largely based on the OECD Model Tax Convention, they cannot be applied to pre-1977 treaties with beneficial owner not included following the Model.

The starting point for defining beneficial ownership in UK tax treaty practice is the nominee concept. In general, these negotiations define beneficial ownership as a measure taken to prevent claims (of the treaty benefit) by a resident in a third state through a nominee in a contracting state in a similar manner to the references made by the UK before the OECD or by the USA during the negotiations or explanation of the 1966 Protocol.[236] In most British negotiations held during the 1960s, wherein the counterparty asks the meaning of the concept of beneficial owner, the UK underpinned its intention of including such a clause by providing an explanation based on nominees and the problem created by its potentially abusive nature, which the country aimed to combat.[237] Little or no other references on beneficial ownership are found in discussions of the rule, while the word nominee appears repeatedly.

In the negotiation of the treaty with Spain during the 1960s, British negotiators argued that the beneficial owner is the true owner alone who can establish a claim, which, as a definition and compared to beneficial owners' words, adds little.[238] Could it be that the context requires beneficial ownership in relation to nominees to be included, as all negotiations point to them? To the author, this must be the case, as the only other reference recognises that the concept has to be adapted to its context.

As stated above, nominee is used in the UK in a loose sense to refer to intermediaries in arrangements where the debtor has very little or no power at all, such as custodians or bare trustees.[239] The main issue, again, is whether nominee wording in UK law covers both common law arrangements, such as agency or custodian contracts, and equity law arrangements, such as bare trusts.[240] In contrast to US scholars, who largely consider nominees closer to agency arrangements, it seems there is a large tendency in UK private law to refer nominees to trust law, even though it is likely to be in an improper way.[241] Moreover, the nominee wording is usually connected to little or no power, so in the UK the concept could largely refer to bare trusts, where the trustee has little or no choice but to follow creditor instructions. However, this result may be imprecise. Many agency arrangements may be considered to underly an implied bare trust in equity, so the concept would also cover agency contracts, where property is transferred or held in equity, even though no explicit settlement exists. In addition, the tax treaty context again makes private law results unable to directly define beneficial owner rules for tax

[236] '[I]n the United Kingdom, however, the nominees who were the legal owners of the dividends would be in a position if the OECD wording were adopted to make a claim which could not be turned down on any legal grounds': Double Taxation Negotiations in Oslo – 4th–8th March 1968, marginal numbers 24 and 72, in Double Taxation Agreement with Norway (TNA Ref IR 40/17262); 'The new United Kingdom wording was designed to prevent claims by a resident of a third state via a nominee in a contracting State': Negotiation of New Double Taxation Convention with Finland, Helsinki – 27th February to 11th March 1968, marginal number 13, in Origin Papers of the Renegotiation of Double Taxation Agreement with Finland (TNA Ref IR 40/17812). The UK's similar proposal at the OECD will refer likewise to nominees. See Report on Suggested Amendments to Articles 11 and 12 of the Draft Convention, Relating to Interest and Royalties Respectively, Working Party 27, Fiscal Committee, OECD, 16 February 1970, [FC/WP27(70)1], p 13; Double taxation agreement with New Zealand (TNA 40/17426), as quoted by Vann (n 33).

[237] ibid.

[238] Double Taxation Negotiations in Madrid, Monday 25th–Friday 29th November, 1968, in Double taxation agreement with Spain Board of Inland Revenue, m no 26 (TNA Ref IR 40/18058).

[239] See fns 170 et seq and accompanying text in ch 2 above.

[240] See fns 170 et seq and accompanying text in ch 2 above.

[241] See fn 174 and accompanying text in ch 2 above.

treaty purposes. From this viewpoint, no conclusions can be reached regarding how beneficial ownership should be interpreted, not even in a negative sense.

As many of the negotiations pay attention to financial and bank custodians, consideration of how nominee accounts worked in the UK may be of help:

> Under the British nominee arrangement, securities are kept in the name of a responsible individual or firm located in the financial district of London. This nominee may continue for several years as the registered holder of certain securities even though owners have changed several times. The nominee receives the dividends, annual reports, and similar information usually sent to stockholders. In the UK when a stock certificate is transferred it requires the signature of the buyer as well as the seller. Under the nominee arrangement certificates are put out in specific denominations which are endorsed in blank by the nominee. The nominee's signature is guaranteed by a member of the London Stock Exchange. Such certificates then pass from hand to hand as they are purchased and sold, the certificates remaining in the name of the nominee. The holder of a nominee's certificate files a claim with the nominee for the dividend when it is declared. The nominee then pays the dividend to the certificate holder – but deducts a charge for handling the transaction.[242]

The facts seem clear, but it is not clear what type of legal arrangement a nominee in financial cases refers to. Again, as in the USA, nominee may refer to a registered owner whose register may serve as a presumption of legal ownership, even though no claim can be made against the actual owner in common law or equity law.[243] In any case, a clear-cut definition of nominee cannot be achieved.

Whatever nominee means, the concept in this international tax law context may be taken as a specific rule, but excluding such nominees in a private law sense, or as an example of a broader range of excluded arrangements. This leaves the options for defining nominee as being excluded from treaty benefits by the beneficial ownership rules, as:[244]

(a) a contract in common law similar to an agency contract in which the subject does not have the legal ownership but has record ownership, and the *intermediary* is absolutely or very largely bound to the principal's orders in what is referred to as the control of the asset and enjoyment of the fruits;

(b) a contract in common law similar to an agency contract in which the subject has both the legal and record ownership of the asset, and the *intermediary* is absolutely or very largely bound to the principal's orders in what is referred to as the control of the asset and enjoyment of the fruits;

(c) an arrangement resulting from common or equity law in which the subject does not have the legal ownership[245] but has the record ownership of the asset, and the *intermediary* is absolutely or very largely bound to the orders of the principal/beneficiary and/or settlor in what is referred to as the control of the asset and enjoyment of the fruits;

[242] Kamm (n 64) 411.

[243] See distinctions on title ownership, record ownership, substantive ownership and colloquial ownership in fn 241 in ch 3 above.

[244] Idem.

[245] Note that legal ownership is not referred to as ownership in common law but substantive law ownership, including the best outweighing right both in equity and common law.

(d) an arrangement resulting from equity or common law in which the subject has legal ownership and has the record ownership of the asset, and the *intermediary* is absolutely or very largely bound to the orders of the principal/beneficiary and/or settlor in what is referred to as the control of the asset and enjoyment of the fruits;
(e) a general term for intermediaries, in which the role of the intermediary is absolutely or very largely limited to the orders of the principal-beneficiary in what is referred to as the control of the asset and to define the enjoyment of the assets.

The explanations given by British negotiators signed in the period from the 1960s to the 1970s does not lead to any of these options, and to take any of them is absolutely arbitrary, as there is little explanation other than to define the beneficial owner as the 'true owner', excluding 'nominees', which could support any and all of the above-mentioned options.[246]

The 'true owner' definition provided by British negotiators may lead to consideration of substance over form principles.[247] There are also other comments by British negotiators, such as the assertion that the problem towards which beneficial ownership is aimed is solved in most continental countries by resorting to the 'reality' of the transactions.[248] This could have made beneficial ownership a sort of general anti-avoidance rule or substance over form rule, but this was not the case.

The treaty negotiation between the UK and Finland shows that the UK's concern was that, as the treaty only required the income to be 'paid to' a resident in the other contracting state, any person legally entitled to the income, or even merely receiving the income, may access treaty benefits insofar as the income was delivered to him or her.[249] Moreover, in the negotiations with Norway, the British argued that intermediaries who were 'legally entitled' to income were entitled to treaty benefits without a beneficial owner test and their treaty benefits could not be turned on 'legal grounds'.[250]

This could probably be better understood if framed within the literalism upon which tax rules were interpreted until the 1980s as a consequence of the *Duke of Westminster* case.[251] As tax treaty rules on dividends, interest and royalties only allowed reduced

[246] Double Taxation Negotiations in Madrid, Monday 25th–Friday 29th November 1968, in Double taxation agreement with Spain Board of Inland Revenue, m no 26 (TNA Ref IR 40/18058); Double Taxation Negotiations in Oslo – 4th–8th March 1968, m no 24, in Double taxation agreement with Norway (TNA Ref IR 40/17262); Negotiation of New Double Taxation Convention with Finland, Helsinki, 27th February to 11th March 1968, marginal number 13, in Origin Papers of the Renegotiation of Double Taxation Agreement with Finland (TNA Ref IR 40/17812).

[247] Double Taxation Negotiations in Madrid, Monday 25th–Friday 29th November 1968, in Double taxation agreement with Spain Board of Inland Revenue, m no 26 (TNA Ref IR 40/18058).

[248] Double Taxation Negotiations in Oslo – 4th–8th March 1968, m no 24, in Double taxation agreement with Norway (TNA Ref IR 40/17262).

[249] Negotiation of New Double Taxation Convention with Finland, Helsinki, 27th February to 11th March 1968, marginal number 13, in Origin Papers of the Renegotiation of Double Taxation Agreement with Finland (TNA Ref IR 40/17812).

[250] Double Taxation Negotiations in Oslo – 4th–8th March 1968, m no 24, in Double taxation agreement with Norway (TNA Ref IR 40/17262).

[251] The *Duke of Westminster* case crystallised from 1936 the principle that every man or woman is entitled to order his or her affairs so that the tax attaching under the appropriate acts is less than it would otherwise be. This principle led to decades of what has been called the literal approach to tax statutes in the UK. Only in 1985 did the *Ramsay* case add nuances to such principles and give grounds for a contextual and purposive interpretation that served to prevent tax avoidance. However, and even though the new *Ramsay* principle served to tackle many tax avoidance schemes, the lack of general anti-avoidance rules left the UK approach

rates upon payment, if such wording had been challenged before a UK court at the time, it seems likely to this author that the court would have ruled in favour of the entitlement of an intermediary with a legal right to the income but bound under a trust or agency agreement to pass all the income, and the trustee would have no other power. However, other countries in Europe could tackle the problem through substance over form principles or by interpreting the rules in their context, as was suggested by the UK in several negotiations.[252] The lack of substance over form or anti-avoidance principles and a literal interpretation of the law may be the problems the UK was trying to overcome.

In this regard, limitation of taxation at source in articles on dividends, interests and royalties normally requires the relevant income to qualify as the respective type of income, and the income to be paid.[253] The income will normally only qualify as a dividend, interest or royalty for tax treaty purposes if it falls within the specific company–shareholder, debtor–creditor or lessor–lessee relationship.[254] As the person holding the creditor position in such arrangements normally has to be the legal owner of the asset from which the income derives, income derived by a subject who is not the legal owner of the shares, securities or an intangible right cannot – in principle – be regarded as dividends, interests or royalties for tax treaty purposes.[255] It follows that agents and nominees who do not hold the legal ownership cannot qualify for reduced withholding rates under dividends, interests and royalties articles.

In the case of trustees, if a trustee is acting in its own name and has the legal right, as would happen in most cases, its income could be considered as qualifying as the

to tax avoidance still a long way from other countries' hard use of anti-avoidance doctrines. This ultimately led in 2013 to the introduction of a statutory anti-avoidance rule. See *Commissioner v Duke of Westminster* [1936] AC 1 (HL); *Commissioner v Duke of Westminster* [1935] All ER 259; *Ramsay v Inland Revenue Commissioner* (1981) 1 All ER 865 (HL). See J Tretola, 'The Interpretation of Taxation Legislation by the Courts – a Reflection on the Views of Justice Graham Hill' (2006) 16 *Revenue Law Journal* 6674; J Freedman, 'Defining Taxpayer Responsibility: In Support of a General Anti-Avoidance Rule' [2004] 4 *British Tax Review* 332; N Preston, 'The Interpretation of Taxing Statutes: The English Perspective' (1990) 7 *Akron Tax Journal* 43.

[252] Double Taxation Negotiations in Oslo – 4th–8th March 1968, m no 24, in Double taxation agreement with Norway (TNA Ref IR 40/17262).

[253] See articles on dividends, interest and royalties of 1963 OECD Draft Model Tax Convention, and 1945 United Kingdom–United States Income Tax Treaty, 1946 Australia–United Kingdom Tax Treaty, 1947 New Zealand–United Kingdom Tax Treaty and 1951 United Kingdom–Norway Tax Treaty. See contemporary extended wording in the same articles of the 1977 and subsequent OECD Model Tax Convention versions, as well as and subsequent UK treaties. Regardless of the 1977 wording changes, almost all treaties have used the wording 'paid to' and the dividend concept to define the scope of application of the treaty, including limitation of withholding at source.

[254] See Arts VIII.1, IX.1 and X.1 of the 1946 London Model Tax Convention. See Arts 10.3, 11.3 and 10.2 of the Model, in its different versions since 1963. In all of them, dividends are considered as income from shares, interest as income from bonds, debentures and similar, and royalties as income from property. UK treaties until 1963 generally do not provide for a definition of dividends. However, as normally those articles provide for an interpretation rule similar to the current Art 3(2), dividends, interests and royalties have to be interpreted in the sense of the laws of the contracting state applying the treaty, leading to UK domestic law in cases where the UK was the source country, where such concepts are defined by reference to the income deriving from the relevant arrangement. However, many nuances arise on presumed income, controlled-foreign corporations rules, etc. See Vogel (n 235) 653; M Helminen, *The Dividend Concept in International Tax Law* (Kluwer 1999) 160–61; JM Castro Arango, *El Concepto de Dividendo En Los Convenios de Doble Imposición* (Universidad Externado de Colombia, 2016) 348 et seq; Reimer and Rust (n 4) 839. See also JF Avery Jones et al, 'The Definitions of Dividends and Interest in the OECD Model: Something Lost in Translation?' [2009] *British Tax Review* 406.

[255] Some nuances may arise regarding presumed or imputed income, CFC rules, transparent entities, usufruct split of ownership, etc. See references in previous note.

relevant type of income, even though beneficial ownership may be with the beneficiary. However, if an absolute entitlement is with the beneficiary, tax rules would tax the income on the latter, and not the intermediary. This will not happen in intermediary situations in civil law countries, as an intermediary acting in its own name and on its own account would be entitled to the treaty as creditor and the income would be taxed on his or her hands.[256] Also, in the case of intermediaries acting in the name and on behalf of others, both domestic tax allocation and tax treaties would be directed at the beneficiary. In continental law, in all cases domestic allocation of income is on the only person vesting the creditor rights.

In agency cases, the issue at stake probably involves both private law and civil law considerations. On the private law side, UK law generally does not distinguish between disclosed and undisclosed principals as the contract binds the principal in both cases.[257] However, a nineteenth-century principle stated that foreign principals under undisclosed agency contracts were not bound by the agent's acts, unless proved to the contrary.[258] This presumption seemingly lost its value during the first half of the twentieth century, and was finally dismissed by the Queen's Bench Division in 1968.[259]

The point is, however, that at the time beneficial ownership was introduced into British tax treaty policy to deal with intermediaries and other subjects, it was doubtful

[256] The non-existence of trust or division of ownership in civil law countries makes it impossible to split ownership in intermediary situations. The full ownership is either in the intermediary or in the creditor; it cannot be in both of them. Tax law would normally rely on the subject with the only possible ownership, so there is no divergence with the treaty. This makes legal ownership applicable to both domestic allocation and treaty allocation. See A Hudson, *Equity and Trusts* (Routledge, 2013) 60; S Martín Santisteban, *El Instituto Del 'Trust' En Los Sistemas Legales Continentales y Su Compatibilidad Con Los Principios de 'Civil Law'* (Aranzadi, 2005) 90–103; LA Wright, 'Trusts and the Civil Law – A Comparative Study' (1967) 6 *Ontario Law Review* 114, 118. On the mere obligational or personal nature of continental law *fiducia* given the single and unique shaping of ownership in continental law countries versus the possible division of ownership into two types within common law legal systems, see JG Díaz-Cañabate, *Negocios Fiduciarios En Derecho Mercantil* (Real Academia de la Jurisprudencia y Legislación, 1955) 30. In the case of the Germanic *Treuhand*, even though its shaping is in general similar to that of continental law *fiducia* in that the fiduciary creditor is denied any real right, there are some regulatory or case law exceptions that grant rights *quasi in rem* to the beneficiaries or creators of the *Treuhand* vis-à-vis the fiduciary debtor or third parties: P Claret y Martí, *De La Fiducia y Del 'Trust'* (Bosch 1946) 91; S Grundmann, 'Trust and Treuhand at the End of the 20th Century. Key Problems and Shift of Interests' (1999) 47 *American Journal of Comparative Law* 401, 410, 424.

[257] Although it is considered an anomaly for a person to enter into a contract without knowing the other party. However, some exceptions apply depending on the country, such as the agent showing himself absolutely and in everything as the party to the contract, explicit exclusion of the principal, or when the matter of the contract is inconsistent with the existent of the principal. See *Rabone v Williams* (1785) 7 T R 360. See also *Scrimshire v Alderton* (1743) 2 Stra 1182, as quoted by Tan Cheng-Han, 'Undisclosed Principals and Contract' (2004) 120 *LQR* 480. In US law, see ss 2.06 and 6.03 of American Law Institute, The Restatement (Third) of Agency; W Seavey, *Law of Agency* (West, 1964) 6–7, 201–03; HG Reuschlein and WA Gregory, *The Law of Agency and Partnership* (West, 1990) 176–77; W Seavey, 'The Rationale of Agency' (1920) 29 *Yale Law Journal* 859, 877–78. See also the references to AMES in ibid and GHL Fridman, *The Law of Agency* (Butterworths 1960) 165. In the UK see Tan Cheng-Han; W Müller-Freienfels, 'The Undisclosed Principal' (1953) 16 *MLR* 298; F Pollock, *Principles of Contract: Being a Treatise on the General Principles Concerning the Validity of Agreements in the Law of England* (R Clarke & Company 1885) 104 et seq. It seems that in the USA the rule is excepted if it is unfair to the parties. See Seavey, *Law of Agency* 6–7. Analysing the effects of undisclosed common law agency and continental agency in tax law, see JF Avery Jones and DA Ward, 'Agents as Permanent Establishments under the OECD Model Tax Convention' [1993] *European Taxation* 154, 154–58; JF Avery Jones and J Lüdicke, 'The Origins of Article 5 (5) and 5 (6) of the OECD Model' [2014] *World Tax Journal* 203, 203, 205–06.

[258] Jones and Ward (n 257); Jones and Lüdicke (n 257), and sources quoted therein.

[259] *Teheran-Europe Co Ltd v ST Belton (Tractors)* (1968) 2 QB 545 (CA).

whether the foreign undisclosed principal doctrine was still in force; consequently, it was unclear whether the legal effects of arrangements subscribed to by undisclosed agents acting on behalf of non-residents – even from common law countries – were attributable to the principal or to the agent him- or herself.[260] Even though it was unclear if the foreign principal doctrine was already dead and the 1968 ruling was merely court recognition, if such undisclosed agents for non-residents held shares or securities under an agency agreement, all the effects would be presumed to be assigned to the agent unless it was proved to the contrary that the arrangement provided for all the effects to pass to the principal. For tax treaty purposes, this mean that such intermediaries fulfilled the creditor requirement in a shareholder–corporation, creditor–debtor or lessor–lessee arrangement. Were domestic tax rules allocating tax effects to the principal in both undisclosed and disclosed agencies, and for resident and non-resident subjects?[261] If this were the case, there may have been a huge mismatch between tax treaty allocation and domestic tax law allocation.

On the second requirement, the income *to be paid*, three interpretations may be followed. The first one, a strict interpretation, is that the income has to be effectively transferred. The second is that the income has to be allocated in the hands of the subject under the law of the contracting state, in the same way as the subject to tax test was interpreted by the USA as meaning the income was within the scope of charge but was not effectively taxed.[262] This option can also be divided into allocation of the income under the law of residence, under the law of source and under the law of the state applying the treaty according to Article 3(2). Finally, the third interpretation is that the income is put at the disposal of the recipient under the conditions set in the relevant legal arrangement.[263] In the 1960s, the interpretation of paid was not clear until the commentary clarified that the last option was the correct one.[264] However, if it were to be interpreted by a British court, it was again likely that the first option could have been taken.[265] The substitution of 'paid to' by 'derived by' in some UK tax treaties

[260] Considering the effect of this uncertainty on the agency permanent establishment and *mutatis mutandis* for our analysis, Jones and Lüdicke (n 257) 207.

[261] *William v Singer* (n 211) may suggest so.

[262] See Belgium comments in 'Observations of Member Countries on difficulties raised by the OECD Draft Convention on Income and Capital' [TFD/FC/216], Fiscal Committee, OCDE, 9 May 1967, p 14, OECD Archives, Paris.

[263] See para 4 of the Commentary to Art 10.1 of the 1977 OECD Model Tax Convention and matching paragraphs on Arts 11 and 12: 'The term "paid" is capable of very wide construction, since the concept of "payment" means "the fulfilment of the obligation to put funds at the disposal of the creditor in the manner required by contract or by custom."' This had been drafted since 1971. Revised Articles 11 and 12 of the OECD Draft Convention and Commentaries thereon, Working Party 27, Fiscal Committee, OECD, 17 January 1971, [FC(71)1], pp 4 and 13. This seems to be the position taken by the Canadian Tax Review Board in *MacMillan Bloedel v MNR*. See Van Weeghel (n 64) 61–62.

[264] See commentary to Arts 10, 11 and 12 of the 1963 OECD Draft Tax Convention, lacking any definition of 'paid to', and compare to the commentary on such wording in 1977 OECD Model Tax Conventions.

[265] In the negotiation with Finland that led to the introduction of the beneficial ownership test in the UK-Finland Treaty, UK treaty negotiators said in relation to the beneficial owner test: 'The OECD wording was very difficult for the United Kingdom because the word "paid" opened the way to a claim by any person who received the dividend unless it was qualified by a phrase such as "beneficial owner"': Negotiation of new Double Taxation Convention with Finland, Helsinki – 27th February to 11st March 1968, m no 13 and 60–62, in Origin papers of the renegotiation of double taxation agreement with Finland (TNA Ref IR 40/17812); 'The United Kingdom would prefer to see the benefit of these Articles made available only where the recipient

may suggest so.[266] Even if the above-mentioned last option was the interpretation given, again the income received by a trustee or nominee would qualify as paid as far as the income is submitted, recognised or paid as agreed to the person who holds the legal right to the credit.

Was this the reason why the UK suggested the inclusion of beneficial owner? If this were to be the case, beneficial ownership could not be regarded at the time as referring to substance over form, as it was precisely the opposite direction from the one that UK tax law was taking under the *Duke of Westminster* doctrine. In this sense, beneficial ownership could be a sign of the *Duke of Westminster* doctrine posing several inconveniences that ultimately led to the *Ramsay* doctrine.[267] The assertions from the UK that other countries solved the issue by looking at the substance may confirm the author's viewpoint, suggesting that the UK was not able to do so.[268] This confirms that beneficial ownership was not a substance over form or anti-avoidance principle, but a consequence of the lack thereof. The beneficial owner rule was probably a literal solution to the literal approach to tax rules, namely the 'paid to' wording.

Given that the true owner definition is of little help and that it did not refer to a substance over form principle, the discussions of British representatives at the OECD offer some clues about the meaning of the term, and the beneficial owner test in tax treaties may have a narrower scope than originally thought. The minutes of the meetings held for the preparation of the 1977 OECD Model show the initial proposal by the UK delegation:

> In our view the relief provided for under these Articles ought to apply only if the beneficial owner of the income in question is resident in the other contracting State, for otherwise the Articles are open to abuse by taxpayers who are resident in third countries and who could, for instance, put their income into the hands of bare nominees who are resident in the other contracting State.[269]

From these initial words, two main points arise. First, the delegates refer to potential abuse without clarifying whether they are referring to a specific issue, or if they are pointing to a more general broader problem of which the nominee issue is just an example.[270] Although dubious, it is the use of 'for instance' that suggests the latter.[271] The other point is that the word nominee is accompanied by 'bare', which, without precluding that the rule may refer to a broader group of transactions, may suggest that the type of intermediaries the UK was concerned about had rather limited powers, and

of the income is also the beneficial owner and the reseident in the other contracting state': OECD Fiscal Committee Working Party on permanent establishment (TNA Ref IR 40/17059).

[266] Many treaties from the 1960s signed by the UK substituted the wording 'paid to' for 'derived by', suggesting paid to was weak in certain cases. Reimer and Rust (n 4) 813. See the 1975 Treaty with Spain and the 1969 treaty with Austria.

[267] See, s II.B.ii.a in ch 3 above.

[268] See above, n 216.

[269] 'Observations of Member Countries on difficulties raised by the OECD Draft Convention on Income and Capital' [TFD/FC/216], Fiscal Committee, OCDE, 9 May 1967, p 14, OECD Archives, Paris.

[270] On the same issue, but regarding the discussion at the OECD, see Du Toit (n 68) 215.

[271] Regarding the later OECD Commentary, on the words 'such as' before the examples of agents and nominee, and recognising them as examples of a broader meaning, see ibid; S Van Weeghel, *The Improper Use of Tax Treaties* (Kluwer 1998) 72; H Pijl, 'Beneficial Ownership and Second Tier Beneficial Owners in Tax Treaties in the Netherlands' (2003) 31 *Intertax* 353, 355.

was not just any type of intermediary or complex intermediary structure. Therefore, it seems that the term 'bare' entails a reduction in the scope of application of the beneficial owner rule. However, this consideration still does not shed light onto the meaning of beneficial ownership, and all of the above considered meanings fall within the requirement of have few or no powers or discretion.

A later discussion at the OECD in 1970 added new nuances to the UK view:

> 25. The United Kingdom Delegation considers that as they stand Articles 10, 11 and 12 are defective in that they would apply to dividends, interests and royalties paid to an agent or a nominee with a legal right to the income. To remedy this situation, it proposes either that a 'subject to tax clause' be introduced, under which the country of source would give up its right to tax only if the country of residence taxed the income, or else that these Articles be made to apply only to income paid to the 'beneficial owner'.[272]

Here, the British representatives refer to nominees as subjects legally entitled to the income. Similarly, in the negotiation of the tax treaty with Norway, British negotiators held that beneficial ownership dealt with nominees who are 'legal owners', so their entitlement under the tax convention cannot be turned 'on any legal ground' without the beneficial owner or subject to tax tests.[273] It follows that intermediaries with mere record ownership probably did not fall within the concerns of the UK.[274] Subsequent OECD discussions on the issue, holding that the main problem was persons acting in their own name but on the account of a principal and that agents manifestly acting as such posed no problem, also backed this idea.[275]

In addition, some final interesting comments from internal Treasury documents and treaty negotiations on how the concept was understood by officers at the Treasury at the time may help to clarify what the UK perspective on the terms was.

In 1975, a report from the Treasury Department held that beneficial ownership and the subject to tax test were of little help for stepping-stone and conduit companies:

> The copyright royalty field where nowadays very substantial sums pass to pop stars and artistes from recording companies and to the authors of best sellers illustrates the weakness of the 'subject to tax' (para 37) and the 'beneficial ownership' test (para 31) on which claims for exemption or reduction of tax are conditional.[276]

[272] 'Report on suggested amendments to Articles 11 and 12 of the Draft Convention, relating to interest and royalties respectively' [FC/WP27 (70) 1], Working Party 27, Fiscal Committee, OECD, 16 February 1970, p 14; OECD Archives, Paris.

[273] Double Taxation Negotiations in Oslo – 4th–8th March 1968, m no 13, in Double taxation agreement with Norway (TNA Ref IR 40/17262).

[274] Even though record ownership may serve as presumption of legal ownership, it cannot be regarded as legal ownership as the holder of the latter, if different, overrides the former. The record ownership presumption thus falls within evidence functions and not ownership legal title.

[275] 'The second solution consists in taking into consideration the state of residence of the beneficial owner, the dividends, interest or royalties and in disregarding the state of residence of the person having the receipt of such income, whether so doing in the name and on behalf of the beneficial owner, or in his own name but on behalf of the beneficial owner. There is no reason to think that the case of the person acting manifestly as an agent in the name and on behalf of the beneficial owner gives rise to any difficulties': 'Report on suggested amendments to Articles 11 and 12 of the Draft Convention, relating to interest and royalties respectively' [FC/WP27 (70) 1], Working Party 27, Fiscal Committee, OECD, 16th Feb 1970, p 14; OECD Archives, Paris.

[276] 'OECD Working Group No 21 of Working Party No 1: Tax Avoidance' in OECD Fiscal Committee Working Party on Tax Avoidance (TNA Ref IR 40/17049).

The report added:

> It would however be comforting if we could construct a practice which denied beneficial ownership of income in respect of which there was a collateral agreement – oral or written – to pay an equivalent or similar amount on to a third party and which was rigorously policed so that the onus was upon the claimant to disclose all facts relevant to a demonstration that the claim was not offensive.[277]

In principle, nothing precludes the possibility that an entity whose shares are held by third parties, as an independent legal person, performs functions proper to bare trusts, agents or any other intermediary. The beneficial owner clause should in principle be applicable and deny access to treaty benefits relating to dividends, interest and royalties insofar as the income is passed by the entity under a nominee arrangement.

The problem arises where the income is received by the company under an arrangement – loan, shares or lease – and distributed under a different arrangement – dividend, a different loan, etc. In these cases, there is no direct connection between the beneficiary and the income received by the intermediary. This is valid for both conduit companies and for intermediaries acting independently under the relevant creditor arrangement and a collateral arrangement with a third party which is not related. For example, an intermediary which is the owner of some financial instruments, being fully entitled thereto, enters into a derivative product that replicates the income and values of such instruments.[278] In this case, while the beneficiary of the derivative could be considered as factually receiving the flows generated by the income, they cannot be considered entitled to the income received by the alleged intermediary as in a nominee arrangement. This is because their claims regarding compliance with the derivative contract are barely contractual or personal, and they cannot enforce their ownership against third parties, and if said economic intermediary alienates the financial instrument, the beneficiary could do nothing to constrain the will of such intermediary. The latter could only claim the fulfilment of the obligation towards the intermediary, requiring the amounts corresponding to the contract. The same applies to conduit companies where the shareholder receives the income upon the corporation distribution, while the corporation is receiving income from the debtor in its own right.

Those statements from the UK clearly show that beneficial ownership at the beginning of its treaty use did not cover these conduit and other transactions at all where the obligation to pass the income was independent from the arrangement upon which the intermediary obtained the assets deriving the income or upon which such assets were subsequently acquired.

In addition, the introduction of other provisions to deal with conduit companies in treaties with the Netherlands, Switzerland and Luxembourg, where beneficial ownership was included, also suggests the inability of the term to cope with them.[279]

[277] ibid.

[278] Even though dealing with a beneficial ownership test derived from the Model, this is the case in *Bank A v Federal Tax Authority* (swaps), where a financial institution acquired shares and entered into a collateral agreement, but an independent swap contract referred to the income of such shares. However, the court ruled against the taxpayer following an anti-avoidance principle: *Undisclosed companies v Federal Tax Administration (Swaps case)* [2012] Bundesverwaltungsgericht A-6537/2010.

[279] 'United Kingdom/Switzerland Double Taxation Protocol', 10 July 1980; 'United Kingdom/Netherlands Double Taxation Agreement', 7 November 1979; 'United Kingdom/Switzerland Double Taxation Protocol', 10 July 1980, in Luxembourg (TNA IR 40/18362).

This limited early scope also matches how the concept has been progressively broadened as tax authorities needed tools to tackle other avoidance schemes, even though the term was not initially aimed as such arrangements.[280] Perhaps the 1970s winds of change in UK tax law that ultimately led to the *Ramsay* doctrine was also felt with regard to how beneficial ownership was understood in tax treaties, widening its scope on the justification of the battle against tax avoidance. If this is true, it is ironic that a rule introduced to solve the rigour of the *Duke of Westminster* doctrine but within a literal viewpoint eventually ended up spreading its effects beyond its wording and primary aim.

A second comment – one repeated in several documents – stated that beneficial owner weakness needed to be supplemented with other anti-avoidance rules for cases such as dividend stripping, bond washing or possible use of liability under remittance basis taxation to access treaty benefits without actual taxation in the UK.[281] This also confirms that the beneficial owner test was a rather narrow one.

Additionally, in the negotiations with New Zealand, a rather limited reference to nominees in the sense of *agents* indicates that New Zealand considered that the tax implications in these cases would be redirected to principals, so that the concept of beneficial ownership would not be relevant for the purposes of these intermediaries.[282] However, it is not specified whether this refers to ordinary agents, so that if one were speaking about all types of agents – both disclosed and undisclosed – the concept of beneficial ownership would be irrelevant, or whether this irrelevance refers only to disclosed agents. The relevance of the concept of beneficial ownership could be understood for the purposes of undisclosed agents if the existence of an implicit trust is taken into account, since, in the event that the agent does not pass on the transaction effects to the principal, the principal could exercise and claim their equitable ownership on the basis of this breach of trust.

Finally, some negotiations refer to banks and custodians, which suggests that treaty negotiators were thinking about intermediaries holding shares or securities just to manage them and receive the income on behalf of the actual owner, who was the client of the bank or custodian entity.[283] In addition, the use of nominee wording, which is widely referred to in these financial intermediary transactions, may suggest that beneficial ownership at the time was confined to these type of transactions.[284]

[280] The 1986 conduit company report seemingly expanded the use of the beneficial ownership test in the Model. See OECD, 'Double Taxation Conventions and the Use of Conduit Companies' in *International Tax Avoidance and Evasion: Four Related Studies* (OECD 1987) 93. On this point see S Jain and J Prebble, 'Conceptual Problems of Beneficial Ownership in Respect of Agents and Nominees' (2018) 73 *World Tax Journal* 3. However, Jain and Prebble missed the combination of beneficial ownership and anti-avoidance rules on intermediary companies from US case law, which had already existed for decades before the 1986 Report.

[281] See above, n 199. See also '2. Article 6 (Limitation of Relief)'; 'Main points arising out of the talks with a Spanish delegation on 23 July 1974 on which we have undertaken to write to the Spaniards', T. 1169/207/71, p 3, in Double Taxation Agreement with Spain Board of Inland Revenue (TNA Ref IR 40/18058); Art 3(2) of the 1969 United Kingdom–Austria Tax Convention. Art 3(2) of the 1967 United Kingdom–Luxembourg Tax Convention. Double Taxation Negotiations in Oslo – 4th–8th March 1968, m no 11, in Double taxation agreement with Norway (TNA Ref IR 40/17262); Negotiation of new Double Taxation Convention with Finland, Helsinki – 27th February to 11st March 1968, m no 7, in Origin papers of the renegotiation of double taxation agreement with Finland (TNA Ref IR 40/17812).

[282] See Negotiation of the United Kingdom–New Zealand DTT included in TNA IR 40/17246, cited and within the limitations of the citation therein stated in Vann (n 9) 276–79.

[283] See above, n 231.

[284] See above, n 242.

Taking into account those considerations by the UK at the OECD and in the negotiations that the aim of the rule was to tackle intermediaries with a legal right to income but not to deal with conduit corporations, dividend stripping or other arrangements, and that it was primarily aimed at custodians and banks, it is very likely that beneficial ownership had, in this first instance and from the UK's point of view, a very narrow scope. The application would be limited to custodians, nominees and agents under equity or common law arrangements who held legal ownership of shares or securities but were acting in their own name and on behalf of a third party with few or no powers.

Looking at the assumed views of both the USA and the UK, a number of questions arise. On the US side, complex or non-fixed trusts, partnerships and estates were considered unable to access treaty benefits even if acting on their own.[285] Conversely, taking the UK view into account, one might argue they could access treaty provisions. Two options can be considered: (i) the UK definition was a strict one, so any other arrangement sharing the characteristics but not being an agency or bare trust cannot be considered as excluded from treaty benefits within the scope of beneficial ownership; and (ii) the definition was an example, and any arrangement sharing such characteristics was excluded from treaty benefits under such a rule.

On this point, the negotiations with New Zealand over the 1967 Tax Treaty might suggest that discretionary trusts without a specific beneficiary may also be excluded from the scope of application of the rule under the treaty's beneficial owner rule.[286] Accordingly, in the author's view, the above-mentioned second option is correct, and all types of arrangements were excluded if displaying the defined characteristics. However, most discretionary trusts, active partnerships and estates would not be denied beneficial owner status, as those arrangements normally imply an active role for the intermediary, and not limited duties, and is normally taxed in the hands of the trustee.[287] A different issue is that an arrangement providing all the control and decision powers with a certain beneficiary is hidden behind an apparently active trust, partnership or estate. In that case, the intermediary arrangement is obviously excluded from the treaty benefits on its own residence conditions, though this is because it is actually a bare trust or nominee arrangement itself, not because it is one of these fiduciary arrangements with few or no powers.

Similarly, as the UK was including the beneficial ownership rule in treaties with civil or continental law countries, one might argue about which arrangements fall within the exclusion. Continental agencies and *fiducia* could be the ones that share the greatest resemblance to bare trust and nominee arrangements. There is little problem under continental laws with direct agency, as income and tax effects will normally be allocated to the principal if the agent is acting in the name and on behalf of the principal.[288] For agencies acting in their own name and on behalf of the principal, continental law normally states that the tax consequences will be allocated to the agent unless the

[285] See above, n 87 and accompanying text.

[286] File IR 40/17246, 14 February 1966, The National Archives (UK) Public Record Office. Quoted by Vann (n 33) n 27, by reference to John Taylor. See also accompanying text.

[287] See above, ch 3.

[288] 'Report on suggested amendments to Articles 11 and 12 of the Draft Convention, relating to interest and royalties respectively' [FC/WP27 (70) 1], Working Party 27, Fiscal Committee, OECD, 16 February 1970, p 14; OECD Archives, Paris.

transaction hides the ownership of the principal, in which case, under the sham or simulation principle – in the sense of defining actual facts, not in the sense of anti-avoidance doctrine[289] – the tax consequences will be allocated to the principal.

To sum up, in the author's view, the UK definition of beneficial owner at this early stage between the 1960s and 1970s excluded reduced tax rates at source on dividends, interest and royalties by subjects resident in the other contracting holds: (i) they hold the legal ownership of the asset, including the title ownership and record ownership, but not the absolute substantive law ownership; (ii) they transfer the income to a third party with a direct and accrued right that arises as soon as derived by the intermediary, in the form of a substantive legal ownership, to the income; (iii) their decision-making powers with regard to the asset and/or income are virtually non-existent; (iv) the beneficiary's interest on the income is quantified in a precise manner from the beginning of the legal relationship, be it a set amount or defined in abstract terms as having the whole or partial right to a certain right of the intermediary, so the right of the beneficiary can be quantified as soon as the income arises to the intermediary; and (v) they are bound by law to comply with the instructions received. In positive terms, for tax treaty purposes, beneficial owners: (i) may have or lack legal ownership, record ownership and/or title ownership, but always enjoy all powers of control and enjoyment thereof; (ii) receive the income from the legal, record and/or title owner in their own right and not at the discretion of the legal, record and/or title owner; (iii) have the full or almost full power to decide on the asset and/or the income; (iv) hold an interest which is quantified in a concrete manner (even if in relation to an undefined credit), so their right can be quantified *ab initio* as soon as the income arises to the intermediary, and not abstractly or conditional; and (v) are entitled to enforce the rights pertaining to their ownership against the intermediary and in some cases against third parties.

Very briefly, using Miller's terms, the beneficial owner will be the substantive law owner in common law or equity law who can claim the greatest proprietary rights before the courts, which perfectly matches what was said by the UK in its negotiations with Spain defining the beneficial owner as the true owner alone who can establish a claim.[290] In this regard, it seems beneficial ownership in tax treaties from the British perspective in the 1960s followed the equity law definition of beneficial ownership of the time, which matches the case law interpretation of the term in domestic tax law of the time.[291]

However, it should be borne in mind that this is the interpretation of the UK, and treaties have to be interpreted by deriving the common intention from the views of both countries, so beneficial ownership may not always be interpreted in this sense in all the UK treaties agreed in the 1960s and 1970s.[292] Moreover, dynamic interpretation may account for the broadened interpretation of beneficial ownership in these treaties that has since developed.

[289] See fn 204 and accompanying text in ch 3 above.

[290] Beneficial owner is defined as the 'True Owner alone who could establish a claim': Double Taxation Negotiations in Madrid, Monday 25th–Friday 29th November, 1968, in Double taxation agreement with Spain Board of Inland Revenue, m no 26 (TNA Ref IR 40/18058). See Miller (n 83) 216–18.

[291] See above, II.B.ii.a in ch 3, namely cases in n 233 above.

[292] J Avery Jones, 'The "One True Meaning" of a Tax Treaty' [2001] *Bulletin for International Taxation* 220, 222.

What also had to be taken into account was the UK's thinking on how its domestic tax system dealt with intermediaries, so it is doubtful how the rule would apply to an agent acting in its own name and on its own account. Probably the UK's viewpoint was that the mentioned case fell within the scope of the beneficial owner rule.

In the case of the United States–United Kingdom 1966 Protocol, the author argued that the USA considered any trust, estate or partnership to be unable to access treaty benefits, while the UK may have considered them able to do so in some circumstances. In this sense, it is likely that the US understanding of the term was broader than the UK's, as the former had longer experience in the use of the rule that led it to use it as a tool to tackle other structures. As the interpretation of a treaty in theory has to be construed by matching the intentions of both parties and the minimum common understanding was the narrow UK view, it could be said that the 1966 United Kingdom–United States Protocol only excluded nominees and bare trusts in the very narrow sense of those intermediaries with little or no power, and left open the access to treaty benefits to other – actual – active fiduciaries or intermediaries. In this sense, Treasury decisions regarding the application of the treaty could be considered as overriding the treaty, and should be interpreted as excluding only those arrangements where the intermediaries have little or no power.

In the case of the United Kingdom–New Zealand Tax Treaty, New Zealand seemingly did not see any problem at all with the allocation of tax consequences to principals in nominees and agents cases, so for them the concept created a number of controversies rather than adding a solution, such as in the case of active or discretionary trusts.[293] This was seen by Vann as a sign of New Zealand considering the concept as already implicitly contained in tax treaties.[294] Taking both views, the term beneficial owner in the 1967 United Kingdom–New Zealand Tax Treaty could be regarded as largely following the UK view, because New Zealand considered the concept irrelevant, covering active trusts, bare trusts and nominees with few powers, and posing problems with other active trusts where intermediaries held more abilities or powers.

In the case of other treaties, such as UK's treaties with Norway, Finland, Spain and Austria from the 1960s and 1970s, there is no information on how the UK's counterparties understood the beneficial owner rule apart from the assertions attributed to them and contained in the UK minutes. It may be conceded that as the term beneficial owner was incorporated at the suggestion of the UK, the counterparty just agreed with the UK's proposal, so the definition incorporated was the UK view. However, it is also likely that many nuances could be derived from what was understood by the other party and from what the other party bore in mind from its domestic understanding of intermediaries and their tax treatment.

[293] See above, n 286.
[294] Vann (n 33) 277.

5

Changing Skin in the OECD Model: What do Intermediaries in Continental Law and Common Law have in Common?

I. The Wording and the 1977 OECD Original Meaning of the Terms

In 1977, beneficial ownership was included in Articles 10, 11 and 12 of the OECD Model Tax Convention (the Model) on interests, dividends and royalties. From there, it moved into most treaties within the world tax treaty network.[1] However, despite its move from UK and US tax treaty policy to global tax treaty policy, its meaning has never been clear, and tax authorities and courts have been interpreting it inconsistently.[2] Worse still, compared with its previous use being limited to just the USA and UK, the interaction of the concept with more legal systems, most of which were not familiar with such common law wording, added more difficulties. The UK's proposal, limited to exclude nominees, changed in the OECD to include continental law intermediaries acting in their own name but on account of the beneficiary.[3] What do the two types of arrangement have in common?

A. The Interpretation of Tax Treaties and Beneficial Ownership

It is unanimously accepted that the beneficial owner test in tax treaties has to be interpreted according to international tax treaty interpretative rules.[4] This includes the rules

[1] The beneficial owner requirement is included with that wording or beneficially owned in at least 3,380 tax treaties on income and capital taxes, according to the IBFD Tax Research Platform. On Arts 10, 11 and 12 it seems to be included in at least 1,790 tax treaties (as of 3 May 2019).

[2] Update of the UN Model Double Taxation Convention between Developed and Developing Countries–Beneficial Ownership (E/C.18/2019/CRP.10), 2 April 2019, Committee of Experts on International Cooperation in Tax Matters, United Nations, p 2, para 3; D Oliver et al, 'Beneficial Ownership' (2000) 54 *Bulletin for International Taxation* 310, 310.

[3] See the answers of other countries to the UK proposal concerning such agents *proprio nomine* in 'Report on suggested amendments to Articles 11 and 12 of the Draft Convention, relating to interest and royalties respectively' [FC/WP27 (70) 1], Working Party 27, Fiscal Committee, OECD, 16 February 1970, p 14; OECD Archives, Paris.

[4] Oliver et al (n 2) 317–18; C Du Toit, *Beneficial Ownership of Royalties in Bilateral Tax Treaties* (IBFD 1999) 21.

codified in Articles 31 and 32 of the Vienna Convention of the Law of Treaties and, specifically in tax treaties, Article 3(2) of the Model.[5]

The first article sets the treaty terms – beneficial ownership in this case – which have to be interpreted in good faith on the ordinary meaning of the term, taking into account the intrinsic and extrinsic context, which would give it a special meaning if this was the purpose of the parties, and taking into account supplementary sources, such as preparatory works, if needed.[6] In the end, the interpretation of beneficial ownership, as with any other treaty rule, has to depart from the ordinary sense of the wording, and considering

[5] On tax treaties as international treaties being interpreted following international interpretative rules, see M Lang and F Brugger, 'The Role of the OECD Commentary in Tax Treaty Interpretation' (2008) 23 *Australian Tax Forum* 95; P Wattel and O Marres, 'The Legal Status of the OECD Commentary and Static or Ambulatory Interpretation of Tax Treaties' (2003) 43 *European Taxation* 222. However, the specific object and characteristics of tax treaties have to be taken into account to interpret them, which in the author's view is not a deviation from public international law principles but to take into account its object, purpose and context. Du Toit (n 4) 49–52; Lang and Brugger 103 et seq; E Van der Bruggen, 'Unless the Vienna Convention Otherwise Requires: Notes on the Relationship between Article 3(2) of the Model and Articles 31 and 32 of the Vienna Convention on the Law of Treaties' (2003) 43 *European Taxation* 142, 270. On the customary nature of the interpretative rules of the Vienna Convention, which makes irrelevant whether the state is party to the Vienna Convention or not, see R Bernhardt, 'Interpretation in International Law', *Encyclopedia of Public International Law*, vol 7 (Elsevier, 1984) 321; I Sinclair in JF Avery Jones, 'Interpretation of Tax Treaties' (1986) 40 *Bulletin* 75, 75; ME Villiger, *Commentary on the 1969 Vienna Convention on the Law of Treaties* (Martinus Nijhoff, 2009) 439 et seq. For case law, see *Guinea-Bisseau v Senegal* [1991] International Court of Justice Reports 53 (ICJ); *Territorial Dispute (Libyan Arab Jamahiriya v Chad)* [1994] International Court of Justice Reports 6. In the USA, it is argued that the Vienna Convention's interpretative criteria do not lay down customary law criteria, but are somehow generally accepted principles. Lower courts commonly resort to the Vienna Convention, and the Department of State recognises it as an authoritative guide, but the Supreme Court only very vaguely resorts to its interpretative criteria. The US position probably accepts it, but states its willingness to retain its power to add nuances: American Law Institute, *Restatement (Third) Foreign Relations of the United States*, vol 1 (American Law Institute Publishers, 1986) 196; R Kysar, 'Interpreting Tax Treaties' (2016) 101 *Iowa Law Review* 1387, 1402. On the need to overcome domestic interpretative rules see Bernhardt 319. On the interpretation of tax treaties in the USA as compared to other countries see Kysar 1404 et seq. See also Robert Thornton Smith, 'Tax Treaty Interpretation by the Judiciary' (1995) 49 *Tax Lawyer* 845; JA Townsend, 'Tax Treaty Interpretation' (2001) 55 *Tax Lawyer* 219; RK Osgood, 'Interpreting Tax Treaties in Canada, the United States, and the United Kingdom' (1984) 17 *Cornell International Law Journal* 255. On Art 3(2), see JF Avery Jones et al, 'The Interpretation of Tax Treaties with Particular Reference to Article 3 (2) of the OECD Model – I' [1984] *British Tax Review* 14; JF Avery Jones et al, 'The Interpretation of Tax Treaties with Particular Reference to Article 3 (2) of OECD Model – Part 2' [1984] *British Tax Review* 90; MN Kandev, 'Tax Treaty Interpretation: Determining Domestic Meaning under Article 3 (2) of the OECD Model' (2007) 55 *Canadian Tax Journal* 31; F Engelen, *Interpretation of Tax Treaties under International Law* (IBFD, 2004) 473 et seq; HA Shannon, 'United States Income Tax Treaties: Reference to Domestic Law for the Meaning of Undefined Terms' (1989) 17 *Intertax* 453; E Reimer and A Rust (eds), *Klaus Vogel on Double Taxation Conventions*, vol 1, 4th edn (Kluwer, 2015) 206 et seq.

[6] On the interpretation criteria see Bernhardt (n 5) 322 et seq; I Brownlie and J Crawford, *Brownlie's Principles of Public International Law*, 8th edn (Oxford University Press, 2012) 379–84; GG Fitzmaurice, 'Law and Procedure of the International Court of Justice: Treaty Interpretation and Certain Other Treaty Points' (1951) 28 *British Yearbook of International Law* 1; R Bernhardt, 'Interpretation and Implied (Tacit) Modification of Treaties, Comments on Arts. 27, 28, 29 and 38 of the ILC's 1966 Draft Articles on the Law of Treaties' (1967) 27 *Zeitschrift für Ausländisches Öffentliches Recht un Völkerrecht* 491; I Sinclair, *The Vienna Convention on the Law of Treaties*, 2nd edn (Manchester University Press, 1984); Engelen (n 5) 111 et seq; 'Annual Report of the International Law Commission' (1966) II *Yearbook of the International Law Commission* 169, 217 et seq. On the application of the Vienna Convention to tax treaties see Engelen (n 5) 425 et seq; D Ward, 'Principles to Be Applied in Interpreting Tax Treaties' [1977] *Canadian Tax Journal* 263; M Edwardes-Ker, *Tax Treaty Interpretation* (Queen Mary University of London Theses, 1994) https://qmro.qmul.ac.uk/xmlui/handle/123456789/1679; Reimer and Rust (n 5) 37 et seq; Engelen (n 5) 425 et seq; Reimer, E, 'Interpretation of Tax Treaties' (1999) 39 *European Taxation* 458; JM Calderón Carrero and MD Piña Garrido, 'Interpretation of Tax Treaties' (1999) 39 *European Taxation* 376.

the rest of the treaty, other related treaties signed together (subsequently or after), domestic law of the states, negotiation materials and any other source related to the treaty, must try to unravel the meaning intended by the contracting parties. But that meaning has to take into account the case at stake by balancing all such available materials in accordance with their value and their relation to the specific treaty and not in general to the models, and without exceeding the limit of the possible meaning of such wording contained of the treaty.[7] This will include taking into account all of the relevant protocols, annexes, domestic law, other treaties, models, commentaries, practices, administrative guidance, case law and any other material, and using them in accordance with their value in relation to the treaty.

To interpret beneficial ownership on its wording and within a specific treaty means to interpret the treaty jointly with the other sources specifically connected to such treaty, and not in relation to other treaties or model in general. That said, other treaties or models, the materials related to them and state practice arising out of them may play a role in the interpretation of the specific applicable treaty[8] – but their influence will depend on their relevance to that treaty. In addition, general principles of international law could be applicable to the treaty insofar as they are generally accepted and without objection.[9] In this regard, it has been suggested that international principles such as the prevention of abuse may help to interpret the term.[10]

All materials related to beneficial ownership that somehow connect to the relevant treaty have to be taken into account and properly weighed against their relationship with

[7] See Sinclair (n 6). A relevant controversy was whether there is a hierarchy between interpretative methods, as literal and purposive interpretation had taken place for decades. However, the International Law Commission rejected any hierarchy, even though the text has to be respected as a starting point. Bernhardt points to a more relevance of the text, context and object. Dixon suggests there is some prevalence of the text. See some of these views in M Dixon, R McCorquodale and S Williams, *International Law*, 5th edn (Oxford University Press, 2011) 87; Bernhardt (n 5) 322; 'Annual Report of the International Law Commission' (n 6) 220. Recent case law seems to suggest there is sort of a primacy of the text as the starting interpretative point: *Territorial and Maritime Dispute (Nicaragua v Colombia)* (2007) 2007 International Court of Justice Reports 832 (ICJ) 867–69. Probably the most correct view is that the interpretative process forms a single process that includes all criteria, and even though it may go through different steps and sources, it is a matter of logic, not a matter of hierarchy. This, of course, includes departing from the text and respecting its limit, but without implying that the text is above the rest. Thus, all sources and criteria have to be properly balanced against each other: 'Annual Report of the International Law Commission' (n 6) 220; Brownlie and Crawford (n 6) 381; *Land, Island and Maritime Frontier Dispute (El Salvador/Honduras: Nicaragua intervening)* (1992) International Court of Justice Reports 1992 351 (ICJ) 718. In the USA, calling for a substantive interpretation taking into account extrinsic material, see Kysar (n 5).

[8] The OECD Commentary plays a major role in treaty interpretation, both as the starting point for negotiations of most countries and because it reflects practices and consensus to some extent. However, its value in relation to a specific treaty has to be carefully balanced against other sources. On the role of the Commentary see Lang and Brugger (n 5); Wattel and Marres (n 5); H Ault, 'The Role of the OECD Commentaries in the Interpretation of Tax Treaties' (1994) 22 *Intertax* 144; Reimer and Rust (n 5) 45 et seq; C Garbarino, *Judicial Interpretation of Tax Treaties: The Use of the OECD Commentary* (Edward Elgar Publishing, 2016). On subsequent practice and whether commentaries to the Model may prove administrative practice: Van der Bruggen (n 5) 270; Lang and Brugger (n 5) 103; Reimer and Rust (n 5) 49–52; Engelen (n 5) 435.

[9] Brownlie and Crawford (n 6) 33–34.

[10] D Ward, 'Abuse of Tax Treaties' (1995) 23 *Intertax* 176, 178–79; K Vogel, *Klaus Vogel on Double Taxation Conventions*, 3rd edn (Kluwer, 1997) 66, 125; L De Broe, *International Tax Planning and Prevention of Abuse* (IBFD, 2008) 301–76. On the connection between beneficial owner and the international principle of abuse, see R Danon, 'Le Concept de Bénéficiaire Effective Dans Le Cadre Du MC OCDE' [2007] *IFF Forum Für Steuerrecht* 38, 50–51 and 53; RA De Mooij, *The OECD Model Convention – 1998 and Beyond, the Concept of Beneficial Ownership in Tax Treaties, vol 52, Congress* (Kluwer, 2000) 32.

the treaty at stake. However, as the beneficial owner clause is normally taken in most treaties from the Model without any specific discussion, interpretation would generally follow the Commentary to the OECD Model Tax Convention and its wording, unless there are other sources providing a different definition or nuances.[11]

(i) The Ordinary Meaning of Beneficial Ownership: The OECD Wording

First of all, beneficial owner is made up of two words. The first question to ask is whether the two words should be interpreted jointly or separately. The proper meaning is the one derived from a joint consideration, even though separate interpretations may serve as a starting point.[12]

Beneficial, according to the *The New Oxford English Dictionary*, means 'resulting in good; favourable or advantageous'.[13] In addition, *The Oxford English Dictionary* also notes a second definition, related to its legal meaning, as 'law of or relating to right to the use or benefit of the property, other than legal title'.[14] *Black's Law Dictionary* defines beneficial as 'tending to the benefit of a person; yielding a profit, advantage or benefit; enjoying or entitled to a benefit or profit. This term is applied both to estates (as a "beneficial interest") and to persons (as the "beneficial owner").'[15]

Owner, in turn, refers to the person to whom something belongs or by whom something is possessed by.[16] In a technical sense, *Black's Law Dictionary* defines owner as the subject 'holding ownership, dominion or title of property; or proprietor'.[17] In a more specific way, the dictionary defines owner as:

> He [or she] who has dominion of a thing, real or personal, corporeal or incorporeal, which he has a right to enjoy and do with as he pleases, even to spoil or destroy it, as far as the law permits, unless he be prevented by some agreement or covenant which restrains his right.[18]

In any case, *Black's Law Dictionary* itself recognises it is a general concept that must be related to its context.[19]

[11] For instance, the USA normally defines beneficial ownership with reference to domestic allocation rules in their technical explanation, which clearly does not follow the Model. The issue would be what effect has this approach to its counterparty if its counterparty is basing its negotiation on the Model. Other examples are found in the 1989 Germany–Italy, the 1991 Germany–Norway and the 1992 Germany–Sweden Tax Conventions, where beneficial ownership is also defined in its protocol by domestic allocation rules.

[12] Rejecting the separate interpretation, even though in relation to Art 3(2), MN Kandev, 'Tax Treaty Interpretation: Determining Domestic Meaning under Article 3 (2) of the OECD Model' (2007) 55 *Canadian Tax Journal* 31, 57.

[13] J Pearsall (ed), *The New Oxford Dictionary of English* (Oxford University Press, 1998) 162.

[14] ibid.

[15] HC Black, *Black´s Law Dictionary*, 6th edn (West Publishing Company 1990) 156.

[16] '[U]sed with a possessive to mean that someone or something belongs or is possessed by the person mentioned': Pearsall (n 13) 1326.

[17] 'Owner. The person in whom is vested the ownership, dominion, or title of property; proprietor. He who has dominion of a thing, real or personal, corporeal or incorporeal, which he has a right to enjoy and do with as he pleases, even to spoil or destroy it, as far as the law permits, unless he be prevented by some agreement or covenant which restrains his right': Black (n 15) 1105.

[18] ibid.

[19] 'The term is, however, a nomen generalissimum, and its meaning is to be gathered from the connection in which it is used, and from the subject-matter to which it is applied. The primary meaning of the word as applied to land is one who owns the fee and who has the right to dispose of the property, but the term also includes one having a possessory right to land or the person occupying or cultivating it': ibid.

As owner can be understood in a narrow sense as regarding the full right to dispose, use and enjoy, or in a broad sense as related to a set of rights upon which the subject can occupy, use and have different abilities in relation to an object, owner in beneficial owner may lead the latter to also be understood in a narrow or broad sense. However, whatever the case, the word beneficial points to benefiting, leading to some extent to use and enjoyment.

It follows that beneficial ownership has to refer to a proprietary right on a thing with more or less broad abilities to benefit or get advantage from it, namely to use and enjoy it. Considering that owner is a word of some strength, as opposed to, for instance, title, the abilities of an owner should comprise the core abilities to benefit from an object derived from the ownership condition, especially use and enjoyment.[20] Similarly, it could be interpreted as the ownership right to use and enjoyment.

The problem becomes how to determine to what extent the subject has to benefit and have strong proprietary rights in order to qualify as beneficial owner in such sense. The above meanings remain significantly vague and may include almost any possession right, usufruct or beneficiary interest, and many others.

An interesting point in this regard relates to how such definition of rights of use and enjoyment may be interpreted in civil law countries. The term could easily be related to civil law usufruct, as civil law countries recognise the division of ownership into the abilities to use and enjoy, on the one hand, and to sell and dispose of the thing, lacking the right to use or control, on the other.[21] One of the first translations of beneficial owner at the OECD used the precise word *l'usufrutier*.[22] However, this first translation was dismissed, and the wording *bénéficiare effectif* was used instead.[23] The change in wording strongly suggests that the term beneficial owner was not absolutely equivalent to the beneficiary in a usufruct, and that civil law countries did not want to use the rule for usufructs, or not only usufructs.[24] Was the meaning broader or narrower, then?

[20] 'The term "owner" is used to indicate a person in whom one or more interests are vested for his own benefit. The person in whom the interests are vested has "title" to the interests whether he holds them for his own benefit or for the benefit of another. Thus the term "title", unlike "ownership"' is a colourless word; to say without more that a person has title to certain property does not indicate whether he holds such property for his own benefit or as a *trustee*': ibid (emphasis added).

[21] See G Venezian, *Usufructo, Uso y Habitación*, vols I and II (V Suarez, 1928); F Rivero Hernández, *Usufructo, Uso y Habitación*, 2nd edn (Civitas, 2016).

[22] '[N]otre sens, l'allègement prévu par ces articles ne devrait être accordé que si le propriétaire ou l'usufruitier (beneficial owner) des revenus en question réside dans l'autre Etat contractant': 'Observations des pays membres sur les difficultes soulevées par le projet de convention de l'OCDE sur le revenu et la fortune', Fiscal Committee [TFD/FC/216], OCDE, 2 mai 1967. Liste consolidee des questions a examiner relatives au projet de convention de double imposition concernant le revenue et la fortune [TFD/FC/218], OCDE, 21 juillet 1967.

[23] The wording *l'usufruitier* as translation of beneficial owner was substituted by *bénéficiare*, which was used in an intermediary report in 1968; after 1969, *bénéficiare effective* was definitively used. See 'Rapport preliminaire sur les amendments à apporter eventuellement à l'article 11 du projet de convention rélative aux interest et a l'article 12 du projet de convention rélative aux redevances' [FC/WP27(68)1], Fiscal Committee, OCDE, 30 December 1968: 'selon laquelle le pays de la source ne renoncera à son droit d'imposition que si le pays de résidence impose les intérêts, ou bien prévoir que les dispositions des articles ne s'appliquent qu'aux intérêts, etc., payés au "bénéficiaire effectif", comme dans la Convention Pays-Bas-Royaume-Uni). Les délégués de la Suisse et des Etats-Unis préfèrent tous deux la solution du "bénéficiaire effectif"' (above, note sur les debats qui ont eu lieu lors de la 31ème session du comite fiscal, tenue du 10 au 13 juin 1969, sur le premier rapport du groupe de travail nº 27 de ce Comité [DAF/FC/69.10], Fiscal Committee, OCDE, 4 July 1969).

[24] Baker argues that *bénéficiare effectif* should not be used in the sense of any similar technical term of civil law countries: P Baker, *Double Taxation Conventions*, loose-leaf edn (Sweet & Maxwell) 10–17.

Turning to consideration of the meaning of the words jointly, it has already been argued that beneficial owner refers to the person with the present right in equity against the world at large over assets or property of a trust outweighing any other rights and usually including the primary right to control and the primary right to income.[25] It is important to bear in mind that beneficial ownership may arise as result of an implied trust – such as one derived from equitable claims in an agency or any other fiduciary relationship – and not necessarily an express one, even though identification is more complex in such cases.[26] In a loose way, it may be argued that beneficial ownership could comprise any equitable right granted in equity on a thing related to use, benefit or enjoyment to a certain degree.

Article 3(2) of the Model, which is contained in most treaties, could lead to the use of the same definition in those countries that recognise beneficial ownership in equity law. Under such an article, terms not defined in the Model itself, such as beneficial owner, shall be defined by the meaning it has under the laws of the state applying the treaty, unless the context requires otherwise.[27] This would leave the treaty term for common law countries to be defined according to its domestic definition in equity law or in tax law,[28] and these definitions, particularly the equity law meaning and the meaning under the certainty principle in tax law, largely match the above-mentioned definition derived from the wording. In addition, other similar meanings contained in the domestic law of several states, such as beneficial owner definitions for purposes of money laundering, rightful recipient and economic allocation, may be used to define the treaty term in each state's respective treaties under this approach.[29] Finally, domestic anti-avoidance rules have been considered by some as applicable to the treaty under the beneficial owner interpretation following Article 3(2).[30]

However, the majority of authors and courts accept beneficial ownership to be one of the cases where the context requires otherwise, so it cannot be understood under any of those meanings as the definition of the law of the state applying the treaty.[31]

[25] See s II.B in ch 2 above.

[26] See s II.C.viii in ch 2 above.

[27] See the literature on Art 3(2) quoted above in n 5.

[28] ibid. Some authors note that submission is to domestic law related to the treaty, and resort to domestic private law or other tax rules is limited: see Shannon (n 5) 457 et seq; K Vogel and R Prokisch, 'General Report' in K Vogel and R Prokisch (eds), *Interpretation of Double Taxation Conventions*, vol a (Kluwer, 1993) 80; Vogel (n 10) 210. Others note that rules from other taxes or private law may be used, at least after the 1995 clarification: Engelen (n 5) 485; Kandev (n 5) 55; Kandev (n 12) 55. However, if it is used in both tax law related to the treaty and other areas, the first one shall prevail: Reimer and Rust (n 5) 207.

[29] See the definition on beneficial ownership regarding money laundering in Art 3(6) of Directive (EU) 2015/849 of the European Parliament and of the Council of 20 May 2015 on the prevention of the use of the financial system for the purposes of money laundering or terrorist financing [2015] OJ L141/73, derived from Recommendations 10, 24 and 25 of the Financial Action Task Force. The same rule is applicable in most countries. On its relationship to beneficial ownership in tax treaties, rejecting its use, see W Eynatten, K De Haen and N Hostyn, 'The Concept of "Beneficial Owner" under Belgian Tax Law: Legal Interpretation Is Maintained' (2003) 31 *Intertax* 523, 533. On economic ownership, see s 39(2) of the German Abgabenordnung; D Killius, 'The Concept of "Beneficial Ownership" of Items of Income under German Tax Treaties' (1989) 17 *Intertax* 340. On beneficial ownership and a similar concept in Nordic countries, namely Denmark and Sweden, which is sometimes misunderstood as its domestic definition, see J Bundgaard and N Winther-Sorensen, 'Beneficial Ownership in International Financing Structures' (2008) 50 *Tax Notes International* 587, 607–08; D Kleist, 'First Swedish Case on Beneficial Owner' (2013) 41 *Intertax* 159.

[30] Rejected in Du Toit (n 4) 178.

[31] Baker, *Double Taxation Conventions* (n 24) 10–7; Vogel (n 10) 562; A Martín Jiménez, 'Beneficial Ownership: Current Trends' (2010) 2 *World Tax Journal* 35, 50, 55; Libin in Oliver et al (n 2) 316;

First, the concept is unknown to most countries, so no definition is provided in them.[32] Moreover, in those countries familiar with the wording, it has no specific meaning but several variable meanings, as shown in previous chapters, so the interpretation would remain inconsistent.[33] Secondly, some definitions, such as that for anti-money laundering rules, do not fit the object and purpose of the rule in tax treaties.[34] The same may be argued for meanings such as beneficial ownership regarding discretionary trusts, which may pose significant problems in relation to such objects and purposes.[35] Thirdly, differences in domestic meanings would lead to variable and inconsistent results, and would leave allocation of taxing powers in the hands of domestic authorities.[36] A variable domestic allocation can hardly be in line with the object and purpose of allocating tax jurisdiction of tax treaties, which is to provide for certainty in cross-border

De Broe (n 10) 456, 490; Danon (n 10) 40; S Van Weeghel, *The Improper Use of Tax Treaties* (Kluwer, 1998) 70; J Avery Jones et al, 'The Origins of Concepts and Expressions Used in the OECD Model and Their Adoption by States' (2006) 60 *Bulletin for International Taxation* 220, 249. See also Du Toit (n 4) 178, even though he seemingly suggests that there might be a domestic meaning if the term is found within domestic law related to tax treaties and domestic law upon which it refers. In favour of a domestic meaning following Art 3(2), even though accepting the need for some contextual adjustments, C Eliffe, 'The Meaning of "Beneficial Ownership" in Double Tax Agreements' [2009] *British Tax Review* 276, 297–98. In favour of a domestic meaning, Eynatten et al (n 29) 538. Pijl claims a domestic definition for the Netherlands, but because the country enacted a specific definition that overrides the context upon which beneficial owner would normally be internationally defined under Art 3(2): H Pijl, 'Beneficial Ownership and Second Tier Beneficial Owners in Tax Treaties of the Netherlands' (2003) 31 *Intertax* 353. In case law, almost all cases support an autonomous international tax definition of the term, even though some of them then combine it with domestic anti-avoidance rules or principles. To mention a few, see *Indofood International v JPMorgan* [2006] EWCA Civ A3/2005/2497, 8003 BTC 158; *Prevost v The Queen* [2009] FCA A-252-08, FCA 57; *Real Madrid v Resolución del TEAC [1]* [2006] Audiencia Nacional Rec 1099/2003, 2007 JUR 8915; *Real Madrid v Resolución del TEAC [2]* [2006] Audiencia Nacional Rec 174/2006, 2006 JUR 284679; *Real Madrid v Resolución del TEAC [3]* [2006] Audiencia Nacional Rec 247/2006, 2006 JUR 284618; *Real Madrid v Resolución del TEAC [4]* [2006] Audiencia Nacional Rec 1096/2003, 2007 JUR 16549; *Real Madrid v Resolución del TEAC [5]* [2006] Audiencia Nacional Rec 1099/2003, 2007 JUR 8915; *Real Madrid v Resolución del TEAC [6]* [2006] Audiencia Nacional Rec 1106/2003, 2007 JUR 16526; *Real Madrid v Resolución del TEAC [7]* [2006] Audiencia Nacional Rec 1110/2003, 2006 JUR 204307; *Real Madrid v Resolución del TEAC [8]* [2006] Audiencia Nacional Rec 280/2006, 2007 JUR 101877.

[32] P Baker, *Double Taxation Conventions* (Sweet & Maxwell, 2018) 10–17; Avery Jones et al (n 31) 249; Vogel (n 10) 562; Committee of Experts on International Coperation in Tax Matters, 'Update of the UN Model Double Taxation Convention between Developed and Developing Countries – Beneficial Ownership' (United Nations, 2019) E/C.18/2019/CRP.10 2; L De Broe, *International Tax Planning and Prevention of Abuse* (IBFD, 2008) 668.

[33] Committee of Experts on International Coperation in Tax Matters (n 32) 2; Avery Jones et al (n 31) 246; C Brown, 'Symposium: Beneficial Ownership and the Income Tax Act' (2003) 51 *Canadian Tax Journal* 401; MD Brender, 'Symposium: Beneficial Ownership in Canadian Income Tax Law: Required Reform and Impact on Harmonization of Quebec Civil Law and Federal Legislation' (2003) 51 *Canadian Tax Journal* 311, 353; R Speed, 'Beneficial Ownership' (1997) 26 *Australian Tax Review* 34.

[34] Dismising the use of the beneficial ownership definition contained in the Savings Directive as being aimed at a different purpose and framed in a different context, F Avella, 'Using EU Law To Interpret Undefined Tax Treaty Terms: Article 31 (3)(c) of the Vienna Convention on the Law of Treaties and Article 3 (2) of the OECD Model Convention' (2012) 4 *World Tax Journal* 95. This has been explicitly recognised in the 2014 amendments to the Commentary on the OECD Model Tax Convention on beneficial ownership. See the footnote to para 12.6 of the Commentary to OECD Model Tax Convention 2014.

[35] See the discussion in Eliffe (n 31) 295; JF Avery Jones et al, 'The Treatment of Trusts under the OECD Model Tax Convention – II' (1989) 51 *British Tax Review* 65, 69–70; Du Toit (n 4) 164; J Prebble, 'Accumulation Trusts and Double Taxation Conventions' [2001] *British Tax Review* 69. On the several outcomes of beneficial ownership in different countries, see Avery Jones et al. See also discretionary trusts in chs 2 and 3 above.

[36] Oliver et al (n 2) 315. Even though not specifically regarding different domestic definitions, the UN report notes that different interpretations may lead to double taxation or double non-taxation: Committee of Experts on International Coperation in Tax Matters (n 32) 2.

investment. Fourthly, the translation of beneficial owner has several nuances in different countries.[37] The submission to domestic law on different wordings may lead to several conflicts, whereas a broad international meaning could allow the encapsulation of all wordings in different languages to make it and its function coherent.[38] Finally, in most tax treaties, the only reason for including the beneficial owner wording is that the treaty follows the Model. Given that the Commentary provides for a definition, it cannot be held that the countries understood the term differently from the international meaning.[39]

The rejection of a domestic meaning has been confirmed by courts, and by the majority of international tax authors, including the most highly reputed, from common law countries.[40] Even though sustaining the interpretation of the term in the sense of their domestic meaning would be easy and appealing, they have argued strongly in favour of an international meaning.[41] Having said that, other specific sources related to the specific treaty being applied may override this sense and specifically refer to the interpretation in the domestic law.[42]

With interpretation in accordance with domestic law under Article 3(2) being widely rejected, some authors argue that the international meaning is imported from the meaning that beneficial ownership has in common law countries.[43] This must be rejected for treaties deriving the concept solely from the Model and with no other reference. The wording in French is *bénéficiare effectif*, which has nothing to do with the common law countries' concept. It is highly doubtful whether the equity law concept was intended. If it was, it could be argued another wording would have been used in the French version, or beneficial owner would even have been maintained. In contrast, no reference to ownership is found in the versions of the Romance languages, but to actual or factual benefit.[44] Such a difference between the use of the word ownership, which has some strength, and the word *effectif* can only mean that the wording of the rule was adapted to the civil law context, where ownership could not be split as in common law countries. This probably shows that civil law countries intended to connect such wording not to legal entitlement or ownership rules, but to some facts. Their not wanting to use either ownership or usufruct could mean that they intended to develop a meaning different from anything known to both legal traditions, or at least, a broader concept that may cover issues regarding intermediaries derived from arrangements of both legal traditions.

The commentaries since 1977 define beneficial owner as excluding intermediaries, such as agent or nominees, which clearly does not absolutely match beneficial ownership

[37] See translations in Oliver et al (n 2) 311–12 and the discussion above in this chapter.

[38] Eliffe (n 31) 297.

[39] Committee of Experts on International Cooperation in Tax Matters, 'Progress Report of Subcommittee on Improper Use of Tax Treaties: Beneficial Ownership' (United Nations, 2008) E/C.18/2008/CRP.2/Add.1 9; Du Toit (n 4) 183 et seq.

[40] *Indofood International Finance Ltd v JP Morgan Chase Bank NA* 158 (EWCA Civ) [42]; *Prevost v The Queen* (n 31) para 12; Baker (n 32) 10–17; Avery Jones et al (n 31) 249.

[41] P Baker, 'Beneficial Ownership: After Indofood' (2007) 6 *GITC Review* 22.

[42] Such as the case of the Technical Explanations to US treaties. See s I.B in ch 4 above.

[43] Du Toit (n 4) 236–37; Eliffe (n 31) 304.

[44] Danon suggests this indicates to look to reality – in his argument, economic reality: Danon (n 10) 41. Similarly, Vogel (n 10) 562.

in equity.[45] If that had been the case, mention of trusts or the equitable meaning would at least have been included in the OECD Commentaries. Indeed, many discussions at the OECD on the inclusion of the beneficial owner test focus on trustees, and even an early draft version of the OECD Commentaries defined beneficial owner in a negative sense in relation to trustees.[46] However, such wording was dropped in the final, approved version of the OECD Commentaries, and was substituted in the last version by agents.[47] In the latter case, trustees was used as an example and was supplemented by the expression 'any other intermediaries', and do not define the whole scope to which the rule applies, suggesting that the concept also covered arrangements conferring rights not necessarily in equity.

In sum, the common law meaning cannot be the international tax law meaning derived from the OECD Model. This has been recently confirmed by the OECD in its 2014 amendment to the Commentary, which claims that the trustee of a discretionary trust could qualify as a beneficial owner for tax treaty purposes despite perhaps not being considered so in equity.[48] This does not mean that beneficial ownership in tax treaties has nothing to do with its common law origins, but it has certainly departed from them, and was significantly modified in order to be applicable to the different legal traditions present at the OECD. Thus, the current content of the OECD Model meaning derived from common law may be uncertain but is also very limited.

This view is confirmed by the amendments to the OECD Model Tax Conventions introduced in 2003 and 2014, stating that beneficial owner in tax treaties has no legal or technical meaning, nor does it refer to the domestic meaning of any country.[49] This does not, however, mean that there is no relationship, as trusts–beneficial ownership cases in common law countries could fall within the scope of application of the rule. But it is clear that beneficial ownership in international tax treaties differs from that of common law countries. The use of the term in international rules on exchange of information, though different from the term in tax treaties, also clearly departs from equity law meanings.[50] This is not surprising, given the malleable sense of the term in the domestic law of common law countries and its colloquial origin. What is surprising is that some authors still insist on such an equity law meaning, which does not provide an actual reference.

Turning to the phrase used in the already mentioned French version of the OECD Model, *bénéficiare effectif*, the first word refers to the subject who obtains a benefit,

[45] See paras 12, 8 and 4 of Commentaries to Arts 10 to 12 of the OECD Model Tax Convention versions from 1977 to 2017.

[46] 'Report on suggested amendments to Articles 11 and 12' (n 3) pp 13–14; 'Proposals for the amendment of articles 11 and 12 of the draft convention, relating to interest and royalties respectively, and of the commentaries thereon' [FC/WP27 (70) 2], Working Party 27, Fiscal Committee, OECD, 4 November 1970, pp 2, 9; OECD Archives, Paris.

[47] See paras 12, 8 and 4 of Commentaries to Arts 10 to 12 of the 1977 OECD Model Tax Convention.

[48] See fn 1 to paras 12.1, 9.1 and 4 of Commentaries to Arts 10, 11 and 12 of the 2014 OECD Model Tax Convention.

[49] See paras 12, 8 and 4 of Commentaries to Arts 10 to 12 of the 2003 OECD Model Tax Convention and paras 12.1, 9.1 and 4 of Commentaries to Arts 10 to 12 of the 2014 OECD Model Tax Convention.

[50] Broadly speaking, the use of the term in exchange of information corresponds to the individual controlling an entity or arrangement irrespective of their legal relationship. See para 5.b of the Interpretative Note to Recommendation 10 of the Financial Action Task Force.

advantage, right or privilege;[51] so far, the wording largely matches the English version. The conflict derives from the second word, *effectif*, which means real, effective, actual or true, as opposed to chimeric, abstract, apparent, fictitious, imaginative, unreal, possible, potential, virtual or nominal.[52] Here the difference with the English version is clear, as the French refers to the facts or reality, probably as opposed to something apparent, fictitious or unreal, while the English seems to derive a meaning at least closer to a legal right.[53]

Some authors relate the French version to a redefinition of the facts, such as substance over form or sham doctrine, which in turns leads to thoughts of anti-avoidance rules or principles.[54] This is seemingly in opposition to the English version, which links the issue to a legal beneficiary. To the author, the anti-avoidance view in the French version recalls how beneficial ownership doctrine in tax law is combined with anti-avoidance principles in the USA. Not surprisingly, case law from countries using wording directly translated from the French version usually arrives at the conclusion that beneficial ownership is a sort of anti-avoidance rule.[55]

Are these terms referring to anti-avoidance principles? While common law countries may reach anti-avoidance solutions through judiciary roles, civil law countries – in theory – with limited judiciary powers, need to resort to codified anti-avoidance doctrines. Is beneficial ownership importing to tax treaties the solutions of both legal traditions to avoidance or sham-simulation schemes?

To some authors it is.[56] However, the vagueness of both the English and French versions does not permit such a conclusion to be reached, at least not without taking into account any context specific to the relevant treaty. The reconciliation of the two versions raises even more doubts than it resolves, as it seems that both lead to different paths – legal and factual – leaving an enormous gray area in between. At this point, some authors wonder whether one of the versions – presumably the English one as the original – may take precedence over the other,[57] but this cannot be the case as even the English version leaves many issues open, and it is clear that the OECD discussions

[51] 'Le possesseur d'un bénéfice …, relative à un benefice …, Personne qui bénéfice d'un avantage, d'un droit, d'un privilège': A Rey and J Rey-Debove (eds), *Le Robert, Dictionnaire Alphabétique & Analogique de La Langue Française* (Société du Nouveau Littré, 1978) 451.

[52] 'Qui produit un effet réel, d'où Qui existe réelement, qui est de fait. … ANT. Abstrait, apparent, chimérique, fictive, hypotétique, soire, imaginaire, irréel, nominal, possible, potenttiel, virtual': Rey and Rey-Debove (n 51).

[53] This was the argument by the Tax Authorities in *Prevost v The Queen* (n 31) para 15. Resort to reality being derived from the use of the word *efectivo* was also argued by the Court of Justice of the European Union, although the translation in the directive does not match in all languages that of treaties in the Danish cases, Court of Justice of the European Union (Grand Chamber) Joined Cases C-115/16, C-118/16, C-119/16 and C-299/16 *N Luxembourg 1 and others v Skatteministerie (and joined cases)* [2019] ECLI:EU:C 134 [10]. The directive, in the case of Spain, uses *beneficiario efectivo* as derived from *bénéficiare effectif*.

[54] See Vogel (n 10) 562.

[55] See *Royal Bank of Scotland* [2006] Conseil d'Etat 283314; *Real Madrid v Resolución del TEAC [1]–[8]* (n 31); *Mobel Línea v Reino de España [Goldman Sachs]* [2006] Audiencia Nacional Rec 389/2007, 2010 JUR 413691.

[56] See Vogel (n 10) 562. Other authors see it as an economic ownership test, which makes it close to an anti-avoidance rule. See S Jain, *Effectiveness of the Beneficial Ownership Test in Conduit Company Cases* (IBFD, 2013) 191; Kemmeren in Reimer and Rust (n 5) 726; Danon (n 10) 43. Kemmeren states that its definition as economic owner follows its anti-avoidance nature.

[57] Du Toit (n 4) 167.

slightly modified the meaning claimed by the UK proposal, such nuances being reflected in the use of the wording *bénéficiare effectif.*

In any case, if one or both terms are broadly taken, any legal or factual entitlement to control, use and enjoyment would exclude the application of source tax limits contained in Articles 10–12 of the Model.[58] More sources from the context surrounding the Model will be needed to narrow the scope of the terms, but before doing so, a brief review of the wording used in different countries may be helpful to map out how the terms were initially understood in the different legal traditions.

(ii) Beneficial Ownership Wording in Different Legal Traditions

The OECD Model, where beneficial owner is included in both the French and English versions, is not a legally binding instrument, but simply a starting point for negotiations. The actual applicable rules are the relevant tax treaties, and, in many cases, for tax treaties signed by countries whose official language is different from French or English, the authentic language of the treaty is usually a different one into which beneficial owner is translated.[59] However, the French or English OECD Model version is usually also signed as a third or fourth authentic version in cases where both contracting states have different languages to those. Interpretation of beneficial owner in such tax treaties must, in theory strictly departing from the VCLT, depart from the wording of the authentic versions. Reconciliation of the wording of all such tax treaties, with their nuances and the specific definition of beneficial ownership in each translation, makes the duty of defining beneficial ownership, in principle, much more complex.[60]

Just at the OECD level, beneficial ownership is translated into at least 22 languages.[61] In addition, because the model is used by many non-OECD countries, the translations of beneficial ownership may number many more than this. The main outcome of the analysis of different translations is that countries with similar legal systems and/or languages tend to use similar wording.

[58] Baker argues that defining beneficial owner as excluding anything less than a legal obligation to pass the income would imply that none of us would be beneficial owners of income received: P Baker, 'The Meaning of "Beneficial Owner" as Applied to Dividends under the Model' in *Taxation of Intercompany Dividends under Tax Treaties and EU Law* (IBFD, 2012) s 6.3.

[59] See different wordings in Du Toit (n 4) 165.

[60] On the reconciliation and interpretation of multilingual treaties, see CB Kuner, 'The Interpretation of Multilingual Treaties: Comparison of Texts versus the Presumption of Similar Meaning' (1991) 40 *International & Comparative Law Quarterly* 953; P Arginelly, *Multilingual Tax Treaties: Interpretation, Semantic Analysis and Legal Theory* (IBFD, 2015); D Shelton, 'Reconcilable Differences – The Interpretation of Multilingual Treaties' (1996) 20 *Hastings International and Comparative Law Review* 611; M Lang, 'The Interpretation of Tax Treaties and Authentic Languages', *Essays on Tax Treaties. A Tribute to David A Ward* (IBFD, 2013).

[61] Beneficial owner in Australia, Canada, Ireland, New Zealand the UK and the USA; *Nutzungsberechtigter* in Austria, Germany and Switzerland; *bénéficiaire effectif* in Belgium, Canada, Switzerland, France and Luxembourg; *beneficiario efectivo* in Chile, Colombia, Mexico and Spain; *prïõâjemce je skutecïnyâm* in the Czech Republic; *Retmaessige ejer* in Denmark; *Tosiasiallinen edunsaaja* in Finland; *saaja* in Estonia; *πραγματικός δικαιούχος* in Greece; *Haszonhúzója* in Hungary; *raunverulegur eigandi* in Iceland; *Bealim She'Bayosher* in Israel; *Uiteindelijk gerechtigde* in Netherlands and Belgium; *virkelige rettighetshavera* in Norway; *Wla´sciciel* in Poland; *beneficiário efetivo* in Portugal; *skutocny vlastník* in the Slovak Republic; *upravičeni lastnik* in Slovenia; *verklige innehavaren* or *Har rätt till* in Sweden. Respective translations are also found in Japanese, Latvian and Turkish. However, some treaties of such countries deviate from those translations and use other expressions.

The first group, of the Roman–Germanic legal tradition, including Germany, Switzerland and Austria, employ the word *Nutzungsberechtigter*, which is connected to entitlement – not ownership – use or benefit.[62] However, it is unclear whether such entitlement refers to a strict direct legal entitlement, a broad entitlement or even an economic entitlement. It seems that the use of a term related to economic entitlement, such as *wirtschaftlicher Eigentümer* in German domestic tax law, was intentionally avoided, as Switzerland did not recognise economic allocation rules as Germany did, and Germany wanted to differentiate the term from its domestic attribution rules.[63] Still, in the case of Germany, the possibility of applying beneficial ownership in the sense of economic allocation remains unclear, as some treaties explicitly interpret the term by submission to domestic allocation rules, which would include economic allocation.[64] Some authors seemingly claim that the term has to be interpreted in that sense.[65] One of the first German treaties to include the beneficial owner test, the 1972 treaty with Australia, used the German economic ownership (*wirtschaftlicker Eigentümer*) as equivalent, as well as economically entitled (*wirtschaftlich bezugsberechtigt*), which may suggest that German negotiators early on related the term to their domestically known economic allocation.[66] However, most authors claim beneficial ownership in tax treaties has nothing to do with German domestic economic allocation rules.[67]

A second group, of continental–Napoleonic legal tradition, and specifically those of the Romance languages, use a translation matching the French version of the Model, such as *beneficiario efectivo* in Spanish, *beneficiario effettivo* in Italian, *beneficiário efetivo* in Portugese or *beneficiarului efectiv* in Romanian.[68] As they are derived from the French version, the comments above for the French version may apply.

As with the French version, the term's ordinary meaning refers to the person who factually, actually or really benefits or takes advantage from the income – *bénéficiaire* – and may relate to sham simulation or anti-avoidance doctrines.[69] This wording is probably the reason why case law in some of these countries resorts to anti-avoidance doctrines when applying the terms.[70]

In a third group, of Nordic countries, the translation of beneficial owner refers to the person with the right.[71] Sweden uses the wording *verklige innehavaren* or *Har rätt till*,

[62] Du Toit (n 4) 165. See, eg Art 10.2 of the 2000 Germany–Austria Tax Convention and Art 10.2 of the 1977 United Kingdom–Switzerland Tax Convention.

[63] Killius (n 29) 341.

[64] See s 10 of the Protocol to the 1989 Germany–United States Tax Convention; s 9 of the Protocol to the 1989 Germany–Italy Tax Convention; and s 4 of the Protocol to the 1991 Germany–Norway Tax Convention, where beneficial ownership is defined by submission to domestic rules on allocation of income.

[65] Vogel, as quoted in F Vega Borrego, *Limitation on Benefits Clauses in Double Taxation Conventions* (Kluwer, 2006) 83. The IBFD also apparently claimed so in the 1980s: see Vogel (n 10) 561.

[66] See s 7 of the German version of the Protocol to the 1972 Australia–Germany Tax Convention.

[67] A Meindl-Ringler, *Beneficial Ownership in International Tax Law* (Kluwer, 2016) 173; A Rust, 'Germany' in G Maisto (ed), *Multilingual Texts and Interpretation of Tax Treaties and EC Tax Law* (IBFD, 2005) ch 11, s 11.2.2; Killius (n 29) 341; Fischer, as quoted by Meindl-Ringler.

[68] See, eg the Spanish versions of Art 10.2 of the 1975 and 2015 United Kingdom–Spain Tax Conventions; Art 10.2 of the 1988 United Kingdom–Italy Tax Convention; Art 10.2 of the 1993 Spain–Portugal Tax Convention; and Art 10.2 of the 2016 Bosnia-Herzegovina–Romania Tax Convention.

[69] Above, nn 44, 51 and 52 and accompanying text.

[70] Above, nn 54 and 55.

[71] Du Toit (n 4) 165.

Norway the words *virkelige rettighetshavera*, and Denmark *Retmaessige ejer.*[72] In these cases, the wording seems to adopt a legal approach towards the person who is entitled, owner or with the right. Contrary to its literal meaning, it seems the tax authorities of these countries attempted to adopt an economic or factual interpretation of the term that was combined with their domestic rightful recipient theories.[73] Nevertheless, the Danish Courts narrowed it down to a legal approach in line with their wording and the OECD origins, and distinguished it from such domestic doctrines.[74] The Swedish Supreme Administrative Court has, in turn, sustained a broad interpretation of beneficial owner in tax treaties in line with the domestic principles.[75]

A fourth group, comprising countries such as Netherlands and Belgium, the latter in its Flemish version, use the wording *uiteindelijk gerechtigde*, similar to ultimately entitled.[76] This inclines the interpreter to look at who is the very last to be entitled behind a certain contract or arrangement, which may be somehow biased. However, the terms are somehow contradictory, as *entitled* refers to a right to some extent, while *ultimately* seems to surpass such purely legal approach. In the case of the Netherlands, domestic law defines beneficial owner in relation to dividends close to an economic sense, which somehow relates to the wording used, even though it also requires acquiring a tax reduction.[77] Conversely, and despite the wording of the Flemish version,

[72] See Art 10 of the Swedish text of the 2016 Azerbaijan–Sweden Tax Convention; Swedish Text of Art 10.3 of the 1996 Nordic Convention; Art 10.2 of the Norwegian text of the 2013 United Kingdom–Norway Tax Convention; Art 10.2 of the Danish text of the 1980 United Kingdom–Denmark Tax Convention.

[73] In Danish and Swedish tax law, the theory of rightful recipient – *rette indkomstmodtager* in Denmark and *den som faktiskt har rätt till inkomsten* in Sweden – allows reallocation of income where the facts show that a person different to someone with formal legal entitlement has factual right. This, even though inconsistent, has been frequently understood as economic entitlement or substance over form. Moreover, tax authorities have considered beneficial ownership in tax treaties is connected to such a concept and even preparatory works of domestic legislation using rightful recipient or beneficial owner equate both terms. Bundgaard and Winther-Sorensen (n 29); Kleist (n 29); *X AB* [2015] Skatterättsnämnden 108-13/D, 46-15; *X AB 2* [2012] Skatterättsnämnden 71-10/D, 6063-11. It seems that, more recently, tax authorities have abandoned the attempts to equate both wordings. HS Hansen, LE Christensen and AE Pedersen, 'Denmark – Danish "Beneficial Owner" Cases – A Status Report' (2013) 67 *Bulletin for International Taxation* 192, 194.

[74] *H1 A/S (Lux Hold Co2)* [2010] Skatteankestyrelsen SKM2010.729.LSR-09-01483; *H1 ApS* [2010] Skatteankestyrelsen SKM 2011.57 LSR-09-00640; *H1 Ltd (Cayman)* [2011] Skatteankestyrelsen SKM 2011.485 LSR-09-03189; *Ministry of Taxation v FS Invest II Sàrl (formerly ISS Equity A/S)* [2011] Ostre Landsret SKM 2011.121-B-2152-10, 14 ITLR 703; *Cyprus Co* [2011] Skatteankestyrelsen SKM 2012.26; *S A/S (Lux Holdco)* [2010] Skatteankestyrelsen SKM 2010.268 LSR-09-01478. In Sweden, see Kleist (n 29).

[75] Kleist (n 29).

[76] See, eg Art 10.2 of the Dutch version of the 2013 Netherlands–United Kingdom Tax Convention, and Art 10.2 of the Flemish version of the 1987 United Kingdom–Belgium Tax Convention. Du Toit (n 4) 165.

[77] Article 25(2) CITA 1969 reads: '… A person is not considered to be beneficial owner if such person in connection with the received proceeds has paid a consideration as part of a combination of transactions, in which it is plausible that: (a) the proceeds have wholly or partially, directly or indirectly, benefited an individual or an entity who is entitled to a reduction, refund, or credit of dividend withholding tax that is less than that to which the person having paid the consideration is entitled; and (b) such individual or entity [as meant in sub-paragraph(a)] directly or indirectly remains to hold or acquires a position in shares, profit-sharing certificates or [hybrid] loans as meant in Article 10(1)(d) of the CITA 1969 that is similar to its position in similar shares, profit-sharing certificates, or [hybrid] loans before the start of the combination of transaction [as meant above]'. The negative definition of beneficial owner in Art 4(7) DWTA 1965 reads substantially the same. Pijl (n 31); R De Boer and F Boulogne, 'Netherlands' in G Maisto (ed), *Taxation of Intercompany Dividends under Tax Treaties and EU Law* (IBFD, 2012) ch 19, s 19.3.2.3.

the Belgian tax authorities seemingly interpret the term in a narrow sense of legal entitlement.[78]

Another group, including Japan, Hungary (*Haszonhúzója*) and South Africa (*Vir eie voordeel besit*), although not necessarily sharing a common legal background, place the spotlight on the benefit, using wordings that refer to who benefits, or the party which is the beneficiary.[79] The latter seems to be in line with the common part of the definition of almost all translations, specifically the two official OECD ones, but lacks any other counter-reference, leaving it broadly open without specifying what type of benefits leads to a denial of the application of the relevant treaty articles.

The diversity of wordings reflects the difficulty in reaching a single meaning. As pointed out by Du Toit, if the words to be interpreted are different, it is unlikely that interpreters – especially those with little background in international tax and knowledge of the term, it should be added[80] – will reach similar results.[81] In some cases, the wording seems to guide the interpreter to legal entitlements, or even ownership; in others, it refers to the facts or economic benefit. However, what are common in the different wordings used are, first, that all of them point to the person benefiting to some extent from the income in order to be considered beneficial owner, which, of course, relates to the OECD wording common to the English and French versions. What is less clear is what is required by and the intensity of such benefit.

Secondly, the specific wording used in each language does not necessarily correspond to the interpretation used by the relevant country or countries. This is the case with Belgium and the Nordic countries, where wordings reflect a factual or legal approach respectively, but other interpretations are given by other authorities and courts. In this context, the OECD and other countries' texts override the direction indicated by the literal wording of beneficial ownership in the national language, which is relatively easy because of the vagueness of any wording related to beneficial ownership.

Nevertheless, almost all cases leave unclear whether or not negotiators included a specific wording to reflect their point of view on the issue and that subsequent overriding interpretations are deviations, or whether translations were just the incorporation into the treaties of the OECD concept carrying the meaning it had from the Commentary and with no other adjustment. The author's view is that the latter is correct, unless other materials referring to the specific treaty suggest otherwise. In the end, different translations can only be a starting point as, being translations, the main burden of interpretation still lies with the Model. If the contracting parties attempt to vary specific definitions in the Treaty, other materials shall be explicitly included.[82] In other words, deviations of wording are just indicia of the view of the contracting state. However, the OECD Commentary being the main interpretative source, such indicia cannot be absolute statements unless other materials about the specific treaty require otherwise.

[78] Eynatten et al (n 29).
[79] Du Toit (n 4) 165.
[80] Baker (n 58) s 6.3.
[81] Du Toit (n 4) 267.
[82] Such as technical explanations in the USA, or Protocols in German treaties mentioned in n 64 above and references to Technical Explanations in ch 4 above.

B. The Factual Event of Articles 10–12: 'Paid to' and Qualification of Income under the Model. Nominees, Direct and Indirect Agency, Civil Law Fiducia and Abusive Intermediaries

One of the main questions regarding beneficial ownership in the Model is why the terms are only included in articles referring to dividends, interests and royalties, and not in articles referring to any other type of income.[83] Actually, the first UK proposal also suggested including the requirement for beneficial ownership as a general clause, as an alternative to only including it in these articles.[84] Recent studies have also dealt with the possibility of extending the rules to other articles.[85] However, the requirement was only included in Articles 10–12, and remains unchanged, which has been seen by some as indicating that it was unnecessary for other articles. So, what is the difference between such articles and the rest of the allocation of jurisdiction rules in the Model?

As mentioned, the main difference with other articles seems to be the fact that such articles use the connector 'paid'.[86] Conversely, most articles of the Model use the connector 'derived by' or 'accruing', or even directly require the income to be 'of a resident'.[87]

The OECD discussions on the introduction of the term confirm that the interpretation of paid was the key issue for the introduction of the test, following the UK arguments.[88] In addition, UK's modification of the 'paid to' wording of the Model in most of their treaties to 'derived by', jointly with the subject to tax test or beneficial owner, confirms this.[89] Also, the Belgian delegation suggested the amendment of Articles 10–12 by changing pay to *attribuer* or 'allot'.[90] This Belgian proposal is contained in the minutes immediately after the beneficial owner proposal.

The term 'paid to' was not defined in the Commentary at the time,[91] probably because at an early stage the discussion was focused on allocating tax rights and defining types of income, so subject–object connectors were not subject to an in-depth analysis.[92] As mentioned above, paid to could be interpreted in the sense of domestic allocation rules in accordance with Article 3(2), or in an international sense.[93] The latter seems preferable, matching the aim of allocation of jurisdiction, related to some extent

[83] R Vann, 'Beneficial Ownership: What Does History (and Maybe Policy) Tell Us' in M Lang et al (eds), *Beneficial Ownership: Recent Trends* (IBFD, 2013) 284.

[84] 'Note on the discussion of the first report of Working Party No 27 of the fiscal committee on interest and royalties during the 31st session of the fiscal committee held from 10th to 13th june, 1969 [DAF/FC/69.10]', Fiscal Committee, OECD, 4 July 1969, p 6; OECD Archives, Paris.

[85] Committee of Experts on International Cooperation in Tax Matters (n 39).

[86] See a II.B in ch 4 above, namely fn 266 and accompanying text.

[87] J Wheeler, 'The Attribution of Income to a Person for Tax Treaty Purposes' (2005) 59 *Bulletin for International Taxation* 477, 478.

[88] R Fraser and JDB Oliver, 'Beneficial Ownership: HMRC's Draft Guidance on Interpretation of the Indofood Decision' (2007) 1 *British Tax Review* 39, 44–45.

[89] See fn 266 and accompanying text in ch 4 above.

[90] 'Observations of Member Countries on difficulties raised by the OECD Draft Convention on Income and Capital' [TFD/FC/216], 9 May 1967, Fiscal Committee, OCDE, p 14; OECD Archives, Paris.

[91] Compare commentary to Art 10 of the 1963 OECD Draft Model Convention; and para 7 of the Commentary to Art 10 of the 1977 OECD Model Tax Convention. Also, respective commentaries to Arts 11 and 12.

[92] J Wheeler, *The Missing Keystone of Income Tax Treaties* (IBFD, 2012) s 2.4.2.

[93] Supporting a domestic interpretation of 'paid to': P Pistone, 'Italy: Beneficial Ownership and the Entitlement to Treaty Benefits in the Presence of Transparent Entities' in Lang et al (n 83) 213.

to the definition of the subjective elements of the relevant arrangement, as those define ability to pay.[94]

Under an international interpretation, there are three ways to define 'paid to': (i) to interpret it in a literal way, as transferring funds from one person to the other; (ii) to define it in accordance with domestic allocation rules, whether residence, source or the state applying the treaty; and (iii) to fulfil the conditions of payment under private law following the conditions of the relevant arrangement.[95] As has been stated, probably because the UK understanding followed the first approach, this led to mismatches with intermediaries, as the income was allocated for tax purposes to one person while tax treaties were applied in relation to another person; probably the appropriate view was the last one.[96]

However, once the proposal reached the OECD, the rest of the countries understood the problem of beneficial ownership, paid to and intermediaries in accordance with their understanding of intermediaries. In this sense, the scope was broadened to intermediaries 'acting in his [or her] own name'.[97]

This new problem introduced at the OECD probably had little to do with the UK issue. Drafts confirm the change to the UK proposal at the OECD. In a first draft, the Commentary stated that the concept was aimed at an intermediary acting for a 'beneficiary holding legal right to the income'.[98] However, in the final draft, this wording was eliminated, indicating that the concept was not limited to the original problems – legal entitlement as opposed to equitable entitlement – which were only problems to the UK. As intermediaries in continental law were holding in their own name and have the legal right, the beneficiaries have no actual direct legal right, and the beneficial owner would not serve them. Such reference to the legal right was eliminated. Also, the term could not serve for conduit companies, to whom the UK later proposed extension.

Treaties based on the Model's scope of application require a subject (resident) and an object (income) to be related in very specific ways to the contracting states. Because tax treaties refer to personal taxes, and they are defined by reference to a subject obtaining income, income needs to be in the hands of a person – in this case, in the hands of a resident. In tax treaties, on the residence side, income is required to be connected to a subject who is a resident for the treaty to apply in relation to such income.[99] This is done in an explicit way through tax treaties' allocation rules, such as 'paid to', and through the implicit subjective element of the qualification of income. Still, both allocation rules – explicit and implicit – are probably connected.

Treaty jurisdiction allocation rules only apply if the income qualifies as the relevant type of income, and different types of income require the recipient/creditor to hold a specific legal position in relation to the payee.[100] As an example, for income to qualify as an interest, Article 11.3 of the OECD Model Tax convention requires it to derive from

[94] Reimer and Rust (n 5) 710 et seq.
[95] See s II.B in ch 4 above.
[96] On the proper interpretation being a creditor–debtor relationship, see Van Weeghel (n 31) 58.
[97] 'Report on suggested amendments to Articles 11 and 12' (n 3) p 14.
[98] 'Revised Articles 11 and 12 of the OECD Draft Convention and Commentaries thereon', Fiscal Committee [FC (71) 1], 14 January 1971, pp 4 and 13.
[99] See Art 4 of the OECD Model Tax Convention and definitions of relevant types of income in Arts 6–21.
[100] See fns 253 and 254 and accompanying text in ch 4 above.

debt claims.[101] If, for instance, the creditor sells his or her right to the interest or the coupon to a third party but retains the debt claim, it would be questionable whether the income, once received by the third party and if paid by the debtor, would still retain its interest qualification.

Two views may be advocated on this issue. Following an isolated analysis of each transaction or a direct qualification requirement, the income is not derived from a debt claim for the buyer of the coupon but from a credit he or she bought.[102] A second view providing for comprehensive analysis, or an indirect qualification effect, would hold that the income received by a third party qualifies as an interest because globally the income derives from a debt claim, and the OECD does not require such income to be in the same person who holds the creditor position, but to come from shares/debt/lease in a broad sense, and the income, though paid to a different person, is paid on such consideration.[103] The fact the creditor does not derive directly from a debt claim but from the acquisition of the credit becomes irrelevant.

To this author, the first view is correct.[104] Only if directly derived from the specific creditor position would the income qualify as the relevant type of income.[105] This is because treaty allocation of taxing powers is done taking into account the economic relationships between the countries in order to encourage or disincentivise certain types of relations. Also, the definitions take into account the role as an intra-group creditor or corporate holding to minimise economic double taxation in some cases. If the second interpretation is held, treaty advantages or disadvantages would be applicable to persons who do not hold the legal and economic condition the relevant rule was aimed at, and economic double taxation may be improperly mitigated. This view is confirmed by the statement introduced by the 1977 Commentary defining 'paid to' as 'the disposal of the creditor in the manner required by contract or by custom'.[106] To connect the term 'paid' to the requirements of the contract or private law links the object–subject connection to the subjective element of the qualification of income. The consequence is that treaties are generally applied on the condition of the creditor under the relevant arrangement.[107]

In the EU, the Court of Justice of the European Union (CJEU) confirmed this view in the *Scheuten Solar* case, where it held that to qualify as an interest under the

[101] ibid.

[102] The Commentary states that the creditor bearing the risk of the participation is one of the key elements – though not the only one – to qualify income under the first definition contained in Art 10.3. Strictly speaking, a third party acquiring the coupon would thus not bear the risk and would not qualify. See para 25 of the Commentary to Art 10 of the OECD Model Tax convention. See also M Helminen, *The International Tax Law Concept of Dividend* (Kluwer, 2017) 103; Reimer and Rust (n 5) 836.

[103] Helminen (n 102) 104.

[104] Vogel (n 10) 653. For Helminen (n 102) 104, either interpretation seems a proper application of the treaty.

[105] Except in the case of limb 3 of the Art 10.3 definition, where other subjects may qualify in relation to a certain income if provided by domestic law.

[106] See para 7 of the Commentary to Art 10 of the 1977 OECD Model Tax Convention. See also the respective commentaries to Arts 11 and 12.

[107] However, in the case of submission of the type of income to domestic tax law qualification, such as the case of presumptive income or the limb 3 definition of dividends, would 'paid to' be disconnected from such condition? In many of these latter cases the 'paid to' connector becomes irrelevant as there are no funds to put at disposal with presumptive income. In these cases, it is obvious the treaty's subjective element is substituted by a complete submission to domestic rules governing presumptive income.

Interest and Royalties Directive (which was enacted following the patterns of the 1996 Model), the income has to be credited or allocated to the creditor in a debt-claim relationship.[108]

It becomes clear that the issue of the interpretation of 'paid to' was just for the UK at the beginning, as stated in the previous chapter. Because of the split of ownership, the creditor position was vested in a subject – the nominee – while domestic tax rules were taxing the income in the hands of the beneficiary. In the case of agency, because the UK rules always redirect the effects to the principal, no issue arises as both the creditor position and the allocation of income under domestic law were directed at the same person. As stated in the previous chapter, only with foreign indirect agencies might an issue arise at some time, but this seems to have lost significance at the time beneficial ownership was discussed.[109] In any case, some reminiscences of the old concept of foreign indirect agency principal may have reinforced the issue of trustees and nominees. And for the UK, paid to was seemingly to be interpreted in a very literal, improper way that did not solve the problem of the legally entitled having creditor status and qualifying for the treaties.

This creditor view on qualification of income and split of ownership explains why, even though the UK repeatedly expressed its concern with the 'paid to' terms, the beneficial ownership test was not included in relation to other types of income. For instance, in the case of pensions, if the income was not derived in consideration of past employment, it could not qualify as a pension under the treaty, so treaty rules would not be applicable to the case.[110] Because of the very personal condition of the pensioner, it is highly difficult to allocate the creditor condition to a third person's hands or, if done, income could not qualify as income from past employment. The result is that no mismatch arises between allocation under domestic law and treaties.

Conversely, creditor status on debt claims, shares and intangibles is easily movable from one subject to another, while beneficiary rights may be retained in another and, in many cases, is even the usual commercial way of doing such business. What may also be interesting is whether the evolution of beneficial ownership in equity law would today have redirected the creditor status to the beneficiary in many cases or would do so in the future, which would render this issue irrelevant.[111]

Leaving aside the evolution of ownership in the UK, such a split of the creditor status and the person to whom income was allocated was unusual for civil law countries on dividends, interests and royalties. An intermediary acting in its own name but for the benefit of a third party – an indirect agency – holds the creditor position, and income would normally be allocated to him or her under domestic law as the person showing the ability to pay.[112] Equally, a creditor who collaterally acts as a debtor in favour

[108] Even though the reasoning is unclearly combined with beneficial ownership: *Scheuten Solar Technology GmbH v Finanzamt Gelsenkirchen-Süd* [2011] CJEU C-397/09, 2011 ECR I [24 et seq].

[109] See fn 257 et seq and accompanying text in ch 4 above.

[110] Article 18 of the OECD Model tax Convention. See E Reimer and A Rust (eds), *Klaus Vogel on Double Taxation Conventions*, vol 2, 4th edn (Kluwer, 2015) 1445; Committee of Experts on International Cooperation in Tax Matters (n 39) para 74.

[111] See s II.A.iv in ch 2 above.

[112] De Haen and Eynatten claim a nominee may be beneficial owner: Eynatten et al (n 29) 539. On allocation in agency in *propio nomine*, see J Wheeler, 'General Report' in *Conflicts in the Attribution of Income to a*

of the beneficiary as a civil law *fiducia* is considered to hold the creditor position, and the income would be allocated to him or her under domestic tax law.[113] Conversely, an intermediary to whom the income is paid – in a colloquial sense – but acting in the name and on the account of a third party – a direct agency – would not qualify as the creditor in the relevant type of income, nor would income be considered as paid to him either in the sense of the treaty or in domestic law. This is why, when the UK proposed the introduction of the beneficial owner test, some countries saw no problem, while other redirected the issue to a substance over form analysis and a third group probably held it might be helpful for certain types of intermediaries,[114] but they were talking about different issues.

Whereas the UK issue was a mismatch between domestic allocation and treaty allocation that would leave the treaty open to improper exploitation, there was no such mismatch for civil countries, but a pure abuse of the treaty through stepping stone arrangements. For civil law countries, the problem was likely to be subjects putting rights from which the income raises in the hands of residents in a low tax jurisdiction or in a country with advantageous tax treaties who will act in their own name and on their own account, but who will, under the same or a different arrangement, transfer the income or equivalent economic effect to residents in other countries. In this case, there is no mismatch because the intermediary would be taxed on the income in accordance with being the creditor in the relevant arrangement and will respectively obtain treaty advantages. The issue is the transaction is legitimate, but abusive from the treaty perspective, because it will ultimately benefit residents in a third country because of collateral arrangements. The economic effects make such an intermediary transaction economically closer to an intermediary acting on his or her principal's name and account, but the tax consequences are allocated to the intermediary as opposed to a direct agent. Moreover, the transaction is usually tax driven, although sometimes it might be a common business arrangement. In the absence of tax advantages, that transaction would probably have been arranged as a direct agency.

This is not the case for the UK, where the use of a nominee leads to such a mismatch. Allocation of income under domestic tax law is directed to a person, while, under private law upon which the treaty is applied, the creditor is a different person. This is not necessarily derived from the intention to exploit a more advantageous tax treatment, but is because in common law countries shares and other securities are usually held in the name and account of custodians or nominees.[115]

Person (Kluwer, 2007) 36 et seq. In Belgium, it seems generally that intermediaries who are acting in their own name but on account of third parties are taxed on the income, although there are some exceptions, such as the Administratiekantoor. See Eynatten et al (n 29) 529–30, 540, 545. In the Netherlands, it seems it depends on who bears the risk: H Pijl, 'Netherlands' in J Wheeler, *Conflicts in the Attribution of Income to a Person*, vol b (Kluwer, 2007) 459; J Wheeler, 'The Attribution of Income in the Netherlands and the United Kingdom' (2011) 3 *World Tax Journal* 39, 120.

[113] Even though this may be controversial as different theories consider whether *fiducias* actually transfer ownership or not. See A Baez, *Los Negocios Fiduciarios En La Imposición Sobre La Renta* (Aranzadi, 2009) 130 et seq; V Combarros Villanueva, 'La Interpretación Económica Como Criterio de Interpretación Jurídica (Algunas Reflexiones a Propósito Del Concepto de "Propiedad Económica" En El Impuesto Sobre Patrimonio)' [1984] *Civitas. Revista española de derecho europeo* 485, 528.

[114] 'Report on suggested amendments to Articles 11 and 12' (n 3) p 14.

[115] See above fns 63 and 64 in ch 4 above.

Abusive and non-abusive transactions are carried on in the same way and under a clear mismatch.

Other countries such as the USA interpreted connecting rules such as 'paid to' or 'derived by' in accordance with their domestic law attribution rules, as in shown by the *Aiken* and *NIPSCO* cases.[116] The result was that this issue was hardly a problem for them, even though technically the solution could be seen as controversial.

Because of the different views on the issue, the discussion at the OECD probably mixed up the UK technical mismatch with pure abusive transactions. The UK was probably looking to solve the aforementioned technical mismatch, perhaps not fully understanding civil law countries' intermediary arrangements. It is also possible it was considering abusive transactions, where there was no allocation mismatch but which it was unable to solve through anti-avoidance rules because of the *Duke of Westminster* doctrine, and it mixed up the two issues.[117] Some civil law countries had already developed anti-avoidance rules at the time, while others were at an initial stage of development of such rules or the literal approach to tax rules was still supported.[118] In addition, the controversy over whether they were applicable to tax treaties emerged, so even countries that had anti-avoidance rules had difficulties.[119] Contrary to the technical mismatch in the UK, civil law countries were probably looking more into pure abusive transactions or simulated transactions hiding a different reality, as shown by the fact that some countries argued at the OECD that applying a substance approach would solve the problem.[120]

The result is that beneficial ownership in the OECD Model is slightly broader than in the previous UK view, to encapsulate the different problems that arise. That the concept is broadened is clearly shown by the fact that early discussions dealt mainly with the concept of 'trustees', whereas final versions of the discussions and commentaries expanded the concept to include intermediaries, agents, nominees and *mandataires*.[121] An important issue that remains unclear, though, is to what extent the abusive character of the transactions at which it was aimed entered the beneficial ownership test or remained as a previous policy analysis.

In the author's view, the meaning of 'paid to' was never as critical as the UK argued, it always had a very broad and loose meaning linked to the relevant arrangement, and the UK view was simply a misunderstanding that combined its allocation mismatch and

[116] See *Aiken Industries, Inc v Commissioner* (1971) 56 TC 925; *Northern Indiana Public Service Co v Commissioner* [1997] USCA 7th Circ 96-1659, 96-1758, 115 F3d 506.

[117] See fn 251 in ch 4 above.

[118] France, Germany, the USA and Spain had anti-avoidance rules or principles long before the introduction of the beneficial owner test. In France, Art 1594° of Loi de Vichy du 13 janvier 1941, annexe I, Loi portant simplification, coordination et renforcement des dispositions du Code general des impôts directs (Journal official de l'État français, 3 février 1941); in Germany, 1993, s 5 of the Reichabgabenordnung, 13 December 1919, RGB l, at 1993, 1994; and s 6.1 of the Steueranpassungsgesetz, 16 October 1934 RGBl. I at 925, 926; in Spain, Art 24.2 of Ley 230/1963, de 28 de diciembre, General Tributaria. However, some of these have been amended or substituted later. In the USA, see *Gregory v Helvering* (1935) 293 US 465 (USSC).

[119] See OECD, 'Double Taxation Conventions and the Use of Conduit Companies' in *International Tax Avoidance and Evasion: Four Related Studies* (OECD, 1987) para 44; Commentary to Art 1 of the 1992 OECD Model Tax Convention, para 22 et seq.

[120] 'Report on suggested amendments to Articles 11 and 12' (n 3) p 14.

[121] Compare 'Report on suggested amendments to Articles 11 and 12' (n 3) p 14, locating the issue with 'trustees', and final versions of the Commentary.

the UK's legislative and interpretative limits to tackle avoidance with the very broad and undefined meaning of paid to. Actual treaty allocation was linked to the qualification under the relevant creditor position and the UK issue was one of legal position, and its relationship with domestic allocation rules and their interpretation principles.

C. The Definition of Beneficial Ownership in Treaties Based on the 1977 Model

The Commentary to the 1977 Model defines beneficial ownership in a negative sense as 'an intermediary, such as an agent or nominee'.[122] The first question is whether it is an example of excluded subjects under the beneficial owner test or it is a definition. Within the first approach would fall those authors and case law that argue that beneficial ownership is a broad rule, most of them arguing that it is an anti-avoidance rule, a substance over form test or an economic ownership test.[123] In a similar vein, some courts claim it is a sort of purpose test or activity test.[124] Under such views, the Commentary will (i) just give examples of excluded subjects and will cover any transaction, of an intermediary or any other character, that is considered economically to be equivalent to an agent or nominee, or (ii) to be abusive under the test provided by the anti-abuse rule – artificiality, purpose, etc – or where the subject is not liable to tax, respectively.

(i) Beneficial Ownership as a Broad Anti-avoidance Rule, a Rule Calling for the Definition of Actual Legal Facts or a Subject to Tax Rule?

Probably the main trend in case law is to interpret beneficial ownership as a substance over form or economic substance test.[125] However, the first problem when considering beneficial ownership as a broad anti-avoidance rule or as a rule calling for defining

[122] Paras 12, 8 and 4 of the Commentaries to Arts 10, 11 and 12 of the 1977 OECD Model Tax Convention, respectively.

[123] Jain (n 56) 191; Kemmeren in Reimer and Rust (n 5) 726; Danon (n 10) 43; Vogel (n 10) 562. Advocating for the concept in the sense of an artificiality test, D Guttman, 'The 2011 Discussion Draft on Beneficial Ownership: What Next for the OECD?' in Lang et al (n 83) 342–43. Similarly Vega Borrego (n 65) 86. In case law, see, among others, *Royal Bank of Scotland* (n 55); *Eidgenössische Steuerverwaltung v X Bank* [2015] Bundesgericht/Supreme Court 2C_364/2012 and 2C_377/2012; *V SA* [2001] Commission fédérale de recourse en matière de contributions VPB 65.86; *Vodafone International holdings BV v Union of India & Anr* [2012] Supreme Court of India No 26529 of 2010; *Mobel Línea v Reino de España [Goldman Sachs]* (n 55); *Real Madrid v Resolución del TEAC [1]* (n 31). On the Swiss cases, see Meindl-Ringler (n 67) 238 et seq; P Reinarz, 'Switzerland: Treaty Shopping and the Swiss Withholding Tax Trap' (2001) 41 *European Taxation* 415; P Reinarz and F Carelli, 'Court Rulings on Dividend Stripping and Denial of Swiss Tax Treaty Benefits' (2016) 18 *Derivatives and Financial Instruments*.

[124] Even though often mixed with substance over form, economic ownership or other principles, see the examples of *Hanhwa Total Co Ltd v Head of Seosan District Office of National Tax Service & other* [2016] Supreme Court 2015du2451, 2016ha KSCR 1195; *NPO Cifrovie Televisionnie Systemi v Tax Inspectorate* [2017] Arbitration Court (Kaliningrad region) A21-2521/2017. Both cases are known by the author through the IBFD Tax Treaty Case law Reports.

[125] Martín Jiménez (n 31) 51; R Collier, 'Clarity, Opacity and Beneficial Ownership' [2011] *British Tax Review* 684, 698.

actual legal facts is that most of the authors and courts supporting such an approach mismatch, or do not distinguish properly between, substance over form in a strict sense, anti-avoidance rules and economic ownership.[126]

First of all, substance over form in a narrow sense or legal substance rule refers to definition of the facts of what actually took place before qualifying them.[127] This means before assigning relevant tax, or treaty, consequences, in this case beneficial ownership, the actual legal facts happening must be defined. Under this principle of application of the law, apparent qualification given by the parties or the wording of the contract must be disregarded, and the actual qualification of the arrangement carried must be considered in applying the legal consequences.

However, because the line dividing the definition of the facts and the qualification steps of application of the law are usually blurred, substance over form is also sometimes considered as a proper anti-avoidance rule. Moreover, several countries, especially those based in common law, do not strictly distinguish between the two steps of application of the law. Thus, substance over form doctrines in those countries – or economic substance – usually resort to certain characteristics present in the transaction at stake, such as the purpose or artificiality, to state that the substance of the transaction was different from the one to which the rules at stake were intended to apply.[128] However, those countries are not defining what actually took place from a legal point of view as legal substance, but are redefining the consequence or qualification and/or interpreting the law due to an element at stake in the transaction that rendered the arrangement as abusive or according to its economic substance.[129]

All in all, despite such distinctions, the reality is more complex. Beneficial owner case law, administrative practice and academic works sometimes use substance over form for beneficial ownership in the sense of redefinition of the actual facts that took place and disregard the form or arrangements given by the parties,[130] sometimes use it

[126] Martín Jiménez (n 31) 52 points to the difficulty in differentiating between economic broad interpretation and anti-avoidance rules.

[127] F Zimmer, 'General Report', *Form and Substance in Tax Law* (Kluwer, 2002) 24–25; J Zornoza Pérez and A Báez Moreno, 'The 2003 Revisions to the Commentary to the OECD Model on Tax Treaties and GAARs: A Mistaken Starting Point' in M Lang et al (eds), *Tax Treaties: Building Bridges between Law and Economics* (IBFD, 2010) 133–38; F Zimmer, 'Domestic Anti-Avoidance Rules and Tax Treaties – Comment on Brian Arnold's Article' (2005) 59 *Bulletin for International Fiscal Documentation* 25, 26.

[128] Madison relates substance over form doctrine to disregard the formal application of the law. It subdivides substance over form in the USA in the sham transactions doctrines, including business purpose and economic substance, and recharacterisation doctrines, including step transaction and sham entity. Thus, substance over form under such a view is an anti-avoidance or economic substance principle: AD Madison, 'The Tension Between Textualism and Substance-Over-Form Doctrines in Tax Law' (2002) 43 *Santa Clara Law Review* 699. On the relationship between economic substance and subprinciples in the USA, see, amongst others, WJ Kolarik II and SNJ Wlodychak, 'The Economic Substance Doctrine in Federal and State Taxation' (2014) 67 *Tax Lawyer* 715; WP Streng and LD Yoder, 'United States' in F Zimmer (ed), *Form and Substance in Tax Law* (Kluwer, 2002); L Lederman, 'W(h)ither Economic Substance' (2010) 95 *Iowa Law Review* 389; TA Kaye, 'United States' in *A Comparative Look at Regulation of Corporate Tax Avoidance* (Springer, 2012).

[129] Zornoza Pérez and Báez Moreno (n 127) 137–38; Zimmer, 'Domestic Anti-Avoidance Rules' (n 127) 25–26.

[130] An example is *Samsung Electronics Ltd v National Tax Service of Korea* [2018] Supreme Court 2016 du 42883, according to the report in the IBFD Tax Treaty Case Law Reports, stating that the court considered the 'effective' beneficial owner.

in the sense of an anti-avoidance rule requalifying the consequence of a certain legal arrangement,[131] and sometimes as a mix of both.[132]

Secondly, as already advanced, proper anti-avoidance rules requalify the consequence of a legal fact because certain elements indicating abuse, such as artificiality, activity or purpose, are absent or present.[133] The taxpayers do not hide actual legal facts, but have a different purpose or an economic rationale that is not in line with the tax policy of the applicable rules. However, the legal facts are not necessarily challenged.

Finally, economic ownership has no precise definition, but refers to the abilities that different economic theories attach to ownership. In this regard, the concept may be as broad as to refer to any person economically benefiting from an arrangement. Some countries, such as Germany, differ in that they use an economic interpretation of the law or economic allocation rules to which beneficial ownership may be linked to some extent.[134] However, this does not necessarily mean beneficial ownership is economic ownership in a broad sense, but that beneficial ownership refers to certain allocation or anti-avoidance rules that are defined upon certain economic characteristics. Moreover, because, in several cases, anti-avoidance rules point towards the economic beneficiary if elements of abuse are at stake, economic ownership and anti-avoidance doctrines are usually mismatched. In this regard, to use the wording economic ownership to define beneficial owner is misleading. What may be consistent, though controversial, is whether in some countries the concept equates to such domestic principles.

Beneficial ownership is frequently defined under any of those approaches, some of them or all of them, which adds confusion to the term, as if the obscurity of the terms was not enough. Although most authors equate economic understanding of beneficial ownership to substance over form, this author advocates not using the former because it may lead to consideration of a broad economic understanding and may mistakenly lead to domestic economic allocation rules. As stated, beneficial ownership in most treaties based on the Model does not depend on domestic meanings, so using that word would lead to a mistaken result. Similarly, to consider an international economic meaning does not relate to the development of the rule, as will be seen. Conversely, the substance over form approach, as a legal principle known in different forms in different legal traditions, may fit its meaning, though it is probably limited to its use in a legal substance test, and not in an economic substance sense.

[131] *Royal Bank of Scotland* (n 55). Despite mentioning that the arrangements are hiding a simulated arrangement, it takes into account the purpose of taking a tax advantage, which suggest that it was applying an actual requalification.

[132] *Eidgenössische Steuerverwaltung v X Bank* (n 123); *Futures* [2015] Bundesgericht/Supreme Court 2C_895/2012. According to Reinarz and Carelli, and based on their analysis of the ruling, the court decided on beneficial ownership blended with a sort of substance over form test, but, recognising the validity of the transactions, they were actually applying an anti-avoidance rule and requalifying the transaction.

[133] Zornoza Pérez and Báez Moreno (n 127) 136.

[134] See s 39(2) of the German Abgabenordnung. On the difference between an early broad economic interpretation in Germany and the current legal economic ownership principle, see Baez (n 113) 33–34.

(a) Beneficial Ownership as an Economic Substance or Anti-avoidance Requalification Test

The first group of cases look into beneficial owner as a substance over form test in the sense of a proper anti-avoidance rule requalifying the consequence to the legal facts as shown by the taxpayer, without challenging these facts.

In Spain, the National Court ruled that beneficial ownership implied a sort of business purpose test or anti-avoidance substance over form principle in the *Real Madrid* set of cases, involving conduit companies set up to receive football players' royalties, and in the *Goldman Sachs–Mobel Linea* case.[135] The French Conseil D'Etat also ruled in the *Royal Bank of Scotland* case, which involved a usufruct of shares, that beneficial ownership was somehow related to an abuse of law test or an artificiality test.[136] In France, such a view has seemingly permeated to lower courts, such as in the *Société Innovation et Gestion Financière* case.[137]

(b) Beneficial Ownership as a Blend of Legal Substance, Definition of Facts or Simulation Rule, and Economic Substance or Requalification Anti-avoidance Rule

Other countries, although they could be seen as arguing that beneficial ownership is a sort of substance over form test, mix the definition of facts and anti-avoidance rules, redefining the consequence of the legal facts.

In Switzerland, courts, including the Supreme Court, have apparently combined a substance over form analysis, in the sense of defining actual legal facts taking place, with anti-avoidance principles, such as activity or purpose tests, to define beneficial ownership.[138] Moreover, the Swiss Federal Administrative Court – mistakenly – considered that the beneficial owner in exchange of information and regarding income tax treaties, although performing different objects, has a similar or identical meaning, leading to an economic substance over form understanding.[139]

In India, the Supreme Court grouped the beneficial owner with the substance over form doctrine, the lifting of the corporate veil doctrine or the alter ego doctrine, the latter two as proper requalifying anti-avoidance rules.[140] However, it left unresolved whether the court considered them as equivalent, similar or different but referring to the same facts. Nevertheless, the court connected all of them to some extent. However, that case dealt with domestic law and not with tax treaty law. The High Court of Bombay in the

[135] *Mobel Línea v Reino de España [Goldman Sachs]* (n 55); *Real Madrid v Resolución del TEAC [1]–[8]* (n 31); Martín Jiménez (n 31) 39.

[136] See above, n 131.

[137] *Société Innovation et Gestion Financière* [2009] Administrative Tribunal of Paris 05-8263, 8-9/99 Revue Jurisprudence Fiscale 961; D Guttman, 'Beneficial Ownership without Specific Beneficial Ownership Provision' in Lang et al (n 83) 164–65.

[138] *V SA* (n 123); *Non Disclosed Taxpayer v Eidgenössische Steuerverwaltung (UBS Case)* [2011] BVGE A-6053/2010; *X Holding* [2005] Eidgenössiscge Steuerrekurskommission SKR 2003-159; *Undisclosed companies v Federal Tax Administration (Swaps case)* [2012] Bundesverwaltungsgericht A-6537/2010; *X Sàrl v Administration Fédérale des Contributions AFC* [2014] Bundesverwaltungsgericht A-4689/2013; *Lux Partnership* [2015] Bundesgericht/Tribunal fédéral 2C_752/2014; *Eidgenössische Steuerverwaltung v X Bank* (n 123); *Futures* (n 132). The analysis of these cases is based on Meindl-Ringler (n 67) 238 et seq and the IBFD Tax Treaty Case Law Database.

[139] *Non Disclosed Taxpayer v Eidgenössische Steuerverwaltung (UBS Case)* (n 138). See below, ch 7.

[140] *Vodafone International holdings BV v Union of India & Anr* (n 123) para 67.

Aditya Birla Nuvo case, however, somehow equated beneficial ownership to equitable owner, but subsequently applied anti-avoidance reasoning, leaving unclear whether the term has an anti-avoidance meaning or if the result derives from the application of the two rules (or principles, as considered in chapter three) separately.[141] The Authority for Advanced Rulings, in turn, assumed beneficial ownership in a very formal way in some cases, sometimes in the sense of equitable ownership, while in most cases it adopted a substance over form view, although it was not clear whether it took a redefinition of the facts approach or a requalifying approach.[142]

In Korea, the *Winiamando* case was resolved on a substance over form basis considering activity and substance.[143] Because the tax authorities raised the issue of beneficial ownership but the court did not analyse it, some authors suggest that the court somehow considered beneficial ownership as similar or identical to the applied substance over form test.[144] Also, the Supreme Court of Korea held in the *Hanwha Total* case that the beneficial owner is in principle the receiver, unless the other person is defined as the beneficial owner under substance over form analysis.[145] However, this does not seem to equate beneficial ownership and substance over form; rather, the latter serves to define the facts which the beneficial owner would only subsequently apply.

In Argentina, the Tax National Court ruled in the *Molinos del Rio de la Plata* case that beneficial ownership is defined as an anti-avoidance rule[146] or as an economic substance test.[147] In addition, one of the members of the Tax Court mismatched beneficial ownership in tax treaties with the definition proposed by the Financial Action Task Force for measures to prevent money laundering or the use of vehicles for illicit purposes.[148]

A final group of cases seemingly use beneficial ownership in the sense of substance over form as a pure definition-of-facts rule. In the UK, the well-known *Indofood* case

[141] *Aditya Birla Nuvo Ltd v Union of india* [2011] Bombay High Court No 730 of 2009 and No 345 of 2010. See an analysis of the case in DP Sengupta, '*Aditya Birla Nuvo v DDIT High Court of Bombay*' in Lang et al (n 83).

[142] *Ar dex Investments Mauritius Ltd* [2011] Authority for Advance Rulings No 866 of 2010; *Foster's Australia Limited* [2008] Authority for Advance Rulings No 736/2006. Considering beneficial ownership in relation to the object of the device to obtain an advantage, see *KSPG Netherlands Holding BV* [2010] Authority for Advance Rulings No 818/2009. In a formal sense, accepting the Mauritian certificate of beneficial ownership on the basis of a circular issued for dividends giving presumptive value to such certificates, although the case dealt with capital gains, see *E*Trade Mauritius Ltd* [2010] Authority for Advance Rulings No 826 of 2009. The Income Tax Appelate Court also considered beneficial ownership in a very formal way in the sense of accepting a certificate from the foreign tax authority: *Universal International Music BV* (Income Tax Appellate Tribunal). Considering beneficial ownership in relation to the residence requirement, see *Abdul Razak A Meman In re* [2005] Authority for Advanced Rulings No 637 of 2004. The ABC case seemingly adopt a 'common sense' approach, which may be seen as an equitable ownership or anti-avoidance view. *ABC* [1995] Authority for Advance Rulings P No 13 of 1995. Sengupta (n 141) 126.

[143] *Winiamando* [2012] Supreme Court 2010 du 25466.

[144] Ji-Hyun Yoon, 'An End of a Journey or a New Beginning? The 2012 Trilogy of Supreme Court Decisions on International Tax' [2013] *Asia-Pacific Tax Bulletin* 190, 196.

[145] *Hanhwa Total Co Ltd v Head of Seosan District Office of National Tax Service & other* (n 124). On the IBFD Tax Treaty Case Database.

[146] Even though unclear, mixing arguments and bringing together different mismatching sources, see Gómez in *Molinos Río de la Plata* [2013] Tribunal Fiscal de la Nación 34.739-I and 35.783-I [VII]. See also M Screpante, 'Treaty Abuse and Beneficial Ownership – the Molinos Case' in E Kemmeren et al (eds), *Tax Treaty Case Law around the Globe 2017* (IBFD, 2018).

[147] Magallón in *Molinos Río de la Plata* (n 146) para IV.

[148] Gómez in ibid para VII.

related beneficial ownership and a substance test.[149] However, it remains unclear whether the test is a legal substance test or an economic substance test.

In Indonesia, *PT Transportasi Gas* and *PT Indostat* also seemingly applied a substance over form test, possibly in the sense of an economic substance anti-avoidance test.[150]

(c) Beneficial Ownership as a Legal Substance, Definition of Facts or Simulation Rule

In Spain, the well-known, relevant *Real Madrid* ruling by the Supreme Court on intermediary companies established by football players to channel royalties seemed to relate beneficial ownership to simulation or definition of the actual legal facts.[151]

(d) Unclear Cases Mixing Definition of Facts, Substance Over Form and Beneficial Ownership

Some of these cases relating beneficial ownership and substance over form, such as the *Royal Bank of Scotland* case, *X Holding* and *Re V SA*, based their decisions jointly on their domestic anti-abuse rules and on beneficial ownership, so it is unclear whether such rulings actually meant that beneficial ownership is a substance over form test.[152]

Other cases, even though collaterally connecting beneficial owner and substance over form or anti-avoidance principles, do not actually equate them. The Federal Court of Appeal of Canada, in the *Prevost* case, linked case conduits and piercing the corporate veil, which relates to a substance analysis.[153] Still, this author's view is that the court states that piercing the corporate veil works at first instance, then, once the facts are set, beneficial ownership would test if the entity is a nominee, but this does not equate beneficial ownership with substance over form. Similarly, in India, the Authority for Advance Rulings ruled in the *XYZ* case that after a proper analysis of the facts, the beneficial owners of a company activity may be the shareholders,[154] but this is only after the facts are defined in a first and separate step following domestic economic substance.

The view that the beneficial owner test implies a substance over form analysis is also borne by several administrative circulars. The tax authorities of China and Vietnam hold such an approach in public notes.[155] In the case of the UK, HMRC issued two

[149] *Indofood International Finance Ltd v JP Morgan Chase Bank NA* (n 40) para 44. The case, being one of the leading cases on beneficial ownership coming from a common law jurisdiction, has been analysed several times. See Baker (n 41); Fraser and Oliver (n 88); Kemmeren in Reimer and Rust (n 5) 754; Meindl-Ringler (n 67) 111 et seq; S Jain, *Effectiveness of Beneficial Ownership Test in Conduit Companies Cases* (IBFD, 2013) 133 et seq.

[150] *PT Transportasi Gas Indonesia v Direktur Jenderal Paiak* [2008] Pengadilan Pajak (Tax Court) Put-13602/PP/M.I/13/2008; *PT Indosat, Tbk v Direktur Jenderal Paiak* [2010] Pengadilan Pajak (Tax Court) Put-23288/PP/M.11/13/2010. See J Gooijer, 'Beneficial Owner: Judicial Variety in Interpretation Counteracted by the 2012 OECD Proposals?' (2014) 42 *Intertax* 204, 210; P Baker, 'Editor's Note Re PT Transportasi Gas Indonesia' (2008) 11 *International Tax Law Reports* 407; Meindl-Ringler (n 67) 282–283.

[151] *Real Madrid v Administración General del Estado* [2011] Tribunal Supremo/Supreme Court 5016/2006, 2011 RJ 515 FJ 5.

[152] Martín Jiménez (n 31) 50; for the Swiss cases, see Meindl-Ringler (n 67) 240.

[153] *Prevost v The Queen* (n 31) para 16.

[154] *XYZ* [1995] Authority for Advance Rulings P-9 of 1995.

[155] In China, Guo shui han (circular) [2009] No 601, as supplemented by SAT Public Notice [2012] No 30 and Public Notice [2018] No 9, points at, among other factors: submitting income to a third jurisdiction in a

notes following the *Indofood* case, which relates the term to the object and purpose of the treaties and to prevention of abuse.[156] As derived from the *Indofood* case, one may expect what lays behind the reasoning is a subject over form analysis. However, the notes remain ambiguous and refer more to the facts to look at in order to define whether there is an obligation to pass the income, rather than whether beneficial ownership enables an anti-avoidance requalification or whether this is limited by the tax treaty.[157] To this author, it is likely that the former option is sustained.

(e) Beneficial Ownership as an Anti-avoidance Requalification Rule Based on an Activity and/or Purpose Test[158]

Previous chapters have already shown the use of beneficial owner in the USA as a business purpose test. *Aiken Industries, Northern Indiana Public Service Companies* and *SDI Netherlands* were some of the first cases in which beneficial ownership in tax treaties was interpreted in such a sense, and they set a consistent pattern in US tax treaty practice.[159] In those cases, however, beneficial ownership was derived from an intertwining of tax treaties and domestic allocation rules – including a purpose test – and was not derived from the treaty beneficial owner test itself, as it was not contained in them. Similarly, in Denmark, the *H1 Aps, NetApp* and *Cyprus Co* cases interpreted beneficial ownership as a sort of business purpose test. Those cases also considered the activity, assets and premises of corporations in a sort of business activity test, though concluding that the term had to be interpreted narrowly.[160]

Tax authorities in Russia have also seemingly taken the approach that beneficial ownership is an economic entitlement or substance over form test.[161] More recently,

certain period; the lack of or little business activities; the reduced size of assets, employees or operations; lack of or little control or risk; whether the company enjoys a reduced tax burden; back-to-back loans; and back-to-back royalties payments. The first criteria are clearly close to an activity, purpose or anti-avoidance test. However, Public Notice 30 clearly states that the beneficial owner has to be assessed in relation to substance over form. See C Pellone, 'China-Tax Authorities Issue Circular on Interpretation of Double Tax Treaties' (2011) 18 *International Transfer Pricing Journal* 143; Dongmei Qiu, 'The Concept of "Beneficial Ownership" in China's Tax Treaties – the Current State of Play' (2013) 2 *Bulletin of International Taxation*. In Vietnam, Circular 205/2013/TT.BTC of 24 December 2013 provides in its Art 6 the exclusion from beneficial owner condition in relation to transfer of income, business activities, resources, control and risk, intermediaries in technical services, low tax rate, and a general statement to agent or intermediary. Both circulars are available at the IBFD Tax Research Database.

[156] See HMRC INTM332000 and INTM504000, www.gov.uk/hmrc-internal-manuals/international-manual/intm332000 and www.gov.uk/hmrc-internal-manuals/international-manual/intm504000.

[157] See the analysis of the guidance in Fraser and Oliver (n 88).

[158] On how beneficial owner relates to an activity test, see S Jain, J Prebble and K Bunting, 'Conduit Companies, Beneficial Ownership, and the Test of Substantive Business Activity in Claims for Relief under Double Tax Treaties' (2013) 11 *eJournal of Tax Research* 386.

[159] *Aiken Industries, Inc v Commissioner* (n 116) 934; *Northern Indiana Public Service Co v Commissioner* (n 116); *SDI Netherlands v Commissioner* [1996] Tax Court No 23747-94, 107 TC 161, 175.

[160] *H1 ApS* (n 74); *Nycomed* [2012] National Tax Tribunal SKM 2012.409 LSR; *Cyprus Co* (n 74). See commentaries in Meindl-Ringler (n 67) 251 et seq; Bundgaard and Winther-Sorensen (n 29); Jakob Bundgaard, 'The Notion of Beneficial Ownership in Danish Tax Law: The Creation of a New Legal Order with Uncertainty as a Companion' in Lang et al (n 83); Hansen et al (n 73).

[161] Letter 03-00-RZ/16236 of 9 April 2014. See Reimer and Rust (n 5) 745–46. The ruling takes into consideration that Russian dividends are routed to third countries where there is no treaty or treaties are less beneficial, back-to-back loans and back-to-back royalties agreements.

the authorities' precise beneficial owner substance over form test is derived from the company actually carrying out business or a sort of economic activity test.[162] The Kaliningrad Arbitration Court, even though seemingly using the concept in a much narrower way than the tax authorities, also put the spotlight on the activity of the corporation in the *NPO Cifrovie Televisionnie Systemi* case, dealing with interests paid to a Cyprus intermediary entity.[163] The same approach was followed by the Arbitration Court of the Vladimirskaya Oblast in the *ZAO* case, albeit in relation to capital gains, where no beneficial owner test was found in the treaty.[164] The Federal Arbitration Court of Moscow also tested beneficial ownership against the activity of the entity in *INTESA*.[165]

In *Prevost* and *Velcro*, the Supreme Court of Canada also took into account the activity of the corporation. However, in such Canadian cases, the analysis does not act as an anti-avoidance activity test, but aims to define the fact to which the test applies.[166] In Korea, the Supreme Court analysed the beneficial owner test, in the *Hanhwa Total* case, in relation to the business purpose and the economic activity of the intermediary entity.[167] The same approach was followed in the *Samsung Electronics* case.[168] In Italy, the Supreme Court distinguished in the *Aptar South Europe Sarl* case how the test should be applied to active and passive holdings, stating for the former that an activity test may define beneficial ownership, and that for the latter an autonomy test may be applied, although it also indicates the artificiality of the entity as commanding to some extent.[169] In *ECO-BAT BV*, the court also held that the activity of the corporation is commanding in defining beneficial ownership.[170]

What is unclear in most of these cases is whether such activity analysis is taken as an indication of whether the corporation is a 'fake' arrangement where the parties give a different shape or name, or is an actual business activity test. In the first case, it would be a step to define the facts upon which, once settled, beneficial ownership will be tested – similar to substance over form in the sense of definition of the facts – while in the latter it will be a proper anti-avoidance requalification rule.[171]

Contrary to all those cases, the Tax Court of Canada, in the *Alta Energy Luxembourg* case, explicitly denied beneficial ownership to be a general anti-avoidance rule (GAAR) and stated that it was of very limited application compared with other rules.[172]

[162] Letter CA-4-9/8285@ of 28 April 2018, taking into account assets and employees, income being passed, control and the existence of operating business.

[163] *NPO Cifrovie Televisionnie Systemi v Tax Inspectorate* (n 124). Analysed through the IBFD Tax Treaty Case Law Database.

[164] *ZAO Vladimirsky torgoviy dom v Federal Tax Service* [2017] Arbitration Court of the Vladimirskaya Oblast A11-6602/2016. Analysed through the IBFD Tax Treaty Case Law Database.

[165] *Intesa v Federal Tax Service* [2016] Federal Arbitration Court of Moscow A40-241361/2015.

[166] *Prevost v The Queen* (n 31) para 16(d); *Velcro v The Queen* [2012] TCC 57 (TCC) [35].

[167] *Hanhwa Total Co Ltd v Head of Seosan District Office of National Tax Service & other* (n 124). Analysed through the IBFD Tax Treaty Case Law Database.

[168] *Samsung Electronics Ltd v National Tax Service of Korea* (n 130). Analysed through the IBFD Tax Treaty Case Law Database.

[169] *Aptar South Europea SARL v Agenzia delle Entrate* [2016] Corte di Casazzione 27113/2016.

[170] *ECO-BAT BV v Agenzia delle Entrate* [2016] Corte Suprema di Cassazione 10792/2016. Analysed through the IBFD Tax Treaty Case Law Database.

[171] See above, n 127 et seq and accompanying text.

[172] *Alta Energy Luxembourg SARL* [2018] Tax Court of Canada 2014-4359(IT)G, 2018 TCC 152 [93 et seq].

(f) Moving from Beneficial Owner as the Person to Whom Income has to be Allocated for Tax Purposes to the Person Economically and Legally Controlling the Income: The Italian View

Italian tax authorities traditionally took the view that the beneficial owner was the person to whom income had to be allocated for tax purposes, probably because of the influence of the 1989 Germany–Italy Tax Treaty defining beneficial ownership, and in line with the Partnership Report but not with the commentaries to the Model.[173] This approach has also been taken to the domestic implementation of the Interest and Royalties Directive. Although the directive only defines beneficial owner as subject to tax in relation to permanent establishments, Italian domestic law also provides such a definition for companies.[174]

The main problem in Italy is that many cases not explicitly dealing with beneficial ownership are considered as beneficial owner cases, adding confusion to the already complex matter.[175] A minor line of some administrative rulings have been mistakenly identified or related to beneficial owner cases, but were actually resolved under a substance over form anti-avoidance approach and with little or no grounds in the term.[176] Most of the cases mentioned, considered by scholars as beneficial owner cases, are probably not beneficial owner cases but allocation cases. On the one hand, because the main approach in Italy links beneficial owner and subject and liability to tax, any case on such matters is considered a beneficial owner case; on the other hand, some pure conduit cases led to the blending of treaty shopping abusive cases and beneficial owner analysis.

However, more recently, the Supreme Court has aligned the Italian view with the OECD Commentary view on the concept and has acknowledged that the beneficial owner is the person who has the legal and economic entitlement and control of the income.[177] In this regard, the Supreme Court has explicitly rejected beneficial ownership as being a sort of activity test, and does not require premises, employees or assets to be present for a person to be considered a beneficial owner. An interesting argument

[173] Ruling 12/431 of 7 May 1987; Ruling 104/E of 6 May 1997; Ruling 86/E of 12 July 2006. Other cases considered by some authors relating to beneficial ownership are 26/E of 21 May 2009, No 47/E of 2 November 2005 and 32/E of 8 July 2011, even though they do not discuss beneficial ownership but liability to tax in order to apply exemption. See M Gusmeroli, 'The Supreme Court Decision in the Government Pension Investment Fund Case: A Tale of Transparency and Beneficial Ownership (in Plato's Cave)' (2010) 64 *Bulletin for International Taxation* 198, 199; L Banfi and F Mantegazza, 'An Update on the Concept of Beneficial Ownership from an Italian Perspective' (2012) 52 *European Taxation* 57, 57; M Rossi, 'An Italian Perspective on the Beneficial Ownership Concept' (2007) 45 *Tax Notes International* 1117, 1127. See also s 9 of the Protocol to the 1989 Germany–Italy Tax Convention; OECD, *The Application of the OECD Model Tax Convention to Partnerships* (OECD Publishing, 1999) para 54. On the mistaken approach of the Partnership report, biased by their drafters, see s III.A below.

[174] Compare Art 1.4 and 1.5 of the Council Directive 2003/49/EC of 3 June 2003 on a common system of taxation applicable to interest and royalty payments made between associated companies of different Member States [2003] OJ L157/49, and its implementation in Italy in Legislative Decree 143 of May 30, 2005. See Rossi (n 173) 1128–29.

[175] See, eg Banfi and Mantegazza (n 173) 58; Pistone (n 93) 181.

[176] Eg *Credito Emiliano Holding v Ag delle Entrate* [2010] Commissione Tributaria Provinciale of Reggio Emilia 242-01-10 13 et seq.

[177] *Aptar South Europea SARL v Agenzia delle Entrate* (n 169) 3.2; *Q BV v Agenzia delle Entrate* [2916] Corte di Cassazione 10792/2016 9. See M Rossi, '"Sede Di Direzione Effettiva" e "Beneficiario Effettivo" Nel Quadro Dei Rapporti Italo-Francesi' [2017] *Corriere Tributario* 1270.

of the Supreme Court is the distinction between active and passive holdings, whereby if the test applicable in the sense of activity test would be applicable to the latter, no holding would be a beneficial owner.[178]

(g) Beneficial Ownership in the OECD Model is not a Substance Over Form Rule or a General Anti-avoidance Rule, nor Submits to Domestic Attribution of Income Rules

It is the author's view that approaches considering beneficial ownership as a broad rule to call for a redefinition of the facts upon legal reality or as an actual anti-avoidance rule are flawed.

From a historical point of view, the discussions at the OECD put the spotlight on a specific type of arrangement and their characteristics, not on their abusive characteristics, nor do they mention the reality as the relevant element.[179] It is true that the comments by the representatives at the OECD mentioned the improper character of the access to treaty source limits of these arrangements. However, in the author's view, this shows precisely there was an *ex ante* analysis in the development of the beneficial owner test that did not transfer the abusive analysis to the elements defining the event of the rule.[180]

The transactions are *ex lege* excluded from the consequence of the treaty because it was considered that such transactions shall not access treaty benefits as they are abusive, but there is no analysis of abuse as we currently understand anti-avoidance rules in the event of the rule. There is no argument in the 1977 Commentary or in any other document suggesting an abusive analysis shall be performed to deny access to relevant treaty rules dependent on beneficial ownership.[181] If it were the case, there is no reference upon which such rule could be construed. Anti-avoidance rules may be defined by purpose, artificiality, economic effects and several other factors, so to try to define beneficial ownership as such without any other reference would be impossible and against the rule of law and legal certainty.[182]

Moreover, most of these anti-abuse concepts were developed or clarified later. At the time of introduction of the term, some countries had anti-avoidance rules, some had them but they were still at an early stage of development and some did not have such rules at all.[183] If countries did not know how to deal with them and were adopting literal interpretations in many cases, it can hardly be said that there was a consensus on such a controversial topic so far as to include it in all tax treaties. If there was no clear legal abusive concept at the time, they could not resort to it. It is probable that the translation of beneficial owner to effective beneficiary by several countries, trying to avoid the

[178] *Aptar South Europea SARL v Agenzia delle Entrate* (n 169) 3.2.

[179] 'Report on suggested amendments to Articles 11 and 12' (n 3) p 14.

[180] Walser in *Ifa: The OECD Model Convention – 1998 & Beyond: The Concept of Beneficial Ownership in Tax Treaties (IFA Congress Series Set)* (Kluwer, 2000) 17 et seq.

[181] See paras 12, 8 and 4 of commentaries to Arts 10, 11 and 12 of the 1977 OECD Model Tax Convention and documents in nn 3, 46 and 98 above.

[182] O Ryynänen, 'The Concept of a Beneficial Owner in the Application of Finnish Tax Treaties' (2003) 44 *Scandinivian Studies in Law* 359.

[183] See above, n 118.

common law distinction between equitable ownership and legal ownership, led to the mistake many years later, when the concept started to be applied, of mixing the concept with anti-avoidance considerations.[184] It should be taken into account that the concept was introduced in the 1970s but only started to be applied repeatedly at the end of the 1990s and beginning of the 2000s, once general anti-avoidance rules had been developed and consolidated.

Some may argue whether consistent practice would have rendered beneficial ownership a substance over form test after evolving through the years and despite its origin. It is true, as argued, that a significant amount of countries interpret beneficial ownership as such. However, there are so many deviations and inconsistencies that this author cannot see that there is an *opinio iuris*, and consistent practice as required by international law.[185] Each of the countries interpreting beneficial ownership in such a sense does it in a different way, normally backed by their own domestic understanding of avoidance, combined with other rules and in different cases. As stated earlier, they especially use substance over form reasoning, but in several different ways, including definition of the facts or, despite recognising the facts as presented by the taxpayer, requalifying the consequence of them. In addition, there is also a significant number of countries interpreting beneficial ownership in a narrow way. Only in cases where both contracting states adopt a similar substance over form interpretation, consistently and with no or only a small deviation, which is not normally the case, could such practice be adopted, but this would be specifically for their treaty and not a general understanding as derived from the Model.

Moreover, if this were the case, the OECD's Base Erosion and Profit Shifting (BEPS) Action 6 resulting in the introduction of a principal purpose test (PPT) as a minimum standard would be irrelevant in relation to Articles 10, 11 and 12 of the Model.[186] Not surprisingly, nobody raised the question of whether the PPT was already implicit in the beneficial owner test. Moreover, as will be analysed later, the 2014 Commentary implicitly recognises that the term is not an anti-avoidance rule by recognising it is compatible with them and it does not limit its use, recognising they have different results.[187]

In the *Cayman Holdco* and *ISS* cases, the National Tax Court of Denmark and the Eastern High Court of Denmark clearly drew a line between the rightful recipient theory, which somehow relates to an artificiality or substance over form test, and

[184] Eynatten et al (n 29) 578.

[185] Just to mention a few main rulings: the *Velcro* and *Prevost* cases in Canada adopt a narrow legal view; the *Indofood* case an economic substance approach; and the Danish cases seemingly an economic ownership or artificiality approach. This shows there is no consistency at all, and the differences could not be wider. *Velcro v The Queen* (n 166); *Prevost v The Queen* (n 31); *N Luxembourg 1 and others v Skatteministerie (and joined cases)* (n 53).

[186] See Art 29.9 of the 2017 OECD Model Tax Convention, and respective commentary. On its content, see A Báez Moreno, 'GAARs and Treaties: From the Guiding Principle to the Principal Purpose Test. What Have We Gained from BEPS Action 6?' (2017) 45 *Intertax* 432; V Chand, 'The Principal Purpose Test in the Multilateral Convention: An In-Depth Analysis' (2018) 46 *Intertax* 18; M Lang, 'BEPS Action 6: Introducing an Antiabuse Rule in Tax Treaties' [2014] 7 *Tax Notes International* 658; S Van Weeghel, 'A Deconstruction of the Principal Purposes Test' (2019) 11 *World Tax Journal* 3.

[187] See paras 12.5, 10.3 and 4.4 of the Commentary to Arts 10, 11 and 12 in the 2014 OECD Model Tax Convention. See J Avery Jones, R Vann and J Wheeler, 'OECD Discussion Draft "Clarification of the Meaning of „Beneficial Owner" in the OECD Model Tax Convention"' (2012), http://www.oecd.org/tax/treaties/48420432.pdf, 5.

the treaty beneficial owner test.[188] If beneficial ownership does not match the rightful recipient test, and the latter refers to a substance over form or artificiality test in the splitting of assets and income, it could be argued that beneficial ownership does not imply a substance over form test or an artificiality test.[189]

Similarly, but understanding substance over form in the sense of the definition of legal facts, the CJEU, in the set of Danish cases ruling affirmed beneficial ownership, diverges from substance over form as understood in the sense of redefining legal facts by recognising that 'the reality principle' was not enough to resolve the issue, which was also acknowledged by the parties to the case.[190] Similarly, it argued that the rightful recipient test was not applicable to the case as the income was actually paid, recognising it as a rule for definition of the facts.[191] If income is actually paid to a conduit company as the actual creditor, substance over form or rightful recipient may not solve the problem, while beneficial ownership under the court's view points to the economic owner as the subject behind the conduit entity.[192]

On the other hand, it is clear that beneficial ownership cannot be interpreted in the sense of a subject to tax test, because this solution was explicitly rejected during the OECD discussions.[193] However, the rejection was based on the early misinterpretation of subject to tax as effective taxation.[194] What could be more controversial is whether it could be interpreted as a subject to tax or liability to tax in the sense of being within the scope of charge, even though not effectively taxed, as suggested by some authors.[195]

This does not seem to be the case.[196] It is absolutely clear that tax treaties operate on the subject being subject to general liability to tax, and not the income being subject in the hands of somebody, even if not effectively taxed, as subject to tax in that sense would imply.[197] The discussions at the OECD and the Commentary did not discuss tax liability of intermediaries but only to whom treaty rules were applicable as an independent issue from domestic allocation.[198] At the time, allocation of jurisdiction and attribution

[188] *H1 Ltd (Cayman)* (n 74) s 6; *Ministry of Taxation v FS Invest II Sàrl (formerly ISS Equity A/S)* (n 74). Meindl-Ringler (n 67) 252.

[189] Bundgaard argues that the rightful recipient theory is not always clear and varies from a substance over form test to a matter of interpretation. See Bundgaard and Winther-Sorensen (n 29) 600.

[190] *N Luxembourg 1 and others v Skatteministerie (and joined cases)* (n 53) 25.

[191] See Advocate General Kokkot Opinion in the C-115/16 case, para 100.

[192] *N Luxembourg 1 and others v Skatteministerie (and joined cases)* (n 53) 88.

[193] Note that they reject it because they do not want to introduce an effective taxation test: 'Report on suggested amendments to Articles 11 and 12' (n 3) p 13.

[194] See above section II.A in Ch 4.

[195] As argued by Libin in Oliver et al (n 2) 322 et seq; Ault in JL Walser, 'The OECD Model Tax Convention – 1998 and Beyond' in *The Concept of Beneficial Ownership in Tax Treaties*, vol a (Kluwer, 2000) 21–22; De Broe (n 32) 722, even though blended with other tests; Meindl-Ringler (n 67) 385; Avery Jones et al (n 187), though mixed with a control test. However, De Broe mismatches subject to tax with effective taxation, as understood in very early times, and argues that beneficial owner refers to within the scope of charge, even if exempted, as subject to tax was more recently understood.

[196] Martín Jiménez (n 31) 63.

[197] M Lang, *The Application of the OECD Model Tax Convention to Partnerships, a Critical Analysis of the Report Prepared by the OECD Committee on Fiscal Affairs* (Kluwer, 2000) 52, 63.

[198] 'Report on suggested amendments to Articles 11 and 12' (n 3) p 13. In some treaties, however, such as the 1989 Italy–Germany Tax Convention, beneficial owner may be understood in such sense because it explicitly says so, but not as derived from the Model.

of income at the domestic level were located at two different levels. Of course, treaties depended to some extent on domestic rules, but this was mainly in the definition on the type of income and general liability of subjects. The point was not whether or how domestic allocation rules operate, but how intermediaries access jurisdiction rules that were largely disconnected from specific domestic allocation rules, despite being connected to general liability.

An additional argument for rejecting the term as a subject to tax test is that the Interest and Royalties Directive requires both the income to be subject to tax and the beneficial owner to access directive provisions.[199] If beneficial ownership was meant to be an attribution of income rule, such dual requirement would be nonsense.[200] Because the Interest and Royalties Directive is based on the 1996 OECD Model, the directive added the subject to tax test, implicitly recognising that the Model did not reach the requirement of the income being subject.

(ii) Beneficial Ownership as a Narrow Anti-avoidance Rule Preventing Access to Treaty Rules of Intermediaries having Certain Characteristics: Economic and Legal Characteristics of Common Law and Civil Law Intermediaries

(a) Narrow Exclusion of Agents and Nominees or Examples?

The only definition of the term is the exclusion of intermediaries from access to relevant treaty rules provided in the Commentary. The problem is how to define which intermediaries are excluded. The term may be understood in a broad sense as excluding subjects economically acting as intermediaries, including any arrangement with characteristics similar to an intermediary, or intermediaries from a more or less strict legal perspective.

The first point will result in the exclusion of arrangements such as swaps or conduit companies, which, economically, act as a mere intermediary receiving and giving equivalent payments.[201] Even though the discussion is similar to the above-mentioned one, it is different, as it dismisses the point of considering beneficial ownership as a general anti-avoidance rule applicable to any case, narrowing it down to intermediaries. Considering it in the sense of excluding economic intermediaries, it certainly becomes close to an anti-avoidance rule. In relation to conduit companies or back-to-back arrangements, the consequences will be similar, but not in the case of, for instance, dividend stripping or bond washing. Moreover, even though the consequences might be similar, the contents when interpreting it as a GAAR or in the sense of economic ownership are clearly different. In the case of considering it a GAAR, they focus on the substance, purpose or artificiality, while in the latter they focus on the economic effect similar to one defined example.

[199] See Art 1(5) of the Council Directive 2003/49/EC of 3 June 2003 on a common system of taxation applicable to interest and royalty payments made between associated companies of different Member States.
[200] M Greggi, 'Taxation of Royalties in an EU Framework' (2007) 47 *Tax Notes International* 1149, 1159.
[201] Such as in the Swiss swap cases, *Eidgenössische Steuerverwaltung v X Bank* (n 123); *Futures* (n 132); *Undisclosed companies v Federal Tax Administration (Swaps case)* (n 138).

A group of scholars, including Van Weeghel, argue that only agents/*mandataires* and nominees are excluded, including agents in common law and in civil law countries.[202] For the Dutch scholar, the beneficial owner is the creditor, and in the case of agency or nomineeship, it is the principal.[203] In other words, the beneficial owner is the creditor/owner under the relevant legal system. Similarly, De Haen, Hostyn or Eynatten claim beneficial ownership only denies treaty benefits to intermediaries acting in the name of third parties, but does not in all cases exclude intermediaries acting in their name but on the account of a third party.[204]

Conversely, a second group of scholars argue that the reference to agents or nominees is a list of examples of a category of excluded transactions.[205] The author's view is that considering beneficial ownership as the creditor is flawed because it simply repeats the implicit connection of subject–object already contained in the definition of income, and it may be misleading because under such a view nominees and trustees acting in their own name would be beneficial owners, even though clearly the intention was to exclude them.[206] This would make the beneficial ownership test redundant. It is true that the proposal by Van Weeghel clearly says nominees are excluded, but this contradicts the creditor definition without indicating if such exclusion is a single exception or again opens the door to exclusions, which would again leave the question open. In addition, the elimination of the original draft Commentary of the wording 'having the legal right to receive the income' suggests that other arrangements beyond mere creditors are covered.[207]

Consequently, the second and majority view of agents and nominees being examples seems correct, confirmed by the fact that the Commentary uses the wording 'such as', indicating they are examples of excluded intermediaries.[208] This does not, however, mean that any intermediary transaction is excluded because the list remains open. Substitution of the reference 'any trustee or other intermediary' by 'any intermediary, such as an agent or nominee' suggests that the OECD was targeting specific types of intermediaries, and not any and all.[209]

All discussions at the OECD were dealing with trustees, agents and nominees, which of course shows the focus was on the intermediaries, and not on any type of economically alike transaction.[210] Furthermore, though usufruct was first used in the

[202] See Van Weeghel (n 31) 89, 91, although he adjusts the meaning of exclusion of agents and nominees in relation to the cases where there is a mismatch in allocation between source and residence.

[203] ibid 91.

[204] Eynatten et al (n 29) 539.

[205] Du Toit (n 4) 216–17; Danon (n 10) 41; De Broe (n 32) 683.

[206] As suggested by Eynatten et al (n 29) 539, but clearly against 'Report on suggested amendments to Articles 11 and 12' (n 3) p 13. The 2003 version of the Commentary also confirms that mere formal owners or creditors would not qualify. See para 12.1 of the Commentary to Art 1 of the 2003 OECD Model Tax Convention.

[207] '[R]esidence there by any intermediary such as an agent or nominee, … having the legal right to receive the income': 'Revised Articles 11 and 12 of the OECD Draft Convention and Commentaries thereon' (n 98) pp 4 and 13.

[208] Above, n 205.

[209] Compare 'Proposals for the amendment of articles 11 and 12 of the draft convention' (n 46) p 9 and 'Revised Articles 11 and 12 of the OECD Draft Convention and Commentaries thereon' (n 98) pp 4 and 13.

[210] 'Observations of Member Countries on difficulties raised by theOECD Draft Convention on Income and Capital' [TFD/FC/216], 9 May 1967, Fiscal Committee, OCDE, p 14; 'Report on suggested amendments to Articles 11 and 12' (n 3) pp 13–14; 'Proposals for the amendment of articles 11 and 12 of the draft convention'

translation to the French version, it was later eliminated, which may suggest that other arrangements where there was no actual intermediation were not covered by the beneficial owner rule.[211] In addition, one of the first drafts of the 1977 Commentary defined beneficial ownership as denying access to relevant treaty rules to 'any intermediary'.[212] However, 'any' was eliminated and substituted by 'an', which indicates the intention was not to exclude any intermediary or similar arrangement, but to exclude a group of intermediaries with specific common characteristics.

Also, earliest versions of the Commentary defined the exclusion in relation to *trustees or other intermediaries*.[213] Such definition probably provided a joint view of both sides, common law and civil law, excluding common law's trustees and civil law's similar intermediaries. However, the final version substituted the word 'trustees' with 'nominees'. This substitution suggests that the negative definition was narrowed down only to certain types of trustees, such as nominees, and not any trustee. This could support discretionary trusts possibly accessing treaty provisions. In addition, the reference to other intermediaries located on an equal footing to excluded trustees was turned into the general definition, albeit limited by the examples of agents and nominees. Would an equal footing definition as *nominee or other intermediaries* being used lead to the consideration of any intermediary being excluded? Was this the reason for the change?

An intermediary draft also pointed out that 'intermediaries, such as an agent or nominee, interposed between the payer and the beneficiary having the legal right to receive the income'.[214] The dropping of the last part on the legal right to the income also indicates to some extent that the concept was not limited to the original problems, which were only those of the UK.[215]

In the author's view, the exemplification of agents or nominees, read together with 'intermediaries', performs two functions. First, it limits the exclusion of intermediaries performed by the beneficial ownership test to refer only to certain types of intermediaries and not to any intermediary.[216] Secondly, it defines the characteristics of the excluded transactions by providing examples of agent and nominees.[217]

The result is a sufficiently open definition that includes different intermediary arrangements from different legal traditions. Otherwise, if the exemplification is taken

(n 46) p 9; 'Revised Articles 11 and 12 of the OECD Draft Convention and Commentaries thereon, (n 98) 4 and 13.

[211] '[N]otre sens, l'allègement prévu par ces articles ne devrait être accordé que si le propriétaire ou l'usufruitier [beneficial owner] des revenus en question réside dans l'autre Etat contractant': 'Observations des pays membres sur les difficultes soulevées par le projet de convention de l'OCDE sur le revenu et la fortune' [TFD/FC/216], 2 May 1968, Fiscal Committee, OCDE; OECD Archives, Paris. Compare this to the final draft of the French version of the 1977 OECD Model Tax Convention.

[212] Compare 'Proposals for the amendment of articles 11 and 12 of the draft convention' (n 46) p 9, 'Revised Articles 11 and 12 of the OECD Draft Convention and Commentaries thereon' (n 98) pp 4 and 13, and 'Revised Commentary of the 1963 draft convention' [DAF/CFA/WP1/76.19], 5 November 1976, Committee on Fiscal Affairs, Working Party 1, pp 49 and 73. In the first one, 'any trustee or other intermediary' was used, in the second, 'any intermediary', while in the latter 'any' was dropped and just 'an intermediary' was left.

[213] 'Proposals for the amendment of articles 11 and 12 of the draft convention' (n 46) p 9.

[214] 'Revised Articles 11 and 12 of the OECD Draft Convention and Commentaries thereon' (n 98) pp 4 and 13.

[215] See s I.B above; see also s II in ch 4.

[216] Ryynänen (n 182) 354–55.

[217] Above, n 205.

too strictly, not even trustees with narrow powers, but not as narrow as nominees' arrangements, would be excluded from the beneficial owner effect, which is clearly not in line with the aim of the introduction of the test.[218] In addition, it contains a sufficiently defined concept not to bar all transactions where economic effects in a loose sense are transferred – such as usufructs or sale of assets – from the beneficial ownership condition, absolutely threatening legal certainty and outside the original aim. Only those arrangements qualifying as intermediary arrangements with similar characteristics to agency and nomineeship that the Model puts the spotlight on would be excluded from the application of the relevant treaty rules – but similar to what extent and on what characteristics?

(b) Passing the Economic Effect

Again, a broad versus narrow approach discussion arises on how to interpret beneficial ownership, in this case on whether the analogy to agency and nomineeship shall refer to economic or legal abilities. One group of scholars argue that the economic abilities or functions of agency or nomineeship are what matter in defining analogous contracts subject to beneficial ownership limitation.[219] A second approach would be to define the core of the negative definition of beneficial ownership in relation to some legal characteristics of agents, nominees and *mandataires*.

The economic view has to be rejected for several reasons. First, a plain economic understanding would leave the concept without any precise meaning, resulting in almost nobody being considered a beneficial owner.[220] Secondly, if taken in an economic sense, beneficial ownership would imply an economic substance test as an anti-avoidance rule, and the above-mentioned reasons rejecting the approach from a historical and practical perspective would deny value to such interpretation.[221] This, though, would be limited to intermediaries rather than any arrangement, and would pose the same inconveniences mentioned above but in the specific case of intermediaries. Thirdly, as argued, the economic benefit of third parties was part of the diagnosis but did not enter the rule. Fourthly, it is clear, and has been confirmed by the OECD, that the beneficial owner in tax treaties is different from the beneficial owner in anti-money laundering and exchange of information rules.[222] Those rules try to find the ultimate individual behind a legal person because they try to unveil the criminals hiding behind corporations.[223] If the anti-money laundering rule refers to the person economically controlling the income or asset, and they are not necessarily the same, this means that in tax treaties beneficial owner does not have that meaning. In addition, in some countries, such as

[218] Early discussions were largely focused on trustees: 'Report on suggested amendments to Articles 11 and 12' (n 3) p 14.

[219] Danon (n 10) 43.

[220] Baker (n 58) s 6.3; *Prevost v The Queen* (n 31) para 15; R Collier, 'Clarification of the Meaning of Beneficial Owner in the OECD Model Tax Convention' (PwC 2011) CT06/RSC.

[221] Collier (n 220).

[222] See fn 1 to paras 10.4, 12.6 and 4.5 of Commentaries to Arts 10, 11 and 12 of the 2014 OECD Model Tax Convention.

[223] See para 5(b) of the Interpretative Note to Recommendation 10 of the Financial Action Task Force; OECD Steering Group on Corporate Governance, *Behind the Corporate Veil: Using Corporate Entities for Illicit Purposes* (OECD Publishing, 2001).

the Netherlands, economic ownership may be vested in different subjects, which could make none of them able to access treaty benefits.[224] This clearly goes against its original purpose. Even in common law jurisdictions, where beneficial ownership is held jointly by two different subjects, it could lead to severe mistakes.[225]

Finally, rejection of the economic approach to beneficial ownership is also implicitly confirmed by the early OECD discussions of the term and the Commentary itself. All comments in the minutes refer to legal arrangements transferring income to third parties, and not to economic effects. Discussions surround legal concepts such as trustee, agent, *mandataire* and similar terms.[226] The continental law view puts the spotlight on the fact that some are acting 'in its own name but on behalf of', which is clearly a legal qualification.[227] The elimination of the reference to 'any intermediary, such as an agent or nominee', leaving the exclusion to 'an intermediary, such as an agent or nominee', also suggests that the intention is to narrow down the definition and not apply to any intermediary in an economic sense.[228] The use of agent or nominee as examples of excluded intermediaries, the former with heavier legal implications than intermediary, suggests that legal characteristics were the key points.

In addition, the Commentary resorts to economic ownership in other parts, such as in the definition of an independent agent in relation to permanent establishment.[229] If this was clearly used in such a case which also deals with intermediaries, why was it not used in relation to beneficial ownership? If the intention was to define beneficial ownership as economic ownership, such wording would have been used in the model itself, or at least in the Commentary or discussions. This was not the case, and all references point to legal terms.

But to take the second above-mentioned view defining beneficial ownership in a purely legal and narrow sense and to render the economic effect as irrelevant is to deny the significance granted by the OECD representatives to the fact that the problem was to the benefit of residents in third countries. It is clear that discussions at the OECD put the spotlight on nominees, agents, trustees and *mandataires* acting 'in [their] own name but on behalf' of the beneficial owner.[230] And on behalf of means the person to whom economic effects are allocated.[231] The statements of the OECD make clear that economic effects or economic entitlement cannot be irrelevant in defining beneficial ownership. Clearly, the problem was, economically, that income subject to the treaties was benefiting third parties under such arrangements. Considering its inability to fill the whole definition, but also its importance in defining the issue, the transfer of economic effects can only be rendered as the first characteristic of beneficial ownership in a negative

[224] Aleksandra van Boeijen-Ostaszewska et al, 'Clarification of the Meaning of "Beneficial Owner" in the OECD Model Tax Convention Response from IBFD Research Staff' (IBFD, 2012) 3–4.

[225] See above, chs 2 and 3.

[226] See documents in n 210 above.

[227] 'Report on suggested amendments to Articles 11 and 12' (n 3) p 14.

[228] See above, n 212.

[229] See para 37 of the Commentary to Art 5 of the 1977 OECD Model Tax Convention.

[230] 'Report on suggested amendments to Articles 11 and 12' (n 3) p 14.

[231] Minervini indicates that the origin of the wording 'on behalf' is in accountancy, where the arrangements carried out for the benefit of third parties were reflected as in 'others' account'. Later law acknowledged acting 'on behalf' or 'in account' of other person as one of the characteristics of agency: G Minervini, *El Mandato* (Bosch 1959) 11.

sense, subject to other legal characteristics.[232] The economic transfer includes both the effective payment and the accrual of an economic right in payment or kind. However, as a legal connection is needed, such payments need to be related to the second requirement, and mere factual payments without any legal connection will not exclude the beneficial ownership condition.

(c) Obligation to Pass the Income within the Same Legal Obligation

Most scholars define legal characteristics that define beneficial ownership on the abilities to control or enjoy the assets and/or income. In this regard, Du Toit points at ownership characteristics as outweighing those of any other person, clearly following a philosophical–economical common law view.[233] Similarly, Eliffe points to outweighing ownership attributes and indicia such as use, enjoyment and control.[234] Vogel, in turn, defines the legal characteristics of who is free to decide on the use of an asset and/or the income derived from it.[235] Danon, in a similar vein and following Vogel to some extent, points to the power of the economic control of the attribution of the income.[236]

Similarly, the Federal Court of Appeal of Canada in *Prevost* and *Velcro* held that use, enjoyment, risk and control were the commanding factors in defining beneficial ownership.[237] In *Indofood* in the UK, in turn, references are made to direct benefit or enjoyment.[238] In the *ISS* case in Denmark, the control of the income seemingly was the key point.[239] Also, in the *H1 Aps* and the *Cayman Holdco* cases in Denmark, the power to decide on the income was considered as commanding.[240] In the *Danish Derivatives* case and the *Futures* case, the Federal Supreme Court of Switzerland points to the power of disposal and the risk in relation to the income as some of the key indicators of beneficial ownership, although it is unclear whether this supplements an economic analysis as legal characteristics or if it is derived from a broad economic view.[241] In Russia, the Arbitration Court of Kaliningrad, in the *NPO Cifrovie Televisionnie Systemi* case, looked at the risk and responsibility, as well as control, to check whether a Cyprus intermediary entity in a loan was the beneficial owner.[242] In Italy, the Supreme Court pointed to control and autonomy as the beneficial owner characteristics for passive holdings in the *Aptar South Europe Sarl* case, albeit mixed with artificiality.[243] In India, the Income Tax Appellate Tribunal held in *Qad Europe BV* that risk and responsibility were the

[232] In case law, see, eg 'direct benefit' in *Indofood*: *Indofood International Finance Ltd v JP Morgan Chase Bank NA* (n 40) para 44; *Prevost v The Queen* (n 31) 13, basing the argument on 'whose behalf'; Danon (n 10) 43–44, though he combines an economic test with a sort of activity test, which makes it close to an anti-avoidance rule. Many other rulings and authors use the economic test, albeit in a broad sense and without limiting in a joint use with a legal test. See s I.C.(i) (b) above.

[233] Du Toit (n 4) 248–49. Compare with the ownership definition in ch 2 above.

[234] Eliffe (n 31) 304–05.

[235] Vogel (n 10) 562.

[236] Danon (n 10) 43.

[237] *Velcro v The Queen* (n 166) para 27.

[238] *Indofood International Finance Ltd v JP Morgan Chase Bank NA* (n 40) 44.

[239] *Ministry of Taxation v FS Invest II Sàrl (formerly ISS Equity A/S)* (n 74).

[240] *H1 Ltd (Cayman)* (n 74); *H1 ApS* (n 74).

[241] *Eidgenössische Steuerverwaltung v X Bank* (n 123); *Futures* (n 132). See Reinarz and Carelli (n 123).

[242] *NPO Cifrovie Televisionnie Systemi v Tax Inspectorate* (n 124).

[243] *Aptar South Europea SARL v Agenzia delle Entrate* (n 169).

commanding characteristics in relation to beneficial ownership of royalties.[244] In Korea, the Supreme Court, in the *Hanhwa Total* case, seems to look at the control, despite considering the activity of the corporation.[245]

But if such approaches are followed in a plain way, these reasonings enter the classic beneficial ownership trap. If such control, enjoyment or abilities are understood from a purely legal view, they will not solve nominee cases, as nominees acting in their own name have the legal right to decide on control and enjoyment. It is clear that such cases fall within the scope of the rule. Moreover, control and/or enjoyment does not significantly differ from the abilities attained by the ordinary concept of ownership.[246] And if economic enjoyment and control, or the power to decide on them, are referred to, as is done by many of the authors and rulings mentioned, it will bring us back to the starting point, as it broadens the concept in the sense of an anti-avoidance rule, or if in a plain economic sense, it would have no specific meaning.[247] Indeed, most of those authors and rulings do not see such abilities as legal abilities; rather, they seem them as an economic or purely factual matter.

The main common characteristic of agents, nominees, trustees and *mandataires* in the discussions at the OECD is that the receipt of income by the intermediary is connected to the obligation to pass the income.[248] For instance, in the case of a bank custodian or nominee, the bank would not buy the shares unless there was a custodian, mandate or agency agreement with the client. This leads to two requirements.[249]

The first one is the legal or contractual obligation to pass the income. In this regard, a legal claimable right has to exist, so discretionary or factual passing of the income will fall outside the scope of the rule.[250] However, what some authors have called a 'factual obligation' is unclear.[251] It could be understood as an actual legal obligation derived from the facts or as a mere factual event, even in cases of some 'commitment' with no legal effect. In the author's view, the first understanding is the only one covered, as otherwise one is led again to an open-ended story.

However, not every obligation will lead to the lack of beneficial ownership, as, in the author's view, it has to be directly connected to the receipt of the income as a second requirement to qualify. In other words, the obligation to pay to the beneficiary accrues on the receipt of the income. If the third person cannot claim the income before a court, or such a claim does not arise on the receipt of the income by the intermediary, then such potential intermediary is the beneficial owner.

[244] *Qad Europe BV v DDIT* [2016] Income Tax Appelate Tribunal Mumbai ITA Nos 83 & 84/Mum/2007 [7].
[245] *Hanhwa Total Co Ltd v Head of Seosan District Office of National Tax Service & other* (n 124).
[246] See above, ch 2.
[247] See above, n 58 and s I.C(i).
[248] Similarly Baker (n 58) s 6.3. See also B Baumgartner, *Das Konzept Des Beneficial Owner Im Internationalen Steuerrecht Der Schweiz* (Zurich, 2010), https://www.zora.uzh.ch/id/eprint/47601/; Meindl-Ringler (n 67) 92–93.
[249] Baumgartner argues for a similar test, even though suggesting it is derived from a substance over form test. See Baumgartner (n 248); Meindl-Ringler (n 67) 92–93.
[250] Avery Jones et al (n 187) 6; Baker (n 58) s 6.3; Kemmeren in Reimer and Rust (n 5) 723; De Broe (n 32) 687. In case law, *Prevost v The Queen* (n 31) 15.
[251] Vogel (n 10) 562; Baumgartner (n 248) 136, 410; Meindl-Ringler (n 67) 93.

This is confirmed by cases such as *Prevost* and *Velcro*, where it was held that, because there was no automatic flow, the articles of incorporation or shareholders' agreements did not oblige the passing of income and the decision to distribute dividends was subject to Dutch law requirements, the conduit entity was the beneficial owner.[252] In a negative sense, such rulings link the lack of beneficial ownership to the existence of an automatically accrued obligation, and not to factual payments.

Similarly, the Federal Supreme Court of Switzerland held in the Danish Derivatives case that the interconnection set where the obligation to pass the income is determined by the reception of the income defines the exclusion of beneficial ownership.[253] In such cases, where a bank obliged to make certain payments under a derivative arrangement has not hedged its derivative position, it will still be obliged to pay the respective amounts under the derivative. The independence of such payment from the dividend that may be derived from acquiring underlying shares proves the bank could be regarded as the beneficial owner of such dividend. However, the Supreme Court in the Danish Derivatives case added nuances to this view to give a more comprehensive and less strict view, where income being factually passed and the derivative passing the risk to a third party may disregard the beneficial owner status.[254] The court nevertheless considers the connection between the obligations to be a point to take into account, but broadens, as compared to the test being proposed here, the facts to take into account in order to determine whether such a connection exists or not.

In addition, in the above-mentioned example of the custodian, which was probably the main original problem the UK was trying to deal with, the recipient of the income acquires the right from which the income is derived precisely in connection with the duty to pass the income to the client. To this author, the second legal characteristic of the negative definition of beneficial ownership, which is the reason for acquiring the creditor position from which the income is derived, must be precisely the arrangement or obligation to pass the income received. This includes such cases as an order to the bank to acquire in its own name certain shares but for the benefit of a client, but also the case where the beneficial ownership transfers the rights to an intermediary with the obligation to hold it for the benefit of, and to pass the income to, the beneficiary, in exchange for the payment of a fee for the service.[255]

Regarding this requirement, it is controversial whether independent arrangements could fall within the scope of the rule. An example would be the case in which a beneficial owner mandates an intermediary to buy certain rights from third parties in its own name and on its own account, and to pass the income or equivalent amounts in a second arrangement to the principal–beneficial owner, such as in the case of a swap agreement hedged against the shares. In this case, clearly the acquisition by the intermediary of the shares derives from the mandate of the client to buy the rights and pass the income. However, the acquisition of such a right needs a second step that falls under the free will

[252] *Prevost v The Queen* (n 31) 16; *Velcro v The Queen* (n 166) 28.

[253] Reinarz and Carelli (n 123) 2.3.

[254] ibid.

[255] In the derivatives case of the Supreme Court of Switzerland, the court points to the interdependance between the acquisition and financing of the shares. ibid.

of the intermediary.[256] He or she may not buy the shares but will still be obliged to pay the amount equivalent to the performance of the financial assets.[257]

Conversely, in the case of direct financial agencies or custodians, the intermediary acquiring the rights is the same in which the obligation to pass the income is laid down, and is precisely the legal reason or object for such an arrangement. A step further is the case where a subject, such as a bank, already holds a right, such as shares, and in a later agreement is obliged to pay an amount equivalent to the income received from such assets in exchange for a payment from the client. It could even be possible that the obligation to pay equivalent amounts remains, irrespective of the intermediary maintaining the shares or not, such as in the case of a swap agreement.

As argued by the Federal Administrative Court of Switzerland in the Danish Bank Derivatives Case, under the same line of reasoning of Baumgartner, beneficial ownership implies a dual dependence test.[258] To disregard beneficial ownership, the obligation to pass the income must derive from the receipt of the income, and the receipt of the income must be derived from the obligation to pass the income. Although Baumgartner seemingly links the concept to a sort of substance over form and factual test, which had already been rejected, the reference to the interdependence of obligations is absolutely correct. The only flaw in Baumgartner's argument in the author's view is that, to Baumgartner, not only does income not need to be effectively passed, but also an economic effect such as the mere accrual would be covered. What the court – and probably Baumgartner – does not deal with is whether such interconnection has to be within a single or successive arrangements, that is, does one have to be the direct reason for the other, or do arrangements with different timing qualify to deny beneficial ownership if the obligation to pass the income, or the acquisition of the position from which the income is derived, has the other indirect, but not direct, reason or object.

In the author's opinion, at the very early stage of the 1977 Model and its commentary, the beneficial ownership exclusion only covered cases where the intermediary acquires its creditor position within the same arrangement from which the obligation to pass the income is derived,[259] or at least subsequent or simultaneous arrangements that may show that the acquisition of the creditor position is based on the obligation to pass the income. This is indicated by the initial discussion pointing to beneficial owners who 'put their income into the hands of bare nominees', as well as the fact that the 1986 Conduit Companies report needed to clarify this point.[260] No source suggests that such cases were covered, so to consider it so would be imprudent. Moreover, some documents from the UK close in time to the OECD discussions clearly showed that the test was considered weak by its proponent for cases of independent arrangements.[261]

[256] Collier (n 220).

[257] *Non Disclosed Taxpayer v Eidgenössische Steuerverwaltung (UBS Case)* (n 138). See R Mateotti and FM Sutter, 'Switzerland: Broad v Narrow Interpretation of the Beneficial Owner Concept' in Lang et al (n 83) 58.

[258] Reinarz and Carelli (n 123) 2.3.

[259] Rejecting independent arrangements where income is factually passed leads to beneficial ownership being disregarded: Collier (n 220).

[260] 'Observations of Member Countries on difficulties raised by the OECD Draft Convention on Income and Capital' [TFD/FC/216], 9 May 1967, Fiscal Committee, OCDE, p 14; OECD Archives, Paris.

[261] See fn 276 and accompanying text in ch 4 above.

However, as will subsequently be shown, the case may have changed after the 1986 conduit companies report for treaties based on it.

Another question is the types of arrangements covered. It is clear that the real or obligational character of the duty is irrelevant insofar as in nomineeships the beneficiary's right has all the characteristics of a real entitlement, while in an agency or mandate the principal has just a contractual right. Both nominees and agents are explicitly excluded.

More controversial is whether the legal obligation to pass the income without any contractual or real right falls within the beneficial ownership exclusion.[262] It would be controversial to exclude a father or mother as not being a beneficial owner of his or her salary because he or she is obliged to pay alimony to his or her spouse, or to pay child support for the benefit of his or her sons or daughters.[263] Also, it would be odd to deny beneficial ownership where a person's right to income is seized by a court or tax authority order to pay his or her tax debts or creditors.[264] This could lead to conflict especially in cases of equitable remedies or implicit trusts where another subject has the right to income.[265] The second requirement mentioned above solves the issue. As the obligation to pay the income is not connected to the reason why the intermediary acquired the creditor position in these cases, beneficial ownership status will not be denied.

(d) Discretionary Trusts

A relevant and controversial type of arrangement for beneficial ownership qualification is trustees. Comments have been raised around the observation that New Zealand had about the Model, holding that trustees were to be treated as beneficial owners under the Model if they were subject to tax on the income in the country of which they were residents.[266] Avery Jones held that this reservation showed that trustees were not ordinarily considered as beneficial owners, as the observation stated that they were 'to be treated as', not 'are', implicitly excluding them from the ordinary meaning.[267] Du Toit, following his proposed definition of beneficial owner as the person who is the owner in equity, also supported beneficial ownership in tax treaties ordinarily excluding trustees.[268]

However, as previously stated, one of the first drafts of the Commentary to the beneficial ownership condition related the rule to the exclusion of 'any intermediary, such as

[262] The CJEU argued that obligations 'in substance' may lead to beneficial ownership status being disregarded. However, such a view is probably derived from the application of an economic substance or anti-avoidance rule, and not a pure factual test: *N Luxembourg 1 and others v Skatteministerie (and joined cases)* (n 53) para 132. Rejecting factual passing of the income: Collier (n 220).

[263] As argued by some participants in the conference on beneficial ownership that took place at the Vienna University of Economics in 2012.

[264] Denying lack of beneficial ownership in the use of payments received to pay its funding obligations: Collier (n 220).

[265] See implied trusts in chs 2 and 3 above.

[266] See para 9 of the Commentary to Art 3 of the 1977 OECD Model Tax Convention, and para 14 of Commentary to Art 3 on Models from 1992 to 2000. The wording is similar to that adopted in 2014 in fn 1 to paras 12.1, 9.1 and 4 of Commentaries to Arts 10, 11 and 12 of the 2014 OECD Model Tax Convention.

[267] Avery Jones et al (n 35) 70.

[268] Du Toit (n 4) 164.

agents or trustees'. As suggested by Prebble, the substitution of 'trustees' by 'nominees' can only mean that not all trustees are excluded.[269] In the author's view, the substitution by nominees indicates only certain types of nominees, ie those with very limited powers, or at least limited power, are excluded from the beneficial ownership condition in tax treaties. Conversely, other type of trusts or trustees, such as those of accumulation or discretionary trusts, may qualify as such.[270]

Moreover, as mentioned above, the US technical explanations consistently took the view that discretionary and accumulation trusts could qualify as beneficial owners for tax treaty purposes if acting on their own.[271] Even the UK told the Australian negotiators in the discussion of the 1967 Tax Convention that accumulation trusts were regarded as beneficial owners for tax treaty purposes in such cases.[272]

In addition to the Prebble argument, because there is no beneficial owner in discretionary trusts, the context would require the beneficial owner to be interpreted as the person with the largest interest, that is, the trustee.[273] Still, it could be said that beneficial ownership, though attenuated, could be in potential beneficiaries in a negative sense.[274] In addition, beneficial ownership tax principles will qualify trustees as beneficial owners for tax purposes if the concept in tax law is understood as the set of principles defining upon whom taxes have to be assessed, namely under the uncertainty principle.[275] Applying such a view to treaties, Prebble's view would be fully consistent. In any case, the historical view seems sufficient to sustain this approach.

(e) Cash Poolings and Syndicated Loans

Another interesting type of arrangement is cash poolings. In a case heard before the Supreme Administrative Court of Poland in 2016, the court held that the leader of a cash pooling cannot be regarded as the beneficial owner because, irrespective of the private law rights on the income that may formally regard them as having the right to decide on the use of the income, they are bound to distribute the results of the pooling in accordance with the cash pooling agreement.[276] This author does not fully share that view. In most cases, the leader will use the cash in accordance with the instructions, and if, within such instructions, they acquire shares, credits or intangibles and receive income therefrom, they are bound to put all the income into the cash pool. However, it may be the case that the cash pooling continues for a long time and is not liquidated after such income has been reinvested, mixed with other capitals, etc. In this case, if, under the cash pooling agreement, the income does not immediately accrue to the participants, I think the beneficial owner under the treaties would be the leader.

[269] Prebble (n 35) 77–78.

[270] Currently recognised in fn 1 to paras 12.1, 9.1 and 4 of Commentaries to Arts 10, 11 and 12 of the 2014 OECD Model Tax Convention.

[271] See ss I.B(ii) and (iii) in ch 4 above.

[272] See Negotiation of the United Kingdom–New Zealand DTT included in TNA IR 40/17246, cited and within the limitations of the citation therein stated in Vann (n 83) 276–79.

[273] See discretionary trusts in ch 2.

[274] See Nolan in fn 148 in ch 2 above, and accompanying text.

[275] See discretionary trusts in ch 3 above.

[276] *Undisclosed taxpayer v Ministerstwo Finansów (Cashpooling Case)* [2016] Naczelny Sąd Administracyjny II FSK 3666/13 FSK 1693/14. On the IBFD Tax Treaty Case Law Database.

In addition, if another view is taken, the cash pooling position of each participant has to be liquidated at all times for tax purposes, which also seems impractical. The case is similar to investment funds, where an arrangement gives the property to a person to manage it, even though he or she is not the owner. In such cases, it is clear, as will be analysed in relation to the Collective Inivestment Vehicles Report, that the fund is the beneficial owner for tax treaty purposes.[277] Or take the case of a corporation, where, although independent persons, the directors are obliged to manage it in the best interests of the shareholders. In the case of cash pooling, insofar as the leader would be free to manage the pool it at its discretion in order to fulfil the objective of the pooling, even though limited by the objectives and conditions of the arrangement, the leader would appear to me to be the beneficial owner.

Similarly, the *ABN Amro* case in India dealt with a syndicated loan where payments of interest were made from India to the ABN branch in Sweden as the leader of the syndicate.[278] In the case, the court ruled that ABN was only the beneficial owner of its part of the loan and not that of the rest of the lenders, as it was acting as a mere collector or conduit for their part.[279] In the author's view, insofar as the income automatically accrues to the other banks, this view is correct. However, if the income is accumulated and subject to other considerations and no automatic accrual is given, further examination is needed. If the income is only distributed once, the loan has been liquidated, and there are high chances that the leader is the beneficial owner under the proposed test.

(f) Timing

A final question relates to timing. Is timing relevant to the beneficial ownership condition?[280] Would an earlier or later payment passing the income imply or exclude the beneficial ownership condition? In the author's view, timing is irrelevant; what defines exclusion of beneficial ownership is that the beneficiary obtains an economic benefit legally accruing from the reception of the income by the intermediary. Even if paid years late or even if it is not effectively paid but raises a credit of economic content, the intermediary may be excluded as not being the beneficial owner and such condition is determined on the beneficiary.

In the *E*Trade Mauritius Ltd* case, the Authority for Advance Rulings of India argued: 'The short interval within which the dividends were paid and capital reduction were affected in October, 2008 is not a factor which establishes the beneficial ownership of the shares or the gains resting with the holding company.'[281] However, the case dealt with Article 13 of the Model, on capital gains, which does not explicitly use the concept and may depart from the OECD understanding, leaving the value of this case unknown.

[277] See s III.B.

[278] *Bharti Airtel Ltd v ACIT (ABN Amro)* [2014] Income Tax Appellate Tribunal (ITAT) Delhi ITA No 5636/Del/2011.

[279] ibid 26.

[280] F Navisotschnigg, 'The Beneficial Ownership Test' in *Tax Treaty Entitlement* (Amsterdam 2019) ch 4, s 4.2.3.

[281] *E*Trade Mauritius Ltd* (n 142) 11.1.

In *Velcro*, the court dealt with the fact that a shareholders' agreement was obliged to pass the income within a certain time frame.[282] The court dismissed the argument because the corporation was not a party to the agreement and there was no predetermined flow of income.[283] However, it is unclear whether, if the payment had been automatic, the immediate submission of the income would have been required.

(g) Definition of Beneficial Ownership for Treaties Based on the 1977 OECD Model

In sum, beneficial ownership in treaties based on the 1977 Model without taking into account the 1986 conduit companies report will only deny access to limited taxation at source provided in Articles 10–12 of the Model, given that: (i) the subject transfers the economic effect to a third party in payment, kind or through any other economic effect; (ii) the subject is constrained or obliged to pass the income, and it is not merely a discretionary decision or a matter of fact; (iii) the accrual of such secondary obligation arises on the accrual of the income by the intermediary; (iv) the reason for the acquisition of the right from which income derives is linked or is the obligation to pass the income itself; and (v) the obligation to pass the income and the reason for the acquisition of the right were contained in the same arrangement or two simultaneous or subsequent and connected arrangements.

(h) The Problem with Sham or Anti-avoidance Rules

A possible different scenario, and the reason for frequent misunderstandings, is that in some cases such contracts may be hidden or may be arranged in an artificial way. In these cases, definition of the facts and qualification should be followed carefully. First, the actual facts must be defined. Only when facts are precisely defined can the beneficial ownership rule be applied upon qualification of such facts.[284]

For example, in a pure simulated or fake transaction, a client could agree with a financial intermediary his or her willingness to buy shares, but in order to avoid taxation, they agree to sign a contract on a derivative replicating the dividend and capital gains and losses of the share, while the bank buys the shares in its own name and on its own account. In a second hidden document, both parties agree that the bank must actually hold the shares and declare that the actual owner having full rights to control and income is the client. Following the proposed definition of beneficial owner, disclosed documents would lead to the bank being considered as the beneficial owner. In this case, the correct solution is to first disregard the apparent legal facts – the first shown arrangements – and to set out the facts regarding the hidden document. Obviously, under such facts, the bank would not be the beneficial owner.

A different scenario would be the same case of a client subscribing to a derivative replicating the dividend and capital gains and losses of a share, but without any

[282] *Velcro v The Queen* (n 166) para 28.

[283] ibid 45. Also in *Prevost v The Queen* (n 31) 15.

[284] It seems to be the case in some cases, where the facts are first defined on substance over form – legal substance – and then beneficial owner is applied: *Hanhwa Total Co Ltd v Head of Seosan District Office of National Tax Service & other* (n 124).

hidden arrangement. In this case, the bank will be obliged to pay equivalent amounts in any case and irrespective of holding the shares or not. There are no undisclosed facts and the law is applicable to them. In such a case, the bank would qualify as beneficial owner if it receives any income from owned shares irrespective of paying equivalent amounts.[285]

However, anti-avoidance rules may requalify the consequence of those facts in the qualification step. If a principal purpose or artificial test is applicable, eg Article 29.9 of the Model, and the arrangement's only purpose is to reduce the tax burden or it is arranged in an artificial way, the legal consequence of such facts – that are real and defined – will be redirected to the ones defined in the law for the ordinary transaction. The facts are actual and defined, and there are no hidden facts. The parties simply choose the optimal tax arrangement to achieve the economic objective they are aiming for, but because of artificiality or the purpose of tax avoidance in those facts, the consequence is redirected and the consequence would be the one that would be applied if the shares had been bought directly by the client. That is, the beneficial owner is the client. However, this derives from the application of the anti-avoidance rule, not from the beneficial owner test itself. Here the beneficial owner is just part of the consequence by submission of another rule, not part of the applicable rule.

As mentioned before, in the Swaps case and the Danish Derivative case, the Federal Administrative Court of Switzerland held that the independence of the derivatives' obligation to pay from the possibility of hedging them or holding the underlying assets made it possible to consider the banks as beneficial owners.[286] The Federal Supreme Court confirmed this under the interdependence test. However, the Supreme Court also considered that beneficial ownership implies a substance over form test, and concluded that the derivative arrangements were hiding the actual transaction because the banks were hedging such derivatives against holding the underlying assets, making the transaction economically equivalent to holding the shares under a custody arrangement. What they were actually doing was to apply an anti-avoidance rule, not the beneficial owner test as defined by the OECD Commentary. The problem then is to define whether a domestic anti-avoidance rule is applicable to the treaty.

D. Beneficial Ownership, Conduit Companies and the 1986 Report: Independent and Unconnected Arrangements and Beneficial Ownership

Parallel to the discussions of the 1977 Model, the Fiscal Committee held discussions and drafted reports on the improper use of tax treaties until 1986.[287] Because beneficial

[285] *Undisclosed companies v Federal Tax Administration (Swaps case)* (n 138). See Mateotti and Sutter (n 257) 58.

[286] *Futures* (n 132); *Eidgenössische Steuerverwaltung v X Bank* (n 123). See Reinarz and Carelli (n 123).

[287] 'Draft report on tax avoidance through the improper use or abuse of tax conventions' [CFA/WP1(75)3], 21 May 1975, Working Party 1, Fiscal Committee, OECD; 'Draft report on tax avoidance through the improper use or abuse of tax conventions' [CFA/WP1(76)5], 28 April 1976, Working Party 1, Fiscal Committee, OECD; 'Revised second draft report on tax avoidance through the improper use and abuse of tax conventions'

ownership covered some types of improper use of tax conventions, the rule was discussed again. However, the discussion did not limit itself to restating the clause, but seemingly broadened its scope of application.

The concept was discussed in the frame of conduit corporations – companies interposed in a third country to obtain the advantage of a tax treaty. The problem is that conduit corporations are not always agents or nominees in a strict sense, nor do they fall within the proposed definition in most cases, so if the author's interpretation is right, beneficial ownership had little effect in those cases.[288] Arrangements where the conduit or intermediary was acting on its own account and the obligation to pass the income does not automatically accrue on receipt of the income, subject to discretion or where the creditor position of the recipient was not dependent on the arrangement upon which it had the obligation to make the payments, were not covered by the beneficial owner exclusion. But economically, they pose similar consequences to intermediaries explicitly covered and excluded from treaty benefits.

In the cases of conduit companies, three different set of cases are distinguished.[289] First, where a corporation acts as an agent, nominee, trustee or other intermediary arrangement for a third party: a third party income conduit. In these cases, where the income is not distributed under the corporation object, beneficial owner applies in the above-mentioned ordinary meaning.

Secondly, where income is passed as a dividend or other remuneration to the shareholders because of such condition and under the discretion of the corporation: an entity conduit. Unless included as a right/obligation in the articles of incorporation, or shareholders' agreements to which the entity is a party, the decision to distribute income is absolutely discretionary for the shareholders and/or board of directors. Then the distribution of received income fails to fulfil the requirement of the recipient to be obliged to pass the income, and the accrual of the right of the beneficiary arising directly from the accrual of the income by the intermediary.

In the *YUM Restaurants* case, the Income Tax Appellate Tribunal of Delhi tried to draw an analogy between conduit or intermediary entities and agents, nominees or trusts. To do so, it resorted to the sample of a minor subject to a guardian, where if the guardian buys property with the money of the minor, irrespective of doing it in its own name and on its own account, beneficial ownership will be vested in the minor.[290]

[CFA/WP1(76)5 (1st revision)], Working Party 1, Working Group 21, OECD; 'Draft progress report to the committee on the improper use of tax conventions' [DAFFE/CFA/WP1/82.4], Working Party 1, Committee on Fiscal Affairs, OECD; 'The Improper Use of Tax Conventions by persons not entitled to their benefits through 'conduit companies'' [DAFFE/CFA/WP1/82.5], Working Party 1, Committee on Fiscal Affairs, OECD; all in the OECD Archives, Paris.

[288] Collier argues that the report recognises that beneficial owner was not an adequate response for conduits: Collier (n 125) 688. Vega Borrego points if interpreted in a narrow sense beneficial owner would not solve conduits, which makes him advocate for a broad interpretation: Vega Borrego (n 65) 84. See also the argument by the UK stating that a new interpretation of beneficial owner was needed to cover conduits in fn 276 and accompanying text in ch 4 above.

[289] Wheeler distinguishes two cases: entity conduits and income conduits. Here, I have divided them into three, as I distinguish between income conduits for third parties and income conduits for related parties. Wheeler (n 87) 482.

[290] *Yum Restaurants (India) Pvt Ltd v ITO* [2014] Income Tax Appellate Tribunal (Delhi) ITA No 1097/Del/2014 22.5.

Comparing such a case with intermediary entities, the court stated that such entities have independent status and rights, and cannot be considered as intermediaries for the ultimate holding company.[291] Implicitly, it was recognising that the economic and controlling rights of the ultimate holdings to the company are independently exercised from the rights of the subsidiary company holding the property to the property itself.

Similarly, the Suprema Corte di Cassazione in Italy held in the *Aptar* case that requiring passive holdings to develop an activity or purpose, as compared to active holdings, would mean no holding would ever be a beneficial owner, and thus would never access treaties.[292] Their objective is simply to hold and is fulfilled.

In *Prevost*, the Supreme Administrative Court of Canada held that a conduit company cannot be disregarded as a non-beneficial owner because the shareholders subscribed to an agreement to distribute most of the income if the corporation is not party to the agreement.[293] This confirms the author's view that only where the intermediary entity-payer is legally bound to pass the income, and both obligations are connected and derived from the position upon which the creditor acquire such status, will it not be considered the beneficial owner. However, when the decision to distribute the income is based on a different and independent legal basis, such as the shareholders' political and economic rights, the beneficial owner status is vested in such intermediary. As stated and historically confirmed by documents from the UK, beneficial ownership would not resolve the conduit companies case at an early stage unless it was clearly acting as an agent or nominee, like any other custodian or bank.[294] The application to them was probably a later construction.

The case where articles of incorporation or shareholders' agreements to which the company is a party are bound to distribute all received income may also fall outside the scope of the early 1977 OECD Model Tax Convention beneficial owner test. In this case, even though the requirements to distribute the income and direct accrual are fulfilled, the intermediary corporation may have obtained the rights from which the income is derived from a third party and without any connection to the obligation to distribute the income. Only where the corporation obtained the rights in connection to the obligation to pass the income, for instance at the time of incorporation, would the corporation not be considered beneficial owner.

Finally, the third group is where corporations pass the income to the shareholders under arrangements different to that of the corporation object itself, such as under a loan, licence or any other arrangement: an own shareholders' income conduit. Preferred shares may also fall within this group. These cases, unless the connection of the receipt of the income and the duty to pay such income are explicitly laid down in relevant arrangements, would also fall outside the scope of beneficial ownership limitation.

[291] ibid.

[292] It does, however, suggest an artificiality or abusive test may be applied to holdings, but it does not apply it to the case: *Aptar South Europea SARL v Agenzia delle Entrate* (n 169) para 3.2.

[293] *Prevost v The Queen* (n 31) para 15.

[294] See the argument by the UK stating that a new interpretation of beneficial owner was needed to cover conduits in n 276 above and accompanying text.

The *Velcro* case concerned a Canadian company paying royalties to a Dutch corporation that was a licensor and subsidiary of a Netherlands Antilles corporation.[295] The case was decided following the *Prevost* case reasoning, arguing that the facts that (i) the Dutch corporation had the use, enjoyment, risk and control, (ii) was not obliged to pass the income, (iii) the income was not automatically passed, and (iv) despite the Netherlands Antilles corporation being entitled to claim the rights against the sublicensor if the intermediary failed to do so, the rights to authorise assignments or claims remain in the intermediary entity, led to consider the Dutch corporation as beneficial owner.[296]

In all these cases, the main issue is the overlap of the economic rights of the shareholder because of his or her stock owner or any other right holder condition, and his or her ability to control the behaviour of the conduit company through his or her political rights regarding the corporation.[297] Through the first, he or she receives income on his or her own account; through the second, he or she can decide if a different person transfers the income that the person making the decision will receive under its previously mentioned character. But even though control of the legal actions of both persons fall on the same person, when he or she exercises his or her political right, the legal consequences are performed by a different person, which makes both the receipt of the income and its submission legally independent from one another. Moreover, political and economic rights of shares may be divided.

Those cases mentioned that do not fit within the beneficial owner test, especially those where income is distributed as a dividend, are probably the reason why the 1986 conduit companies report readdressed the issue again and broadened the scope of application of beneficial ownership. If these cases were not excluded from the beneficial owner action, there were certainly major doubts regarding its application that needed explicit clarification.

(i) Transfer of Economic Effects

The 1986 conduit company report first recasts beneficial ownership as it stood in the 1977 Commentary.[298] It is clear that a corporation acting as an 'intermediary' – this being understood as an agent or trustee, whether explicit, implicit or sham – falls within the agent or nominee exclusion and is not the beneficial owner. The only new addition is that the conduit company report refers to 'the economic benefit' of the third party as a characteristic of agency, and nomineeship arrangements are excluded under the beneficial owner rule.[299] To this author, this was simply a clarification of the economic transfer already implicitly contained in the previous definition provided in the Commentary to the 1977 OECD Model.

[295] *Velcro v The Queen* (n 166).

[296] ibid 45.

[297] The conduit companies report pointed to the difficulties arising from the relationships between shareholders, the corporation and other parties, and the decision-making process to define whether it is beneficial ownership. See OECD (n 119) 93.

[298] ibid.

[299] 'Thus the limitation is not available when, economically, it would benefit a person not entitled to it who interposed the conduit company as an intermediary between himself and the payer', ibid.

(ii) Independent Arrangements

The real novelty in the conduit companies report is that it explicitly recognises that beneficial ownership may also exclude source taxation limits from other arrangements under which a subject has a similar function to that of an agent or nominee.[300] Specifically, it points out that a conduit company formally holding ownership but with very narrow powers, acting on the account of the interested parties, thus rendering it a mere fiduciary or administrator, does not qualify as a beneficial owner.[301] In a negative way, it holds that the mere fact that the corporation's main function is to hold assets is not enough to bar its beneficial owner status.

The main question is whether the conduit companies report retains the previous interpretation as derived from the 1977 Commentary, and so is a mere clarification, or if it broadens the concept to cover cases lacking some of the requirements. And if it retains or broadens the concept, the question that arises is what elements define the analogy of the conduit as compared to an agent or nominee, or the lack of beneficial ownership.

Jain, Prebble and Crawford suggest that the conduit analogy to agents or nominees in the conduit companies report is based on what they call the dominion test.[302] The authors claim that the conduit companies report is mismatching beneficial owner and dominion/ownership,[303] which leads to any conduit company being a beneficial owner. They also argue that the obligation to pass the income does not solve the issue because all entities acting in their own name and on their own account would be beneficial owners. To solve the problem they see, they advocate for interpreting beneficial ownership in an economic substance sense, but their argument fails. First, they do not consider the test to be composed of several elements and not only ownership abilities, as shown here. Secondly, the conduit companies report was modifying the content of the test to adapt it to conduit companies' situations and resolve its flaw.

In the *Royal Dutch Shell* case, a classic dividend coupon stripping case, the court decided that the recipient of the dividends of the coupon that a corporation bought from the owner of the shares was the beneficial owner.[304] The court concluded that the ownership of the underlying assets was not needed and that the subject was free to benefit from the dividends.

For Jain et al, the case was formally decided on the company holding the coupons having 'dominion' over the income and should have been defined by reference to substantive economic ownership.[305] In the author's view, the court did not resolve the case on a 'dominion test' but on the proper beneficial owner test. That is, the holder of the coupons did not have the obligation to pass the income or equivalent amount, and

[300] 'The provisions would, however, apply also to other cases where a person enters into contracts or takes over obligations under which he has a similar function to those of a nominee or an agent', ibid.

[301] ibid.

[302] S Jain, J Prebble and A Crawford, 'Conduit Companies, Beneficial Ownership, and the Test of Dominion in Claims for Relief under Double Tax Treaties' (2014) 11 *WU International Taxation Research Paper Series*.

[303] The authors use a blend of philosophical, economical and legal definitions of ownership and dominion, as well as assuming there is a sort of absolute ownership, which this author has already rejected in favour of different sets of abilities in relation to properties. Compare that approach with ch 2 above.

[304] *Royal Dutch Shell (Market Maker)* [1994] Hoge Raad 28.638 BNB 1994/217.

[305] Jain et al (n 302) 46.

its position was not acquired within the same obligation from which he was obliged to pass the income, as in the agent case, simply because he had no obligation to pass the income. The case was resolved in this sense because the coupon buyer had ownership 'and' because they did not have the obligation to automatically pass the income, not because they had ownership/dominion. Jain et al claim the result of the *Royal Dutch Shell* case is derived from an 'inverse error' because not being an agent or nominee does not imply being the beneficial owner.[306] But in the case of beneficial owner in tax treaties, this is the case. This is probably influenced by Jain et al domestic common law view of beneficial ownership in its positive sense, but the evolution of the concept of the OECD made it operate in a negative sense and not to provide a comprehensive definition, which would have been extremely difficult to achieve, given the different legal systems all around the world. The concept was born to exclude certain intermediaries, not to qualify some of them. Finally, the authors claim the *Royal Dutch Shell* case is a conduit company case, which is obviously not the case, or at least not a pure income or entity conduit case. The case could have involved an individual and the same result would have been achieved. For a dividend coupon stripping, a different controlled person is not needed, and in the case the coupon holder was not controlled by the other company, which is one of the elements of conduits.

Another case criticised by Jain et al is the *Prevost* case. Here, two independent companies, one British and the other Swedish, acquired a Canadian company. To that end, they incorporated a joint venture holding corporation in the Netherlands.[307] Jain et al claim the case was resolved on the ability of not being accountable, which equates to dominion.[308] Again, the case was decided on the fact that the intermediary entity was owner 'and' was not obliged to pass the income automatically.[309] Income was not accruing to the shareholders automatically, but under an independent legal decision, which left the entity functionally as the beneficial owner. However, for these authors, beneficial owner in the case meant owner. They argue that if it is understood as dominion, beneficial owner resolves agent and nominee cases, but this is not true, as agents in *nomine proprio* have full dominion while the principal has not. Their relationship is obligational. And it is clear that the OECD was targeting such cases. If beneficial owner were ownership, this would add nothing to the treaty, as normally definitions of dividends or interests provide for allocation rules dependent on the owner of the credit or right. The problem is that Jain et al do not see beneficial ownership in a negative sense as comprising all the above-mentioned elements. Also, with regard to the conduit cases, precisely the OECD was trying to modify it through the conduit companies report so it would cover them and overcome its narrow scope.

What these authors suggest is that beneficial ownership is a sort of broad economic anti-avoidance rule, which I have already rejected for historical and practical reasons.[310] Their proposal would either leave almost no single holding company as beneficial owner or would introduce a broad anti-avoidance rule with an unknown meaning – artificiality,

[306] ibid 47.
[307] *Prevost v The Queen* (n 31).
[308] Jain et al (n 302) 53.
[309] *Prevost v The Queen* (n 31) para 15.
[310] Jain et al (n 302) 60. Vega Borrego also supports this view: Vega Borrego (n 65) 86. See also Danon (n 10).

purpose, activity? – that was never intended. Specifically, the OECD recognises in the Conduit Companies Report that beneficial ownership deals with conduit entities in a very limited way, which is incompatible with the interpretations of Jain et al.[311] It is the author's view that dividend coupon stripping cases or usufruct cases, such as *Royal Bank of Scotland* or *Royal Dutch Shell*, would not fall within beneficial ownership as considered by such authors, and that *Prevost* or *Velcro* would be solved differently to the way they propose – and also to what the court proposes.

It may be argued that the concept did not carry this meaning before, as suggested by Vega or Jain, but was expanded to an economic substance by the conduit companies report.[312] This is not the case, however, because the reasoning deals with 'functions' and 'powers' as being similar to those of an agent or nominee. Claiming the functions or powers, the report is clearly indicating some economic characteristics of such arrangements, but also their legal characteristics. The report is turning the beneficial owner test, which already posed both characteristics, to conduits.

To the author, the conduit company report slightly expanded the beneficial ownership definition as it was intended by some countries in order to cover conduit companies and other arrangements that at the beginning were a doubtful fit within the beneficial owner test, especially regarding the single or successive arrangement requirement.

It may be doubted whether the reasoning applies just to conduits or also to other arrangements. The wording of the conduit companies calls for 'other cases' in general terms, suggesting that the reasoning does apply to other arrangements. The relevant added points are 'functions' being similar to those of an agent or nominee and that the intermediary remains with few 'powers'. This could be the case for conduits, but also for other arrangements.

On the functions being similar, it is this author's view that this has to be interpreted in relation to conduit companies in the sense of the obligation to pass income.[313] On the limited powers, the interpretation has to be that the obligation is automatic, linked and accrues because of the receipt of the income.[314] So what is the difference from the previous definition of the Commentary?

Under the conduit companies report, the cases where the intermediary has the obligation to pass the income, but this is not linked to the accrual of the income and not within the same arrangement – a similar legal and economic function to a nominee, but a different legal qualification – as well as its power being limited by a different arrangement – few powers, but not by the same arrangement – are also subject to beneficial ownership limitation. In other words, the conduit companies report extended the exclusion of beneficial ownership to intermediary cases where the obligation to pass the income was derived from an arrangement different to the one upon which the creditor acquired the right from which the income arises.

[311] OECD (n 119) para 15.

[312] Though unclear, this seems to be the view of Eynatten et al (n 29) 537.

[313] *Prevost v The Queen* (n 31) 15; *Velcro v The Queen* (n 166) 44. Baumgartner (n 248) 130, 409; Meindl-Ringler (n 67) 92–93. Although Baumgartner improperly matches beneficial ownership with substance over form.

[314] Baumgartner (n 248) 139, 410; Meindl-Ringler (n 67) 93. The same commentary to previous note applies.

(iii) Meaning of Beneficial Ownership for Treaties Drawn Up Taking into Account the Conduit Companies Report

If what has been argued were the case, beneficial ownership in tax treaties drawn up taking into account the conduit company report[315] would have to be interpreted in the sense of excluding the limitation to source taxation in cases where: (i) economic effects are transferred to third parties in payment, kind or any other effect; (ii) the subject is constrained or obliged to pass the income and is not merely a discretionary decision or a mere fact; (iii) the accrual of this second obligation arises on the accrual of the income by the intermediary; (iv) the reason for the acquisition of the right from which income derives is linked to or is the obligation to pass the income itself; and (v) the obligation to pass the income and the reason for the acquisition of the right derive from the same or different, simultaneous, subsequent or independent, but connected, arrangements.

This leaves conduit companies distributing income as a dividend because of shareholders agreements to which the corporation is not a party, or because of the vote of a shareholders meeting, as non-beneficial owners. The key is that this second arrangement is based on or refers to the existence of income received by the entity. It could be possible that such a reference is omitted or hidden in the distribution agreement and a proper analysis of the facts leads to consideration as to whether such a connection exists or whether the arrangement is performed in an artificial way. The former would be the case where general reference to the profits is made in holding companies where little or no other income is received and few expenses are made. The latter would lead to the application of anti-avoidance rules upon their requirements, but does not involve beneficial ownership directly.

In the above-mentioned *Prevost* case, the Dutch intermediary company was paying the majority of the income received to its shareholders because of a shareholders' agreement to which the corporation was not a party.[316] It is the author's view that this case shows precisely the facts that the conduit company report is trying to cover and were doubtful under the 1977 commentary. Because the obligation is contained in an independent agreement, the case would escape the beneficial owner test and the conduit company report wants to be given analogous treatment by considering all the obligations at stake. As the shareholders' agreement refers to the income received – the profits were largely the dividends received from Prevost – and the shareholders have the ability and duty to trigger the payment, the conduit cannot be said to be the beneficial owner. However, the court decided that the intermediary corporation was the beneficial owner because it was not a party to the shareholders' agreement, it had full use, enjoyment, control and risk abilities, and there were no automatic payments.[317] Moreover, the fact that only a certain amount falls within the obligation to pass does not preclude

[315] Eynatten et al seemingly reject the use of the conduit companies report. De Broe points out that the conduit companies report has to be taken into consideration in interpreting beneficial ownership, although he does not state precisely whether this would be applicable to treaties before the report was approved. In the author's view, this only applies to treaties that used the document to negotiate it. See Eynatten et al (n 29) 537; De Broe (n 32) 683.

[316] *Prevost Car Inc v The Queen* (2008) 2008 TCC 231 (Tax Court of Canada) [12].

[317] ibid 100, 102; *Prevost v The Queen* (n 31) 15.

the consideration that the entity is partially not a beneficial owner.[318] It would be the beneficial owner on the amount without obligation to pass, but not the beneficial owner on the rest.

In the *Velcro* case, as mentioned, the fact that the court took into account was that there was no automatic flow of income.[319] It is the author's view that the fact that the intermediary entity was obliged to pass 90 per cent of the received income, that such obligation was connected to the acquisition of the right from which the income is derived and that the income accrued directly to the Netherlands Antilles entity renders the intermediary a non-beneficial owner.[320] This is in addition to the fact that an anti-avoidance rule based on artificiality or purpose would also be applicable, not as beneficial owner test, but in parallel.

For this author, although the argument of the Supreme Administrative Court that holding beneficial ownership was dependent on the existence of an automatic obligation to pass the income is absolutely right, its application to the cases was probably flawed.

In the *Intesa San Paolo* case, the Russian subsidiary of the Italian Intesa Bank was financed through a loan given by its parent company, a Luxembourg corporation. This was financed, in turn, by the ultimate parent company, Intesa San Paolo in Italy.[321] The court analysed the activity of the corporation in Luxembourg, the tax burden and the transactions carried on, and concluded it was not the beneficial owner. However, the author's view is that this case should have been resolved by paying attention to whether the arrangements obliged the passing on of the interest received by the Luxembourg company to the Italian parent. Only if the income accrued directly to the Italian corporation should the intermediary company not be regarded as the beneficial owner. However, one question could be whether the arrangements as shown by the taxpayers are actual or hide other arrangements, but this will apply to defining the facts beforehand, and only once that is done will beneficial ownership apply.

In the *Real Madrid* set of cases, football players were transferring their image rights to foreign corporations that, in turn, were licensing them to Hungarian companies that, again in turn, were licensing them to Real Madrid Football Club.[322] Royalties were paid from Spain to Hungarian corporations, and after a few days the income was paid in turn to the ultimate companies in Cyprus, Netherlands and elsewhere. The case was resolved by resorting to a general anti-avoidance principle and on the basis of presumptions. However, in the author's view, the arrangements should have been analysed. It is likely that the arrangements between the Hungarian and ultimate corporations made the payments received by such intermediaries accrue directly to their licensors. In addition, the Hungarian companies were probably obliged to transfer the income because of the acquisition of the licence. If this were the case, such corporations would not be considered beneficial owners under the proposed test. However, in the author's view, there was no need to resort to substance over form or anti-avoidance principles.

[318] Navisotschnigg (n 280) s 4.2.3.
[319] *Velcro v The Queen* (n 166) para 45.
[320] ibid 44.
[321] *Intesa v Federal Tax Service* (n 165). On the IBFD Tax Treaty Case Law Database.
[322] *Real Madrid v Resolución del TEAC [1]–[7]* (n 31).

In sum, most of the cases concerning conduit entities, such as the several Danish cases or the *Indofood* case, should have been solved by checking whether the receipt of the income and accrual to the next tier are connected, and if such obligation is connected to the acquisition of the right from which the income is derived within a single arrangement, successive arrangements or separate arrangements. In those cases, there was little need to resort to substance or commercial analysis if such obligations exist.

However, dividend cases would be more difficult to solve if no shareholders' agreement exists or if the articles of incorporation do not oblige the distribution of all the income received. This is the case of, for instance, *Molinos de la Plata.*[323] In such cases, disconnection of the receipt of the income, the acquisition of the rights, the obligation to pass the income and accruals would render the intermediary the beneficial owner. Resort to anti-avoidance rules such as purpose, activity or artificial test, if applicable, would be needed.

In the *International Power* case, the Supreme Administrative Court of the Czech Republic held that treaty benefits were not available if an intermediary conduit in the Netherlands for the benefit of a UK corporation 'did not exercise its shareholder rights and the dividends only "flowed through" it in order to avoid withholding tax'.[324] It is unclear from the summaries available if this was done as a sort of purpose test or if it analysed the exercise of shareholders' rights as a proof of independence of obligations. If it were the latter case, the ruling would be in accordance with the test the author supports.

However, the definition the author sustains does not serve to deny treaty benefits to usufruct arrangements, dividend stripping and other similar arrangements. Cases such as *Goldman Sachs*, *Royal Bank of Scotland* and *Royal Dutch Shell* would fall outside the scope of the beneficial owner test.[325] As mentioned, the rulings on those cases mix beneficial ownership with substance over form, purpose tests and other anti-avoidance rules. Precisely because beneficial ownership does not serve to that end, tax authorities and courts needed to reinterpret it or resort to anti-avoidance rules. The problem is such an outcome was reached at the cost of certainty and legality.

It is important to restate at this point that beneficial ownership does not consider whether the interposition of the corporation is simulated or abusive. Because of the dual condition of shareholders in relation to corporations mentioned above, abuse of law is frequent in conduit companies, but this does not mean beneficial ownership in relation to conduit companies cases implies its abusive character, nor that abusive conduit companies will never pass the beneficial owner test.[326] Both considerations are independent, and the above-mentioned considerations on definition of the facts, abuse and beneficial ownership remain applicable for conduit companies.

The sham case, for instance, is mentioned in the Conduit Companies Report, where it states that cases in which the assets from which the income derives are not transferred to the intermediary corporation cannot access treaty provisions on the status of the

[323] *Molinos Río de la Plata* (n 146).

[324] *Elektrárny Opatovice, a s v Finanční ředitelství v Hradci Králové (International Power)* [2011] Nejvyšší Správní Soud (Supreme Administrative Court) 2 Afs 86/2010-141.

[325] *Mobel Línea v Reino de España [Goldman Sachs]* (n 55); *Royal Bank of Scotland* (n 55); *Royal Dutch Shell (Market Maker)* (n 304).

[326] Although the ruling is highly inconsistent: *N Luxembourg 1 and others v Skatteministerie (and joined cases)* (n 53) para 138. See below, ch 6.

entity.[327] However, in these cases there is no need to resort to beneficial ownership, even though the report mentions that the corporation is a nominee, but just to define the proper facts under which the creditor is the principal. The treaty then becomes applicable on the principal conditions.

On this point, the author argues, in line with Collier, that the Conduit Companies Report did not change beneficial ownership in the sense of converting it into a general anti-avoidance rule, because it was never conceived as a broad anti-avoidance rule.[328] It only broadened the concept to cover some conduits and independent arrangements where income was passed. The rule did not cover all conduit companies' transactions, but just some of them with the above-mentioned characteristics. This is confirmed by the fact that the report and the Commentary recommended the introduction of other rules to deal with such abusive conduits not covered by beneficial ownership.[329] If it were a general anti-avoidance rule, no other rules would be needed. Closing the discussion, the report itself claims that beneficial ownership only covers conduit companies 'in a very rudimentary way'.[330] General anti-avoidance rules for conduits cannot be regarded as rudimentary, but as complex and advanced.

E. Beneficial Ownership as an Implicit Rule

Some commentators argue that beneficial ownership was already implicitly in all treaties and its inclusion made no change.[331] This is normally derived from the US position that used the beneficial ownership principle in tax treaties even before it was made explicit in the 1966 Protocol to the 1945 United Kingdom–United States Tax Convention.[332] In US case-law it is known that the beneficial ownership implicit reasoning was behind the *Aiken* and *NIPSCO* cases.[333]

French courts have supported the inclusion of beneficial owner in all tax treaties. In the *Diebold* case, the Conseil D'Etat ruled that beneficial ownership is implicit in all treaties irrespective of whether they contain the wording or not.[334] The case does not delve deeper into the meaning of the concept, and it is resolved with a sort of arm's length reasoning. However, the Conseil D'Etat later established in an interpretative general ruling that beneficial ownership is implicit in all treaties except those made after 1977 that omit the term.[335] Because the term was included in the 1977 OECD Model, the Conseil D'Etat assumes that if it is omitted it is because the parties did not want the principle to apply. The *Royal Bank of Scotland* case, again supported the implicit

[327] OECD (n 119) pt 13.
[328] Collier (n 125) 688.
[329] OECD (n 119) para 16.
[330] ibid 15.
[331] Walser (n 195) 17–18; Vega Borrego (n 65) 88.
[332] See 'Article 4. Dividends' in the Technical Memorandum of Treasury Department Concerning Proposed Protocol Amending the Income Tax Convention between the United States and the United Kingdom, 1966-2, Cumulative Bulletin 1127, Senate Report No 89-3.
[333] Y Brauner, 'Beneficial Ownership in and Outside US Tax Treaties' in Lang et al (n 83) 146; PN James, 'Aiken Industries Revisited' (1986) 64 Taxes 131, 137; Meindl-Ringler (n 67) 201–02.
[334] *Diebold Courtage SA v Ministre de l'Economie* [1999] Conseil D'Etat 191191, 8 and 9; Guttman (n 137).
[335] Guttman (n 137) 163–64.

character of the concept, but now sustained a meaning combined with an abuse of rights clause.[336]

Leaving aside the meaning of the term, the implicit beneficial owner principle of the *Diebold* case permeated down to the lower courts in France. In this regard, the *Société Innovation et Gestion Financiére* case followed the *Diebold* reasoning, although its meaning follows the *Royal Bank of Scotland* combination of the term with an anti-avoidance meaning.[337] The *Atlantique Negoce* case also apparently considers beneficial owner as implicit in treaties, as the treaty at stake in the case did not contain such wording.[338]

In Switzerland, the Federal Tax Court argued in the rulings on the *X holding* case, the Swaps case, the Danish Derivatives case and several others that beneficial ownership is implicit in all tax treaties in a sort of substance over form combined with activity and purpose test.[339] The Federal Supreme Court also confirmed this in cases such as the Swaps case and the Danish Derivatives case.[340]

The Supreme Administrative Court of the Czech Republic also considered beneficial owner to be implicit in all tax treaties in the *International Power* case, concerning dividends received through a Dutch intermediary corporation by a UK corporation.[341]

In practice, Russian tax authorities have taken the view that beneficial ownership is implicit in all tax treaties.[342] However, in some cases, the courts denied the possibility of applying beneficial ownership if it is not contained in the treaty.[343]

Probably the place where most countries have considered that beneficial ownership is implicit is in Article 13 of the Model, on capital gains. Because of the lack of a beneficial owner test in that article, countries needed to resort to anti-avoidance rules or principles to tackle certain intermediary holding structures, and to claim implicit beneficial ownership was an easy solution, especially if considered on its broad anti-avoidance meaning.

In Russia, the Arbitration Court of the Vladimirskaya Oblast took this approach in the *ZAO* case to deny treaty application to a Cyprus intermediary entity holding shares in a Russian entity and deriving capital gains.[344] In Korea, the *Samsung* case held that beneficial ownership is implicit in the capital gains article.[345]

[336] *Royal Bank of Scotland* (n 55).

[337] *Société Innovation et Gestion Financière* (n 137); Guttman (n 137) 164–65.

[338] *Atlantique Negoce v Ministre de l'Economie, des Finances et de l'Industrie* [2018] Cour administrative d'appel (Administrative Court of Appeal) Versailles 17VE03170.

[339] *X Holding* (n 138); *Futures Case* [2012] Bundesverwaltungsgericht A-1246/2011; *Undisclosed companies v Federal Tax Administration (Swaps case)* (n 138). See Meindl-Ringler (n 67) 238 et seq; Reinarz and Carelli (n 123).

[340] *Futures* (n 132); *Eidgenössische Steuerverwaltung v X Bank* (n 123).

[341] *Elektrárny Opatovice, a s v Finanční ředitelství v Hradci Králové (International Power)* (n 324). According to the IBFD Tax Treaty Case Law Database.

[342] Letter 03-00-RZ/16236 of 9 April 2014.

[343] *Eastern Value Partners v Federal Tax Service* [2012] Ninth Arbitration Court of Appeal A40-60755/12-20-388.

[344] *ZAO Vladimirsky torgoviy dom v Federal Tax Service* (n 164). According to the IBFD Tax Treaty Case Database.

[345] *Samsung Electronics Ltd v National Tax Service of Korea* (n 130). According to the IBFD Tax Treaty Case Database.

However, the country where beneficial ownership has been applied most by courts according to Article 13 on capital gains is India, albeit with inconsistent results.[346]

The author's view is that beneficial ownership is not to be considered implicit in all treaties, especially if the meaning hereby supported is given.

A first argument, derived from the US practice, is that beneficial ownership is implicit by applying domestic allocation principles, including beneficial ownership, to tax treaties. This is the case in the *Aiken* and *NIPSCO* cases.[347] However, this does not sustain implicit beneficial ownership for two reasons. The first reason is that if the beneficial owner principle were applicable to all treaties understood as application of the beneficial owner domestic principle, most countries would not be able to apply it, except common law countries; the rest of the countries normally lack a domestic beneficial owner allocation principle. Under that logic, it is obvious that if they do not know it, it cannot be applicable to their tax treaties.

The second reason is that it is highly doubtful that domestic allocation principles of the source or residence countries apply to allocate income at the treaty level. Even the USA had to explicitly lay down this view in its Technical Explanation because it was not obvious to other countries and international practice. Moreover, the USA changed its view on this point several times.[348]

As said elsewhere in this book, the object–subject connection in the treaty is mainly made through the qualification of the relevant income, that is, it is normally made under private law because it defines the ability to pay and the transfer pricing rules, and only in exceptional cases is it made through submission to domestic law, such as in the case of presumptive income. Reasons to reject general submission of allocation include divergences in the application of tax treaties and the subjection of the treaty to legislation in one of the states which may change its domestic law in order to change the jurisdiction rules. In any of these cases, many scholars reject the idea that treaty allocation absolutely depends on domestic rules as attempted by some countries and the OECD. Even though recent works, such as the Partnerships Report, and more recently some outcomes of the BEPS Action Plan, are heading in that direction, it remains an exception in an evolving scene. Although it could be the general rule in the future, it was certainly not the case at the time beneficial ownership was introduced.

A similar approach considers beneficial ownership to be implicit in the 'paid to' and other allocation terms used in tax treaties. Again, this is not the case. Those terms, as argued before, simply refer to fulfilment of the arrangement as required by the law in accordance with custom or the relevant arrangement.[349] Connecting the issue to the definition of the relevant income, the issue namely refers to the relevant arrangement conditions. This leaves the issue of nominees, agents acting in their own name and conduit companies within the scope of application of the treaties. Only in relation to submission of the relevant income definition, such as in the case of the third limb of the dividend definition, may the object–subject connection be submitted to domestic law,

[346] In some cases it ruled in a very formal sense, while in others it ruled in an economic or substance over form sense. See as examples *E*Trade Mauritius Ltd* (n 142); *KSPG Netherlands Holding BV* (n 142).

[347] *Aiken Industries, Inc v Commissioner* (n 116); *Northern Indiana Public Service Co v Commissioner* (n 116).

[348] See above, n 99 et seq and accompanying text.

[349] See above, n 91 et seq and accompanying text.

which in turn may suggest another allocation of income rule. However, this is not an implicit beneficial ownership rule. Another approach would even go against the definition of such terms proposed by the OECD, which intended a broad term to cover any transaction, as otherwise several mismatches would arise.

Yet another approach is that beneficial ownership is implicit as an international practice. This has two different sub-approaches. The first one is that beneficial ownership is internationally applied as a narrow allocation principle to agents, nominees and similar intermediaries. This is again rejected because beneficial ownership was precisely introduced to solve the problem several countries had on applying the treaty to intermediaries acting in their own name but on account of others. If it was introduced because several countries have such a problem, it cannot be said there was a common understanding of the rule as implicit. Even if it was claimed to be so, it could not be said to be an international practice and is not implicit. It could be said that after a number of decades it has turned into a practice, but again, different views do not show practice and *opinio iuris*.

The second sub-approach is that beneficial ownership is implicit as a general anti-avoidance rule or principle derived from good faith and international practice, or because of the guiding principle or factual approaches supported by the OECD.[350] This might be the case of the *Diebold* case. In the author's view, this is not the case for two reasons. First, beneficial ownership does not mean a general anti-avoidance rule or principle, as has already been argued. Secondly, there is, as yet, no consensus, consistent practice or *opinio iuris* on an internationally accepted broad anti-avoidance rule, nor on the meaning of beneficial ownership.[351]

F. The Extension of Beneficial Ownership Rules Other than Articles 10–12

If beneficial ownership is not considered as implicit, there are doubts as to whether the problem of Articles 10–12 of the Model in relation to intermediaries may also arise in

[350] Those supporting the existence of an international principle of prevention of abuse in tax law based their arguments on: (i) good faith as a general principle of international law; (ii) because prevention of abuse is recognised by the Statutes of the International Court of Justice; (iii) a customary rule in taxation derived from practice of States; and (iv) because the object and purpose of tax treaties includes prevention of double non-taxation and prevention of abuse. All of them remain controversial. Vogel (n 10) 123–25; Ward (n 10) 178–79. See para 9.3 of the Commentary to Art 1 of the 2003 OECD Model Tax Convention and para 59 of the Commentary to Art 1 of the 2017 OECD Model Tax Convention. Against the existence of such principle, see De Broe (n 32) 306–08; Van Weeghel (n 31) 100–01, 107; V Chand, 'The Interaction of the Principal Purpose Test (and the Guiding Principle) with Treaty and Domestic Anti-Avoidance Rules' (2018) 46 *Intertax* 115, 116. As well as his viewpoint, De Broe provides a comprehensive analysis of the issue. Considering beneficial ownership is implicit in such general anti-avoidance, see Walser (n 195) 17–18. Vogel considering the existence of a general principle based on substance over form, and interpreting beneficial owner in this sense seemingly considers beneficial ownership to be implicit in all treaties. Vogel (n 10) 123–25, 562. See also Vega Borrego (n 65) 88.

[351] Though recent developments on the principal purpose test may be construing a general principle that would be consolidated in practice in forthcoming years. On the differences on tax policy among states and their tolerance to abusive practices, see De Broe (n 32) 346–62; Zornoza Pérez and Báez Moreno (n 127) 152. Denying the existence of an anti-avoidance principle, see De Broe (n 32) 306–08; Van Weeghel (n 31) 100–01, 107.

relation to other articles. The UN Committee of Experts on International Cooperation in Tax Matters asked in 2007–2008 for a report on whether beneficial ownership was needed in other articles of the Model.[352]

Under the report elaborated by Professor Baker at the request of the Committee, three types of treaty shopping by interposing intermediaries may be distinguished.

The first one is to use tax treaties to limit a residence state's ability to tax the income. This would usually happen by interposing an entity in an intermediary state so the treaty between the intermediary state and the source country, and the treaty between the intermediary state and the residence country, preclude taxation by the residence state.[353] Under this scheme, the taxpayer may argue that under such treaties income is not allocated to him or her, but to the corporation in the intermediary state, and thus can only be taxed in accordance with those treaties in the residence state of the intermediary state and/or in the source state. He or she may even argue that such treaties limit the application of the domestic anti-avoidance rules of the residence state intending to catch income allocated to the intermediary state from escaping residence taxation.[354] This treaty shopping could be especially attractive if there is no treaty between the beneficial owner's resident state and the source country.

In Baker's view, the articles susceptible to such treaty shopping are Articles 7, 13(6), 21 and 22(4).[355] It seems that Baker puts the spotlight on those articles not because of their ability to limit residence taxation of the beneficial owner through treaty shopping, but because of their ability to limit source taxation. However, through his arguments, he also recalled this 'reflexive' arrangement or avoidance of beneficial owner residence taxation by interposition of an entity.

A solution to such issue could be derived from applying an anti-avoidance rule and the income being obtained by the beneficial owner taxpayer directly from the source country, so income is not considered by the residence country as being obtained from the intermediary state and treaties do not limit taxation at residence. This could increasingly be the case after the introduction of the principal purpose test after the BEPS Action Plan. But in the author's view, the issue of the 'reflexive' avoidance and the solution to it through anti-avoidance rules also applies to any of the other articles of the treaty in addition to Articles 7, 13(5/6) and 21.

The second type of treaty shopping involves using treaties to limit source taxation. A resident of a state that has no treaty in force with the source country may transfer his or her rights to an entity or person in an intermediary country with a treaty with that country so that the source country could not tax it.[356] The report considers this type of treaty shopping in relation to Article 7, where there is no permanent establishment, Article 8 on income from operation of international traffic of ships and aircraft, Article 13(3) on capital gains from alienation of ships and aircraft operated in international traffic, Article 13(5) and (6) on capital gains of movable property other than those whose tax rights are allocated to the situs, Article 14 on independent work where there is no permanent establishment, Article 15 on income from employment, Article 16 on

352 Committee of Experts on International Cooperation in Tax Matters (n 39).
353 ibid 38, 50, 65.
354 ibid 39.
355 ibid 38, 50, 64 and 75.
356 ibid 36.

pensions and Article 21 on other income.[357] However, Article 21 will only have a risk of treaty shopping regarding limitation of tax powers of the source country in the case of the Model, as, under the UN Tax Convention, the source country retains its taxing powers. Article 22, in turn, may also be susceptible to treaty shopping by interposing an intermediary as a way of limiting the tax power of the state of situs in case of movable property whose taxing powers on them are not attributed to the situs country. However, the UN Report notes that Articles 8 and 13(3) on income and capital gains from aircraft and ships operated in international traffic have no such risk, and for Articles 15 and 16, even though shopping might be possible, it may not be frequent.

In relation to Article 13(3), the report sees no treaty shopping risk by interposing a subject because the rule allocates tax jurisdiction to the state of the place of effective management.[358] Baker states that there is no risk of tax avoidance if the treaty limits the tax jurisdiction of, for instance, the state where the aircraft is located because the effective management is in another state. In principle, the rule is not weak with regard to treaty shopping because it is based on a factual test, and not a presumption, as residence is. The report also holds that no treaty shopping may operate in relation to Article 8 on income from international shipping and transport for the same reasons.[359] The reasoning may also be applicable in relation to the current 2017 Model, because even though Articles 8 and 13(3) no longer refer to the place of effective management, they depend on the residence of the corporation, which in turn depends on mutual agreement, which will take into account the facts.[360]

Regarding Article 15, for the report it seems possible a subject may transfer his or her income rights to a company in an intermediary state. Baker considers this a minor issue, even though implicitly recognising it is possible.[361] The author's view is that, in addition to such arguments, if the income is attributed to a corporation, it cannot be regarded as employment services and in such a case, if beneficial ownership is included in Article 7, it is likely the source country will retain its taxation powers if the work is performed in the other country.[362] Moreover, if an actual employment relationship is hidden through an intermediary corporation, mere definition of actual legal facts would lead to the application of Article 15 between the source and residence countries. An employment relationship implies a specific and very personal relationship between the employee and the employer that, despite allocating the income to a third party, would still qualify under Article 15. A different issue is the case of fake or sham self-employed persons. In such cases, the problem is a matter of evidence in order to ascertain whether there is subordination or whether the person works under the direction of the other person.[363] But this is an evidence issue under labour law, not a tax treaty issue. Mere proper qualification would allow the residence country to retain taxation rights. In sum, there is no need at all to include beneficial ownership in Article 15.

[357] ibid 36, 49, 64, 75. Though Baker seemingly only considers there is actual risk in relation to Arts 7, 13(6) and 22.

[358] ibid 60.

[359] ibid 62.

[360] See Arts 8, 13(3), and 4(3) of the 2017 OECD Model Tax Convention.

[361] Committee of Experts on International Cooperation in Tax Matters (n 39) para 73.

[362] As recognised in relation to pensions, see above, n 110.

[363] Although the term seemingly has to follow domestic interpretation. See Reimer and Rust (n 110) 1142 et seq.

Article 16, on pensions, also seems resistant to treaty shopping through agents or nominees. The UN Report sustains a reasoning similar to that above in relation to employment. If a person transfers his or her rights to a corporation, it can hardly be income from past employment and turns into financial income.[364] Moreover, pension funds and management firms are subject to surveillance by financial authorities and could face regulatory consequences if they attempt to change the beneficiary of a pension scheme to a corporation, especially if the contributions to such pensions implied tax benefits or were related to a specific regulated labour regime. In the author's view, there seems little risk of tax avoidance in relation to Article 16.

Even though the report does not discuss it, it would seem the same reasoning applies to directors' fees, government service and students, as the qualification of all of them depends on a specific personal status of the creditor.

The final type of treaty shopping concern through interposition of intermediaries involves taxation of third countries.[365] The case involves a subject resident in a country that obtains income from a source country. A third country taxes the income obtained because even though it is not the source country, it may somehow be connected to it. There is no tax treaty between that third state and the residence country. This case does not refer to dual source cases but to a third country. In such a case, a subject may put his or her income in the hands of an intermediary entity in a country with a treaty with the above-mentioned third state, so the treaty prevents taxation by that third country. In the case of the report, it deals with this case in relation to Article 21. The report dismisses this case, reasonably arguing that third countries taxing such income is an infrequent issue.[366]

However, although the Report considers Articles 7, 13(5) and (6) and 21 to be susceptible to treaty shopping, Baker considers it better not to introduce beneficial ownership into such articles of the treaty.

The first reason to dismiss the introduction of the rule is because Articles 7 and 13 do not refer to income streams, unlike Articles 10–12.

In relation to capital gains, Baker points out that there is the 'theoretical difficulty of applying the beneficial ownership concept not to a stream of income but to a capital gain or the proceeds of the disposal of an asset'.[367] However, the report does not delve into the legal and economic differences between them, probably because in a general sense they seem obvious. The problem is explained with a few examples.

The first one states that if taxes are imposed on a capital gain realised on a gift, there is no actual gain benefiting the person behind or the intermediary person on the body.[368] Baker wonders whether the recipient of the gift would be considered the beneficial owner as benefiting from such gain.[369] To my view, this reasoning is flawed. The definition of income in contemporary personal taxation comprises any increase of net wealth, no matter whether it is realised or unrealised.[370] Different to that, because of

364 Committee of Experts on International Cooperation in Tax Matters (n 39) para 74.
365 ibid 40, Example 3.
366 ibid 36.
367 ibid 88.
368 ibid 57.
369 ibid.
370 See RA Musgrave, 'In Defense of an Income Concept' (1967) 81 *Harvard Law Review* 44, 49; HC Simons, *Personal Income Taxation* (University of Chicago Press, 1938) 100.

administrative and liquidity reasons, capital gains are postponed until the assets are sold.[371] In the example, the gain has been to the benefit of the person behind the body corporate when occurring, by, for instance, an increase in the stock market value if listed. Such increase was available to him or her, even though it was not liquid. The intermediary corporation could have sold the asset and made it liquid before, could have exchanged it for another asset or could have distributed it to the person behind. The fact that the asset was gifted including the unrealised capital gain should not make it different, from a tax perspective, from the case in which the corporation first sells the asset, so the gain is taxed, and then gifts the money. Because of equality and equivalence of transactions, the unrealised gain is taxed on the gift as in the case of prior selling before donating the cash. And in the latter case, nobody would doubt the gain has benefited the corporation in the first instance. However, this still does not mean the shareholder is necessarily the beneficial owner. Just from a technical income tax point of view, including tax treaties, a corporation or person benefits from capital gains no matter whether they are realised or unrealised.[372] The flaw seems to be that the report assumes the capital gain 'rises' at the time of the disposal, but the capital gain is generated during the tenancy of the asset, and what happens upon sale is its realisation.

Moreover, the income of a person or the beneficial owner behind a corporation – the unrealised gain that is realised upon gifting – must be distinguished from the income of the receiver of the gift – the whole value of the income. If a person earns a certain object as salary in kind, then increases its value and then pays it as salary in kind to another person, nobody would doubt that the first person earns salary as income and has a capital gain as income, and that the second person receives the whole value as income. A gift is not significantly different.

Turning to a second issue, it seems that Baker considers it difficult to define who is the beneficial owner because a gain realised by a corporation would increase the value of both the corporation and the shares held by the shareholder, or the value of the parent company if the former is a subsidiary.[373] The gain could be paid to a third person, but may also benefit the same or other persons in several other ways. Again, the author sees no difficulty on this point. Where a corporation receives a dividend or any other income flow, its value increases, but so does the value of its parent company, if there is one. Also, this issue arises in domestic law and allocation principles solve it under beneficial owner tax principles, though not in exactly the same way as in tax treaties.

The problem is probably that beneficial ownership as understood here falls into the beneficial ownership trap, by somehow being equated to a broad economic benefit – 'ultimate effective beneficiary'. If one interprets beneficial ownership as defined in

[371] W Andrews, 'A Consumption-Type or Cash Flow Personal Income Tax' (1974) 87 *Harvard Law Review* 1113, 1141–43; ML Fellows, 'A Comprehensive Attack on Tax Deferral' (1990) 88 *Michigan Law Review* 722, 724; Simons (n 370) 56. However, some authors point out that the liquidity problem is a false argument, as it is not an issue in most cases, so they argue in favour of taxing non-realised income: Fellows 724; ECCM Kemmeren, 'A Global Framework for Capital Gains Taxes' [2018] *Intertax* 268, 272; D Shakow, 'Taxation without Realization: A Proposal for Accrual Taxation' (1986) 134 *University of Pennsylvania Law Review* 1111, 1167–76.

[372] See para 5 of Commentary to Art 13 of the OECD Model Tax Convention. See Reimer and Rust (n 5) 1077. 1.

[373] Committee of Experts on International Cooperation in Tax Matters (n 39) 55.

this book, there is no such a problem. The intermediary corporation would have the beneficial ownership if it has no obligation to pass the income on or give equivalent economic benefit that accrues upon receipt of the income, and such obligation is related to the reason why the intermediary corporation held the asset. Thus, the mere fact that the gain indirectly benefits the parent company would not render the intermediary company a beneficial ownership. Only where the corporation is obliged to pass the gain or equivalent economic effect outside the increase in value of the shares and under the above-mentioned characteristics would the corporation be disqualified as the beneficial owner.

The misunderstanding of beneficial ownership, ownership and economic ownership may also be seen in the argument claiming that there are legal problems if one says the legal owner of an asset is not the beneficial owner of the gain arising from it. The problem is exactly the same as the one of the legal owner or creditors of shares, debts or the leasing of intangibles acting for the account of a third party. Of course, he or she is the legal owner of the dividends, interests or royalties, but the rule is precisely aimed at preventing such legal ownership being argued to claim the application of the treaty to bar taxing rights of the states involved if this benefits a third person not entitled to treaty provisions. If one thinks that beneficial ownership is a type of legal ownership of entitlement, there is certainly a problem. But beneficial ownership in tax treaties precisely tries to override formal ownership interpretations in such cases through the elements of definition provided above, so no conflict can be found.

Maybe what the report is trying to argue is that it would be odd to say that the gain is beneficially owned by the third party while the asset is owned or beneficially owned by the intermediary. It may be the case from a private law point of view, but from the tax treaty point of view what matters is the gain, and that is the reason why the beneficial ownership test in tax treaties refers to the income and not to the asset. If beneficial ownership was added to Article 22, this would also add consistency to the tax treaty treatment of both the asset and the income derived from it.

On business profits, the report states that to define the beneficial owner would be difficult because business profits are the result of computation of sales or income less expenses.[374] In addition, expenses could be in one entity while sales could be in a different one. However, the report itself recognised that although determining beneficial ownership could be harder because of computation, it is not impossible. Computation would just be a matter of defining the taxable bases involved according to domestic law and transfer pricing rules. And beneficial ownership would simply define that part of the income that would not be subject to treaty tax jurisdiction limits. It would certainly increase the complexity of the application of the treaty, but is not necessarily impossible.

From a formal viewpoint, the report also considers that beneficial ownership only relates to income streams, as those types of income are the only ones related to the problems of income 'paid to'.[375] As capital gains and business profits are not 'paid to', ie the problem at which the beneficial ownership was aimed, it does not necessarily arise. The issue, however, is not as clear as it seems. As gains are not defined in the treaty and are considered from an international point of view as a very broad concept,

[374] ibid 68.
[375] ibid 56.

domestic law plays an important role defining them.[376] Thus, if domestic law is based on legal ownership, then the problem of the mismatch between domestic allocation and treaty allocation with nominees in common law countries appears, as well as with agents acting in their own name but on the account of third parties.

Also, the problem of nominees and continental agents acting on account of others may appear in relation to business profits. Again, the treaty does not define business profits, which are left open to be defined as any income related to a business or enterprise in a broad sense. Because of this broad sense, it seems that, as in the rest of the articles in the Model, the subject–object connection required refers to the legal entitlement under the relevant arrangements, so the possibility of setting up an intermediary remains, despite paid to not being included.

As stated, the 'paid to' problem was probably a misunderstanding by the UK, who gave it a mistaken interpretation and a greater role than the one it was meant to have.[377] Consequently, the fact that the articles do not include paid to does not limit the possibility of exploiting them through treaty shopping by interposing an intermediary. The problem is not the term 'paid to' but that the intermediary may have legal and full ownership, and can transfer similar economic effects to a third party.[378] And with capital gains, it is possible to put assets in the hands of an intermediary and take advantage of tax treaties so that taxation of income derived from a sale, or from unrealised gains, is limited.

However, despite the report recognising some risk of treaty shopping in such cases, Baker ultimately doubts the adequacy of the introduction of the term because of its lack of clarity.[379] Because the concept was subject to so much discussion, its introduction would raise conflicts around the articles in which it is introduced. This is why Baker recommends in the first instance only to introduce it in Article 21, probably because to him this is the article with the highest risk of treaty shipping, and as a second option to do nothing.[380]

In addition, the UN Committee of Experts on International Cooperation in Tax Matters also raised concerns that its introduction in other articles would somehow highlight that previous versions, or articles that remain without the term, are weak in relation to such treaty shopping structures.[381] However, the report states that the issue is already there to a certain extent, because beneficial ownership only appears in Articles 10–12 and, because the risk is higher in relation to the income to which such articles refers, this justifies it being in some articles but not in others.[382]

Having said this, this author believes that beneficial ownership would be helpful in relation to the rest of the articles, either introducing it into each article or including it as a general clause.

Once the term has been narrowed down and clarified by the OECD 2014 amendments, the argument about its lack of clarity cannot be fully upheld. Of course, there

[376] See para 3 of Commentary to Art 13 of the OECD Model Tax Convention.
[377] See above, s I.B; see also UK section in ch 4.
[378] Similarly Meindl-Ringler (n 67) 316.
[379] Committee of Experts on International Cooperation in Tax Matters (n 39) para 84 et seq.
[380] ibid 91.
[381] ibid 77.
[382] ibid 78.

might be certain misinterpretations of the new commentary, but a proper interpretation, as will be defended later, avoids misconceptions, is in line with its historical origin and resolves issues in relation to intermediaries. Thus, it may now be introduced without various concerns that the conflicts it might raise might outweigh its benefits.

In relation to the recognition of the weakness of previous versions, not to include it does not mean that the issue is not there. Just stating in the Commentary that the articles are not open to treaty shopping does not solve the problem. If those articles are open to treaty shopping through intermediaries and beneficial ownership is not implicit, as has been argued, its introduction does not declare an issue that was already there but fixes it.

However, the introduction of the PPT and limitation on benefits (LOB) clauses following the BEPS Action Plan may have left the clause superfluous,[383] especially as the PPT will also cover the cases covered by beneficial ownership with the same consequences, although the former, in the author's view, has greater scope. This being the case, to introduce beneficial ownership into other articles would make little or no difference if the treaty has a PPT. Still, as will be argued later, beneficial ownership may play a role in some very specific cases where PPT and LOB could fail.

II. Broadening the Rule: Is Beneficial Ownership a GAAR under the 2003 Commentary?

After more than a decade since 1986 without readdressing the meaning of beneficial ownership, the OECD again dealt with the topic in a 2002 report entitled 'Restricting Entitlement to Treaty Benefits'. This was the result of three milestones. First, some cases put the spotlight on the beneficial ownership test, which had received almost no attention for decades, and attracted the attention of academics.[384] Secondly, the IFA Congresses held in London in 1998 and in Eilat in 1999 devoted respective seminars to the topic.[385] Finally, and connected to the first two milestones, some scholars published significant work on the issue.[386] In addition, the early-1990s crisis led the OECD to develop studies on tax evasion and avoidance.

The four main new ideas added to the Commentary by the report were: (i) beneficial ownership clarifies paid to, so it becomes clear that the source tax limit is not dependent on a person just receiving the income; (ii) beneficial owner is not used in a narrow technical sense; (iii) the rule has to be understood in the light of the object and purpose of the convention of eliminating double taxation and preventing evasion and avoidance; and (iv) beneficial owner excludes persons, other than agents or nominees, who act as a conduit for another person who in fact receives the benefit of the income.[387]

[383] Chand (n 350) 119.

[384] *Royal Dutch Shell (Market Maker)* (n 304); *Diebold Courtage SA v Ministre de l'Economie* (n 334); *V SA* (n 123).

[385] The outcome of the 1998 IFA London seminar on beneficial ownership is available in Walser (n 195); the result of the 1999 IFA Eilat seminar is available in Oliver et al (n 2).

[386] The most significant works were Du Toit (n 4); Van Weeghel (n 31).

[387] See OECD, 'Restricting the Entitlement to Treaty Benefits' in *2002 Reports Related to the OECD Model Tax Convention* (OECD Publishing, 2003) paras 21–24. See also paras 12, 12.1 and 12.2; 8, 8.1 and 8.2; 4,

The first and second points above simply confirm what has already been analysed from the basis of historical documents. Few additional comments are needed, and the author submits the reader to the points made previously. On the first point, however, it should be noted that, as argued elsewhere in this book, paid to has to be analysed in relation to the qualification of the subject–object connection under the relevant income definition.[388]

The second point, stating the concept has no narrow technical meaning, raises two issues. It is unclear what no narrow technical meaning means. It could mean that, in a negative sense, the term is a broad anti-avoidance rule, or that it does not match the specific legal meanings that are usually attributed to that term. It seems to be accepted that it means that the term shall not be understood under the meaning the wording has in the domestic law of any country, nor in other international regulations such as those dealing with exchange of information or prevention of money laundering.[389] The way in which the report 'Restricting Entitlement to Treaty Benefits' tries to achieve a neutral definition has been seen by some scholars as supporting this view. This confirms, as argued in previous chapters, that the concept must be interpreted in an international autonomous sense. Additionally, the phrase states that, in addition to having no narrow technical meaning, it must be interpreted in relation to the object and purpose of preventing avoidance. Because the report tried to satisfy all countries and many intended to apply beneficial ownership on a case-by-case basis, a broad interpretation was needed. But this does not mean that a broad general anti-avoidance rule definition was given; rather, the term was intended to cover divergent practice. This, as developed in greater detail in the next paragraph of the 2003 Commentary, will be analysed later. For the moment, suffice it to say that it cannot be said that the beneficial owner rule in the Commentary has no technical meaning, as the Commentary explicitly said, nor that it has a broad anti-avoidance meaning. Of course the concept has a technical and legal meaning, but this is defined by its interpretation in the international tax context.

In this regard, the 2003 Commentary was of significant importance because, thanks to its ambiguity, it led several authors, authorities and courts to argue that it defined beneficial ownership as a broad anti-avoidance rule.[390] Because the Commentary put the spotlight on a rule that for many countries passed inadvertently, gave it a confusing meaning and connected the term to the objective of the treaty to prevent avoidance, several cases raised in the period after the 2003 Commentary were resolved through the use of the concept. But, as will be seen, such a broad anti-avoidance understanding was not exactly what 'Restricting the Entitlement to Treaty Benefits' had intended.

4.1 and 4.2, of Commentaries to Arts 10, 11 and 12 of the 2003 OECD Model Tax Convention, and compare to previous versions.

[388] See above, s I.B.

[389] Amendments to the Commentary in 2014 modified this phrase from the 2003 Commentary to clarify this sense and under such wording denies that the concept is related to the domestic meaning of any country. See paras 12.1, 9.1 and 4 of the Commentaries to Arts 10, 11 and 12 of the 2014 OECD Model Tax Convention. See Meindl-Ringler (n 67) 48.

[390] Martín Jiménez (n 31) 50. Stating denial of the 'narrow technical meaning' leads to an economic broad interpretation, see *Eidgenössische Steuerverwaltung v X Bank* (n 123) para 5.2. Among authors sustaining the view that beneficial owner is a broad anti-avoidance rule on the basis of the 2003 Commentary, see Vega Borrego (n 65) 86 et seq; Pijl (n 31).

A. Beneficial Ownership, the Object and Purpose of the Model, and the Single Taxation Principle

The 2003 Commentary on the beneficial ownership rule states that it would be inconsistent with the object and purpose of the Model to grant source taxation limits just because a person receives income. The main reason to deny the limit to intermediaries, according to the Commentary, is that domestic tax law does not allocate the income to them, and as income is not taxed in their hands, no multiple taxation arises.[391] According to the Commentary, Articles 10–12 of the Model shall not apply to intermediaries because there is no multiple taxation on them. However, the reasoning is flawed for several reasons.

First, it assumes that intermediaries such as nominees and agents in all cases are not taxed under the domestic law of all countries. This, however, depends on the types of intermediaries, as in several countries and cases disclosed agents and nominees are not taxed unless acting in the name and on the account of third parties, and the income is directed to the principals, depending on the relevant rules.[392] And in the case of undisclosed agents or agents acting in their own name but for the benefit of the third party, it depends on the legislation of the relevant countries, which have a great variety of solutions. In some cases, the income is taxed in the agent's hands and in some cases in the hands of the principal.[393] However, the 2003 Commentary assumes in a general sense that income is never taxed in the hands of agents and nominees, which is not always true. One wonders whether the Commentary is either assuming that the concept only applies to the agents and nominees to whom income is not allocated, which would make the concept a sort of subject to tax test (such meaning in the sense of being within the scope of charge, and not necessarily effectively taxed, has already been rejected because there is no explicit reference supporting that view, and this implicit reference in the 2003 Commentary cannot justify such a major change in how treaties apply) or understands the concept as an effective taxation rule, which has some support as the next paragraph in the Commentary explores this idea.

In that second sense, the reasoning assumes that the treaty does not apply because there is no double taxation. This argument, if taken to its logical conclusion, may lead to the thinking that a condition for the treaty to apply is that there is double taxation.[394] Both outcomes are severely flawed.

In this regard, the object and purpose of tax treaties is not directly to eliminate double taxation, but to facilitate international trade through elimination of multiple taxation, the actual mechanism of the treaty working on allocation of tax jurisdiction.[395]

[391] See paras 12.1, 8.1 and 4.1 of Commentaries to Arts 10, 11 and 12 of the 2003 OECD Model Tax Convention.

[392] Wheeler, 'General Report' (n 112) 36.

[393] See above, n 112.

[394] A Martín Jiménez, 'The 2003 Revision of the OECD Commentaries on the Improper Use of Tax Treaties: A Case for the Declining Effect of the OECD Commentaries?' (2004) 58 *Bulletin for International Fiscal Documentation* 17, 21.

[395] Baker (n 32) B-6; Engelen (n 5) s 10.3; JA Becerra, *The Interpretation and Application of Tax Treaties in North America* (IBFD, 2007) 5.2; K Vogel and R Prokisch, 'General Report' in K Vogel and R Prokisch (eds), *Interpretation of Tax Treaties* (Kluwer, 1993) 72. On the object to facilitate international trade, see K Vogel,

Tax treaties do not have a single objective and purpose, and to discern them is difficult and sometimes conflicting.[396] This author, in line with a large majority of scholars, would argue that tax treaties have different levels of objects and purposes that relate to each other. In this sense, elimination of double taxation is an intermediate policy object, but not the main object, and not the specific object of the treaty through which the objectives are applied. Also, to assume that the object is to eliminate double taxation is close to assuming that the subjective intentions are the object of the parties, which is not what is intended by the principle of interpretation. The object and purpose are defined by the objective purpose of the treaty, not by a subjective intention. Thus, the specific main object of tax treaties is to allocate tax jurisdiction, but leaving states the power to decide whether actual taxation is charged and what the specifics are.[397] To say the object and purpose is to eliminate double taxation is like stating that the object and purpose of the Treaty of the European Union is free movement. This is obviously not true, and freedoms are just policy mechanisms to achieve an area of peace and economic growth and prosperity. Freedoms, though playing a really important role in taxation, are subject to other principles in order to achieve the objects and purposes of the European treaties.

In any case, even if the elimination of double taxation is considered as the object and purpose of the treaty, the Commentary applies the object and purpose of prevention of multiple taxation as a rule on the scope of application of the treaty, and not as a principle of interpretation as it should be. The result of arguing that the treaty only applies where there is double taxation leads to a conflict with the object and purpose of allocation of tax jurisdiction and the derived specific rules defining tax jurisdiction.[398] If one is fulfilled, the other one fails. If one takes the need of being taxed as a prerequisite, then the result of which country has jurisdiction to tax is altered. For instance, in the case of Article 12, it was considered from a policy perspective that the state of residence should be the only one taxing, and it was for that state to decide if the income was actually taxed or not. If one assumes no taxation goes against the object and purpose of the treaty, under that logic, if the residence country does not tax, then the source country may tax. Of course, this is not true, and would be considered a treaty override.[399] To take that object and purpose as a rule, rather than as a principle that helps interpretation, directly attacks the actual object and purpose of the treaty and the relevant rules as seen traditionally.

Contrary to this, the object and purpose assists in interpreting the treaty but cannot fully override the text and the mechanism of the treaty. Where a general principle is

'Steuerumgehung Nach Innerstaatlichem Recht Und Nach Abkommensrecht' 369; U Paschen, *Steuerumgehung Im Nationalen Und Internationalen Steuerrecht* (Deutscher Universitäts-Verlag GmbH 2001) 4. Quoted by V Ruiz Almendral and G Seitz, 'El Fraude a La Ley Tributaria (Análisis de La Norma Española Con Ayudad de La Experiencia Alemana)' [2004] *Estudios Financieros* 3, 31. On avoidance of double taxation to facilitate international trade, see p 7 of Commentary to Art 1 of the 1977 OECD Model Tax Convention and subsequent versions. The aim to eliminate double taxation was in Art 1 of the 1943 Mexico and 1946 London Drafts from the League of Nations. On the aim to allocate tax jurisdiction, see Becerra 5.2; DA Ward, 'Canada's Tax Treaties' (1995) 43 *Canadian Tax Journal* 1719, 1728.

[396] Kysar (n 5) 1409.

[397] Becerra (n 395) 5.2; Ward (n 395) 1728; De Broe (n 32) 358.

[398] Kysar (n 5) 1409.

[399] Lang (n 197) 29.

in conflict with a rule, the rule prevails; the principles of legality and legal certainty prevail when balanced against the principle of interpretation in accordance with the object and purpose because of its importance to the whole system. At most, the object and purpose can push the interpretation within the limits of the ordinary meaning and context a little, but if a treaty rule allocates tax jurisdiction in its conditions, the objective and purpose cannot totally override the consequence of the rule against its ordinary meaning, even in non-taxation cases.[400] In this regard, some authors rightly point out that the object and purpose is of little help, or at least doubtful, in interpretation.[401] As Sinclair argued, the object and purpose is probably a 'secondary and ancillary process in the application of the general rule on interpretation'.[402] Its role is to test whether the interpretation derived from the ordinary meaning and context could be in line with the object and purpose.[403] And even in cases where the ordinary meaning and context do not properly fit with the object and purpose, the latter cannot fully override the former. Here, the ordinary meaning and context of beneficial owner cannot lead to interpretation of it in the sense of denying application of Articles 10–12, where there is no double taxation.

Moreover, the Commentary on beneficial ownership states that beneficial ownership has to be interpreted in the light of the object or purpose of the Model of eliminating double taxation or to achieve a single taxation, including its downside sense of preventing non-taxation,[404] ie that beneficial ownership also has to give effect to the principle that at least one country shall tax. The concept of single taxation is considered to have been consolidated in the USA in the 1980s, and was exported to the OECD Commentary in 1992.[405] This is generally justified by the objectives of preventing tax avoidance and evasion that have been around tax treaties for some time.[406]

However, it is the author's view that there is nothing in treaties based on the OECD Model as such, and where there is no taxation at all because of the application of the treaty, the object of the treaty is precisely fulfilled.[407] Tax treaties developed a single

[400] Edwardes-Ker (n 6) 162. Stating how the rule is in line with the object and purpose, implicitly recognising purpose guides interpretation but does not prevent the use of the rule on its ordinary meaning, see *Maximov v US* (1963) 373 US 49 (USSC).

[401] M Lang, *Introduction to the Law of Double Taxation Conventions*, 2nd edn (IBFD, 2013) 40; Vogel and Prokisch (n 395) 72.

[402] Sinclair (n 6) 130.

[403] ibid.

[404] Shaviro states that the single tax principle has an upside, preventing double taxation; and a downside, preventing non-taxation. See D Shaviro, 'The Two Faces of the Single Tax Principle' (2016) 41 *Brooklyn Journal of International Law* 1293. On the introduction of downside single taxation in beneficial ownership, see paras 12.1, 8.1 and 4.1 of the 2003 OECD Model Tax Convention. The single tax principle in both an upside and downside sense and as a general principle of international tax law was first proposed by Avi-Yonah, based on US practices. See RS Avi-Yonah, 'International Taxation of Electronic Commerce' (1996) 52 *Tax Law Review* 507, 517; R Avi-Yonah, *International Tax as International Law: An Analysis of the International Tax Regime* (Cambridge University Press, 2007) 8 et seq.

[405] RS Avi-Yonah, 'Who Invented the Single Tax Principle: An Essay on the History of US Treaty Policy' (2014) 49 *New York Law School Law Review* 305, 309.

[406] See League of Nations, 'Double Taxation and Tax Evasion – Report Presented by the Committee of Technical Experts on Double Taxation and Tax Evasion' (1927) Doc G. 216 M. 85. II; E Farah, 'Mandatory Arbitration of International Tax Disputes: A Solution in Search of a Problem' (2008) 9 *Florida Tax Review* 703, 711; Avi-Yonah (n 405) 309, fn 21.

[407] Lang (n 197) 29.

taxation principle in its upside sense, that is, to prevent double taxation, but not to prevent no taxation, or a downside single taxation principle. Even though it may have been around tax treaties as a preliminary idea for some time, the single taxation principle has only recently gained a strong support as a supplement to allocation of tax jurisdiction rules, and it is still far from being a complete and consistent applicable rule or principle.[408] Also, tax treaties do not explicitly recognise it as they work on liability, and it is difficult to state that it is a customary principle of international law if several countries do not see a problem with no taxation.[409] It is certainly controversial to say that consistent principles developed for almost a century have changed because of the inconsistent policy of some countries.[410] In addition, from a technical point of view, the single taxation principle still has no specific content as it poses several inconsistencies, such as defining in which cases it is applicable, if there should be a minimum taxation and how it relates to legitimate tax incentives. At most, the principle or rule is being developed, and probably soon will be recognised, but it is still just a desirable policy or objective.[411]

In the author's view, prevention of tax avoidance or evasion in the sense used by the OECD does not necessarily derive from or lead to the single tax principle; rather, it refers to the abuse of allocation of tax jurisdiction rules. If the aim of tax treaties is to allocate tax jurisdiction, irrespective of states effectively taxing or not, abuse of treaties implies a distortion of tax jurisdiction rules and threatens the single tax principle in its upside sense, but does not necessarily imply an attack on the downside single tax principle. In other words, if the object of the treaty is not to guarantee the downside single tax principle, it cannot be abused, so prevention of abuse cannot implicitly be derived from the existence of that downside tax principle.

However, some specific rules suggested by the Commentary are aimed at guaranteeing a downside single tax principle, such as subject to tax rules or limitation on benefits. Such rules have a limited scope and do not apply to the whole Model. Only after the 2017 Model might it be said that a single tax principle starts to be considered as a recognised principle, but most treaties still do not include the new rules proposed by the 2017 Model, so if the large majority of the treaty network does not embrace such a view, it can hardly be said it is a customary practice giving support to such a principle. The fact that

[408] Since the proposal of Avi-Yonah that the single tax principle was a customary principle of international tax law, some scholars have argued in favour of it, although some of them may be seen as supporting it as a desirable objective, but not as an already existent customary principle of international law. See DM Ring, 'One Nation among Many: Policy Implications of Cross-Border Tax Arbitrage' (2002) 44 *Boston College Law Review* 79, 105; Y Brauner, 'An International Tax Regime in Crystallization' (2002) 56 *Tax Law Review* 259, 302. Denying full recognition to the single tax principle on its downside view, see Shaviro (n 404); MTS Roch, 'La Imposición Justa Sobre Las Sociedades En Un Escenario Global: Un Tema Pendiente' [2018] *Derecho & Sociedad* 186, 186. The BEPS project is considered to be the milestone recognising the downside single tax principle as an international desirable policy objective. But by recognising it is an objective, authors, including Avi-Yonah, are implictly recognising it was not and is not an applicable recognised rule or principle. See R Avi-Yonah, 'Full Circle? The Single Tax Principle, BEPS, and the New US Model' [2016] *Global Taxation* 12, 20–21; Y Brauner, 'BEPS: An Interim Evaluation' (2014) 6 *World Tax Journal* 10, 28.

[409] Stating tax treaties do not deal with no taxation, see R Falcón y Tella and E Pulido, *Derecho Fiscal Internacional* (Marcial Pons, 2010) 114.

[410] Shaviro states that there is a considerable variation in countries' tolerance or hostility to overseas tax avoidance because of the ambiguous effects of avoidance in domestic welfare. Shaviro (n 404) 1301.

[411] Avi-Yonah, 'Full Circle?' (n 408) 20–21; Brauner, 'BEPS: An Interim Evaluation' (n 408) 28.

prevention of avoidance or evasion in general is not specifically dealt with in tax treaties, except in the case of abuse of tax treaties or their interaction with domestic law, does not mean that there is no concern about such an issue, just that no general substantive rule – apart from formal exchange of information and assistance in collection and specific anti-avoidance – exists to coordinate actions against avoidance and abuse in general. Several examples exist, but only in relation to abuse of tax treaties, and, as stated, they are still crystallising. And if no rules confirm a practice, such principle cannot exist. The existing principle is prevention of abuse on allocation of jurisdiction, which does not deal with the downside tax principle.

Consequently, beneficial ownership cannot be interpreted in the sense of preventing double non-taxation or supporting a single taxation principle in its downside sense. Not a single source – except the 2003 self-sustaining Commentary – indicates that beneficial ownership has such a meaning; indeed, the historical discussions stated that countries at the OECD were in favour of the introduction of beneficial ownership because they did not want Articles 10–12 to be dependent on effective taxation.[412] If the term was an alternative to avoiding such a consequence, it could not mean it. In addition, if no positive single taxation principle exists in international tax law, beneficial ownership cannot mean something that does not exist.

In the end, tax treaties apply upon liability to tax, not subjection to taxation or effective taxation.[413] This overrides any argument on single taxation or the need for multiple taxation for treaties to be applied. Some may argue that there are general principles that limit the application of the treaties in cases where there is no double taxation irrespective of the treaty explicitly only requiring liability to tax, or that the 2003 Commentary does indeed introduce such a rule. But to try to derive such a rule from a general principle, or to introduce it through the Commentary, goes against elementary legal principles. What might possibly have happened is that international practice has established such rules as customary law, but in the author's view, there is no consistent practice or *opinio iuris* such as to recognise it. A different issue is the applicability of anti-avoidance rules or principles, but this depends on the source of the rules and its applicability.[414]

The absurdity of relating beneficial ownership with no taxation is shown by the case where the residence country does not charge in accordance with its domestic law, and the source country also does not tax according to its domestic law. In such a case, because neither of the countries charge, the subject could not be considered the beneficial owner and the source country would be enabled to tax. The result is obviously absurd.

A conflicting relevant case on beneficial ownership regarding non-taxation is conduit companies receiving income offset against interest expenses. In this case, no tax is charged even if the intermediary country has a high tax rate. Would this be a non-taxation case and excluded from beneficial ownership? What if interest payments are to be paid to an independent third party in a third country? In these cases, the recipient

[412] 'Report on suggested amendments to Articles 11 and 12' (n 3) pp 13–14.

[413] See above, n 197.

[414] On the application of domestic anti-avoidance rules, see Commentary to Art 1 of 1992, 2003 and 2017 Model Tax Conventions. For a comprehensive study, see V Chand, 'Interaction of Domestic General Anti-Abuse Measures with Tax Treaties' in R Danon (ed), *Base Erosion and Profit Shifting: Impact for European and International Tax Policy* (Schulthess, 2016); V Chand, *The Interaction of Domestic Anti-Avoidance Rules with Tax Treaties: (With Special Considerations for the BEPS Project)* (Schulthess, 2018).

is the beneficial owner unless the above-mentioned characteristics are found. The non-taxation requirement does not stand.

What, in reality, seems to lie behind the reasoning of the Commentary are the misleading 2003 amendments to it on the improper use of tax treaties.[415] First, in 2003, the Commentary elevated the objective of preventing avoidance to a main object and purpose of the treaty. Until 2003, the Commentary subordinated prevention of avoidance and evasion to the main objective of facilitating international trade.[416] Secondly, the Commentary switched from an ambiguous position on compatibility of domestic anti-avoidance rules to almost full compatibility.[417] Finally, and most importantly, it introduced a controversial anti-avoidance rule defined as a guiding principle based on a two-pronged subjective – main purpose to reduce taxation – and objective – to be contrary to the object and purpose of the treaty – test.[418] Probably all these measures underlay the objective of the Commentary to introduce the previously mentioned and controversial downside single tax principle.

Leaving aside legality issues, the problem is that such rules enter a sort of circular reasoning.[419] This is especially true regarding the so-called guiding principle. The transaction is considered abusive insofar as it goes against the object and purpose of the rules. But if the object and purpose of the rules is to allocate tax jurisdiction, which of course limits tax jurisdiction and reduces the tax burden, the reduction of taxation is the consequence of the fulfilment of the object and purpose. Similarly, if the object and purpose of prevention of abuse is taken into account, a transaction would be abusive if contrary to such object and purpose, and it is contrary to such object and purpose if it is considered abusive. There is no test against which it could be analysed except the purpose test proposed by the Commentary as a guiding principle,[420] and such a purpose test has no support apart from the Commentary creating it out of thin air.[421] What is different is that new trends after the BEPS Action Plan have led most treaties to contain a PPT, which in turn may lead in the future to a consistent practice.[422] But in that case, there is an actual rule in the treaty itself – from a customary point it is not yet created – and no rule can be conjured up out of thin air from the object and purpose of the treaty.

[415] OECD (n 387). On 2003 amendments see Zornoza Pérez and Báez Moreno (n 127); B Arnold, 'Tax Treaties and Tax Avoidance : The 2003 Revisions to the Commentary' (2004) 58 *Bulletin for International Fiscal Documentation* 244; Martín Jiménez (n 394); Zimmer, 'Domestic Anti-Avoidance Rules' (n 127).

[416] Compare para 7 of the 1977 OECD Model Taxation and the same paragraph in th e2003 OECD Model Tax Convention. See Arnold (n 415) 248.

[417] Compare paras 7 and 10 of Commentary to Art 1 of the 1977 OECD Model Tax Convention; paras 7–26 of the Commentary to Art 1 of the 1992 OECD Model Tax Convention, especially paras 22–26; and paras 7–26, namely Art 9.2 to 9.6, of the 2003 OECD Model Tax Convention.

[418] See para 9.5 of the 2003 OECD Model Tax Convention.

[419] Arnold (n 415) 249; Zornoza Pérez and Báez Moreno (n 127) 156.

[420] Zornoza Pérez and Báez Moreno (n 127) 156.

[421] Arnold argues, as per the Swiss observation to the 2003 Commentary amendments, that the objective of preventing avoidance was taken out of the thin air: Arnold (n 415) 249.

[422] See Art 29.7 of the 2017 OECD Model Tax Convention, Art 7 of the multilateral instrument, and minimum standard in OECD, *Preventing the Granting of Treaty Benefits in Inappropriate Circumstances, Action 6 – 2015 Final Report* (OECD Publishing, 2015) 18–19. On its interpretation, see Báez Moreno (n 186); Chand (n 186); E Pinetz, 'Use of a Principal Purpose Test to Prevent Treaty Abuse' in M Lang et al (eds), *Base Erosion and Profit Shifting (BEPS)* (Linde, 2016); A Báez Moreno and J Zornoza Pérez, 'The General Anti-Abuse Rule of the Anti-Tax Avoidance Directive' in JM Almudí et al (eds), *Combating Tax Avoidance in the EU* (Kluwer, 2019).

That said, the inconsistent view of the 2003 Commentary on the abuse of tax treaties permeates into the beneficial ownership interpretation. This author wonders whether the actual reasoning of the Commentary lies not in the interpretation of the object and purpose of Articles 10–12 within the tax treaty, but in the new approach to abuse, including the guiding principle and the object and purpose of preventing abuse. If this is the case, this leads to a circular reasoning, as stated above. Source taxation limitation cannot be granted because the transaction was aimed at obtaining such treaty limitation, so it is abusive, and it is abusive because it goes against the object and purpose of the Model of preventing abuse. But if the objective is to avoid double taxation, securing limitation of taxation fulfils the objective. If it is to prevent tax avoidance, the transaction is abusive because it goes against the objective of preventing abuse. And if the object and purpose of the relevant articles (ie Articles 10–12) is accepted, they are simply allocating jurisdiction, so once the tax jurisdiction is defined on the content of such rules, it cannot be said their application is abusive on the basis of going against the objective of precisely allocating tax jurisdiction. Non-taxation is the result of allocation of jurisdiction, which means the object and purpose is achieved.[423] Obviously, this reasoning cannot be sustained. What is different is that the taxpayer achieves an advantageous allocation of tax jurisdiction in an artificial manner. But this is not what the OECD Commentary guiding principle states.

The consequence is that beneficial ownership grounds in the 2003 Commentary are inconsistent, limiting its value. The absence of taxation on nominees and the fact that no double taxation arises can only be taken as examples of the reason why the concept was introduced, but without direct relation to the definition of the concept. In some of the cases to which beneficial ownership applies, this might be the case, but beneficial ownership is not defined by the fact that no actual taxation is granted, as no taxation may occur for several reasons. In some cases, non-taxation would simply derive from the fact of being an intermediary (though some intermediaries may be taxed in some instances). Conversely, beneficial ownership is aimed at resolving the issue that the tax jurisdiction would not be limited because of the status of an intermediary. Contracting states wishing to guarantee limited taxation is granted because of the specific economic relations between both states are only benefiting subjects within such economic relations, not third parties. Only the status of the person economically and legally benefiting from the income, under the above-mentioned conditions, defines the limitation on tax jurisdiction of contracting states.

B. Adding the Conduit Companies Report to the Commentary and the Factual Test

The 2003 amendments also introduce the ideas contained in the 1986 conduit companies report to the Commentary.[424] This was probably a good idea, as it increased legal

[423] Lang (n 197) 29.

[424] See paras 12.1, 8.1 and 4.1, in fine, of the Commentary to Arts 10, 11 and 12, respectively, of the 2003 OECD Model Tax Convention. See also OECD (n 119) para 14.b.

certainty. The report was only included in the full version of the Model; the condensed version, as the most frequently used version of the Model, lacks the content of the report. Its inclusion in the Commentary made it available and made clear its application to the Model to all international tax stakeholders.

Nevertheless, the 2003 amendments did not stop at transferring the report's content to the Commentary, and slight but significant changes to the Model were made. The main change was that conduits and other arrangements may be excluded from the beneficial ownership condition if another person 'in fact' receives the income concerned or when 'as a practical' matter they have very narrow powers.[425] Conversely, the conduit companies report mentions 'functions', or 'powers which render'.[426] Clearly, the conduit companies report was using terms that somehow fall between legal and economic facts.[427] However, the 2003 Commentary uses terms referring purely to facts or economic matters.[428] The new wording may be controversial as it could lead one to think that the factual transfer of income leaves an intermediary excluded from the beneficial owner test.[429] The reference to factual transfers cannot be upheld because, considering the French version, which refers to who actually benefits, it seems to refer to the definition of the actual facts taking place.[430] This, together with the object and purpose analysis, leads beneficial ownership to being considered as a sort of general anti-avoidance rule or substance over form test under the 2003 Commentary.[431] The problem is that this pushes several tax authorities to misunderstand beneficial ownership as a substance over form test because of the reference to the facts.[432]

However, the use of the facts in relation to beneficial ownership was probably also derived from the factual approach adopted by the OECD in the 2003 Commentary. Because the OECD confused the steps in its definition of the facts and qualification of rules, the fact that income has been passed – part of the facts – and whether it qualifies under the beneficial owner test may have been mixed up.[433] The result is that the Commentary apparently introduces facts to the qualification of beneficial ownership, which is incorrect and a reason for denying validity to the commentaries.

In addition, the Commentary's use of the example of conduits may be considered to define the concept, while in fact the reverse is true. Conduits are excluded because are not beneficial owners and it is not the case that beneficial owners are excluded because they are similar to conduits. The Commentary's misleading wording apparently takes a frequent fact pattern that is excluded under beneficial ownership as its definition.

[425] See paras 12.1, 8.1 and 4.1, in fine, of the Commentary to Arts 10, 11 and 12, respectively, of the 2003 OECD Model Tax Convention.

[426] See OECD (n 119) para 14.b.

[427] Collier states powers seem to denote a legal test: Collier (n 125) 690.

[428] ibid; C Du Toit, 'The Evolution of the Term "Beneficial Ownership" in Relation to International Taxation over the Past 45 Years' (2010) 64 *Bulletin for International Taxation* 500, 504.

[429] Collier (n 125) 690. See, eg Vega Borrego (n 65) 86. Stating the term as it stands in the 2003 Commentary limits treaty rules for persons who materially receive the income irrespective of another receiving it as the owner.

[430] See paras 12.1, 8.1 and 4.1 of Commentaires Sur Les Articles Du Modèle De Convention Fiscale.

[431] Vega Borrego (n 65) 86.

[432] Collier (n 125) 703.

[433] See above n 127 et seq and accompanying text.

However, it is only an example, and beneficial ownership stands as was interpreted before.

If beneficial owner is taken with reference to the facts, it becomes a substance over form test, which has already been rejected because it does not correspond with the history and function of the term. And if it is not a substance over form test but refers to factual obligations of passing the income, the rule becomes inapplicable as it will deny beneficial ownership in any subsequent payment.[434]

Some may argue that the Commentary may have intended to change the meaning to a broad economic meaning. However, as Collier argues, if that was the objective, then the concept is not explained clearly enough and it did not make any sense to retain the references to agents and nominees.[435] Collier was right, and the point is that the Committee intended to leave it open so that all countries could fit their divergent interpretations on beneficial ownership into it, which, from a technical and legal point of view, should attract much criticism.[436]

Finally, a controversial wording added to the Commentary and related to the definition of intermediary is the use of 'immediate recipient'.[437] However, this may be confusing, as it may be considered to be related to timing requiring an immediate payment; indeed, the Commentary tried to state the irrelevance for the application of the treaty of the income to be paid directly to an intermediary.[438] As stated, timing is not decisive, but the fact that an economic right accrues is legally related to the reception of the income.

C. The Missing Key in the 2003 Amendments

One may wonder why the OECD changed the Commentary on beneficial owner in such a confusing way and, if it tried only to provide examples, it is unclear whether they were actually needed. The key to understand the 2003 amendments to the beneficial owner test is in the 2002 report 'Restricting Entitlement to Treaty Benefits'.

In that document, the Fiscal Committee recognises the lack of consensus on how beneficial ownership interpretation should be drafted.[439] For some countries, the meaning of the concept depends very much on the facts of the case, and a general meaning would be difficult to achieve. But the report states that the majority of representatives concluded that it would still be helpful to try to clarify the concept, even though changes were intended to be neutral and general. The result, as analysed, is confusing, and was probably simply meant to be few examples.

The discussion probably lacked clarity because by stating that the concept depends on the facts of the case, the representatives were mixing definition of the facts and content of the rule. From a technical point of view, and from any constitutional point of

[434] See above n 58.
[435] Collier (n 125) 690–91.
[436] OECD (n 387) 22 et seq.
[437] See paras 12.1, 8.1 and 4.1, in fine, of the Commentary to Arts 10, 11 and 12, respectively, of the 2003 OECD Model Tax Convention.
[438] Changes in the 2014 substituting immediate by direct stated there was no actual change.
[439] OECD (n 387) 22 et seq.

view, it is at least debatable that a legal body should reject defining a rule because it is unsure which cases it should be applicable to. Facts have to be qualified under the law, rather than the law be defined upon the facts. The only place where the facts should influence definition of the law is before enacting the rule or setting the case law that will govern the cases. Of course, reality is continuously adapting the content of the law, but this does not mean that the OECD can leave the rule fully open to any case, as was done in the 2003 Commentary, especially in tax treaties, where the law is defined by two or more countries, so that a consensus on the definition may be construed. They may perhaps have just wanted to leave it open to make it possible to apply it in future cases.

In the author's view, the reference in the 'Restricting Entitlement to Treaty Benefits' report stating that there was no consensus on the meaning of beneficial ownership denies any value in the 2003 approach. An inconsistent and impracticable commentary that cannot be applied cannot be sustained against a taxpayer, and if the intention was to change its meaning, consensus and clarity should have been achieved. Lacking such consensus and clarity, beneficial ownership stands as it was previously defined.

To the author's view, the 2003 changes did not modify the meaning of beneficial ownership in the way defended in this book.[440] The only change is that after 2003, beneficial ownership covers independent arrangements where the acquisition of the creditor status is unconnected to the obligation to pass the income, as in the conduit companies report, for any treaty based on the 2003 Model, and not just on those taking into account the conduit companies report between 1986 and 2003. In the author's view, until 2003, treaties based on the 1977 OECD Model without consideration of the conduit companies report cannot exclude independent arrangements on consideration of the beneficial owner status.

However, the Commentary was approved and published with this misunderstanding included, leading to an increase in the use of the term beneficial owner in an inappropriate sense that was not resolved until the 2014 amendments.[441] Because there were almost no other anti-avoidance rules in the treaties and the 2003 commentaries supported a broad view, it was an unavoidable temptation for tax authorities to resort to the beneficial owner test to tackle almost any arrangement.[442] Moreover, several scholars saw the 2003 Commentary as confirmation of the already existing interpretation of beneficial owner as a general anti-avoidance rule.[443] What they miss is that the interpretation is derived from a turnaround on the part of the OECD in the general approach to abuse under the guiding principle and the factual approach that the OECD itself previously rejected. If such an approach was previously denied, it means that it was newly introduced in 2003, so cannot be a confirmation that beneficial ownership was already an anti-avoidance rule, because, amongst other reasons, anti-avoidance rules were not a matter of consensus in the 1970s and 1980s and several countries lacked them, and the beneficial owner definition also lacked consensus, as recognised in the 'Restricting Entitlement to Treaty Benefits' report but not in the Commentary. As stated

[440] Collier (n 125) 690.
[441] ibid 703. On how the term has been slightly clarified in the 2014 as opposed to previous versions, see Vallada.
[442] ibid.
[443] Vega Borrego (n 65) 86; Pijl (n 31) 354. Martín Jiménez considers if the 2003 amendments give support to an economic substance interpretation, although he rejects it: Martín Jiménez (n 31) 51.

above, the OECD for a long time held the view that beneficial ownership was a very narrow rule, as explicitly recognised in the conduit companies report.

III. Beneficial Ownership and Allocation of Income in Relation to Hybrid Vehicles

A. The Partnerships Report (1998)

The partnerships report of 1998 addressed the beneficial owner test within the analysis of treaty allocation of income to partnerships and other hybrid entities.[444] The main idea in the partnerships report – despite it being full of inconsistencies – is that allocation of income at the treaty level has to follow the allocation of income rules of the state of residence.[445] The justification is based on considering domestic allocation rules of the residence state as part of the context that should be taken into account to interpreting the allocation rules in the treaty, such as paid to, derived by and similar wording.[446] This makes a significant change to the interpretation of the object–subject connectors in tax treaties before that date. As said by the author elsewhere in this book, such connectors historically derived from the subjective element of the definition of income, jointly with the terms paid to or derived by, which in turn were generally defined by the creditor position of the subject, completely opposite to the new partnerships report view.

This change received significant criticism from many scholars for two main reasons: first, because it changed the rules for interpretation of treaties with no legal support, overriding Article 3(2) and the rules of the Vienna Convention of the Law of Treaties;[447] and secondly, because it introduced a subject to tax test – in the sense of theoretical subjection in the hands of a subject, not of effective taxation – which is not in line with the general liability to tax requirement upon which tax treaties work.[448] If the USA introduced specific rules into their tax treaties for looking into the domestic allocation

[444] OECD (n 173) para 54.

[445] ibid 42 et seq. For analysis on the issue and critiques of the report see P Baker, 'The Application of the Convention to Partnerships, Trusts and Other, Non-Corporate Entities' (2002) 2 *GITC Review*; M Clayson, 'OECD Partnerships Report: Reshaping Treaty Interpretation?' [2000] *British Tax Review* 71; R Danon, 'Conflicts of Attribution of Income Involving Trusts under the OECD Model Convention: The Possible Impact of the OECD Partnership Report' (2004) 32 *Intertax* 210; FA Engelen and FPG Potgens, 'Report on "The Application of the OECD Model Tax Convention to Partnerships" and the Interpretation of Tax Treaties' (2000) 40 *European Taxation* 250; Lang (n 197); H Salomé and RJ Danon, 'The OECD Partnership Report – a Swiss View on Conflicts of Qualification' (2003) 31 *Intertax* 190; J Schaffner, 'The OECD Report on the Application of Tax Treaties to Partnerships' (2000) 54 *Bulletin for International Fiscal Documentation* 218.

[446] OECD (n 173) para 53. R Danon, *Switzerland's Direct and International Taxation of Private Express Trusts* (Université de Genève, Schulthess, 2003) 321.

[447] See Engelen and Potgens (n 445) 268; Clayson (n 445) 74. Also, the Netherlands rejected the Partnerships report, implicitly recognising it was not in line with previous practice. See observation of the Netherlands at para 27.1 of the Commentary to Art 1 of the 2003 OECD Model Tax Convention, rejecting the view of the Partnership report.

[448] Lang (n 197) 37–38, 55. Some authors criticise Lang's approach, stating that the submission to domestic law of residence is not a subject to tax test but submission of the terms derived by or paid to. See J Barenfeld, *Taxation of Cross-Border Partnerships: Double Tax Relief in Hybrid and Reverse Hybrid Situations*, vol 9 (IBFD, 2005) s 5.2.4; Danon (n 446) 320–21.

of the income, and the USA being one of the main advocates of such an idea, it can only mean explicit rules were needed. Otherwise, the USA would have achieved their policy objective of linking tax treaties to allocation through interpretation.[449]

Following the same approach, the partnerships report defined the beneficial owner as the person to whom income is allocated under the laws of the state of residence.[450] This approach follows the one advocated by a number of scholars who state that beneficial ownership has always been a sort of subject to tax test in the sense of tax being allocated, but not effectively.[451] This approach is mistaken for several reasons.[452]

First, if both beneficial ownership and treaty allocation requirements refer to allocation rules of the state of residence, there is no need for the introduction of beneficial ownership.[453] This proves that at least one of them does not have that meaning.

Secondly, as stated, when the UK proposed the introduction of a rule to solve the nominee problem, a subject to tax test was explicitly rejected. As many authors have pointed out, to define treaty allocation rules in accordance with the domestic rules of the state of residence is equivalent to introducing a subject to tax test.[454] The meaning is thus incompatible with the historical origins of the concept.

Thirdly, if this is the natural interpretation of the scope of application of the treaty as derives from *paid to*, *derived by* and *achieved* as part of the context in which to consider application of the treaty, it does not make sense that Article 3 or 4 did not explicitly include any reference. Moreover, such an approach would make Article 4 almost irrelevant, as the main issue would be whether the income was allocated to the subject or not. In this regard, if that were the case, beneficial ownership would not be needed at all, and this has already been rejected.

It might be possible, however, that the OECD intended a change in the meaning for subsequent treaties. The subsequent introduction of a sort of subject to tax understanding in the 2003 Model could support the subject to tax understanding seemingly initiated by the partnerships report.[455] However, as stated, the report upon which the 2003 amendments were made explicitly indicates that there was no consensus on the meaning of beneficial ownership, so it was intended to leave it as broad as possible. To define it according to domestic allocation is a very specific meaning that does not correspond to such broad meaning and lack of consensus. There is a huge mismatch between the 2003 Commentary and the 1998 partnerships report, so, in the author's view, such a change in the meaning never actually took place. The content of the 2010 Collective Investment Reports pointing to the discretion of management and without any reference to allocation of income, which is radically incompatible with a meaning following domestic allocation under the laws of the state of residence, also confirms

[449] See Art 4.1(d) MC USA 1996 and 2006.

[450] OECD (n 173) para 54.

[451] Above, n 195.

[452] Lang (n 197) 60.

[453] ibid 52.

[454] ibid 63. Luc De Broe suggests that beneficial ownership means subject to tax as within the scope of charge, but not necessarily effectively taxed. In other words, that the subject is liable to tax on the specific income. See De Broe (n 32) 721–22.

[455] See paras 12.1, 8.1 and 4.1 of the Commentaries to Arts 10, 11 and 12 of the 2003 OECD Model Tax Convention, and our previous analysis on them.

the author's view.[456] Eventually, the 2014 amendments to the commentary on beneficial ownership said nothing about beneficial ownership referring to allocation rules of the residence state. If that was the case, the opportunity to say so was then. That shows that to interpret beneficial ownership in the sense of an attribution of income rule is not the consensual view.

Finally, on the formal side, the value of the documents where this interpretation is defended is doubtful. On the one hand, authors point to some inconsistencies in the Partnerships Report, which put its whole content into doubt to the point of making some countries, such as the Netherlands, reject its content.[457] If the value of OECD documents is that they are sometimes considered to be qualified doctrine, once their content is shown to be technically defective, that value falls. On the other hand, the value of a meaning that is contained in a report that is not part of the Commentary must be even less than if it were in the Commentary itself. Note that the part of the Partnerships Report dealing with beneficial ownership has not been inserted in the Commentary. If the legal status of the Commentary could be regarded as controversial, one might wonder what the report status is. Nevertheless, if the report is taken into consideration during the negotiations as part of the full version of the Model, it must be considered in the interpretation of the treaty.

The Partnerships Report was probably influenced by the view of the USA. In 1996, just two years before the Partnerships Report, the USA changed the meaning it held on beneficial ownership to submit it to the allocation rules of the state of residence.[458] The Partnership Report may reflect this view, but cannot be said to reflect the view of all OECD Members.

B. The Collective Investment Vehicles Report (2010)

The Collective Investment Vehicles (CIVs) report addressed whether, and under which conditions, such entities would access treaty benefits.

First, the report states that to qualify as a beneficial owner it is irrelevant that neither the vehicle nor the investor is the owner of the assets from a legal perspective where the vehicle has no legal personality.[459] This is grounded on three arguments. The first is that the right of investors in a CIV is not comparable to the right of an investor who directly owns an underlying instrument. An investor can obtain the reimbursement of its income, but it is for the managers of the vehicle to decide how this will be done, or whether they can sell its participation. However, in neither case can they take specific decisions on what to do with underlying assets other than through the

[456] See OECD, *The Granting of Treaty Benefits with Respect to the Income of Collective* (OECD Publishing, 2010) para 35.

[457] Danon (n 445) 222.

[458] See the definition of beneficial owner in Commentaries to Arts 10, 11 and 12 of the Technical Explanation to the 1996 United States Model Tax Convention and compare it to the same commentaries in the 1986 US Model Tax Convention.

[459] See OECD (n 456) para 35.

vehicle management conditions. Secondly, the investors in a widely held CIV have no full ability to decide on buying or selling assets, while a direct investor has full discretion on the management of his or her portfolio. The final argument is that in several countries the tax treatment of both investment vehicles and direct ownership of shares is different.

The main point underlying such assertions is that the report tries to distinguish legal ownership in private law and beneficial ownership in tax treaties. This is simply a reminder, given that it has been consistently held since the introduction of the term, that mere legal ownership does not always support beneficial ownership for tax treaty purposes. The last point is a bit more controversial. Because it relates beneficial ownership to tax treatment, it may be argued it leads to beneficial ownership following allocation of income to some extent.[460] This is incorrect. This author thinks the last one is just the domestic enactment recognising the other two. The point the CIVs Report is trying to make is that domestic tax law recognises that legal ownership is not always relevant in relation to this kind of vehicle as a general policy principle.

Regarding the meaning of the term collective investment vehicle, the report held:

> a widely held CIV, as defined in paragraph 4, should be treated as the beneficial owner of the income it receives, so long as the managers of the CIV have discretionary powers to manage the assets on behalf of the holders of interest in the CIV and, of course, so long as it also meets the requirements that it be a 'person' and a 'resident of the State in which it is established'.[461]

Following the report, a CIV is a beneficial owner if the managers are free to manage the assets and if the vehicle is a person and a resident for tax treaty purposes. To some extent, this interpretation resembles the one backed by some authors pointing to control as the defining element of beneficial ownership.[462] However, the CIVs report points to control of assets, while those authors interpret beneficial ownership as referring to control of income or control of assets, or both.

On the first element of freedom of management, the report assesses an element of beneficial ownership that is key in relation to vehicles: discretion. Under the definition this author supports, one of the key issues is whether the potential intermediary is obliged to pass the income. The CIVs report thus changes the obligation to pass the income to discretion. If an entity has no discretion, then it cannot be said that it is not obliged to pass the income or its economic effect. The income's economic effects are enjoyed directly by the person with such control. However, in this author's view, the definition is not fully correct.

The first reason for this is because it only refers to one circumstance that may indicate lack of beneficial ownership. However, a CIV may have discretion and still be obliged to pass some income. Otherwise, certain types of trusts where the trustee has a certain level of discretion to manage the assets but has to pass the income will qualify as

[460] Fibbe argues that the CIVs report confirms the approach given by the Partnership report: G Fibbe, 'Changes to the OECD Commentary on Collective Investment Vehicles Proposed by the OECD Committee on Fiscal Affairs' (2010) 64 *Bulletin for International Taxation* 138, 144.
[461] OECD (n 456) para 35.
[462] Danon (n 446) 340; Vogel (n 10) 562.

a beneficial owner under the CIVs reasoning.[463] Discretion, thus, is just an indication to assess whether a CIV is a beneficial owner under the ordinary test, but the characteristics of the test remain the same.[464] This is confirmed by the draft report that used discretion as an indication to assess beneficial ownership but not to define it, and by the report itself recognising that beneficial ownership is not different from CIVs and that discretion just refers to some economic characteristics, so the definition of the CIVs report has to be supplemented by the commentaries to Articles 10, 11 and 12.[465]

The second reason is because it points to the asset, and the beneficial ownership test in the treaty refers to the income.[466] What the CIVs report probably intended to argue is that discretion in the management of the assets enables the vehicle to be the beneficial owner of the income. Thus, a vehicle that is fully subject to the decisions of its investors would almost never be considered the beneficial owner. Conversely, a vehicle whose managers are free to decide on the investments may be the beneficial owner if the requirements of the test as previously suggested are not fulfilled. This seems logical because if a vehicle has no discretion, and if its participants can decide at any time on the sale or buying of the assets, from a legal point of view, it is unable to perform the investment function it should have, so it cannot be said to have any independent status from the investors. It is not a matter of whether the vehicle is obliged or not to pass the income; rather, it is that it can hardly be said that a proper CIV exists if no distinction can be made between the decisions of the vehicle and the decisions of the investors.

Such discretion on deciding on the assets has to be distinguished from discretion in the distribution of the income to third parties, which indicates a lack of obligation to pass the income as required by the proposed definition of beneficial ownership in order to deny access to treaty limits. Such an obligation is part of the definition, not alone, but in relation to the rest of the above-mentioned characteristics. However, the wording of the report is not the most appropriate and may lead to mistakes. The report itself corrects the definition given and, in dealing with CIVs, states that such references have to be considered in accordance with the general meaning of beneficial ownership, implicitly recognising that they are not an exception to general requirements.[467]

The other two characteristics seemingly required by the Report to be a beneficial owner – to be a person and a resident – are just improper drafting of the CIVs report.[468] A vehicle may be resident but not a beneficial owner, or may be a beneficial owner but not resident. Even though the literal wording suggests otherwise, what the Report obviously intended to say is that access to treaty rules will be granted if the subject is

[463] Avery Jones et al (n 187) 1; R Danon, 'Clarification of the Meaning of "Beneficial Owner" in the OECD Model Tax Convention: Comment on the April 2011 Discussion Draft' [2011] *Bulletin for International Taxation* 437, 439.

[464] J Vittala, *Taxation of Investment Funds in the European Union* (IBFD, 2004) s 4.4.3.3.

[465] OECD (n 456) para 35.

[466] See Arts 10, 11 and 12 of the Model Tax Convention and compare it to ibid. See OECD, 'Meaning of Beneficial Owner, Revised Discussion Draft' (OECD, 2012) [CTPA/CFA(2012)63] 7.

[467] OECD (n 456) para 35.

[468] See B Da Silva, 'Granting Tax Treaty Benefits to Collective Investment Vehicles: A Review of the OECD Report and the 2010 Amendments to the Model Tax Convention' (2011) 39 *Intertax* 195, 201.

a beneficial owner, but also that the rest of the requirements of the treaty have to be fulfilled, including residence and tax personality.

The inconsistencies in the definition provided by the CIVs report can be understood in two ways. First, it could be argued that they are inconsistent wording behind which lies the general definition of the term. Secondly, it could be said to be another improper definition of beneficial owner because of the different views of the term. Note that the definition provided by the CIVs report and the one provided by the 2003 Commentary have coexisted from 2010 onwards.[469]

As stated, the CIVs report recognises that the definition of beneficial owner is no different from the general one recognised in the Commentary.[470] The CIVs report is just a reminder that the test has to be properly assessed in relation to CIVs because their lack of personality and because legal ownership can sometimes be in the participants can produce mismatches. In this regard, insofar as the CIV has legal personality, beneficial ownership will be tested against the vehicle in the above-mentioned defended definition.[471] However, if it has no legal personality, beneficial ownership could still be tested against the vehicle if it has tax personality or is liable to tax. This does not mean that beneficial ownership depends on tax liability, but that recognition of the person depends on liability; once it is established, then the test will be assessed against such subject. In these cases, tax law overrides civil law, which will ordinarily command ability to pay, and allocates ability to pay to the vehicle. For consistency, beneficial ownership should also follow that approach. In the end, the reference to discretion and the recognition of tax liability by the CIVs report points towards this.

IV. Clarifying What has Always been there: The 2014 Changes to the Commentary

Misunderstandings surrounding beneficial ownership were not solved with the 2003 amendments and the partnerships and collective investment reports. On the contrary, controversy increased because of the mixed effect of the inconsistencies of those documents and the new social attitude against tax planning triggered by the Great Recession. In 2011, the OECD opened discussions to clarify the concept that led to the 2014 changes in the wording of the Model itself, and in the Commentary.[472]

A. Must the Beneficial Owner also Receive the Income to Access Source Tax Limitation Rules?

In treaties signed by the UK before 1977 and in the first drafts of the OECD Model containing the rule, the beneficial ownership condition was included in paragraph 1 of

[469] Collier (n 123) 692.
[470] OECD (n 456) para 35.
[471] Vittala (n 464) s 4.4.3.3.
[472] OECD, 'Clarification of The Meaning of "Beneficial Owner" in the OECD Model Tax Convention Discussion Draft' (OECD, 2011); OECD (n 466); OECD, *2014 Update to the Model Tax Convention* (OECD, 2014).

Articles 10 and 11: 'Interest arising in a Contracting State and paid to a resident of the other Contracting State may be taxed in that other State if such resident is the *beneficial owner* thereof.'[473]

As the legal event of the rule in paragraph 2 was defined as 'such' dividends or interests, the requirement applied to both paragraphs 1 and 2, thereby conditioning allocation to tax jurisdiction to residence, source and limitation of taxation at source. Because making residence taxation dependent on the beneficial owner being a resident of the state made no sense, final drafts left the beneficial ownership requirement simply in relation to limitation of taxation at source.

The introduction of the concept of beneficial owner in paragraph 2 of Articles 10 and 11, and in Article 12.1, but leaving the requirement to pay to or to receive, raised the question early on as to whether the subject has to fulfil both tests in order to qualify for reduced taxation at source:[474]

> 2. However, such dividends may also be taxed in the Contracting State of which the company paying the dividends is a resident and according to the laws of that State, *but if the recipient is the beneficial owner* of the dividends the tax so charged shall not exceed ...[475]

If this were the case, source limited taxation would have only been applicable if the person to whom the income was paid or who received the income was also the beneficial owner. This would leave beneficial owners who were not the person to whom income was paid, such as those receiving through custodians, without access to the treaty rules of the country in which they are resident.

The Commentaries since 1977 state that the rules apply on beneficial ownership that fulfils treaty requirements, irrespective of the income being paid directly to the beneficial owner or through a different person.[476] Moreover, they later clarified this specific issue of the relevance of beneficial ownership and the irrelevance of the recipient in the 2003 commentary.[477]

The *Guinness* case involved a loan from a UK corporation to a Mexican entity.[478] However, the UK corporation ordered the Mexican company to pay back the loan to another company of the group that was resident in the UK. Because both companies were residents in the UK, the court held that they had the right to the reduced rate provided in the Model. The ruling does not deal with the fact of one being the payee and the other the beneficial owner, but implicitly recognises that what is relevant is the residence of the beneficial owner.

However, in 1995, Articles 10 and 11 were amended to eliminate references to *receive* and *paid* on the provisions limiting source taxation. Article 12, however, was

[473] See, eg Arts 11.1, 12.1 and 13.1 of the 1969 United Kingdom–Japan Double Tax Convention; 'Proposals for the amendment of articles 11 and 12 of the draft convention' (n 46) p 9.

[474] Vogel (n 10) 563.

[475] See also Art 11 with a similar wording.

[476] See paras 12, 9 and 4 of Commentaries to Arts 10 to 12 of 1977 OECD Model Tax Convention; Vogel (n 10) 563.

[477] See paragraph 12.2 of the Commentary on Article 10 of the 2003 OECD Model Tax Convention.

[478] *Operadora y Controladora Intercontinental, SA de CV v Administración Especial de Recaudación de la SHCP (Guinness))* [1998] Tribunal Fiscal de la Federación Juicio de Nulidad No 100(20)33/97/20328/96.

only amended in 1998 because a controversy arose about what would be the consequence of not being beneficial owner.[479]

From those changes, apparently the only requirement for reduced taxation was that the beneficial owner was a resident of the state. Still the problem was not solved:

> 1. Dividends *paid by* a company which is a resident of a Contracting State *to a resident of the other Contracting State* may be taxed in that other State.
> 2. However, *such dividends* may also be taxed in the Contracting State of which the company paying the dividends is a resident and according to the laws of that State, *but if the beneficial owner of the dividends* is a resident of the other Contracting State, the tax so charged shall not exceed:[480]

Because paragraph 2 of Articles 10 and 11 referred to 'such dividends', pointing at dividends defined by paragraph 1 – dividends paid to a resident of the other contracting state – and paragraph 1 referred to 'dividends paid to', there was still doubt over whether dividends have to be both paid to or received by the beneficial owner resident in the other contracting state.[481] The commentary made clear that the amendment was done to clarify that conditions to access treaty benefits were to be assessed on the beneficial owner, the income to be paid to him or to another person being irrelevant for the purposes of the treaty between the source country and the country of residence of the beneficial owner.[482]

Changes in the 2014 Model made absolutely clear that access to limits to source taxation contained in Articles 10 and 11 is only dependent on the person being the beneficial owner and a resident of the contracting state:[483]

> 2. However, *dividends paid by a company which is a resident of a Contracting State* may also be taxed in that State according to the laws of that *State, but if the beneficial owner* of the dividends is a resident of the other Contracting State, the tax so charged shall not exceed:[484]

In relation to royalties, such clarification was not needed because there is only one paragraph allocating tax jurisdiction to the residence state, so no controversial interaction between the reference of the second paragraph allocating tax jurisdiction to source arises.

[479] Some countries argued whether Art 21 would be applicable instead of 12 if the subject was not beneficial owner: Meindl-Ringler (n 67) 33.

[480] See also Art 11 of the 1995 OECD Model Tax convention and Art 12 of the 1998 OECD Model Tax Convention.

[481] A few commentators raised the issue of how the article applies where the direct recipient and beneficial owner are in two different states. One commentator suggested that 'if the recipient is not considered the beneficial owner of a dividend, it should in our view be made more explicit in the Commentary which party is the beneficial owner': OECD (n 466) paras 29–30.

[482] It is not irrelevant for the treaty between the source country and the intermediary. See paras 12.2, 8.2 and 4.2 of Commentaries to Arts 10, 11 and 12 of the OECD Model Tax Convention from 1995 and 1998 versions onwards.

[483] OECD, *2014 Update to the Model Tax Convention* (n 472) 7. See F Vallada, 'Beneficial Ownership under Articles 10, 11 and 12 of the 2014 OECD Model Tax Convention' in *The OECD Model Convention and its Update 2014*, vol 90 (Linde, 2015).

[484] See also Art 11, which has similar wording.

The new wording omits dividends having to be paid to a resident of the other contracting state in order to access source taxation limitation. The question is how it relates to previous versions. Is this just a clarification or a modification?[485]

To the author, the consistent position of the OECD Commentary from very early on makes clear that this is just a clarification. However, it is unclear why the Commentary, dealing with the meaning, still gives significant importance to the recipient, even after 2014, which contradicts the explicit statements of the Commentary on the relevance of beneficial ownership.[486] To some extent, the Commentary inherited the original view of the UK on the problem.

B. New Definition? Use and Enjoyment without Being Constrained to Pass the Income

The main changes in 2014 to the beneficial owner test in the OECD Model came in the Commentary. Already existing paragraphs were subject to minor adjustments and renumbering.[487]

Some changes to existing paragraphs simply confirmed what was already there. First, 'immediately received by a resident of a State' was substituted with 'paid direct to', and 'immediate recipient' was replaced with 'direct recipient'.[488] These changes were probably made to resolve the controversy of whether timing played a role defining beneficial ownership and to make it clear that the rule was aimed at making irrelevant the payment and the legal creditor status alone for limitation of taxation at source.

The second change was to clarify that where the Commentary said that beneficial ownership had no narrow technical meaning, it meant it was not defined by the law of a specific country, explicitly excluding it from having the definition it has under law of trusts.[489] The clarification resulted in: (i) confirmation that the concept must be interpreted on its context and cannot be interpreted by submission of the law applying the treaty, especially under Article 3(2); and (ii) confirmation that its international meaning is not derived from equity law. This was already implicit in the Commentary and historical documents, as was argued earlier in relation to the 2003 amendments, and was thus confirmed by the 2014 amendments.[490] Beneficial ownership does have a technical meaning, but it is an international tax meaning that does not correspond to any other rule with the same wording.

It is worth noting on this point that the Commentary includes a footnote indicating that a discretionary trust may be a beneficial owner of income for tax treaty purposes

[485] Navisotschnigg (n 280) s 4.2.3.

[486] See, eg paras 12.4, 10.2 and 4.3 of Commentaries to Arts 10, 11 and 12 of the 2014 OECD Model Tax Convention, where references are made to the direct recipient.

[487] OECD, *2014 Update to the Model Tax Convention* (n 472) 12–21. And compare to para 10 and ss 9 and 4 of the Commentary to Arts 10, 11 and 12 of 2003 OECD Model Tax Convention.

[488] See para 4.1 of the Commentary to Art 10 of the 2014 OECD Model Tax Convention and matching paragraphs of the commentaries to Art 11 and 12.

[489] See paras 12.1, 9.1 and 4, and fn 1, of commentaries to Arts 10, 11 and 12 of the 2014 OECD Model Tax Convention.

[490] See above, n 389 and accompanying text.

even though not recognised as a beneficial owner in equity law.[491] Leaving aside the many nuances arising from whether trustees or beneficiaries are beneficial owners in equity or not before discretion is exercised, this simply confirms what could have been interpreted from previous sources: beneficial ownership in international tax law has a different and independent meaning to the same wording in any other regulations. This means it may or may not match other rules with the same words, depending on the case and the rules involved.

Three new paragraphs were introduced to the Commentary, but the fact that the pre-existing content remains indicates that these new paragraphs were intended to clarify its meaning rather than modify it.[492] The name of the consultation process – 'Clarification of the meaning' – further indicates this.

The first of the new paragraphs defines beneficial ownership in a positive way, as opposed to the previous negative definitions.[493] The second distinguishes beneficial ownership from other anti-avoidance rules.[494] The last one states the difference of the rule from other rules using the same wording but in other contexts, such as exchange of information for tax matters or prevention of crimes.[495]

(i) The Positive Definition: Use and Enjoyment

As stated throughout this chapter, the main doubt since 1977, recognised in the 2002 report on entitlement to treaty benefits, was how to define the main characteristics of beneficial ownership or the common characteristic of agents and nominees that defines the exclusion. The 2014 changes attempted to define them. A new added sub-paragraph (12.4 for the dividends article) states that what is characteristic of agents, nominees and conduits acting as fiduciaries is their right to use and enjoy without being legally or contractually constrained to pass the income.[496] Even though a brave attempt at clarification by the OECD, the solution still leaves many questions open.

The heart of the definition is based on both positive and negative characteristics. The positive one is the right to use and enjoy, the negative is that such right is not constrained. The positive one clearly is related to the ownership abilities of the right to use and enjoy, long-standing core abilities of ownership since Roman *ius utendi*

[491] Footnotes to paras 12.1, 9.1 and 4, of commentaries to Arts 10, 11 and 12 of the 2014 OECD Model Tax Convention.

[492] Two commentators requested 'the OECD to explicitly make clear that the proposed changes solely are a clarification and not in any way a change'. In this respect, another commentator expressed the wish that '[h]opefully, tax administrators and courts faced with the issue for earlier years will recognize the changes as a "clarification" and will have no hesitancy in relying on the new language in resolving pending issues' (the Working Party considers that the changes are indeed a mere clarification of the existing guidance): OECD (n 466) 19. See also The Meaning of Beneficial owner, revised Discussion Draft, Unclassified report, CTPA, Committee on Fiscal Affairs, 25 September 2012 [CTPA/CFA(2012)63] p 19.

[493] See paras 12.4, 10.2 and 4.3 of Commentaries to Arts 10, 11 and 12 of the 2014 OECD Model Tax Convention.

[494] See paras 12.5, 10.3 and 4.4 of Commentaries to Arts 10, 11 and 12 of the 2014 OECD Model Tax Convention.

[495] See paras 12.6, 10.4 and 4.5 of Commentaries to Arts 10, 11 and 12 of the 2014 OECD Model Tax Convention.

[496] See paras 12.4, 10.2 and 4.3 of Commentaries to Arts 10, 11 and 12 of the 2014 OECD Model Tax Convention.

et ius fruendi.[497] The flaws are that civil law countries may be tempted to interpret beneficial ownership in the sense of usufruct or full ownership, which of course was not the case, and the concept does not properly fit within common law countries' distinction between legal ownership and beneficial ownership. In addition, commentators stated it was too vague.[498]

An early draft of the 2014 amendments defined beneficial owner as regards 'full use and enjoyment'.[499] The word full was dropped because commentators argued that discretionary trusts have no use and enjoyment, because tax authorities may get confused in cases of usufructs as limited right to property lacks bare ownership and because it may catch several legitimate cases.[500] Those comments indeed show that to refer to use and enjoyment is flawed.

For instance, in a discretionary trust, the trustee does not normally have the right to use and enjoy but has the right to decide on the use and enjoyment. Its right to use is constrained by its duty to decide who has such right, but until he performs his duty, he is clearly the only person with the right to decide, so no other person could be the beneficial owner in terms of tax treaties, simply because there is no other person.[501] It is not a matter of full or partial rights to use and enjoyment. The trustee in principle has no right to use or enjoy at all in most cases. Also, charities pose a similar issue. Until governing bodies of charities decide on how to use resources, the only subjects who have a right to them are the charity trustees, but they do not have rights to use and enjoy. Without prejudice, those powers are limited by the object of the charity. And clearly charities have the right to apply the limited taxation at source contained in tax treaties.

In the case of civil law countries, usufructuaries have full rights to use and enjoyment. Whilst exercising his or her right, no other person can use and enjoy. The bare or naked owner can only control the right to remain, which does not currently include the right to use and enjoy, but does include a potential future right. It is not a matter of full or partial.

Irrespective of the inclusion of the reference to full or not, many cases would have issues with the reference to use and enjoyment. Vallada points to someone:

> (i) who acquires a house and uses the rental income to pay the mortgage or general use of certain income to meet other costs, (ii) individuals legally obliged to make monthly alimony contributions to a former spouse and (iii) a creditor that obtains a judicial order that 'freezes income of the debtor'.[502]

Also, if use and enjoyment are understood in a strict legal sense, conduit companies would not fall within the exclusion of beneficial ownership, which does not match the clear intention that has been in place at least since the conduit companies report.

[497] Vallada (n 483).
[498] Guttman (n 123) 342.
[499] See para 12.4 and for Art 10 and matching paragraphs for Arts 11 and 12 in OECD, 'Clarification of the Meaning of "Beneficial Owner"' (n 472) 4.
[500] OECD (n 466) paras 8, 12 and 14.
[501] In this case, use and enjoyment is in suspense and the person with the greatest right against others is the trustee, despite not being the final person with use and enjoyment. His right would be overridden once he defines who has the right to benefit from the income or assets. But this is a matter of timing. Before he exercises his duty, he has the greatest right. After he exercises his right, if income or assets are absolutely granted, the beneficiary has the greatest right, including the right to use and enjoyment. See ibid 8.
[502] Vallada (n 483).

Because conduit companies have use and enjoyment, and pass the income under different titles, beneficial ownership would be absolutely irrelevant.

A different approach could be to consider use and enjoyment in an economic sense. This does not seem to be the case intended by the 2014 Commentary, as to use two clearly legal concepts for an economic understanding will only cause misunderstandings, which was precisely what the OECD tried to avoid with the clarification, because such definition would lead to the problems mentioned above on economic interpretation of the term and because the Commentary explicitly refers to the 'right'.[503] Also, the Commentary states that beneficial ownership is compatible with economic substance doctrines, which would be superfluous if beneficial ownership referred to economic rights, as that would imply that the two rules refer to similar content, duplicating the test.[504] On the contrary, beneficial ownership has to have a legal meaning. Danon, a strong advocator for an economic meaning, pleaded for a change to that economic sense during the clarification process, which confirms that he interpreted the drafts and final amendments as they stood as referring to legal use and enjoyment.[505]

The definition used by the 2014 Commentary, however, resembles the definition used in the case law of the *Velcro* and *Prevost* cases of Canada, decided a few years before the amendments to the Commentary were made.[506] It also seems similar to the definition contained in the negotiations of the 1967 tax treaty between the UK and Australia.[507] In both cases, however, use and enjoyment is supplemented by other characteristics. In the case of the Canadian case law, they are risk and control, and in the case of the negotiations between UK and Australia, control.

Taking into account such approaches, the first part of the Commentary definition on the right to use and enjoy cannot be regarded as a proper definition, but is just an additional characteristic that has to be subjected to other characteristics to exclude beneficial ownership as defined in sections I.C and I.D above.[508] Moreover, in the view of this author, it is of very little relevance. What matters is the second part of the definition: being constrained by an obligation to pass the income. But, as shown above, this definition in isolation poses several inconveniences.

(ii) The Negative Definition or Forward Test: Not Constrained by Legal or Contractual Obligation

The commentary does not clarify what types of obligation exclude the beneficial ownership condition. Would a guarantee on the income limiting its use and enjoyment constitute a constraint? In the case of a judiciary claim of a debt against a debtor

[503] See paras 12.4, 10.2 and 4.3 of Commentaries to Arts 10, 11 and 12 of the 2014 OECD Model Tax Convention.

[504] See paras 12.5, 10.3 and 4.4 of Commentaries to Arts 10, 11 and 12 of the 2014 OECD Model Tax Convention.

[505] Danon (n 463) 439.

[506] See *Prevost Car Inc v The Queen* (n 316) 100; *Prevost v The Queen* (n 31) 13.

[507] See Negotiation documents of the 1967 United Kingdom–Australia Tax Convention contained in TNA 40/16741, as quoted by Vann (n 83) 278–79.

[508] Bernstein states use and enjoy cannot be interpreted in a legal sense: J Bernstein, 'Thoughts on the OECD Discussion Paper on Beneficial Ownership' [2011] *Tax Notes International* 49, 51–52. Similarly, stating use and enjoy has to be balanced against the rest of the definition, Vallada (n 483).

with a right to dividends already declared in which the judge rules the garnishment or seizure, is the recipient of the dividends a beneficial owner? The link between reception of income and obligation to pass the income, as well as which types of limitations disqualify the beneficial owner, remains doubtful. In quantitative terms, it is unclear what happens if only part of the income is subjected to limitations while the rest is not.

During the consultations about the 2014 amendments, some commentators argued that the negative definition would cause conflicts for CIVs granting guarantees on their investments. Thus, the final drafting excluded 'obligations that are not dependent on the receipt of the payment by the direct recipient', such as those of the debtor in a financial transaction or those of pension funds or CIVs.[509] This addition partially solves the above-mentioned issue.

It is still unclear whether such exclusions refer to cases where the obligation to pay to the third party remains, even in cases where there is no income received, or if it refers to cases in which the creditor position of the potential intermediary is unconnected to the obligation to pay to the third party. In the first case, only general debts or limits to any property of the subject, such as unconnected loans or guarantees to third parties, would be excluded from the scope of limitation of the rule and enable the subject to be the beneficial owner. In the second, arrangements that specifically relate to certain income but that were not involved in the acquisition of the creditor position would still enable the subject to be the beneficial owner of the income.

The first view is correct. Since the conduit companies report, and retained in the 2014 amendment, beneficial ownership excluded treaty limitation of taxation at source for arrangements independent of the acquisition of the right by the intermediary-creditor as long as they fulfil the rest of the requirements.[510] In the cases of guarantees or unconnected loans, the reason is to obtain finance, while in the case of unconnected treaty shopping arrangements such as a swap to which the obligation to hold the shares is attached, the reason is to access certain rights' effects without less favourable tax consequences. The point is whether the acquisition of the shares, credit or assets from which the income raises is dependent on the obligation to pass the income. And in finance agreements this is not usually the case, but the main object is to obtain finance.

The Commentary states that the 'contractual or legal' obligation to pass the income excludes a beneficial ownership condition. But it would be an inappropriate result for tax treaty purposes to exclude from the beneficial owner status a father who has the legal obligation to pass the income to the son or due to court order. The legal obligation to which the Commentary refers is that derived from a real or contractual right linked to the obligation to receive the income, but not pure independent obligations. The reasoning behind the exclusion of guarantees and financial transactions that are independent from the receipt of income also supports this view.[511] Moreover, in most cases, legal obligations to pass the income directly accruing from the receipt would be derived from a previous arrangement or settlement, so the use of the word legal in relation to the obligation excluding beneficial ownership in the Commentary has to be understood in

[509] See paras 12.4, 10.2 and 4.3 of Commentaries to Arts 10, 11 and 12 of the 2014 OECD Model Tax Convention.

[510] See above, section 5.1.4.

[511] See paras 12.4, 10.2 and 4.3 of Commentaries to Arts 10, 11 and 12 of the 2014 OECD Model Tax Convention.

the sense of the legal consequence of such an arrangement or settlement, and not pure legal obligations such as those of alimony or debts.

In sum, the requirement of the absence of an obligation to pass the income results in the need for the obligation to pass the income being connected to the reason why the right from which the income derives was acquired, as advocated by the author above.

(iii) Relevance of Substance and Facts for Determination of Beneficial Ownership

The commentary states that the obligation to pass the income will normally be derived from the legal documents, 'but may also be found to exist on the basis of facts and circumstances showing that, in substance', the subject has no unconstrained right to the income.[512] This wording raises enormous concern, as it may be interpreted so that beneficial ownership may be excluded just because income is transferred in fact, or it may even be inferred that beneficial ownership implies a substance over form test.[513] Some have even argued that the 2014 amendments were elevating the concept to a general anti-avoidance rule or a sort of economic ownership test.[514]

The term cannot be understood in a factual or substance over form test. The consultation documents show that the addition of the requirement of the obligation to pass the income to be connected to the receipt of the income was also due to this threat.[515] The facts or substance do not define the rule, but they do define the fact pattern that has to be tested and qualified against the rule. And the rule requires a legal obligation to pass the income to exist in order to disqualify the subject as a beneficial owner. If no legal or contractual obligation to pass the income exists, the subject cannot be said to be limited on its right to credit and is thus the beneficial owner.

The possibility of misunderstanding the use of the facts and substance in the Commentary is again derived, as in many cases at the OECD, from the mix of the steps of defining the relevant facts and their qualification under the law.[516] What the Commentary intends to say by referring to the facts is that there are several cases where the obligation is not apparent or is hidden, but a proper analysis of the facts may show there is an obligation to pass the income irrespective of non-existent documents on such an obligation. But this is a matter of proof and not one of the rule.

The use of the substance points to the definition of the facts. It does not refer to a substance over form general anti-abuse rule requalifying the legal consequence, but to substance as a matter of legal fact or proof.[517] If the facts show there is an obligation,

[512] See paras 12.4, 10.2 and 4.3 of Commentaries to Arts 10, 11 and 12 of the 2014 OECD Model Tax Convention.

[513] See Comments on Discussion Draft – Clarification of the Meaning of «Beneficial Ownership» in the OECD Model Tax Convention, United States Council for International Business, 2011, p 3; Clarification of the Meaning of «Beneficial Owner» in the OECD Model Tax Convention, Direction des Affairs Fiscales – Mouvement des Enterprises de France, 2011. Pointing to the need to distinguish beneficial owner from the need of activity or economic substance because of the reference to substance, see Comments on the Public Discussion Draft on Clarification of the Meaning of «Beneficial Owner» in the OECD Model Tax Convention, Federation of European Accountants, 2011, p 1; Comments on Clarification of the Meaning of «Beneficial Owner» in the OECD Model Tax Convention – Discussion Draft, Kim & Chang, 2011, p 2.

[514] Bernstein (n 508) 53; OECD (n 466) para 16; Guttman (n 123) 341–43; Meindl-Ringler (n 67) 74.

[515] OECD (n 466) para 17.

[516] See above, n 128 et seq and accompanying text.

[517] Guttman (n 123) 343 fn 3.

then beneficial ownership may be denied. But the obligation has to exist.[518] And such facts may not be clear in the documents, or may be shown in a covert way to distract or make its qualification more complex for the tax authorities. A substance over form rule in the sense of a GAAR, conversely, recognises legal facts as shown by the taxpayer but redirects the consequence to a different one, ie to the consequence corresponding to the event matching the economic substance of the transaction.

That the Commentary itself states that 'such an obligation' may be derived from the facts implicitly recognises that an obligation has to exist, that no factual payment can be taken into account to deny beneficial ownership and that no requalification of consequence is done through beneficial ownership.[519] The fact that subparagraph 12.6 (of the Commentary to the dividends article) distinguishes beneficial ownership from substance over form GAARs also confirms this.[520] It would be unwise to state that beneficial ownership does not preclude the use of substance over form GAARs if they mean the same.

(iv) Beneficial Ownership is Tested on the Income, not on the Assets

The OECD model and the Commentary have always been seemingly clear on the fact that the beneficial owner test refers to the income and not to the assets from which the income is derived.[521] Nevertheless, a minority of scholars referred to the assets to test the beneficial owner.[522] Maybe the mistake is due to the implicit object–subject allocation rule derived from the definition of each type of income that is largely based on the creditor status of the subject within the relevant legal relationship: shareholder–corporation, creditor–debtor and lessor–lessee.[523] But it is precisely the beneficial ownership condition that tries to overcome such limits and is tested on the income. The 2014 amendment simply clarifies this point.[524] The commentary recognises that beneficial ownership of the assets and income is in most cases in the same person, even though in some cases it would be different and the relevant one would be the income.

The problem in such cases is one of qualification of income. If the creditor is a different person from the beneficial owner of the income – such as in the case of a coupon holder – some may question whether the income obtained by such a beneficial owner can qualify as the relevant type of income.[525] For instance, a dividend obtained by an intermediary who is not the beneficial owner for tax treaty purposes is passed to the beneficial owner who is a resident in a third country under a different arrangement

[518] K Van Raad, 'Report on Beneficial Ownership under the OECD Model Convention and Commentaries' (2011) 3; Vallada (n 483).

[519] See paras 12.4, 10.2 and 4.3 of Commentaries to Arts 10, 11 and 12 of the 2014 OECD Model Tax Convention.

[520] See paras 12.6, 10.4 and 4.5 of Commentaries to Arts 10, 11 and 12 of the 2014 OECD Model Tax Convention.

[521] The only apparent divergence is the Report on Collective Investment Vehicles. See above, s III.B.

[522] Vogel, for instance, states that beneficial ownership is defined by the control or decision on the income and/or assets: Vogel (n 10) 562.

[523] See above, n 100 and accompanying text.

[524] See paras 12.4, 10.2 and 4.3 of Commentaries to Arts 10, 11 and 12 of the 2014 OECD Model Tax Convention.

[525] See Helminen (n 102) 103.

connected to the receipt of the income by the intermediary. That second arrangement may not be derived from a debt claim and could qualify as other income. Similarly, the proceeds from the sale of the coupon of a dividend or interest could not be regarded as dividends as it is not income from shares or debts.[526] In those cases, would Article 21 or Article 10 apply?

In the case of Article 10, insofar as domestic law subjects income from such an arrangement to the same tax treatment as dividends, it does not matter that the subject is the creditor within the shareholder–company arrangement.[527] But in the rest of the cases, if the narrow qualification of the strict interpretation of dividends/interests/royalties is taken, qualification fails. From a legal point of view, the principal of an arrangement where an intermediary who is the creditor has to pass the income is not receiving income from shares/debts/lease. The result would be that the treaty between the country where the payer is a resident and the country where the intermediary is a resident would not limit the source ability to tax, but the treaties between the country of residence of the payer and the country of residence of the intermediary, and between the country of residence of the payer and the country of residence of the principal, cannot qualify the income as such, so Article 21 on other income would probably apply. The result is inconsistent. In the author's view, the beneficial ownership test also implies the effect of transferring the qualification of the income from the intermediary to the beneficial owner of the income once he or she has been identified. This does not work in the reverse way, so the creditor cannot borrow the beneficial ownership condition from the final recipient.

A similar problem arises for the intermediary in relation to Article 12, so once it is established that he is not the beneficial owner, it may be argued that the income falls within Article 21, depriving source taxation rights.[528] In this case, Article 21 will not apply but Article 12 remains applicable, but both countries would have the ability to tax without limit, and the country of the intermediary would have to give a credit or exemption in accordance with Article 23. The fact that the recipient is not the beneficial owner does not eliminate qualification of the income as a royalty, but simply deprives the limitation of taxing rights of the source country. Conversely, Article 21 would only applicable where income does not qualify as any other income from the convention, which is not the case here.

A misconception is also found regarding this part of the Commentary as pointing to the beneficial owner of the income 'as opposed to the owners of the assets'.[529] If this is strictly understood in the sense of formal or legal ownership, beneficial ownership of the asset may be inferred negatively and the income has to be in the same person. It is the author's view that beneficial ownership of the asset may be in a different person without limiting the chance of passing the beneficial owner test of Articles 10–12 on its own requirements in relation to the income. However, if beneficial ownership is

[526] ibid 105.

[527] ibid.

[528] 'Working Party No 1 on Double Taxation, Steering Group on the Revision of the Model Tax Convention, Preparing for the 1995+Update' [DAFFE/CFA/WP1/MR(95)2/REV3], 12 September 1995, Working Party 1, Committee on Fiscal Affairs; OECD Archives, Paris. See also Meindl-Ringler (n 67) 33.

[529] See paras 12.4, 10.2 and 4.3 of Commentaries to Arts 10, 11 and 12 of the 2014 OECD Model Tax Convention.

absolutely vested in a different person, that person would borrow the creditor status of the recipient under the beneficial owner rule just for the purposes of qualifying the income.

(v) The Beneficial Owner in Tax Treaties is not the Ultimate Beneficial Owner nor the Controlling Individual

Because the beneficial ownership wording has spread from common law throughout international rules because of its flexibility, some have mismatched the rule contained in tax treaties with that contained in exchange of information rules or instruments for the prevention of international crimes such as the recommendations from the Financial Action Tax Force.[530] All such rules have different meanings.

This is because, first, they have different contexts. As will be shown in a later chapter, the beneficial owner in prevention of crimes is aiming to discover the individuals trying to launder money.[531] In such cases, what is relevant is to look for the individuals behind the corporations, as corporations are just tools to enable them to commit or finance their crimes. This has nothing to do with ability to pay. In the case of exchange of information, in turn, the objective is to have all possible information of the facts to enable tax authorities to properly qualify and assess taxes. Among such information, the information on the subjects involved is of high importance as personal taxes are assessed on subjects, so one of the first steps is to define whether corporations or subjects are the ones to whom income has to be allocated, and information is essential.[532] But such information does not define substantive tax law obligations to pay – or to exempt – taxes; rather, it simply adds to the information used to define the facts so that rules can be applied on them.

In contrast, beneficial ownership in tax treaties is a substantive provision that allocates income as a requirement for access to treaty benefits. The example of a largely held corporation serves as an example. In money laundering or exchange of information, the beneficial owner(s) would be the CEO or managing officers.[533] Obviously to assess qualification for tax treaty provisions on the status of the individuals controlling the entity does not make any sense, although in some cases the controlling persons and the beneficial owner in tax treaties as interpreted in this work may match. But it cannot be said that the two tests are equivalent because in most cases they are not.

Secondly, and moreover, to use definitions provided in exchange of information or anti-money laundering rules would imply an economic ownership test that the 2014

[530] See, eg *Non Disclosed Taxpayer v Eidgenössische Steuerverwaltung (UBS Case)* (n 138); Gómez in *Molinos Río de la Plata* (n 146).

[531] See FATF, *International Standards on Combating Money Laundering and the Financing of Terrorism & Proliferation* (FATF 2017) 6.

[532] See Art 5.4(b) of the OECD Model Agreement on Exchange of Information for Tax Matters. See also A.1, A.1.1, A.1.2, A.1.3, A.1.4 and A.1.5; A.3; B.1.1 in Global Forum on Transparency and Exchange of Information for Tax Purposes, *Terms of Reference to Monitor and Review Progress towards Transparency and Exchange of Information for Tax Purposes* (Global Forum, 2010) 3–9; Global Forum on Transparency and Exchange of Information for Tax Purposes, *2016 Terms Of Reference To Monitor And Review Progress Towards Transparency And Exchange Of Information On Request For Tax Purposes* (Global Forum, 2016) 3–10.

[533] See i.i.iii in Interpretative note to Recommendation 10 in FATF (n 531) 60.

Commentary itself implictly rejected and is technically flawed for the above-mentioned reasons.[534] If such an approach is taken, no corporation, trust, partnership or any other entity would ever qualify for tax treaty purposes because those entities are usually controlled by the shareholders or directors, so the beneficial owner will always be a different person from the entity or arrangement itself, which is clearly not in line with the intention of the clause or how tax treaties work.

(vi) Beneficial Ownership is not a General Anti-avoidance Rule but does not Limit their Use: Action 6 Report

Once the Commentary provides for a definition of beneficial ownership, the issue of its relationship with other rules arises. The Commentary points out that beneficial ownership and other anti-avoidance rules may overlap on the same cases, and the former does not preclude the use of the latter.[535] The first point is clear, but the second needs additional nuances.

In fact, beneficial ownership may overlap in certain cases with other anti-avoidance rules, for example, in the case of an intermediary who is artificially interposed with little substance. In such an event, if the intermediary fulfils the negative definition of beneficial ownership, he or she will not be able to access limited taxation at source. In addition, if a substance or artificiality test is applicable, the case will consequently fall under a different rule.[536] It is true that both beneficial ownership and the anti-avoidance rule are applicable to the same case, but what the Commentary does not specify are the several outcomes that may be the result of such an overlap, and by plainly stating that beneficial ownership does not limit other rules, it may mistakenly lead to the thinking that GAARs are always applicable on top of beneficial ownership. This will depend on whether the results of the two rules are conflicting or not and, if they are, which rule prevails according to the relationship between them.

In this regard, it is relevant that the beneficial ownership amendments explicitly pointed out that the changes in the Commentary on the rule do not preclude or limit the conclusions of what at the time was ongoing work on Action 6 of the BEPS Action Plan, which was approved a year later.[537] This Action, among other issues, established the OECD general framework on the relationship between anti-avoidance rules and introduced two new highly relevant anti-avoidance rules in tax treaties.[538] The analysis of beneficial ownership, then, needs to be supplemented with the analysis of the Action 6 Final Report of 2015.

[534] See paras 12.6, 10.4 and 4.5 of Commentaries to Arts 10, 11 and 12 of the 2014 OECD Model Tax Convention.

[535] See paras 12.6, 10.4 and 4.5 of Commentaries to Arts 10, 11 and 12 of the 2014 OECD Model Tax Convention.

[536] Although with several inconsistencies, this is the approach adopted by the Court of Justice of the European Union, which states that exemption under the Interest and Royalties Directive can be denied on the basis of beneficial ownership or abuse of rights, that both are alternatives and that the one does not presume the other. See *N Luxembourg 1 and others v Skatteministerie (and joined cases)* (n 53) 138.

[537] See OECD, *2014 Update to the Model Tax Convention* (n 472) 2.

[538] See OECD (n 422) 78 et seq. See also paras 54 et seq of Commentaries to Art 1 of the 2017 OECD Model Tax Convention.

However, before turning to the report, the main clear outcome of that paragraph in the 2014 Commentary on beneficial owner is the implicit recognition that beneficial ownership is not a general anti-avoidance rule.[539] The commentary states that it only covers some types of avoidance and that it does not preclude others, such as substance over form, closing a long-standing discussion which had gone on since the introduction of the term.[540] If both rules are applicable and they cover different arrangements, some of them matching and some of them not, then it is recognised that they have different scopes, so beneficial ownership cannot mean substance over form or other anti-avoidance rules.

Despite some authors claiming that the 2014 amendments left open whether beneficial ownership referred to economic substance because of the reference to substance in the definition of obligations excluding beneficial ownership, it becomes clear that beneficial ownership does not refer to such rules.[541] This implicit recognition, together with the above analysis of the role of substance in defining obligations that exclude beneficial ownership, creates a complete clear statement that beneficial ownership is not economic substance.

V. Beneficial Ownership and the Post-BEPS Era: New Rules and Conflicts between Beneficial Ownership and the PPT and LOB Tests

So far, beneficial owner has been the only treaty-based anti-avoidance rule. Moreover, the doubts on the use of domestic anti-avoidance rules in tax treaty cases made it one of the very few anti-avoidance rules applicable in most treaties. The BEPS Action Plan changed the landscape on prevention of what has been called aggressive tax planning.[542]

In the post-BEPS era, beneficial ownership is just another anti-avoidance rule among a significant number, and probably a weak one compared with the others. The BEPS Action Plan has reinforced recharacterisation of transactions within transfer pricing rules, strengthened the resistance of transfer pricing rules themselves against tax planning, introduced a new limitation on benefits and the principal purpose test, consolidated the view that domestic anti-avoidance rules are almost always compatible with treaties, strengthened Controlled Foreign Corporations rules and established

539 Vallada (n 483).

540 See paras 12.6, 10.4 and 4.5 of Commentaries to Arts 10, 11 and 12 of the 2014 OECD Model Tax Convention.

541 See above nn 513 and 514.

542 See the results of the Action Plan on Base Erosion and Profit Shifting and the Inclusive Framework at www.oecd.org/tax/beps/, www.oecd.org/ctp/beps-actions.htm and www.oecd.org/tax/beps/beps-about.htm. For analysis of the Action Plan and outcomes, see R Danon (ed), *Base Erosion and Profit Shifting (BEPS)* (Schulthess, 2016); M Lang (ed), *Base Erosion and Profit Shifting (BEPS)* (Linde, 2016); JM Almudí Cid, JA Ferreras Gutiérrez and PA Hernández González-Barreda (eds), *El Plan de Acción Sobre Erosión de Bases Imponibles y Traslado de Beneficios (BEPS): G20, OCDE y Unión Europea* (Aranzadi, 2017); Brauner, 'BEPS: An Interim Evaluation' (n 408).

several other anti-avoidance measures.[543] This has probably taken the pressure off the beneficial owner rule. While previously states had incentives to interpret beneficial ownership as a broad anti-avoidance rule as the only available rule, now other, more powerful, measures exist.

From a policy perspective, the new scenario will probably help to consolidate the explicit narrow scope of the rule clarified by the 2014 changes as there is less need to resort to it to tackle tax avoidance.[544] Moreover, if beneficial ownership is misinterpreted as a broad anti-avoidance rule in the sense of a purpose or economic test, it would largely duplicate the scope of such new GAARs or principles, which makes little sense.[545] But at the same time, as the pressure will now be on the PPT and domestic GAARs as broad anti-avoidance rules, and to LOBs, beneficial ownership may have lost its significance.[546] As a primitive and narrow rule, beneficial ownership only covers a few treaty-shopping cases, while the PPT would cover many of those covered by beneficial ownership and much more. The result is that even though beneficial ownership would help to solve treaty shopping through intermediaries, new anti-avoidance rules would also solve it, so beneficial ownership may become superfluous for most cases in the new scenario.[547] In this regard, the discussion on whether beneficial ownership should be extended to other articles loses significance.

In some specific cases, however, beneficial ownership may be of help. An example is found in protected cell companies (PCCs). Some authors have raised doubts as to whether LOB and PPT tests will work properly with PCCs, because the whole company can fulfil the criteria of such rules while the relevant cell does not.[548] The problem is that the only existing person fulfilling the criteria is the company, and the cell does not exist *ad extra* in theory, and rules cannot be applied in relation to something that does not exist. In cases where the cell benefits a resident in a third country and passes the income, beneficial ownership may tackle the structure.

From a legal perspective, beneficial ownership now cohabits with other rules, and the relationship between all of them may raise new controversies.

The Action 6 Final Report of the BEPS action plan established the introduction of a principal purpose test and limitation on benefits rules, and defined the OECD viewpoint on interaction between the different anti-avoidance rules.[549] Some issues arise: first, the relationship between beneficial ownership and domestic anti-avoidance rules;

[543] See, among others, OECD (n 422); OECD, *Aligning Transfer Pricing Outcomes with Value Creation, Actions 8–10 – 2015 Final Reports, OECD/G20 Base Erosion and Profit Shifting Project* (OECD Publishing, 2015); OECD, *Designing Effective Controlled Foreign Company Rules, Action 3 – 2015 Final Report* (OECD Publishing, 2015).

[544] Chand (n 350) 119; R Danon, 'Treaty Abuse in the Post-BEPS World: Analysis of the Policy Shift and Impact of the Principal Purpose Test for MNE Groups' (2018) 72 *Bulletin for International Taxation* 31, 35; C Elliffe, 'The Meaning of the Principal Purpose Test: One Ring to Bind Them All?' (2019) 11 *World Tax Journal* 48, 72; Navisotschnigg (n 280) 4.3.6.

[545] Chand (n 350) 119. Danon states even when beneficial owner is interpreted in a broad sense, it does not match the PPT. See Danon (n 544) 32, 54.

[546] Chand (n 350) 119; Meindl-Ringler (n 67) 380.

[547] On how the application of GAARs would make beneficial owner almost irrelevant, see. specifically in relation to PPT, Chand (n 350) 119.

[548] S Swain, 'Can PPT-LOB Clause Plug the Loopholes Inherent in PCC Entities?' (2019) Kluwer International Tax blog http://kluwertaxblog.com/2019/05/29/can-ppt-lob-clause-plug-the-loopholes-inherent-in-pcc-entities/.

[549] See above nn 422 and 538.

and secondly, the interaction of beneficial ownership and the new treaty-based anti-avoidance rules, namely the PPT and LOB.

On the first point, the BEPS Action Plan amendments to the Commentary furthered the 2003 idea that, in general, domestic anti-avoidance rules do not conflict with tax treaties.[550] Four arguments support this approach. First, the 2015 Action 6 Final Report states that as taxes are applied in domestic tax law, abuse of tax treaties can also be seen as abuse of domestic tax law, so domestic rules are applicable.[551] This approach is a development from the criticised factual approach of the 2003 Commentary, which went a step further, stating that the facts upon which treaties are applicable are defined by domestic anti-avoidance rules.[552] Although the new approach seems slightly better, it is still highly debatable. Secondly, treaties authorise the use of domestic anti-avoidance rules in several cases, submit definitions to domestic rules or explicitly authorise them.[553] Thirdly, treaty interpretative rules and other domestic doctrines may include rules or principles that reject the application to abusive cases – the so-called interpretative approach.[554] Among them, the above-mentioned guiding principle should be highlighted.[555] And fourthly, use of domestic anti-avoidance rules is justified if there is a PPT or LOB in the treaty, or on the basis of the existence of the guiding principle.[556]

The consequence for beneficial ownership would be, in the view of the OECD commentaries, that the application of beneficial ownership does not conflict at all with domestic anti-avoidance rules, and both would be applicable to the same case either because beneficial ownership applies once the anti-avoidance rule defines the facts – the factual approach – because submission of definitions through Articles 3(2) or 10.3 leads to domestic anti-avoidance rules, or because international or domestic interpretation rules deny access to the treaty before the beneficial owner test is applied or even after it. But in the author's view, the Commentary view is completely misleading, even though the result stating the compatibility may be correct.

The three arguments can be rejected. The factual approach misunderstands the steps of definition of the facts and qualification, as previously stated, and begins to be a common misconception in the OECD.[557] Simulation rules can of course be applied to define the facts, but those are not anti-avoidance rules.[558] The interpretative reasoning

[550] See OECD (n 422) 82, para 24; para 71 of Commentaries to Art 1 2017 OECD Model Tax Convention.

[551] See ibid 80 and 84, paras 11 and 26.5; paras 58 and 78 of the Commentary to Art 1 of the 2017 OECD Model Tax Convention.

[552] See paras 9.2 and 22.1 of the Commentary to Art 1 of the 2003 OECD Model Tax Convention. See also Zornoza Pérez and Báez Moreno (n 127); Arnold (n 415); Zimmer, 'Domestic Anti-Avoidance Rules' (n 127); S Van Weeghel, 'General Report' in *Tax Treaties and Tax Avoidance: Application of Anti-Avoidance Provisions* (Kluwer, 2010); Chand, *The Interaction of Domestic Anti-Avoidance Rules with Tax Treaties: (With Special Considerations for the BEPS Project)* (n 414) 219 et seq.

[553] See OECD (n 422) 82–83, paras 25–26; paras 72–73 of the Commentary to Art 1 of the 2017 OECD Model Tax Convention.

[554] See OECD (n 422) 80–81, 83–85, paras 12, 26.2 and 26.5; paras 59, 75 and 78 of the Commentary to Art 1 of the 2017 OECD Model Tax Convention.

[555] See OECD (n 422) 81, para 14; para 61 of the Commentary to Art 1 of the OECD Model Tax Convention, para 9.5 of of the Commentary to Art 1 of the OECD Model Tax Convention.

[556] See OECD (n 422) 83–84, paras 26.1 and 26.4; paras 74 and 77 of the Commentary to Art 1 of the OECD Model Tax Convention. See also para 9.5 of the Commentary to Art 1 of the OECD Model Tax Convention.

[557] Zornoza Pérez and Báez Moreno (n 127) 133 et seq; Arnold (n 415) 251–252.

[558] See above n 128 et seq and accompanying text.

also fails because treaties have to be interpreted according to the Vienna Convention on the Law of Treaties and international law that does not (yet) recognise anti-avoidance interpretative rules.[559] Domestic interpretative anti-avoidance rules can be rejected because in most cases they are not interpretative rules applicable to the whole system, but actual rules despite being derived from the judiciary because of their legal tradition. And the guiding principle and good faith principles are built up in the air, with little or no legal support.[560]

Regarding the submission reasoning, it is not that they solve conflicts; rather, if the rules are properly applicable, it is the ordinary application of the treaty.[561] If the treaty itself is submitting, there is no conflict but normal interpretation. Lastly, regarding the PPT and LOB as justification for domestic anti-avoidance rules, again, if they are applied, they are just the ordinary application of the treaty, and not justification of another rule.[562] In addition, it may be the case that such rules and domestic rules do not match in their scope of application, so of course the domestic rule cannot extend denial of treaty rules beyond the limits of the PPT and LOB.

What the Commentary is seemingly trying to do is to create and spread a state of mind where treaties and anti-avoidance rules do not conflict at all. This is clearly shown when the Commentary states that conflicts 'will be avoided'.[563] Is the Commentary inducing an avoidance of conflicts or establishing an 'aggressive conflict avoidance' concept?

Two issues must be distinguished. The first one, depending on the event and scope of the rule, is whether they actually conflict. The second, if both rules are in principle applicable and lead to different results, is how they relate to each other, and how they fit into the relevant or relevant legal systems.

On the first one, conflicts actually exist when two rules are applicable to the same facts and they lead to different solutions,[564] for instance, if an intermediary at the treaty level is excluded from the benefit but a domestic rule provides that intermediaries will always get the same tax treatment of the principal. But is this the case of so-called general anti-avoidance rules and other anti-avoidance rules?

In the author's view, this is not normally the case. Normally, so-called specific anti-avoidance rules put the spotlight on a characteristic of a transaction, while so-called general anti-avoidance rules look at artificiality, purpose or substance. Both refer to

[559] See above n 350 and accompanying text.

[560] See Arnold (n 415) 249; Zornoza Pérez and Báez Moreno (n 127) 156.

[561] Chand, 'Interaction of Domestic General Anti-Abuse Measures with Tax Treaties' (n 414) 122.

[562] ibid.

[563] Baker interprets the Commentary as providing that such conflicts may often be avoided by applying a detailed analysis of the operation of the provisions. This seems to suggest that for the OECD and the UN there is always a way in the treaty to achieve the same result as applying domestic rules. See P Baker, 'Improper Use of Tax Treaties, Tax Avoidance and Tax Evasion', *United Nations Handbook on Selected Issues in Administration of Double Tax Treaties for Developing Countries* (United Nations, 2013) 396.

[564] Even though such distinction is broadly accepted, there is no absolute consensus on their precise definition and content. See ibid; G Hughes, 'Rules, Policy and Decision Making' (1968) 77 *Yale Law Journal* 411, 419; J Raz, 'Legal Principles and the Limits of Law' (1972) 81 *Yale Law Journal* 823, 838; R Dworkin, *Taking Rights Seriously* (Harvard University Press, 1978) 22 et seq; HLA Hart, *The Concept of Law* (Clarendon Press, 1994); SJ Shapiro, 'The "Hart–Dworkin" Debate: A Short Guide for the Perplexed' (2007) Public Law and Legal Theory Working Paper Series 17, fn 32; R Alexy, *A Theory of Constitutional Rights* (Oxford University Press, 2010) 45.

different events. Thus, where some authors suggest that specific anti-avoidance rules prevail over general anti-avoidance rules, this author cannot agree.

The first reason is because in most cases there is no conflict at all, as they are based on different facts. Secondly, in the author's view, the *lex specialis* principle as a rule of conflict is nothing more than a prejudice that is accepted because of its long-standing application over centuries, but with little technical ground.[565] None of the definitions suggested actually have a solid reasoning that may frequently lead to the same result. The result is that if both rules apply, they are based on different factual events and they lead to different results, we will need to resort to conflict rules defined by the relationship between the relevant rules.[566]

The second reason depends on how the relevant legal system defines the relationship between tax treaties and domestic law, and then how the relevant system defines relationships between different conflicting rules.[567] If a specific country defines its system as monistic, then the issue becomes how different rules interact within such a system.[568] If the country is a dualistic one, then the issues are both how the international rules and the domestic system interact, and how the rules interact with each other within each system.[569]

The result is that such conflicts have to be solved under specific conflict rules provided by the relevant rules or legal system (eg Article 21.2 of the Model) or by the constitutional rules involved (*lex superior*, *lex posterior*, etc).[570] The latter will provide general rules to determine which of two rules prevails where there is a conflict between them.

For instance, if constitutional rules provide that treaty rules prevail over domestic law in cases of conflict, domestic anti-avoidance rules are not applicable. The result on the potential conflict (no actual conflict arises) is that the domestic rules do not apply.

The case turns differently if constitutional rules set treaty rules and domestic rules at the same level and part of the same legal system, such as in dualistic countries once the treaty has passed into domestic legislation. In these cases, anti-avoidance rules may be applicable if their scope of application is the whole tax system, including tax treaties if they have passed into domestic legislation.

In these cases, only if rules are based on the same event, completely or partially, but lead to a different result will there be an actual conflict. This is the case in previously

[565] Papinianus is considered one of the first sources supporting the *lex specialis* principle: Papinianus in *Digestus* 50.17.80. Rejecting the *lex specialis* principle or questioning its content in different fields, see A Lindrjoos, 'Addressing Norm Conflicts in a Fragmented Legal System: The Doctrine of Lex Specialis' [2005] *Nordic Journal of International law* 27, 64; N Prud'homme, '*Lex Specialis*: Oversimplifying A More Complex and Multifaceted Relationship?' (2007) 40 *Israel Law Review* 356.

[566] See Dworkin (n 564) 27; Alexy (n 564) 49.

[567] For the systems used in different countries, see MD Evans, *International Law* (Oxford University Press, 2014) 419; MN Shaw, *International Law*, 7th edn (Cambridge University Press, 2014) 94.

[568] See, among monist authors, H Kelsen, *Pure Theory of Law* (University of California Press, 1970); H Lauterpacht, *International Law: Collected Papers of Hersch Lauterpacht*, vol 2 (Cambridge University Press, 1975) 238 et seq.

[569] Among dualistic scholars, see D Anzilotti, *Corso Di Diritto Internazionale Lezioni* (1923). This seems to also be the case for Triepel & Strupp. See also JG Starke, 'Monism and Dualism in the Theory of International Law' (1936) 17 *British Yearbook of International Law* 66; G Sperduti, 'Dualism and Monism' (1977) 3 *Italian Yearbook of international Law* 31.

[570] See Alexy (n 564) 49; Dworkin (n 564) 27 et seq.

mentioned dualistic countries. But if a general anti-avoidance rule and a specific rule refer to different facts, there is no conflict at all. In any case, the point is that specific analysis of the content of the rules involved and the relevant legal systems is needed, and no general statements such as those provided by the OECD can be made in such a broad sense.

In relation to beneficial ownership, in both the cases where the treaty authorises domestic general anti-avoidance rules and where the country's constitutional system puts the treaty at the same level of domestic law, there is no conflict at all. Beneficial ownership denies access to treaty rules because some of the facts – to transfer the economic benefit of the income, be bound to do so, etc – that were considered by the legislator who made the case deserved to be excluded from the legal consequence – treaty rules. Where a principal purpose or artificiality test denies access to treaty rules, it is because other facts – purpose of the arrangement, artificiality – were judged by the legislator as deserving of being excluded from the legal consequence. In both cases, the legislator set a consequence based on some facts and, no matter whether both or just one of them is present, the consequence in this case is their exclusion. Both refer to different facts, and slightly different consequences.[571] Consequently, the author's viewpoint is that if there is no rule excluding the application of either of them, whether constitutional – such as *lex superior* – or specific, and both rules are within the same legal system and level, beneficial ownership and GAARs would be applicable at the same time. As they look to different events, in the author's view, there is no conflict between them at all. And where the treaty does not authorise domestic rules and the treaty prevails, then domestic rules are not applicable, so no actual conflict arises.

If, however, a domestic general rule states that all tax rules have to be applied under an economic ownership view, this does not correspond to beneficial ownership in the tax treaty, and if both that rule and the treaty are constitutionally at the same level, such as in some dualistic countries, there would be an actual conflict. In this case, following Dworkin or Alexy, the conflict has to be resolved by resorting to the rule of conflict, which can either be constitutional or specific, and explicit or implicit.[572] Normally, interpretation will lead one to state which rule shall prevail.

The analysis of the relationship at treaty level between beneficial ownership, the principal purpose test and the limitation on benefits rule will also lead to similar results.

First, on the relationship between beneficial ownership and the principal purpose test, as both are based on the same legal order, ie both are contained in the treaty, in principle both are applicable from a constitutional conflict rule point of view. Then, turning to their legal event, both are clearly referring to different issues: the principal purpose test to the purpose of the transaction, the beneficial owner to the above-mentioned characteristics. Thus, there is no conflict at all and, absent any exclusion set by the legislator, both remain applicable.[573] The limitations to source taxation in Articles 10–12 will

[571] Danon (n 544) 31–32.

[572] See Alexy (n 564) 49; Dworkin (n 564) 27 et seq.

[573] Danon implicitly recognises that there is no conflict by stating beneficial ownership does not match PPT, apparently irrespective of considering it a broad or narrow rule. See Danon (n 544) 54. Also, Meindl-Ringler implicitly recognises this by stating that the LOB and PPT rules have loopholes that beneficial ownership may cover, although interpreting the beneficial owner rule in a different sense to the author's view. Meindl-Ringler (n 67) 348, 379 et seq.

be excluded where a subject does not fulfil the beneficial owner characteristics laid out in Articles 10–12; the arrangement must, as one of the principal purposes, obtain the advantage of such articles, and is not in accordance with the object and purpose of such provisions, if provided by Article 29 – either of the relevant treaty or the Multilateral Instrument (MLI), or both. The legislator considered both facts as deserving denial of treaty rules consequences, and nothing precludes each from operating independently of each other.

Secondly, on the relationship between beneficial ownership and the limitation on benefits rules, the same reasoning applies. As limitation on benefits and beneficial ownership refer to different facts, each of them judged as deserving access or not to the treaty rules by the legislator on their own characteristics, both are applicable at the same time to the same case irrespective of each other.

VI. The 2019 United Nations Update Draft

The UN subcommittee did not include the 2014 amendments to the beneficial ownership meaning because no change in the Model was made between 2011 and 2017.[574] The introduction of Article 12A on technical fees in the United Nations Model (UN Model) in 2017 carried on the 2014 update to the beneficial owner to the UN model.[575] Nevertheless, this was done only in relation to Article 12A because its commentary was new and it made no sense to include old commentary.[576] However, the Commentary on beneficial ownership on Articles 10, 11 and 12 in the UN Model has so far maintained the content it had in the OECD Commentary before 2014.

In 2019, the Committee of Experts on International Cooperation in Tax Matters decided to update the UN Model and Commentary on the beneficial ownership rule in relation to Articles 10–12 following the OECD 2014 update.[577] The changes almost exactly transfer what was amended in the OECD changes. The only significant difference follows the fact that Article 12 of the OECD Model only allocates tax jurisdiction to the residence country, whereas the UN Model establishes that shared taxation with limited taxation at source is established, as in Articles 10 and 12 of both Models.[578] The commentary to Article 12 is adapted in the UN Model to such case.

Because this author considers that the interpretation of beneficial ownership is the same in all models since 1977, except in the issue of unconnected obligations, the update makes no difference, but constitutes a mere clarification.

[574] Committee of Experts on International Coperation in Tax Matters (n 32) 5, para 16.

[575] See paras 52 et seq of Commentary to Art 12A of the UN Model Tax Convention.

[576] Compare paras 52 et seq of Commentary to Art 12A, and para 13 of the Commentary to Art 10 of the UN Model Tax Convention, and respective paragraphs in commentaries to Art 11 and 12.

[577] Committee of Experts on International Cooperation in Tax Matters (n 32).

[578] Compare Art 12 of both the OECD and UN Model Tax Convention.

6

Beneficial Ownership and EU Law

I. Beneficial Ownership in the Interest and Royalties Directive: The Danish Cases

The obstacle of multiple taxation for the internal market, together with divergences in tax rules and treaties between Member States, led to the enactment of the Parent-Subsidiary Directive in 1990, and of the Interest and Royalties Directive (the Directive) in 2003.[1] Because the Interest and Royalties Directive was aimed at eliminating juridical multiple taxation and the OECD Model Tax Convention (the Model) was the long-standing standard for such purpose, the Directive borrowed part of its definitions from the Model.[2] This included the beneficial owner requirement, so the doubts on the meaning of the concept also entered EU Law.

[1] The obstacle of multiple taxation in direct tax matters and divergences in tax rules for the development of the Internal Market has been discussed since the beginnings of the European Communities. Some proposals were issued, but none of them succeeded until 1990 and 2003, on dividends and on interest and royalties, respectively. See *The EEC Reports on Tax Harmonization: The Report of the Fiscal and Financial Committee and the Reports of the Sub-Groups A, B and C (Neumark Report)* (IBFD, 1963); AJ Van der Tempel, *Corporation Tax and Individual Income Tax in the European Communities* (Office for Official Publications of the European Communities, 1970) 3; O Ruding, *Report of the Committee of Independent Experts on Company Taxation.* (Office for Official Publications of the European Communities, 1992) 11–12. See also Proposal of 16 January 1969 for a Directive on the common tax arrangements applicable to parent and subsidiary companies in different Member States; Proposal of 18 July 1978 for a Council Directive on the application to collective investment institutions of the Council Directive concerning the harmonization of systems of company taxation and of withholding taxes on dividends; Proposal for a Council Directive on a common system of taxation applicable to interest and royalty payments made between parent companies and subsidiaries in different subsidiaries in different Member States, COM (90) 571 final of 6 December 1990; Proposal of 4th March 1998 for a Directive to eliminate withholding taxes on payments of interest and royalties between associated companies of different Member States, COM (98) 67; Council Directive 90/435/EEC of 23 July 1990 on the common system of taxation applicable in the case of parent companies and subsidiaries of different Member States, now Council Directive 2011/96/EU of 30 November 2011 on the common system of taxation applicable in the case of parent companies and subsidiaries of different Member States; Council Directive 2003/49/EC of 3 June 2003 on a common system of taxation applicable to interest and royalty payments made between associated companies of different Member States; B Terra and P Wattel, *European Tax Law* (Kluwer, 2005) 601, 757.

[2] COM (98) 67 (n 1) pp 6, 8; Report on the proposal for a Council Directive on a common system of taxation applicable to interest and royalty payments made between associated companies of different Member States, COM (98) 0067 – C4-0195/98 – 98/0087(CNS), p 12. Although the reports mention the use of the Model to draft some definitions, it is not stated in relation to beneficial ownership; however, it is clearly derived from the Model. The final definition of the Directive is not exactly the same as the one in the Commentary to the Model, but the definition contained in the first draft of the Directive used almost exactly the same words from the Commentary of 1977, clearly showing that it was borrowed from there. Article 3 of the Proposal for a

A. The Definition of Beneficial Ownership in the Interest and Royalties Directive

The exemption for source taxation provided by the Interest and Royalties Directive is conditional on the subject or permanent establishment resident or located in a Member State being the beneficial owner of the income.[3] Thus, an important point is to define which relationship is needed to qualify for being a beneficial owner, in order that the exemption is applicable. On this point, although borrowed from the OECD Model and its Commentary, the Directive adds nuances. The main definition given by the Directive, the one provided for corporations, although inspired by the Model, does not fully match it. In addition, the Directive distinguishes between the beneficial owner definition for companies and another one for permanent establishments, while the OECD Commentary only provides one.[4]

The first definition, for corporations, is largely based on the OECD commentary example as it stood prior to 2003, and states that a company shall be treated as beneficial owner if receiving the income for its own benefit and not as an intermediary, such as an agent, trustee or authorised signatory, for another person.[5]

One structural difference with the definition as provided in the OECD Commentary is that the latter defines beneficial ownership only in a negative sense and with examples, while the Directive in the first instance provides a positive open definition of a person receiving the income for their 'own benefit' to qualify as beneficial owner, in addition to the negative example that largely follows the OECD Commentary.[6] The main question is whether the test differs from the OECD Commentary by additionally defining the term 'own benefit' or if this is just a clarification. Also, one might wonder whether the two tests are different, so the positive and the negative terms have to be satisfied in order to qualify, or if they mean the same.

An interesting point on the positive definition is that it links beneficial ownership and the recipient of the income, which raises the question dealt with by the Model and Commentaries in 1995, 1998 and 2014.[7] The issue, as stated elsewhere, was whether the subject must fulfil being both a recipient and a beneficial owner of the income, as well as being a resident, for the exemption to apply; or whether being the beneficial owner and a resident was enough. The author's view is that the issue in the Directive is an import from the OECD that carried the defective wording, but in which it was clear the only relevant person was the beneficial owner. To sum up, there is no need to be both recipient and beneficial owner to obtain the Directive relief.

Another point to note is that the French version says 'les perçoit pour son compte proper', or receiving 'for its own account', which may not be seen exactly as

Council Directive on a common system of taxation applicable to interest and royalty payments made between associated companies of different Member States, COM (98) 67 final.

[3] See Art 1(1) of Council Directive 2003/49/EC (n 1) [2003] OJ L157/49.

[4] The first version of the Proposal of the Directive matched the interpretation given by the OECD Commentary from 1977. See Art 3 in COM (98) 67 final (n 2).

[5] See Art 1(4) of Council Directive 2003/49/EC (n 1).

[6] See Art 1(4) of Council Directive 2003/49/EC (n 1). See M Greggi, 'Taxation of Royalties in an EU Framework' (2007) 47 *Tax Notes International* 1149, 1158.

[7] See s IV.A in ch 5 above.

receiving the income for its own benefit, as in the English version.[8] Also, the French translation of intermediaries is 'intermédiaire' in the OECD, while the Directive refers to 'représentant'.[9]

On the positive definition, the French version could be interpreted in an economic sense as on whose account is done, or could be interpreted in a legal sense as referring to arrangements in which a person is acting in their own name but on account of somebody else.[10] Similarly, the English version could be seen as who economically benefits, or who is legally taking advantage of the interests or royalties. Neither version actually provides a solid reference,[11] but the doubts have led most authors to interpret the concept in an economic sense, with no consensus.[12]

However, because the Directive takes the concept from the Model, the interpretative outcomes reached in previous chapters could, as a starting point and subject to nuances, be applicable here.[13] The comments on the Directive drafts stated that several of the concepts were borrowed from the Model with some adaptations.[14] Although not stated explicitly in such documents in relation to beneficial ownership, the author's view is that, unless there is a clear difference, the Model and Commentaries can be used to interpret the concept. On this point, both the Model and the Commentaries can be interpreted in a legal or economic sense, but this author would argue in favour of the meaning defended above. If both pose the same issue and a solid conclusion is reached in one, the same arguments can be used in the Directive.

The inconvenience of this approach is that most of the documents used to arrive at the definition we give for the Model are already of controversial value when referred to in the interpretation of enacted treaties. They were not directly used in the discussion of tax treaties themselves, but for the Model, which has an indirect value for the interpretation of applicable enacted treaties. But it is even worse in this case, as it could be argued that those documents are totally alien to the Directive discussion and enactment. In the author's view, the argument is sustained, as the Model was used to discuss the Directive, it was explicitly mentioned in the drafts as part of the essence of the Directive, and its content permeated the Directive and was taken into account as

[8] Directive 2003/49/Ce du Conseil du 3 Juin 2003 concernant un régime fiscal commun applicable aux paiements d'intérêts et de redevances effectués entre des sociétés associées d'États membres différents, in its French version.

[9] Compare Arts 1(4) of the Council Directive 2003/49/EC (n 1) in its French and English versions.

[10] Although not referring explicitly to the French version, relating beneficial ownership and acting on its own account, S Martinho and others, 'A Comprehensive Analysis of Proposals to Amend the Interest and Royalties Directive: Part 1' (2011) 51 *European Taxation* 397, 404.

[11] ibid.

[12] Claiming an economic interpretation, ibid; M Distaso and R Russo, 'The EC Interest and Royalties Directive – a Comment' (2004) 44 *European Taxation* 143, 148. This seems to be the majority view in Italy: Association of Italian Companies (Associazione fra le Società Italiane per Azioni – Assonime), communication 10 November 2005; L Banfi and F Mantegazza, 'An Update on the Concept of Beneficial Ownership from an Italian Perspective' (2012) 52 *European Taxation* 57, 58. In contrast, claiming the literal wording gives it a narrow non-economic meaning: D Weber, 'The Proposed EC Interest and Royalty Directive' [2000] *EC Tax Review* 15, 23.

[13] Greggi (n 6) 1159; Martinho et al (n 10) 404. See also A Zalasinski, 'The ECJ's Decisions in the Danish "Beneficial Ownership" Cases: Impact on the Reaction to Tax Avoidance in the European Union' (2019) 2 *International Tax Studies* s 4.7.3.

[14] See above, n 2.

approved in the legislative procedure.[15] Moreover, those OECD historical documents are simply confirmation of the meaning the term had in the Model and Commentary, and not a definition provided *ex novo*. In other words, the term takes its meaning from the Model and the Directive themselves, and those other documents simply help to shed light on what was already there, albeit somewhat obscured.[16]

However, additional arguments contribute to such interpretation. The economic interpretation makes little sense and will extend the meaning *sine die*,[17] the interpretation regarding the permanent establishment indicates that the drafters were thinking about a legal defined reason related to a certain extent to who shows ability to pay or is taxable,[18] and, as will be seen later, the economic meaning is probably incompatible with primary law.[19]

An additional problem regarding the interpretation is that the examples of intermediaries excluded differ from those in the OECD Commentary. While the OECD mentions agents and nominees/*mandataires*, the Directive points to agents, trustees or authorised signatories.[20] Again, the translations of the Directive do not match its English version, and the French version of the Directive uses *administrateur fiduciaire* or *signataire autorisé*.[21] *Administrateur fiduciaire*, referring to continental fiducia, does not match trustee, and the reference to agent is missing.

In the author's view, divergences in the examples do not modify the meaning, because they are just examples of excluded intermediaries.[22] All of them may be taken into account. The actual issue is to define who acts on their own benefit or account in a positive sense, and which intermediaries are excluded.

In this regard, the author's view is that the differences with the Model are not significant enough for the term's meaning to depart from the meaning as understood in the Model. Because the history of the term beneficial ownership shows that the only reason for its inclusion in the Directive was the OECD and its original meaning was directly borrowed from it, and because nuances of meaning do not cause the term to absolutely deviate from its original meaning, it cannot be said to be a different concept. It would certainly be controversial to absolutely ignore the Commentary and Model. Thus, the Model and Commentary help to interpret the term, as confirmed by the Court of Justice of the European Union (CJEU).[23] The only difference, which is a rather formal one, when the documents are compared is that the definition is contained in the Directive itself, while in the Model it is in the Commentary. Its appearance in the Directive itself

[15] Court of Justice of the European Union (Grand Chamber) Joined Cases C-115/16, C-118/16, C-119/16 and C-299/16 *N Luxembourg 1 and others v Skatteministerie (and joined cases)* [2019] ECLI:EU:C 134 [91].

[16] ibid.

[17] See fn 220 and s I.C in ch 5 above. To some extent, recognising such meaning makes the concept unclear: Distaso and Russo (n 12) 148.

[18] See Art 1(5) of Council Directive 2003/49/EC (n 1).

[19] See below, s I.B(ii).

[20] Compare paras 12, 8 and 4 of the commentaries to Arts 10, 11 and 12 of the 1996 OECD Model Tax Convention, on which the Directive is based; and Art 1(4) of Council Directive 2003/49/EC (n 1).

[21] See Art 1(4) of Directive 2003/49/Ce du Conseil du 3 Juin 2003 concernant un régime fiscal commun applicable aux paiements d'intérêts et de redevances effectués entre des sociétés associées d'États membres différents, in its French version.

[22] For Weber, the definition could be closed to those examples: Weber (n 12) 23.

[23] *N Luxembourg 1 and others v Skatteministerie (and joined cases)* (n 15) para 90. Contrarily, Advocate General Kokott stated in the same case that the term has to be adapted to the EU context. See also Zalasinski (n 13) s 4.7.3.

adds legal certainty as compared to the controversial, though certainly valid, value of the Commentaries. Consequently, and because of the previous analysis of the term in the Model, the term cannot be a broad anti-avoidance term nor an economic rule.[24]

The main change in the Directive as compared to the Commentary is that beneficial ownership is also established as a requirement for permanent establishments (PEs), and a specific and different meaning is given in this regard. This second meaning states that a PE shall be considered as a beneficial owner insofar as the interest or royalties are effectively connected to the PE, and that the income is subject to tax in the relevant Member State.[25] The OECD Commentary, for its part, provides no specific beneficial owner requirement, or meaning in the Commentary, for PEs.

The OECD Model does not provide a beneficial owner requirement for PEs because it would be irrelevant. Treaties are not, in principle, applicable to PEs where they are receiving income from a third country.[26] Thus, no treaty shopping through legal and economic attribution to the PE of assets giving rise to the income could be achieved. Even if PEs were able to access treaty provisions, no problem would arise because the income would only be allocated to the PE if it performs functions and bears some risk in relation to it, so no treaty shopping through formal legal attribution could be achieved.

On the other hand, the Directive is applicable to income received in other countries by PEs, but does not deal with allocation of income to PEs. As no private law or tax allocation could be found in the Directive, the condition was added to the beneficial owner meaning.[27] The requirement of effective connection between the PE and the interest or royalties is the translation into the Directive of the PE treaty allocation rules that would be applicable if the Model were applicable to PEs.[28]

The second part of the definition, the subject to tax rule, does not make an actual difference with respect to the treatment provided in the Directive for interest and royalties derived by companies.[29] The subject to tax test actually requires the income to be allocated under domestic law to a subject who is liable to tax, not actual taxation.[30] And liability in the hands of the beneficial owner is also required for interest and

[24] J Lopez Rodriguez, 'Beneficial Ownership and EU Law' in M Lang et al (eds), *Beneficial Ownership: Recent Trends* (IBFD, 2013).

[25] See Art 1(5) of Council Directive 2003/49/EC (n 1).

[26] E Fett, *The Application of Bilateral Income Tax Treaties in Multilateral Situations* (IBFD, 2014) ch 4.

[27] See Greggi (n 6) 1159; J Muller, 'The Interest & Royalty Directive' (BNA Bloomberg, 2005).

[28] Martinho et al (n 10) 404; Greggi (n 6) 149; Terra and Wattel (n 1) 764.

[29] Distaso and Russo (n 12) 149.

[30] 'While most MS [Member States] appear to apply a "subjective" subject to tax requirement – ie it applies to the company as such, rather than to the specific interest or royalty payment – some MS require that the payment itself should be subject to tax (an "objective" subject to tax requirement). According to the survey, one MS requires that the company should not have an option of being exempt. That MS furthermore requires that the company should be subject, in its MS of residence, to a tax that is of the same or similar character as the income tax in the first MS. There is *no support in the Directive for either requirement.* On the contrary, the conditions of Article 3(a) are exhaustive, thus leaving no scope to impose further conditions and restrictions'[emphasis added]: Report from the Commission to the Council in accordance with Article 8 of Council Directive 2003/49/EC on a common system of taxation applicable to interest and royalty payments made between associated companies of different Member States, COM (2009) 179, 17 Apr 2009, 6–7; Lopez Rodriguez (n 24). The Ruding report and early directive proposals referred to 'actually taxed', which may suggest that subject to tax is only theoretical subjection of the income, as the actual taxation wording was abandoned. However, recent case law seemingly requires effective taxation, probably influenced by the OECD's Base Erosion and Profit Shifting (BEPS) state of mind. See *N Luxembourg 1 and others v Skatteministerie (and joined cases)* (n 15) para 146.

royalties allocated to a company.[31] The difference is explained by the fact the PE is not an independent taxpayer from the company, so the subject to tax condition cannot depend on the company if it is not a resident of the country where the PE is. The actual difference is that, for companies, the requirement is contained in a separate condition from the beneficial owner test, while for PEs it is connected to the beneficial owner test.[32] From a technical perspective, it would probably have been better to separate the subject to tax test from the beneficial ownership condition. In this sense, the subject to tax test for PEs could have been eliminated from the beneficial ownership condition and governed under the general subject to tax rule, though clarifying its application to PEs.[33]

Indeed, the definition of beneficial ownership for PEs has nothing to do with how beneficial ownership is understood in the Model, but is a different requirement of arm's length allocation and a subject to tax test. The meaning does not leave the rule related to beneficial ownership as understood in international tax law, but a different requirement, so labelling that rule as beneficial ownership is almost irrelevant.

Finally, a provision states that where a PE is considered beneficial owner, the company owning the PE will not be considered the beneficial owner. This point is controversial and unclear.[34] What it actually means is that insofar as the income is allocated to the PE, the income should not be allocated to the headquarters for purposes of the Directive.[35] However, if the home state does not apply a territorial system or eliminates double taxation on the PE through treaties, problems may arise.[36]

B. The Ruling on the Danish Cases (2019)

For a long time following the approval of the Directive in 2003, the concept of beneficial ownership in the Interests and Royalties Directive did not receive much attention. It was only in academic literature that scholars wondered whether the concept had to be interpreted in the same sense as in the OECD Commentary or adapted to the EU context.[37] However, around 2010, the Danish tax authorities challenged several cases where multinationals and investment funds structured their investments through intermediary holding companies in other EU Member States. The application of the Directive to those holdings provided an exemption to achieve the optimal tax route to repatriate income to third countries.[38] Six of these cases were referred to the CJEU, which provided a

[31] See Art 3(a)(iii) of Council Directive 2003/49/EC (n 1).

[32] For Greggi, the additional tests does not mean the test is strengthen for permanent establishments: Greggi (n 6) 1159.

[33] Distaso and Russo (n 12) 149.

[34] Muller (n 27).

[35] ibid.

[36] ibid.

[37] Martinho et al (n 10) 403–04; Greggi (n 6); Muller (n 27).

[38] J Bundgaard, 'The Notion of Beneficial Ownership in Danish Tax Law: The Creation of a New Legal Order with Uncertainty as a Companion' in Lang et al (n 24); J Bundgaard and N Winther-Sorensen, 'Beneficial Ownership in International Financing Structures' (2008) 50 *Tax Notes International* 587; A Riis, 'Danish Tax Authorities Prevail in Recent Beneficial Ownership Decision' (2011) 51 *European Taxation* 184; A Riis and N Bjornholm, 'First Danish Ruling on Beneficial Ownership' (2010) 50 *European Taxation* 324; B Tolstrup and N Bjornholm, 'Beneficial Ownership – Withholding Tax on Dividends and Interest from the Danish Perspective' (2011) 65 *Bulletin for International Taxation* 503; HS Hansen, LE Christensen and AE Pedersen,

controversial ruling on the meaning of beneficial ownership in the Directive alongside other issues such as the general principle of prevention of abuse in EU law.[39]

(i) Economic Benefit

Concerning the meaning of beneficial ownership, the CJEU directly held that the wording in the Directive should be read as 'who actually benefits' or who 'benefits economically' and who 'accordingly has the power freely to determine the use to which it is put'.[40] This conclusion is grounded in three arguments.

First, based on the *Scheuten Solar Technology* case, the CJEU held that income within the scope of the Directive is 'income from debt claims of every kind'.[41] The second ground was that, because the different translations of beneficial ownership in the different European languages refer to owner, entitlement, effect or benefit, the court upheld the argument that the term has to mean not the formally identified recipient but the person who benefits economically.[42] The third ground was that the legislative history of the Directive shows that it was based on the 1996 OECD Model Tax Convention and the Commentaries conclude that conduit companies must be excluded from reduced taxation at source.

In this last sense, the CJEU, in the Danish cases, took the view that the meaning of beneficial ownership should be chosen from possible meanings in a way that gives effect at the same time to the objects both of avoiding double taxation and preventing evasion and avoidance. At this point in its reasoning, the CJEU refuted the taxpayers' arguments that to interpret the concept in accordance with the Model would be in conflict with the legality principle because of the lack of legitimacy of the international organisation. However, the CJEU concluded that because the OECD documents were part of the explanatory and accompanying materials available to the European Parliament and the Council when the Directive was approved, legality and legitimacy were guaranteed[43] – all the more so because the meaning found was derived not only from the OECD materials, but also from the Directive's wording and context themselves.

The CJEU's arguments nonetheless contain some flaws. First, the CJEU does not properly analyse the Commentary on the Model with regard to its last 2014 update,

'Denmark – Danish "Beneficial Owner" Cases – A Status Report' (2013) 67 *Bulletin for International Taxation* 192; T Booker, 'Recent Developments Regarding Beneficial Ownership in Denmark' (2012) 52 *European Taxation* 67.

[39] *N Luxembourg 1 and others v Skatteministerie (and joined cases)* (n 15); Court of Justice of the European Union (Grand Chamber) Joined Cases C-116/16 and C-117/16 *Skatteministeriet v T Danmark and Y Denmark Aps* [2019] ECLI:EU:C 135. See I Lazarov, '(Un)Tangling Tax Avoidance under the Interest and Royalties Directive' [2018] 11 *Intertax* 873; S Barentzen, 'Cross-Border Dividend and Interest Payments and Holding Companies – An Analysis of Advocate General Kokott's Opinions in the Danish Beneficial Ownership Cases' [2018] *European Taxation* 343; Zalasinski (n 13); AM Ottosen and S Andersen, 'Preliminary Judgments in the EU Beneficial Ownership Cases' (2019) 21 *Derivatives and Financial Instruments*; PA Hernández González-Barreda, 'Holding Companies and Leveraged Buy-Outs in the European Union Following BEPS: Beneficial Ownership, Abuse of Law and the Single Taxation Principle' (2019) 59 *European Taxation* 409.

[40] *N Luxembourg 1 and others v Skatteministerie (and joined cases)* (n 15) paras 88–89, 122. The economic interpretation as a means to achieve the desirable policy objective of tackling conduits was preconised by Dennis Weber: see Weber (n 12) 23.

[41] *N Luxembourg 1 and others v Skatteministerie (and joined cases)* (n 15) paras 86–87.

[42] ibid 89.

[43] ibid 90.

but only refers to the conduit case. Probably because the Directive was approved the same year as the 2003 Commentary, the Court took its view from that Commentary. However, as analysed above, that 2003 Commentary was full of imprecisions. Moreover, it is unclear why the Directive used the 2003 Commentary. If a dynamic interpretation approach was to be taken, why did it not use the 2014 Commentary; and if a static approach was to be taken, why did it not use the 1996 version, which did not contain the conduit references?

Some early authors suggested that it would be tempting for the CJEU to use beneficial ownership in a broad sense, in order to achieve the desirable policy of tackling conduits.[44] Was the CJEU solution policy-oriented?

Secondly, the CJEU derives the meaning of beneficial ownership from translations, some of them formulated in the 1960s, with little knowledge of the issue behind it. The translations are, in the author's view, of little value in interpreting the term.

Finally, it derives an economic meaning from a legal definition of interest in a sort of mish-mash. The CJEU first holds that the beneficial owner is the person who can claim the interest, and then states that the beneficial owner is the economic owner. However, if only the person holding the position of creditor can receive interest, an economic owner in several cases cannot be considered as receiving interest as it is not the creditor. And if beneficial owner means whoever benefits economically, a company that can claim the interest and is not the economic owner, such as in a wholly owned company, cannot be considered the beneficial owner. The Directive would remain inapplicable in both cases, because of the conflict between the interest definition and the beneficial owner definition. The result is absolutely inconsistent, as it provides two different definitions for beneficial ownership. The CJEU probably meant that only the person who can claim an interest in substance could be a beneficial owner. The problem is in the ruling itself, which states that beneficial ownership is not a substance over form rule, at least from a legal substance point of view.[45] To state that beneficial ownership means economic ownership makes it not significantly different from a general anti-avoidance rule, thus overlapping the abuse of rights rule.[46]

By coming back to an economic interpretation of the term, the CJEU resurrected a debate that the OECD closed with a certain degree of success with the modifications included in the 2014 Commentary.[47] It is unclear whether the CJEU interprets beneficial ownership in the sense of economic allocation of income, as used for domestic allocation purposes in several countries,[48] or as an anti-avoidance rule. The CJEU explicitly

[44] Weber (n 12) 23.

[45] The CJEU considered the rightful recipient in Denmark and concluded that this was not applicable to the case, in line with the view of the parties to the case. That principle is based on the substance over form doctrine. Thus, if it was not applicable but beneficial owner was applicable, they cannot mean the same. See Conclusions of Advocate General Kokott in Case C-115/16 *N Luxembourg v Skatteministeriet*, 1 March 2018, para 100; *N Luxembourg 1 and others v Skatteministerie (and joined cases)* (n 15) para 26; Bundgaard and Winther-Sorensen (n 38) 600.

[46] See s I.C.(ii)(b) in ch 5 above. See also the definition of the Italian tax authorities, based on economic benefit, and how it gets really close to an anti-avoidance rule by analysing the purpose of the transaction: Banfi and Mantegazza (n 12) 58–59.

[47] See ch 4 above.

[48] Such as recognized in s 39(2) of DE: Abgabenordnung (Bundesgesetzblatt 2002 – BSBI 72, 2002), 1 October 2002 [Fiscal Code of Germany] (last amendment 2017), National Legislation, IBFD.

draws a line between the term and anti-abuse principles, but in some paragraphs it refers to beneficial ownership as an anti-abuse rule.[49] In the author's view, the CJEU probably intended to achieve a sort of economic attribution of income rule, but the expansion of the EU principle of prevention of abuse does not properly achieve the concept.

More accurately, and in contrast to the CJEU, the Opinion delivered by Advocate-General Kokott considered the beneficial owner under the Directive to be the person who can claim the interest under private law, unless the person is acting as a trustee or agent – possibly hidden – in his or her own name but for the benefit of a third person.[50] In this sense, holding corporations qualify as beneficial owners as they hold the claim and there is no trustee relationship, and also because they benefit from the spread between the interest rates. However, the Opinion leaves the door open for the referring court to define whether a hidden trust exists, and whether the risk is entirely or largely borne by the shareholders of the recipient corporation, in which case beneficial ownership could not be said to be held by the intermediary corporation.[51]

Advocate-General Kokott clearly does not consider it is possible to interpret beneficial ownership in the Directive purely according to the Model or to give it an international fiscal meaning, as allocation of taxing powers within the EU should follow its own principles and conform to primary law; rather, she seems to adapt the interpretation of the term suggested under the OECD materials to the special characteristics of the Internal Market.[52] In the author's view, A-G Kokott's interpretation of beneficial ownership is correct.[53] A single amendment would the author introduce to her definition. In relation to certain conduits or other arrangements, especially in continental countries, may the concept be expanded to include linked contracts where income received accrues automatically to third parties.[54] Regarding her argument on the EU autonomous interpretation, one may add that this does not render the meaning derived from the Commentary irrelevant, but it does have to be adapted to the context, namely subject to primary law limits.

However, the inconsistent outcome of the CJEU's judgment may lead some states to increasingly deny the benefits of the Directive on the grounds of the beneficial ownership clause as the economic benefit definition opens the door to its application to any case. As said in relation to the OECD commentary, economic benefit or actual benefit has no reference upon which any allocation principle can be tested, and almost everybody could be excluded from the condition of beneficial ownership if interpreted in that sense.[55] In contrast to the CJEU's ruling, the intention of the use of the wording in the Directive was to limit the exemption to the above-mentioned specific cases in relation to which it was included, in line with the OECD definition, but not to be an expansive general anti-avoidance or economic ownership rule.[56]

[49] Under the heading of 'The burden of proving the abuse of rights', the ruling discusses the beneficial owner test: *N Luxembourg 1 and others v Skatteministerie (and joined cases)* (n 15) para 140 et seq.

[50] A-G Opinion in Case C-115/16 *N Luxembourg 1* (n 39) paras 36–46.

[51] ibid 42.

[52] ibid 55.

[53] ibid 36–46.

[54] See s I.D(ii) in ch 5 above.

[55] See fn 220 and s I.C in ch 5 above.

[56] Lopez Rodriguez (n 24).

(ii) Beneficial Ownership and Abuse of Law

In addition to considering the beneficial owner to be the person who 'economically benefits', the CJEU somehow establishes in its rulings in the Danish cases a relationship between beneficial ownership and abuse of EU law. It states that the fact that a corporation is not the beneficial owner is a relevant factor or element in establishing the existence of abuse of law.[57] Moreover, the beneficial owner burden of proof is discussed under the heading of 'The burden of proving the abuse of rights'.[58] The relationship between beneficial ownership and abuse, even though logical from the perspective of the CJEU – if the legal creditor is different from the person who economically benefits, there could be an abuse of the Directive by allocating a formal right to a different person – fails if the beneficial owner is not defined as the person who economically benefits. However, such a point is not in line with other statements from the CJEU in the same ruling claiming that there is no absolute direct relationship between abuse and lack of beneficial ownership.[59] The above-mentioned strong connection as an indication of this leaves the issue unclear. If beneficial ownership requires the holding of creditor status except in cases of trustees, nominees and where there is an obligation to pass on the income, the abusive character of a transaction involving a non-beneficial owner creditor who is actually taxed may be more than controversial.

Moreover, because beneficial ownership is used as an indicator of the presence of abuse, tax authorities could regard any transaction as abusive where only one or a few shareholders control a company, or where there is any factual or economic benefit for a third party irrespective of its entitlement. At the very least, beneficial owners being residents in third countries will automatically trigger the abuse analysis. Because of the broad meaning of beneficial ownership and its use as an indicator to define abuse, an improper assessment of the abuse test could result in any transaction economically benefiting a third person being abusive. In this regard, the ruling seems a surprising outcome, conflicting with the *Eqiom* case, where the CJEU held that the fact that the ultimate owners are residents in third countries cannot per se be considered as abusive.[60] On the other hand, in the Danish cases, the CJEU considers the fact that the shareholders are in third countries as indicative of abuse. What the ruling does not say is how strong an indicator this factor is. Perhaps it is precisely because this position contradicts the *Eqiom* ruling that the latter is not quoted at all.

In any case, the unclear relationship between abuse and beneficial ownership is the result of using such an broad economic definition for the term, making it extremely close to an anti-avoidance rule. Still worse, an anti-avoidance rule normally provides certain elements – purpose, artificiality, etc – while economic benefit does not provide any reference to test the case.

[57] *N Luxembourg 1 and others v Skatteministerie (and joined cases)* (n 15) paras 138, 142–43; *Skatteministeriet v T Danmark and Y Denmark Aps* (n 39), paras 117–18.

[58] *N Luxembourg 1 and others v Skatteministerie (and joined cases)* (n 15) para 140 et seq.

[59] ibid 138. Claiming beneficial owner and abuse or substance have no direct relationship, see Martinho et al (n 10) 403; Banfi and Mantegazza (n 12) 65.

[60] Sixth Chamber Case C-6/16 *Eqiom SAS, formerly Holcim France SAS and Enka SA v Ministre des Finances et des Comptes publics* [2017] ECLI:EU:C:2017:641. See A Delgado Pacheco, 'El Tribunal de Justicia de La Unión Europea Trata de Aclarar El Concepto de Elusión Fiscal' Blog Centro de Estudios Garrigues http://blog.centrogarrigues.com/el-tjue-y-el-concepto-de-elusion-fiscal/.

(iii) The Compatibility with EU Primary Law

A surprising gap in the ruling is that the CJEU did not take up the opportunity to test whether beneficial ownership is compatible with primary law.[61] Beneficial ownership restricts directive benefits in several cases, especially in the loose sense favoured by the court. Because it applies to intra-EU cross-border transactions, it might be seen as restricting the exercise of freedom of establishment and free movement of capital.

As consolidated in long-standing case law, anti-avoidance rules restricting or making less favourable intra-EU cross-border transactions are only justified in EU law if proportional as they target (wholly) artificial arrangements.[62] The conflict in the Danish cases derives from the contradiction of the objective of beneficial ownership – to tackle abusive arrangements – and its definition – economic benefit, with no artificiality analysis – so non-artificial transactions economically benefiting residents in third countries would be restricted in a disproportionate manner.

This is further evidence of the unclear connection between abuse and beneficial ownership; the CJEU did not clarify this in the case, but added more confusion.

(iv) The Danish Cases, Consistent Interpretation, Tax Treaties and Contextual Materials

The final point regarding beneficial ownership is that Member States may be considered as obliged to interpret domestic rules on cross-border exemptions as implicitly containing a beneficial ownership expansive meaning. This has been the case of the ruling of the Spanish Central Economic-Administrative Court of 8 October 2019, where the court held the application of the beneficial owner test as interpreted in the Danish case to the Spanish rule providing withholding exception on interests for associated enterprises resident in the European Union, even though the domestic rule did not include the requirement.

But what is worse, authorities and courts may be seen as obliged, or at least tempted, to interpret beneficial ownership in tax treaties in accordance with the Danish case rulings.

It might be wondered whether indirect effect or the consistent interpretation principle gives any support to this approach. Although indirect effect is generally referred to in the implementation of directives and secondary legislation, it would be odd to argue that the domestic implementation of beneficial ownership is subject to indirect effect while beneficial ownership in the treaties is not, if both have the same meaning according to the CJEU.[63] This is especially important for tax treaties between Member States, but also those with third countries. Because the CJEU states that this is the interpretation derived from the OECD, several countries could consider it the correct view

[61] Zalasinski (n 13).

[62] Grand Chamber Case C-196/04 *Cadbury Schweppes plc y Cadbury Schweppes Overseas Ltd v Commissioners of Inland Revenue* [2006] ECLI:EU:C:2006:544 [51]. See G Marín Benítez, 'The European Union, the State Competence in Tax Matters and Abuse of the EU Freedoms' in JM Almudí et al (eds), *Combating Tax Avoidance in the EU* (Kluwer, 2019) 42 et seq; Michael Lang, 'Cadbury Schweppes' Line of Case Law from the Member States' Perspective' in R De La Feria et al (eds), *Prohibition of Abuse of Law: A New General Principle of EU Law?* (Hart Publishing, 2011).

[63] On indirect effect, see P Craig and G De Burca, *EU Law*, 6th edn (Oxford University Press, 2015) 209 et seq.

with regard to tax treaties, or simply a confirmation of the view that they have upheld so far. This may again trigger a discussion on beneficial ownership, and would raise the inconsistency surrounding beneficial ownership again. Although the importance of beneficial ownership after the BEPS Action Plan may be decreasing as other and more powerful anti-avoidance rules are becoming more important, it would give tax authorities a powerful undefined tool again.

Similarly, some authors have wondered whether the meaning of beneficial ownership as with the nuances included in the Directive could be used to interpret the Model. The argument is that the Directive, as relevant rules of international law applicable in relations between the parties, should be used to interpret treaties between Member States where no specific definition departing from the OECD is used.[64] Actually, the issue depends on which position is taken regarding the relationship of the Model and the Directive as regards the meaning of the term.

If, as the CJEU recognises, the term in the Directive is defined, at least to some extent, by the Model, then to use the Directive to interpret the term would be to enter into circular reasoning. The Commentary will be used to interpret the Directive, and the Directive will be used to interpret the Model.

Taking another view, if the Directive has a different meaning from the Model, then the reasoning may work. The issue is whether it makes sense to take a Directive that has some differences from the Model, such as the subject to tax test, even though not connected to beneficial ownership, to interpret a different legal instrument negotiated in different circumstances.

The final option would be to consider both instruments as referring to the same concept, or even not the same but based on the same core. This would lead to the consistent interpretation of both, although subject to minor adaptations according to the context. Both instruments may be taken into account in interpreting both treaties between Member States and third countries and the Directive. Ultimately, in the author's view, this is the right option, but that viewpoint is of course based on considering the terms as referring to the same concept, in the sense argued in this work.[65]

II. Beneficial Ownership in the Parent–Subsidiary Directive

Contrary to the Interest and Royalties Directive, the Parent–Subsidiary Directive does not contain a beneficial owner requirement. The reason is that the former deals with juridical double taxation, while the latter aims to eliminate economic double taxation.[66] While the former is subjected to directive shopping attempts, the latter cannot help to eliminate source taxation through the interposition of an entity. Under the

[64] F Avella, 'Using EU Law to Interpret Undefined Tax Treaty Terms: Article 31 (3)(c) of the Vienna Convention on the Law of Treaties and Article 3 (2) of the OECD Model Convention' (2012) 4 *World Tax Journal* 95, s 5.1. The Italian view on beneficial ownership as an attribution of income rule makes the concept different from the meaning it has under the Model, so it would be odd if the Directive concept could be used to interpret Italian treaties. See A Bavila, 'Italy' in J Wheeler (ed), *Conflicts in the Attribution of Income to a Person*, vol B (Kluwer, 2007) 336. See also s I.A. in ch 5 above.

[65] Zalasinski (n 13) s 4.7.3.

[66] See A-G Opinion in *Skatteministeriet v T Danmark and Y Denmark Aps* (n 39) para 44.

Parent–Subsidiary elimination of economic double taxation rationale, income will be taxed in the entity distributing the income, not affected or eliminated by the Directive, so elimination of source taxation does not take place.

The Danish Group of cases also dealt with some cases concerning the Parent–Subsidiary Directive.[67] In *T Danmark*, the referring court did not ask the meaning of beneficial ownership in the Parent–Subsidiary Directive because there was no such rule. However, it did ask whether beneficial ownership in tax treaties would be an implementation of domestic or treaty-based anti-avoidance rules as authorised by the Parent–Subsidiary Directive and, if so, what was its meaning. The CJEU dismissed the question.

The CJEU answered the case from a different angle by resorting to the primary law anti-abuse principle and dismissed the beneficial owner questions. For the CJEU, because the question on the meaning was conditional on beneficial owner being an implementation of the Parent–Subsidiary Directive's anti-avoidance rules, and such rules were no longer needed if a primary law principle was applied, the beneficial owner question was irrelevant. The result was that the beneficial owner role in the Parent–Subsidiary Directive remained unanswered.[68]

However, the Advocate-General's Opinion stated that beneficial ownership in the Parent–Subsidiary Directive was irrelevant as the directive was aimed at economic double taxation, and not only to juridical double taxation as in the Interest and Royalties Directive. In the latter, the chances of directive shopping on source taxation made beneficial ownership necessary.[69]

However, the CJEU judgment in *T Danmark* states, just a few paragraphs after claiming beneficial ownership is not relevant, that the Parent–Subsidiary Directive enables the exemption to be denied on the grounds of the receiver not being the beneficial owner.[70] In addition, the CJEU puts beneficial ownership as one of the indicators to check when determining whether arrangements at stake are abusive or not.[71] It is unclear if this was a mistake arising from the fact that the CJEU was developing the rulings on the Interest and Royalties Directive and the Parent–Subsidiary Directive in parallel, or if it considered the term as implicit. Could the Court have been referring to considering beneficial ownership as a matter of fact to define the factual pattern to which the Directive applies, but not as a requirement of the Directive itself? In addition, if it is considered implicit in its judgment, the CJEU does not state whether the Parent–Subsidiary Directive requires the term to be adapted to its context or fully follows the meaning provided in the ruling on the cases concerning the Interest and Royalties Directive.

Shockingly, the CJEU has left it unclear whether such an unlimited tool can be applicable in regard to an instrument which contains no reference to it: the Parent–Subsidiary Directive. On this point, again, the Opinion of Advocate-General Kokott differs, suggesting that beneficial ownership is irrelevant to the Parent–Subsidiary

[67] See the ruling and opinion in the *T Danmark* case.
[68] *Skatteministeriet v T Danmark and Y Denmark Aps* (n 39) paras 93–94.
[69] A-G Opinion in Case C-117/16 *Skatteministeriet v Y Danmark* [2018] ECLI:EU:C:2018:145, para 43.
[70] *Skatteministeriet v T Danmark and Y Denmark Aps* (n 39) para 111.
[71] ibid 100.

Directive but that what is relevant is whether economic and juridical multiple taxation arises.[72] Still, the ruling is there, and from a literal point of view makes the application of the exemption conditional on beneficial ownership. Also, beneficial ownership considers that being a resident in a third country is an indicator for defining abuse. Because the ruling explicitly raises the applicability of beneficial ownership and its relation to abuse of law, to wonder whether it is a mistake without the CJEU saying so would be more than controversial. The result is that beneficial ownership could now be considered as a requirement of the Parent–Subsidiary Directive, with unclear results.[73]

An additional issue is what happens to interests or royalties paid in excess of market value. If these are requalified as dividends, the Parent–Subsidiary Directive applies. This has led some authors to argue that there is a loophole, because that excess would not be subject to the beneficial ownership condition.[74] Taking the view of the CJEU, where beneficial ownership is applicable to the Parent–Subsidiary Directive, the issue would not arise. However, in this case, the beneficial owner requirement is not considered to apply to the Parent–Subsidiary Directive, which is probably irrelevant because, as mentioned, the Parent–Subsidiary Directive is aimed at economic double taxation.

III. The Directive of Administrative Cooperation and Beneficial Ownership

Beneficial ownership wording is also contained in EU law in the Directive of Administrative Cooperation.[75] However, its meaning is derived from international instruments on cooperation in prevention of crimes, money laundering and exchange of information for tax matters. Those instruments and the meaning of the term therein will be discussed in the next chapter.

For the moment, it is sufficient to make clear that the meaning of the concept in the Directive of Administrative Cooperation has nothing to do with beneficial ownership in the Interest and Royalties Directives and in tax treaties because of their different contexts and functions.[76] The meaning in each of those instruments cannot serve to interpret the others.

[72] A-G Opinion in Case C-115/16 *N Luxembourg 1* (n 39) para 44.

[73] Zalasinski (n 13) s 4.7.1.

[74] Martinho et al (n 10) 403.

[75] See Council Directive (EU) 2016/2258 of 6 December 2016 amending Directive 2011/16/EU as regards access to anti-money-laundering information by tax authorities in relation to Art 3(6) of Directive (EU) 2015/849 of the European Parliament and of the Council of 20 May 2015 on the prevention of the use of the financial system for the purposes of money laundering or terrorist financing. The previous Savings Directive contained a beneficial owner definition similar to the one in the Interest and Royalties Directive: '1. For the purposes of this Directive, "beneficial owner" means any individual who receives an interest payment or any individual for whom an interest payment is secured, unless he provides evidence that it was not received or secured for his own benefit'. As it has been repealed, it no longer has relevance. See Art 3 of Council Directive 2003/48/EC of 3 June 2003 on taxation of savings income in the form of interest payments.

[76] Avella claims that the different purpose of the concept of beneficial owner in exchange of information makes it unable to relate to the Model meaning. If the meaning in the Interest and Royalties Directive is derived from the Model, it could also be argued that they have different purposes and cannot be used to interpret each other. Avella (n 64) s 5.1.

7

Beneficial Ownership in Exchange of Information for Tax Matters

I. International Instruments of Exchange of Information and Beneficial Ownership

A. The Legal Basis and Scope for Exchange of the Beneficial Ownership Information

(i) Beneficial Ownership as Foreseeable Relevant Information

It must first be briefly mentioned that beneficial ownership has no explicit mention in primary level international instruments enacting exchange of information for tax matters.[1] The legal support for exchanging beneficial ownership information lies in the broad clauses on exchange of information, obliging contracting parties to share information which may be foreseen as relevant or necessary for the purposes of applying administration or enforcement tax conventions, or the application of domestic provisions concerning tax law.[2] Thus, exchange of beneficial owner information is justified on its relevance for application of taxes or for prevention of evasion or abuse.

As personal taxes are defined with reference to persons, information regarding persons involved is relevant.[3] The problem is that in many cases there are several persons

[1] See the OECD Model Agreement on Exchange of Information on Tax Matters; Art 26 of the OECD Model Tax Convention; Multilateral Competent Authority Agreement for the Common Reporting Standard, signed in Berlin on the 29 October 2014. In the case of FATCA agreements, beneficial ownership is mentioned but as an alternative wording for controlling person. See FATCA Model 1 and Model 2 Agreements, and their annexes. On this point see R Offermanns, 'Current Trends Regarding Disclosure Mechanisms: Reporting Ultimate Beneficial Ownership – Part 1' (2019) 59 *European Taxation* 237, 244.

[2] Art 26 of the OECD Model Tax Convention and Art 1 of the OECD Model Agreement on Exchange of Information on Tax Matters.

[3] See Art 5.4(b) of the OECD Model Agreement on Exchange of Information on Tax Matters; paras 5 and 7 of the Commentary to Art 26 of the OECD Model Tax Convention' OECD, *Manual on the Implementation of Exchange of Information Provisions for Tax Purposes* (OECD, 2006) para 26; Global Forum on Transparency and Exchange of Information for Tax Purposes, *Terms of Reference to Monitor and Review Progress towards Transparency and Exchange of Information for Tax Purposes* (Global Forum, 2010) 3–9; Global Forum on Transparency and Exchange of Information for Tax Purposes, *2016 Terms of Reference to Monitor and Review Progress towards Transparency and Exchange of Information on Request for Tax Purposes* (Global Forum, 2016) 3–10.

connected to an object of income, but domestic income only allocates such income to one person. However, to limit exchange of information only to the person to whom income shall be allocated under domestic law would make the process of exchanging information too burdensome, as the authorities submitting the information would have first to assess to whom the income has to be allocated under the laws of the requesting state. It would also imply prejudgement of the outcome of the tax assessments procedure, jeopardising the competence of competent authorities. Moreover, it would limit the application of anti-avoidance rules or misguide the interpretation of allocation rules, as only where all information on subjects is available and their relation to the object is clear might one see whether income has to be attributed to one or the other.

In contrast, it is commonly understood that such information clauses are to be interpreted in a broad sense, so any relevant information related to some extent to the case may be requested.[4] Because almost all countries have anti-avoidance rules or economic allocation rules, subjects economically or functionally related to the object of the income are potentially relevant in assessing the cases. This would cover beneficial ownership in the sense that will later be analysed.

The need to exchange beneficial ownership with such wording is only explicitly contained in G20 communiqués, Global Forum declarations and Recommendations from the OECD Council.[5]

In the case of the automatic exchange of information of financial accounts, the Multilateral Competent Authority Agreement establishing the Common Reporting Standard (CRS) refers to the need to exchange information about the controlling person, which use could be seen in these instruments as equivalent to beneficial ownership.[6] However, the Multilateral Competent Authority Agreement does not use the beneficial owner concept, nor a definition of controlling person.[7] The definition is only contained in the CRS report and its implementation manual.[8]

In the case of exchange of information upon request, covering any type of information, the need to exchange beneficial owner information as part of the foreseeable

[4] See OECD (n 3) para 23 et seq; Commentary to Art 26 of the Model; Grand Chamber Case C-682/15 *Berlioz Investment Fund SA v Directeur de l'administration des contributions directes* [2017] ECLI:EU:C:2017:373 66 et seq.

[5] Among others, see G20 Leaders' Declaration, 6 September 2013, St Petersburg, para 51; G20 Leaders' Declaration, Brisbane, 16 November 2014, para 14; G20 High-Level Principles on Beneficial Ownership Transparency, Brisbane, November 2014; G20 Leaders' Communique, Hangzhou Summit, 4–5 September 2016, para 20; G20 Leaders' Declaration: Shaping an Interconnected World, Hamburg, 8 July 2017; Recommendation of the Council of the OECD on the Standard for Automatic Exchange of Financial Account Information in Tax Matters, 15 July 2014; Declaration from the OECD on Automatic Exchange of Information in Tax Matters, 6 May 2014, para 4.

[6] See ss 1.1(e) and 2.2(a) of the Multilateral Competent Authority Agreement for the Common Reporting Standard, signed in Berlin on 29 October 2014. On the development of the Common Reporting Standard, see A Musilek, 'Change of Paradigm in Administrative Cooperation Directives: Automatic Exchange of Information' in JM Almudí et al (eds), *Combating Tax Avoidance in the EU* (Kluwer, 2019).

[7] See s 1 of the Multilateral Competent Authority Agreement for the Common Reporting Standard, signed in Berlin on 29 October 2014.

[8] OECD, *Standard for Automatic Exchange of Financial Account Information in Tax Matters*, 2nd edn (OECD Publishing, 2017) 57. Note, though, that beneficial ownership is not explictly used but uses controlling person and submits to the definition used by the Financial Action Tax Force.

relevant information is contained in the 2016–2020 Peer Review Handbook (the Handbook) for exchange of information upon request.[9]

The issue is that the definitions of beneficial ownership, both in automatic exchange of financial accounts and exchange of information upon request, are contained in reports and documents of doubtful or controversial legal value.[10] Those instruments are used to assess whether a certain jurisdiction complies with international standards, but have no legal binding value. However, because of the effect of the name-and-shame policy performed by the Global Forum, the result is that almost all countries follow definitions provided by such instruments and establish domestic rules enabling access to such information. And on the exchange side, because the above-mentioned broad scope of exchange of information rules, as well as because the Multilateral Competent Authority Agreement for CRS includes the obligation to exchange information on the controlling person, there is no problem with exchanging such information as it is clearly covered by them. Thus, the problem is not whether such information could be exchanged, which is beyond any doubt, but whether a confusing definition provided by documents of little legal value can set the standard for such an important role. In addition, as will be seen later, in the specific case of automatic exchange, the proportionality and relevance of such information for all cases could be controversial. It is debatable whether the fact that it is derived from a non-binding legal document is taken into account.

In addition, the submission used by those documents to the Financial Action Task Force (FATF) Recommendations to define beneficial ownership reinforces questions of legality, as will be seen later.

With reference to the EU implementation of automatic exchange of information on beneficial ownership of legal persons and arrangements, beneficial ownership

[9] Global Forum on Transparency and Exchange of Information for Tax Purposes, *Exchange of Information on Request: Handbook for Peer Reviews 2016–2020*, 3rd edn (OECD Publishing, 2016) 19.

[10] The value of these documents may be doubtful, as they may be regarded as soft law. This does not mean that their content lacks any value. First, as we already said, Art 26 of the OECD Model Tax Convention and the Multilateral Convention on Assistance in Tax Matters supports exchange of information on 'any information' foreseeable as relevant. Thus, the information these documents note may easily fall within the scope of application of exchange of information agreements, wide as they are. It may also be argued that these recommendations are somehow binding because they can be regarded as reflecting an international consensus. However, both ideas may lack legitimacy as the Global Forum and the OECD agreements are not signed up to in a formal sense as treaties, parliaments do not participate, there is a huge asymmetry on the information and power, and participant states, members, the OECD, the G20 and the Global Forum have different roles and powers. However, if states voluntarily agree to introduce the content of such documents into their domestic rules through their constitutional procedure, as they do, they would guarantee the principle of legality, especially with regard to non-OECD member countries. And as far as different subjects are concerned, information on all subjects related to a certain income or asset may be requested unless there is no connection or no relevance at all for the ongoing investigations. See, *mutatis mutandis*, discussions on the OECD Commentary as they are recommendations, with most of these documents concerned with exchange of information. H Ault, 'The Role of the OECD Commentaries in the Interpretation of Tax Treaties' (1994) 22 *Intertax* 144; HJ Ault, *The OECD Model Convention – 1998 and Beyond, the Concept of Beneficial Ownership in Tax Treaties* (Kluwer, 2000) 145; M Lang and F Brugger, 'The Role of the OECD Commentary in Tax Treaty Interpretation' (2008) 23 *Australian Tax Forum*; DA Ward, 'Principles To Be Applied in Interpreting Tax Treaties' (1977) 25 *Canadian Tax Journal* 263, 268; P Wattel and O Marres, 'The Legal Status of the OECD Commentary and Static or Ambulatory Interpretation of Tax Treaties' (2003) 43 *European Taxation* 222. See, on submission to manuals, s 1, pt 2 of the Mutual Competent Authority Agreement in OECD (n 8) 23. On the possibility of regarding them as reflecting international consensus, see, *mutatis mutandis*, para 35 of the introduction to the Commentary to the OECD Model Tax Convention.

definitions are contained in the Anti-Money Laundering Directive, to which the Directive in Administrative Cooperation submits.[11] In the case of automatic exchange of information on financial information, the Directive on Administrative Cooperation refers to controlling persons, and defines them according to the CRS regulations.[12] Because the definitions themselves are contained in the directive, legality issues are less controversial. However, because it supplements definitions by submitting to the FATF, some doubts may arise.

In the case of the Foreign Account Tax Compliance Act (FATCA) and its agreements, the conventions establish the obligation to share the information of the controlling person and provide a specific definition.[13] This improves legal certainty and avoids legality issues. However, the concept is also defined by submission to the FATF Recommendations and its controversial meaning, so the problem of using such interpretation remains.

(ii) The Scope of Exchange of Information

International instruments currently share information on beneficial ownership for tax matters in relation to bank accounts, and on legal persons and legal arrangements.

Regarding exchange of information upon request, the Handbook requires tax authorities to make available information on subjects including the beneficial owner of any entity or arrangement.[14] This includes: companies and any bodies corporate; bearer shares and custodial accounts; partnerships with income, business activity or limited liability; trusts governed by the law, managed or with trustees in such jurisdiction; foundations; and any other entity or arrangement.[15]

It also requires availability of information on bank accounts, including beneficial ownership of the accounts among other information.[16]

Finally, the Handbook established the obligation of availability of information. Because no information can be exchanged if domestic law does not enable authorities to access information in the hands of private parties, such as bank accounts, it requires states to have domestic provisions that provide access to such information. This is specifically aimed at preventing states from arguing bank secrecy as a reason for limiting access to information.[17] On this point, the Handbook requires authorities to be able to access all relevant information on bank accounts in the hands of any institution

[11] See Art 22(1a) of the Council Directive (EU) 2016/2258 of 6 December 2016 amending Directive 2011/16/EU as regards access to anti-money-laundering information by tax authorities, and Art 3(6) of Directive (EU) 2015/849 of the European Parliament and of the Council on the prevention of the use of the financial system for the purposes of money laundering or terrorist financing.

[12] See Art 8.3a of Directive 2011/16/EU as regards mandatory automatic exchange of information in the field of taxation, as amended by Council Directive 2014/107/EU of 9 December 2014 amending Directive 2011/16/EU as regards mandatory automatic exchange of information in the field of taxation, and para 5 of Part D of Section VII of Annex I of Council Directive 2014/107/EU of 9 December 2014 amending Directive 2011/16/EU as regards mandatory automatic exchange of information in the field of taxation.

[13] See Arts 1.1(mm) and 2.2(a) 1 of FATCA Agreement Model 1A, and matching provisions in models 1B and 2.

[14] A.1 in Global Forum on Transparency and Exchange of Information for Tax Purposes (n 9) 19.

[15] A.1.1, A.1.2, A.1.3, A.1.4 and A.1.5 in ibid 19–20.

[16] A.3 in ibid 21.

[17] ibid 21–23.

within their jurisdiction, namely beneficial ownership of any entity such as companies, partnerships, trusts, foundations and any other body holding bank accounts.[18]

In the case of the CRS and FATCA automatic exchange of information on financial information, the Multilateral Competent Authority Agreement, FATCA agreements and Directive 2014/107/EU implementing CRS in the EU, controlling person or beneficial owner is included in the information that is automatically exchanged on bank accounts.[19]

B. The Definition of Beneficial Ownership in International Instruments for Exchange of Information: Exchange upon Request, CRS and FATCA

(i) CRS, FATCA and Exchange of Information upon Request Submission to FATF

From very early on, administrative cooperation in tax matters has taken the concept of beneficial ownership from definitions of the term as used in the FATF Recommendations.[20] In current instruments, the Handbook, the CRS reports and FATCA agreements submit to the definitions of beneficial owner and controlling person in the FATF Recommendations.[21]

However, in the case of the CRS reports governing the exchange of information on bank accounts, beneficial owner is used in both an explicit and an implicit sense.

As an explicit concept, the exchange of information of the controlling person is required. This is the case of an account in the name of a legal person controlled in the end by a natural person. This last person would be the beneficial owner.[22]

In the CRS instruments, the controlling person is defined as the natural person or persons who exercise control over an entity.[23] Although based on the FATF definitions, it does not mention the person on whose behalf a transaction is carried out, as the FATF Recommendations do, and puts the spotlight on control. In addition, it does not provide the subsidiary provisions as referring to the presumption of ownership control and the manager provision, as will be seen in relation to the FATF. The difference is not highly significant because, as stated earlier, the FATF gives pre-eminence to control. In addition, because the CRS regulations note that the term has to be interpreted

[18] B.1.1 in ibid 21–22.

[19] Section 2.2(a) of the Multilateral Competent Authority Agreement for the Common Reporting Standard, signed in Berlin on 29 October 2014; Art 2.2(a) of FATCA Agreement Model 1A, and matching provisions in models 1B and 2.

[20] For instance, Directive 2003/48/CE of the Council of 3 June 2003 on taxation of savings income in the form of interest payments.

[21] See Global Forum on Transparency and Exchange of Information for Tax Purposes (n 9) 33, paras 20 et seq; para 6 of Part D of Section VII of the Common Reporting Standard in OECD (n 8). Art 1.1. mm) of FATCA Agreement Model 1A, and matching provisions in models 1B and 2. And para 5 of Part D of Section VII of Annex I of the Council Directive 2014/107/EU of 9 December 2014 amending Directive 2011/16/EU as regards mandatory automatic exchange of information in the field of taxation.

[22] OECD (n 8) 24 and 57.

[23] See para 6 of Part D of Section VII of the Common Reporting Standard in OECD (n 8).

consistently with FATF Recommendations, a harmonised interpretation would reconcile the small divergence.

However, in addition to the obligation to share information on the controlling person, the CRS agreements require within the obligation to exchange that account holders disregard nominal holders, implicitly establishing a beneficial owner rule. The CRS reports provide that where the person listed as the client is holding the account as agent, custodian, nominee, signatory, investment advisor or intermediary for the benefit or account of another person, this last person would be regarded as the account holder.[24] This is similarly defined in the OECD Model TIEAs Commentary.[25] The concept is very similar to that definition of beneficial owner in the Commentary of the OECD Model Tax Convention (the Model), regarding tax jurisdiction in relation to dividends, interests and royalties.[26] What is unclear is whether such definitions of persons excluded as account holders are examples of a broader beneficial owner implicit exclusion, similar to the Model, or are strict definitions only excluding the account holder where a strict and formal agency, custodian or above-mentioned arrangement is at stake.

If the broad option is taken, the person holding an account through a controlled corporation who is acting as an agent for him or her could be regarded as the beneficial owner through the controlling person rule, or through this last rule. As a consequence, it could be possible that these rules point to different persons at the same time: the formal account holder, the beneficial owner under the implicit rule, another entity or physical person on account of the exchanging authority considering that the account is being held, and the natural person at the end of the chain of ownership following FATF recommendations. This could definitely lead to several inconsistencies if the role and legal relations of each party are not carefully defined and provided in the information exchange.

(ii) The Beneficial Owner Definition in the FATF Recommendations

The definition of beneficial owner contained in the exchange of information manuals, and then in the domestic rules of most countries that implement FATCA and beneficial ownership in exchange of information upon request, almost exactly matches the content it has in FATF Recommendations.[27]

The glossary to the FATF Recommendations defines the beneficial owner as:

> the natural person(s) who ultimately owns or controls a customer and/or the natural person on whose behalf transaction is being conducted. It also includes those persons who exercise ultimate effective control over a legal person or arrangement.[28]

[24] ibid 60.

[25] Commentary to the Model Agreement on Exchange of Information of Tax Matters, paras 49 and 51.

[26] Commentary to Arts 10, 11 and 12 in the OECD Model Tax Convention, and in particular versions before 2014.

[27] FATF, *Transparency and Beneficial Ownership* (FATF, 2014) 8; Global Forum on Transparency and Exchange of Information for Tax Purposes (n 9) 19; OECD, *Standard for Automatic Exchange of Financial Information in Tax Matters Implementation Handbook* (OECD Publishing, 2015) 47, 80; OECD (n 8) 57 and 198.

[28] FATF, *40 Recommendations* (FATF, 2003) 15.

Three comments may be derived from this definition. First, a beneficial owner is a natural or physical person. The rule is trying to find a person, the potential criminal, hidden behind or part of a corporate structure. Secondly, beneficial owner is used in relation to corporations and other arrangements without legal personality. Thirdly, two definitions are used, seemingly interchangeably. The first one focuses on control, while the second focuses on the person on whose behalf the transaction is conducted.

The problem of the definition based on control is that such a concept is undefined and could be interpreted in two different senses: on the one hand, as referred to legal control or ownership control, and on the other hand, as economic or factual control. As per the FATF Recommendations, it seems the definition gives priority to the person who economically or factually controls the entity, even though it establishes some presumptions as it refers to ownership or legal control through managing positions to make it possible to define a beneficial owner in cases where it is difficult to determine the control of the entity. But these exceptions are operational clauses to prevent the rules from failing in cases where it is impossible to define the controlling person. In the end, it is probable that both legal and economic analyses are needed to reach a conclusion. However, as the concept will greatly depend on the case at stake, the results could be inconsistent.

The second definition, the person on whose behalf a transaction is carried out, poses similar problems. It may be defined in a legal sense as the person to whom legal consequences of a transaction are attributed, or in an economic sense as the person to whom economic benefits of a transaction accrue.

The interpretative notes on FATF Recommendations 10, 24 and 25 actually put the spotlight on control, with priority given to the ultimate controller.[29] These interpretative notes state that beneficial owner for legal entities refers to: (i) the identity of the natural persons who ultimately have a controlling ownership interest in a legal person; (ii) to the extent that there is doubt as to whether the person(s) with the controlling ownership interest is or are the beneficial owner(s) or where no natural person exerts control, the identity of the natural persons (if any) exercising control of the legal person or arrangement through other means; and (iii) where no natural person is identified, the identity of the relevant natural person who holds the position or the senior managing official.[30]

These definitions give enough indication of who is beneficial owner in most cases in relation to corporations. Other cases, however, such as trusts, are more complex. In the case of a trust with several trustees and/or beneficiaries, or foundations, for instance, it would be difficult to identify a single controlling person. In those cases, the FATF Recommendations indicate that all the subjects involved should be identified, including trustees, settlors, protectors, beneficiaries, and any other natural person exercising ultimate effective control over the trust, including through a chain of control or ownership.[31] Another complex case could be widely held investment funds. In this case, the

[29] FATF, *International Standards on Combating Money Laundering and the Financing of Terrorism & Proliferation* (FATF, 2016) 22, 61–62, 86–93.

[30] See para 5(b)(i) of Interpretative Note to Recommendation 10 in ibid 61–62.

[31] ibid 62.

manager would normally be regarded as the beneficial owner as he or she would control the fund, unless a fund investor controls the fund.

The commanding role of control in the definition makes defining who is the beneficial owner really complex in several cases. In addition to the qualitative issue of defining control in a legal or economic sense, there is also the issue of defining the intensity of the control needed to qualify as beneficial owner. For instance, would a person with control over significant organic decisions, but who has a minority stake in relation to ordinary business, qualify as beneficial owner?[32] Different due diligence from different intermediaries obliged to submit information could lead to inconsistencies.

(iii) The Mismatch on the Object of Exchange of Information and FATF Definitions and the Problem of an Open Definition

Because the concepts have been imported to exchange of information rules from FATF with little adaptation, the rules do not fit properly and lead to mismatches.

First, the FATF Recommendations are aimed at implementing and harmonising legal, administrative and regulatory measures to prevent international crimes, namely money laundering, terrorism financing, proliferation and other threats.[33] In this regard, the FATF recommendations were originally aimed at preventing money laundering from drug trafficking, but more recently they have been broadened to money laundering in general.[34] As may be seen, these objectives are aimed at preventing serious international crimes through the control and limiting of their financing. As a consequence, the definition of beneficial owner in the FATF Recommendations is conditioned by such objectives, as they try to unravel the physical or natural person hiding behind or controlling such structure, as they are the persons responsible for such crimes.[35]

Exchange of information on tax matters has a different function, as its aim is to at enable the application of tax rules.[36] In this regard, the application of tax rules requires, among other activities, that ability to pay is quantified and allocated according to the relevant rules. Thus, income allocation may refer to a physical person or a legal person, depending on the case and the rules involved. And the natural persons behind a corporate structure or an arrangement without legal personality could be relevant or absolutely irrelevant, depending on the case and the allocation rules at stake, whether domestic or conventional. This is even clearer in cases where the FATF indicates that the beneficial owner is a managing or senior official controlling the entity, or, in case of funds, the manager controlling the fund.[37] Even though such information may be relevant for administrative purposes, its relevance for the assessment of taxation as

[32] Regarding control in US proposals implementing FATF recommendations, see TE Rutledge, 'Requiring Disclosure of Business Entity Ownership: Proposed New Laws Are Burdensome, but with the Benefit of Being Ineffective' [2010] *Journal of Passthrough Entities* 60.

[33] FATF (n 29) 7.

[34] ibid.

[35] Even though this historical premise has been challenged by several jurisdictions establishing criminal responsibility of legal entities that may even lead to disincorporation.

[36] See Art 26 of the OECD Model Tax Convention, Art 4 on the Multilateral Convention on Assistance in Tax Matters and Art 1 on the Model Treaty on Exchange of Information.

[37] (i.iii) and (ii.ii) in FATF (n 29) 62.

regards the application of the law is doubtful. In this sense, it might be controversial to consider information on beneficial owners, as per managers, as 'foreseeably relevant' for application of taxes, as treaties require. As this information does not aid quantification or attribution of income, it could be regarded as irrelevant, and the state requested to supply the information may deny it, or the subjects involved may challenge the exchange procedure. However, as the concept is included in the Global Forum and OECD manuals, it could be argued that the international consensus considers such information as foreseeably relevant for tax purposes.

The main problem relating to the above-mentioned issues is that once the information has been exchanged, the tax authorities may be tempted to consider the subject as the person to whom income has to be allocated for tax purposes. It is clear that exchange of information rules do not define allocation of income for tax purposes or tax treaties, but once the identification of an individual behind an arrangement is known to the tax authorities, the authorities may be tempted to allocate the income to them or to consider them the beneficial owner for the purposes of tax treaties, in order to define their tax obligations. This is especially true for tax authorities with little expertise in beneficial ownership. Moreover, the use of the wording 'ownership' denotes a strong link to the income that implicitly tells the authorities that this is the person to whom income has to be allocated following ordinary tax law allocation rules that usually follow private law. The result is that allocation rules, requalification rules such as anti-avoidance rules or the redefinition of facts may push to align allocation of income or its consequences upon the individual controlling the entity or arrangement.

In addition, because the definition mixes the controlling person and the person on behalf of whom the transaction is carried out, it could lead to the mistaken consideration that the person controlling is the person to whom the transaction can be legally or economically allocated. The use of 'on behalf of' in the general definition has implicit considerations of allocation that do not relate to the specific definitions used by the interpretation notes.[38] As the specific controlling definitions are directed at persons who may legally have nothing to do with the income for the purposes of tax rules, both considerations jointly considered may allocate income for tax purposes to the controller.

The definitions as used by exchange of information reports by the Global Forum and OECD are misleading because exchange of information rules do not reflect the flexibility they have in FATF regulations. These reports have assumed some examples provided by FATF Recommendations as strict rules, and such rules do not make any sense for tax purposes. As an example, the FATF Recommendations point out in a footnote that it might be useful to use an ownership threshold to identify cases of control, and they mention 25 per cent as a mere example.[39] However, Global Forum exchange of information reports, and consequently many countries' rules on the issue, have considered 25 per cent to be a fixed threshold for defining beneficial ownership for tax information purposes.[40] This may lead to the misapplication of tax rules and has few grounds, as it is not related at all to substantive tax rules. Moreover, a broadly held corporation could be controlled with less participation, and establishing a threshold may lead to it dividing activities and participations to try to avoid characterisation as beneficial ownership.

[38] Global Forum on Transparency and Exchange of Information for Tax Purposes (n 9) 219.
[39] FATF (n 29) 61, fn 32.
[40] OECD (n 27) 47; OECD (n 8) 198.

It is also true that OECD and Global Forum documents point out that the use of FATF definitions should be adapted to the context of the exchange of information and cannot be applied beyond the limits of what is necessary for such purposes.[41] However, this is only made as a general statement, while the FATF's definitions for controlling persons are shown to be absolute in several exchange of information instruments. The problem is that careless appliers may not look at the FATF documents but simply take definitions from the CRS, the Handbook, FATCA and the Directives on Administrative Cooperation and Anti-Money Laundering, reflecting partial aspects of the FATF in an absolute manner and even deriving more specific definitions from them.

Finally, because the concept is undefined and gives a prominent role to control, which remains undefined especially regarding the intensity of control required, the definition of how to identify beneficial owners and, consequently, the information to exchange remains entirely at the will of the countries. Countries may exchange subjects under different criteria, leading to a 'babel' conflict. They will apparently speak the same language under the beneficial owner and control criteria, but under the apparently same meaning there will be different cases. This might not be a significant problem for criminal matters, as they will be taken as indicators that will need further facts to be presented in court. But for tax authorities, careful consideration and additional information on facts will be needed to assert whether the presumed beneficial owner actually is a relevant person in relation to the object of the income subject to taxation.

In sum, the use of beneficial ownership as defined by the FATF on exchange of information for tax matters is a considerable flaw that could lead to several misunderstandings and mismatches in the application of tax rules. The origin of the misunderstanding is the G20 call for the Global Forum to work together with the FATF on exchange of information on beneficial owners.[42] This might make sense because cases involving financing of crimes may also involve tax crimes or are related to avoidance of taxes, but conversely, tax avoidance does not always imply financing crimes. The Global Forum itself calls for FATF Recommendations to be taken into account carefully and adapted to the new context,[43] but such a call is hidden among the significance given by the rules provided by law on exchange of information to the meanings of the FATF Recommendations.

Moreover, the author's view is that the misuse of beneficial ownership in exchange of information is not a matter of intensity or adapting it to the context as if a careful use could fit the concept to its new function, but that the concept should have taken a different wording and not beneficial owner as the term is absolutely misplaced. In addition, many jurisdictions that do not know the concept of beneficial ownership are introducing it into their domestic rules without considering their scope and limits to their use.[44] And these limits may not recommend its use for tax purposes because the

[41] Global Forum on Transparency and Exchange of Information for Tax Purposes (n 9) 18.

[42] See, eg G20 Leaders' Declaration, 6 September 2013, St Petersburg, para 51, calling for the Global Forum to draw on the FATF works. See the rest of the declarations, calling for joint works or drawing attention to FATF, in n 5 above.

[43] Global Forum on Transparency and Exchange of Information for Tax Purposes (n 9) 18.

[44] On the inconsistent implementation of beneficial ownership in Colombia because of the pressure to commit to international standards to access the OECD, see PA Hernández González-Barreda, 'El Concepto de Beneficiario Efectivo En La Reforma Tributaria: Intercambio de Información y Normas Antiabuso' in JR Piza et al (eds), *El Impacto de la Ley 1819 de 2016 y sus Desarrollos en el Sistema Tributario Colombiano* (Universidad Externado de Colombia, 2018).

risk that the use of the concept leads to mismatches on allocation of income is too high to adopt it. Moreover, it is doubtful if this information is relevant or, in the case of automatic exchange, proportional, as will be seen later. In any case, the beneficial ownership rule is there and it has to be applied, so it is essential to remember that the information obtained under the beneficial owner rules simply serves to define the facts, and subsequent careful analysis of the facts and context should be made in order to assess tax obligations and, if information is missing, what additional information on how the beneficial owner relates to the income is required.

Finally, it should not be forgotten that, as mentioned before, beneficial ownership and similar concepts in relation to exchange of information cannot be mismatched with the same wording in tax treaties. Their different contexts, purposes and development clearly show they have to be interpreted separately.[45]

II. Beneficial Ownership in Exchange of Information in EU Law

A. Automatic Exchange of Information on Financial Accounts: Council Directive 2014/107/EU (DAC2)

The Directive of Administrative Cooperation was amended in 2014 to implement the CRS in the European Union.[46] Some EU countries had already implemented the CRS in advance, through their bilateral agreements with the USA, to prevent FATCA from being enacted unilaterally.[47] However, the EU expanded the obligation to coordinate the obligations of exchanges between Member States, but also to third states that are part of the CRS system.

The scope of exchange, the definitions and all the regulations follow the Global Forum and the CRS, so there is no difference with the above-mentioned issues with reference to the definition of beneficial ownership.[48]

What is remarkable is that by enacting the Directive on Administrative Cooperation rules in exchange of information matters regarding financial accounts, the EU has become competent by exercise in such matter. This could be argued in the future if the EU wishes to strengthen exchange of information rules. It may even be argued that the external relations to negotiate this matter with third states are now within EU competences, though this is very much subject to debate.

[45] Pointing to the different contexts of beneficial ownership within the EU in the Interest and Royalties Directive and the Exchange of Information in the Savings Directive, see F Avella, 'Using EU Law to Interpret Undefined Tax Treaty Terms: Article 31 (3)(c) of the Vienna Convention on the Law of Treaties and Article 3 (2) of the OECD Model Convention' (2012) 4 *World Tax Journal* 95, s 5.1.

[46] Council Directive 2014/107/EU of 9 December 2014 amending Directive 2011/16/EU as regards mandatory automatic exchange of information in the field of taxation.

[47] See Joint Statement from the United States, France, Germany, Italy, Spain and the United Kingdom Regarding an Intergovernmental Approach to Improving International Tax Compliance and Implementing FATCA, 7 February 2012; Letter to Commissioner Algirdas Semeta from the Ministers of Finance of Germany, France, United Kingdom, Spain and Italy, 9 April 2013.

[48] See Arts 9 and 13 of the Council Directive 2014/107/EU and compare the content with OECD (n 8).

B. Exchange of Information on Legal Persons and Other Legal Arrangements: Directive (EU) 2016/2258 (DAC5)

In 2015, the so-called G5 – Spain, Italy, France, Germany and the UK – proposed to establish mechanisms on registers and automatic exchange of information regarding the beneficial owner of legal persons and other legal arrangements, which was supported by the G20, the Global Forum and the OECD.[49]

The EU then followed those countries in implementing that policy through Directive (EU) 2016/2258, regarding access to anti-money laundering information by tax authorities.[50] This Directive enables tax authorities to access information collected under Directive (EU) 2015/849 on money laundering, which reflects and transforms the FATF Recommendations into hard law in the EU. Thus, tax authorities have access to information on beneficial ownership of legal persons and other arrangements.

The Anti-Money Laundering Directive, to which Directive 2016/2258 amending the Directive on Administrative Cooperation submits to define access of tax authorities to exchange of information on beneficial owners, is based on the FATF Recommendations, so its beneficial ownership definition is largely based on the FATF definition of the concept. Beneficial owner is defined as any natural person(s) who ultimately owns or controls the customer and/or the natural person(s) on whose behalf a transaction or activity is being conducted.[51] In addition, the Anti-Money Laundering Directive provides more precise definitions as specific projections of the general definition.

In the case of corporate entities, beneficial owner is defined as the natural person(s) who ultimately owns or controls a legal entity through direct or indirect ownership of a sufficient percentage of the shares or voting rights, or ownership interest in that entity, including through bearer shareholdings or through control via other means, excluding listed companies.[52] In addition, it states that direct or indirect ownership of 25 per cent plus one of shall be indicative of ownership, even though it allows Member States to lower that percentage.[53]

For indirect participations, the Anti-Money Laundering Directive, to which the Directive on Administrative Cooperation submits, currently defines indirect participation as referring to a joint 25 per cent plus one ownership by a corporation under the control of the beneficial owner, or by multiple corporate entities which are under the control of the same natural person.[54]

As in the FATF, although the main definition points either to control or the person on whose behalf the transaction is conducted, the specific definitions are largely based

[49] Letter from the Finance Ministers of Germany, France, United Kingdom, Italy and Spain to G20 Finance Ministers, 14 April 2016. This matter was also in a previous declaration, the Declaration on Automatic Exchange of Information in Tax Matters, 6 May 2014.

[50] See Council Directive (EU) 2016/2258 of 6 December 2016 amending Directive 2011/16/EU as regards access to anti-money-laundering information by tax authorities.

[51] Art 3(6) of Directive 2015/849/EU of the European Parliament and of the Council of 20 May 2015 on the prevention of the use of the financial system for the purposes of money laundering or terrorist financing, amending Regulation (EU) No 648/2012 of the European Parliament and of the Council, and repealing Directive 2005/60/EC of the European Parliament and of the Council and Commission Directive 2006/70/EC.

[52] Art 3(6)(a)(i) of Directive 2015/849/EU.

[53] ibid.

[54] ibid.

on control. More specifically, the main definition deals with ownership. However, as ownership is supplemented, especially in indirect participations, with control in a general sense, the definitions provided in the Anti-Money Laundering Directive enable Member States to provide a different definition of control. Among others, it suggests control as defined for consolidated financial reporting in Directive 2013/34/EU.[55] It is unclear whether authorisation for a different control definition only refers to indirect participations or also for the general definition of control. The latter seems preferable because it is at the end of the paragraph and covers the whole content of the paragraph. The fact that the general definition offers a broad definition also supports this view.

Finally, it states that if it is not possible to determine, or there are doubts regarding, such a person, the senior managing official would be regarded as the beneficial owner.[56]

Regarding trusts, beneficial owners include settlors, trustees, protectors, beneficiaries or persons with main interest, and any other person exercising ultimate control.[57]

In the case of legal entities such as foundations or legal arrangements similar to trusts, the beneficial owner is the person holding a similar position to those mentioned regarding trusts.[58]

The meaning of beneficial ownership provided by the Anti-Money Laundering Directive, to which the Directive on Administrative Cooperation for Tax Matters refers, raises several comments. First of all, even though the definition largely follows the definitions provided by the FATF Recommendations, it significantly improves them by specifying that such definitions are normally an indication of beneficial ownership, implicitly assuming they are not absolute and precise definitions. In this sense, there might be other persons controlling the entity that may be regarded as beneficial owners, even though they are not mentioned in the Directive's definition.[59] However, the mentioned cases in the Directive seem to be considered beneficial owners in any case, as the definition includes them as a sort of minimum. All in all, the language used seems to give more leeway for departing from such definitions in certain cases. For instance, when the Directive deals with percentage of ownership, it says a certain level of shareholding 'shall be an indication'.[60] Even though it uses the word shall, the use of 'indication' could be interpreted in the sense that it is not an absolute definition.

Secondly, as the Directive enables a state to reduce the percentage required to consider a person as controlling the entity, there might be several differences among contracting states and with third countries using the 25 per cent rule as contained in the recommendations.[61] This flexibility is a consequence of the more imprecise definition the Directive uses as compared to the FATF Recommendations, which is probably good for anti-money laundering purposes. If, however, as previously stated, defining beneficial ownership with reference to a percentage could be a mistake for

[55] ibid.
[56] Art 3(6)(a)(ii) of Directive 2015/849/EU.
[57] Art 3(6)(b) of Directive 2015/849/EU.
[58] Art 3(6)(c) of Directive 2015/849/EU.
[59] Art 3(6) of Directive 2015/849/EU states beneficial owners include 'at least', suggesting it may cover others and the definition is not closed.
[60] Art 3(6)(a)(i) of Directive 2015/849/EU.
[61] Art 3(6)(a)(i) of Directive 2015/849/EU.

tax purposes, to allow different percentages would be even worse, as it could lead to significant confusion. One state receiving information on subjects from a country with a lower threshold could imply that they are using same percentage. Thus, when exchanging information on beneficial ownership between entities within the EU, and between Member States and third countries, caution should be given to the percentages used by each state.

Thirdly, where different levels of corporations and participations are involved, definition of beneficial ownership could be highly complex and burdensome. This is not a significant problem from a legal point of view, but the issue could be that the complexity makes the results unreliable and leads to misunderstandings. Moreover, because indirect participations depend on a concept of control that is open to Member States, the results could be varied.[62] Also, the fact that states may define beneficial ownership in a different sense, covering more cases, as the Directive states the definition simply includes 'at least' as a minimum rule, would result in an authentic European diversity of beneficial owners. This, in addition to the different possible thresholds, makes the results incredibly complex. Moreover, even if all Member States use the definition of control of the Consolidated Financial Statements Rules, as such control definition remains open-ended, several beneficial owners may be identified in complex structures.[63]

Finally, irrespective of whether the 25 per cent percentage threshold is taken or another lower number, planning schemes based on such a safe harbour may allow the avoidance of reporting.[64] In addition, 25 per cent has been considered for some as a large number, because much lower participations may enable control in large companies, participations that it would be worthwhile to subject to reporting.[65] In addition, if 25 per cent is taken as the threshold, three persons may be considered beneficial owners at the same time, which could mislead the tax analysis of the case. On the other hand, for each state to be able to lower the threshold differently may lead to miscommunications between states if not all countries adopt the same number.

In sum, Directive (EU) 2016/2258's definition of beneficial ownership of corporations and other legal arrangements may be considered an improvement on the FATF definition as it makes it more flexible and probably more able to adequately take into account individual cases for the prevention of money laundering. However, the definition still might be inadequate for tax purposes because the above-mentioned issues are still at stake in that concept.

[62] Commenting on the Anti-Money Laundering Directive, Ganguli discussed different possibilities on how to define indirect participations and control, and its uncertainty, in relation to the previous 2005 Anti-Money Laundering Directive. Even though the current wording provides some more light, the definition in relation to indirect participations might still be highly controversial. See I Ganguli, 'The Third Directive: Some Reflections on Europe's New AML/CFT Regime' (2010) 29 *Banking & Financial Services Policy Report* 1, 5–6.

[63] ibid 5. See Directive 2013/34/EU of the European Parliament and of the Council of 26 June 2013 on the annual financial statements, consolidated financial statements and related reports of certain types of undertakings, amending Directive 2006/43/EC of the European Parliament and of the Council and repealing Council Directives 78/660/EEC and 83/349/EEC.

[64] ibid 5–6.

[65] Open Ownership and Global Witness, 'Learning the Lessons from the UK's Public Beneficial Ownership Register' (2017) 7, https://www.globalwitness.org/documents/19250/Learning_the_Lessons_from_the_UKs_public_Beneficial_Ownership_register.pdf.

III. The UK Registers on Beneficial Ownership

A. The Register of People with Significant Control

In 2015, the UK became one of the first countries in the world to establish a beneficial owner register.[66] The Small Business, Enterprise and Employment Act 2015 established obligations for certain companies regarding the Register of People with Significant Control.[67]

The Act requires companies within the scope of the registration duties to hold a register of: (i) individuals who are people with significant control or beneficial owners; and (ii) relevant legal entities with control over the company.[68]

The Act establish duties of identification and reporting of individuals of people with significant control or beneficial owners, who are: (i) persons that hold, directly or indirectly, more than 25 per cent of the shares in a company; (ii) persons that hold, directly or indirectly, more than 25 per cent of the voting rights; (iii) persons that hold, directly or indirectly, the right to appoint or remove a majority of the board of directors; (iv) persons who exercise, or have the right to exercise, significant influence or control over a company; (v) trustees of a trust or party to other arrangements not being legal persons (partnerships) who exercise, or have the right to exercise, control on the trust or arrangement; and (vi) trustees of a trust or party to other arrangements not being legal persons (partnerships) who fulfil any mentioned condition on ownership, voting rights, rights to appoint directors or significant influence or control.[69]

The rule also states how indirect participations define beneficial ownership through majority stakes.[70] If a person holds a majority stake in an entity, which in turn holds a controlling interest as previously defined in a company, that person would be regarded as the beneficial owner for the purposes of the register. The definition of majority interest includes: (i) holding the majority of voting rights in the company that holds the controlling interest in another company; (ii) being a member of a company and having the right to appoint or remove a majority of the board of the company that holds the controlling interest; (iii) being a member of the company and controlling alone, pursuant to a shareholders' agreement, a majority of votes in the company that holds the controlling interest; and (iv) having the right to exercise, or actually exercising, 'dominant influence or control' over the company that holds the controlling interest. Controlling interest, in turn, is defined by the rules of significant control. In addition, successive chains of ownership will be defined by majority rules in the intermediary companies, while the last controlled company will be defined by previous rules on significant control.

[66] F Mor, 'Registers of Beneficial Ownership' (House of Commons, 2019) 8259 5, http://researchbriefings.files.parliament.uk/documents/CBP-8259/CBP-8259.pdf.

[67] See s 81 of and Sch 3 to the Small Business, Enterprise and Employment Act 2015 c 26.

[68] See ss 790B and 790M of the Companies Act 2006 as amended by Sch 3 to the Small Business, Enterprise and Employment Act 2015 c 26.

[69] See Pt 1 of Sch 1A to the Companies Act 2006 as amended by Sch 3 to the Small Business, Enterprise and Employment Act 2015 c 26.

[70] See s 18 of Sch 1A to the Companies Act 2006 as amended by Sch 3 to the Small Business, Enterprise and Employment Act 2015 c. 26.

Other rules oblige the reporting of interests in companies, although this does not refer to significant persons or beneficial owners.

The definitions of persons exercising significant influence pose the same controversy regarding international instruments as those defining control, interest and the use of the 25 per cent threshold, especially regarding Directive on Administrative Cooperation from which it is derived.

The fourth test, referring to persons who have the right to exercise or actually exercise control, is relevant because it is the closing clause to catch cases that escape thresholds.[71] It actually comprises two different tests: the first one looks at whether an individual has a right, while the second looks at the position in fact.[72]

The right to exercise significant influence or control includes absolute decision rights over matters related to the running of the business.[73] Some examples are powers to decide on adopting or changing business plans, changes in the business, appointment or removal of the CEO, or borrowing.[74] Also, vetoes over business plans or borrowing may imply beneficial ownership.[75] Some authors wonder whether these examples are self-standing, as a person with only the right to veto additional borrowing but with no other power does not seem to have clear control.[76] It also seems that a veto given to minorities does not trigger control, although it might be unclear what is a minority right.[77] Also, control is excluded where an absolute right or control is derived from being a prospective purchaser subject to conditions, such as clearance by competition authorities.[78] This may enable one to argue that there is no control in purchases of companies subject to conditions where the condition is pending.[79]

Examples regarding the second test, the actual control, refer to cumulative effects, such as a director who owns keys.[80] The facts that he or she is a director and owns the keys may lead to the conclusion that he or she is a significant person. Also, a person who is not a member of the board of directors, but who regularly directs or influences decisions of the board, or a person whose recommendations always or almost always are followed by shareholders with a majority of voting rights would fall within such definition.[81]

Several roles are excluded, such as lawyers, accountants, consultants, tax advisors, regulators, suppliers, liquidators and managing directors.[82] The reason is obvious:

[71] A Turner and T Follet, 'Tangled up in Chains? Making Sense of the New UK Requirement to Keep Registers of "people with Significant Control"' (2016) 22 *Trusts and Trustees* 537, 542–43.

[72] ibid 543.

[73] ibid.

[74] See s 2.6 of the Statutory Guidance on the Meaning of 'Significant Influence or Control' over Companies in the Context of the Register of People with Significant Control (Department for Business, Energy and Industrial Strategy, June 2017).

[75] ibid s 2.7.

[76] Turner and Follet (n 71) 543.

[77] See s 2.8 of Statutory Guidance (n 74); Turner and Follet (n 71).

[78] See 2.8 of Statutory Guidance (n 74).

[79] In a case similar to *Wood Preservation Ltd v Prior (Commissioner)* (1969) 1 WLR 1077. However, in that case, the position of the court was that because the condition was available to the purchaser, beneficial ownership was fully available to him. One wonders what would happen in terms of control reporting.

[80] See s 3.2 of Statutory Guidance (n 74).

[81] ibid s 3.3.

[82] ibid s 4.

clearly they influence decisions at the request of the persons controlling the entity, but on an independent or quasi-independent basis and not because of their own interest in the business.

The problem of the rules governing the register, as well as the statutory guidance, is that the definitions and examples are very broad, vague and subject to the facts, which would raise great uncertainty.

In the case of the right to exercise or the actual exercise of rights in relation to trusts or other arrangements, similar reasoning applies. The right to exercise may be derived from: the right to appoint trustees, partners, etc, except by court or by breach of fiduciary duty; the right to direct the distribution of funds or assets; the right to direct investments; the right to amend the deeds; or the rights to revoke or terminate.[83] In these cases, analysing the functions of settlors or protectors may be of significance.[84] For instance, the powers of a settlor to revoke a trust may be an indication of settlor control.

In the case of actual exercise in relation to trusts, it seems that regular involvement and active exercise are needed.[85]

All these catch-all rules supplementing thresholds and based on the rights to exercise or actual exercise are highly related to the facts, whether legal or effective, which may lead to inconsistencies pending further guidance.[86]

The problem of using this information for tax purposes is that, because they depend on factual analysis, they will assign beneficial owner status to completely different cases. A person holding 50 per cent of shares in a company would be regarded as a significant person in the same way as a person holding the keys and being a director would. Once a beneficial owner is reported, such information without its full context would be misleading once incorporated into tax assessment files. Of what importance would a director with keys be for tax purposes? Careful checking of the facts that lead to the assignment of beneficial owner status should be given to tax authorities.

The definition of majority, in turn, is not fully in line with the Directive on Administrative Cooperation, although the authorisation to the Member States to define control in a different sense gives support to such definition.

In addition, the implementation of the register in the UK had some practical issues. To mention just a few, the use of name, surname, and month and year of birth make it unlikely, if not impossible, to be able to match different records from the same person.[87] Another significant challenge is the management and checking of such an amount of information.[88] Again, if this information is used for tax purposes, there may be significant challenges to fulfilling its purpose of helping to tackle tax avoidance if it is not complete and accurate. In some cases, there is the very great possibility that the information will misdirect the assessment rather than help it.

[83] ibid s 5.3 et seq.
[84] Turner and Follet (n 71) 544.
[85] See s 5.6 of Statutory Guidance (n 74).
[86] Turner and Follet (n 71) 544.
[87] Open Ownership and Global Witness (n 65) 7.
[88] ibid 8.

B. The Commissioner Register of Beneficial Ownership in Relation to Trusts

Following the enactment of the Fourth Anti-Money Laundering Directive, the UK enacted a public register of beneficial owners of trusts known as the Trusts Registration Service (TRS) as the implementation of the directive. The register is governed by the Money Laundering, Terrorist Financing and Transfer of Funds Regulations 2017 (the Regulations).[89]

In the case of trusts, the Regulations define beneficial owner as each settlor, trustee, beneficiary, class of person in whose main interest the trust is set up and any individual who has control over the trust.[90] The definition largely follows the Fourth Anti-Money Laundering Directive, although the Register does not include the protector and eliminates indirect control (in practice, they are, however, included within the scope of the Regulations).

Where the interest in a trust is held by a corporation, which is in turn held by an individual, he or she will be considered as having an interest in or control of the trust.[91] The regulations for beneficial ownership of a trust refer to the beneficial owners of companies. The definition of beneficial ownership of corporations includes indirect participations and indirect control, so beneficial owners of corporations with interest in a trust will be consider beneficial owners of the trust.[92]

In addition, the regulations provide for a precise definition of control. This includes the abilities to: (a) dispose of, advance, lend, invest, pay or apply trust property; (b) vary or terminate the trust; (c) add or remove a person as a beneficiary or to or from a class of beneficiaries; (d) appoint or remove trustees or give another individual control over the trust; and (e) direct, withhold consent to or veto the exercise of a power mentioned in sub-paragraphs (a) to (d).[93] The definition is part of the authorisation of the Fourth Anti-Money Laundering Directive to Member States to define control and includes almost any significant powers in relation to the trust.

The same definitions are provided for foundations, as stated by the directive, although referring to equivalent or similar positions. It is assumed that control also refers to functions analogous to those stated in relation to trusts of disposing, advance, vary or terminate, etc, although this is only stated in relation to the persons involved.

In addition, the Regulations state that individuals holding consent, discretion or power, in relation to power of advancement, power of investigation, power of delegation, or appointment and retirement of a trustee at will of beneficiaries, as well as the joint power of extinction by all beneficiaries who are full of age and capacity, do not define control.[94]

[89] See s 45 of The Money Laundering, Terrorist Financing and Transfer of Funds (Information on the Payer) Regulations 2017, No 692. See also Trust Registration Service (Trs) – Frequently Asked Questions, HMRC Guidance, 9 October 2017.

[90] See s 6(1) of The Money Laundering Regulations (n 89).

[91] ibid s 6(4)(a).

[92] ibid s 6(4)(a).

[93] See s 6(2) of The Money Laundering, Terrorist Financing and Transfer of Funds (Information on the Payer) Regulations 2017, No 692.

[94] ibid s 6(4)(b).

In relation to deceased estates, beneficial owner is defined with reference to the executor (the original or by representation) or administrator for the time being of a deceased person.[95] In Scotland, it is defined in reference to the executor.[96]

For other legal arrangements not falling within the previous definitions, the Regulations state that the beneficial owner is any individual benefiting from the property and, if not defined, the class of persons who may benefit.[97] In the case of indirect benefit through a corporation, similar rules to those above apply.[98] These rules are reiterative as, following interpretation of the rule for foundations and other arrangements, the same conclusion will probably be reached.

Finally, as a catch-all clause, beneficial owner is defined in general as 'the individual who ultimately owns or controls the entity or arrangement or on whose behalf a transaction is being conducted'.[99] This undefined provision would catch almost any case not defined within previous cases as referring to control or the allocation of the effects of a transaction. What could be controversial is whether cases escaping the previous rules, if any, could be subject to the catch-all rule. If those cases were implicitly excluded, it cannot be said that the catch-all rule could cover them. The legislator's intention was not to cover them. However, if they are missing because of a mistake, of course it can cover them. This could raise specific controversial cases, although, because of the broad definition of previous cases, it is difficult to imagine a case that could escape.

All definitions match the Fourth Anti-Money Laundering Directive's definitions, although the meanings are adapted to the specific institutions of England, Wales and Scotland.

The Regulations also provide definitions of beneficial ownership for body corporates and partnerships. Although subjected to the commissioner trust register in a different manner to trusts, they are subject to some obligations regarding information.

In these cases, beneficial owner is defined for bodies corporate as: an individual exercising control over the management of the body corporate; an individual owning or controlling directly or indirectly more than 25 per cent of the shares or voting rights; or an individual who controls the body corporate.[100] The definition of control is submitted to Schedule 1A to the Companies Act 2006, so the definition in this part is harmonised with the beneficial owner definition of the Register of People with Significant Control.[101] In addition, the subsidiary definition of Companies Act 2006 is also used.[102]

In relation to partnerships, the definition also follows the 25 per cent control and ultimate control of the management criteria.[103] However, it does not define control for partnerships by submission to Schedule 1A of the Companies Act 2006. In turn,

[95] ibid s 6(6)(a).
[96] ibid s 6(6)(b).
[97] ibid s 6(7).
[98] ibid s 6(8).
[99] ibid s 6(9).
[100] ibid s 5(1).
[101] ibid s 5(2)(a).
[102] ibid s 5(2)(b).
[103] ibid s 5(3)(a).

it adds the criterion of satisfying the beneficial ownership conditions set out in Part 1 of Schedule 1 to the Scottish Partnerships (Register of People with Significant Control) Regulations 2017,[104] although these are essentially the same as in Schedule 1A of the Companies Act 2006.

IV. Data Protection, Privacy and Beneficial Ownership Registers: The Relevance of Beneficial Ownership in Exchange of Information for Allocation of Income

One of the main concerns regarding exchange of information for tax matters is privacy rights and data protection of the information exchanged, including beneficial ownership.[105] The huge amount of information that is being collected by tax authorities following international developments triggered by tax scandals raises the risk of having such an amount of sensitive information concentrated in just a few databases.

From a practical point of view, some hackings of large international financial databases have raised the question of whether it is safe to concentrate the personal information of taxpayers, bank information and amounts into a single database such as under the CRS.[106]

From a legal perspective, the first concern is whether amassing such information is proportionate regarding its effect on the right to privacy.[107] In this regard, some authors wonder whether exchanges of information under the CRS follow right to privacy case law, because: they allow authorities to access and store content on a general basis, compromising the essence of the fundamental right to a private life; the storage of data on a generalised basis without any differentiation or exception is not limited to what is necessary; and it does not provide for remedies to access, modify or erase data relating to them.[108]

On the subject of regulation of right to privacy, authors have also wondered whether exchange of information is compatible with data protection regulations.[109]

An additional concern is whether these automatic exchanges are compatible with treaties establishing exchange of information, as it is questionable in many cases whether the information could be regarded as foreseeably relevant.[110]

[104] ibid s 5(3)(b).

[105] See, among others, F Noseda, 'Common Reporting Standard and EU Beneficial Ownership Registers: Inadequate Protection of Privacy and Data Protection' (2017) 23 *Trusts and Trustees* 404; P Baker, 'Privacy Rights in an Age of Transparency: A European Perspective' [2016] *Tax Notes International* 583; AEFI Expert Group, 'First Report of the Commission AEFI Expert Group on the Implementation of Directive 2014/107/EU for Automatic Exchange of Financial Account Information' (AEFI Group, 2015); V Wöhrer, *Data Protection and Taxpayers' Rights: Challenges Created by Automatic Exchange of Information* (IBFD, 2018).

[106] Noseda (n 105) 405; Wöhrer (n 105) s 5.2.

[107] Baker (n 105) 584; Noseda (n 105) 407; Wöhrer (n 105) s 6.

[108] See, among others, *X v Belgium*, *Fs v Germany*, *Janyr v Czech Rpeublic*, *Sabou v Czech Republic*, the *Schrems* cases and others quoted in Baker (n 105) 584; Noseda (n 105) 407. See also cases quoted and commentaries in Offermanns (n 1) 407; Wöhrer (n 105) s 6.

[109] Wöhrer (n 105) s 7; Baker (n 105) 585–86.

[110] Wöhrer (n 105) s 4.7; Noseda (n 105) 407.

In this sense, authors raise doubts as to whether information is relevant, and to some extent if the massive exchange of such information is proportionate, putting the spotlight on the object. Examples include exchange of information on assets while the home state does not charge capital or wealth taxes,[111] as well as exchange of information to home states applying special tax regimes on a territorial basis, as information from abroad does not feature in the assessment.[112] Other challenged cases include the exchange of information of persons related to any type of entity or arrangement, on the basis of relationships to the vehicle that have little to do with ownership or tax entitlement,[113] the report of assets where there is no increase in gains or income,[114] and reporting in relation to charities.[115]

The fact that a huge amount of non-relevant information is exchanged is attributed by some authors to the fact that the CRS is copied from FATCA, which was more or less adapted to the US tax system, but does not fit every tax system.[116]

In the author's view, the above-mentioned facts, such as a country not charging wealth tax or that a taxpayer does not have a capital gain or income within the period, does not undermine the foreseeable relevance of the information. In fact, only once the information is obtained and compared to previous years may the capital gain be considered as non-existent. For the purpose of checking whether a capital gain exists or not, it is undoubtedly relevant. Also, in cases of special tax regimes, information may be relevant as certain requirements apply in some cases which without such information could not be assessed.

Also, it does not seem to be disproportionate, as other means would not guarantee proper assessment in several cases.

The problem, rather than being in the relevance of the objects of information exchanged, lays in the definition of the subjects. Why would a certain state need to know that a director with the keys is a relevant person for tax purposes? Cases such as this which concern partially controlling persons, or persons with a veto on borrowing, etc, can be seen as disproportionate and not relevant for the purposes of tax assessment. These cases correspond to the UK system, but almost all countries have issues because of the open control definition proposed by the FATF Recommendations, the CRS and Anti-Money Laundering Directive and the Directive on Administrative Cooperation.

While, in the USA, FATCA defines controlling persons more or less in relation to their economic attribution rules, although also subject to criticism, the implementation by other countries is expanding the terms way beyond their original scope.[117] In relation to trusts, for instance, to exchange information on settlors, trustees, beneficiaries and other persons involved is relevant only because, in the assessment of a trust, the principles detailed in chapter three above define to whom the income is allocated. However,

[111] Noseda (n 105) 407.
[112] ibid.
[113] ibid 408.
[114] ibid.
[115] ibid.
[116] ibid.
[117] ibid.

that information has to be properly balanced against the certainty, uncertainty and anti-abuse principles.

The principles of proportionality and subsidiarity challenge the burden of disclosure charged on entities and taxpayers, especially within the European Union, and also question exchange of information obligations between Member States.[118]

Ultimately, the important point in proportionality is whether the definitions provided regarding beneficial ownership match their purpose, ie to assess taxes. Because most states normally impose taxes in a personal sense, the subject is highly relevant.[119] However, most states charge taxes on the legal owner.[120] Because the concepts of control and participation in entities and arrangements are based on economic concepts, it is highly debatable whether they are generally relevant for tax assessment. Domestic allocation under economic ownership is normally done under anti-avoidance rules or economic qualification rules,[121] but in several countries, probably a majority, the use of such rules is an exception, as there is a presumption of validity of private rules, at least as a starting point, including allocation of income.[122] The result is that the relevance and proportionality of exchange of information on beneficial ownership is highly debatable because the application of taxes upon economic ownership, to which such ownership refers, should be exceptional and not the general rule for the allocation of income. However, there are some cases in which it may be useful.

In some cases, arrangements and entities may be purely simulated, while the actual ownership is hidden. In those cases, exchange of information may serve to define who under the actual legal facts is the legal owner. Also, some cases may be arranged in an artificial manner, so the facts exchanged under these beneficial ownership rules could help to define what the tax consequences should be following its economic substance. However, the author is unsure whether a significant amount of those cases would justify the vast amount of information that will be exchanged, or whether to reinforce information upon request would have been more proportional. On the point of proportionality, an argument is that the objective of prevention of tax avoidance or evasion may justify exchange measures. However, to some authors this is not the case, as a general presumption of tax avoidance or evasion is insufficient.[123]

Even a pre-filed information system, where information is available upon a simple request but not automatically exchanged, could have been an interesting option to explore.

Finally, there is a significant risk of what has been called risk of false information exchange.[124] If the wrong information is submitted by a country, the second country could assess on the basis of such information, and challenging the information in the administrative processes of the two countries is not an easy task, and may lead to *devil's proof*. Moreover, because subjects are not party to exchange of information, they cannot

[118] See R Offermanns, 'Current Trends Regarding Disclosure Mechanisms: Reporting Ultimate Beneficial Ownership – Part 1' (2019) 59 *European Taxation* 162, 168.
[119] See above, ch 3.
[120] ibid.
[121] See J Wheeler, 'General Report', *Conflicts in the Attribution of Income to a Person* (Kluwer, 2007).
[122] ibid.
[123] Offermanns (n 1) 242.
[124] See Wöhrer (n 105) s 5.3.

discuss the information except in the assessment procedure. Where this happens within a country, authorities or the taxpayer can easily request the person submitting the information, such as a bank, to confirm it. However, where this happens in a cross-border case, expenses, administrative burdens and so on make it almost impossible, or at least highly complex, to challenge it.[125] In the case of beneficial ownership, because the concepts are blurred, the risk of wrong or wrongly interpreted information is significant.

[125] ibid.

8

Final Remarks

Beneficial ownership in recent times could be considered as a myth. As with the seahorse on the cover, some use it to run, some use it to swim. However, the term is probably just an early twentieth-century horse that has been forced to work in post-industrial and digital environments for which it was not invented, especially in the area of tax and international tax law.

Probably because it has always been seen as an imprecise myth, divergent opinions have been extending the concept into areas where it has not been considered before. Over time, social and economic challenges have reshaped the term in equity, tax and international taxation.

At the beginning, the term had no legal meaning, but was a colloquial term to define the intense legal ability regarding an object by the beneficiary in equity, because of the social importance attached to ownership at the end of the nineteenth century. Later, the increasing importance of ownership, the also increasing use of equity instruments for estate and tax planning, and the development of the tax system, the latter largely based upon ownership, caused the concept to increase in importance. More recently, the social concern regarding avoidance has made the term gain relevance. As a blurred term but one still based on ownership, it has enabled cases to be caught where subjects have enjoyed property without being strictly caught by ordinary ownership rules.

Still, these developments have drawn approximate lines on what beneficial owner is in each area. But in any case, beneficial ownership is probably the consequence of *the myth of ownership* as argued by Murphy and Nagel, permeating into equity and tax law, improperly claiming that there should always be a person with an almost absolute entitlement to the income or assets.

I. Beneficial Ownership in Equity

In equity, beneficial ownership has become a term of some strength. The French Revolution brought about an absolute understanding of ownership that it did not have before. The word ownership being inserted in beneficiary rights in equity progressively sneaked an absolute conception of ownership into equity rights. *Saunders v Vautier*, *Baker v Archer-Shee* and, more recently, *FHR European Ventures, Shell UK Ltd and others* and *Twinsectra v Yardley*, among others, have progressively approximated beneficiary rights to continental quasi-absolute legal ownership rights. This does not mean beneficiary rights are always equivalent, not even in the strongest cases. However, in cases where beneficiaries have the broadest beneficiary rights, beneficial ownership is really close to absolute legal ownership.

Consequently, beneficial ownership in equity is at the intersection where beneficiary rights approximates the closest to the main characteristics of absolute legal ownership. Beneficial ownership in equity could be defined as the present right in equity against the world at large over assets or property of a trust outweighing any other rights and usually including a primary right to control and a primary right to income. In addition, it is important to bear in mind that beneficial ownership is a subtype of beneficial interest in a broad sense.

Beneficial interest in a broad sense, in turn, would be a right in equity, normally for the future, including an expectation or right to be taken into consideration, a vested right and beneficial ownership. Thus, only when beneficiary interest qualifies as a proprietary interest may one speak about beneficial ownership.

Beneficial ownership could be jointly held, such as in joint ownership or ownership in common, and it could be possible that a subject is the beneficial owner of just a part of the assets or income from a trust, such as an interest in possession, where it can be said that the subject is the beneficial owner of the income but not of the assets.

In cases of discretionary trusts or suspension of beneficiary rights, such as implicit trusts, where beneficiary rights are subject to conditions, it is the author's view that there could be a negative beneficial ownership right in the potential beneficiaries. In addition, the greatest ownership against the world would be in the trustee as legal owner. This is a minority view, as most authors would consider it is in suspension. In the author's view, it is a matter of timing, as currently the person with the greatest rights is the trustee, while in the future another person will fully acquire them. Still, the issue is probably a matter of label rather than an actual issue. The problem arises where statutes attach consequences to being the beneficial owner.

II. Beneficial Ownership in Tax Law

Because contemporary tax law was built upon the allocation of ability to pay or an object of wealth to a subject, and this depends on ownership, beneficial ownership jumped into tax law. As part of the ownership system of common law countries, beneficial ownership became a necessary tool to define ability to pay. However, because of the flexibility of equity law, beneficiary rights are significantly different, so tax law had to adapt tax rules to such flexibility in order to fulfil the collection of taxes objective. In parallel to the increase in the use of equity instruments for estate and tax planning, as well as jurisdictional remedies, tax law developed some principles, namely two main substantive principles and some additional ideas.

The first principle is what in this book has been called the certainty principle. Under this principle, taxes will be charged on a subject if the subject can be identified as the beneficial owner in equity. This principle follows substantive ownership as, if a defined subject holds an absolute and non-contingent right to income and control either in equity or in common law, that could be claimed against the world – even the trustee and third parties – before a court, irrespective of certain limitations, such as third parties' bona fide rights.

From such principle, there is a second subprinciple or what has been called the uncertainty principle. If nobody can be identified as holding an absolute and non-contingent right to income and control, either in equity or common law, that could be claimed before a court, then taxes will be charged upon the trustee. Because he or she holds the greatest rights in the world in relation to the asset or income, he or she will be regarded as the beneficial owner for tax purposes, despite being unable to enjoy the asset or income or benefit him- or herself.

The second principle is the anti-avoidance principle. If certain conditions are fulfilled, taxes will be charged upon the person controlling the assets or income, the person with revoking powers or the person in whom the economic substantive abilities are vested.

An additional interpretative idea is that beneficial ownership has to be interpreted in the context in which it appears. The above-mentioned principles are subject to nuances depending on the case, so ability to pay, collection of taxes, the objectives of certain reliefs and property rights are balanced.

It must also be taken into account that beneficial ownership may refer to partial items of income, or could be vested in different subjects jointly at the same time. If a subject has an absolute right to income but not to the assets, then he or she will be charged on the income, but will not be considered entitled to the assets for tax purposes. In the case of joint ownership, partial beneficial ownership could be considered.

Finally, and as a consequence of the development of those principles to fit equitable rights and tax objectives, beneficial ownership in tax law does not fully equate to beneficial ownership in equity. Beneficial ownership is not a single concept in tax law, as some have argued, claiming that it is a term of art; rather, it is a set of principles inspiring how income should be allocated, taking into account the principles of equity law balanced against the principles of tax law. These principles are not absolute, but subject to the specific and normally complex rules governing taxation in each country. Indeed, those rules are a reflection of such principles, although they provide several exceptions.

III. Beneficial Ownership in Tax Treaties

Beneficial ownership entered international tax law because the USA started to use its domestic principles on allocation of income in international tax treaties, considering them implicit. However, the concept soon acquired relevance in the UK, which had problems dealing with intermediaries in equity, probably because of the narrow approach to interpreting tax statutes derived from the *Duke of Westminster* case.

From that issue, the wording found its way into Articles 10–12 of the OECD Model Tax Convention (the Model) and spread into the global tax treaty network. Because the negotiations at the OECD reshaped the term, beneficial ownership no longer carried the meaning it had in common law domestic law, either in equity or in tax law.

The concept changed for tax treaties based on the 1977 Model to deny access to treaty provisions in cases where: (i) the subject transfers the economic effect to a third party in payment or kind, or through any other economic effect; (ii) the subject is constrained or obliged to pass the income and it is not merely a discretionary decision or a mere fact; (iii) the accrual of that second obligation arises on the accrual of the income by the intermediary; (iv) the reason for the acquisition of the right from which income derives is linked or is the obligation to pass the income itself; and (v) the obligation to pass the income and the reason for the acquisition of the right were contained in the same arrangement or two simultaneous or subsequent arrangements.

The main problem of such a definition is that the concept does not cover the case in which a subject signs up to two unconnected fully independent agreements, one upon which they receive income and another upon which they pay certain amounts – equivalent to the received ones but not referring to the arrangement upon which income is received by the intermediary. The 1986 Conduit Companies Report and the 2003 Model took these cases into account. The result is that treaties signed following the 1977 Model and taking into account the Conduit Companies Report, or treaties signed following the 2003 Model, exclude the application of treaty provisions in cases where: (i) economic effects are transferred to third parties in payment, kind or any other effect; (ii) the subject is constrained or obliged to pass the income and it is not merely a discretionary decision or a mere factual payment: (iii) the accrual of that second obligation arises on the accrual of the income by the intermediary; (iv) the reason for the acquisition of the right from which income derives is linked or is the obligation to pass the income itself; and (v) the obligation to pass the income and the reason for the acquisition of the right are derived from the same or different, simultaneous, subsequent or independent arrangements, although mutually referenced.

Beneficial ownership cannot be regarded as a broad anti-avoidance rule, nor as an economic ownership rule. First, there is no reference – artificiality, purpose, etc – upon which it could be built. Secondly, without any reference, it may exclude almost any person from the qualification as beneficial owner, as most payments received are used, in turn, to pay providers, family, needs, etc. Finally, at the time the concept was proposed, several countries did not have general anti-avoidance rules, had anti-avoidance rules that were in an early stage of development or had directly rejected them.

Neither could beneficial ownership be regarded as referring to attribution of income rules or subject to tax rules, whether interpreted as requiring effective taxation or merely meaning within the scope of charge and without needing effective taxation. Those views were rejected early on by the OECD, and are in opposition to how treaties allocate tax jurisdiction, although applicable by some countries if specifically providing for income sources relevant to the specific applicable treaty.

The concept of beneficial ownership in international tax treaties refers to the income, not to the asset. In addition, its meaning has nothing to do with beneficial ownership in domestic law or in other international instruments, such as those providing for exchange of information for tax matters or for the prevention of crimes. Another significant point is that beneficial ownership is not implicit in tax treaties.

IV. Beneficial Ownership in Exchange of Information for Tax Matters

The need to exchange beneficial ownership information is not explicitly contained in international instruments governing exchange of information with such wording. It is only in the Common Reporting Standard, the Foreign Account Tax Compliance Act and the EU Directives transposing such instruments that controlling person is used as being similar to beneficial ownership. The need for exchange of information on beneficial ownership/controlling person is contained in reports and documents from the OECD and the Global Forum, which are of controversial legal value.

In those instruments, the use of beneficial ownership wording is misleading, because it relates the term to ownership attributes and, in tax law, to allocation of income principles, and it may improperly be equated to the term in tax treaties. Thus, the first point to note is that such wording should be avoided.

Secondly, beneficial ownership/controlling person is defined by reference to the Financial Action Task Force Recommendations. However, the definitions provided therein do not fit the objective of application of tax rules properly. Because they are aimed at preventing crimes, they wish to identify the individuals behind corporate structures used for financing crime. However, tax law aims at defining the ability to pay on the persons involved. As domestic tax rules normally allocate income on legal ownership, at least as a starting point, the last person in a chain of ownership is not ordinarily relevant. Only in avoidance and fake arrangements may the ultimate controlling person be relevant. The problem is that a massive exchange of information may incentivise the tax authorities to directly apply anti-avoidance rules once a person identified as the ultimate person is on the file. The use of the wording ownership in beneficial ownership contributes to this idea of mismatching the controlling person and the person to whom the income shall be allocated.

Thirdly, definitions provided in different instruments do not match, and are largely based on broad concepts, such as control. This may lead to divergences, which, taking into account that the same wording is used, may lead to the false feeling of speaking on the same terms. In addition, the use of certain thresholds may allow exchange of information planning.

Finally, because exchange of information instruments increasingly perform on an automatic basis, it is controversial whether they are proportionate to the aim of preventing the international tax avoidance and evasion at which they are aimed. Because the information exchanged only matches domestic tax rules in avoidance and fake cases, it is controversial whether exchanging such a massive amount of information is proportionate in justifying such a restriction on the privacy of individuals.

V. Recommendations and Future of Beneficial Ownership

As seen, beneficial ownership is not a single concept, but is a wording with several nuances depending on the context. Because of the false feeling of being a term of art, and the misinterpretations it may lead to for lawyers with little expertise in the area, the author would suggest avoiding the use of the term in statutory law. Instead, specific ownership or beneficiary interests or incidents should be used.

Regarding registers and exchange of information, the author would suggest not using the term and instead trying to adapt international instruments to the domestic allocation rules of different states. Because the term is already spread throughout exchange of information materials and because those rules are already in force, it is alternatively suggested that domestic rules not use beneficial ownership or controlling person words, but ultimate controller. This would enable tax authorities to have a clear picture of the role of such information: to provide facts to then assess the application of taxes but without prejudging to whom such income or assets shall be allocated.

Finally, regarding international tax treaties, it is the author's view that the 2014 amendments to the Model have significantly clarified the meaning of the concept in line with the definition proposed in this book. However, the recent ruling of the Court of Justice of the European Union calling for an economic anti-avoidance interpretation and considering it as derived from the Model may raise the controversy again. Still, the introduction of the Principal Purpose Test (PPT) and the Limitation on Benefits (LOB) clause in the Multilateral Instruments and new treaties would take the pressure off the beneficial owner concept. Previously, as beneficial ownership was the only anti-avoidance rules in treaties, tax authorities were tempted to interpret beneficial ownership in a broad sense. Now, the Principal Purpose Test may serve that objective with much more legal certainty as providing a more consistent reference based on the purpose of the transactions. However, beneficial ownership may still be a useful term for certain transactions that may pass PPT and LOB tests, as might be the case for protected cell companies, and for treaties that do not contain such new anti-avoidance rules. In any of the cases, beneficial ownership should be interpreted in the narrow sense supported here, so that it corresponds to its history and its interpretative materials, and does not conflict with legal certainty.

BIBLIOGRAPHY

'Annual Report of the International Law Commission' (1966) II *Yearbook of the International Law Commission* 169.

'*Schlosberg v United States*: Straw Corporations and the Interest Deduction' (1982) 2 *Virginia Tax Review* 131.

'Trust Shares and the Nominee Problem in New York' (1938) 48 *Yale Law Journal* 106.

Aaronson, G (ed), 'GAAR Study: A Study to Consider Whether a General Anti-Avoidance Rule Should Be Introduced into the UK Tax System' (2011) https://webarchive.nationalarchives.gov.uk/20130402163458/, www.hm-treasury.gov.uk/d/gaar_final_report_111111.pdf.

AEFI Expert Group, 'First Report of the Commission AEFI Expert Group on the Implementation of Directive 2014/107/EU for Automatic Exchange of Financial Account Information' (AEFI Group, 2015).

Alexy, R, *A Theory of Constitutional Rights* (Oxford University Press, 2010).

Almudí Cid, JM, Ferreras Gutiérrez, JA and Hernández González-Barreda, PA (eds), *El Plan de Acción Sobre Erosión de Bases Imponibles y Traslado de Beneficios (BEPS): G20, OCDE y Unión Europea* (Aranzadi, 2017).

American Law Institute, *Restatement (Third) Foreign Relations of the United States*, vol 1 (American Law Institute Publishers, 1986).

Ames, JB, 'The Origin of Uses and Trusts' (1908) 21 *Harvard Law Review* 261.

Ames, JB, *Lectures on Legal History* (Harvard University Press, 1913).

Andrews, W, 'A Consumption-Type or Cash Flow Personal Income Tax' (1974) 87 *Harvard Law Review* 1113.

Anzilotti, D, *Corso Di Diritto Internazionale Lezioni* (1923).

Arginelly, P, *Multilingual Tax Treaties: Interpretation, Semantic Analysis and Legal Theory* (IBFD, 2015).

Arnold, B, 'Tax Treaties and Tax Avoidance: The 2003 Revisions to the Commentary' (2004) 58 *Bulletin for International Fiscal Documentation* 244.

Ault, H, 'The Role of the OECD Commentaries in the Interpretation of Tax Treaties' (1994) 22 *Intertax* 144.

Ault, HJ, *The OECD Model Convention – 1998 and Beyond, the Concept of Beneficial Ownership in Tax Treaties* (Kluwer, 2000).

Austin, J, *Lectures on Jurisprudence*, vol 1, 5th edn (John Murray, 1911).

Austin, J, *Lectures on Jurisprudence*, vol 2, 5th edn (John Murray, 1911).

Avella, F, 'Using EU Law to Interpret Undefined Tax Treaty Terms: Article 31 (3)(c) of the Vienna Convention on the Law of Treaties and Article 3 (2) of the OECD Model Convention' (2012) 4 *World Tax Journal* 95.

Avery Jones, J, 'The "One True Meaning" of a Tax Treaty' [2001] *Bulletin for International Taxation* 220.

Avery Jones, J, 'The History of the United Kingdom's First Comprehensive Double Taxation Agreement' in J. Tiley (ed), *Studies in the History of Tax Law*, vol 3 (Hart Publishing, 2009).

Avery Jones, J, 'Interpretation of Tax Treaties' (1986) 40 *Bulletin for International Fiscal Documentation* 75.

Avery Jones, J, 'The Beneficial Ownership Concept Was Never Necessary in the Model' in M Lang et al (eds), *Beneficial Ownership: Recent Trends* (IBFD, 2013).

Avery Jones, J, 'The United Kingdom's Influence on the Model' (2011) 6 *British Tax Review* 653.

Avery Jones, J, 'The UK's Early Tax Treaties with European Countries' in P Harris and D de Cogan (eds), *Studies in the History of Tax Law*, vol 8 (Hart Publishing, 2017).

Avery Jones, J, '*Weiser v HMRC*: Why Do We Need "Liable to Tax" and "Subject to Tax" Clauses?' [2013] *British Tax Review* 9.

Avery Jones, J and Lüdicke, J, 'The Origins of Article 5 (5) and 5 (6) of the OECD Model' [2014] *World Tax Journal* 203.

Avery Jones, J and Ward, DA, 'Agents as Permanent Establishments under the Model' [1993] *European Taxation* 154.

Avery Jones J, Vann R and Wheeler J, 'OECD Discussion Draft "Clarification of the Meaning of „Beneficial Owner" in the Model"' (2012), http://www.oecd.org/tax/treaties/48420432.pdf.

Avery Jones, JF et al, 'The Definitions of Dividends and Interest in the OECD Model: Something Lost in Translation?' [2009] *British Tax Review* 406.

Avery Jones, JF et al, 'The Interpretation of Tax Treaties with Particular Reference to Article 3 (2) of OECD Model – Part 2' [1984] *British Tax Review* 90.

Avery Jones, JF et al, 'The Interpretation of Tax Treaties with Particular Reference to Article 3 (2) of the OECD Model – I' [1984] *British Tax Review* 14.

Avery Jones, J et al, 'The Treatment of Trusts under the OECD Model Convention – II' [1989] *British Tax Review* 65.

Avery Jones, J et al, 'The Origins of Concepts and Expressions Used in the OECD Model and Their Adoption by States' (2006) 60 *Bulletin for International Taxation* 220.

Avi-Yonah, R, *International Tax as International Law: An Analysis of the International Tax Regime* (Cambridge University Press, 2007).

Avi-Yonah, R, 'Full Circle? The Single Tax Principle, BEPS, and the New US Model' [2016] *Global Taxation* 12.

Avi-Yonah, R, 'Globalization, Tax Competition, and the Fiscal Crisis of the Welfare State' [2000] *Harvard Law Review* 1573.

Avi-Yonah, R, 'International Taxation of Electronic Commerce' (1996) 52 *Tax Law Review* 507.

Avi-Yonah, R, 'Who Invented the Single Tax Principle: An Essay on the History of US Treaty Policy' (2014) 49 *New York Law School Law Review* 305.

Bacon, F, *The Reading Upon the Statute of Uses* (William Henry Rowe, 1804).

Báez Moreno, A, 'GAARs and Treaties: From the Guiding Principle to the Principal Purpose Test. What Have We Gained from BEPS Action 6?' (2017) 45 *Intertax* 432.

Báez Moreno, A, *Los Negocios Fiduciarios En La Imposición Sobre La Renta* (Aranzadi, 2009).

Báez Moreno, A and Zornoza Pérez, J, 'The General Anti-Abuse Rule of the Anti-Tax Avoidance Directive' in JM Almudí Cid, JA Ferreras Gutiérrez and PA Hernández González-Barreda (eds), *Combating Tax Avoidance in the EU* (Kluwer, 2019).

Baker, JH, *An Introduction to English Legal History* (Butterworths, 2002).

Baker, P, *Double Taxation Conventions*, loose-leaf edn (Sweet & Maxwell, 1993).

Baker, P, 'Beneficial Ownership: After Indofood' (2007) 6 GITC review.

Baker, P, 'Editor's Note re *PT Transportasi Gas Indonesia*' (2008) 11 *International Tax Law Reports* 407.

Baker, P, 'Improper Use of Tax Treaties, Tax Avoidance and Tax Evasion' in *United Nations Handbook on Selected Issues in Administration of Double Tax Treaties for Developing Countries* (United Nations, 2013).

Baker, P, 'Privacy Rights in an Age of Transparency: A European Perspective' [2016] *Tax Notes International* 583.

Baker, P, 'The Application of the Convention to Partnerships, Trusts and Other, Non-corporate Entities' (2002) 2 *GITC Review* 1.

Baker, P, 'The Meaning of "Beneficial Owner" as Applied to Dividends under the Model' in G Maisto (ed), *Taxation of Intercompany Dividends under Tax Treaties and EU Law* (IBFD, 2012).

Banfi, L and Mantegazza, F, 'An Update on the Concept of Beneficial Ownership from an Italian Perspective' (2012) 52 *European Taxation* 57.

Barenfeld, J, *Taxation of Cross-Border Partnerships: Double Tax Relief in Hybrid and Reverse Hybrid Situations*, vol 9 (IBFD, 2005).

Barentzen, S, 'Cross-Border Dividend and Interest Payments and Holding Companies – An Analysis of Advocate General Kokott's Opinions in the Danish Beneficial Ownership Cases' [2018] *European Taxation* 343.

Baumgartner, B, *Das Konzept Des Beneficial Owner Im Internationalen Steuerrecht Der Schweiz* (Zurich, 2010), https://www.zora.uzh.ch/id/eprint/47601/.

Bavila, A, 'Italy' in J Wheeler (ed),*Conflicts in the Attribution of Income to a Person*, vol B (Kluwer, 2007).

Becerra, JA, *The Interpretation and Application of Tax Treaties in North America* (IBFD, 2007).

Bernhardt, R, 'Interpretation and Implied (Tacit) Modification of Treaties, Comments on Arts. 27, 28, 29 and 38 of the ILC's 1966 Draft Articles on the Law of Treaties' (1967) 27 *Zeitschrift für Ausländisches Öffentliches Recht un Völkerrecht* 491.

Bernhardt, R, 'Interpretation in International Law' in *Encyclopedia of Public International Law*, vol 7 (Elsevier, 1984).

Bernstein, J, 'Thoughts on the OECD Discussion Paper on Beneficial Ownership' [2011] *Tax Notes International* 49.

Bertane, LG, 'Tax Problems of the Straw Corporation' (1975) 20 *Villanova Law Review* 735.
Birks, P, 'The Roman Law Concept of Dominium and the Idea of Absolute Ownership' [1985] *Acta Juridica* 1.
Black, HC, *Black's Law Dictionary*, 6th edn (West, 1990).
Blackstone, W, *Commentaries on the Laws of England*, vol 1 (Bancroft-Whitney, 1915).
Blackstone, W, *Commentaries on the Laws of England*, vol 2 (Bancroft-Whitney, 1915).
Blattmachr, JG, Gans, MM and Lo, AH, 'A Beneficiary as Trust Owner: Decoding Section 678' [2009] *ACTEC Journal* 106.
Bogert, GG and Bogert, GT, *Trust and Trustees*, vol 16, 2nd edn (West, 1995).
Bogert, GG and Hess, AM, *Trust and Trustees*, vol 1, 3rd edn (West, 2007).
Bogert, GG and Shapo, HS, *Trust and Trustees*, vol 3 (2rd Ed, West, 2012).
Booker, T, 'Recent Developments Regarding Beneficial Ownership in Denmark' (2012) 52 *European Taxation* 67.
Brabazon, M, 'BEPS Action 2: Trusts as Hybrid Entities' [2018] 2 *British Tax Review* 211.
Brake, ME, 'The Vested vs. Contingent Approach to Future Interests: A Critical Analysis of the Michigan Cases' 9 (1945–46) *University of Detroit Law Journal* 61.
Brauner, Y, 'An International Tax Regime in Crystallization' (2002) 56 *Tax Law Review* 259.
Brauner, Y, 'Beneficial Ownership In and Outside US Tax Treaties' in M Lang et al (eds), *Beneficial Ownership: Recent Trends* (IBFD, 2013).
Brauner, Y, 'BEPS: An Interim Evaluation' (2014) 6 *World Tax Journal* 10.
Brender, MD, 'Symposium: Beneficial Ownership in Canadian Income Tax Law: Required Reform and Impact on Harmonization of Quebec Civil Law and Federal Legislation' (2003) 51 *Canadian Tax Journal* 311.
Bross, SR, 'The United States Borrower in the Eurobond Market – A Lawyer's Point of View' (1969) 34 *Law and Contemporary Problems* 172.
Brown, C, 'The Taxation of Trusts: Reconciling Fundamental Principles' (2001) 21 *Estates, Trusts and Pensions Journal* 1.
Brown, C, 'Symposium: Beneficial Ownership and the Income Tax Act' (2003) 51 *Canadian Tax Journal* 401.
Brown, C, 'Tax, Trusts and Beneficial Ownership: Perils for the Unwary Practitioner' (2003) 23 *Estates, Trusts and Pensions Journal* 9.
Brown, C and Rajan, CL, 'Constructive and Resulting Trusts: Challenging Tax Boundaries' (1997) 45 *Canadian Tax Journal* 659.
Brownlie, I and Crawford, J, *Brownlie's Principles of Public International Law*, 8th edn (Oxford University Press, 2012).
Buckle, S, *Natural Law and the Theory of Property: Grotius to Hume* (Oxford University Press, 1993).
Buehler, AG, 'Ability to Pay' (1945) 1 *Tax Law Review* 243.
Bundgaard, J and Winther-Sorensen, N, 'Beneficial Ownership in International Financing Structures' (2008) 50 *Tax Notes International* 587.
Bundgaard, J, 'The Notion of Beneficial Ownership in Danish Tax Law: The Creation of a New Legal Order with Uncertainty as a Companion' in M Lang et al (eds), *Beneficial Ownership: Recent Trends* (IBFD, 2013).
Burrows, A (ed), *English Private Law* (Oxford University Press, 2007).
Calderón Carrero, JM and Piña Garrido, MD, 'Interpretation of Tax Treaties' (1999) 39 *European Taxation* 376.
Carroll, MB, 'New Tax Convention between the United States and Canada' (1942) 20 *Taxes* 459.
Carroll, MB, 'Tax Convention with France' (1948) 26 *Taxes* 952.
Carroll, MB, 'Evolution of US Treaties to Avoid Double Taxation of Income Part II' [1968] *The International Lawyer* 129.
Case, R, 'Disregard of Corporate Entity in Federal Taxation – The Modern Approach' (1943) 30 *Virginia Law Review* 398.
Castán Tobeñas, J, *Derecho Civil Español, Común y Foral*, vol 2, decimocuarta edn (Reus, 1992).
Castro Arango, JM, *El Concepto de Dividendo En Los Convenios de Doble Imposición* (Universidad Externado de Colombia, 2016).
Chand, V, 'Interaction of Domestic General Anti-Abuse Measures with Tax Treaties' in R Danon (ed), *Base Erosion and Profit Shifting: Impact for European and International Tax Policy* (Schulthess, 2016).
Chand, V, 'The Interaction of the Principal Purpose Test (and the Guiding Principle) with Treaty and Domestic Anti-Avoidance Rules' (2018) 46 *Intertax* 115.
Chand, V, 'The Principal Purpose Test in the Multilateral Convention: An In-Depth Analysis' (2018) 46 *Intertax* 18.

Chand, V, *The Interaction of Domestic Anti-Avoidance Rules with Tax Treaties (With Special Considerations for the BEPS Project)* (Schulthess, 2018).

Cheng-Han, T, 'Undisclosed Principals and Contract' (2004) 120 *LQR* 480.

Chow, G and Pryor, I, *Taxation of Trusts and Estates* (Thomson Reuters, 2018).

Christman, J, *The Myth of Property: Toward an Egalitarian Theory of Ownership* (Oxford University Press, 1994).

Claret y Martí, P, *De La Fiducia y Del 'Trust'* (Bosch, 1946).

Clayson, M, 'OECD Partnerships Report: Reshaping Treaty Interpretation?' [2000] *British Tax Review* 71.

Cleary, GE, 'The Corporate Entity in Tax Cases' (1945) 1 *Tax Law Review* 3.

Cleave, B, 'The *Weiser* Case: UK Pension Income Not Subject to Tax in Israel under the Israel–United Kingdom Income Tax Treaty (1962)' (2013) 67 *Bulletin for International Taxation* 280.

Clements, R and Abass, A, *Equity and Trusts*, 2nd edn (Oxford University Press, 2011).

Colin, A and Capitant, H, *Cours Élementaire de Droit Civil Français*, vol 2, dixième edn (Dalloz, 1948).

Collier, R, 'Clarity, Opacity and Beneficial Ownership' [2011] *British Tax Review* 684.

Collier, R, 'Clarification of the Meaning of Beneficial Owner in the Model' (PwC, 2011) CT06/RSC.

Combarros Villanueva, V, 'La Interpretación Económica Como Criterio de Interpretación Jurídica (Algunas Reflexiones a Propósito Del Concepto de "Propiedad Económica" En El Impuesto Sobre Patrimonio)' [1984] *Civitas. Revista española de derecho europeo* 485.

Committee of Experts on International Cooperation in Tax Matters, 'Progress Report of Subcommittee on Improper Use of Tax Treaties: Beneficial Ownership' (United Nations, 2008) E/C.18/2008/CRP.2/Add.1.

Committee of Experts on International Cooperation in Tax Matters, 'Update of the UN Model Double Taxation Convention between Developed and Developing Countries – Beneficial Ownership' (United Nations, 2019) E/C.18/2019/CRP.10.

Coombes, J, 'A Beneficial Decision? *Ayerst v C&K Construction Ltd*' [1975] *British Tax Review* 302.

Cope, M, *Constructive Trusts* (Law Book Co, 1992).

Craig, P and De Burca, G, *EU Law*, 6th edn (Oxford University Press, 2015).

Cuena Casas, M, 'La Validez de La Venta de Cosa Ajena Como Exigencia de Sistema' [2008] *Nul: estudios sobre invalidez e ineficacia* 1.

Da Silva, B, 'Granting Tax Treaty Benefits to Collective Investment Vehicles: A Review of the OECD Report and the 2010 Amendments to the Model Tax Convention' (2011) 39 *Intertax* 195.

Danon, R, 'Le Concept de Bénéficiaire Effectif Dans Le Cadre Du MC OCDE' [2007] *IFF Forum für Steuerrecht* 38.

Danon, R (ed), *Base Erosion and Profit Shifting (BEPS)* (Schulthess, 2016).

Danon, R, *Switzerland's Direct and International Taxation of Private Express Trusts* (Université de Genève, Schulthess, 2003).

Danon, R, 'Conflicts of Attribution of Income Involving Trusts under the OECD Model Convention: The Possible Impact of the OECD Partnership Report' (2004) 32 *Intertax* 210.

Danon, R, 'Clarification of the Meaning of "Beneficial Owner" in the Model: Comment on the April 2011 Discussion Draft' [2011] *Bulletin for International Taxation* 437.

Danon, R, 'Treaty Abuse in the Post-BEPS World: Analysis of the Policy Shift and Impact of the Principal Purpose Test for MNE Groups' (2018) 72 *Bulletin for International Taxation* 31.

Dari-Mattiacci, G and Guerriero, C, 'Law and Culture: A Theory of Comparative Variation in Bona Fide Purchase Rules' (2015) 35 *OJLS* 543.

Dart, JH and Barber, W, *A Treatise on the Law of and Practice Relating to Vendors and Purchasers of Real Estate*, 5th edn (Stevens & Sons, 1876).

Davies, PS and Virgo, G, *Equity and Trusts* (Oxford University Press, 2016).

De Broe, L, *International Tax Planning and Prevention of Abuse* (IBFD, 2008).

De Boer, R and Boulogne, F, 'Netherlands' in G Maisto (ed), *Taxation of Intercompany Dividends under Tax Treaties and EU Law* (IBFD, 2012) ch 19.

De Mooij, RA, *The OECD Model Convention – 1998 and Beyond, the Concept of Beneficial Ownership in Tax Treaties, vol 52, Congress* (Kluwer, 2000).

Delgado Pacheco, A, 'El Tribunal de Justicia de La Unión Europea Trata de Aclarar El Concepto de Elusión Fiscal' Blog Centro de Estudios Garrigues http://blog.centrogarrigues.com/el-tjue-y-el-concepto-de-elusion-fiscal/.

Dewar, JL, 'The Development of the Remedial Constructive Trust' (1982) 60 *Canadian Bar Review* 265.

Distaso, M and Russo, R, 'The EC Interest and Royalties Directive – a Comment' (2004) 44 *European Taxation* 143.
Dixon, M, McCorquodale, R and Williams, S, *International Law*, 5th edn (Oxford University Press, 2011).
Du Toit, C, *Beneficial Ownership of Royalties in Bilateral Tax Treaties* (IBFD, 1999).
Du Toit, C, 'The Evolution of the Term "Beneficial Ownership" in Relation to International Taxation over the Past 45 Years' (2010) 64 *Bulletin for International Taxation* 500.
Dworkin, R, *Taking Rights Seriously* (Harvard University Press, 1978).
Eastaway, N, Kimber, J and Richards, I, *Tax Advisers' Guide to Trusts* (Bloomsbury, 2016).
Edwardes-Ker, M, *Tax Treaty Interpretation* (Queen Mary University of London Theses, 1994) https://qmro.qmul.ac.uk/xmlui/handle/123456789/1679.
Ehrenzweig, AA and Koch, FE, *Income Tax Treaties* (Commerce Clearing House, 1949).
Eliffe, C, 'The Meaning of "Beneficial Ownership" in Double Tax Agreements' [2009] *British Tax Review* 276.
Eliffe, C, 'The Meaning of the Principal Purpose Test: One Ring to Bind Them All?' (2019) 11 *World Tax Journal* 48.
Engelen, F, *Interpretation of Tax Treaties under International Law* (IBFD, 2004).
Engelen, FA and Potgens, FP, 'Report on "The Application of the Model to Partnerships" and the Interpretation of Tax Treaties' (2000) 40 *European Taxation* 250.
Evans, MD, *International Law* (Oxford University Press, 2014).
Eynatten, W, De Haen, K and Hostyn, N, 'The Concept of "Beneficial Owner" under Belgian Tax Law: Legal Interpretation Is Maintained' (2003) 31 *Intertax* 523.
Falcón y Tella, R and Pulido, E, *Derecho Fiscal Internacional* (Marcial Pons, 2010).
Falk, CE, 'Nominees, Dummies and Agents: Is It Time for the Supreme Court to Take Another Look?' (1985) 63 *Taxes* 725.
Farah, E, 'Mandatory Arbitration of International Tax Disputes: A Solution in Search of a Problem' (2008) 9 *Florida Tax Review* 703.
FATF, *40 Recommendations* (FATF, 2003).
FATF, *Transparency and Beneficial Ownership* (FATF, 2014).
FATF, *International Standards on Combating Money Laundering and the Financing of ——, Terrorism & Proliferation* (FATF, 2016).
FATF, *International Standards on Combating Money Laundering and the Financing of Terrorism & Proliferation* (FATF, 2017).
Fearne, C, *An Essay on the Learning of Contingent Remainders and Executory Devises* (RH Small, 1845).
Fellows, ML, 'A Comprehensive Attack on Tax Deferral' (1990) 88 *Michigan Law Review* 722.
Ferris, G, 'How Should a System of Registered Title to Property Respond to Fraud and Sharp Practice?' in H Conway and R Hickey (eds),*Modern Studies in Property Law*, vol 9 (Hart Publishing, 2017).
Fett, E, *The Application of Bilateral Income Tax Treaties in Multilateral Situations* (IBFD, 2014).
Fibbe, G, 'Changes to the OECD Commentary on Collective Investment Vehicles Proposed by the OECD Committee on Fiscal Affairs' (2010) 64 *Bulletin for International Taxation* 138.
Fisher, H, *The Collected Papers of Frederik W Maitland* (Cambridge University Press, 1911).
Fitzmaurice, GG, 'Law and Procedure of the International Court of Justice: Treaty Interpretation and Certain Other Treaty Points' (1951) 28 *British Yearbook of International Law* 1.
Frankel, T, *Fiduciary Law* (Oxford University Press, 2010).
Franklin, M, 'Security of Acquistion and of Transaction: La Possession Vaut Titre and Bona Fide Purchase' (1931) 6 *Tulane Law Review* 589.
Fraser, R and Oliver, J, 'Beneficial Ownership: HMRC's Draft Guidance on Interpretation of the Indofood Decision' (2007) 1 *British Tax Review* 39.
Freedman, J, 'Defining Taxpayer Responsibility: In Support of a General Anti-Avoidance Rule' [2004] *British Tax Review* 332.
Freedman, J, 'Interpreting Tax Statutes: Tax Avoidance and the Intention of the Parliament' (2007) 123 *Law Quarterly Review* 53.
Freedman, J, 'The UK GAAR', General Anti-Avoidance Rules (GAARs) – A Key Element of Tax Systems in the Post-BEPS Tax World? (IBFD, 2016).
Fridman, GHL, *The Law of Agency* (Butterworths, 1960).
Fuller, H, 'Business Purpose, Sham Transactions and the Relation of Private Law to the Law of Taxation' (1962) 37 *Tulane Law Review* 355.

Gammie, M, 'The Origins of Fiscal Transparency in UK Income Tax' in J Tiley, *Studies in the History of Tax Law*, vol 4 (Hart Publishing, 2010).

Gammie, M, 'The Archer-Shee Cases (1927): Trusts, Transparency and Source', in J Snape and D de Cogan (eds), *Landmark Cases in Revenue Law* (Hart Publishing, 2019).

Ganguli, I, 'The Third Directive: Some Reflections on Europe's New AML/CFT Regime' (2010) 29 *Banking & Financial Services Policy Report* 1.

Garbarino, C, *Judicial Interpretation of Tax Treaties: The Use of the OECD Commentary* (Edward Elgar Publishing, 2016).

Garner, B (ed), *Black's Law Dictionary*, 10th edn (West – Thomson Reuters, 2009).

Garrigues Díaz-Cañabate, J, *Negocios Fiduciarios En Derecho Mercantil* (Real Academia de la Jurisprudencia y Legislación, 1955).

Geny, F, *Méthode d'interpretation Eet Source En Droit Privé Positif: Essai Critique*, vol II (Librairie générale de droit et de jurisprudence, 1919).

Getzler, J, 'Morice v Bishop of Durham (1805)' in C Mitchell and P Mitchell (eds), *Landmark Cases in Equity Law* (Hart Publishing, 2012).

Getzler, J, 'Transplantation and Mutation in Anglo-American Trust Law' (2009) 10 *Theoretical Inquiries in Law* 355.

Global Forum on Transparency and Exchange of Information for Tax Purposes, *Terms of Reference to Monitor and Review Progress towards Transparency and Exchange of Information on Request for Tax Purposes* (Global Forum, 2010).

Global Forum on Transparency and Exchange of Information for Tax Purposes, *Exchange of Information on Request: Handbook for Peer Reviews 2016–2020*, 3rd edn (OECD Publishing, 2016).

Global Forum on Transparency and Exchange of Information for Tax Purposes, *2016 Terms of Reference to Monitor and Review Progress towards Transparency and Exchange of Information on Request for Tax Purposes* (2016), http://www.oecd.org/tax/transparency/about-the-global-forum/publications/terms-of-reference.pdf.

Godefroi, H, *The Law of Trusts and Trustees* (Stevens & Sons, 1879).

Gooijer, J, 'Beneficial Owner: Judicial Variety in Interpretation Counteracted by the 2012 OECD Proposals?' (2014) 42 *Intertax* 204.

Greenberg, D, Banaszak, K and Greenberg, Y (eds), *Jowitt's Dictionary of English Law*, vol 1, 4th edn (Sweet & Maxwell, 2015).

Greenberg, D, Banaszak, K and Greenberg, Y (eds), *Jowitt's Dictionary of English Law*, vol 2, 4th edn (Sweet & Maxwell, 2015).

Greggi, M, 'Taxation of Royalties in an EU Framework' (2007) 47 *Tax Notes International* 1149.

Grey, TC, 'The Disintegration of Property' (1980) 22 *Nomos* 69.

Griffiths, LJ, 'New Life for the Agency Theory: *Commissioner v Bollinger*' (1989) 17 *Florida State University Law Review* 127.

Grimm, C, 'Das Steuerrecht Im Spannungsfeld Zwischen Wirtschaftlicker Betrachtungsweise Und Zivilrecht' [1978] *Deutsche Steuer-Zeitung* 283.

Grundmann, S, 'Trust and Treuhand at the End of the 20th Century. Key Problems and Shift of Interests' (1999) 47 *American Journal of Comparative Law* 401.

Gusmeroli, M, 'The Supreme Court Decision in the Government Pension Investment Fund Case: A Tale of Transparency and Beneficial Ownership (in Plato's Cave)' (2010) 64 *Bulletin for International Taxation* 198.

Guttman, D, 'Beneficial Ownership without Specific Beneficial Ownership Provision' in M Lang et al (eds), *Beneficial Ownership: Recent Trends* (IBFD, 2013).

Guttman, D, 'The 2011 Discussion Draft on Beneficial Ownership: What Next for the OECD?' in M Lang et al (eds), *Beneficial Ownership: Recent Trends* (IBFD, 2013).

Hanbury, HG, 'Periodical Menace to Equitable Principles' (1928) 44 *Law Quarterly Review* 468.

Hansen, HS, Christensen, LE and Pedersen, AE, 'Denmark – Danish "Beneficial Owner" Cases – A Status Report' (2013) 67 *Bulletin for International Taxation* 192.

Hardy, A, 'Trusts: United Kingdom' [2012] *IBFD* 48.

Harris, JW, *Property and Justice* (Oxford University Press, 1996).

Hart, HLA, *The Concept of Law* (Clarendon Press, 1994).

Hegel, GWF, *Hegel's Philosophy of Right* (Oxford University Press, 1952).

Helminen, M, *The International Tax Law Concept of Dividend* (Kluwer, 2017).

Helminen, M, *The Dividend Concept in International Tax Law* (Kluwer, 1999).
Hensel, A, *Steuerrecht* (NWB Verlag, 1986).
Hensel, A, *Derecho Tributario* (Marcial Pons, 2005).
Hernández González-Barreda, PA, 'El Concepto de Beneficiario Efectivo En La Reforma Tributaria: Intercambio de Información y Normas Antiabuso' in JR Piza and JM Castro (eds), *El Impacto de la Ley 1819 de 2016 y sus Desarrollos en el Sistema Tributario Colombiano*, Tomo 3, (Universidad Externado de Colombia, 2018).
Hernández González-Barreda, PA, 'Holding Companies and Leveraged Buy-Outs in the European Union Following BEPS: Beneficial Ownership, Abuse of Law and the Single Taxation Principle' (2019) 59 *European Taxation* 409.
HMRC, 'General Anti-Abuse Rule (GAAR) Guidance' www.gov.uk/government/publications/tax-avoidance-general-anti-abuse-rules.
Holmes, OW Jr, 'Early English Equity' [1885] *Law Quarterly Review* 162.
Honoré, AM, 'Ownership' in P Smith (ed), *The Nature and Process of Law: An Introduction to Legal Philosophy* (Oxford University Press, 1993).
Hudson, A, *Equity and Trusts* (Routledge, 2013).
Hudson, A, *Equity and Trusts* (Routledge, 2017).
Hughes, G, 'Rules, Policy and Decision Making' (1968) 77 *Yale Law Journal* 411.
Hulsey, BH, 'Tax Aspects of the Nominee Corporation: *Roccaforte v Commissioner of Internal Revenue*' (1986) 22 *Tulsa Law Journal* 61.
IFA, *The OECD Model Convention – 1998 & Beyond: The Concept of Beneficial Ownership in Tax Treaties*, IFA Congress Series Set (Kluwer, 2000).
Jain, S, *Effectiveness of the Beneficial Ownership Test in Conduit Company Cases* (IBFD, 2013).
Jain, S and Prebble, J, 'Conceptual Problems of Beneficial Ownership in Respect of Agents and Nominees' (2018) 73 *World Tax Journal* 10.
Jain, S, Prebble, J and Bunting, K, 'Conduit Companies, Beneficial Ownership, and the Test of Substantive Business Activity in Claims for Relief under Double Tax Treaties' (2013) 11 *eJournal of Tax Research* 386.
Jain, S, Prebble, J and Crawford, A, 'Conduit Companies, Beneficial Ownership, and the Test of Dominion in Claims for Relief under Double Tax Treaties', (2014) 11 *WU International Taxation Research Paper Series*.
James, PN, 'Aiken Industries Revisited' (1986) 64 *Taxes* 131.
Jenks, E, *A Short History of English Law* (Methuen & Co, 1949).
Joint Committee on Internal Revenue Taxation, *Legislative History of United States Tax Conventions, vol 1 – Income Tax Conventions Sec 1–11* (US Government Printing Office, 1962).
Joint Committee on Internal Revenue Taxation, *Legislative History of United States Tax Conventions, vol 2 – Income Tax Conventions Sec 12–25* (US Government Printing Office, 1962).
Kaiser, TE, 'Property, Sovereignty, the Declaration of Rights of Man, and the Tradition of French Jurisprudence' in D Van Kley (ed), *The French Idea of Freedom: The Old Regime and the Declaration of Rights of 1789* (Stanford University Press, 1994).
Kamm, JO, 'American Trading in Foreign Securities' (1951) 6 *Journal of Finance* 406.
Kandev, MN, 'Tax Treaty Interpretation: Determining Domestic Meaning under Article 3 (2) of the OECD Model' (2007) 55 *Canadian Tax Journal* 31.
Katz, L, 'The Concept of Ownership and the Relativity of Title' (2011) 2 *Jurisprudence* 191.
Kaye, TA, 'United States' in K Brown (ed), *A Comparative Look at Regulation of Corporate Tax Avoidance* (Springer, 2012).
Kelsen, H, *Pure Theory of Law* (University of California Press, 1970).
Kemmeren, ECCM, 'A Global Framework for Capital Gains Taxes' [2018] *Intertax* 268.
Killius, D, 'The Concept of "Beneficial Ownership" of Items of Income under German Tax Treaties' (1989) 17 *Intertax* 340.
King, EP, 'Fiscal Cooperation in Tax Treaties' [1948] *Taxes* 889.
King, EP, 'Tax Conventions to Which United States Is a Party' (1960) 1 *Proceedings of the Institute on Private Investments Abroad* 479.
Kleist, D, 'First Swedish Case on Beneficial Owner' (2013) 41 *Intertax* 159.
Kleist, D, 'Sweden: Trusts and Foreign Foundations in Swedish Tax Law' (2011) 17 *Trusts and Trustees* 622.
Knight, RA and Knight, LG, 'Disregard of the Corporate Entity and Nominee Corporations after Bollinger' (1989) 21 *University of Toledo Law Review* 203.

Kolarik, WJI and Wlodychak, SNJ, 'The Economic Substance Doctrine in Federal and State Taxation' (2014) 67 *The Tax Lawyer* 715.

Kozolchyk, B, 'Tranfers of Personal Property by a Nonowner: Its Future in Light of Its Past' (1986) 61 *Tulane Law Review* 1453.

Kozusko, DD and Vetter, SK, 'Trusts: United States' [2012] *IBFD* 16.

Kuner, CB, 'The Interpretation of Multilingual Treaties: Comparison of Texts versus the Presumption of Similar Meaning' (1991) 40 *ICLQ* 953.

Kurtz, J and Kopp CG, 'Taxability of Straw Corporations in Real Estate Transactions' (1968) 22 *Tax Lawyer* 647.

Kysar, R, 'Interpreting Tax Treaties' (2016) 101 *Iowa Law Review* 1387.

Lainoff, S, Bates, S and Bowers, C, 'Attributing the Activities of Corporate Agents under US Tax Law: A Fresh Look from an Old Perspective' (2003) 38 *Georgia Law Review* 143.

Lang, M, *The Application of the OECD Model Tax Convention to Partnerships, a Critical Analysis of the Report Prepared by the OECD Committee on Fiscal Affairs* (Kluwer, 2000).

Lang, M, 'Cadbury Schweppes' Line of Case Law from the Member States' Perspective' in S Vogenenauer and R de la Feria (eds), *Prohibition of Abuse of Law: A New General Principle of EU Law?* (Hart Publishing, 2011).

Lang, M, 'The Interpretation of Tax Treaties and Authentic Languages' in G Maisto et al (eds), *Essays on Tax Treaties. A Tribute to David A Ward* (IBFD, 2013).

Lang, M, *Introduction to the Law of Double Taxation Conventions*, 2nd edn (IBFD, 2013).

Lang, M, 'BEPS Action 6: Introducing an Antiabuse Rule in Tax Treaties' [2014] *Tax Notes International.*

Lang, M, (ed), *Base Erosion and Profit Shifting (BEPS)* (Linde, 2016).

Lang, M and Brugger, F, 'The Role of the OECD Commentary in Tax Treaty Interpretation' (2008) 23 *Australian Tax Forum* 95.

Langbein, J, 'The Secret Life of the Trust: The Trust as an Instrument of Commerce' (1997) 107 *Yale Law Journal* 165.

Lauterpacht, H, *International Law: Collected Papers of Hersch Lauterpacht*, vol 2 (Cambridge University Press, 1975).

Lawson, F and Rudden, B, *The Law of Property* (Clarendon Press, 1982).

Lazarov, I, '(Un)Tangling Tax Avoidance under the Interest and Royalties Directive' [2018] 11 *Intertax* 873.

League of Nations, 'Double Taxation and Tax Evasion – Report Presented by the Committee of Technical Experts on Double Taxation and Tax Evasion' (1927) Doc G. 216 M. 85. II.

Lederman, L, 'W(h)ither Economic Substance' (2010) 95 *Iowa Law Review* 389.

Lewin, T, *A Practical Treatise on The Law of Trusts and Trustees*, 2nd edn (Maxwell and Son 1842).

Libin, J, 'Congress Should Address Tax Avoidance Head-On: The Internal Revenue Code Needs a GAAR' (2010) 30 *Virginia Tax Review* 339.

Liebmann, BN, 'Disregarding the Corporate Nominee: *Commissioner v Bollinger*' [1989] *The Tax Lawyer* 371.

Likhovski, A, 'The Duke and the Lady: *Helvering v Gregory* and the History of Tax Avoidance Adjudication' (2004) 25 *Cardozo Law Review* 953.

Likhovski, A, *The Story of Gregory: How Are Tax Avoidance Cases Decided?*, Business Tax Stories (Foundation Press, 2005).

Lindrjoos, A, 'Addressing Norm Conflicts in a Fragmented Legal System: The Doctrine of Lex Specialis' [2005] *Nordic Journal of International Law* 27.

Locke, J, *Second Treatise of Government* (Harlan Davidson, 1982).

Lopez Rodriguez, J, 'Beneficial Ownership and EU Law' in M Lang et al (eds), *Beneficial Ownership: Recent Trends* (IBFD, 2013).

Loutzenhiser, G, *Tiley's Revenue Law*, 8th edn (Hart Publishing, 2016).

Lupoi, M, *Trusts: A Comparative Study* (Cambridge University Press, 2000).

M, JG, 'Relief from Stamp Duty on Inter Company Transfers' [1956] *British Tax Review* 184.

M, JG, 'Transfers between Associated Enterprises' [1959] *British Tax Review* 142.

M, JG, 'Beneficial Owner' [1962] *British Tax Review* 343.

M, JG, 'Conditional Contracts and Beneficial Ownership' [1968] *British Tax Review* 267.

M, JG, 'Beneficial Ownership' [1969] *British Tax Review* 64.

Madison, AD, 'The Tension Between Textualism and Substance-Over-Form Doctrines in Tax Law' (2002) 43 *Santa Clara Law Review* 699.

Maitland, FW, 'The Origin of Uses' (1894) 8 *Harvard Law Review* 127.
Maitland, FW and Brunyate, J, *Equity* (Cambridge University Press, 1936).
Marín Benítez, G, 'The European Union, the State Competence in Tax Matters and Abuse of the EU Freedoms' in JM Almudí Cid, J Ferreras Gutiérrez and PA Hernández González-Barreda (eds), *Combating Tax Avoidance in the EU* (Kluwer, 2019).
Marín Benítez, G, *¿Es Lícita La Planificación Fiscal?* (Lex Nova, 2013).
Martín Jiménez, A, 'Beneficial Ownership as a Broad Anti-Avoidance Provision: Decisions by Spanish Courts and the OECD's Discussion Draft' in M Lang et al (eds), *Beneficial Ownership: Recent Trends* (IBFD, 2012).
Martín Jiménez, A, 'Beneficial Ownership as an Attribution-of-Income Rule in Spain: Source and Residence Country Perspectives' in M Lang et al (eds), *Beneficial Ownership: Recent Trends* (IBFD, 2012).
Martín Jiménez, A, 'The 2003 Revision of the OECD Commentaries on the Improper Use of Tax Treaties: A Case for the Declining Effect of the OECD Commentaries?' (2004) 58 *Bulletin for International Fiscal Documentation* 17.
Martín Jiménez, A, 'Beneficial Ownership: Current Trends' (2010) 2 *World Tax Journal* 35.
Martín Santisteban, S, *El Instituto Del 'Trust' En Los Sistemas Legales Continentales y Su Compatibilidad Con Los Principios de 'Civil Law'* (Aranzadi, 2005).
Martinho, S et al, 'A Comprehensive Analysis of Proposals to Amend the Interest and Royalties Directive: Part 1' (2011) 51 *European Taxation* 397.
Maston, I, *Tolley's UK Taxation of Trusts 2018–2019* (Relx – Tolley, 2018).
Mateotti, R and Sutter, FM, 'Switzerland: Broad v Narrow Interpretation of the Beneficial Owner Concept' in M Lang et al (eds), *Beneficial Ownership: Recent Trends* (IBFD, 2013).
Matthews, P, 'All about Bare Trusts: Part 1' [2005] *Private Client Business* 266.
McAree, C, 'United Kingdom' in J Wheeler (ed), *Conflicts in the Attribution of Income to a Person* (Kluwer, 2007).
McFarlane, B and Stevens, R, 'The Nature of Equitable Property' (2010) 4 *Journal of Equity* 44.
Meindl-Ringler, A, *Beneficial Ownership in International Tax Law* (Kluwer, 2016).
Miller, DS, 'Taxpayers' Ability to Avoid Tax Ownership: Current Law and Future Prospects' (1998) 51 *The Tax Lawyer* 279.
Miller, JA and Maine, JA, *The Fundamentals of Federal Taxation*, 4th edn (Carolina Academic Press, 2017).
Miller, JE, 'The Nominee Conundrum: The Live Dummy Is Dead, but the Dead Dummy Should Live' (1978) 34 *Tax Law Review* 213.
Minervini, G, *El Mandato* (Bosch, 1959).
Møllin Ottosen, A and Andersen, S, 'Preliminary Judgments in the EU Beneficial Ownership Cases' (2019) 21 *Derivatives and Financial Instruments.*
Mor, F, 'Registers of Beneficial Ownership' (House of Commons, 2019) 8259.
Muller, J, 'The Interest & Royalty Directive' (BNA Bloomberg, 2005).
Müller-Freienfels, W, 'The Undisclosed Principal' (1953) 16 *MLR* 298.
Munzer, S, *A Theory of Property* (Cambridge University Press, 1990).
Murphy, L, and Nagel, T, *Myth of Ownership* (Oxford University Press, 2002).
Musgrave, RA, 'In Defense of an Income Concept' (1967) 81 *Harvard Law Review* 44.
Musilek, A, 'Change of Paradigm in Administrative Cooperation Directives: Automatic Exchange of Information' in JM Almudí Cid, JA Ferreras Gutiérrez and PA Hernández González-Barreda (eds), *Combating Tax Avoidance in the EU* (Kluwer, 2019).
Navisotschnigg, F, 'The Beneficial Ownership Test' in M Lang et al (eds), *Tax Treaty Entitlement* (Amsterdam, 2019) ch 4.
Niehuss, JM, 'Foreign Investment in the United States: A Review of Governmental Policy' (1975) 16 *Virginia Journal of International Law* 65.
Nock, RS, '"Hiving off" and Stamp Duty Exemption' [1971] *British Tax Review* 254.
Nolan, R, 'Equitable Property' (2006) 122 *LQR* 232.
Noseda, F, 'Common Reporting Standard and EU Beneficial Ownership Registers: Inadequate Protection of Privacy and Data Protection' (2017) 23 *Trusts and Trustees* 404.
OECD, 'Double Taxation Conventions and the Use of Conduit Companies' in *International Tax Avoidance and Evasion: Four Related Studies* (OECD Publishing, 1987).
OECD, *The Application of the Model to Partnerships* (OECD Publishing, 1999).

OECD, 'Restricting the Entitlement to Treaty Benefits' in *2002 Reports Related to the OECD Model Tax Convention* (OECD Publishing, 2003).

OECD, *Manual on the Implementation of Exchange of Information Provisions for Tax Purposes* (OECD Publishing, 2006).

OECD, *The Granting of Treaty Benefits with Respect to the Income of Collective* (Center for Tax Policy and Administration, 2010), https://www.oecd.org/tax/treaties/45359261.pdf.

OECD, 'Clarification of the Meaning of "Beneficial Owner" in the Model Discussion Draft' (OECD, 2011).

OECD, 'Meaning of Beneficial Owner, Revised Discussion Draft' (OECD, 2012) CTPA/CFA(2012)63.

OECD, *2014 Update to the Model Tax Convention* (OECD, 2014).

OECD, *Action 2. Neutralising the Effects of Hybrid Mismatch Arrangements – Final Report* (OECD Publishing, 2015).

OECD, *Aligning Transfer Pricing Outcomes with Value Creation, Actions 8–10 – 2015 Final Reports, OECD/G20 Base Erosion and Profit Shifting Project* (OECD Publishing, 2015).

OECD, *Designing Effective Controlled Foreign Company Rules, Action 3 – 2015 Final Report* (OECD Publishing, 2015).

OECD, *Preventing the Granting of Treaty Benefits in Inappropriate Circumstances, Action 6 – 2015 Final Report* (OECD Publishing, 2015).

OECD, *Standard for Automatic Exchange of Financial Information in Tax Matters Implementation Handbook* (OECD Publishing, 2015).

OECD, *Standard for Automatic Exchange of Financial Account Information in Tax Matters*, 2nd edn (OECD Publishing, 2017).

OECD Steering Group on Corporate Governance, *Behind the Corporate Veil: Using Corporate Entities for Illicit Purposes* (OECD Publishing, 2001).

Offermanns, R, 'Current Trends Regarding Disclosure Mechanisms: Reporting Ultimate Beneficial Ownership – Part 1' (2019) 59 *European Taxation* 162.

Offermanns, R, 'Current Trends Regarding Disclosure Mechanisms: Reporting Ultimate Beneficial Ownership – Part 2' (2019) 59 *European Taxation* 237.

Oliver, D et al, 'Beneficial Ownership' (2000) 54 *Bulletin for International Taxation* 310.

Open Ownership and Global Witness, 'Learning the Lessons from the UK's Public Beneficial Ownership Register' (2017).

Osgood, RK, 'Interpreting Tax Treaties in Canada, the United States, and the United Kingdom' (1984) 17 *Cornell International Law Journal* 255.

Owens, EA, 'United States Income Tax Treaties: Their Role in Relieving Double Taxation' [1962–63] 17 *Rutgers Law Review* 428.

Parada, L, *Double Non-Taxation and the Use of Hybrid Entities: An Alternative Approach in the New Era of BEPS* (Kluwer, 2018).

Partridge, D, 'Simplification of Securities Transfers by Trustees' [1958] *ABA Section Real Property Probate & Trust Proceedings* 44.

Paschen, U, *Steuerumgehung Im Nationalen Und Internationalen Steuerrecht* (Deutscher Universitäts-Verlag GmbH, 2001).

Pearce, R, Stevens, J and Barr, W, *The Law of Trusts and Equitable Obligations*, 5th edn (Oxford University Press, 2010).

Pearsall, J (ed), *The New Oxford Dictionary of English* (Oxford University Press, 1998).

Pellone, C, 'China-Tax Authorities Issue Circular on Interpretation of Double Tax Treaties' (2011) 18 *International Transfer Pricing Journal* 143.

Pijl, H, 'Beneficial Ownership and Second Tier Beneficial Owners in Tax Treaties in the Netherlands' (2003) 31 *Intertax* 353.

Pijl, H, 'Netherlands' in J Wheeler (ed), *Conflicts in the Attribution of Income to a Person*, vol B (Kluwer, 2007).

Pinetz, E, 'Use of a Principal Purpose Test to Prevent Treaty Abuse' in M Lang (ed) *Base Erosion and Profit Shifting (BEPS)* (Linde, 2016).

Pistone, P, 'Italy: Beneficial Ownership and the Entitlement to Treaty Benefits in the Presence of Transparent Entities' in M Lang et al (eds), *Beneficial Ownership: Recent Trends* (IBFD, 2013).

Pollock, F, *Principles of Contract: Being a Treatise on the General Principles Concerning the Validity of Agreements in the Law of England* (R Clarke & Co, 1885).

Pollock, F and Maitland, FW, *History of English Law*, vol 1, 2nd edn (Cambridge University Press, 1968).

Pollock, F and Maitland, FW, *History of English Law*, vol 2, 2nd edn (Cambridge University Press, 1968).
Postlewaite, PF, 'The Status of the Judicial Sham Doctrine in the United States' (2016) 15 *Revenue Law Journal* 140.
Prebble, J, 'Accumulation Trusts and Double Taxation Conventions' [2001] *British Tax Review* 69.
Preston, N, 'The Interpretation of Taxing Statutes: The English Perspective' (1990) 7 *Akron Tax Journal* 43.
Prud'homme, N, 'Lex Specialis: Oversimplifying A More Complex and Multifaceted Relationship?' (2007) 40 *Israel Law Review* 356.
Qiu, D, 'The Concept of "Beneficial Ownership" in China's Tax Treaties – The Current State of Play' (2013) 2 *Bulletin of International Taxation* 98.
Rado, AB, 'The Tax Conventions Between the United States and Italy' (1959) 14 *Tax Law Review* 203.
Ramallo Massanet, J, 'Derecho Fiscal Frente a Derecho Civil: Discusión En Torno a La Naturaleza Del Derecho Fiscal Entre L Trotabas y F Geny' [1973] *Revista de la Facultad de Derecho de la Universidad Complutense de Madrid* 7.
Raz, J, 'Legal Principles and the Limits of Law' (1972) 81 *Yale Law Journal* 823.
Reimer, E, 'Interpretation of Tax Treaties' (1999) 39 *European Taxation* 458.
Reimer, E and Rust, A (eds), *Klaus Vogel on Double Taxation Conventions*, vol 1, 4th edn (Kluwer, 2015).
Reimer, E and Rust, A (eds), *Klaus Vogel on Double Taxation Conventions*, vol 2, 4th edn (Kluwer, 2015).
Reinarz, P and Carelli, F, 'Court Rulings on Dividend Stripping and Denial of Swiss Tax Treaty Benefits' (2016) 18 *Derivatives and Financial Instruments*.
Reinarz, P, 'Switzerland: Treaty Shopping and the Swiss Withholding Tax Trap' (2001) 41 *European Taxation* 415.
Reinhard-DeRoo, M, *Beneficial Ownership* (Springer, 2014).
Reuschlein, HG and Gregory, WA, *The Law of Agency and Partnership* (West, 1990).
Rey, A and Rey-Debove, J (eds), *Le Robert, Dictionnaire Alphabétique & Analogique de La Langue Française* (Société du Nouveau Littré, 1978).
Ribes Ribes, A, *Convenios Para Evitar La Doble Imposición: Intepretación, Procedimiento Amistoso y Arbitraje* (Edersa, 2003).
Riis, A, 'Danish Tax Authorities Prevail in Recent Beneficial Ownership Decision' (2011) 51 *European Taxation* 184.
Riis, A and Bjornholm, N, 'First Danish Ruling on Beneficial Ownership' (2010) 50 *European Taxation* 324.
Ring, DM, 'One Nation among Many: Policy Implications of Cross-Border Tax Arbitrage' (2002) 44 *Boston College Law Review* 79.
Rivero Hernández, F, *Usufructo, Uso y Habitación*, 2nd edn (Civitas, 2016).
Roch, MTS, 'La Imposición Justa Sobre Las Sociedades En Un Escenario Global: Un Tema Pendiente' [2018] *Derecho & Sociedad* 186.
Rose, CM, 'Property as the Keystone Right' (1995) 71 *Notre Dame Law Review* 329.
Rossi, M, '"Sede Di Direzione Effettiva" e "Beneficiario Effettivo" Nel Quadro Dei Rapporti Italo-Francesi' [2017] *Corriere Tributario* 1270.
Rossi, M, 'An Italian Perspective on the Beneficial Ownership Concept' (2007) 45 *Tax Notes International* 1117.
Roth, ES et al, *Canadian Taxation of Trusts* (Canadian Tax Foundation, 2016).
Rotman, L, 'Deconstructing the Constructive Trust' (1999) 37 *Alberta Law Review* 133.
Rowland, A, 'Beneficial Ownership in a Corporate Context: What Is It? When Is It Lost? Where Does It Go?' [1997] *British Tax Review* 178.
Ruding, O, *Report of the Committee of Independent Experts on Company Taxation* (Office for Official Publications of the European Communities, 1992).
Ruiz Almendral, V and Seitz, G, 'El Fraude a La Ley Tributaria (Análisis de La Norma Española Con Ayudad de La Experiencia Alemana)' [2004] *Estudios Financieros* 3.
Ruiz Almendral, V, *El Fraude a la Ley Tributaria a examen* (Aranzadi, 2006).
Rust, A, 'Germany' in G Maisto (ed), *Multilingual Texts and Interpretation of Tax Treaties and EC Tax Law* (IBFD, 2005) ch 11.
Rutledge, TE, 'Requiring Disclosure of Business Entity Ownership: Proposed New Laws Are Burdensome, but with the Benefit of Being Ineffective' [2010] *Journal of Passthrough Entities* 59.
Ryynänen, O, 'The Concept of a Beneficial Owner in the Application of Finnish Tax Treaties' (2003) 44 *Scandinavian Studies in Law* 345.

Salmons, D, 'Claims against Third-Party Recipients of Trust Property' (2017) 76 *CLJ* 399.
Salomé, H and Danon, RJ, 'The OECD Partnership Report – a Swiss View on Conflicts of Qualification' (2003) 31 *Intertax* 190.
Schaffner, J, 'The OECD Report on the Application of Tax Treaties to Partnerships' (2000) 54 *Bulletin for International Fiscal Documentation* 218.
Schwartz, A and Scott, RE, 'Rethinking the Laws of Good Faith Purchase' (2011) 111 *Columbia Law Review* 1332.
Scott, AW, 'The Nature of the Rights of the Cestui Que Trust' (1917) 17 *Columbia Law Review* 269.
Scott, AW, Franklin Fratcher, W and Ascher, M, *Scott and Ascher on Trusts*, vol 3, 4th edn (Aspen, 2007).
Scott, AW, Franklin Fratcher, W and Ascher, M, *Scott and Ascher on Trusts*, vol 5, 4th edn (Aspen, 2007).
Screpante, M, 'Treaty Abuse and Beneficial Ownership – the Molinos Case' in M Lang et al (eds), *Tax Treaty Case Law around the Globe 2017* (IBFD, 2018).
Seavey, W, 'The Rationale of Agency' (1920) 29 *Yale Law Journal* 859.
Seavey, W, *Law of Agency* (West, 1964).
Seiler, M, *GAARs and Judicial Anti-Avoidance in Germany, the UK and the EU* (Linde, 2016).
Sengupta, DP, '*Aditya Birla Nuvo v DDIT High Court of Bombay*' in M Lang et al (eds), *Beneficial Ownership: Recent Trends* (IBFD, 2013).
Shakow, D, 'Taxation without Realization: A Proposal for Accrual Taxation' (1986) 134 *University of Pennsylvania Law Review* 1111.
Shannon, HA, 'United States Income Tax Treaties: Reference to Domestic Law for the Meaning of Undefined Terms' (1989) 17 *Intertax* 453.
Shapiro, SJ, 'The "Hart–Dworkin" Debate: A Short Guide for the Perplexed' (2007) 77 Public Law and Legal Theory Working Paper Series.
Shaviro, D, 'The Two Faces of the Single Tax Principle' (2016) 41 *Brooklyn Journal of International Law* 1293.
Shaw, MN, *International Law*, 7th edn (Cambridge University Press, 2014).
Shelton, D, 'Reconcilable Differences – the Interpretation of Multilingual Treaties' (1996) 20 *Hastings International and Comparative Law Review* 611.
Simons, HC, *Personal Income Taxation* (University of Chicago Press, 1938).
Simpson, AWB, *An Introduction to the History of Land Law*, reprint of 1st edn (Oxford University Press, 1964).
Sin, KF, *The Legal Nature of the Unit Trust* (Oxford University Press, 1997).
Sinclair, I, *The Vienna Convention on the Law of Treaties*, 2nd edn (Manchester University Press, 1984).
Smith, A, *Wealth of Nations: An Inquiry into the Nature and Causes of The Wealth of Nations* (Mobilereference.com, 2009).
Smith, RJ, *Plural Ownership* (Oxford University Press, 2005).
Smith, RT, 'Tax Treaty Interpretation by the Judiciary' (1995) 49 *The Tax Lawyer* 845.
Speed, R, 'Beneficial Ownership' (1997) 26 *Australian Tax Review* 34.
Sperduti, G, 'Dualism and Monism' (1977) 3 *Italian Yearbook of International Law* 31.
Starke, JG, 'Monism and Dualism in the Theory of International Law' (1936) 17 *British Yearbook of International Law* 66.
Stevens, D, 'Taxation of Trusts in Canada' https://store.lsuc.on.ca/Content/pdf/2017/CLE17-00205/CLE17-00205-pub.pdf.
Stone, HF, 'The Nature of the Rights of the "Cestui Que Trust"' (1917) 17 *Columbia Law Review* 467.
Stone, M and Lesnie, V, 'Some Thoughts on Beneficial Interests and Beneficial Ownership in Revenue Law' (1996) 19 *University of New South Wales Law Journal* 181.
Streng, WP and Yoder, LD, 'United States' in F Zimmer (ed), *Form and Substance in Tax Law* (Kluwer, 2002).
Summers, R, 'A Critique of the Business Purpose Doctrine' (1961) 41 *Oregon Law Review* 38.
Surrey, S, 'Assignments of Income and Related Devices: Choice of the Taxable Person' (1933) 33 *Columbia Law Review* 791.
Surrey, S, 'The United States Tax System and International Tax Relationships' (1964) 17 *Tax Executive* 104.
Swain, S, 'Can PPT-LOB Clause Plug the Loopholes Inherent in PCC Entities?' (2019) Kluwer International Tax blog http://kluwertaxblog.com/2019/05/29/can-ppt-lob-clause-plug-the-loopholes-inherent-in-pcc-entities/ accessed 18 June 2019.
Terra, B and Wattel, P, *European Tax Law* (Kluwer, 2005).
The EEC Reports on Tax Harmonization: The Report of the Fiscal and Financial Committee and the Reports of the Sub-Groups, A, B and C (Neumark Report) (IBFD, 1963).

Thomas, AVW, 'Note on the Origin of Uses and Trusts – WAQFS' (1949) 3 *Southwestern Law Journal* 162.
Thomas, GW and Hudson, A, *The Law of Trusts* (Oxford University Press, 2004).
Tolstrup, B and Bjornholm, N, 'Beneficial Ownership – Withholding Tax on Dividends and Interest from the Danish Perspective' (2011) 65 *Bulletin for International Taxation* 503.
Townsend, JA, 'Tax Treaty Interpretation' (2001) 55 *Tax Lawyer* 219.
Tretola, J, 'The Interpretation of Taxation Legislation by the Courts – a Reflection on the Views of Justice Graham Hill' (2006) 16 *Revenue Law Journal* 6674.
Turner, A and Follet, T, 'Tangled up in Chains? Making Sense of the New UK Requirement to Keep Registers of "People with Significant Control"' (2016) 22 *Trusts and Trustees* 537.
Turner, MA, 'Agent vs Nominee: A Suspended Decision for Dummy Corporations' (1989) 67 *Taxes* 263.
Vallada, F, *Beneficial Ownership under Articles 10, 11 and 12 of the 2014 Model*, The OECD-Model-Convention and its Update 2014, 90 (Linde, 2015).
van Boeijen-Ostaszewska, A et al, 'Clarification of the Meaning of "Beneficial Owner" in the Model Response from IBFD Research Staff' (IBFD, 2012).
Van der Bruggen, E, 'Unless the Vienna Convention Otherwise Requires: Notes on the Relationship between Article 3(2) of the Model and Articles 31 and 32 of the Vienna Convention on the Law of Treaties' (2003) 43 *European Taxation* 142.
Van der Tempel AJ, *Corporation Tax and Individual Income Tax in the European Communities* (Office for Official Publications of the European Communities, 1970).
Van Erp, S and Akkermans, B (eds), *Property Law* (Hart Publishing, 2012).
Van Raad, K, 'Report on Beneficial Ownership under the OECD Model Convention and Commentaries' (2011), http://ibdt.org.br/material/arquivos/Atas/jfb_20111020093958.pdf.
Van Weeghel, S, *The Improper Use of Tax Treaties* (Kluwer, 1998).
Van Weeghel, S, 'General Report' in S Van Weeghel (ed), *Tax Treaties and Tax Avoidance: Application of Anti-Avoidance Provisions* (Kluwer, 2010).
Van Weeghel, S, 'A Deconstruction of the Principal Purposes Test' (2019) 11 *World Tax Journal* 3.
Vann, R, 'Beneficial Ownership: What Does History (and Maybe Policy) Tell Us' in M Lang et al (eds), *Beneficial Ownership: Recent Trends* (IBFD, 2013).
Vasey, V, 'Fideicommissa and Uses: The Clerical Connection Revisited' (1982) 17 *The Jurist* 201.
Vega Borrego, F, *Limitation on Benefits Clauses in Double Taxation Conventions* (Kluwer, 2006).
Venezian, G, *Usufructo, Uso y Habitación*, vols I and II (V Suarez, 1928).
Villiger, ME, *Commentary on the 1969 Vienna Convention on the Law of Treaties* (Martinus Nijhoff, 2009).
Virgo, GJ and Burn EH, *Trusts and Trustees*, 7th edn (Oxford University Press, 2008).
Vittala, J, *Taxation of Investment Funds in the European Union* (IBFD, 2004).
Vogel, K, *Klaus Vogel on Double Taxation Conventions*, 3rd edn (Kluwer, 1997).
Vogel, K, 'Steuerumgehung Nach Innerstaatlichem Recht Und Nach Abkommensrecht' (1985) Steuer und Wirtschaft 369.
Vogel, K and Prokisch, R, 'General Report' in K Vogel and R Prokish (eds), *Interpretation of Double Taxation Conventions*, vol a (Kluwer, 1993).
Walser, JL, 'The Model – 1998 and Beyond' in *The Concept of Beneficial Ownership in Tax Treaties*, vol a (Kluwer, 2000).
Ward, D, 'Principles To Be Applied in Interpreting Tax Treaties' [1977] 25 *Canadian Tax Journal* 263.
Ward, D, 'Canada's Tax Treaties' (1995) 43 *Canadian Tax Journal* 1719.
Ward, D, 'Abuse of Tax Treaties' (1995) 23 *Intertax* 176.
Ward, DA et al, 'The Business Purpose Test and Abuse of Rights' [1985] *British Tax Review* 68.
Ward, DA et al, 'A Resident of a Contracting State for Tax Treaty Purposes: A Case Comment on Crown Forest Industries' (1996) 44 *Canadian Tax Journal* 408.
Waters, DWM, 'The Nature of the Trust Beneficiary's Interest' (1967) 45 *Canadian Bar Review* 219.
Waters, DWM, *Constructive Trusts: Case for a New Approach in English Law* (Athlone Press, 1964).
Wattel, P and Marres, O, 'The Legal Status of the OECD Commentary and Static or Ambulatory Interpretation of Tax Treaties' (2003) 43 *European Taxation* 222.
Weber, D, 'The Proposed EC Interest and Royalty Directive' [2000] *EC Tax Review* 15.
Wheeler, J, 'The Attribution of Income to a Person for Tax Treaty Purposes' (2005) 59 *Bulletin for International Taxation* 477.
Wheeler, J, 'General Report' in J Wheeler (ed) *Conflicts in the Attribution of Income to a Person* (Kluwer, 2007).

Wheeler, J, 'The Attribution of Income in the Netherlands and the United Kingdom' (2011) 3 *World Tax Journal* 39.

Wheeler, J, *The Missing Keystone of Income Tax Treaties* (IBFD, 2012).

Wilson, RA, 'Unincorporated Business Activity for 1980' (1982) 2 *Statistics of Income Bulletin* 15.

Wöhrer, V, *Data Protection and Taxpayers' Rights: Challenges Created by Automatic Exchange of Information* (IBFD, 2018).

Wright, LA, 'Trusts and the Civil Law – A Comparative Study' (1967) 6 *Ontario Law Review* 114.

Yoon, J-H, 'An End of a Journey or a New Beginning? – the 2012 Trilogy of Supreme Court Decisions on International Tax' [2013] *Asia-Pacific Tax Bulletin* 190.

Zalasinski, A, 'The ECJ's Decisions in the Danish "Beneficial Ownership" Cases: Impact on the Reaction to Tax Avoidance in the European Union' (2019) 2 *International Tax Studies* 2.

Zimmer, F, 'General Report' in F Zimmer (ed), *Form and Substance in Tax Law* (Kluwer, 2002).

Zimmer, F, 'Domestic Anti-Avoidance Rules and Tax Treaties – Comment on Brian Arnold's Article' (2005) 59 *Bulletin for International Fiscal Documentation* 25.

Zornoza Pérez, J and Báez Moreno, A, 'The 2003 Revisions to the Commentary to the OECD Model on Tax Treaties and GAARs: A Mistaken Starting Point' in M Lang et al (eds), *Tax Treaties: Building Bridges between Law and Economics* (IBFD, 2010).

INDEX

www.ingramcontent.com/pod-product-compliance
Ingram Content Group UK Ltd.
Pitfield, Milton Keynes, MK11 3LW, UK
UKHW020906190926
475560UK00010B/299

9 781509 923076